EDITORIAL BOARD

UNIVERSITY TREATISE SERIES

INTERPRETING LAW

A PRIMER ON HOW TO READ STATUTES AND THE CONSTITUTION

William N. Eskridge Jr.
Yale Law School

Foreword by
John Paul Stevens

FOUNDATION
PRESS

444 Cedar Street, Suite 700
St. Paul, MN 55101
1-877-888-1330

Printed in the United States of America

ISBN: 978-1-63459-912-2

Dedicated to the Memory of

Philip P. Frickey
(1953–2010)

and

Elizabeth Garrett
(1963–2016)

Foreword

by John Paul Stevens

When I served as Associate Counsel to a Subcommittee of the House Committee on the Judiciary in 1951, Members of the Subcommittee occasionally asked me to explain provisions in bills being considered for possible enactment. On one such occasion, I was asked about a proposed bill that suspended the statute of limitations for private treble damages actions during the pendency of government antitrust proceedings. I recall noting that the draft of the bill failed adequately to explain when a plaintiff whose cause of action had arisen before the government action commenced must file his complaint in order to avoid the limitations bar. After discussing alternatives, the Member responded: "I think we should let the judges decide this one." That incident persuaded me that thoughtful legislators occasionally conclude that it is wiser to postpone the final resolution of ambiguous statutory provisions until after the decision-maker has had an opportunity to consider the impact of the statute in future cases. Legislators sometimes rely on judges to fill gaps in new statutes. It never occurred to me that a so-called "canon" of statutory construction might have provided an answer to the ambiguity.

In both my years in private practice and my work as a judge, I have been influenced by Karl Llewellyn's observation that "there are two opposing canons on almost every point."[1] For that reason I have always been reluctant to place primary reliance on any canon of statutory construction when confronted with a question about the correct interpretation of an ambiguity. Statutes are commands issued by legislatures, sometimes to the general public and sometimes to narrower audiences. When misunderstood, as the Charge of the Light Brigade into the "valley of Death" demonstrated, such commands can have disastrous consequences.[2] For that reason, it is often necessary to seek all available information about the reasons for the legislature's command, before deciding exactly what it means. In the

[1] Karl N. Llewellyn, Remarks on the Theory of Appellate Decision and the Rules or Canons About How Statutes Are to be Construed, 3 Vanderbilt L. Rev. 395, 401 (1950).

[2] Alfred, Lord Tennyson, "The Charge of the Light Brigade," reprinted in English Poetry in Three Volumes from Tennyson to Whitman 1005 (Charles W. Eliot ed., 1910).

overwhelming majority of cases the meaning that an ordinary reader would derive from the text of the law provides the proper answer. The relatively few difficult cases, however, justify the extensive scholarship surrounding statutory interpretation, which has generated an increasing volume of "canons."

In their recent book, *Reading Law: The Interpretation of Legal Texts*, my friends Justice Antonin Scalia and linguist Bryan Garner have favorably identified 57 canons that they believe will constrain "the tendency of judges to imbue authoritative texts with their own policy preferences."[3] Those authors oppose any consideration of legislative history in statutory construction on the ground that it "greatly increases the scope of manipulated interpretation, making possible some interpretations that the traditional rules of construction could never plausibly support."[4]

I do not share their assessment. Although admittedly there is a risk that elected judges may be tempted to adopt positions that will enhance their chances of reelection—being "tough on crime" by imposing harsh sentences in criminal cases, for example—in my view federal judges, as well as appointed state judges, are remarkably consistent in trying to conform their rulings to the policy preferences expressed by the legislatures rather than those they espouse. It is for that reason that they often (and wisely) spend time reviewing legislative history before deciding close cases, a point Professor Eskridge cogently demonstrates in Chapter 4 of his book. Indeed, one of the benefits that the judge obtains by simply relying on the legislature's policy choices is eliminating the often difficult task of deciding whether a statute is, in fact, a wise choice. Not having to decide whether a statute represents sound policy saves busy judges valuable time. As Thurgood Marshall often remarked, there is nothing in the Constitution that prevents legislatures from enacting stupid laws.

While Eskridge does not endorse the Scalia-Garner justification for canons, he has provided us with an appendix listing as many as 200 different canons of statutory interpretation endorsed by the Supreme Court during the 30 Terms that Bill Rehnquist and John Roberts have served as Chief Justice. The appendix is a useful and orderly collection of Supreme Court rulings in statutory cases, though

---

[3] Antonin Scalia & Bryan A. Garner, Reading Law: The Interpretation of Legal Texts xxviii (2012).

[4] Scalia & Garner, Reading Law at 378.

I'm not sure whether any special purpose is served by describing them as "canons."

The book uses a hypothetical statute banning vehicles in Lafayette Park, opposite the White House in Washington, D.C., and various hypothetical amendments to that law, to explain the author's approach to statutory interpretation. A similar hypothetical has been used by other authors writing about statutory construction, but none as comprehensively or as persuasively as Professor Eskridge. Each of the chapters in his book is well written and informative, though two are especially illuminating: Chapter 5 dealing with *Agency Interpretation and Regulatory History*, and his conclusion entitled *Canons and Norms in Constitutional Interpretation.*

Agency practice often provides the practical answer to questions of statutory interpretation that might be decided differently by scholars or linguists, because in many instances the agency's administration of a statute is never challenged in court. Moreover, under what has become known as the "*Chevron* doctrine," when an agency resolves an ambiguity in a statute that it administers, courts are required to accept the agency's answer whenever it "is based on a permissible construction of the statute."[5] As a matter of fact agencies usually are intimately familiar with the legislative history of their governing statutes, and therefore—despite some scholars' and jurists' criticism of reliance on legislative history—the *Chevron* doctrine ensures that such history will often play a decisive role in construing federal statutes. Chapter 5 of Eskridge's book, discussing this point, is well worth careful reading.

The conclusion demonstrates an important point about constitutional interpretation, though one that the author does not make explicitly. The Supreme Court's majority's decision in *Obergefell v. Hodges*[6] upholding the right to same-sex marriage as an aspect of liberty protected by the Due Process Clause of the Fourteenth Amendment has implicitly—but unquestionably—rejected the central argument advanced by many "originalist" scholars.[7] Those scholars do not merely support studying the original

---

[5] Chevron, U. S. A., Inc. v. Natural Resources Defense Council, Inc., 467 U. S. 837, 843 (1984).

[6] 135 S.Ct. 2584 (2015).

[7] See, e.g., id. at 2598 ("The generations that wrote and ratified the Bill of Rights and the Fourteenth Amendment did not presume to know the extent of freedom in all of its dimensions, and so they entrusted to future generations a charter protecting the right of all persons to enjoy liberty as we learn its meaning. When new insight reveals a discord between the Constitution's central protections and a received

intent of the Framers or the original public meaning of the Constitution as a source of guidance in constitutional interpretation. Rather, in their view, that original intent or meaning permanently defines the constitutional text unless and until that text is amended pursuant to a procedure authorized by Article V.[8] In Eskridge's discussion of the constitutionality of a hypothetical statute enacted in 1956 making it a crime for a "homosexual" to enter Lafayette Park, he convincingly demonstrates that such a statute would have been adjudged valid at that time. During the past half-century there has been no change in the relevant intent of the Framers or the public meaning of the constitutional text at the time of the Founding, but the law is now different than it was then. For reasons that the Framers certainly did not anticipate, we now have a "more perfect union" than we did in 1956.

JUSTICE JOHN PAUL STEVENS

December 17, 2015

legal stricture, a claim to liberty must be addressed."); id. at 2603 ("[I]n interpreting the Equal Protection Clause, the Court has recognized that new insights and societal understandings can reveal unjustified inequality within our most fundamental institutions that once passed unnoticed and unchallenged.").

[8] See, e.g., Randy E. Barnett, The Gravitational Force of Originalism, 82 Fordham L. Rev. 411, 418 (2013) ("[T]he proper way to change 'this Constitution' is provided in Article V. Judges are not allowed to update the text of the Constitution by changing the meaning it had at the time of the enactment."); Thomas B. Colby, Originalism and the Ratification of the Fourteenth Amendment, 107 Nw. U. L. Rev. 1627, 1672 (2013) ("To an originalist . . . the Constitution can be changed when the people collectively act to change it, but the people must act in compliance with the original meaning of Article V—the constitutional text that dictates the procedures for effectuating constitutional change.").

Acknowledgments

My greatest debt is to recently departed colleagues: Phil Frickey (1953–2010), my first co-author and the smartest man I have ever known, and Beth Garrett (1963–2016), a later co-author and the smartest woman I have ever known. Phil and Beth were the parents of many of the ideas and insights in the present volume.

I also owe a great debt to Nino Scalia (1936–2016), whom I dubbed "the Conscience of the Court" in the wake of his death this year. He was a legal giant whose new textualist legisprudence inspired me to write this particular book.

Valuable feedback came to me from Abbe Gluck, Bob Katzmann, Dorothy Landsberg, Brian Landsberg, Victoria Nourse, Dick Posner, Brian Slocum, Kate Shaw, Larry Solan, David Souter, Ed Stein, John Paul Stevens, as well as the participants in faculty workshops at Cardozo, Duke, McGeorge, and Yale Law Schools. Dean Robert Post of the Yale Law School provided generous funds and a sabbatical that enabled me to complete this book. Ryan Pfeiffer not only guided me through the publication process, but influenced the content of this book at every stage. Thank you, valued colleagues.

Critical to the completion of this manuscript has been the work of my invaluable research assistants at the Yale Law School: Josh Divine (Class of 2016), Natalie Hausknecht (Class of 2015), Paul Henderson (Class of 2017), Chris Pagliarella (Class of 2016), Lise Rahdert (Class of 2015), Theo Rostow (Class of 2017), and Marissa Roy (Class of 2017). Much gratitude for your excellent work.

All but one of the illustrations in this volume were taken from public domain websites sponsored by the Library of Congress and by the Wikimedia Commons; I am grateful to both.

WILLIAM N. ESKRIDGE JR.
WASHINGTON, D.C.

Table of Contents

INTERPRETING LAW

A PRIMER ON HOW TO READ STATUTES AND THE CONSTITUTION

Introduction

CANONS AND NORMS IN STATUTORY INTERPRETATION

Lafayette Park, Washington, D.C.

America is a republic of statutes. That is, most of the law Americans must obey originates in legislation—either direct statutory commands or regulatory requirements issued by agencies implementing statutes. This is a big change from the founding era, when most of the rules followed by businesses, individuals, and governmental officials were judge-made rules, namely, the "common law." Over time, statutes and agency regulations have displaced the common law. Since World War II, statutes have swept the field of applicable law.

Not only are statutes America's main source of law, but they are battlegrounds for our most serious values. Thus, family values find their legal foundation in statutory rules enforcing or rewarding marital commitments and parental duties to their children. Education codes are loaded with public goals and lessons schools should inculcate in our youth. Our collective disgust is most often expressed in criminal statutes. Legislation and agency implementing rules ensure cleaner air and water, protect biodiversity, and require companies to clean up their waste. Even the equality norm, traditionally associated with the Constitution, is increasingly implemented through anti-discrimination super-statutes. Workplace equality for older persons, people with disabilities, and lesbian and gay persons receives little constitutional protection but is strongly protected by federal and state statutes.[1]

No one questions the central role that statutes play in our polity and our culture—but there is a lot of dispute over the way those statutes ought to be interpreted. I'd like to start with a high-profile battle of books authored by two Supreme Court Justices, offering what appear to be competing theories of statutory interpretation. As we shall see, the debate between "textualism" and "purposivism" is both a contrived debate and an incomplete one. The best way to think about statutory interpretation is not to focus on a single foundational rule, but is instead to consider a variety of sources, each having a different valence dependent upon the particular statutory text, structure, and history. The complexity of statutory analysis is reflected in the much-criticized "canons of statutory construction."

Before turning to discussion of the debate and the canons, let me set the stage for the (hypothetical) statute that will be the playground for our exploration of American statutory interpretation. Once part of the White House grounds, Lafayette Square (so named in 1824) is several acres of beautifully landscaped park along "H" Street, between Fifteenth and Seventeenth Streets in Northwest Washington, D.C. At the center of Lafayette Park, as it is known today, is an equestrian statue of President Andrew Jackson, which is the centerpiece of the illustration at the beginning of this introduction. The Marquis Gilbert de Lafayette and three other European-born Revolutionary War heroes adorn the four corners of the park. This is a major tourist attraction, as it is right across the street from the White House. Assume that Congress in 1992 adopts a statute providing that "[n]o vehicles will be allowed in Lafayette

---

[1] William N. Eskridge Jr. & John Ferejohn, *A Republic of Statutes: The New American Constitution* (2010); Ernest A. Young, *The Constitution Outside the Constitution*, 117 Yale L.J. 408 (2007).

Park." Does this statute prohibit kids from riding their bicycles through the park?[2]

Textualism vs. Purposivism

The Supreme Court's rule of law conscience for more than a quarter century, the late Justice Antonin Scalia maintained that the alpha and the omega of statutory interpretation is the enacted text of the statute. "The meaning of terms on the statute books ought to be determined, not on the basis of which meaning can be shown to have been understood by a larger handful of the Members of Congress; but rather on the basis of which meaning is (1) most in accord with context and ordinary usage * * * and (2) most compatible with the surrounding body of law into which the provision must be integrated."[3] Judges applying statutes should ignore legislative deliberations and other context extrinsic to the enacted legal text. Appealing directly to *rule of law values* in our polity, Justice Scalia claimed that his "new textualism" makes statutory interpretation more predictable and constrains judicial discretion better than other approaches, including the eclectic approach long followed by his predecessors and colleagues on the Supreme Court of the United States.[4]

In his recent book *Reading Law* (2012), Justice Scalia teamed up with linguist Bryan Garner to endorse fifty-seven textualist canons of statutory interpretation that will help judges and lawyers follow the foregoing approach, thereby delivering on the promise that textualism is the only methodology that can ensure predictability and objectivity to the application of laws to facts. The authors address a much-discussed hypothetical law: "No *vehicles* shall be allowed in the

---

[2] The vehicles in the park hypothetical is inspired by the classic articulation in H.L.A. Hart, *The Concept of Law* 126–29 (1961); H.L.A. Hart, *Positivism and the Separation of Law and Morals*, 71 Harv. L. Rev. 593, 607–11 (1958); see generally Frederick Schauer, *A Critical Guide to Vehicles in the Park*, 83 N.Y.U. L. Rev. 1109 (2008) (situating the vehicles in the park hypothetical within the jurisprudential debate between Hart and Fuller). For an exploration of a hypothetical "no animals in the park" law, see Robert E. Keeton, *Statutory Analogy, Purpose, and Policy in Legal Reasoning: Live Lobsters and a Tiger Cub in the Park*, 52 Md. L. Rev. 1192 (1993).

[3] *Green v. Bock Laundry Mach. Co.*, 490 U.S. 504, 528 (1989) (Scalia, J., concurring in the judgment).

[4] *Chisom v. Roemer*, 501 U.S. 380, 404 (1991) (Scalia, J., dissenting); Antonin Scalia, *A Matter of Interpretation* (1997); Antonin Scalia & John F. Manning, *A Dialogue on Statutory and Constitutional Interpretation*, 80 Geo. Wash. L. Rev. 1610, 1617–18 (2012). See generally William N. Eskridge Jr., *The New Textualism*, 37 U.C.L.A. L. Rev. 621 (1990); John F. Manning, *Textualism as a Nondelegation Doctrine*, 97 Colum L Rev 673, 728 (1997).

park." Does such a statute prohibit bicycles? Scalia and Garner work their way through a variety of dictionary definitions of "vehicle" and contemplate how that term is used in ordinary parlance. Perform this exercise for yourself: As a matter of ordinary language, does this law apply to bicycles? If simple textualism creates a more predictable rule of law, you ought to be able to figure this out easily—and your answer ought to match the one reached by Scalia and Garner. Jot down your answer in the margin (or, if this is not your book, on a scrap of paper).

Now consider the conclusion reached by the distinguished jurist and the learned linguist: "The proper colloquial meaning [of 'vehicle'] in our view (not all of them are to be found in dictionaries) is simply a *sizable* wheeled conveyance (as opposed to one of any size that is motorized)." According to Justice Scalia and Professor Garner, the scrupulous textualist would have to apply the statutory prohibition to automobiles, golf carts, and mopeds—but can safely assume that the vehicles in the park law cannot apply to "airplanes, bicycles, roller skates, and toy automobiles."[5] Is this the answer you derived from the statutory language? Is this a predicable application of dictionaries, ordinary parlance, and grammar to this rather simple statutory problem? Does a simple textualist methodology always deliver the predictability its authors promise? Many scholars are dubious.[6]

One reason that the Scalia and Garner exercise may not generate a predictable rule of law is that their analysis does not seem to consider the broader statutory context for the vehicles in the park law. For example, if the law were a federal statute regulating activity in Lafayette Park (pictured and described above), the thorough textualist would be well-advised to consult the Dictionary Act of 1947, which provides a definition that applies everywhere in the U.S. Code: "The word 'vehicle' includes every description of carriage or other artificial contrivance used, or capable of being used, as a means of transportation on land."[7] As we shall see below, most state codes have almost as capacious a definition of "vehicle." Why is this not relevant

---

[5] Antonin Scalia & Bryan A. Garner, *Reading Law: The Interpretation of Legal Texts* 37–38 (2012) (both quotations in text).

[6] William N. Eskridge Jr., Book Note, *The New Textualism and Normative Canons*, 113 Colum. L. Rev. 531 (2013); Joseph Kimble, *The Rule of the Last Antecedent, the Example in* Barnhart, *Why Both Are Weak, and How Textualism Postures*, 16 Scribes J. Leg. Writing 5–43 (2015); Richard A. Posner, *The Incoherence of Antonin Scalia*, The New Republic, Aug. 28, 2012.

[7] Dictionary Act of July 30, 1947, ch. 388, § 4, 61 Stat. 633, codified at 1 U.S.C. § 4 (defining land "vehicles" for purposes of the U.S. Code); cf. id. § 3 (defining water "vehicles").

context for a textualist approach? If so, does it not suggest the possibility that bicycles are "vehicles"?

More important, before a textualist analysis settles on the ordinary meaning of "vehicle," it ought to consider the background and purpose of the statute, considerations that typically clarify the issues and often solve the statutory puzzle. For example, if Congress adopted this precise vehicles in the park law in order to make Lafayette Park safer for elderly persons and small children—the most likely reason—then Scalia and Garner seem too quick to say that the statute cannot cover bicycles, as a matter of ordinary meaning. If I told you that bicyclists and skateboarders had been causing accidents in the park and that the legislature responded with a "no vehicles" ordinance to reduce accidents, you would assume, as a matter of ordinary meaning, that the "vehicles" covered by the ordinance include bicycles and skateboards. Likewise, if the relevant congressional committee reports described the Lafayette Park statute as responsive to a series of accidents in which bicyclists and skateboarders had run into children and knocked over elderly visitors, the rule of law is not well-served by an abstract textualist approach that reads bicycles and skateboards out of the statute. At least in some circumstances, the predictable rule of law may be undermined, rather than advanced, by a context-denying stance asserting that bicycles are simply not "vehicles" subject to a law banning vehicles from the park.[8]

Justice Stephen Breyer adds another concern about the new textualism's inattention to legislative and policy context. He worries that "an overemphasis on text can lead courts astray, divorcing law from life—indeed, creating law that harms those whom Congress meant to help."[9] Thus, he argues, the judge in the case of the bicycle in the park ought to interpret "vehicle" in light of the statutory purpose. His approach is responsive to rule of law concerns, in some cases more so than Justice Scalia's approach. One hundred judges given the statutory text *and* the committee reports might be more likely to deliver the same interpretation than one hundred judges given just the statutory text. More important, Justice Breyer believes that his approach is more *legitimate,* because it is more consistent

---

[8] Lon L. Fuller, *Positivism and Fidelity to Law—A Reply to Professor Hart*, 71 Harv. L. Rev. 630, 661–69 (1958); accord, Abbe R. Gluck & Lisa Schultz Bressman, *Statutory Interpretation from the Inside—An Empirical Study of Congressional Drafting, Delegation and the Canons: Part I,* 65 Stan. L. Rev. 901 (2013).

[9] Stephen Breyer, *Active Liberty: Interpreting Our Democratic Constitution* 85 (2006).

with our nation's democratic premises. "Legislation in a delegated democracy is meant to embody the people's will," either directly or indirectly. Thus, "the interpretation of a statute that tends to implement the legislator's will helps to implement the public's will and is therefore consistent with the Constitution's democratic purpose."[10]

Because democratically elected and accountable legislators deliberate about how to address social and economic problems and enact statutes to solve those problems, Justice Breyer maintains that the process of interpretation should be informed and driven by study of the discussions, purposes, and other context within which the legislature acted—apparently evidence of "the legislator's will" and therefore "the people's will." Thus, judges interpreting the vehicles in the park law should ask how a "reasonable member of Congress" would have wanted judges to apply the statute to particular facts, in light of the "language, structure, and general objectives" adopted by Congress.[11] Although Breyer does not challenge the primacy of statutory text, he insists that a fair reading of statutory text consider the underlying legislative expectations and problem-solving purposes.[12]

Purposive readings of statutory text seem to be a sounder approach to the bicycle case: Interpret "vehicle" in light of the deliberations that produced the statute and the purpose it was expected to advance. In everyday, ordinary parlance, it is certainly possible to refer to a bicycle as a vehicle, and if the purpose of the statute is public safety, it makes sense of the legislators' goal to say that bicycles might be "vehicles" excluded from Lafayette Park. Especially if bicycle accidents were a specific occasion for the public demand for the statute, the fair reading of the statutory text is that

---

[10] Id. at 99 (both quotations in text); accord, William W. Buzbee, *The One Congress Fiction in Statutory Interpretation*, 149 U. Pa. L. Rev. 171, 180–203 (2000); Daniel A. Farber, *Statutory Interpretation and Legislative Supremacy*, 78 Geo. L.J. 281 (1989). For examples of Breyer's critique in particular cases, see, e.g., *Utility Air Regulatory Group v. EPA*, 134 S.Ct. 2427, 2452–53 (2014) (Breyer, J., concurring in part and dissenting in part); *Arlington Cent. Sch. Dist. Bd. of Educ. v. Murphy*, 548 U.S. 291, 308–16, 323–24 (2006) (Breyer, J., dissenting).

[11] Breyer, *Active Liberty*, 88 (quotation in text); Stephen Breyer, *Making Our Democracy Work: A Judge's View* 94–96 (2010); accord, Robert A. Katzmann, *Judging Statutes* (2014). Justice Breyer's approach is, for the most part, an update of the purpose-oriented approach classically developed in Henry M. Hart Jr. & Albert M. Sacks, *The Legal Process: Basic Problems in the Making and Application of Law* (William N. Eskridge Jr. & Philip P. Frickey eds., 1994) (tent. ed. 1958).

[12] Compare Commencement Address of Justice David Souter, Harvard University, May 27, 2010 (offering a "fair reading" approach to legal interpretation).

the statute covers bicycles—precisely the opposite result from that suggested by Justice Scalia and Professor Garner. Because a purposive approach to statutes is responsive to both rule of law and democracy values, most academics and many judges prefer this kind of theory.[13]

But the diligent interpreter will not resolve all of the "hard cases" through Justice Breyer's approach, which is in tension with both rule of law and democracy values if applied simplistically. Recall that Justice Breyer seeks to carry out the "people's will" and implement the "legislator's will" or purpose. Rhetorically, this language ties Breyer's purposivist approach tightly to democratic legitimacy, but this is a rhetorical coup resting upon assumptions about voters and their legislators that are not obviously correct. Do We the People have a "will" regarding a statutory policy, and does that will match up with the "legislator's will"? Apart from the mystical metaphysics of these metaphors, they suffer from an ill fit with the constitutional lawmaking process, which does not rest statutory policy upon the "will" of either the people or particular legislators. Article I, Section 7 of the Constitution says that Congress expresses its collective "will" when the House and the Senate vote for the identical statutory text, which is then presented to the President and signed into law. To be sure, when Justice Breyer talks about the "will" of Congress, he is probably referring to committee reports and speeches by legislative floor managers—but he does not explain why these subgroups and individuals reflect a collective "will," or how the congressional "will" represents the "people's will."[14]

If the "public will" is rather murky, perhaps legislative "purpose" may be more useful. After all, we presume legislation to be purposeful activity, and so it may seem natural to supposed that statutes have

---

[13] E.g., Aharon Barak, *Interpretation in Law* 85–86, 340–41 (2006); Kent Greenawalt, *Statutory and Common Law Interpretation* (2012); Katzmann, *Judging Statutes*; Richard A. Posner, *The Problematics of Moral and Legal Theory* 208–10, 257–58 (1999); T. Alexander Aleinikoff, *Updating Statutory Interpretation*, 87 Mich. L. Rev. 20, 26–27 (1988); Lawrence Lessig, *Understanding Changed Readings: Fidelity and Theory*, 47 Stan L Rev 395, 407–08 (1995); Daniel B. Rodriguez & Barry R. Weingast, *The Positive Political Theory of Legislative History: New Perspectives on the 1964 Civil Rights Act and Its Interpretation*, 151 U. Pa. L. Rev. 1417 (2003); Cass R. Sunstein, *Interpreting Statutes in the Regulatory State*, 103 Harv. L. Rev. 405 (1989).

[14] Jeremy Waldron, *Law and Disagreement* (1999); Max Radin, *Legislative Intent*, 43 Harv. L. Rev. 863 (1930). For a sophisticated and insightful approach to collective legislative "intent," see Victoria F. Nourse, *Elementary Statutory Interpretation: Rethinking Legislative Intent and History,* 55 B.C.L. Rev. 1613 (2014), drawing from Christian List & Philip Pettit, *Group Agency: The Possibility, Design, and Status of Corporate Agents* (2011).

purposes. Unfortunately, statutory purpose does not always resolve hard cases. The purpose that one might fairly attribute to Congress as a whole is often set at such a high level of generality that it could support a variety of interpretations. Moreover, statutes usually have more than one purpose, and often a constellation of purposes, cutting in different directions. Consider how these difficulties play out in the case of the bicycle in the park.[15]

Thus, the Senate sponsor of the vehicles in the park law might have pitched the bill on safety grounds: Speedy vehicles will often injure tourists visiting the park. But other senators might have announced their support for other reasons, such as aesthetic ones: Noisy, fume-generating vehicles disrupt the tranquility and family atmosphere desirable for the park's visitors. Some senators might have invoked security concerns: Because Lafayette Park is right in front of the White House, the park should not have vehicles of any sort. If the Senate votes for the bill, even if by a large margin, who is to say what the purpose is?[16] And whatever legislative purpose or expectations the Senate adopts has to be matched up with that of the House. Assume that the House sponsor only mentions the aesthetic purpose. As applied to bicycles, the House sponsor's purpose cuts in a different direction (exempting bicycles from regulation) from the Senate sponsor's purpose (the law targets bicycles). Which purpose represents the "intent" or "will" of Congress? Often, there is no neutral way to figure this out. Indeed, members of Congress might have agreed with *both* purposes, which would only deepen the difficulty purposivist theory encounters with the simple cases such as our bicycle hypothetical. While theoretically superior to a simple textualist approach, a purely purposivist approach may be more malleable and less predictable, in practice, than a purely textualist approach.[17]

---

[15] For balanced critiques of purposivism, see Richard A. Posner, *How Judges Think* 324–42 (2008); William N. Eskridge Jr. & Philip P. Frickey, *Legislation Scholarship and Pedagogy in the Post-Legal Process Era,* 48 U. Pitt. L. Rev. 691 (1987); Michael Herz, *Purposivism and Institutional Competence in Statutory Interpretation,* 2009 Mich. St. L. Rev. 89; *United States v. Pino-Perez,* 870 F.2d 1230, 1231–35 (7th Cir., en banc, 1989) (Posner, J).

[16] For a classic example of conflicting statements of purposes by different Senate sponsors, compare *United Steelworkers v. Weber,* 443 U.S. 193, 202–03 (1979) (Sen. Humphrey and other liberals, invoked by the majority opinion), with id. at 254 (Sen. Dirksen, a conservative co-sponsor of the final bill, invoked by the dissenters).

[17] Posner, *How Judges Think,* 80–81, 197–98, 253–54; John F. Manning, *What Divides Textualists from Purposivists?,* 106 Colum. L. Rev. 70 (2006); Damien M. Schiff, *Purposivism and the "Reasonable Legislator": A Review Essay of Justice Stephen Breyer's* Active Liberty, 33 Wm. Mitchell L. Rev. 1081 (2007).

The foregoing criticisms of a strict textualism or a popular purposivism do not suggest that either text or purpose is irrelevant to statutory interpretation. Indeed, *both* statutory text *and* legislative purpose are critically important to a proper application of statutes—and they naturally operate together and not as competing approaches. That is, statutory interpretation is the application of enacted texts to new and often unanticipated circumstances in light of the legislature's design and purposes. For a more detailed statute than the simple one I have presented thus far, the statutory purpose can best be understood or refined by study of the statutory structure as well as its legislative history. Text and purpose are like the two blades of a scissors; neither does the job without the operation of the other.[18]

More important, statutory text and legislative purpose do not exhaust the context that is relevant for the proper application of statutes. The operation of the rule of law depends, critically, on context that goes beyond and sometimes against the plain meaning precepts of textualism, and the democracy values hailed by purposivists may require something more than attention to legislative history. Indeed, there are other considerations that ought to inform responsible statutory interpretation.

To take the most obvious example, the rule of law requires the judge to consider practice and precedent before she confidently declares statutory meaning. If the Supreme Court has already applied the vehicles in the park law to bicycles, then the Court's statutory precedent is binding unless it is overruled, a super-high hurdle. Thus, however he views the ordinary meaning of vehicle in the abstract, the strict textualist would—and should—follow a binding precedent holding that bicycles are vehicles for purposes of this law, and might even follow such a precedent interpreting a similar statute. Likewise, even if she were persuaded that the legislative purpose of the law were park safety and that bicycles are big threats to safety, the purposive jurist would—and should—follow a binding precedent holding that bicycles are *not* vehicles for purposes of this law, and might even follow such a precedent

---

[18] E.g., *Ransom v. FIA Card Servs., N.A.*, 562 U.S. 61 (2011) (starting opinion with statutory purpose, analyzing text, and confirming ordinary meaning by reference back to purpose); *Carr v. United States*, 560 U.S. 438, 444–48, 450–58 (2010) (similar); William N. Eskridge Jr., *Dynamic Statutory Interpretation* ch. 1 (1994); Posner, *How Judges Think*, 253–54. The scissors metaphor is inspired by L.L. Fuller, *American Legal Realism*, 82 U. Pa. L. Rev. 429, 452–61 (1934) (suggesting that Law and Society are like two blades of a scissors).

interpreting a similar statute. Rather than an afterthought, as it is treated in almost all the textualist and purposivist theories, *stare decisis* is central to statutory interpretation, largely because it strongly serves the rule of law values of predictability, generality, and coherence in the ongoing application of statutes. Less obviously, a court's respect for its own precedents may serve democratic accountability in at least one way: It vests the legislature with responsibility for correcting erroneous or outdated statutory decisions.[19]

Even when there is no judicial precedent on point, there will typically be administrative practice that is relevant to the statutory issue. Few issues reach the U.S. Supreme Court or state supreme courts that do not carry with them years of administrative experience. If Congress enacted the vehicles in the park law as a safety measure fifty years ago and the police had never applied the law to bicycles, does that administrative practice have bearing on the proper interpretation of the statute? Even if a purposivist judge believed that the law was enacted for safety reasons and that bicycles are safety hazards, she would—and should—be reluctant to apply the law to a bike rider after fifty years of administrative practice to the contrary, especially if the allowance for bicycles had not led to serious accidents. Conversely, if the police and prosecutors had been applying the vehicles in the park law to bicycles for the last fifty years and offered their experience that bicycles in the park would lead to injuries and trouble, a textualist judge would not—and should not—be so certain that "vehicle" has a plain meaning that excludes bicycles. Indeed, two generations of administrative application would suggest a stable rule of law regime that the textualist ought not disrupt—just as two generations of administrative nonapplication would suggest to a purposivist that the statutory safety goal is not necessarily served by barring bicycles from the park.

No satisfactory theory of statutory interpretation can ignore statutory precedents or administrative practice. Although their general theories give these sources short shift, the judicial opinions of Justices Scalia and Breyer over the decades devoted many more

---

[19] *Michigan v. Bay Mills Indian Community*, 134 S.Ct. 2024, 2037, 2040 (2014) (majority and concurring opinions); Edward Levi, *An Introduction to Legal Reasoning*, 15 U. Chi. L. Rev. 501, 540 (1948); William N. Eskridge Jr., *Overruling Statutory Precedents*, 76 Geo. L.J. 1361 (1990). Although neither has emphasized the role of precedent front and center nor explained how precedent plays into their respective theories, Justices Scalia and Breyer have both endorsed *stare decisis*. Breyer, *Making Our Democracy Work*, 149–56; Scalia & Garner, *Reading Law*, 42–43.

pages of analysis to precedent and practice than to plain meaning and purpose (respectively). To this complexity, consider a third, and very important, value critical to any complete theory of statutory interpretation: the practical purpose of law to provide effective governance for a socially diverse and institutionally complex society.[20] Before exploring this third normative foundation of statutory interpretation, let us consider the relevance of the canons of statutory construction, a vast array of presumptions, precepts, principles, clear statement rules, and background norms that courts apply to interpret statutes.

Canons of Statutory Construction

Most statutory opinions by state and federal judges, as well as many academic theories of statutory interpretation, situate judges as neutral interpreters, hewing carefully to textual plain meanings or legislative purposes (depending on your favored theory) and making no substantive or strategic judgments when they apply statutory text to concrete controversies adjudicated in court. One popular metaphor is that judges in statutory cases are nothing more than the "honest" or "faithful" agents of the legislature.[21] Another popular metaphor is that the judge is the neutral umpire who just calls balls and strikes. These metaphors reflect a partial understanding of the enterprise. Consistent with rule of law aspirations, judges ought to be neutral and ought to follow an objectively determinable method. Consistent with our representative democracy, judges ought to be faithful agents of the legislative plan. But judges are not just umpires or faithful agents—they are partners in governance and are fiduciaries of We the People. To the extent they are agents of the legislature, judges are "relational agents," charged with applying a statutory scheme dynamically over time.[22] And appellate judges, in particular, do a lot more than call balls and strikes—they also mold and sometimes adjust the strike zone, as well as structure the duties of the umpire

---

[20] Eskridge, *Dynamic Statutory Interpretation*, ch. 6; Posner, *Problematics of Legal Theory*, 256–57.

[21] Frank H. Easterbrook, *The Supreme Court, 1983 Term—Foreword: The Court and the Economic System,* 98 Harv. L. Rev. 4, 60 (1984); accord, Daniel A. Farber, *Statutory Interpretation and Legislative Supremacy,* 78 Geo. L.J. 281 (1989); John F. Manning, *Textualism and the Equity of the Statute,* 101 Colum. L. Rev. 1 (2001).

[22] William N. Eskridge Jr., *Spinning Legislative Supremacy,* 78 Geo. L.J. 319 (1988), responding to Farber, *Statutory Interpretation and Legislative Supremacy.*

who does call the balls and strikes.[23] These expanded metaphors suggest the two faces of governance. Substantively, courts play a role in the evolution of statutory directives. Procedurally, courts play a more important role in assuming, assigning, or arbitrating institutional responsibilities.

This is a striking claim, one to which not all judges would openly confess. But the canonical practice of federal as well as state courts suggests its accuracy. An appendix to this volume lists the federal canons of statutory interpretation that have been applied in the last thirty years by the Rehnquist and Roberts Courts, whose Chief Justices celebrate their umpireal role and often deny any other role for judges. As the appendix reveals, there are a few dozen textualist canons that provide guidance for a judge to interpret the ordinary meaning of statutory text, as illuminated by the statutory scheme and the larger code of laws into which the text is embedded. And there are a number of canons that relate to statutory purpose and legislative intent. But the textualist and purpose/intent canons in the appendix are dwarfed in sheer numbers by governance canons that the U.S. Supreme Court openly and repeatedly invokes. Governance canons include those that apportion institutional responsibilities, where the Court sets forth the duties of umpires (courts) and other players (agencies and legislators) in the ongoing elaboration of statutory schemes.[24]

Most of the governance canons, however, are substantive canons—common law traditions, statutory policy norms, constitutional principles, and international law doctrines that fill the gaps or resolve the ambiguities left by Congress when it creates statutes.[25] As Amy Coney Barrett has demonstrated, the dozens of substantive canons negate the claims of both textualist and

---

[23] Posner, *How Judges Think*, 369–72. For a thoughtful counter-statement regarding American legal traditions and the practice of judges, see Jeffrey S. Sutton, *A Review of Richard A. Posner*, How Judges Think, 108 Mich. L. Rev. 859 (2010).

[24] On institutional competence and context in statutory interpretation, see Hart & Sacks, *The Legal Process* (Eskridge & Frickey eds.); Henry M. Hart Jr. & Herbert Wechsler, *The Federal Courts and the Federal System* (1953) (updated through seven editions as of 2016), as well as William N. Eskridge Jr. & Philip P. Frickey, *Cases and Materials on Legislation: Statutes and the Creation of Public Policy* (1988) (updated through five editions as of 2016).

[25] On normative context in statutory interpretation, see *Michigan v. Bay Mills Indian Community*, 134 S.Ct. 2024, 2040 (2014) (Sotomayor, J., concurring); William N. Eskridge Jr., *Public Values in Statutory Interpretation*, 137 U. Pa. L. Rev. 1007 (1989); Francis Mootz III, *Ugly American Hermeneutics*, 10 Nev. L.J. 587 (2010); Cass R. Sunstein, *Interpreting the Regulatory State*, 103 Harv. L. Rev. 405 (1989).

purposivist judges that they are nothing more than the faithful agents of legislatures or umpires calling balls and strikes.[26] In 1997, Justice Scalia agreed with Professor Barrett: "To the honest textualist, all of these preferential rules and presumptions are a lot of trouble," and "increase the unpredictability, if not arbitrariness of judicial decisions."[27] Yet Justice Scalia joined or authored hundreds of opinions for the Court that centrally relied on these "preferential rules and presumptions" and signed on to virtually all of the substantive canons in the appendix.

Especially as reflected in these substantive canons, the governance norm is deeply influenced by the ongoing project of assuring the legitimacy of law, which entails not only the willingness of citizens to follow it (or not openly disobey it), but also encourages citizens to cooperate actively in the great projects of the law. Our nation's traditions and commitments influence statutory interpretation both generally and in particular cases. In the application of law to particular facts and to the lives of human beings, the law is concerned with fairness, justice, and a wide array of other values. At the more general level, namely, judicial treatment of broad categories of statutes, the law is concerned with systemic principles and policies that have been considered legitimate and desirable for much of our history. Somewhere in between the general and the particular is the fact that each area of law operates in a normative context of principles and policies distinctive to that area of law.[28]

For governance-based reasons, it would be significant if the vehicles in the park law were a criminal statute (a matter left elliptical in my report of the law's brief language). That a citizen violating the statute would be subject to social censure and punitive sanctions affects the interpretive process. As I shall explore in more detail in chapter six, if the no-vehicles rule were a crime, judges would and should be stingier in their application of the term "vehicle." Why? Substantively, more is at stake, especially if the rule-violator might go to jail. Institutionally, stingy interpretations rein in much-feared prosecutorial discretion and, more important, prod the legislature (the only appropriate forum for creating new criminal

---

[26] Amy Coney Barrett, *Substantive Canons and Faithful Agency*, 90 B.U.L. Rev. 109, 138–43 (2010).

[27] Antonin Scalia, *A Matter of Interpretation* 28 (1997). Canons such as the rule of lenity are given a pass, due to their "sheer antiquity," Scalia says. Id. at 29.

[28] Jonathan R. Siegel, *Textualism and Contextualism in Administrative Law,* 78 B.U.L. Rev. 1023 (1998), and *Guardians of the Background Principles,* 2009 Mich. St. L. Rev. 123.

prohibitions) to take responsibility for expanding or revising the statute. Philosophically, the legitimacy of law depends upon a judicious application of criminal sanctions; if they are too aggressively deployed, the law loses some of its credibility. For example, if the criminal law were so aggressive as to turn onto productive, cooperative citizens (and not just those who harm their neighbors), such a legal regime would not only be wasteful and unjust, but it would undermine the rule of law and the viability of our pluralist democracy.

Constitutional concerns also motivate a narrow reading of "vehicle" in a criminal version of the Lafayette Park law. The Due Process Clause requires that citizens have adequate notice of what actions are subject to criminal sanctions. Even if a bicycle is often considered a vehicle and even if bicycles may be safety hazards in parks, judges will tend to confine the terms of criminal statutes to their core, prototypical meanings, perhaps from an excess of caution. If you told them that a criminal statute bars "vehicles" from the park, a lot of kids and their parents would not be aware that such a bar includes bicycles. Without researching the matter thoroughly, the thirteen-year-old bike rider would very likely think that automobiles, motorcycles, and maybe mopeds were subject to the vehicular ban. Many minors and their parents would be shocked to learn that bicycles fall within the offense. And how about the six year-old riding her tricycle? Would a parent think twice about whether a no-vehicles rule sweeps up his kid?

Other constitutional values are relevant to the construction of criminal statutes. Thus, constitutional separation of powers bars judges from creating "common law crimes." (Common law regimes are those where judges make the specific rules through case-by-case adjudication.) Article I, Section 1 of the Constitution vests Congress with all the "legislative" powers; Article III vests federal judges with "judicial" power only. One legislative power is the authority to specify certain conduct as criminal; because criminal penalties reflect social opprobrium and often impose liberty as well as monetary penalties, Congress, as the organ most broadly accountable to We the People in all Our Variety, is particularly responsible for making the rules of criminal law. Hence, federal judges would violate Article I if they recognized criminal behaviors without a statutory basis. The same precept also entails a constitutional aversion to judicial case-by-case adjudication that reads generally phrased criminal laws with ever-expanding capacity. Thus, judges are careful not to read vague terms (like "vehicle") more broadly than legislators have directed, through the statutory structure or their own deliberations, lest they create criminal liability common-law style, without the democratic sanction of the legislative process.[29]

Finally, the larger normative context of society pervasively influences the application of statutory text to particular circumstances (a process that often operates subconsciously). An example is the *absurdity canon*, discussed in chapter one: Judges will not apply the literal reading of a statutory text when it would be "absurd" to do so. Thus, archtextualist Justice Scalia not only embraced the anti-absurdity feature of ordinary meaning, but filled his opinions and (especially) his dissents with normative evaluation sounding the alarm of absurdity and outrage.[30] Assume the vehicles in the park law mobilizes only civil sanctions and includes a broad definition of "vehicle" to mean "any mechanism for conveying a person from one place to another." Does the law bar baby carriages from the park? Almost no one would apply the statute to bar baby carriages. Why not?

Although such contraptions might fall under the literal terms of the statute, judges would fall over one another finding reasons to exempt them from the statutory definition. Some judges would say that baby carriages do not fall under the ordinary meaning of the law; others would say that they do not pose the safety problems that bicycles and motor vehicles do; yet others would say that they are beyond the intent of the legislators. Most judges would say that applying the law to baby carriages would be reading the statute "literally" (rather than "reasonably"). All of these arguments have merit, yet none of these arguments completely explains why virtually all judges would rule that baby carriages are not regulated vehicles. No explanation would be complete without an understanding of the value-based concerns with such a rule. Not only do baby carriages seem like a far cry from the prototypical vehicles the statute targets, but they also symbolize the family values Americans claim to cherish, and they fit snugly into the whole purpose of a park.

---

[29] *United States v. Wiltberger*, 18 U.S. 76, 92 (1820) (Marshall, C.J.) (leading case); Daniel M. Kahan, *Lenity and Federal Common Law Crimes*, 1994 Sup. Ct. Rev. 345.

[30] On Justice Scalia's tendency to read text in light of his normative commitments, see *Brown v. Plata*, 131 S.Ct. 1910, 1950–51 (2011) (Scalia, J., dissenting); Miranda Oshige McGowan, *Do as I Do, Not as I Say: An Empirical Investigation of Justice Scalia's Ordinary Meaning Method of Statutory Interpretation*, 78 Miss. L.J. 129 (2008); Jane S. Schacter, *Text or Consequences?*, 76 Brooklyn L. Rev. 1007 (2011). For a textualist objection to the absurdity canon, see John F. Manning, *The Absurdity Doctrine*, 116 Harv. L. Rev. 2387 (2003).

There is a larger point to be made about the role of substantive evaluation in statutory interpretation. How one reads words, how one understands the statutory purpose(s), or how one applies statutory or regulatory precedents is not completely independent of how one understands and evaluates the factual context to which the statute is being applied. This is a point that many judges are loathe to admit, because it is a concession that statutory interpretation is not simply a mechanical application of preexisting rules to cases and controversies. Yet that is what statutory interpretation amounts to in the hard cases that are the best learning experiences. And the reason the Constitution vests federal judges with life tenure is so that they can exercise *judgment* of the sort I am suggesting for the case of the baby carriage.[31]

The role of norms in judicial decisionmaking does not mean that statutory interpretation is unconstrained judicial legislation. Judges are constrained by the proper sources of guidance, and an important purpose of this volume is to lay out and illustrate the variety of considerations outside pure political preferences that guide and constrain judges when they apply statutes to factual circumstances that are often unanticipated by the enacting legislators. Before embarking on this ambitious project, I should explain that I understand the traditional sources of guidance—the so-called "canons of statutory interpretation"—differently from many other theorists.

Some judges and scholars view the canons as strong rules and presumptions that, if followed religiously, would ensure predictability, neutrality, objectivity, and transparency in statutory interpretation. Justice Scalia and Professor Garner take this position in *Reading Law*. Following the fifty-seven canons that they identify (and avoiding legislative history that they denounce) "will curb—even reverse—the tendency of judges to imbue authoritative texts with their own policy preferences" and "will provide greater certainty in the law, and hence greater predictability and greater respect for the rule of law."[32] Unfortunately, this strong stance rests upon

---

[31] *The Federalist* No. 78 (Hamilton) (defending life tenure for federal judges on the ground that it assures them independence from normal politics and frees them up to exercise "judgment" [not "will"], such as a judgment "mitigating" the effect of "partial and unjust" laws); Posner, *How Judges Think*, 259–60, 369; Commencement Address by Justice David Souter, Harvard University, May 27, 2010 (importance of reasoned judgment, rather than mechanical rules, in judicial interpretation of the Constitution).

[32] Scalia & Garner, *Reading Law*, xxvii–xxix. Nineteenth century Anglo-American treatises took this position as well. E.g., Joel Prentiss Bishop, *Commentaries on the Written Laws and Their Interpretation* § 2, at 3 (1882).

improbable assumptions about judges and no statistical or systematic evidence that it can deliver on its ambitious promise of greater determinacy and predictability. Indeed, evidence from several fields of law suggests that a stringent canons-based textualism generates *less* certainty in the law and constrains judges *less* reliably than more context-based approaches to interpretation.[33]

Other theorists focus on legislative expectations, suggesting that at least some of the canons "reflect the probabilities generated by normal usage or legislative behavior. These represent either * * * judgments of how legislatures tend to use language and its syntactical patterns, or descriptions of how legislatures tend to behave. They serve as useful presumptions of supposed actual legislative intent and are, therefore, modestly useful in carrying [out] legislative meaning."[34] Einer Elhuage has advanced this faithful agent approach to cover not only canons that reflect likely legislative preferences, but also those designed to induce legislators to reveal their preferences by passing override legislation.[35] Like the rule of law justification, this democracy-based justification sounds persuasive in the abstract, but founders in the light of real experience and data. Until recently, no one had bothered to survey legislative conventions and practices to check the accuracy of these

---

[33] E.g., James J. Brudney & Corey Ditslear, *Liberal Justices' Reliance on Legislative History: Principle, Strategy, and the Scalia Effect*, 29 Berkeley J. Emp. & Lab. L. 117, 121 (2008) (empirical analysis of Supreme Court labor cases, demonstrating that textualism is less constraining than an approach that also considers legislative history); Catherine L. Fisk, *The Last Article about the Language of ERISA Preemption? A Case Study of the Failure of Textualism*, 33 Harv. J. Legis. 35 (1996) (pension law); Deborah A. Geier, *Commentary: Textualism and Tax Cases*, 66 Temp. L. Rev. 445 (1993) (tax law); Bradford C. Mank, *Is a Textualist Approach to Statutory Interpretation Pro-Environmentalist? Why Pragmatic Agency Decisionmaking Is Better than Judicial Literalism*, 53 Wash. & Lee L. Rev. 1231 (1996) (environmental law); C. Robert Morris, *Bankrupt Fantasy: The Site of Missing Words and the Order of Illusory Events*, 45 Ark. L. Rev. 265 (1992) (bankruptcy law); James P. Nehf, *Textualism in the Lower Courts: Lessons from Judges Interpreting Consumer Legislation*, 26 Rutgers L.J. 1 (1994) (consumer law); Richard J. Pierce, Jr., *The Supreme Court's New Hypertextualism: An Invitation to Cacophony and Incoherence in the Administrative State*, 95 Colum. L. Rev. 749 (1995) (administrative law).

[34] Reed Dickerson, *The Interpretation and Application of Statutes* 228 (1976); accord, *McNary v. Haitian Refugee Center*, 498 U.S. 479, 496 (1991) (presuming that "Congress legislates with knowledge of our basic rules of statutory construction"); Einer Elhauge, *Preference-Estimating Statutory Default Rules*, 102 Colum. L. Rev. 2027 (2002) (assuming that many canons are rough reflections of probable congressional preferences).

[35] Einer Elhauge, *Statutory Default Rules: How to Interpret Unclear Legislation* (2008) (proposing that most of the canons are "preference-estimating" reflections of probable congressional preferences *or* are "preference-inducing" baselines that will stimulate legislators to reveal their current preferences through override legislation).

presumptions. Scholars are now testing these judgments empirically and are reporting that many of the canons do *not* reflect legislative expectations and/or practice.[36] The current volume will augment these studies (which have focused on congressional drafting) with a systematic examination of state legislative drafting manuals and statutory codifications of canons (the latter drawing from Jacob Scott's important survey).[37] Most of the ordinary meaning, whole act, purpose, legislative history, and agency deference canons reflect the aspirations of the legislative drafting process—but few of the whole code, *stare decisis*, or substantive canons reflect aspirations of state or federal legislative drafting offices and personnel.

A third group of scholars emphasize the governance features of the canons. The late Phil Frickey and I understood many of the substantive canons as judicial efforts to give vitality to underenforced constitutional norms such as nondelegation, federalism, and even some individual rights.[38] Pressing further along these lines, Cass Sunstein has argued that judges ought to create a wide range of substantive canons designed to offset what law professors consider dysfunctions in the political process.[39] Governance theories such as these do not pretend to explain the textual and institutional canons, and so they are by definition incomplete theories. Professor Sunstein's theory, for example, has languished because judges do not consider themselves competent to identify substantive dysfunctions in the political process, and law professors have not revealed sufficient

---

[36] Empirical studies of legislative drafting and the canons suggest highly uneven knowledge. Compare Gluck & Bressman, *Statutory Interpretation from the Inside: Part I*, 65 Stan. L. Rev. at 926–28, 949, 1016 (summarizing the authors' findings that few of the canons reliably guide congressional drafting), with Jarrod Shobe, *Intertemporal Statutory Interpretation and the Evolution of Legislative Drafting,* 114 Colum. L. Rev. 807 (2014) (suggesting that the canons have somewhat greater influence).

[37] For a state-by-state survey of legislatively codified canons, see Jacob Scott, *Codified Canons and the Common Law of Interpretation*, 98 Geo. L.J. 341 (2010). I shall augment Scott's useful survey with my own examination of the legislative drafting manuals made available to the public by the U.S. House and Senate and by almost half of the state legislatures. The National Conference of State Legislatures provides web links to almost half of the state legislative drafting manuals, available at http://www.ncsl.org/legislators-staff/legislative-staff/legal-services/bill-drafting-manuals.aspx (viewed Jan. 1, 2016).

[38] William N. Eskridge Jr. & Philip P. Frickey, *Quasi-Constitutional Law: Clear Statement Rules as Constitutional Lawmaking*, 45 Vand. L. Rev. 593, 636–40 (1992); see also William N. Eskridge Jr. & Philip P. Frickey, *The Supreme Court, 1993 Term—Foreword: Law as Equilibrium*, 108 Harv. L. Rev. 26, 81–87 (1994).

[39] Sunstein, *Interpreting Statutes in the Regulatory State*, 103 Harv. L. Rev. at 506–08 (appendix listing proposed canons, most of which do not reflect judicial practice and many of which are directly contrary to federal judicial practice).

competence to establish both the existence of uncontroversial dysfunctions and the ability of canons to correct for them.

The foregoing theories find the canons potentially valuable—but it must be admitted that most law professors have embraced more cynical theories. That is, many scholars and judges view the canons as completely unconstraining—and therefore unhelpful to the rule of law, unfaithful to democratic decisionmaking, and a hindrance to effective governance. By their account, the canons are window-dressing for judicial opinions that pretend to be neutral application of law but that are actually creative applications of old law to unforeseen circumstances. As Karl Llewellyn famously put it, "the courts pretend that there has been only one single correct answer possible," and the vocabulary of "that foolish pretense" is the canons. Because "there are two opposing canons on almost every point," the canons are neither directive nor constraining, and judges appropriately consider their own sense of the situation (rather than the canons) when deciding cases.[40] Some scholars press Professor Llewellyn's point further, to denounce the canons as not only unconstraining but positively obfuscating or downright dishonest, deployed by ideological judges to smuggle their own partisan values into statutes.[41] Unlike the commentators who insist that the canons effectively constrain judges, these cynical commentators find some empirical support for their view that the canons are not inevitably constraining but have not demonstrated that the canons exercise no constraint whatsoever.[42] Indeed, there is preliminary empirical

---

[40] Karl Lewellyn, *Remarks on the Theory of Appellate Decision and the Rules or Canons About How Statutes Are to Be Construed,* 3 Vand. L. Rev. 395, 399, 401 (1950) (quotations in text); see id. at 401–05, famously arraying twenty-eight "canons" and their "counter canons" to demonstrate that almost any *conclusion* can be reached in hard statutory cases by application of widely accepted canons. See also Quentin Johnstone, *Evaluating the Rules of Statutory Interpretation*, 3 Kan. L. Rev. 1 (1954); Kimble, *The Rule of the Last Antecedent*; Stephen F. Ross, *Where Have You Gone Karl Llewellyn? Should Congress Turn Its Lonely Eyes to You?,* 45 Vand. L. Rev. 561 (1992); Edward L. Rubin, *Modern Canons, Loose Canons, and the Limits of Practical Reason: A Response to Farber and Ross*, 45 Vand. L. Rev. 579 (1992).

[41] Frank C. Newman & Stanley S. Surrey, *Legislation: Cases and Materials* 654 (1955); James J. Brudney, *Canon Shortfalls and the Virtues of Political Branch Interpretive Assets,* 98 Calif. L. Rev. 1199 (2010); Richard A. Posner, *Statutory Interpretation in the Classroom and in the Courtroom,* 50 U. Chi. L. Rev. 800 (1983).

[42] James J. Brudney & Corey Ditslear, *Canons of Construction and the Elusive Quest for Neutral Reasoning,* 58 Vand. L. Rev. 1 (2005).

evidence that canonical rule of law factors do play a role in judicial decisionmaking.[43]

A thesis of this volume is that the canons are *neither* mechanical rules that by their own force assure the rule of law or democratic accountability or good governance, *nor* cynical instruments for result-oriented judges to decorate judicial opinions like ornaments on a Christmas tree. Rather, the canons constitute an *interpretive regime*, namely, a set of conventional considerations relevant to statutory interpretation that ought to be laid out systematically in one volume available to students, attorneys, judges, agencies, and legislative drafting offices.[44]

As an interpretive regime, the value of the canons is largely positive rather than normative. As a collection, the canons cannot be conclusively defended based upon any single norm—a predictable rule of law, fidelity to democratically accountable legislators, or good governance—but they can be surveyed and understood. Most of the canons are longstanding foundations of judicial vocabulary for talking about statutory application. That the Supreme Court and state high courts cite them pervasively means that lower court judges as well as private attorneys need to pay close attention to the canons. Congressional and state legislative drafters take most of them seriously; they are reflected in state codifications of interpretive principles and presumptions, treatises and handbooks available to congressional and state legislative staff, official legislative drafting manuals that are publically available for both chambers of Congress and about half the state legislatures, and Congressional Research Service reports and other guidances for legislators and their staffs.[45] For this reason, even skeptical pragmatists cannot ignore the brute

---

[43] Connor N. Raso & William N. Eskridge Jr., Chevron *as a Canon, Not a Precedent: An Empirical Study of What Motivates Justices in Agency Deference Cases*, 110 Colum. L. Rev. 1727 (2010) (empirical demonstration that Justices are influenced by both their political preferences and rule of law canons in statutory cases).

[44] See William N. Eskridge Jr. & John Ferejohn, *Politics, Interpretation, and the Rule of Law*, in *The Rule of Law: Nomos XXXVI* (Ian Shapiro ed., 1993); Michael Herz, *Rediscovering Francis Lieber: An Afterword and Introduction*, 16 Card. L. Rev. 2107, 2117–18 (1995). Cf. Larry M. Eig, American Law Division, Congressional Research Service, Report, *Statutory Interpretation: General Principles and Recent Trends* 1–2 (updated Dec. 19, 2011) (cited in this volume as CRS Report. *Statutory Interpretation*) (summarizing legislative branch assumptions about the canons but omitting most of the canons and failing to explain how they work together).

[45] See CRS Report, *Statutory Interpretation* (updated 2011); Lawrence E. Filson & Sandra Strokoff, *The Legislative Drafter's Desk Reference* 367–85 (2d ed. 2008).

fact that the canons saturate statutory interpretation. Indeed, the canons are the vocabulary of statutory interpretation.

Is description all that can be done with the canons? I think not, for the canons are also America's common law of statutory interpretation—the nation's ongoing experience with applying statutes to concrete circumstances. Like the common law of contracts (which of course have developed interpretive conventions), the canons reflect centuries of judicial practice, at both the state and federal levels, and reflect norms of continuity and incrementalism. Also like the common law, the canons are codified and sometimes modified by legislatures, digested by administrative and legislative staff, scrutinized by academics, and subjected to treatise-like surveys by scholars in the field. For this reason, the canons (again echoing the common law) evolve through a process of critical deployment in case after case, by a wide variety of judicial minds. This process of critical deployment is normative and can be evaluated: Does a particular canon contribute to a predictable rule of law through its widespread acceptance and ease of application? Does it reflect the assumptions of the legislative process and, thereby, help interpreters implement statutes consistent with legitimate democratic expectations? Does the canon reflect an important and productive governance norm?

In the chapters that follow, I shall try to synthesize and evaluate the common law of the canons by bringing together Supreme Court and state high court statutory opinions, state and federal statutory codifications of some canons, and insights gleaned from legislative and administrative practice. Although I shall give some emphasis to U.S. Supreme Court practice (e.g., the appendix), the common law of statutory interpretation entails legislative and administrative as well as judicial practice at both the state and federal levels. Particularly helpful are not only the extensive state legislative codifications of the canons, but also the drafting manuals prepared by the Legislative Counsel for the U.S. House and Senate and by similar offices working for state legislatures, with particular attention to the publicly available manuals used in Alabama, Alaska, Arizona, Colorado, Delaware, Florida, Illinois, Indiana, Kentucky, Maryland, Minnesota, Missouri, Ohio, Pennsylvania, Texas, Utah, and Wisconsin.[46] Legislative practice is useful, because it helps us see which canons

---

[46] B.J. Ard, Comment, *Interpreting by the Book: Legislative Drafting Manuals and Statutory Interpretation,* 120 Yale L.J. 185 (2010) (examination of U.S. House and Senate drafting manuals); http://www.ncsl.org/legislators-staff/legislative-staff/legal-services/bill-drafting-manuals.aspx (viewed Jan. 1, 2016) (websites for drafting manuals for almost half of the state legislatures).

are consistent with the aspirations of our representative democracy, but also because it provides a basis for evaluation of the canons from a rule of law perspective, as Justice Samuel Alito has suggested.[47] If the states are laboratories of statutory interpretation, the codified canons and drafting manuals are important parts of that process of fifty-state experimentation and refinement.[48]

Accordingly, yet another similarity to the common law is that each state or the federal government has its own set of canons, reflecting distinctive regimes. Thus, the canons codified in the Texas Code Construction Act of 1985, reflected in the drafting manual prepared by the Texas Legislative Council, and recognized or applied by the Texas Supreme Court are not the same as those codified by the Florida Legislature, reflected in the drafting manuals used in the Florida House and Senate, and recognized or applied by the Florida Supreme Court. Indeed, canonical regimes evolve within each jurisdiction, none more dramatically than in Michigan. The Michigan Supreme Court in the new millennium has followed a very different canonical regime than the same Court did before the textualist revolution accomplished through four transformative appointments on the seven-Justice bench in 1998–99.[49] And Texas, Florida, and Michigan follow canonical regimes markedly different from the one followed by the U.S. Supreme Court, in part because of the distinctively national perspective of the nation's highest tribunal (reflected in the canons reported in my appendix). The governance structures of Florida, Michigan, Texas, and the United States are different along many dimensions—and one important dimension is the regime of canons followed in each jurisdiction.

Consider a final similarity between the canons and the common law. Notwithstanding these local differences for various state and federal interpretive regimes, the canonical convergence across jurisdictions and across time is even more remarkable. Virtually all of the textual canons have their roots in English law and represent

---

[47] For an excellent examination of legislative drafting manuals as a source for statutory interpretation common law, see *Carr*, 560 U.S. at 463–65 (Alito, J., dissenting).

[48] Abbe R. Gluck, *The States as Laboratories of Statutory Interpretation: Methodological Consensus and the New Modified Textualism*, 119 Yale L.J. 1750 (2010) (describing the variety of interpretive regimes followed by different states).

[49] Id. at 1803–11 (describing the textualist revolution in Michigan after 1998–99); Robert A. Sedler, *The Michigan Supreme Court,* Stare Decisis, *and Overruling the Overrulings*, 55 Wayne L. Rev. 1911 (2009) (highly critical account of the Michigan textualist revolution).

centuries of practical wisdom applied by state and federal judges; pretty much the same ordinary meaning and whole act canons are recognized in all the states and at the federal level. Statutory purpose, plan, or design is codified everywhere and also has been canonical for hundreds of years. The institutional canons (involving statutory precedents, legislative history, and administrative construction) reveal a great deal of variety as regards detail and presentation but not as much variety when it comes to overall practice. While the substantive canons are more heterogeneous, the best-known such canons—the rule of lenity, presumptions against retroactivity and extraterritorial reach, a presumption of severability, and the common law and international law canons—are rooted in tradition and pervasively recognized by state and federal courts as well as in drafting manuals. In short, there is a general common law of statutory interpretation, and it is synthesized and evaluated in this volume (with notation of major state and federal variations).

Methodological Pluralism (Funnel of Abstraction)

A deeper appreciation of the canons must consider the larger contours of the interpretive regime that the canons, as a group, constitute. On the one hand, the canons reflect the methodological pluralism of American statutory interpretation—the variety of sources that judges do consider and ought to consider when they interpret statutes. Contrary to single-minded textualists or resolute purposivists, there is no one foundation for resolving all statutory cases. Any accurate description of statutory practice ought to include ordinary meaning, the whole statute and related statutes, statutory precedents, legislative history, administrative constructions, and constitutional and other background norms as relevant factors to consider.[50] A drawback of these compendiums of canons and sources is that they provide little guidance through the haze of complexity.

On the other hand, the primary canons do enjoy a gently unifying theme, one that unites the rule of law, democratic accountability, and governance criteria. As David Shapiro opined a

---

[50] For examples of complex, multi-factor approaches to statutory interpretation, see Texas Code Construction Act, 1985 Tex. Acts, 69th Leg., ch. 479, codified at Tex. Govt. Code § 311.023 (list of "matters" courts can consider when interpreting statutes); 2A *Sutherland Statutes and Statutory Interpretation* ch. 45 (7th ed. 2015) (introductory essay, followed by dozens of chapters on particular canons in volumes 2A, 2B, and 3A); CRS Report, *Statutory Interpretation* (updated 2011) (report made available to Congress as well as the public).

generation ago, the canons reflect the wisdom that "close questions of construction should be resolved in favor of continuity and against change," when judges are interpreting statutes.[51] I should expand Professor Shapiro's normative analysis to emphasize *coherence* with legal rules and principles, both backward in time (Shapiro's idea) and across the wide range of legal obligations and rights currently. The former is a *vertical* understanding of coherence, the latter is a *horizontal* understanding.[52] The former seeks continuity with our legal *traditions* even as new rules emerge, and the latter seeks *harmonization* of current legal rights and duties even as particular exceptions and innovations abound.

Consider this meta-norm underlying the canons as you read the chapters that follow. Most of them are rooted, at least in part, in the fundamental value of presuming continuity—both vertical continuity over the course of time (tradition) and horizontal coherence with other legal rules and public norms (harmonization). Importantly, of course, both kinds of coherence are subject to new statutes that are generated by the lawmaking process, as well as subject to rules created by agencies to which legislatures have delegated lawmaking authority. This tension between stable, harmonizing coherence and dynamic, problem-solving particularity is a great theme of the modern regulatory state. The canons reflect the institutional role of courts to weigh in on the coherence side of the equation—sometimes insisting upon continuity or harmonization and resisting institutional efforts to change things and create new rules, while at other times serving as a confirmation that a big change has been made and that new rules are legitimately part of an updated coherence that the polity is creating or entrenching.

The assumption of continuity and coherence is well-suited to the limited competence and legitimacy of judges in our system. It is also broadly consistent with the three normative criteria for any system of statutory interpretation, identified and discussed above. Not only does the rule of law famously value coherence and continuity (and abhor surprises), but continuity is a value undergirding the particular structure of statute-creation in our federal and state

---

[51] David L. Shapiro, *Continuity and Change in Statutory Interpretation*, 67 N.Y.U. L. Rev. 921, 925 (1992); see Anita S. Krishnakumar, *Passive-Voice References in Statutory Interpretation*, 76 Brooklyn L. Rev. 941 (2011); Amanda L. Tyler, *Continuity, Coherence, and the Canons*, 99 Nw. U. L. Rev. 1389, 1418–21 (2005).

[52] The different kinds of coherence are taken from William N. Eskridge Jr., *Interpreting Legislative Inaction*, 87 Mich. L. Rev. 67 (1988).

constitutions.[53] Perhaps most surprising is that continuity and overall coherence of legal rules contribute, modestly at least, to the overall legitimacy of our republic of statutes. Philosophers as well as empiricists maintain that a community of principle (where people follow rules because they find them coherent and rational) is more legitimate and produces more engagement from the citizenry than a rulebook community (where people follow the rules because they fear penalties).[54]

A focus on the canons as traditional practice, rooted in notions of continuity and coherence, and evolving common law style, is in striking contrast to completely cynical theories such as Professor Llewellyn's, as well as to one-size-fits-all normative theories such as that of Justice Scalia and Professor Garner. Judges have revealed neither interest in nor competence for these kinds of revolutionary projects, which would also require a much more detailed and empirical (systematic) understanding of the legislative process and the capabilities of legislative as well as judicial administration than these scholars have been able to muster.[55]

Rather than forcing the canons into procrustean roles they cannot perform, this volume suggests the opposite tack—understand and apply the canons actually used by judges in light of the proper goals of statutory interpretation, namely, the inculcation of a stable and coherent system of rules that are linked to democratic deliberation and advance the project of practical governance. Understood this way, the canons might even help guide the neutral judge toward the relevant considerations that contribute to a predictable rule of law, to the projects launched by our democratically elected legislators and implemented by executive officials, and to the community of principle that binds us together as a nation.[56]

---

[53] John F. Manning, *Continuity and the Legislative Design*, 79 Notre Dame L. Rev. 1863 (2004); see William N. Eskridge Jr. & John Ferejohn, *The Article I, Section 7 Game*, 80 Geo. L.J. 523 (1992).

[54] Ronald Dworkin, *Law's Empire* (1986) (originating the contrast between a community of principle and a rulebook community). For empirical support, consider Tom R. Tyler, *Why People Obey the Law* (2d ed. 2006); Tom R. Tyler & Jonathan Jackson, *Popular Legitimacy and the Exercise of Legal Authority: Motivating Compliance, Cooperation and Engagement*, 20 Psychol. Pub. Pol'y & Law 78 (2014).

[55] See Elizabeth Garrett, *Preferences, Laws, and Default Rules*, 122 Harv. L. Rev. 2104 (2009) (criticizing Professor Elhauge from the perspective of Congress, whose preferences are not accurately reflected in most of the canons and which would be unfriendly to the currentist regime favored by the professor).

[56] *Astoria Fed. Sav. & Loan v. Solimino*, 501 U.S. 104, 108–09 (1991); William N. Eskridge Jr., *Dynamic Statutory Interpretation* ch. 9 (1994).

Ironically, my sharpest disagreement with Justices Breyer and, especially, Scalia goes to their emphasis on the incoherence of American statutory interpretation practice. Their books focus on cases and precepts from which they dissent, and their tone is one of dissatisfaction. Justice Scalia, in particular, evidenced a contempt for what he considered the chaotic, incoherent practice of statutory interpretation by the Supreme Court and other courts. But do not mistake complexity for chaos. Lack of simplicity is not the same as incoherence. In fact, the practice of American judges is coherent and is defensible. And the interpretive regime presented in this book is an understandable, widely accepted, and cogent approach to statutes.[57]

Likewise, this volume transcends the textualism versus purposivism debate, which is a misleading debate, because text and purpose are intertwined so completely that they cannot compete so much as work together. Working with more detailed versions of a hypothetical vehicles in the park law, each of the following chapters will introduce the gentle reader to a fundamental precept of statutory interpretation and will explain why that precept contributes to the larger goals of our legal system. Recall these larger goals: We the People believe that the official application of statutes to new circumstances ought (1) to be both neutral and largely predictable, (2) to respect the democratic accountability of their elected representatives, and (3) to operate to advance (or at least not defeat) the purposes of the law and the public values of the community. Please note that these goals will sometimes be in tension or open conflict with one another. One argument of this volume is that these tensions and conflicts cannot (and will not) be resolved through a one-size-fits-all rule and must be approached with an appreciation of particular context.

American statutory interpretation is not a simple exercise—but neither is it unguided. The longstanding judicial practice of statutory interpretation aptly considers the ordinary meaning of the statutory text, in the context of the statutory scheme, judicial precedent, legislative purpose, administrative practice, and constitutional and other public values. The practice is not simply a laundry list of considerations, however. Like Justice Scalia, we are all textualists: The starting point and usually the answer to a statutory problem is a fair reading of the statutory text on point. Like Justice Breyer, all of

[57] For a most thoughtful critique of efforts, including mine, to bring order to statutory interpretation and impose upon judges a uniform methodology, see Glen Staszewski, *The Dumbing Down of Statutory Interpretation*, 95 B.U. L. Rev. 209 (2015).

us engage in a practice whereby we do not know whether there is a single fair reading until we have considered the legal context of that text. That context includes the whole statute, precedent, legislative purpose, administrative practice, and public values. Statutory interpretation has always been, and ought to be, a pragmatic exercise in textual exegesis in light of democratic projects and the larger norms that bind together our community. This is true in state as well as federal courts—and legislators as well as judges have appreciated this complexity, as evidenced by the codifications of canons accomplished by every state legislature.

The remainder of this book will demonstrate how this works, but here is a preview. Professor Frickey and I once proposed that statutory interpretation is a matter of structured practical reasoning.[58] Our pragmatic model was inspired by the Supreme Court's longstanding approach to statutory interpretation, but it also captures the pluralist approach followed by almost all state courts. In the chapters that follow, I shall be working from a federal law barring vehicles from Lafayette Park (pictured at the beginning of this introduction). Accordingly, the focus will be the U.S. Supreme Court, but with notation of state court practice and variation. (Footnotes will reference canons codified by state legislatures and found in state legislative drafting manuals, but will focus on judicial practice in five big states that reflect the methodological variety uncovered by my colleague Abbe Gluck: California, Florida, Michigan, New York, and Texas.)

There is no foundational theory or practice of statutory interpretation, but the rule of law, democratic accountability, and governance features of the enterprise all support the traditional rule that gives primacy to the ordinary meaning of a statute's relevant text, what judges sometimes call everyday or commonsense meaning. Ordinary meaning is the anchor for statutory interpretation, and chapter one of this volume is devoted to this concept and its associated canons. Ordinary meaning is how the statutory provision would be understood by a competent speaker of the English language, in the context of the statute and the facts to which it is applied. (That context includes the purpose attributed to the statute or the particular provision.)

---

[58] William N. Eskridge Jr. & Philip P. Frickey, *Statutory Interpretation as Practical Reasoning*, 42 Stan. L. Rev. 321 (1990); see also Glen Staszewski, *Statutory Interpretation As Contestatory Democracy*, 55 Wm. & Mary L. Rev. 221, 245–49 (2013); Nicholas S. Zeppos, *The Use of Authority in Statutory Interpretation: An Empirical Analysis*, 70 Tex. L. Rev. 1073 (1990).

Chapter one will present ordinary meaning as a continuum, starting with circumstances that fall within the prototypical or core of the statutory rule, moving along the continuum to circumstances that are similar to the core but peripheral, and rounding out the continuum with circumstances that are so distant from the core as to be clearly excluded. The ordinary meaning continuum depends on legal context, however, and the next chapters will show how the legal context—namely, the entire statute (chapter two) and authoritative judicial precedents (chapter three)—can and ought to affect a judge's understanding of a statute's core, periphery, and beyond. Thus, chapter two focuses on the statutory scheme—namely, the whole act and sometimes other provisions in the entire statutory code—for understanding the legal text that is on point. Even when the relevant statutory language is ambiguous, reading it in light of the rest of the statute and its purpose or plan may decisively support one reading. Such statutory context may establish a plain meaning for the statute. Notice the contrast between *ordinary meaning* that a statutory provision may or may not have for the regular speaker of English, and the *plain meaning* that a judge may impose upon the provision, based upon larger statutory context.[59]

Ordinary meaning and statutory context are not the only hard evidence of legal meaning, however. If the Supreme Court has authoritatively construed particular statutory language, that precedent will control interpretation in subsequent cases—even if the earlier interpretation is not the one that the current interpreter believes to reflect the law's ordinary meaning or its plain meaning in light of the whole act. Chapter three will explore the role that *stare decisis* ("the decisions stand") plays in statutory interpretation.

Judicial opinions are usually structured around the question whether a statute has a plain meaning justified by ordinary meaning, the whole act, and precedent. When judges say the law has a plain meaning, they typically say that their inquiry is complete. Yet those same judges often continue their analysis, usually concluding that various other considerations confirm the plain meaning they have already declared. This is a central dividing practice among judicial opinions: Some simply stop once they announce a plain meaning, while others explore further contextual evidence, usually finding

---

[59] See Brian G. Slocum, *Ordinary Meaning: A Theory of the Most Fundamental Principle of Legal Interpretation* ch. 1 (2015) (distinguishing between largely descriptive "ordinary meaning" and prescriptive "plain meaning" in statutory interpretation).

confirmation of plain meaning. Chapters four through six suggest that these additional considerations have a role to play before as well as after a judge considers ordinary as well as plain meaning arguments. In other words, judges for generations have not separated larger context from ordinary or plain meaning, nor should they, for reasons developed in these chapters.

Legislative materials, the focus of chapter four, are controversial among judges and legal academics—much more controversial than they ought to be. Such materials are often highly relevant to the ordinary meaning of a statute, because they can reveal ways in which language is used by contemporary speakers and groups (such as legislative committees) and because they help the interpreter understand the statute's purpose and plan more deeply. Like *The Federalist Papers* in constitutional interpretation, moreover, legislative materials also help render statutory interpretation better accountable to the democratic deliberation that produced the statute. One does not need to ground statutory interpretation in some theory of legislative intent to consider legislative materials relevant to that enterprise.

Generally speaking, the whole act, judicial precedent, and legislative history will tend to focus the ordinary meaning inquiry in ways that improve predictability and objectivity in statutory application. But the whole act might have little to say about an interpretive issue, there may be no authoritative judicial decision for a wide range of reasons, and legislative history is often repetitive of the statutory language. Surprisingly, the rule of law is often most advanced by clear administrative rules and practices—sources of legal understanding that have the additional virtues of indirect democratic accountability and good governance by administrators who are relatively expert. Chapter five considers the relevance of administrative practice and how it interacts with ordinary meaning.

Finally, constitutional norms and substantive norms pervasively affect statutory interpretation. Chapter six and the conclusion offer several dramatic examples where constitutional, common law, and international norms provide the answer to hard statutory cases. Most of the time, these norms provide gapfilling rules that judges apply, often without any deep analysis. A statute criminalizing vehicles in Lafayette Park does not have to assure defendants of jury trials if the government seeks jail time, as the Sixth Amendment makes certain that everyone will assume a jury trial, without any further thought. In most of the examples explored at the end of this volume, not only do these background norms fill in gaps, but they create new gaps and fill them. That is, they trump ordinary meaning. Widely accepted substantive canons support interpretations not suggested by the enacted text, unanticipated by the legislative history, and untouched by statutory precedents. Tradition and harmonization often operate in powerful and anti-democratic ways, even in statutory cases.

The six chapters of this volume suggest the following hierarchy of sources for statutory interpretation, which Professor Frickey dubbed a "funnel of abstraction" and which I have refined in the following manner:

Least Concrete **Norms & Values**

Agency Practice

Legislative Materials

Judicial Precedent

Whole Act & Purpose

Most Concrete Sources of Statutory Meaning **Ordinary Commonsense Meaning**

THE FUNNEL OF ABSTRACTION

[Each line of the Funnel reflects canons instantiating that factor.]

Although developed in the context of the U.S. Supreme Court's statutory practice, the funnel of abstraction also reflects state court practice almost everywhere in the country, from New York and other states in the Northeast, to Texas and Florida as well as other states in the South, to California anchoring the West, to most of the states of the Midwest, with the current exception of Michigan, whose Supreme Court in the last two decades has, for the most part, implemented Justice Scalia's playbook. (Ironically, the Michigan Supreme Court takes the new textualism further than Justice Scalia did, in practice.)

The conclusion to this volume will apply the funnel approach to constitutional interpretation, framed around a slightly different hypothetical statute—one barring "homosexuals" (rather than "vehicles") from Lafayette Park. As we shall see, the basic techniques of statutory interpretation are also applicable to constitutional cases, with some practical differences noted and discussed in the conclusion. More important, the exercise in constitutional interpretation will reveal how the different interpretive sources—ordinary meaning, structure of the legal regime, precedent, legislative history, executive department application and legislative response, and larger background norms—interact in the interpretive enterprise. The lesson here is that judges do not apply the canons mechanically, moving up the funnel as they fill in answers at the various levels of abstraction (from concrete text to abstract international and constitutional norms). Instead, each funnel factor interacts with the others that are relevant. Thus, a text that seems to have a clear ordinary meaning sometimes becomes ambiguous when read in light of the statutory scheme or the legislative history. Conversely, a text that can mean one thing or another frequently assumes greater clarity in light of the statute's purpose or decades of judicial or administrative application.

Chapter 1

ORDINARY MEANING

1897 Léon Bollée Voiturette

The prime directive in statutory interpretation is to apply the meaning that a reasonable reader would derive from the text of the law. This is often referred to as the plain meaning rule, but is better considered to be the *ordinary meaning rule*. "Plain meaning" ought to be reserved for a judicial declaration that there is a clear legal meaning for the provision in question, a point developed most usefully by Brian Slocum.[1]

Most questions of statutory interpretation are never litigated, because they are settled by a straightforward application of ordinary meaning. For example, assume that Congress enacts the Lafayette Park Safety Act of 1992. It has one substantive provision:

---

1 For the most useful explanation of "ordinary meaning," contrasted with "plain meaning," see Brian G. Slocum, *Ordinary Meaning: A Theory of the Most Fundamental Principle of Legal Interpretation* (2015). See also Victoria F. Nourse, *Two Kinds of Plain Meaning*, 76 Brooklyn L. Rev. 997, 1004 (2011); Frank H. Easterbrook, *Statutes' Domains*, 50 U. Chi. L. Rev. 533, 536 (1983). For a related distinction between "linguistic" or "semantic" meaning of a text and its "legal" meaning, see Lawrence B. Solum, *The Interpretation-Construction Distinction*, 27 Const. Comm. 95 (2010).

> Because vehicles create safety problems, no person is permitted to drive a vehicle of any kind in Lafayette Park.

Park police, citizens, and judges would understand the law simply by applying the ordinary meaning rule, without any further inquiry.

Thus, if the police saw a person driving a small truck through Lafayette Park, they would conclude that the driver was violating our Park Safety Act. Almost any speaker of the English language would conclude that the person driving a motorized truck, even small one, was "driv[ing] a vehicle." Conversely, if the police saw a kid carrying a small plastic model car through the park, they would just as easily conclude that the kid was not in violation of the statute. Almost any speaker of the English language would conclude that a child carrying a small plastic model car was not "driv[ing] a vehicle" in the park.

To be sure, other situations would not be so straightforward. The police might scratch their heads for a minute if an antiquarian came into the park driving her 1897 Léon Bollée Voiturette, a three-wheel tandem powered by a single-cylinder two horsepower engine and belt drive. Illustrated by the photo at the front of this chapter, this Voiturette looks like something adapted from a horse-drawn buggy, but is somewhat faster, capable of reaching maximum speeds of twenty-eight miles per hour (slower than today's car or moped). But it is motorized and is a precursor to the modern automobile. Even in this harder case, the police and other officials, as well as the persons in the park, would know that the most relevant inquiry is to consider whether a fair reading of the statutory language covered the activity in question.[2] As to *that* question, I am inclined to say that the 1897 Léon Bollée Voiturette falls within the ordinary meaning of the statutory language. The French word for automobile is *voiture*, and a *Voiturette* connotes a small automobile. Although I am not as certain the Léon Bollée is a "vehicle" as I am that my Toyota Camry is a "vehicle," ordinary meaning suggests that it falls within the statute.

In short, for hard cases as well as easy ones, the *ordinary meaning* (or the "everyday meaning" or the "commonsense" reading[3])

---

[2] Commencement Address by Justice David Souter, Harvard University, May 27, 2010 (discussing the notion of a "fair reading" of legal texts).

[3] *Lopez v. Gonzales*, 549 U.S. 47, 53 (2006) (quotations in text); accord, *Moncrieffe v. Holder*, 133 S.Ct. 1678, 1693 (2013) ("commonsense" understanding); *Mohamad v. Palestinian Auth.*, 132 S.Ct. 1702, 1707 (2012) ("everyday parlance"); *Carachuri-Rosendo v. Holder*, 560 U.S. 563, 574–75 (2010) ("commonsense conception" and "everyday" understanding); *Voices of the Wetlands v. State Water Resources Control Bd.*, 257 P.3d 81, 93 (Cal. 2011) (anchor for statutory interpretation is the "plain, commonsense meaning" of the statutory text, understood in the context of the whole

of the relevant statutory text is the anchor for statutory interpretation.[4]

There are excellent reasons for the primacy of the ordinary meaning rule. To begin with, ordinary meaning matches up well with our understanding of what the *rule of law* entails. A polity governed by the rule of law aspires to have legal directives that are known to the citizenry, that are predictable in their application, and that officials can neutrally and consistently apply based upon objective criteria.[5] A polity without the rule of law is tragic and sad. If citizens and companies cannot rely on predictable application of legal rules, they are less likely to invest in productive activities and spend more time scheming, cheating, and defaulting on their obligations. A lawless polity is one where citizens' rights are unstable and, hence, relatively worthless.[6]

For this reason, there is perhaps no more important role for legislators and administrators than to generate well-understood rules that guide people's conduct into productive channels, and no more important role for judges than to enforce those rules through a method that is objective, general, and predictable. Consistent with this goal, the Park Safety Act's text is accessible to everyone (through signs, the Internet, and the U.S. Code), and the judge's greatest duty is to interpret that statute in a neutral, nonpartisan manner that

---

statute), quoted and followed in *People v. Leiva*, 297 P.3d 870, 874 (2013); *Commissioners Ct. of Titus Cnty. v. Agan*, 940 S.W.2d 77, 80 (Tex. 1997) ("common everyday meaning").

[4] For a sampling of some excellent, nuanced examples of ordinary meaning as the anchor for statutory interpretation, see, e.g., *Adoptive Couple v. Baby Girl*, 133 S.Ct. 2552, 2559–62 (2013); *Levin v. United States*, 133 S.Ct. 1224, 1231–33 (2013); *Mohamad v. Palestinian Auth.*, 132 S.Ct. 1702, 1706–07 (2012); *Bilski v. Kappos*, 561 U.S. 593, 601–05 (2010); *Massachusetts v. EPA*, 549 U.S. 497, 528–32 (2007); *Moskal* v. *United States*, 498 U. S. 103, 108 (1996); *Richards v. United States*, 369 U.S. 1, 9 (1962) (leading case). For some excellent representative state cases, see, e.g., *Apple, Inc. v. Superior Court*, 292 P.3d 883, 885 (Cal. 2013); *Cassel v. Superior Court*, 244 P.3d 1080, 1087–88 (Cal. 2011); *People v. Albillar*, 244 P.3d 1062, 1067–69 (Cal. 2010); *Williams v. State*, 121 So.3d 524, 529–34 (Fla. 2013); *Hampton v. State*, 103 So.3d 98, 110–13 (Fla. 2012); *Smitter v. Thornapple Township*, 833 N.W.2d 875, 880–83 (Mich. 2013); *Barr v. City of Sinton*, 295 S.W.3d 287, 297–99 (Tex. 2009).

[5] Lon L. Fuller, *The Morality of Law* (1964); Friedrich Hayek, *The Constitution of Liberty* 205–16 (1960); see also H.L.A. Hart, *Essays in Jurisprudence and Philosophy* 347 (1983); Colleen Murphy, *Lon Fuller and the Morality of the Rule of Law*, 24 L. & Phil. 239 (2005).

[6] Hayek, *Constitution of Liberty*; Joseph Raz, *The Authority of Law* 210–29 (2009).

honors the text and renders it intelligible to the public. Ordinary public meaning is the method that best fits this aspiration.[7]

Although ordinary meaning does not always yield predictable answers to statutory issues,[8] it seems to yield greater predictability than any other *single* methodology. Thus, if you took 100 people and asked them whether a person behind the wheel of a Toyota Camry is violating a law forbidding any one to "drive a vehicle of any kind" into a park, all of those people would probably agree that the activity falls within the statute. You could probably get a large majority (perhaps not unanimity) for the application of the law to the slower-moving, buggy-like Léon Bollée Voiturette. Conversely, our 100 jurors would readily agree that a fair reading of the text does not cover the kid carrying a small plastic model car. One could add other examples where almost everyone would agree about what the statutory text means. These examples create a predictable application of the statute—and they do a better job than a methodology that considers only "legislative intent" or "statutory purpose" or "best result from a utilitarian perspective."[9]

The ordinary meaning rule also facilitates (though does not guarantee) a neutral and fair application of the statute to particular activities. That is, a sharp focus on the ordinary meaning of statutory language helps judges separate legal interpretation from their personal reaction to the situation being adjudicated. Accordingly, the judge applying the law to the automobile driver who is a snarky juvenile delinquent from a poor background is likely to interpret the statute the same way as another judge applying the same law to a rich, straight-A college student driving a fancy car. The latter judge will apply the same rules of vocabulary and grammar that the first judge will use to interpret the law to sustain liability for the juvenile

---

7 See generally Lawrence M. Solan & Peter M. Tiersma, eds., *The Oxford Handbook of Language and Law* 13–26 (2012); Slocum, *Ordinary Meaning*, ch. 1; Peter M. Tiersma, *Legal Language* (1999); Victoria F. Nourse, *Misunderstanding Congress: Statutory Interpretation, the Supermajoritarian Difficulty, and the Separation of Powers*, 99 Geo. L.J. 1119, 1172–75 (2011); Amy Widman, *The Rostrum Principle: Why the Boundaries of the Public Forum Matter to Statutory Interpretation*, 65 Fla. L. Rev. 1447, 1447–50 (2013); Note, *Textualism as Fair Notice*, Harv. L. Rev. 542 (2009).

8 Compare the majority and dissenting opinions in *Circuit City Stores, Inc. v. Adams*, 532 U.S. 105 (2001), for an engaged debate on what meaning was "ordinary" for a 1926 statute. Compare also the majority and dissenting opinions in *Taniguchi v. Kan Pacific Saipan, Ltd.*, 132 S.Ct. 1997 (2012); *Lindh v. Murphy*, 521 U.S. 320 (1997); *Senne v. Village of Palatine, Illinois*, 695 F.3d 597, 609 (7th Cir. 2012).

9 The proposition in text has not been rigorously tested, but some preliminary evidence is provided by Ward Farnsworth et al., *Ambiguity About Ambiguity: An Empirical Inquiry Into Legal Interpretation*, 2 J. Legal Analysis 257 (2010).

offender. Because the judge is considering evidence that is external to her views on the character of the defendants and that is subject to falsification by outside observers, this methodological discipline ought to facilitate equal treatment of the two offenders.[10]

Rule of law values are more than sufficient to justify the ordinary meaning rule, but a second value also supports the primacy of ordinary meaning—namely *democratic legitimacy*. That is, applying the ordinary meaning of the enacted text of the statute both respects and (possibly) induces accountability of our elected representatives for the statutes they adopt. This value has a formal dimension and a functional one, and they are closely related. Article I, Section 7 of the Constitution provides that congressional bills do not become "law" unless the House of Representatives and the Senate have voted for the same language and have presented that text to the President, whose assent is usually needed unless supermajorities in each chamber override a presidential veto. This constitutional structure, augmented by procedures constitutionally adopted by each chamber, normally assures a great deal of deliberation and compromise for any measure that becomes the law of the land. The *normal* operation of the legislative process is one where text is supposed to matter a great deal, because the only thing that the House and Senate vote on is statutory text, the best evidence of any reconciliation of House and Senate versions is the text ultimately adopted, and the only thing presented to the President is the text of the proposed legislation.[11]

Consistent with this structure, empirical studies of the federal lawmaking process have reported that congressional drafters take the ordinary meaning idea seriously and draft federal statutes under the assumption that courts will apply their ordinary meaning.[12] Likewise,

---

[10] See id. at 257–59 (empirical foundation for the assertion in text); Frederick Schauer, *Statutory Construction and the Coordinating Function of Plain Meaning*, 1990 Sup. Ct. Rev. 231, 232 & 250–56. On the importance of neutrality and consistency in the application of law, see Tom R. Tyler, *Why People Obey the Law* (1990, 2d ed. 2006); Tracey L. Meares & Tom R. Tyler, *Justice Sotomayor and the Jurisprudence of Procedural Justice*, 123 Yale L.J. Forum 525 (2014).

[11] *Immigration & Naturalization Service v. Chadha*, 462 U.S. 919 (1983) (leading opinion on the structure and purpose of Article I, § 7). Compare Jeremy Waldron, *Law and Disagreement* (1999) (applying this structure to argue for a strict plain meaning rule), with Widman, *Rostrum Principle*, 65 Fla. L. Rev. at 1447–50 (arguing that public discourse best supplies evidence of ordinary meaning that allows this method to link statutory interpretation to democratic accountability).

[12] See Victoria F. Nourse & Jane S. Schacter, *The Politics of Legislative Drafting: A Congressional Case Study*, 77 N.Y.U. L. Rev. 575, 594–97 (2002) (empirical survey of congressional drafting practices, reporting that drafters try to provide clear,

state legislative drafting manuals emphasize common usage, ordinary meaning, and everyday meaning as prime directives for drafters of state laws.[13] Not surprisingly, Jacob Scott's survey of state legislative codifications of canons of statutory interpretation reports that a large majority of state legislatures have codified the ordinary meaning rule in some form, as the anchor for their codified canons of statutory interpretation.[14] This is evidence that democratically accountable legislatures, from a wide array of states, consider the ordinary meaning rule the background against which they legislate.

The ordinary meaning rule accords with the constitutional structure for national lawmaking (similar to the structure in most state constitutions): If the statutory text is the only thing the Constitution requires the House, Senate, and (usually) the President to agree on, then a fair reading of the text they agreed on is a natural way to interpret statutes adopted under the constitutional process for adopting statutes in our representative democracy. As discussed below, there may not be an entirely clear and undisputed meaning of the enacted text as applied to circumstances that would not have occurred to legislators and congressional drafting staff. That is fine—but out of respect for the language adopted by our democratically elected and accountable representatives, a judge needs to explain why her interpretation is a plausible application of the statutory text. In other words, judges ought never ignore the statutory text, and in almost all cases the text narrows the range of interpretations that are plausible. If the text is dead against an interpretation, there is a

---

ordinary meaning, directives, except when time does not permit or legislators want to leave ambiguities for interpreters to resolve or gaps to fill in); Jarrod Shobe, *Intertemporal Statutory Interpretation and the Evolution of Legislative Drafting*, 114 Colum. L. Rev. 807 (2014) (similar account from a former legislative drafter). See also Larry M. Eig, American Law Division, Congressional Research Service, Report, *Statutory Interpretation: General Principles and Recent Trends* 4, 6–18 (updated Dec. 19, 2011) (hereinafter cited as CRS Report, *Statutory Interpretation*) (drafting guidance for congressional staff, emphasizing ordinary meaning and its associated canons).

[13] For drafting manuals emphasizing ordinary meaning, see, e.g., Office of the Legislative Counsel, U.S. Senate, *Legislative Drafting Manual* § 107 (Feb. 1997); Alabama Legislative Reference Serv., *Legislative Reference Service Drafting Style Manual* Rule 7 (on-line, viewed Jan. 1, 2016); Florida Senate, *Manual for the Drafting of Legislation* ch. 2, at 12 (6th ed. 2009); Kentucky Legislative Research Comm'n, *Bill Drafting Manual, Kentucky General Assembly* §§ 302, 306 (rev. 2011); Texas Legislative Council, *Texas Legislative Council Drafting Manual* § 3.07(d) (Jan. 2015).

[14] For a state-by-state survey of legislatively codified canons, see Jacob Scott, *Codified Canons and the Common Law of Interpretation*, 98 Geo. L.J. 341 (2010). Table 1 of Scott's article reports the states' overwhelming endorsement of plain or ordinary meaning as the anchor for statutory interpretation. Id. at 357; see, e.g., Mich. Comp. Laws § 8.3a (codification of the concept that statutory words should be interpreted according to their "common usage"); Tex. Govt. Code § 311.011(a) (similar).

strong presumption against it, because the Constitution vests Congress-and-the-President with the authority to add new text to the U.S. Code or revise old text already in the Code.[15]

On top of these dynamite reasons to hew to the ordinary meaning rule, there is a third kind of potential justification for it—everyday-language readings of statutory text tend to advance the *purposes of governance*. The role of government is to promote the public welfare through statutory and regulatory rules and standards, adopted after democratic deliberation. The role of governmental institutions is to coordinate the many plans that we make to advance the lives of citizens and the values of the community. Planning is a collective activity, and in our representative democracy Congress and the President enact statutes that create the frameworks for our great national plans. The Park Safety Act, discussed in this chapter, is one of a series of statutes and regulations governing Lafayette Park and other federal lands in the District of Columbia. Taken together, these (hypothetical) laws reflect an extensively considered collective plan for the use and enjoyment of these public lands.[16]

Statutes can be viewed as coordinating mechanisms for collective plans. On the whole, the ordinary meaning rule is not only a plausible mechanism for making sure the legislative plans are implemented in a manner that reflects the collective judgment of the community, but also enjoys considerable support as the best mechanism, compared to other approaches considered singly. Apart from the obvious reason, that the enacted words best reflect the compromises involved in and the ambit of the national plans adopted by Congress, there is also a practical reason why the ordinary meaning rule is the best approach. Most statutory interpretation is quick and dirty. The police officer wants to know whether she should stop or even arrest a kid riding a bike in Lafayette Park, the young perpetrator's parents want to know whether they should fight the charge or just pay the fine, the congressional staff attorney wants to know whether Congress ought

---

[15] Office of Legal Policy, Department of Justice, *Using and Misusing Legislative History: A Re-Evaluation of the Status of Legislative History in Statutory Interpretation* (1989) (booklet prepared by Assistant Attorney General Stephen Markman, now on the Michigan Supreme Court); Waldron, *Law and Disagreement*; William N. Eskridge Jr., *The New Textualism*, 37 U.C.L.A. L. Rev. 621 (1990); John F. Manning, *Textualism as a Nondelegation Doctrine*, 97 Colum. L. Rev. 673 (1997).

[16] Henry M. Hart Jr. & Albert M. Sacks, *The Legal Process: Basic Problems in the Making and Application of Law* (William N. Eskridge Jr. & Philip P. Frickey eds., 1994) (1958 tent. ed.); Scott Shapiro, *Legality* 128, 195–200 (2011); see Jeremy Waldron, *Planning for Legality*, 109 Mich. L. Rev. 883, 888–91 (2011) (explaining how laws as plans involve the entrenchment of public norms as well).

to consider amending the statute so that it does not sweep up bike-riding youth, the newspaper commentator wants to know whether this is a good story about the law gone awry, and so forth. None of these interested persons has a lot of time to do more extensive statutory research—and the least time-consuming and, therefore, least expensive method for interpreting statutes is to apply a fair reading of the statutory text.[17]

Another powerful reason effective governance favors ordinary meaning is institutional. Administrators and executive branch officials do most of the official statutory interpretation in this country, and a recent empirical examination reports that federal administrative officials start with and focus on the ordinary meaning of the statutory text.[18] Ordinary meaning is even more central to interpretation by judges, who are, theoretically, the authoritative interpreters of statutes. Given their legal education and limited resources, judges are not institutionally competent to make judgments about matters of economic policy, political philosophy, or even current affairs. In both relative and absolute terms, most federal judges and state appellate judges are competent and often excellent in their ability to apply ordinary language to facts that they have found after adjudication, as well as their ability to relate this application to the statutory scheme (chapter two) and to precedents binding on them (chapter three). I am not providing a footnote for this claim, because it rests upon a rough consensus within the legal profession (and has not been empirically questioned).

For all these reasons, the ordinary meaning of the relevant statutory language ought to be the anchor for statutory interpretation by judges. To be sure, the subsequent chapters in this book will explore ways in which the rule of law, democratic legitimacy, and purposive governance support consideration of other kinds of evidence when a judge is interpreting a statute. Even if the ordinary meaning rule supplies the right answer in the large majority of the statutory matters that surface in American public law, other kinds of evidence are often relevant to determine ordinary meaning, to figure

---

[17] On the practical advantages of the ordinary (or plain) meaning rule, see Schauer, *Coordinating Function of Plain Meaning*, 1990 Sup. Ct. Rev. at 250–56; David A. Strauss, *Why Plain Meaning?*, 72 Notre Dame L. Rev. 1565, 1565, 1579–82 (1997); see also Reed Dickerson, *The Interpretation and Application of Statutes* (1975); Waldron, *Law and Disagreement*.

[18] See Christopher J. Walker, *Inside Agency Statutory Interpretation*, 67 Stan. L. Rev. 999, 1030–31 (2015) (reporting that federal agencies interpreting statutes focus on the "ordinary meaning" of the words enacted into law).

out the right interpretation when there is no ordinary meaning, and sometimes to reconsider an apparent ordinary meaning. More important for purposes of this chapter, how, exactly, does a judge determine whether there is an "ordinary meaning"? To address this matter, let's start with some basic intuitions, then introduce the most helpful canons or guideposts, and conclude with some canons that require cautious application.

Ordinary Meaning Rule

Synthesizing the wisdom of the giants of American law, from the framing generation through the nineteenth century, Justice Oliver Wendell Holmes Jr. said that the primary task for the statutory interpreter is to determine "what [the statutory] words would mean in the mouth of an ordinary speaker of English, using them in the circumstances in which they were used."[19] Like the "reasonable person" in the law of torts, the "normal speaker" is "simply another instance of the externality of law."[20] Justice Holmes's articulation has been widely influential and has enjoyed a tremendous revival in the last generation.[21]

This foundational rule for America's republic of statutes is a strong presumption that We the People as well as government officials ought to read statutes in accord with the ordinary meaning their words and phrases would have for the typical English-speaking citizen. For lay people and many lawyers, ordinary meaning is unconscious. Recall our hypothetical Park Safety Act: "Because vehicles create safety problems, no person is permitted to drive a vehicle of any kind in Lafayette Park." Without much thought, almost everyone would conclude that the statute applies to automobiles of all shapes and sizes, but not to small plastic model cars.

Not all applications of the Park Safety Act are easy cases, however. Does this statute cover mopeds, namely, motorized versions

---

[19] Oliver Wendell Holmes Jr., *The Theory of Legal Interpretation*, 12 Harv. L. Rev. 417, 417–18 (1899). For similar statements by earlier giants of American law, see, e.g., *Gibbons v. Ogden*, 22 U.S. 1, 71 (1824) (Marshall, C.J.); James Kent, *Commentaries on American Law* 432 (1826); Joseph Story, *Commentaries on the Constitution of the United States* 157–58 (1833).

[20] Holmes, *Theory of Legal Interpretation*, 12 Harv. L. Rev. at 418.

[21] For early commentators leading the modern revival of Holmes's focus on an objective, external focus for statutory interpretation, see Office of Legal Policy, Dep't of Justice, *Using and Misusing Legislative History* (January 5, 1989); Antonin Scalia, A *Matter of Interpretation* (1997) (published version of informal addresses the author had been giving at law schools and elsewhere since 1985); Frank H. Easterbrook, *The Role of Original Intent in Statutory Construction*, 11 Harv. J.L. & Pub. Pol'y 59, 65 (1988).

of the bicycle? Classical mopeds have pedals and are like bicycles, but with motors. But the term has come to include mechanisms without pedals, where all the propulsion is achieved through the motor, as illustrated below:

Mopeds Without Pedals
[Edgar Jiménez, Photographer (2012)]

Does the Park Safety Act bar this moped without pedals? How does an interpreter determine whether the statute's ordinary meaning includes these mechanisms?

There are a number of ways to understand the process of determining whether a statute has an ordinary meaning as applied to particular facts, such as a person's riding this moped through the park. To begin with, the ordinary meaning rule requires the interpreter to reflect on her own experience and that of others she has observed. My experience as a reasonable speaker suggests that you "drive a vehicle" when you operate an automobile of any sort—but not when you carry a toy into the park. The moped case is closer. Because it can be speedy, zipping along at forty miles per hour, the moped is in some ways more like a "vehicle" that needs to be regulated than the pokier Léon Bollée Voiturette pictured in the front of the chapter. But a moped is not necessarily the kind of vehicle one "drives." The same kind of intuitive process might be expressed socially. Justice Scalia once put it this way: "[T]he acid test of whether a word can reasonably bear a particular meaning is whether you could use the word in that sense at a cocktail party without having people look at you funny."[22]

Admittedly, the precise cocktail party metaphor is an incomplete one, because the judge ought not focus on the linguistic practices of the crowd she parties with. Instead, judges interpreting statutes need to be exceedingly cautious about their process of self-reflection, lest it represent idiosyncratic language customs and practices, rather than the language customs and practices of We the People more generally. In the great run of cases, the rule of law (the strongest justification for the ordinary meaning rule) demands a pluralistic attention to the language practices of *everyone* in the country, rich or poor alike, people with little formal education as well as those with advanced degrees, both manual workers and cocktail partiers. This notion is older than the Constitution and is constitutionally entrenched in the Due Process and Equal Protection Clauses. Specifically, the original meaning of the due process and equal protection language in the Constitution entails rules of law that are, presumptively, knowable by (due process) and applicable to (equal protection) everyone equally.[23]

The ordinary meaning rule requires that the judge provide a fair reading of statutory language, as it would be understood by the audience for the statute (usually, the general population). In most cases, this can usefully be called "everyday meaning" or "common and approved usage," as some judicial and legislative branch officials have done.[24] Thus, the judge should check her or his intuitions against

---

[22] *United States v. Johnson*, 539 U.S. 694, 718 (2000) (Scalia, J., dissenting) (quotation in text).

[23] William N. Eskridge Jr., *Original Meaning and Marriage Equality*, 52 Hous. L. Rev. 1067 (2015); Melissa Lamb Saunders, *Equal Protection, Class Legislation, and Colorblindness*, 96 Mich. L. Rev. 245 (1997).

[24] *Lopez v. Gonzales*, 549 U.S. at 53–54 ("everyday" and "commonsense" meaning); Office of Legislative Research & General Counsel, Utah Legislature, *Legislative Drafting Style Manual* ch. 1, § 1(b) (updated Oct. 24, 2014) ("common and approved usage"). See also Delaware Legislative Council, Division of Research, *Delaware Legislative Drafting Manual* pt. VI, ch. 2, Rule 1(b) (2015) ("commonly understood words").

general, objective evidence about how words and phrases are used and what they mean in our society. Increasingly, judges are turning to dictionaries as external evidence of what words might mean. Dictionaries are most useful to determine what *possible* meanings a word might have, but they are not as useful for reaching closure on what words might mean in different contexts, nor are they always useful for determining the ordinary meaning of word clusters (like "driving a vehicle") or phrases and clauses or entire sentences. Because many of the established dictionaries are old and not regularly updated, they also have a conservative bias that impedes understanding of what words, phrases, and sentences mean today.[25]

For example, *Webster's Third International Dictionary of the English Language* and other leading dictionaries define *vehicle* as "a means of carrying or transporting something, * * * a conveyance." If this definition is applied categorically, an automobile can be a vehicle—but so might a motorcycle, a moped, a bicycle, and even a tricycle. This does not mean that tricycles are within the coverage of the Park Safety Act, however. Indeed, *Webster's Third* and other dictionaries define a *wheelbarrow* as a "small vehicle with handles and one or more wheels for carrying small loads"—but this dictionary evidence is far from dispositive in figuring out whether wheelbarrows are prohibited from Lafayette Park. That one might correctly describe a wheelbarrow as a vehicle in typical conversation does not mean that every sentence using the term vehicle automatically includes wheelbarrows.[26]

Think about the wheelbarrow example from the vantage point of language theory. Classical language theory understands linguistic categories in a mechanical way: There is a definition of "vehicle," with itemized requirements, and any mechanism meeting those requirements must be considered a vehicle.[27] Classical theory might say that a wheelbarrow is a "vehicle" because it hits all the features identified in a dictionary (wheelbarrows are (1) mechanisms (2) conveying people or things (3) from one place to another). But this is not the way people actually process word meaning. Influenced by the theoretical work of Ludwig Wittgenstein and the empirical

---

[25] James J. Brudney & Lawrence Baum, *Oasis or Mirage: The Supreme Court's Thirst for Dictionaries in the Rehnquist and Roberts Eras*, 55 Wm. & Mary L. Rev. 483 (2013).

[26] *Taniguchi*, 132 S.Ct. at 2003–04.

[27] For a leading account of classic (Aristotelian) categorization theory of language, and contrasting it with prototype theory discussed below, see John R. Taylor, *Linguistic Categorization* (3d ed. 2003).

decisionmaking studies of Eleanor Rosch, most language theorists understand linguistic categories more functionally, defined around core *prototypical* applications of statutory words, phrases, and sentences. "By prototypes of categories we have generally meant the clearest cases of category membership defined operationally by people's judgments of goodness of membership in the category."[28] Technical terms (like carbon dioxide or twenty degrees Celsius) are well understood in light of classical theory, but most words and phrases are better understood as fuzzier categories defined by interlinked prototypical illustrations.[29]

To figure out what are prototypical "vehicles" regulated by the Park Safety Act, linguists would start with items that everyone believes are vehicles (such as cars and trucks) and compare them with items that no one believes are vehicles in the park context (such as the plastic toy car). Reasoning from properties found in the prototypical vehicles and by analogy to those accepted vehicles, the linguist would also consult larger empirical sources—not just dictionaries, but also language corpuses and even the Internet. Hence, a bicycle is like a car in some respects (people use it to get from one place to another) and different in other respects (it has no motor and cannot go as fast). One might also consult the Internet to see if bicycles are routinely deemed to be vehicles.[30] More ambitiously, Brigham Young University has created a corpus consisting of more than 400 million words; the corpus is easily searchable for words, word clusters and phrases, and word correlations.[31] A corpus search reveals that bicycles are commonly considered vehicles—a quantitative result in striking contrast to the understanding advanced by linguist Bryan Garner, who joined

---

[28] Eleanor Rosch, *Principles of Categorization*, in Rosch & Lloyd, eds., *Cognition and Categorization* 27, 38 (1978); Eleanor Rosch, *Cognitive Representations of Semantic Categories*, 104 J. Experimental Psychol. 192 (1975). See Lawrence M. Solan, *Law, Language, and Lenity*, 40 Wm. & Mary L. Rev. 57, 134–41 (1998), for excellent analysis and application of prototype theory to issues of statutory interpretation.

[29] See Ludwig Wittgenstein, *Philosophical Investigations* (1953) (germinal work for prototype theory of language); see also Patrick Hanks, *Lexical Analysis: Norms and Exploitations* chs. 4–5, 11 (2013) (an important application and elaboration of prototype theory); Taylor, *Linguistic Categorization*, 38–58 (important authority on categorization theory, contrasting it with prototype theory). See generally Lawrence M. Solan, *The Language of Judges* (1993), and *The Language of Statutes* (2010).

[30] For application of prototype analysis by linguists, consider Dirk Geeaerts, *Theories of Lexical Semantics* (2009); Slocum, *Ordinary Meaning*, ch. 5; Solan, *Language of Statutes*, 38–40, 63–65.

[31] Stephen C. Mouritsen, Comment, *The Dictionary Is Not a Fortress: Definitional Fallacies and a Corpus-Based Approach to Plain Meaning*, 2010 B.Y.U. L. Rev. 1915.

Justice Scalia in opining that the ordinary meaning of "vehicles" excludes bicycles.[32]

Prototype analysis of a statute is not complete, nor in my view has it even seriously launched, without an understanding of the statutory purpose(s). (Dictionaries, the Internet, and corpus linguistics do not necessarily tell us how to read a term in the context of its normative purpose.) As is often the case in modern statutes, the Park Safety Act, in both its title and its initial "because" clause, announces that its purpose is to improve park safety and to prevent accidents occurring because "vehicles" run into park users. Once purpose becomes a factor, prototypical "vehicles," as understood by a reasonable speaker of the English language who is addressing park safety, take on more overlapping mechanisms—quite probably bicycles as well as other speedy modes of transportation.

Prototype analysis would presume that inclusion of an item within statutory language depends on how close the item is to the core exemplars of the statutory coverage. Although this concept has long interested law professors, it has had little explicit currency among appellate judges, with notable exceptions such as Chief Judge Robert Katzmann of the Second Circuit, former Chief Judges Richard Posner and Frank Easterbrook of the Seventh Circuit, and Justice Thomas Lee of the Utah Supreme Court, all of whom have consciously engaged in prototype analysis in statutory cases.[33] Similarly, many widely admired Supreme Court decisions have, implicitly, followed something like that approach.[34] Judge Posner and

---

[32] Antonin Scalia & Bryan A. Garner, *Reading Law: The Interpretation of Legal Texts* 37–38 (2012).

[33] For exemplary opinions deploying prototype theory, see, e.g., *United States v. Soler*, 739 F.3d 226, 230 (2d Cir. 2014) (Katzmann, C.J.); *United States v. Costello*, 666 F.3d 1040 (7th Cir. 2012) (Posner, J.); *Fitzgerald v. Chrysler Corp.*, 116 F.3d 225 (7th Cir. 1997) (Posner, J.); *Secretary of Labor v. Lauritzen*, 835 F.2d 1529, 1536 (7th Cir. 1987) (Easterbrook, J.). See also *Continental Can Co. v. Chicago Truck Drivers*, 916 F.2d 1154 (7th Cir. 1990) (Easterbrook, J.). Consider the recent debate between Justice Lee (searching an internet mechanism to do linguistic corpus research that was decisive for him in finding ordinary meaning) and his skeptical colleagues in *State v. Rasabout*, 2014 Utah 72 (2014).

[34] E.g., *Yates v. United States*, 135 S.Ct. 1074 (2015) (both plurality and dissenting opinions) (whether a red grouper is a "tangible object" for purposes of destruction of evidence law); *Taniguchi*, 132 S.Ct. 1997 (both majority and dissenting opinions); *Muscarello v. United States*, 524 U.S. 125 (1998) (both majority and dissenting opinions) (whether a drug dealer with a gun in the trunk of his car "carries a firearm"); *MCI Telecommunications Corp. v. AT&T*, 512 U.S. 218 (1994) (what regulatory exceptions might be said to "modify" statutory requirements); accord, *POM Wonderful LLC v. Coca-Cola Co.*, 134 S.Ct. 2228, 2237–38 (2014); *United States v. X-Citement Video, Inc.*, 513 U.S. 64, 69–70 (1994).

Justice Lee have deployed computer search programs to discern patterns of ordinary usage for statutory terms, providing trial runs, of sorts, for professional linguistics analysis using the corpus. For the rule of law, democratic accountability, and even governance reasons developed above for the ordinary meaning rule, prototype analysis ought to anchor judicial analysis of what a statutory text means to the ordinary speaker of the English language.

Now apply this analysis to wheelbarrows. They are far from the prototypical "vehicles" targeted by a park safety law. If I say "vehicles pose safety hazards to park users," it is very unlikely I am referring to wheelbarrows; the prototypical "vehicles" covered by this law are automobiles and motorcycles, and wheelbarrows are a far cry from these prototypes. Indeed, wheelbarrows are much closer to the prototypical conveyances that are surely not "vehicles," namely, nonmotorized mechanisms that cannot go very fast, such as baby carriages,

Here is another wrinkle, originally presented by linguists as a qualification to prototype theory.[35] Words travel in clusters. That is another reason why something that might, linguistically, be a *vehicle* in many contexts is not a vehicle in all contexts. Recall that the statute says that no one can "drive a vehicle" in Lafayette Park. Can a laborer pushing a wheelbarrow across Lafayette Park be said to "drive a vehicle"? Ordinary parlance does not speak of "driving" an ordinary wheelbarrow; instead, you "push" the wheelbarrow around the park. People would look at you funny (and not just people inebriated from too many cocktails at a party). That is not a fair reading of the statutory language—unless you were referring to an electric or motorized wheelbarrow, which kids of all ages have "driven" around their backyards.

How about a youth on a moped, such as the one pictured above? Again, a wide variety of dictionaries define *moped* as a "vehicle"—but, again, a further question is whether a person operating a moped is "driving" it. Jot down your intuition about this in the margin (or if this is not your book, on a piece of scrap paper).

As a matter of ordinary parlance, it may seem odd to say that a person "drives" a moped, and I should not fault the gentle reader who dismisses this possibility as a matter of her experience. But this is

[35] Jerry A. Fodor & Ernest Lepore, *The Compositionality Papers* 35–42 (2002); Daniel N Osherson & Edward E. Smith, *On the Adequacy of Prototype Theory as a Theory of Concepts*, 9 Cognition, 35, 45 (1981).

precisely the kind of issue where a judge needs to look outside her own experience and that of her inner circle; she and her assistants need to do research. As it turns out, most states require people to have a *driver license* before they can operate a moped as well as a motorcycle. Almost all the states have patterned their vehicle codes on the 2000 Uniform Vehicle Code, which includes mopeds as "motor vehicles," and says that "drive" means "to operate or be in physical control of a vehicle." The administrative regulations and handbooks advising the public in most states say that you can "drive" a moped or motorcycle in the same way you "drive" a car. Thus, the California Department of Motor Vehicles uses "drive" as well as "ride" and "operate" to describe moped use.[36]

Given this widespread practice, does it now make linguistic sense to say that a person "drives" a moped across Lafayette Park? Such a reading is plausible, but I am not sure this research creates an ordinary meaning that is so clear that it excludes other meanings. In other words, there is linguistic pluralism for this issue. Like California, Georgia requires "motorcycle licenses" for mopeds as well as for regular motorcycles—but unlike California's regulations and unlike the Uniform Vehicle Code, Georgia's administrative guidance says that one "operates" rather than "drives" a moped or a motorcycle. Indeed, the special license in Georgia is called a "motorcycle operator's license." Other states follow Georgia in this regard.[37] Does this state practice change your thinking about whether the Lafayette Park Safety Act bars mopeds from the park? Is it important that even

---

[36] National Committee on Uniform Traffic Laws and Ordinances, Uniform Vehicle Code §§ 1–554 and 1–156 (2000) (definitions of "moped" and "motor vehicle"); ibid., § 1–123 (definition of "drive"); id., § 6–101 (identifying "drivers" who need to be licensed, including moped users). Consistent with the Uniform Code, California has separate "driver license" requirements for "driving" automobiles, motorcycles, and mopeds. See California Department of Motor Vehicles, Driver License and Identity Card Information, available at http://www.dmv.ca.gov/dl/dl_info.htm#two505 (viewed March 1, 2016); California Department of Motor Vehicles, Motorcycle (Supplement to the California Driver Handbook), at 3 (2015), available at https://www.dmv.ca.gov/portal/pubs/dl655/dl655mcycle.pdf (viewed March 1, 2016). For similar language, see also New York Department of Motor Vehicles, Get a Motorcycle License, available at http://dmv.ny.gov/driver-license/get-motorcycle-license (viewed March 1, 2016); Texas Department of Public Safety, Motorcycle Licenses, available at http://www.txdps.state.tx.us/DriverLicense/motorcyclelicense.htm (viewed March 1, 2016).

[37] Georgia Department of Driver Services, Applying for a Motorcycle License, available at http://www.dds.ga.gov/drivers/dldata.aspx?con=1749319514&ty=dl (viewed March 1, 2016); see also Alabama Department of Public Safety, Motorcycle Operator Manual, available at http://dps.alabama.gov/Documents/Manuals/MotorCycleManual.pdf (viewed March 1, 2016); Florida Department of Motor Vehicles, Florida Motorcycle License, available at http://www.dmvflorida.org/motorcycle-license.shtml (viewed March 1, 2016).

states, like California, that use the term "drive" in their regulations, use the terms "ride" and "operate" much more frequently in their handbooks? Finally, recall that Lafayette Park is federal land located in the District of Columbia. The District requires a driver license to operate a motorcycle, but its regulations use the word "operate" rather than "drive." Most relevant, however, the District excludes mopeds altogether from its driver-licensing requirement.[38] Does that affect your thinking?

At this point, consider this precept: The linguistic range of applications of a statutory text typically generates a *continuum of applications*, with no sharply defined line between the applications clearly covered by the statute and those clearly not covered. That is, for most regulatory directives, there is a range of meanings the statutory words might bear. Some of those meanings are close to the "core" of the statute; it is very clear to almost anyone that the statutory language covers these meanings. The Park Safety Act clearly covers automobiles and trucks, which the statutory text suggests are the central concern of the statute. Other meanings are further from the core and are more debatable, but meanings in this *penumbra* might fairly be included in the statutory domain. The Act might well apply to such penumbral objects as mopeds and bicycles. Yet other meanings might be conceivably within the statutory language, but upon brief reflection clearly do not fit with the statutory coverage. Although defined as "vehicles" in the dictionaries, wheelbarrows and toy cars would certainly be outside the domain of our vehicles statute. Figure 1, below, is a visual representation of such a continuum, with a few other mechanisms added to the ones discussed above.[39]

FIGURE 1

Ordinary Meaning Continuum: "Vehicles" in the Park

Core Coverage		Penumbra			Outside the Statute	
Cars	Motorcycles	Mopeds	Bicycles	Tricycles	Wheelbarrows	Toy Cars
Trucks	Motor Scooters		Skateboards		Wheelchairs	Baby Carriages

[38] District of Columbia Department of Motor Vehicles, Motorcycle Endorsement, available at http://dmv.dc.gov/service/get-motorcycle-endorsement (viewed March 1, 2016).

[39] On the contrast between activities falling within the "core" of a statute, and those falling within the statute's "penumbra," see H.L.A. Hart, *The Concept of Law* (1961).

The continuum idea is intuitive. Recall Justice Scalia's witty observation that the litmus test for plain meaning is "whether you could use the word in that sense at a cocktail party without having people look at you funny." Set aside the precise cocktail party metaphor and recast the test as whether you could use the word or phrase in that sense in a more pluralistic *conversation* without having people look at you funny. Either formulation suggests a continuum of ordinary meaning. Consider this hypothetical. You are having a conversation with another parent, and both of you are worried because motorcycle riders have been taking short cuts through the park and running into or brushing aside kids playing in the park. Your colleague says, emphatically, "This city needs to keep vehicles out of the park!" If you say, "Yes, motorcycles, in particular, have got to GO," your interlocutor will shake his head in agreement. In contrast, your interlocutor would think you were sarcastically making fun of his suggestion, if you were to say, in response to his demand for vehicle limitations, "Yes, and give the heave ho to those infernal baby carriages!"

Statutory interpretation can learn something from imagined conversations like this one. Both involve communication whereby the speaker and recipient operate under widely shared assumptions about word meaning, conventions of grammar, and cultural background. Both assume a common goal of fair mutual understanding. To be sure, statutory interpretation is different from ordinary conversation in several important ways. For example, the statutory speaker's words are delivered to a general audience of recipients whose members are not personally known to the speaker, and the speaker does not have an immediate opportunity to observe and to correct the response (or interpretation) of the speaker's words by an immediate audience. It is important to understand that statutory interpretation is more external and objective than a personal conversation would be.[40]

But an important way that statutory interpretation is very much similar to a conversation is that the precise language makes a

---

[40] The analogy of statutory interpretation to a conversation is developed by Geoffrey P. Miller, *Pragmatics and the Maxims of Interpretation*, 1990 Wis. L. Rev. 1179 (drawing from Grice). See also John David Ohlendorf, *Against Coherence in Statutory Interpretation*, 90 Notre Dame L. Rev. 735, 745, 750–57 (2014). The analogy between conversational and written communication is criticized in Bernard S. Jackson, *Making Sense in Law: Linguistic, Psychological, and Semiotic Perspectives* (1995), and its application to statutory ordinary meaning is rejected in Slocum, *Ordinary Meaning*, ch. 2.

difference. Recall that our Park Safety Act provides that no one shall "drive a vehicle of any kind" in Lafayette Park. Although "vehicle of any kind" presumably suggests a broader ambit for the statute than simply "vehicle," the more important addition is the introduction of the verb "drive." So the continuum of ordinary meaning now assumes a new shape, because ordinary parlance does not treat most potential "vehicles" as mechanisms that one "drives." One "drives" a car or truck, so these vehicles remain in the core coverage of the Park Safety Act. One also "drives" the Léon Bollée, as suggested by the illustration at the front of the chapter. Conversely, most mechanisms, like wheelbarrows and baby carriages, that were already outside the statutory ambit, are even more clearly outside. It is not a fair reading of the statute to say that one "drives a wheelbarrow."

In partial contrast, one might "drive" motorcycles and motor scooters. To be sure, we usually say that a person "rides" or "operates" a motorcycle or motor scooter or anything else that one straddles (like a horse), while we usually say the person "drives" a mechanism that cannot be straddled. So "ride" or "operate" is the normal locution in everyday parlance, but it is not grammatically incorrect to say the person "drives" a motorcycle. Most state vehicle laws require a "driver license" to operate motorcycles and motor scooters, and regulations as well as other public documents often say that someone "drives" a motorcycle or motor scooter.[41] It is a bigger stretch to say he that one "drives" a bicycle or tricycle, and so those potential vehicles are also lower in the continuum of plain meaning. Figure 2 provides a rough illustration of the continuum for the statutory bar to "driv[ing] a vehicle of any kind." Notice how the statutory core is smaller and the area outside the statute larger, because the language is more confining.

---

[41] Thus, state DMVs typically use "drive" interchangeably with "ride" and "operate" in discussing the operation of motorcycles and mopeds. *E.g., Motorcycles, Mopeds, and Scooters Defined*, California Department of Motor Vehicles (2011), available at https://www.dmv.ca.gov/portal/dmv/detail/motorcycles/motorcycles (viewed March 1, 2016); *Register a Moped*, New York Department of Motor Vehicles (2015), http://dmv.ny.gov/org/registration/register-moped (viewed March 1, 2016).

FIGURE 2

Ordinary Meaning Continuum: "Driving a Vehicle" in the Park

Core Coverage	**Penumbra**			**Outside the Statute**	
Cars	Motorcycles	Mopeds	Bicycles	Tricycles	Wheelbarrows
Trucks	Motor Scooters			Skateboards	Baby Carriages

Yet another way that statutory interpretation is like a conversation is that both operate under what linguistic philosopher H.P. Grice terms the *cooperative principle.* Conversations are cooperative enterprises; participants not only operate under shared conventions and assumptions about language, but also a shared purpose or purposes. Given this assumption, each participant seeks to be helpful in her communications and in her understanding of her partner's communication. Grice puts it this way: "Make your conversational contribution such as is required, at the stage at which it occurs, by the accepted purpose and direction of the talk exchange in which you are engaged."[42] A corollary to the cooperative principle is that the meaning of a sentence is often more than what can be understood by parsing the semantic meaning of its words within ordinary rules of syntax. Meaning is often inferential, and proper inference depends upon knowing the background assumptions of the conversation (which include conventions of semantics and syntax).[43]

More specifically, the appropriate inference of meaning in a conversation depends upon the point of the conversation. Like conversations, statutes tend to have a point—or what we should call a purpose (or purposes). As before, the analogy between face-to-face conversation and statutory interpretation is not perfect, but here the difference between face-to-face conversations and statutory interpretation amplifies rather than limits my point. That is, statutes are almost always directive, much more consistently so than conversations; statutes purport to solve problems or address public issues. Although the process by which statutes are created and

---

[42] H.P. Grice, *Logic and Conversation*, in William James Lecture 41, 45 (1975) [1967], and *Studies in the Way of Words* 26 (1991). On Grice's theory, see Gerald Gazdar, *Pragmatics: Implicature, Presupposition, and Logical Form* (1979); Scott Soames, *Drawing the Line Between Meaning and Implicature—and Relating Both to Assertion*, 42 Nous 440 (2008).

[43] Robert C. Stalnaker, *Context and Content: Essays on Intentionality in Speech and Thought* (1999). See also Teun A. Van Dijk, *Discourse and Ideology*, in *Discourse Studies: A Multidisciplinary Introduction* 379–407 (Teun A. Van Dijk 2d ed., 2011).

applied involves contention, competition, and often ire, the constitutional assumption is that Congress enacts public-regarding laws and executive and judicial branch officials "take Care" to enforce and faithfully interpret those laws. This is a super-strong instantiation of Grice's cooperative principle. The first speaker in statutory interpretation is not just a colleague, but is the constitutionally empowered Congress-with-the-President, and so the duty of the listener/interpreter to think along lines of the cooperative principle is powerful, *both* because the Constitution vests special authority in that speaker, *and* because that speaker has an additional legitimacy that derives from its members' representation of, and accountability toward, We the People. An interpreter who does not approach statutes with a thorough dedication to this principle is behaving in a way that is undemocratic, and her interpretation requires especially strong justification.[44]

While the point of a conversation is often rather banal and limited, such as sharing information and feelings, the point of a statute is typically quite normative and directive. Sometimes, the statutory point is a grand aspiration or a fundamental norm. Also, many statutes set forth their purpose on the face of the statute. The Park Safety Act has that feature, for the preface to its command is that "vehicles create safety problems." *Because* of that fact, accepted by the legislature, "it shall be a federal offense for anyone to drive a vehicle of any kind into Lafayette Park."

The point, or purpose, of a conversation makes a difference. If a fellow parent expresses concern to you that "vehicles" are creating safety problems in the park, you will view "vehicles" more broadly than you would if the parent's concern were fumes and other kinds of pollution. Indeed, even the phrase "drive a vehicle" would be understood more liberally if safety were the point of the conversation. For example, motorcycles can go just as fast as cars and are more likely to fit onto a park lane—so that I am much more likely to say this: "Your safety concern certainly means that we should not allow people to drive motorcycles through the park!" Most concerned citizens would not look at you funny. Hence, motorcycles might move into the core coverage of the statute, up from the more ambiguous regulatory spot in which we placed them in Figures 1 and 2.

---

[44] James J. Brudney, *Congressional Commentary on Judicial Interpretation of Statutes: Idle Chatter or Telling Response?,* 93 Mich. L. Rev. 1 (1994); Daniel A. Farber, *Statutory Interpretation and Legislative Supremacy*, 78 Geo. L.J. 281 (1989).

Likewise, once the point of a statute is understood to be park safety, motor scooters, mopeds, and bicycles are more likely to fall within the ordinary meaning of the directive. The reason is that all these "vehicles" can go pretty fast and therefore pose dangers for park users. Although we usually do not say we "drive" motor scooters and mopeds, it may be a fair reading of the statute to include these as regulated vehicles; the Internet offers a number of examples of this usage.[45] Importantly, an ordinary speaker of the language would find that locution more acceptable if she knew the point of the conversation was park safety. Motor scooters and mopeds can go pretty fast. But so can bicycles—yet we should still place them in the statutory penumbra, because it is exceedingly odd to say, in either conversation or in statutory interpretation, that anyone "drives" a bicycle.[46] Because slower-moving tricycles, wheelbarrows, and baby carriages are unlikely to harm third parties and are not vehicles that anyone "drives," those mechanisms fall out of the statutory ambit even more clearly than they did before. Figure 3 illustrates the conversational insights once we consider that statutes, like conversations, have a point.

FIGURE 3

Ordinary Meaning Continuum: Because "Vehicles Create Safety Problems," Do Not "Drive a Vehicle of Any Kind" in the Park

Core Coverage	Penumbra	Outside the Statute
Cars Motor Scooters	Bicycles Tricycles	Wheelbarrows
Trucks Mopeds	Skateboards	Baby Carriages
Motorcycles		

The continuum in Figure 3, including the process by which it has been generated, suggests a number of important lessons for text-based statutory interpretation. To begin with, "ordinary meaning" is

[45] Using "Google Trends"—which measures and graphs the frequency of word or phrase searches on Google—my research associate Marissa Roy (Yale Law School Class of 2017) compared "drive a moped" to "ride a moped" as well as "drive a scooter" to "ride a scooter." Search strings with "drive" were used as often or more often than search strings with "ride," showing that the lay person uses that phrase. However, using "drive" in a Google search string turned up less results than "ride" (53,600 vs. 83,700 for drive/ride a moped; 106,000 vs. 449,000 for drive/ride a scooter), suggesting that most webpages cater to the use of "ride."

[46] If you Google Trends "drive a bicycle," you do generate some examples, but they are far less common than "ride a bicycle." Thanks again to Marissa Roy (Yale Law School Class of 2017) for this evidence.

a function of the precise statutory text, conventions of word use and grammar, and statutory purpose (its "point"). Once one has engaged in this kind of analysis, the tail ends of the continuum provide many easy answers. The Park Safety Act has an ordinary meaning that includes cars, trucks, and motorcycles and that excludes wheelbarrows, baby carriages, and dozens of other items that could conceivably be called "vehicles" (such as pogo sticks).

Additionally, the ordinary meaning rule, standing alone, does not tell the statutory interpreter exactly where the draw the line. As Figure 3 indicates, the ordinary meaning of the Park Safety Act might include bicycles and might exclude tricycles, but I am not as confident of those judgments as I am of the judgments reflected in the tail ends of the continuum in Figure 3. What this analysis suggests is that the operation of the ordinary meaning rule depends not only on the considerations previously examined, but (ultimately) on other context. By "operation," I mean *both* the points at which the statute no longer has an "ordinary meaning" *and* which way to go (inclusion in or exclusion from the statute) for the applications for which there is no "ordinary meaning."

Finally, the foregoing analysis may be expressed in a more formal manner. This will illustrate the proper understanding of the *textual canons of statutory construction*, as actors in our legal system actually deploy them. The textual canons are neither hard-and-fast rules that mechanically limit judges, nor ought they be mushy indeterminate considerations with which a judge embellishes a written decision reached on other grounds. Properly presented, the textual canons (like other kinds of canons examined in this volume) reflect decades or even centuries of statutory reasoning and help the interpreter structure as well as reflect upon her inquiry. As illustrated above, the inquiry itself must focus primarily on the precise language of the statute, widely accepted and understood conventions of word usage and grammar, and the point or purpose of the statute.[47]

---

47 For instructive deployments of the textual canons, see the debates among the Justices in *Yates v. United States*, 135 S.Ct. 1074 (2015); *Circuit City Stores, Inc. v. Adams,* 532 U.S. 105 (2001); *Babbitt v. Sweet Home Chap. of Communities for a Great Oregon,* 515 U.S. 687 (1995). See also *Astoria Fed. Sav. & Loan Ass'n v. Solimino,* 501 U.S. 104 (1991).

Ordinary Meaning Canons

This part shall situate the primary textual canons in the inquiry and suggest how the questions raised by each canon help produce a relatively disciplined and productive approach to statutory interpretation. Judges often discuss the textual canons as "presumptions," a term avoided here. Instead, the present account starts with the canonical *anchor*—the ordinary meaning rule, applied through the lens of prototype analysis—and then examines a number of canons that help the interpreter apply, or sometimes adjust, the anchoring rule. The other textual canons support or help us apply that anchor—typically helping the interpreter determine whether there is an ordinary meaning. Recall some of the powerful normative reasons why ordinary meaning ought to be the anchor for statutory interpretation. Ordinary meaning renders the statute more accessible to the citizenry, a great rule of law value. And ordinary meaning best reflects the likely expectations of Congress and the President, a great democracy value.[48] As further confirmation of its democracy value, more than two-thirds of the state legislatures have explicitly codified the "ordinary usage" canon as the starting point for statutory interpretation,[49] and legislative drafting manuals overwhelmingly aspire to create statutes using "plain and commonly understood words," as the Delaware manual puts it.[50]

On the whole, the main value of the textual canons is that they suggest or demand potentially relevant inquiries that help us explore a statute's ordinary meaning. This ordinary meaning must be the linchpin for the textual canons. Specifically, the textual canons ought to be applied through the lens of prototype analysis, and not mechanically. This chapter, therefore, is doing something more than reporting a list of textual canons; it is pitching the traditional canons

---

[48] For support in the legislative process for the ordinary meaning canon, see Abbe R. Gluck & Lisa Schultz Bressman, *Statutory Interpretation from the Inside: An Empirical Study of Congressional Drafting, Delegation, and Statutory Interpretation: Part I*, 65 Stan. L. Rev. 901, 938–39 (2013). For administrative reliance on ordinary meaning as the anchor, see Walker, *Inside Agency Statutory Interpretation*, 67 Stan. L. Rev. at 1030–31.

[49] Scott, *Codified Canons*, 98 Geo. L.J. at 357 (Table 1) (reporting that 34 states have codified the canon that interpreters must follow "ordinary usage" unless the legislature deploys a technical or specialized term of art).

[50] Delaware Legislative Council, Division of Research, *Delaware Legislative Drafting Manual* pt. VI, ch. 2, Rule 1(b) (2015) (quotation in text). The Legislative Counsel for both the U.S. House and the U.S. Senate similarly aspire to drafting in clear, understandable English, and the same was true, either explicitly or by implication, in all the state legislative drafting manuals I examined.

in a way that fits with the underlying normative justifications for them, especially the rule of law and democratic legitimacy justifications.

As you work through the various canons, consider how they help you apply the text of the Park Safety Act to bicycles:

> Because vehicles create safety problems, no person is permitted to drive a vehicle of any kind in Lafayette Park.

In the case of the bicycle, arising under the hypothetical Park Safety Act, the ordinary meaning inquiry is not limited to whether a bicycle is a "vehicle" (Figure 1 above) nor even to whether a person "drives a vehicle" when she rides a bicycle (Figure 2 above). Most completely, the inquiry asks whether the bicyclist "drives a vehicle" of the sort that "create[s] safety problems" (Figure 3 above). My tentative view is that the Park Safety Act does not have a completely clear, unambiguous ordinary meaning, as applied to bicycle riders. While a reasonable speaker of the English language would be justified in calling a bicycle a vehicle that creates safety problems, a bicycle is not the first thing that comes to mind when you hear the word "vehicle," and one would usually not say, in ordinary conversation, that someone "drives" a bicycle. For this reason, more deliberation and research are needed before deciding whether a bicycle is a statutory vehicle.[51]

Dictionary Canon. Dictionaries may help the interpreter apply the ordinary meaning rule, but in a particular and narrow way—usually by confirming that what the judge considers an ordinary, common meaning of a word is actually a "linguistically permissible" meaning for that word.[52] This commonsense utility of dictionaries helps explain why a dictionary canon appears so often in state legislated canons and legislative drafting manuals.[53] And it may help

---

[51] For examples of internet searches to figure out ordinary meaning, compare the majority and dissenting opinions in *Muscarello v. United States*, 524 U.S. 125 (1998), as well as *United States v. Costello*, 666 F.3d 1040 (7th Cir. 2012).

[52] Hart & Sacks, *The Legal Process*, 1375–76 (Eskridge & Frickey eds.); CRS Report, *Statutory Interpretation*, 11–12 (updated 2011). For a (small) sample of recent cases where Supreme Court majorities have relied on dictionaries to help figure out ordinary meaning, see *Taniguchi*, 132 S.Ct. 1997; *Chamber of Commerce v. Whiting*, 131 S.Ct. 1968 (2011); *New Process Steel L.P. v. NLRB*, 560 U.S. 674 (2010); *Crawford v. Metro. Gov't of Nashville & Davidson Co.*, 555 U.S. 271 (2009). Compare *People v. Laidler*, 817 N.W.2d 517, 522–23 (Mich. 2012) (relying on a dictionary), with *People v. Tennyson*, 790 N.W.2d 354, 359–62 (Mich. 2010) (consulting dictionaries but finding legislative intent inconsistent with the dictionary meaning).

[53] "A drafter should know or check the commonly accepted dictionary definition," as a "court will generally apply the common dictionary definitions of words

explain why federal courts, especially the U.S. Supreme Court, have increasingly looked to dictionaries to help them determine the ordinary meaning of statutory terms.[54] Linguists as well as law professors, however, have been quite critical of judicial decisions that quote a definition from a dictionary and then categorize an item based upon whether it fits the dictionary criteria.[55] Most legislative staff who draft statutes and agency staff who draft interpretive regulations do not (for the most part) even consult dictionaries, and most of them are surprised or shocked to hear that federal judges rely on them so heavily.[56]

These criticisms are well-taken. Ordinary conversation does not operate in this way, as prototype theorists have established. If I tell you, "we need to prohibit vehicles from the park, to ensure safety," you have no proper understanding of my sentence if you just consult a dictionary, without further analysis. Dictionaries define vehicle to mean "mechanisms for transporting [or conveying] a person or thing." If applied literally, that definition is capacious enough to include "wheelbarrows," a notion reinforced by dictionary definitions of "wheelbarrow" as a form of vehicle. Not only is it unlikely that I am referring to wheelbarrows when I talk about vehicles in Lafayette Park, but it is even more unlikely that I am doing so in the context of a conversation about how to improve park safety.[57]

Dictionaries have value, however, as both evidence of usage and, sometimes, as a barometer of usage. For example, if the primary

---

that are not specifically defined by statute." Florida Senate, *Manual for Drafting Legislation* ch. 2, at 12 (6th ed. 2009).

[54] Brudney & Baum, *Oasis or Mirage*; Jeffrey L. Kirchmeier & Samuel A. Thumma, *Scaling the Lexicon Fortress: The United States Supreme Court's Use of Dictionaries in the Twenty-First Century*, 94 Marq. L. Rev. 77, 103 (2010).

[55] On the pitfalls of excessive reliance on dictionaries, see, e.g., Scalia & Garner, *Reading Law*, 419–24; Brudney & Baum, *Oasis or Mirage* (finding more of the latter than the former); Ellen P. Aprill, *The Law of the Word: Dictionary Shopping in the Supreme Court*, 30 Ariz. St. L.J. 275, 278 (1998); Craig Hoffman, *Parse the Sentence First: Curbing the Urge to Resort to the Dictionary When Interpreting Legal Texts*, 6 N.Y.U. J. Legis. & Pub. Pol'y 401, 402 (2003). For an example of a judicial opinion that rejects this kind of dictionary fetishism, see *Caraco Pharmaceutical Labs., Ltd. v. Novo Nordisk*, 132 S.Ct. 1670, 1680–83 (2012).

[56] See Gluck & Bressman, *Statutory Interpretation from the Inside: Part I*, 65 Stan. L. Rev. at 938–40 (reporting the views of congressional drafting staff, that they do not consult dictionaries and are surprised that judges rely on them); Walker, *Inside Agency Statutory Interpretation*, 67 Stan. L. Rev. at 1030–31 (reporting that federal agencies interpreting statutes focus on the "ordinary meaning" of the words enacted into law, and not on dictionaries).

[57] *MCI Telecomm. Corp. v. AT&T Co.*, 512 U.S. 218 (1994) (skeptical treatment of an idiosyncratic dictionary understanding of "modify").

dictionaries—*Webster's Third, Oxford English, American Heritage, Random House*, and *Black's*—all define "vehicle" as a motorized mechanism for transporting persons and things from one place to another, that would be evidence that Congress in the Park Safety Act used "vehicle" to signify motorized mechanisms only.[58] In fact, all of these dictionaries define "vehicle" more broadly—and that relative consensus would discourage an interpreter from confining the word to motorized mechanisms. Nonetheless, this is not decisive evidence that a judge interpreting the Park Safety Act *must* read the statutory term that broadly, for the reasons advanced above. Thus, dictionaries are often useful in clarifying or narrowing our understanding of statutory terms.[59] On the other hand, dictionaries may also reveal a linguistic pluralism: A word or cluster of words has a broad range of possible meanings.[60]

One interesting issue is whether the statutory interpreter should examine only the dictionaries in use at the time Congress enacted the statute. This might be very useful to figure out the meaning of terms that are today arcane but that had a readily understandable meaning when the law was enacted; contemporary dictionaries might also provide some information about the statute's purpose.[61] But the rule of law underpinning of the ordinary meaning rule suggests that the dictionary meaning of any term should normally be informed by current as well as historic dictionaries. For example, Noah Webster's 1828 *Dictionary of the English Language* defines "vehicle" as "any kind of carriage moving on land, either on wheels or runners. This word comprehends coaches, chariots, gigs, sullies, wagons, carts of every kind, sleighs and sleds."[62] If Congress had enacted the Park Safety Act in 1828, that contemporary definition would provide no

---

[58] For a list of the most popular dictionaries used by Supreme Court Justices, see Brudney & Baum, *Oasis or Mirage*, 55 Wm. & Mary L. Rev. at 529–32.

[59] For examples where judges were reluctant to find an ordinary meaning that went beyond most of the definitions found in the leading dictionaries, see, e.g., *Taniguchi*, 132 S.Ct. 1997; *Gross v. FBL Fin. Servs., Inc.*, 557 U.S. 167 (2009); *MCI Telecomm. Corp.*, 512 U.S. 218; *United States v. Costello*, 666 F.3d 1040 (7th Cir. 2012) (Posner, J.).

[60] E.g., *Roberts v. Sea-Land Servs., Inc.*, 132 S.Ct. 1350, 1356–57 (2012) (variety of definitions for "award"); *Kasten v. Saint-Gobain Performance Plastics Corp.*, 563 U.S. 1, 7–8 (2011) (finding a variety of different uses for "filing a complaint").

[61] Cf. Scalia & Garner, *Reading Law*, 78–92 (extended defense of a "fixed-meaning canon," but unclear or at least flexible as to how an original meaning is to be applied to new circumstances).

[62] Noah Webster, *American Dictionary of the English Language* (1828) (the relevant definition of "vehicle"), available at http://1828.mshaffer.com/d/word/vehicle (viewed Nov. 1, 2014).

legitimate reason to exclude automobiles from the Act's regulatory ambit in this day and time. On the other hand, the early dictionary definition would lend some support to applying the statute to the 1897 Léon Bollée Voiturette, which seems to fit much more snugly with the notion of "vehicle" in 1828 than perhaps it does today.

Term of Art Canon. "[W]here Congress borrows terms of art in which are accumulated the legal tradition and meaning of centuries of practice, it presumably knows and adopts the cluster of ideas that were attached to each borrowed word in the body of learning from which it was taken and the meaning its use will convey to the judicial mind unless otherwise instructed."[63] Congressional as well as state legislative drafters understand the term of art canon to be a valid but limited exception to the ordinary meaning rule. The Massachusetts Legislature has done so in a particularly apt manner: "Words and phrases shall be construed according to the common and approved usage of the language; but technical words and phrases and such others as may have acquired a peculiar and appropriate meaning in law shall be construed and understood according to such meaning."[64]

An exception for technical terms is strongest and most relevant for *intransitive statutes*, namely, those addressed to particular public or private officials and not to the general population.[65] When Congress is using legal terms of art in laws directing officials, presumably advised by lawyers, it makes sense to focus on the specialized meaning reflected in legal sources such as *Black's Law Dictionary*, rather than general sources such as *Webster's Third*. But when Congress is using ordinary language in laws directed at the general population, ordinary usage, and therefore *Webster's*, is a usually better anchor than technical legal usage, such as that reflected in *Black's*. The Park Safety Act is addressed to all users of

---

[63] *Morissette v. United States*, 342 U.S. 246, 253 (1952) (leading case); see, e.g., *United States v. Castleman*, 134 S.Ct. 1405, 1410–11 (2014); *Sekhar v. United States*, 133 S.Ct. 2720, 2724 (2013); 2A *Sutherland Statutes and Statutory Construction* §§ 47:27, 47:29 (7th ed. 2015); CSR Report, *Statutory Interpretation*, 6–6–7 (updated 2011); Scalia & Garner, *Reading Law*, 320–21 (related canon of imputed common-law meaning). On the relationship between ordinary and technical meaning, see Mary Jane Morrison, *Excursions into the Nature of Legal Language*, 37 Clev. St. L. Rev. 271 (1989).

[64] Mass. Gen. Laws ch. 4, § 6 (Third) (added 1967); see Mich. Comp. Laws § 8.3a; Tex. Govt. Code § 311.011(b) (added 1985); Scott, *Codified Canons*, 98 Geo. L.J. at 357 (Table 1) (reporting that state codifications of the ordinary usage canon almost always have a caveat for "terms of art" or "technical" meanings).

[65] On the distinction between transitive and intransitive statutes, see Edward R. Rubin, *Law and Legislation in the Administrative State*, 89 Colum. L. Rev. 369 (1989).

Lafayette Park—young and old, adventurous and staid, highly educated and uneducated alike. The predictable rule of law is poorly served by interpreting the Act according to a technical legal dictionary rather than one of more general usage. Fortunately, as is usually the case, the definition of "vehicle" in *Black's* is not different from the definitions in *Webster's* and other leading dictionaries of general usage.

As the Massachusetts codification (quoted above) suggests, ordinary meaning and term-of-art meaning are not necessarily inconsistent with one another. Not only might an ordinary meaning be the same as a technical meaning, but ordinary meaning might be elusive or ambiguous in ways that legal terms of art might clear up. In figuring out the prototypical core of a statute, an interpreter ought to examine specialized usage of the relevant statutory language elsewhere. Consider an example of this point.

Black's mainly reflects common law use of terms of art—but terms of art are not limited to the common law. Terms of art can also be gleaned from patterns of statutes and agency regulations.[66] Indeed, "vehicle" is a good example of that. All fifty states and the District of Columbia require registration of "vehicles" in their motor vehicle codes, and so a consensus practice by the states might be a form of statutory common law that can inform statutory interpretation. As it turns out, there is a statutory common law applicable to the issue in the case of the bicycle. Recall that most state vehicle-regulation laws are based upon the 2000 Uniform Vehicle Code ("UVC"). The UVC defines "vehicle" as "[e]very device in, upon or by which any person or property is or may be transported or drawn upon a highway, excepting devices used exclusively upon stationary rails or tracks." The Code defines "bicycle" as "[e]very vehicle propelled solely by human power upon which any person may ride, having two tandem wheels and except scooters and similar devices." While not dispositive, this "statutory common law" supports the argument that the ordinary meaning of "vehicle" includes "bicycles."[67]

Pet Fish Canon. Although not explicitly canonized by judges or legislatures, what linguists call the "pet fish" precept is one that

---

66 *Kasten v. Saint-Gobain*, 563 U.S. at 8–9 (finding a broad term of art by examining a wide range of state statues, agency rules, and judicial decisions).

67 Uniform Vehicle Code § 1–215 (2000) (defining "vehicle"); id., § 1–109 (defining "bicycle"). I appreciate the research of Chris Pagliarella, Yale Law School Class of 2016, who did a 50-state survey to document the point made in text.

judges often follow as a matter of common sense and should therefore understand canonically. The "pet fish" phenomenon occurs when two words combine to produce a meaning that is not the mechanical composition of the two words separately. (Larry Solan first suggested this linguistic insight to me.) Thus, the prototypical "pet" is a dog or a cat; the prototypical "fish" is a salmon or cod—but the prototypical "pet fish" is neither a dog nor a salmon, but is clearly the goldfish. The prototypical pet fish is not linguistically a product of the two terms, but is instead a category of its own, with its own prototype strikingly different from those of its component words. Pet fish is a dramatically smaller category than either component term.[68]

Statutory interpretation practice recognizes the same kind of concept. For example, prototypical "violence" involves great force and the possibility of severe physical harm, and "domestic" involves localized household or relationship activities—but when you put the two words together, as "domestic violence," the meaning is *more* than that of the two words combined. Rather than meaning just aggressive and physically harmful conduct within the household, "domestic violence" as a phrase also includes conduct consisting of oppressive touching and threatening words that create fear.[69]

The Park Safety Act provides an illustration of the pet fish precept, namely, "drives a vehicle." *Webster's Third* defines "drive" as "affect[ing] the movement of" something; "vehicle" means "any mechanism for transporting persons or things." When you put these two broad, open-textured words together, as in "drive a vehicle," the pet fish canon warns us that the meaning of the two words together may not be a function of applying the meaning of each word separately. Like "pet fish," the term "drive a vehicle" has a distinctive meaning that is less than the sum of its parts. For example, a wheelbarrow is a "vehicle," and pushing it certainly "affect[s] its movement"—but your conversational partners would find it very funny indeed for you to talk about "driving a wheelbarrow" across the yard. (There are electric and motorized wheelbarrows that one can imagine "driving," but without that modification we are just referring to a regular wheelbarrow that you push.)

---

[68] For a linguistics-based explication of the pet fish canon, consult Fodor & Lepore, *Compositionality Papers* 35–42; V. Evans, The Evolution of Semantics, in *The Concise Encyclopedia of Philosophy of Language and Linguistics* 196, 201–02 (Alex Barber & Roger J. Stainton, eds., 2010).

[69] *Castleman*, 134 S.Ct. at 1411–12.

The pet fish canon can work together with the term of art canon, as illustrated by our discussion of state regulatory discussions of "driving" such "vehicles" as motorcycles, motor scooters, and even mopeds. Recall that most state motor *vehicle* codes typically provide that people need a "driver license" to operate motorcycles, motor scooters, and (usually) mopeds. The publicly available regulatory materials in most jurisdictions suppose that people can "drive" these kinds of vehicles and use the term "drive" as though it were synonymous with "ride" or "operate." The pet fish canon causes the interpreter to hesitate, however, before concluding that "drives a vehicle" includes "pedaling a bicycle." Although one naturally understands bicycle as being a vehicle and pedaling a bicycle does "affect the movement" of that "vehicle," it is not a natural use of the English language to say that one "drives" a bicycle. (Nor does the Uniform Vehicle Code support that locution.)

As the foregoing analysis suggests, the pet fish canon can suggest either a narrower ("drives a vehicle") or broader ("domestic violence") understanding of a word phrase than would be suggested by combining the definitions of each word. A fair number of Supreme Court cases invoke the concept behind this canon, and at least one decision has recognized this as a principle that should guide statutory interpreters. "[T]wo words together may assume a more particular meaning than those words in isolation. We understand a golden cup to be a cup made of or resembling gold. A golden boy, on the other hand, is one who is charming, lucky, and talented."[70] To the extent that judges recognize as canons the prudent linguistic practices they follow and respect, they should acknowledge the pet fish canon as a useful guide for statutory interpretation.

Grammar Canons. The pet fish canon reminds us that clusters of words and phrases may have meanings that are different from the aggregation of their dictionary definitions of each word. Statutory interpretation requires an understanding not only of word meaning, but also of the meaning of words put together in phrases, clauses, and sentences. The grammar canon becomes highly relevant in understanding how words work together to suggest an ordinary meaning. The grammar canon tells the interpreter to follow our

---

[70] *FCC v. AT&T, Inc.*, 562 U.S. 397, 406 (2011) (holding that "personal privacy" connotes something more particular than the sum of the two words). For other decisions applying the pet fish concept, see *Yates*, 135 S.Ct. 1074 (Ginsburg, J., for a plurality); *Castleman*, 134 S.Ct. at 1411–12; *Muscarello*, 524 U.S. at 143 (Ginsburg, J., dissenting). See also *Kasten v. Saint-Gobain*, 563 U.S. at 8–11 (finding that "filing a complaint" is a composite term of art).

society's accepted rules of grammar when figuring out whether the statute has an ordinary meaning.[71] This canon reflects the aspirations of statutory drafters. As the Florida Senate's drafting manual puts it, the "drafter should always follow rules of standard English grammar and usage when drafting bills."[72]

For a popular example reflected in many state codes and almost all legislative drafting manuals, mandatory words like "shall" or "must" grammatically suggest the addressee is obliged to do something, while permissive words like "may" vest her with discretion.[73] Hence, when our one-sentence vehicles in the park law says that it "shall" be a federal offense, the statute's choice of verbs is significant. Likewise, when a statute or regulation says it "includes" automobiles as "vehicles" rather than says "vehicles are limited to automobiles," the statute is not providing an exhaustive list of vehicles.[74]

For a less well-known example of a grammar canon, consider the role that active versus passive voice might play in statutory

---

[71] E.g., *Carr v. United States*, 560 U.S. 438, 448–49 (2010) (verb tense); *State v. Bodden*, 877 So.2d 680, 685–86 (Fla. 2004) (modification); Tex. Govt. Code § 311.012(a) (1985 codification) (verb tense). On the grammar canon and its importance, see CRS Report, *Statutory Interpretation*, 9–10 (updated 2011); Robert C. Farrell, *Why Grammar Matters: Conjugating Verbs in Modern Legal Opinions*, 40 Loy. U. Chi. L.J. 1 (2008).

[72] Florida Senate, *Manual for Drafting Legislation* ch. 2, at 11 (6th ed. 2009); accord, Ira B. Forstater, Office of Legislative Counsel, U.S. House of Representatives, *House Legislative Counsel's Manual on Drafting Style* § 351(a) (Nov. 1995); State of Illinois, *Illinois Bill Drafting Manual* § 90–5 (Dec. 2012); Kentucky Legislative Research Comm'n, *Bill Drafting Manual* §§ 301–302. All of the state legislative drafting manuals I examined had a rule similar to the Florida grammar rule, and all of the manuals focused much of their attention on specific grammar rules and variations from ordinary grammar (such as the canon that "person" includes corporations).

[73] *Lexecon, Inc. v. Milberg Weiss Bershad Hynes & Lerach*, 523 U.S. 26, 35 (1998) (applying the "may/shall canon"); Tex. Govt. Code § 311.016 (1985 codification); Forstater, Office of Legislative Counsel, U.S. House of Representatives, *Manual on Drafting Style* § 351(i)(2)(A); Florida Senate, *Manual for Drafting Legislation*, ch. 2, at 16–17 (representative state legislative drafting manual, sharply distinguishing may/shall); 2A *Sutherland Statutes and Statutory Construction* § 47:7 (7th ed. 2015) (classic statement of the may-shall canon). See also Delaware Legislative Council, *Legislative Drafting Manual* pt. VI, ch. 2, Rule 11 (an especially elaborate explication of the may/shall distinction, as well as other related ones).

[74] E.g., *Christopher v. SmithKline Beecham Corp.*, 132 S.Ct. 2156, 2170 (2012); *Burgess v. United States*, 553 U.S. 124, 131 n.3 (2008); Tex. Govt. Code § 311.005(13) (codification of the idea that "including" is a term of "enlargement" and not exhaustion); National Conference of Commissioners of Uniform State Laws, *Drafting Rules* Rule 301(d) (2012) (same); see 2A *Sutherland Statutes and Statutory Construction* § 47:7 (7th ed. 2015) ("including" or "includes" connotes a nonexhaustive list).

interpretation. Recall that our Park Safety Act says that "no person is permitted to drive a vehicle of any kind in Lafayette Park." This passive locution would be interpreted differently from an active voice alternative, such as this: "It shall be a federal offense for anyone to drive a vehicle of any kind in Lafayette Park." For reasons explored in chapter six, courts would probably read into this latter version of the statute a scienter requirement, that the accused person knew she was driving a vehicle in that park. But for the law as I have reported it, a court is less likely to require that the violation be a knowing one. "The passive voice focuses on an event that occurs without respect to a specific actor, and therefore without respect to any actor's intent or culpability."[75]

Naturally, the grammar canon follows from the same premises as the ordinary meaning canon, which it supports. When a grammar rule reflects a consensus of correct usage within this country, its application renders statutory interpretation somewhat more predictable. State and federal legislators and their drafting and policymaking staffs say that they follow these rules of grammar, with some widely accepted exceptions; indeed, in the last generation, congressional and most state legislative drafting has become highly professionalized and more consistent, making this assumption even more realistic.[76]

For example, the Park Safety Act says that people cannot "drive vehicles *of any kind*" in Lafayette Park. That locution suggests that the statute reaches more broadly than the core or prototypical understanding of vehicle. If I told you to name "vehicles," you might stop with cars, trucks, and motorcycles; but if I told you to name "vehicles of any kind," you would think more broadly and come up with a more capacious list, including mopeds, bicycles, and maybe even tricycles. This locution does not, however, require that the interpreter read the statute to include anything that might be called a vehicle, in part because it would be ungrammatical to say that someone "drives" a wheelbarrow, a tricycle, or a baby carriage—all

---

[75] *Dean v. United States*, 556 U.S. 568, 572 (2009) (leading case); see *Watson v. United States*, 552 U.S. 74 (2007); Anita S. Krishnakumar, *Passive-Voice References in Statutory Interpretation*, 76 Brooklyn L. Rev. 941 (2011).

[76] Shobe, *Intertemporal Statutory Interpretation*. There is no systematic study of state legislative drafting, but most states have in recent years developed drafting manuals that reflect a professional and sophisticated approach. Many of these manuals are collected on the website of the National Conference of State Legislatures, available at http://www.ncsl.org/legislators-staff/legislative-staff/legal-services/bill-drafting-manuals.aspx (viewed Jan. 1, 2016).

mechanisms that are "vehicles" as that term is used in its broadest sense.

Additionally, the grammar canon ought to yield to the cooperative principle, the idea that the interpreter needs to cooperate, sympathetically, even when the directive is grammatically odd. Thus, many state legislatures have codified a *bad grammar allowance* where strict adherence to grammar rules would undermine the statute's intended operation or its purpose. Minnesota has the most elaborate statement:

> Grammatical errors shall not vitiate a law. A transposition of words and clauses may be resorted to when a sentence is without meaning as it stands. Words and phrases which may be necessary to the proper interpretation of a law and which do not conflict with its obvious purpose and intent nor in any way affect its scope and operation may be added in the construction thereof.[77]

For example, the grammatical oddity of saying one "drives" a moped is not a conclusive argument supporting the exclusion of mopeds from the Park Safety Act.

Several particular locutions have been carved out of the grammar canon, usually by statute. Thus, both Congress (in the Dictionary Act) and most state legislatures have said that singular terms also include the plural and that gendered personal pronouns must be read to be gender neutral.[78] The Dictionary Act and state statutory analogues also define "person," very broadly and somewhat ungrammatically, to presumptively include corporations, partnerships, and other forms of business organization.[79] Legislative

---

[77] Minn. Stat. § 845.18 (quotation in text); accord, Tex. Govt. Code § 312.012(a); 2A *Sutherland Statutory Construction* § 47.1 (7th ed.); Scott, *Codified Canons,* 98 Geo. L.J. at 358–59 (detailed analysis of the "bad grammar rule" and state codifications that recognize it as an exception to the grammar canon). For an example of bad grammar allowance, see *U.S. National Bank of Oregon v. Independent Insurance Agents of America, Inc.*, 508 U.S. 439, 454 (1993).

[78] The Dictionary Act, 1 U.S.C. § 1 (statutory references to the singular include the plural and vice-versa; where statute refers just to "the masculine," courts will infer that "the feminine" are also included). For state practice treating gender and number flexibly rather than strictly according to grammar, see Cal. Civ. Proc. Code § 17(a); Fla. Stats. § 1.01(1)–(2); Tex. Govt. Code § 311.012(b)–(c); 2A *Sutherland Statutes and Statutory Construction* §§ 47:32 (gender), 47:34 (singular/plural) (7th ed. 2015).

[79] The Dictionary Act, 1 U.S.C. § 1 (broad definition of "person," to include corporations etc.), applied to assure close corporations of religious free exercise rights in *Burwell v. Hobby Lobby Stores, Inc.*, 134 S.Ct. 2751 (2014); accord, Cal. Civ. Proc. Code § 17(a); Fla. Stats. § 1.01(3); Tex. Govt. Code § 311.005(1); Scalia & Garner,

drafters are aware that "person" has a statutory meaning that is far broader than its ordinary meaning.[80]

The bad grammar allowance also applies to punctuation. Most authorities recognize a punctuation canon, which calls upon the interpreter to apply accepted rules of punctuation.[81] Most states have not codified this particular canon, and the minority with statutes are ambivalent about its weight. About as enthusiastic as any is the Pennsylvania Legislature, which enacted this rule: "In no case shall the punctuation of a statute control or affect the intention of the General Assembly in the enactment thereof but punctuation may be used to aid in the construction thereof if the statute was finally enacted after December 31, 1964."[82] Although most legislative drafting manuals admonish drafters to "punctuate carefully,"[83] a few follow the example of the Florida Senate: "The drafter should construct each sentence so that its meaning does not depend upon punctuation."[84]

The Last Antecedent Canon. "Referential and qualifying words and phrases, where no contrary intention appears, refer solely to the last antecedent. The last antecedent is the 'last word, phrase, or clause that can be made an antecedent without impairing the meaning of the sentence.'" The rule of the last antecedent can be trumped by punctuation: "A qualifying phrase separated from antecedents by a comma is evidence that the qualifier is supposed to apply to all the antecedents instead of only to the immediately

---

Reading Law, 273–77 (proposing an "artificial-person canon," based on legislative expectations).

[80] E.g., National Conference of Commissioners on Uniform State Laws, *Drafting Rules*, Rule 305.

[81] For usefully cautionary statements of the punctuation canon, see 2A *Sutherland Statutes and Statutory Construction* § 47:15 (7th ed. 2015); CRS Report, *Statutory Interpretation*, 12–13 (updated 2011); Scalia & Garner, *Reading Law*, 161–66; Raymond B. Marcin, *Punctuation and the Interpretation of Statutes*, 9 Conn. L. Rev. 227, 240 (1977). The leading case for a punctuation canon is *United States v. Ron Pair Enterprises*, 489 U.S. 235 (1987), but punctuation was merely a supporting reason in that case. Id. at 241.

[82] 1 Pa. Cons. Stat. § 1923 (quotation in text); accord, Tex. Govt. Code § 312.012(b); Scott, *Codified Canons*, 78 Geo. L.J. at 360–61 (reporting the variety of punctuation canon laws, none of which reveals great enthusiasm for the canon).

[83] Delaware Legislative Council, Division of Research, *Delaware Legislative Drafting Manual* pt. VI, ch. 2, Rule 23(a) (quotation in text).

[84] Florida Senate, *Manual for Drafting Legislation* ch. 2, at 21 (quotation in text); accord, Alabama Legislative Reference Serv., *Drafting Style Manual* Rule 11(a) (same approach). But see Kentucky Legislative Research Comm'n, *Bill Drafting Manual* § 308 (admonishing drafters to "punctuate carefully").

preceding one."[85] This canon is a specialized application of the grammar canon and, frankly, of common sense. Thus, when the vehicles in the park law says that "it shall be a federal offense for anyone to drive a vehicle *of any kind* in Lafayette Park," everyone knows that the prepositional phrase modifies "vehicle" and not "anyone" or "Lafayette Park."

Like the grammar canon more generally, the last antecedent canon must be applied with an eye to reasonable ordinary meaning, in light of the statutory purpose.[86] Consider this alternate version of the vehicles in the park law:

> Because vehicles create safety problems, no person is permitted to drive a vehicle of any kind in Lafayette Park that poses a significant safety problem.

Admittedly, this is a badly drafted statute. According to legislative drafting manuals, clauses not set off by commas and beginning with "that" modify the closest antecedent; clauses set off by commas and beginning with "which" can modify a more remote antecedent.[87] But poorly drafted statutes are enacted every day, and they must be interpreted. What does the clause "that poses a significant safety problem" modify? Legislative drafting practice and the rule of the last antecedent suggest that it modifies "Lafayette Park"—but such a reading would be absurd as a matter of ordinary meaning and would confuse the point of the statute. The clause modifies "vehicle," and the last antecedent canon would not say otherwise, given its caveat, "without impairing the meaning of the sentence." Like the other textual canons, this one must always be applied with an eye on statutory context and purpose—and for this reason the last antecedent canon is sometimes honored in the breach.[88]

---

[85] 2A *Sutherland Statutes and Statutory Construction* § 47:33 (7th ed. 2015) (both quotations in text); accord, *Lockhart v. United States,* 136 S.Ct. 958 (2016); *Jama v. Immigration & Customs Enforcement*, 543 U.S. 335, 342–43 (2005); *Barnhart v. Thomas*, 540 U.S. 20, 26 (2003) (leading case); Scalia & Garner, *Reading Law*, 144–46.

[86] Commentators have been highly critical of dogmatic, acontextual applications of the rule of the last antecedent. See Joseph Kimble, *The Rule of the Last Antecedent, the Example in* Barnhart, *Why Both Are Weak, and How Textualism Postures*, 16 Scribes J. Legal Writing 5–43 (2015); Jeremy Ross, *A Rule of Last Resort: A History of the Doctrine of the Last Antecedent in the United States Supreme Court*, 39 Sw. L. Rev. 325 (2009).

[87] E.g., Delaware Legislative Council, *Legislative Drafting Manual*, pt. VI, ch. 2, Rule 13 (that/which rule discussed in text).

[88] Thus, most commentators would be much friendlier to then-Judge Alito's practical, purpose-based approach to referential words in the Social Security Act, than to Justice Scalia's reliance on the last antecedent in *Barnhart v. Thomas*, 540 U.S. 20.

Absurdity and Scrivener's Error Canons. "All laws are to be given a sensible construction; and a literal application of a statute, which would lead to absurd consequences, should be avoided whenever a reasonable application can be given to it, consistent with the legislative purpose."[89] Many scholars treat this absurdity canon as a permissible exception to the ordinary meaning rule, while others disapprove of its departure from the ordinary or plain meaning rule.[90] As the foregoing quotation suggests, the absurdity canon, like the other textual canons discussed here, is a refinement of and is consistent with the ordinary meaning rule as explained above.[91]

Assume that in 1992 Congress had enacted a different version of the Park Safety Act, containing the following text:

> Because vehicles create safety problems, any person who brings a vehicle of any kind into Lafayette Park commits a felony offense.

See Kimble, *Rule of the Last Antecedent, the Example in* Barnhart. See also *Paroline v. United States*, 134 S.Ct. 1710, 1720–21 (2014) (declining to apply the rule of the last antecedent); *Duffy v. Michigan Dep't of Natural Resources*, 805 N.W.2d 399, 411–12 (Mich. 2011) (similar); Scalia & Garner, *Reading Law*, 152–53 (posing as a sibling canon the "nearest-reasonable-referent canon," because sometimes it is unreasonable to apply a modifying phrase to the last antecedent).

[89] *United States v. Katz*, 271 U.S. 354, 357 (1926) (Stone, J.); accord, *Utility Air Regulatory Group v. EPA*, 134 S.Ct. 2427 (2014) (plurality and concurring opinions); *McNeill v. United States*, 131 S.Ct. 2218, 2223–24 (2011) (unanimous Court); *Zuni Pub. Sch. Dist. No. 89 v. Department of Educ.*, 550 U.S. 81 (2007); *United States v. Wilson*, 503 U.S. 329, 334 (1992); *Green v. Bock Laundry Mach. Co.*, 490 U.S. 504, 509–11 (1989).

The absurdity canon is also very popular among state judges. E.g., *Campbell v. State*, 125 So.3d 733, 741–42 (Fla. 2013). California judges "reject a literal construction that is contrary to the legislative intent apparent in the statute or that would lead to absurd results," *Simpson Strong-Tie Co., Inc. v. Gore*, 230 P.3d 1117, 1127 (Cal. 2010), or "would result in absurd consequences that the Legislature could not have intended." *In re J.W.*, 57 P.3d 363, 369 (Cal. 2013); accord, *State v. Long*, 852 N.E.2d 1150, 1153 (N.Y. 2006); 2A *Sutherland Statutes and Statutory Construction* § 45:12 (7th ed. 2015) (citing many state cases supporting the assumption that the legislature intends for "reasonable interpretation").

[90] E.g., John F. Manning, *The Absurdity Doctrine*, 116 Harv. L. Rev. 2387 (2003). For a response, see Glen Staszewski, *Avoiding Absurdity*, 81 Ind. L.J. 1001, 1012–14 (2006).

[91] For defenses of the absurdity canon as consistent with textualism, consider Scalia & Garner, *Reading Law*, 234–39 (absurdity canon is consistent with textualism only if the text is so absurd that no reasonable person could have intended its result *and* the court can correct the error without undue violence to the text); Veronica M. Dougherty, *Absurdity and the Limits of Literalism: Defining the Absurd Result Principle in Statutory Interpretation*, 44 Am. U. L. Rev. 127, 127–28 & 132–34 (1994); Andrew Gold, *Absurd Results, Scrivener's Errors, and Statutory Interpretation*, 75 U. Cin. L. Rev. 25, 28 (2006).

A sixteen-year-old youth rides his moped through the park. Because this version of the statute prohibits people from "bringing" rather than "driving" vehicles in the park and because a moped is very probably a vehicle that creates safety problems, the youth seems to have violated the statutory command. But has he committed a *felony offense*? That is an unusual, perhaps unprecedented, penalty in our society for a licensed, sober person riding a moped. And it is very odd for a statute to announce a felony without specifying the range of punishment; punishment for federal felonies can range from a few years in prison to lifetime imprisonment to the death penalty.

This is a classic occasion for invoking the absurdity canon: A literal application of the statutory language runs so clearly athwart basic conceptions of fairness and proportionality that one thinks twice before taking the statement literally—and the interpreter can readily see that this language was probably a scrivener's error, namely, an elementary drafting mistake. In ordinary conversation, if one speaker said it was a "felony offense" to bring a bike into Lafayette Park, the other speaker would probably assume that the first speaker had misspoken. What she meant to say was that it was a "federal offense" to bring a bike into the park. Like the interlocutor in a conversation, the statutory interpreter ought to assume the reasonableness of the legislature when it issues commands and ought to correct scrivener's errors.[92]

The absurdity canon also has bite for statutory formulations that are not apparent scrivener's errors. Consider the broadened statute without the error: "Because vehicles create safety problems, any person who brings a vehicle of any kind into Lafayette Park commits a federal offense." As before, "bring" has replaced "drive" in this version of the statute. Because "bring" is a more inclusive term than "drive" and because "vehicle of any kind" remains a very broad term, this is a sweeping statutory directive whose ordinary meaning may well include bicycles as well as motorcycles. While it might be debatable whether bicycles are statutory vehicles under this

---

[92] For instances where the Supreme Court has applied the absurd results canon, or something like it, to statutes with obvious scrivener's errors, see *King v. Burwell*, 135 S.Ct. 2480 (2015); *Koons Pontiac GMC, Inc. v. Nigh*, 543 U.S. 50, 62–64 (2004) (majority and concurring opinions); *Bock Laundry*, 490 U.S. at 509–11 (majority, concurring, and dissenting opinions). See also Michael Fried, *A Theory of Scrivener's Error*, 52 Rutgers L. Rev. 589 (2000); Jonathan Siegel, *What Drafting Errors Teach Us About Statutory Interpretation*, 69 Geo. Wash. L. Rev. 309, 333–44 (2001); David Sollars, *The Scrivener Error Doctrine and Textual Criticism: Confronting Errors in Statutes and Literary Texts*, 49 Santa Clara L. Rev. 459 (2009).

provision, it is far from absurd, for reasonable legislators could justifiably say that bicycles are included.

Does the revised version of the vehicles in the park law include wheelbarrows? Figures 1–3 above suggest that this meaning (wheelbarrows as excluded vehicles) is far from clear—even though dictionaries define wheelbarrows as "vehicles," even though such usage shows up a fair amount on the Internet, even though the grammar canon suggests a broad reading of "vehicle of any kind," and even though the pet fish canon is inapplicable to narrow the phrase "brings a vehicle of any kind."

So does this version of the Park Safety Act have an ordinary meaning that includes wheelbarrows as vehicles? No, it does not. One reason is linguistic and reflects the limitation of dictionaries as definitive sources for understanding statutory language. If you gesture toward a wheelbarrow and say, "bring that park-maintenance vehicle to me," your interlocutor would look around for a truck or riding lawnmower and would not immediately think, "wheelbarrow," even if you were pointing right at it. As a matter of language precision, the dictionary refers to wheelbarrows as vehicles, for indeed they are conveyances for carting stuff from one place to another. But as a matter of general usage, speakers of the English language rarely mean "wheelbarrows" when they are making statements about "vehicles." As linguists would say, wheelbarrows are so distant from prototypical "vehicles," as the term is used in the regulatory sentence, that including them would be absurd.

The clinching reason a wheelbarrow is an absurd application of a vehicles in the park law is that the purpose of the statute—the point of the statutory conversation—is park safety, and it is completely unreasonable (absurd) to think that carting dirt around the park in a wheelbarrow is the kind of activity that endangers park users.[93] Relatedly, wheelbarrows belong in parks and are useful (perhaps even necessary) for parks to carry out their function. Under the cooperative principle that underwrites both personal conversations and statutory interpretations, it is not sensible to understand the statutory language as sweeping wheelbarrows into the blanket prohibition. Shorthand that to say that it would be "absurd" to apply the statutory language to wheelbarrows—or to baby carriages or toy cars, which like wheelbarrows are vehicles that pose virtually no

---

[93] Cf. *People v. Orange Cnty. Fire Auth.*, 354 P.3d 346, 354–56 (Cal. 2015) (Cuéllar, J., concurring) (absurd results must be evaluated from the perspective of the statutory purpose).

safety danger and are a valuable feature of parks.[94] Admittedly, a closer case would be presented by a small motorized wheelbarrow. If they were essentially the same as regular wheelbarrows, but with a little motor to make pushing easier, they could fall under the absurdity exception—but a larger wheelbarrow with a powerful motor allowing it to be driven at a considerable speed would not necessarily trigger an absurdity exclusion.

The public purposes involved in statutory interpretation strongly support my understanding of the absurdity canon as an implementation of (rather than as an exception to) the ordinary meaning rule. As a rule of law matter, most park users would be astounded that a judge would apply a no-bringing-vehicles-into-the-park law to bar ordinary wheelbarrows. Parents would not expect a judge to apply such a law to baby carriages (for another absurd application). Just like a Gricean conversation operating under the cooperative principle, predictable statutory interpretation under the rule of law would be loathe to apply the words ("bring a vehicle") to mechanisms that belong in a park and do not implicate the safety concerns of the Park Safety Act.

Legitimacy and democratic accountability, likewise, support this understanding of the absurdity canon. The legislative history of the no-bringing-vehicles-into-the-park law would not contain any example close to wheelbarrows, baby carriages, and the like; not only would application of the statute to baby carriages not advance the goal of the law, but it would undermine the law by drawing police resources and public attention away from the real problems addressed by the statute. For precisely this kind of reason, legislators do not want their statutes applied in a wild and unlimited manner. State legislatures have codified this understanding. Although a few provide that absurdity is only relevant when the statutory words are ambiguous, most states follow the approach announced by Minnesota: "The legislature does not intend a result that is absurd, impossible of execution, or unreasonable."[95] The Texas Legislature goes even further: "In enacting a statute, it is presumed that * * * a just and reasonable result is intended."[96] The point is that most legislators would go even further than the absurdity canon takes them, as they

---

[94] *Koons Pontiac GMC, Inc.*, 543 U.S. at 62–64.

[95] Minn. Stats. § 645.17(1); cf. id., § 645.16 (basic rule of interpretation is "to ascertain and effectuate the intention of the legislature").

[96] Tex. Govt. Code § 311.021(3) (enacted 1985).

would oppose interpretations that are "unreasonable," from the perspective of the statutory plans they adopt.[97]

Finally, a broad understanding of the absurdity canon is consistent with the substantive purposes of governance. Implicit in a well-ordered republic is the notion that agents and officials of the law should apply statutes reasonably. Recall, again, the analogy to a conversation, a notion common to philosophers of language, legal process theorists, and even many strict textualists. What is the point of a statute barring any and all vehicles from Lafayette Park? Whether the purpose is the safety of older folks and children using the park or maintaining the park as a quiet place (or any other plausible purpose of such a law), its application to wheelbarrows or baby carriages is so far afield and counterproductive as to be an absurd application of the statute. Even though the broad statutory language was not a scrivener's error and its application to a wheelbarrow or baby carriage would not be unconstitutional, the application is so far from the purposes of both the Park Safety Act and the laws creating and regulating Lafayette Park, that it would be ridiculous. It would impose costs and inconvenience on park maintenance personnel, without benefiting anyone, really.

Other Ordinary Meaning Canons

The principles and maxims discussed above do not exhaust the panoply of textual canons. Each of the following canons rests upon a common sense approach to ordinary meaning, and a recent empirical study by Abbe Gluck and Lisa Schultz Bressman suggests that these particular canons also reflect the assumptions of the congressional drafting process,[98] a finding consistent with the Congressional Research Service's drafting guidance provided to congressional staff and with the leading treatise, readily available to (albeit not necessarily mastered by) legislative staff at both the state and federal

---

[97] In his state-by-state survey of the legislatively codified canons of statutory construction, Jacob Scott found that legislatures generally codified the absurd results canon along the lines noted in text, suggesting to implementing judges that the legislature does not intend for statutes to be applied in ways that render its rules so odd that the ordinary legislator would be astounded that her statute should applied *unreasonably*. Scott, *Codified Canons*, 98 Geo. L.J. at 355; see 2A *Sutherland Statutes and Statutory Construction* § 45:12 (7th ed. 2015) (assembling state cases positing that the legislature expects that its statutes receive a "reasonable interpretation").

[98] Gluck & Bressman, *Statutory Interpretation from the Inside: Part I*, 66 Stan L. Rev. at 932–33 (associated words and negative implication canons), 939 (definition of terms canon).

levels.[99] Interestingly, these other ordinary meaning canons have rarely been codified by state legislatures and are usually not mentioned in legislative drafting manuals, either.[100] Consider how these other ordinary meaning canons might apply to the question whether the Lafayette Park Safety Act includes skateboards as "vehicles" barred from the park.

Statutory Definition Canon. Related to the term of art canon is the statutory definition canon: When a statute defines a word or phrase, interpreters should follow the ordinary meaning of the statutory definition.[101] Binding statutory definitions frequently appear at the beginning of an enacted law, in provisions applicable to several laws and codified at the beginning of a particular title or subtitle of the United States Code or the relevant state code, or sometimes as provisions applicable everywhere in the Code. As it turns out, the Dictionary Act of 1947 provides a definition for "vehicle" that applies throughout the U.S. Code: "The word 'vehicle' includes every description of carriage or other artificial contrivance used, or capable of being used, as a means of transportation on land."[102] Because the Park Safety Act bans the bringing of "any and all vehicles" into the park, the grammar canon teams up with the definition canon to make a very strong case for regulatory inclusion of bicycles and even skateboards as statutory "vehicles."

Set aside the Dictionary Act, for it may be superseded by a definition particular to the statute in question. Most major statutes have introductory sections setting forth definitions of key statutory terms, either because legislators are using terms in a specialized sense not captured by ordinary meaning or because they want to

---

[99] CRS Report, *Statutory Interpretation*, 4–6 (definitions), 10–12 (associated words), and 17–18 (*inclusio unius*); 2A *Sutherland Statutes and Statutory Construction* §§ 47.07 (definitions), 47.17 et seq. (associated words), and 47.23 et seq. (*inclusio unius*) (7th ed. 2015).

[100] Scott, *Codified Canons*, 98 Geo. L.J. at 357 (Table 1).

[101] *Babbitt v. Sweet Home Chap. of Communities for a Great Oregon*, 515 U.S. 687 (1995) (leading case for the definition canon); *McWilliams v. City of Long Beach*, 300 P.3d 886, 890 (Cal. 2013); *Baker v. State*, 636 So.2d 1342 (Fla. 1994); *Kuznar v. Raksha Corp.*, 750 N.W.2d 121, 126–28 (Mich. 2008); Scalia & Garner, *Reading Law*, 225–33 (endorsing the definition canon, but dissenting from *Sweet Home*'s application of the statutory definition more broadly than the common law foundations would allow).

[102] Dictionary Act of July 30, 1947, ch. 388, § 4, 61 Stat. 633, codified at 1 U.S.C. § 4 (defining land "vehicles" for purposes of the U.S. Code); cf. id. § 3 (defining water "vehicles").

make sure a recurring term has a standard meaning.[103] Assume, for example, that the Park Safety Act has a statutory definition of "vehicle" that supplants the highly inclusive definition provided by the Dictionary Act:

> Because vehicles create safety problems, any person who brings a vehicle of any kind into Lafayette Park commits a federal offense. For purposes of this law, "vehicle" includes automobiles, motorcycles, and other mechanisms for conveying persons or things.

Echoing the dictionary definition of "vehicle" but less sweeping than the definition in the Dictionary Act, this statutory definition confirms the core coverage of the Park Safety Act, as reflected in Figures 1–3.

Beyond that confirmation, the statutory definition provided here raises more questions than it answers, ironically. Thus, the statutory definition seems very broad ("other mechanisms for conveying persons or things") but lists motor vehicles as particular items included in the definition, a move that suggests a possibly narrower meaning for the term "vehicle" than is contained in the Dictionary Act, for example. As language in the statute, the definition is, itself, subject to interpretation, based upon the ordinary meaning of the words Congress has used, viewed in light of the safety purpose Congress has identified. Happily, there are several textual canons, each appealing to a linguistic common sense shared by the citizenry and congressional drafters, that assist our understanding of the definition. For example, the grammar canon tells us this: The statute's statement that the statutory term "includes" automobiles and so forth suggests that this is a nonexhaustive list and so might be enlarged by interpretation.[104] But what else should be included, in addition to the listed mechanisms? Consider, now, some additional text-based canons relevant to this definition. I caution that these final textual canons, like the ones that surveyed above, require value judgments grounded in public purposes and democratic accountability in order to resolve ambiguities.

---

[103] For drafting advice on when to define terms within the statute, see, e.g., Delaware Legislative Council, *Legislative Drafting Manual* pt. VI, ch. 2, Rule 25(a) Kentucky Legislative Research Comm'n, *Bill Drafting Manual* § 310.

[104] Office of Legislative Research & General Counsel, Utah Legislature, *Legislative Drafting Style Manual* ch. 2, § 3(f) (updated Dec. 24, 2014) (contrasting statutory definitions that start with "means," which tends to reflect an exclusive list, with those starting with "includes," which leaves room for additional items); accord, Delaware Legislative Council, *Legislative Drafting Manual* pt. VI, ch. 2, Rule 26.

Noscitur a Sociis *and* Ejusdem Generis *Canons.* Like many other statutory definitions, the one I have provided for "vehicle" contains a list of terms. Might the meaning of each term in a series be informed by the meaning of other words in the series? Thus, if the statute prohibited anyone from bringing "any automobile, motorcycle, motor scooter, or other vehicle into the park," one would be justified to interpret the general term "vehicle" in light of the series of terms preceding it. The New Mexico Legislature has codified the general principle most aptly:

> In considering the text of a statute or rule * * * the following aids to construction may be considered in ascertaining the meaning of the text: (1) the meaning of a word or phrase may be limited by the series of words or phrases of which it is a part; and (2) the meaning of a general word or phrase following two or more specific words or phrases may be limited to the category established by the specific words or phrases.[105]

Likewise, Professors Gluck and Bressman report that congressional drafters understand and follow the same basic precept. (Oddly, federal and state legislative drafting manuals have little to say about associated words.) Although not widely known to statutory drafters by name, there are two canons that are derived from the associated words precept; those canons are so hoary that they are still cited by their Latin (old law English) tags.[106]

The broader associated words canon is *noscitur a sociis* ("it is known from its associates"). "Thus, when two or more words are grouped together, and ordinarily have a similar meaning, but are not equally comprehensive, the general word will be limited and qualified by the special word[s]."[107] This canon would be squarely applicable if the statutory definition of "vehicle" (quoted above) provided that the term includes "automobiles, motorcycles, motor scooters, and

---

[105] N. Mex. Stat. § 12–2A–20(A) (quotation in text); accord, Minn. Stat. § 645.08(3). For applications of this general precept, see *Yates*, 135 S.Ct. 1074 (plurality and concurring opinions); *Gutierrez v. Ada*, 528 U.S. 250, 254–255 (2000).

[106] See generally Francis Bennion, *Bennion on Statute Law* 195–96 (1990).

[107] 2A *Sutherland Statutes and Statutory Construction* § 47:16 (7th ed. 2015) (quotation in text); see *Yates*, 135 S.Ct. at 1085–86 (plurality and concurring opinions); *Bullock v. BankChampaign, N.A.*, 133 S.Ct. 1754, 1760 (2013); *Freeman v. Quicken Loans, Inc.*, 132 S.Ct. 2034 (2012); *United States v. Williams*, 553 U.S. 285, 294 (2008); *Gustafson v. Alloyd Co.*, 513 U.S. 561, 575 (1995); *Jarecki v. G. D. Searle & Co.*, 367 U.S. 303 (1961) (leading case); *People v. Hill*, 786 N.W.2d 601 (Mich. 2010); CRS Report, *Statutory Interpretation*, 10–11 (updated 2011); Scalia & Garner, *Reading Law*, 195–98.

conveyances." The last item ("conveyances") is the most general, and *noscitur a sociis* would be applicable to presume that the general item is limited to mechanisms similar to the specific items. The limiting idea might be to confine "conveyances" to motorized mechanisms. If that were the limiting idea, then the Park Safety Act would not apply to bicycles and skateboards, though it might apply to motorized bicycles.

As a technical matter, there is a different but related canon that applies to the particular locution I have chosen for the statutory definition of vehicle, namely, *ejusdem generis* ("of the same kind, class, or nature"). "[W]here general words follow specific words in an enumeration * * * the general words are construed to embrace only objects similar in nature to those objects enumerated by the preceding specific words. The doctrine applies equally to the opposite sequence, i.e., specific words following general ones, to restrict application of the general term to things that are similar to those enumerated."[108]

Although judges often use these two Latin canons interchangeably, it is *ejusdem generis* (rather than *noscitur a sociis*) that more squarely applies to figure out how to read the general term at the end of the series "automobiles, motorcycles, and other mechanisms for conveying persons or things." As before, one might say that the statutory bar to "vehicles" applies only to *motorized* vehicles: The common feature of the specific items preceding the general term is that they are both motorized; pursuant to the *ejusdem generis* canon, one might infer that the residual term, likewise, refers only to motorized mechanisms. As a result, the statutory definition would include motor scooters and mopeds—but not bicycles, skateboards, and other non-motorized mechanisms.

While the associated words canons reflect both common sense as well as congressional (and perhaps some state legislative) drafting practices, they can be tricky to apply. When the interpreter faces a

---

[108] 2A *Sutherland Statutes and Statutory Construction* § 47:17 (7th ed. 2015) (quotation in text); see *Yates*, 135 S.Ct. at 1086–87 (plurality and concurring opinions); *SmithKline Beecham Corp.*, 132 S.Ct. at 2171–72; *Begay v. United States*, 553 U.S. 137, 142–43 (2008); *Circuit City Stores, Inc. v. Adams*, 532 U.S. 105, 114–15 (2001) (leading case for *ejusdem generis*); *Sterling Park LP v. City of Palo Alto*, 310 P.3d 925 (Cal. 2013); *Graham v. Haridopolos*, 108 So.3d 597 (Fla. 2013); *Neal v. Wilkes*, 685 N.W.2d 648 (Mich. 2004); CRS Report, *Statutory Interpretation*, 10–11 (updated 2011). But see Scalia & Garner, *Reading Law*, 203–05 (discussing *ejusdem generis* and disagreeing with Sutherland's view that the canon applies to series where specific words follow a general term).

list of specific terms and a more general one, application of the associated words canons requires the interpreter to determine what the specific terms have in common.[109] In the preceding discussion, I suggested that the common feature of the specific items is that they are motorized—but is there not another common feature, namely, that the specific items pose a danger to people in the park? Some motorized mechanisms, such as motorized wheelbarrows, do not go fast enough to pose safety risks. So should a motorized wheelbarrow be considered "[an]other mechanism for conveying persons or things"?

The risk-to-park-users commonality dovetails nicely with the statutory purpose, but the motorized-vehicle commonality is a tighter fit with the two specific items that precede it on the list. Is there a neutral way for the interpreter to choose between the two forms of commonality? This is an ongoing feature that may prevent ordinary meaning inquiries from reaching closure. On the other hand, sometimes there is more statutory context that helps the interpreter resolve this level of generality question. For example, the interpreter might consider the statutory purpose: In light of the statutory policy, what do the statutory terms have in common?[110]

Perhaps what the terms have in common is *both* motorization *and* safety risks. In that event, motorized wheelbarrows would be excluded from the definition, because they are too slow to pose safety risks. But what about bicycles and skateboards? They lack motors but pose big safety risks. So maybe the common element is just risk to public safety, a commonality that would bring bicycles and skateboards within the statutory scheme but still omit motorized wheelbarrows. Note that these applications would bring the Park Safety Act's definition of "vehicle" closer to, but not as sweeping as, the definition found in the Dictionary Act. But without knowing more about the statutory scheme and its legislative background, it is hard to choose among the various commonalities posed by the short list of vehicles in the definition sentence.

Inclusio (Expressio) Unius *Canon*. Another textual canon is *inclusio* (or *expressio*) *unius est exclusio alterius* ("the inclusion [or

---

[109] For an excellent analysis of the common-element requirement for *ejusdem generis*, where the Court rejected the common element identified by both parties, see *SmithKline Beecham Corp.*, 132 S.Ct. at 2171–72.

[110] *Yates*, 135 S.Ct. at 1085–86 (Ginsburg, J., for a plurality) (invoking both *noscitur a sociis* and *ejusdem generis* with reference to the statutory purpose); *Circuit City Stores*, 532 U.S. at 138–40 (Souter, J., dissenting) (applying a statutory purpose analysis to criticize the majority for an unduly narrow deployment of the associated words canon).

expression] of one thing suggests the exclusion of all others").[111] This is a simple intuition that often informs ordinary conversation and is a notion that ought to be readily accessible to legislators and their staffs (though it is largely absent from legislative drafting manuals). If Mother tells Sally, "You may have one cookie and a scoop of ice cream," Sally knows that she is not supposed to scarf up that candy bar on the table. *Inclusio unius*: Allowing Sally to have two tooth-decaying sweets implies that Sally cannot have other goodies that might be within reach.[112]

Like the associated word canons, this one is tricky and requires serious attention to the statutory purpose or a more general baseline of value. For example, Mother tells Sally, "Stop pinching your little sister Anne!" If Sally then starts biting her sister, Mother can properly admonish her. If the misbehaving daughter invokes *inclusio unius,* that is an abuse of logic as well as of the sister. The reason the negative implication canon is not applicable is that the normative baseline, the point of the family conversation, is that each family member should refrain from hurting (or torturing) other family members or persons. Against *that* baseline, Mother would properly interpret her original admonition broadly. Contrast the cookie hypothetical above: The reason *inclusio unius* is appropriate in that context is that the normative baseline, the point of the family conversation, is that sweets-loving children need to exercise restraint for reasons of dental hygiene and overall health. Given *that* baseline, Sally appropriately knows that the tasty candy bar is off limits.[113]

If applied under a proper understanding of this canon, *inclusio unius* is sometimes quite helpful to the interpreter trying to apply a general text to an unanticipated problem. Recall the deep uncertainty about how broadly to apply the statutory definition of "vehicle" in the

---

[111] *Barnhart v. Sigmon Coal Co., Inc.,* 534 U.S. 438, 452–53 (2002); *Russello v. United States*, 464 U.S. 16, 22 (1983) (leading case); *Smitter v. Thornapple Township,* 833 N.W.2d 875, 884–85 & n.34 (Mich. 2013); *Pittsfield Charter Township v. Washtenaw Co.,* 664 N.W.2d 193 (Mich. 2003); 2A *Sutherland Statutes and Statutory Construction* § 47:23 (7th ed. 2015); Scalia & Garner, *Reading Law,* 107–11. See generally John Mark Keyes, Expressio Unius: *The Expression that Proves the Rule*, 10 Statute L. Rev. 1 (1989).

[112] The example in text is taken from William N. Eskridge Jr., Philip P. Frickey, Elizabeth Garrett, and James J. Brudney, *Cases and Materials on Legislation and Regulation: Statutes and the Creation of Public Policy* 669 (5th ed. 2014).

[113] *Barnhart v. Peabody Coal Co.,* 537 U.S. 149, 168 (2003); *Lindh v. Murphy,* 521 U.S. 320 (1997); William N. Eskridge Jr., *The New Textualism and Normative Canons,* 113 Colum. L. Rev. 531 (2013). For a balanced discussion of the *inclusio unius* canon, see *Chevron U.S.A., Inc. v. Echazabal,* 536 U.S. 73 (2002).

previous section. Consider how much easier our task would be if the Park Safety Act consisted of the following text:

> Because vehicles create safety problems, any person who brings a vehicle of any kind into Lafayette Park commits a federal offense. For purposes of this law, "vehicle" means automobiles, motorcycles, motor scooters, and bicycles.

The definitional sentence is more directive when phrased this way. Because the definition uses the limiting term "means" (rather than "includes") and offers a closed list, the negative implication canon suggests that the interpreter ought not find "vehicles" anything outside of the listed mechanisms.[114] Even though skateboard riding can cause accidents, we should be inclined to exclude those devices from the statute, unless there is further context of the sort explored in the next several chapters. Am I 100 per cent certain that the statutory text excludes skateboards? No, I am not. This is yet another illustration of the manner in which plain meaning is a continuum, not a bright line in the center of the road.

Should the interpreter include mopeds without pedals, such as the ones pictured above? They are not items in the statutory list: Does the negative implication canon suggest that the statute does not regulate them? I should include those vehicles within the statute's ordinary meaning, because mopeds are very similar to the listed items. Indeed, one might consider mopeds souped-up bicycles or rudimentary motorcycles, both included in the list. Recall the analogy to conversations. If I tell a group of parents that I am going to keep all "vehicles" out of the park and, further, that by "vehicles," I mean automobiles, motorcycles, motor scooters, and bicycles, then my audience probably expects me to keep out mopeds, which most would consider very similar to motorcycles and motor scooters, and some would consider a kind of bicycle (namely, a motorized bicycle). The point of the conversation is park safety, and mopeds threaten safety almost as much as motor scooters and more than bicycles.

Would a judge include children's tricycles among the "vehicles" subject to the statutory bar? Some people might use the term "bicycle" to include mechanisms with three or more wheels, but that is a decidedly odd usage. Complementing this textual point, the threat posed to park safety by children's tricycles is pretty low, so the safety purpose augurs against a broad reading of "vehicle," especially as

---

114 Office of Legislative Research & General Counsel, Utah Legislature, *Legislative Drafting Style Manual* ch. 2, § 3(f).

defined above. The tricycle case is an easy case, but it offers us an opportunity to reflect more broadly on the exercise we have been performing.

The Park Safety Act not only prohibits, but it also constructs: What is the point of Lafayette Park itself (not just the Park Safety Act)? Based upon the statutory language, one might read the vehicles prohibition as imagining a peaceful space where people can rest and children can play, without the distraction of fumes and noise and without the risk of injury posed by the enumerated vehicles and a few other mechanisms (very few if we take the negative implication canon seriously). Not only do child's tricycles pose little risk to bystanders, but such tricycles epitomize the kind of park Congress was apparently trying to create—one where children can play in peace.

* * *

We are all textualists. That means that a judge must relate all sources of and arguments about statutory interpretation to a text the legislature has enacted. Most statutory issues are solved, often quite easily, by reference to the ordinary meaning rule. As explained in the introduction to this chapter, there are three overlapping normative arguments for the ordinary meaning rule: It helps judges create a predictable and objective rule of law, enjoys great legitimacy because it is faithful to the premises of the legislative drafting process, and is the most reliable way to carry out the great plans to which legislators have committed our society. The values served by the ordinary meaning rule then drive its application. This chapter makes three important points about how that works.

To begin with, the linchpin of statutory interpretation is *ordinary meaning*, for that is going to be most accessible to the citizenry desirous of following the law *and* to the legislators and their staffs drafting the legal terms of the plans launched by statutes *and* to the administrators and judges implementing the statutory plan over times. No responsible scholar or judge rejects the ordinary meaning rule—but statutory interpretation consistently tempts judges to assume that their own language practices, and those of their cocktail-party friends, reflect ordinary meaning throughout the country and among legislators.[115] Notice that the deployment of

[115] The über-textualist (post-1999) Michigan Supreme Court has sometimes succumbed to the temptation of finding a plain meaning when reasonable ambiguity exists. Compare the majority and dissenting opinions in, for example, *Duffy v. Michigan Dep't of Natural Resources*, 805 N.W.2d 399 (Mich. 2011) (lengthy debate over whether a partially paved trailway is a public "highway"); *People v. Gardner*, 753

ordinary meaning requires the responsible judge to open her mind to broader evidence than dictionaries—evidence that includes internet searches and other evidence discussed in subsequent chapters of this volume.

Moreover, ordinary meaning is a *continuum*, and not an on-off switch. Although this notion is consistent with centuries of American judicial practice that cuts across eras and political ideologies, it has recently been disputed by the Michigan Supreme Court. A majority of the Court insists that few statutory provisions are truly ambiguous and claims that ambiguity only exists when two provisions are irreconcilably in conflict or there is a grammatical tie. In particular, ambiguity does *not* exist simply because ordinary speakers of the language might "reasonably differ" in their understanding of the statutory text.[116] That is too narrow a view to take in statutory interpretation, especially for a court (such as the Michigan Supreme Court) that generally does not consult legislative history and takes a relaxed approach toward *stare decisis*.[117]

The Michigan Supreme Court's error is apparent by considering the thousands of statutes that use broad terminology such as "vehicles." An ordinary speaker of English might plausibly consider hundreds, perhaps thousands, of items to be "vehicles" under a variety of circumstances. But no version of the Park Safety Act is going to regulate each and every imaginable vehicle. Depending on the precise terms the drafters chose and the ordinary understanding of the sentences in the statute, statutory interpreters (judges) will place different items into the "core" of the statute, its "penumbra," and its "exclusions." The continuum of plain or ordinary meaning constructed by the judge includes one other contextual feature, namely, the statutory purpose(s). To say that mechanisms such as

---

N.W.2d 78 (2008) (for purposes of a three-strikes law, do separate felony convictions for the same conduct count as separate strikes?); *National Pride at Work, Inc. v. Governor*, 748 N.W.2d 524 (Mich. 2008) (astounding debate over whether collective bargaining "domestic partnership" benefits amount to government "recognition" of a "marriage or other similar union"). Not only was there legitimate question about whether the text admitted some ambiguity in each case, but if I had to find an ordinary meaning, I'd have gone with the one sensibly announced in Justice Marilyn Kelly's dissenting opinion in each of these cases.

[116] *Gardner*, 753 N.W.2d at 85 n.12, quoting *Lansing Mayor v. Public Serv. Comm'n*, 680 N.W.2d 840 (Mich. 2004).

[117] Marilyn Kelly & John Postulka, *The Fatal Weakness in the Michigan Supreme Court's Majority's Textualist Approach to Statutory Construction*, 10 T.M. Cooley J. Prac. & Clinical L. 287 (2008) (documenting the Michigan Supreme Court's post-1999 disinclination to recognize statutory ambiguity and sharply criticizing the majority's offbeat understanding of ordinary meaning).

skateboards and motorized wheelbarrows are "vehicles" as a matter of ordinary meaning, perhaps because they fall within the dictionary definition, turns statutory interpretation into a high-stakes game of Scrabble. Scrabble is fun and educational, but it is a model for statutory interpretation that trivializes the rule of law.[118]

Thus, text-based interpretation is not a mechanical exercise that avoids value judgments. Just as ordinary conversations have a point that affects the way the interlocutors understand one another, so statutes have a purpose that ought to affect the way judges understand the legislated text. I have applied this idea to various items potentially regulated by the Park Safety Act—mopeds, bicycles, tricycles, wheelbarrows, and baby carriages, to name the main ones. This extended thought experiment confirms the truism that words tend to be value-laden, and statutory words are almost always value-laden. If that is so, value judgments are unavoidable. That they are unavoidable, however, does not mean that they are undisciplined or even unproductive.

---

[118] For a biting critique, from a Michigan law school, of a Scrabble-based approach to statutory interpretation, see Staszewski, *Avoiding Absurdity,* 81 Ind. L.J. at 1064–65 (responding to Professor Nagle's analogy of statutory interpretation to Scrabble).

Chapter 2

WHOLE ACT, STATUTORY PURPOSE, AND WHOLE CODE

Bill's 1995 Camry

In figuring out how to apply a statute to particular circumstances, the primary inquiry ought to be the ordinary meaning of the words, phrases, and sentence(s) relevant to those circumstances. If that inquiry yields a clear and definitive answer, the judge will often say there is a *plain meaning* that must be applied, regardless of arguments based upon legislative intent, fairness, or even constitutional concerns. Recall that there is for every statute a continuum of ordinary meaning, which suggests that the judge will often be unsure that the statute has an unambiguous meaning in these circumstances. Ultimately, the judge might still declare a plain meaning—frequently by resolving any doubts by reference to other provisions in the statute or in the U.S. Code. Conversely, even textualist judges will reconsider an apparent ordinary meaning for a statutory word, phrase, or sentence if the whole act suggests more than one reading of the text that is on point.[1]

---

1 E.g., *King v. Burwell*, 135 S.Ct. 2480 (2015) (Roberts, C.J.); *Department of Transportation v. Association of American Railroads*, 135 S.Ct. 1225 (2015) (Kennedy, J.); *Entergy Corp. v. Riverkeeper, Inc.*, 556 U.S. 208 (2009) (Scalia, J.).

Thus, in determining whether a statute has a plain meaning, the interpreter must consider the whole act, and not just one particular provision. "Statutory interpretation * * * is a holistic endeavor. A provision that may seem ambiguous in isolation is often clarified by the remainder of the statutory scheme—because the same terminology is used elsewhere in a context that makes its meaning clear, or because only one of the permissible meanings produces a substantive effect that is compatible with the rest of the law."[2]

Thus, one sentence in a statute, read in isolation, might be ambiguous as a matter of ordinary meaning—but, read in the context of the remainder of the statute, the sentence might have a plain meaning. Like the ordinary meaning rule examined in the previous chapter, the whole act rule is consistent with conventions of ordinary conversation. If Bill says, "I want to buy a vehicle," it is not clear from this sentence, standing alone, whether Bill is in the market for an automobile, motorcycle, moped, or bicycle (or all of the above); indeed, as a linguistic matter it is not even clear whether Bill has a particular vehicle in mind or whether he is just shopping around or even just thinking about the prospect.[3]

In situations like this one, however, the larger conversation typically enables the listener to know exactly what Bill wants. Thus, Bill might preface his remarks with the observation, "I need to retire my twenty-plus-year-old Camry," the vehicle pictured at the front of this chapter. "Although the trusty car is still running fine and I hate

---

[2] *United Savings Ass'n of Texas v. Timbers of Inwood Forest Assocs.*, 484 U.S. 365, 371 (1988); accord, *King v. Burwell*, 135 S.Ct. 2480; *Perez v. Mortgage Bankers Ass'n*, 135 S.Ct. 1199 (2015); *Hobby Lobby Stores, Inc. v. Burwell*, 134 S.Ct. 2751 (2014); *Ledbetter v. Goodyear Tire & Rubber Co.*, 550 U.S. 618 (2007); *Babbitt v. Sweet Home Chap. of Communities for a Great Oregon*, 515 U.S. 687 (1995); *Kokoszka v. Belford*, 417 U.S. 642, 650 (1974); *United States v. Fisher*, 6 U.S. 358 (1805) (Marshall, C.J.); accord, *Sharon S. v. Superior Court*, 73 P.3d 554 (Cal. 2003); *Larimore v. State*, 2 So.3d 101 (Fla. 2008); *Department of Environmental Quality v. Worth Township*, 814 N.W.2d 646 (Mich. 2012); *TGS-NOPEC Geophysical Co. v. Combs*, 340 S.W.3d 432 (Tex. 2011). See P. St.J. Langan, *Maxwell on the Interpretation of Statutes* 47–64 (12th ed. 1969) (English background for the whole act rule); 2A *Sutherland Statutes and Statutory Construction* § 46:5 (7th ed. 2015); Antonin Scalia & Bryan A. Garner, *Reading Law: The Interpretation of Legal Texts* 167–82 (2012).

[3] For a linguistic analysis of the ambiguities in the sentence "Bill wants to buy a vehicle," see Jill C. Anderson, *Just Semantics: The Lost Readings of the Americans with Disabilities Act*, 117 Yale L.J. 992 (2008), and *Misreading Like a Lawyer: Cognitive Bias in Statutory Interpretation*, 127 Harv. L. Rev. 1521 (2014). For a recent Supreme Court case presenting this "de re/de dicto" ambiguity, see *Fowler v. United States*, 131 S.Ct. 2045, 2053 (2011) (Scalia, J., concurring the judgment) (federal crime to kill someone to prevent his/her communication "to a law enforcement officer," a phrase that is ambiguous as to whether the communication would be to a particular officer or to any officer).

change of any sort, it is banged up from other cars (and the occasional post), and my devoted caregiver insists that this beloved vehicle has become an embarrassment." The sentence "I want to buy a vehicle" assumes greater clarity and specificity in light of these previous sentences. It is still ambiguous whether Bill has a particular vehicle in mind—but not if later in the conversation Bill says, "I have been looking at a whole range of Toyota cars but am not sure which one I want." The conversational context makes it clear that the "vehicle" Bill wants to buy is a car—not a motorcycle, moped, or bicycle, but an automobile—and that he would like to buy another Toyota but has not found a particular car just yet.

As suggested by our Camry example, the whole act rule ought to carry forth the project suggested by the ordinary meaning rule and its associated canons. The anchor for whole act analysis is the plan, objective, or scheme that addresses the problem the legislature was addressing. Accordingly, the whole act rule directs that the judge should interpret statutory provisions in light of the purpose of the statutory plan or scheme.[4]

Especially where the ordinary meaning of the statutory provision on point is open to more than one interpretation, the whole act can help us understand what the ordinary meaning of a statutory provision might be. Indeed, the entire statute might not only resolve ambiguities but might also, occasionally, suggest that the meaning of a provision is not as plain (or clear) as we thought upon first reading.[5] Recall Bill's statement, "I want to buy a vehicle." Many readers may believe that the ordinary meaning of that directive is that Bill wants to buy a car, and I have no quarrel with that intuition. What I should

---

[4] For recent elaborations of the whole act rule as advancing the statutory plan, scheme, or structure, see *King v. Burwell*, 135 S.Ct. at 2489; *Abramski v. United States*, 134 S.Ct. 2259, 2269–70 (2014); *POM Wonderful LLC v. Coca-Cola Co.*, 134 S.Ct. 2228, 2237–39 (2014); *Paroline v. United States*, 134 S.Ct. 1710, 1720–21 (2014); *Adoptive Couple v. Baby Girl*, 133 S.Ct. 2552, 2559–62 (2013); *Abbott v. United States*, 562 U.S. 8, 20–21 (2010); *Babbitt v. Sweet Home*, 515 U.S. 687; 2A *Sutherland Statutes and Statutory Construction* § 46:5 (7th ed. 2015). For the classic articulation of the purposive approach to the whole act rule, see Henry M. Hart Jr. & Albert M. Sacks, *The Legal Process: Basic Problems in the Making and Application of Law* (William N. Eskridge Jr. & Philip P. Frickey eds., 1994) (tent. ed. 1958). Accord, Stephen Breyer, *Active Liberty: Interpreting Our Democratic Constitution* 85 (2006); Scalia & Garner, *Reading Law*, 63–66.

[5] *Michigan v. EPA*, 135 S.Ct. 2699, 2707–08 (2015) (considering the statutory scheme and particular provisions to narrow the phase "appropriate and necessary" to require the agency to consider the cost of different regulatory alternatives); *Entergy Corp. v. Riverkeeper*, 556 U.S. at 233 (similar narrowing of the Clean Air Act Amendments in light of the statutory scheme).

insist upon, however, is that the reader must consider the entire conversation, which will tell her more about the overall plan, into which that statement fits. The larger context might reveal that Bill already has a new Toyota but is desirous of adding an antique automobile, such as a Léon Bollée Voiturette (pictured and described in chapter one), to his vehicular warehouse.

Because the whole act rule, properly understood, serves primarily to illuminate or clarify the ordinary meaning of statutory language, the rule and its associated canons ought not be applied in a hypertechnical manner, especially when the statute is one that is long and complicated or is the product of many amendments over the years. These cautions apply more emphatically to the extension of the whole act rule that might be called the *whole code rule*. "Every new act takes its place as a component of an extensive and elaborate system of written laws." Construing those laws to be in harmony, as much as other sources allow, advances the legal system's goals of "impartiality and minimiz[ing] arbitrariness."[6] The whole code rule is most useful when the interpreter is able to compare statutes that are closely related to one another, and is highly useful when there is evidence that the legislature actually considered the statutes *in pari materia* or borrowed language from an earlier statute when it adopted a subsequent one.[7] Under those circumstances, the whole code evidence is most like the whole act evidence, and its rule of law relevance is supported by the premises of our representative democracy.[8]

Unlike the ordinary meaning rule and the whole act rule, the whole code rule and its associated canons usually do not reflect the assumptions of the legislative process. Many state legislatures have codified the ordinary meaning rule and some version of the whole act rule and its associated canons, but no state legislature has codified

---

6 2A *Sutherland Statutes and Statutory Construction* § 53:1 (7th ed. 2015) (both quotations in text); see also id. § 51.1 (harmonization of related statutes); *Robinson v. City of Lansing*, 782 N.W.2d 171 (Mich. 2010) (similar).

7 2A *Sutherland Statutes and Statutory Construction* ch. 51 (7th ed. 2015) (interpreting statutes in light of related statutes). For thoughtful applications of the whole code rule, see *Hobby Lobby Stores,* 134 S.Ct. at 2772; *Samantar v. Yousuf*, 560 U.S. 305, 319 (2010); *Gonzales v. Oregon*, 546 U.S. 243, 273–74 (2006); *Babbitt v. Sweet Home*, 515 U.S. at 696–704; *West Virginia University Hospitals, Inc. v. Casey*, 499 U.S. 83, 100–01 (1991); *Pavelic & Leflore v. Marvel Entertainment Group*, 493 U.S. 120, 123–24 (1989); *Massachusetts v. Morash*, 490 U.S. 107, 114–15 (1989).

8 *Lorillard v. Pons*, 434 U.S. 575 (1978) (leading case, where the Court skillfully compared two related statutory schemes to illuminate the ordinary meaning of the more recent statute).

any version of the whole code rule (caveat: many legislatures have codified the *in pari materia* canon).[9] Although they take a holistic view of drafting individual statutes and often encourage drafters to research the entire statutory terrain for bills they draft, federal as well as state legislative drafting manuals say little about checking the whole code for consistency or variation.[10] Abbe Gluck and Lisa Schultz Bressman's empirical study of congressional drafters found little knowledge of the whole code rule and its associated canons and even less practical drafting in light of the rule.[11] Because the whole code rule and its associated canons introduce considerations legislators and their staff are unaware of and could not easily anticipate, these guidances operate under a greater need for rule of law justification. Do they significantly improve law's coherence and predictability, without unduly upbending assumptions made by legislators? In most instances, I am dubious.

In contrast, the whole act rule finds support or confirmation in the same democracy-respecting considerations that motivate my skepticism about the whole code rule. For example, the whole act rule reflects the prime directive of state and federal legislative drafting manuals, namely, to create an integrated statutory scheme that addresses the problem and advances the purpose(s) identified by the legislative sponsor (the drafter's "client," in drafting manual argot).[12]

---

[9] Jacob Scott, *Codified Canons and the Common Law of Interpretation*, 98 Geo. L.J. 341, 374–78 & Table 6 (2010) (reporting state-by-state codifications of some canons of statutory interpretation).

[10] See Delaware Legislative Council, Division of Research, *Delaware Legislative Drafting Manual* pt. II, chs. 2–3 (2015) (requiring drafters to master the subject matter of the proposed bill and related statutes); Kentucky Legislative Research Comm'n, *Bill Drafting Manual, Kentucky General Assembly* §§ 103 & 205 (rev. 2011) (admonishing legislative drafters to research the substantive law pertaining to a bill and to check for conflicts with other laws); Wisconsin Legislative Reference Bur., *Wisconsin Bill Drafting Manual 2011–2012*, § 2.01(24)(a) (admonishing legislative drafters that bills "should be tailored to blend as well as possible with existing law and to leave no loose ends that will create ambiguity or redundancy"). None of these drafting manuals, however, explicitly mentions the whole code rule or its associated canons as a reason to learn about related statutes.

[11] Abbe R. Gluck & Lisa Schultz Bressman, *Statutory Interpretation from the Inside: An Empirical Study of Congressional Drafting, Delegation, and the Canons: Part I*, 65 Stan. L. Rev. 901, 933–34 (2013); accord, Christopher J. Walker, *Inside Agency Statutory Interpretation*, 67 Stan. L. Rev. 999, 1029–30 (2015) (similar empirical study of agency rule drafters, finding little knowledge and virtually no reliance on the whole code rule).

[12] E.g., Alabama Legislative Reference Service, *Legislative Reference Service Drafting Style Manual*, Introduction (on-line, viewed Jan. 1, 2016) (drafter's goal is to implement the "intent of the author"); Delaware Legislative Council, *Legislative Drafting Manual*, pt. II, ch. 2 & pt. III, ch. 2, § 2(F) (drafter's goal is to work with the

And the various whole act canons well reflect widely followed drafting manual directives that the text needs to be parsimonious and brief, terms must be used consistently and synonyms avoided unless a different meaning is intended, exceptions ought to be laid out explicitly, and the provisions ought to work together in an integrated whole.[13]

Recall that the ordinary meaning rule advances the rule of law because it renders statutory interpretation more transparent to those subject to the law and more predictable and neutral as applied by judges and other government officials. Where other provisions of the statute help the reasonable reader resolve ambiguities in a provision that is on point, the whole act most clearly advances the rule of law. In the last two generations, as Congress and most state legislatures have steadily professionalized the drafting process through expansion of legislative counsel and similar offices, statutes have become more like carefully integrated codes, following the civil law model of an integrated set of rules.[14] At the state level, uniform laws adopted by multiple states have that feature even more clearly. For such integrated laws, it is especially important for the lawyer or the judge to understand the whole statute as well as particular provisions that are on point.[15] It is notable that the drafting rules for the National Conference of Commissioners on Uniform State Laws are indistinguishable from the rules followed by state and federal legislative drafting offices.[16]

The complexity of modern legislation prevents me from a full-fledged contrast between a democracy-respecting whole act rule and a

---

"client" [the bill's sponsor] to understand the statutory purpose, the problem to be solved, and the mechanics as well as nature of the statutory solution).

[13] The drafting admonitions in text are taken straight out of the Alabama Legislative Reference Service, *Legislative Reference Service Drafting Style Manual* (online, viewed Jan. 1, 2016), especially Rules 5 (consistency and meaningful variation), 6 (brevity and no duplication), 14 (exceptions), and 21 (purpose). These rules and goals are typical of those in state legislative drafting manuals, e.g., Delaware Legislative Council, *Legislative Drafting Manual* pt. VI, ch. 2, Rules 1–3, 9; Wisconsin Legislative Reference Bur., *Bill Drafting Manual 2011–2012*, §§ 2.0001(2), 2.01(3), (15) & (24), and 2.06(3), as well as those in the drafting manuals used by the Legislative Counsel for both the U.S. House and the U.S. Senate.

[14] Jarrod Shobe, *Intertemporal Statutory Interpretation and the Evolution of Legislative Drafting*, 114 Colum. L. Rev. 807, 851–54, 857–59 (2014).

[15] 2B *Sutherland Statutes and Statutory Construction* § 52:5 (7th ed. 2015) (harmonizing interpretive strategy for applying uniform multi-state codes).

[16] Compare National Conference of Commissioners on Uniform State Laws, *Drafting Rules: 2012 Edition* (July 2012), with the rules described for Alabama and Delaware and referenced in note 13, above.

democracy-impeding whole code rule. At the federal level, the typical statute is now the omnibus law, a hodge-podge of loosely related (and sometimes completely unrelated) titles and provisions put together by a diverse legislative coalition. For omnibus statutes, the whole act rule and the whole code rule tend to merge, because the statute is, itself, a collection of numerous statutory schemes, some interrelated but others not.[17] The more complicated and the less integrated the statute, and the more committees involved in deliberating and drafting different portions of the omnibus law, the less likely will the whole act rule contribute to a knowable, predictable rule of law.[18] It is reasonable to think that a citizen, her lawyer, or a judge can read and understand a short statute, or a single title in an omnibus law, as an integrated set of rules. It is less likely that a citizen, her lawyer, or a judge can work through a lengthy omnibus statute or would think that different titles will offer guidance for interpretation for each other. We shall return to interpretation of sprawling omnibus statutes in chapter six.

Some judges and scholars have endorsed, as a "benign fiction," the assumption that an omniscient Congress (or state legislature) is always aware of the details of statutory schemes and of related statutes.[19] No one has ever explained why such a "fiction" is "benign" or justified. If an unelected court imposes its own fictions upon the legislative product, the court needs to justify such an imposition, because it is, on its face, in tension with the democratic premises of our system. If the court justifies the fiction on the ground that it reflects the probable views of legislators, it must provide convincing evidence that is the case *or* that some other reason justifies infidelity to legislative assumptions. The burden is on the court announcing or applying the fiction.

---

[17] On omnibus statutes, the leading source is Barbara Sinclair, *Unorthodox Lawmaking: New Legislative Processes in the U.S. Congress* 71 (4th ed. 2011). See also William J. Keefe & Morris S. Ogul, *The American Legislative Process: Congress and the States* (10th ed. 2000); Walter J. Oleszek, *Congressional Procedures and the Policy Process* (9th ed. 2013); Gregory J. Wawro & Eric Schickler, *Filibuster: Obstruction and Lawmaking in the U.S. Senate* (2007).

[18] Shobe, *Intertemporal Statutory Interpretation and the Evolution of Legislative Drafting*, 114 Colum. L. Rev. at 858–59 (suggesting that the whole act rule does not work well for omnibus statutes, where different titles are drafted by different committees, but does work well for modern statutes drafted by the same committee in each chamber).

[19] E.g., *Green v. Bock Laundry Mach. Co.*, 490 U.S. 504, 528 (1989) (Scalia, J., concurring in the judgment); John F. Manning, *The Supreme Court, 2013 Term: Foreword—The Means of Constitutional Power*, 128 Harv. L. Rev. 1, 8–30 (2014).

This is a burden courts cannot bear for some of the whole act canons and most of the whole code canons, as William Buzbee has argued in his analysis of the "one Congress fiction."[20] Empirical research by legislation scholars has established that legislative staff, who do almost all of the bill drafting and who explain proposed legislation to members of Congress, do not know about some of the whole act canons. And they do not follow some of the ones they do know. The politics of legislation requires drafters and sponsors to sacrifice drafting consistency, brevity, and coherence in order to attract and hold the votes of needed legislative allies, and especially those who control one of the vetogates potentially blocking the legislation.[21] But the Gluck and Bressman survey found that many congressional drafters who themselves did not follow whole act canons when writing statutes did not object if judges followed such canons consistently and without partisan slant.[22] For this kind of reason, a large majority of state legislatures have codified rules that invite interpreters to consider not just the words of a statutory provision and not just the larger statute, but also statutory context "similar" as a matter of statutory text or policy.[23]

As for the whole code canons, they are more likely to be "fictions" and less likely to be "benign" or justified. As a matter of legislative practice, statutes are less likely to be drafted with an eye to the whole corpus of law. The Congressional Research Service, for example, does not include the whole code rule in its advice to congressional staff for their participation in statutory drafting.[24] Hence, the whole code rule

---

[20] William W. Buzbee, *The One Congress Fiction in Statutory Interpretation*, 149 U. Pa. L. Rev. 171, 180–203 (2000).

[21] For the leading studies of the assumptions made by congressional drafters, and their tendency to view whole act considerations as impractical, see Gluck & Bressman, *Statutory Interpretation from the Inside: Part I*, 65 Stan. L. Rev. at 934–37; Victoria F. Nourse & Jane S. Schacter, *The Politics of Legislative Drafting: A Congressional Case Study*, 77 N.Y.U. L. Rev. 575, 590–600, 614–16 (2002).

[22] Lisa Schultz Bressman & Abbe R. Gluck, *Statutory Interpretation from the Inside: An Empirical Study of Congressional Drafting, Delegation, and the Canons: Part II*, 66 Stan. L. Rev. 725, 749–50, 770–71, 774–75 (2014) (reporting that congressional drafting staff would be okay with whole act canons if judges applied them consistently).

[23] See Scott, *Codified Canons*, 98 Geo. L.J. at 364, 374–76 (reporting that as many as 30 state legislatures have codified the canon that larger statutory "context" is relevant to interpreting a particular provision).

[24] The CRS Report on statutory interpretation for congressional staff says nothing about the whole code rule and mentions such considerations only to suggest consideration of how terms are used in interrelated statutory programs. Larry M. Eig, American Law Division, Congressional Research Service, Report, *Statutory Interpretation* 14 & n.83 (updated Dec. 11, 2011) (hereinafter cited as CRS Report,

is more often at odds with the premises of our representative democracy than the whole act rule.[25] Accordingly, judges should be cautious before they deploy whole code arguments to transform an ambiguous provision into one with a plain meaning that closes off further inquiry. Indeed, the democratic premises of congressional drafting and deliberation require that judges not treat the whole code rule as dispositive if other evidence cuts another way.[26]

Perhaps surprisingly, some support for a strong whole act rule and even the whole code rule (with qualifications) might be the purposes of governance. If law is purposive and statutes are the means by which our polity formulates and carries forth its great public plans, then the interpreter ought *not* view various provisions in isolation and ought to consider the entire statutory scheme whenever she must apply a particular provision. This point has much greater bite for well-integrated code-like statutes, such as the Model Penal Code or the Uniform Commercial Code, than it has for omnibus measures that are almost random collections of unrelated statutory plans.[27] Study of the whole act to figure out, in a precise way, the plan and objectives of the statutory scheme is, importantly, a task that judges are well-trained to perform. Generalists well-schooled in the broad canvass of the law, judges can and do perform an integrative function in statutory interpretation.

Political philosophy also lends some support to the whole act and whole code rules, and the philosophical argument for such canons ties in with the legitimacy anchor. Thus far, the discussion has relied on democracy-based understandings of legitimacy: We the People have agreed to be bound by rules and plans adopted by our elected representatives acting through the constitutional procedures for lawmaking. That is a procedural foundation for legitimacy, but it may be a thin one, motivating citizens to obey the law, but not necessarily

---

Statutory Interpretation), citing *Sullivan v. Stroop*, 496 U.S. 478, 484 (1990) ("child support" as used in the Child Support program under the Social Security Act points toward the same use of "child support" in the closely related AFDC program, and thus "child support" as used in the AFDC program does not include OASDI payments under title II of the Social Security Act).

25 See Buzbee, *One Congress Fiction*, 149 U. Pa. L. Rev. at 177–79; Gluck & Bressman, *Statutory Interpretation from the Inside: Part I*, 65 Stan. L. Rev. at 934–37.

26 Gluck & Bressman, *Statutory Interpretation from the Inside: Part I*.

27 2B *Sutherland Statutes and Statutory Construction* § 52.5 (7th ed. 2015) (harmonizing interpretation for uniform and model state laws); see, e.g., Minn. Stat. § 645.22: "Laws uniform with those of other states shall be interpreted and construed to effect their general purpose to make uniform the laws of those states which enact them."

to engage with the law or to lend it affirmative support. But there is also a thicker, purpose-based foundation for legitimacy. That thicker foundation rests upon citizens' belief that the law treats everyone the same and that statutory rules represent widely shared values.[28] In many (but not necessarily most) circumstances, this argument provides support for the whole code and whole rules, the canons preferring interpretations of ambiguous provisions because they consistent with other statutes and their policies.

Abstractions, of course, do not resolve cases. As I shall now show, the whole act rule can be most valuable in helping the interpreter ascertain the ordinary meaning of statutory language, as can the whole code rule if one deploys it cautiously. To see how the whole act rule and, sometimes, the whole code rule help understand how statutory interpretation should operate, we now turn to an expanded version of the vehicles in the park law.

Whole Act and Whole Code Rules

To see the whole act rule in action, we need to expand the simple vehicles in the park law beyond the single sentence we analyzed in the previous chapter. Consider this more elaborate statutory scheme:

> **An Act to ensure public safety in Lafayette Park**
>
> **Sec. 1. Findings and Purpose.** Finding that vehicles operating in Lafayette Park have contributed to several serious accidents requiring hospitalization in the last five years, and finding further that vehicles create risks of serious injury to park users, Congress resolves that there is an urgent public need to ban any and all vehicles from Lafayette Park.
>
> **Sec. 2. No Vehicles in the Park.** No vehicles of any kind shall be allowed in Lafayette Park. Any person who drives a vehicle into Lafayette Park may be assessed a fine not exceeding $500 for each violation.

---

[28] Ronald Dworkin, *Law's Empire* 209–15 (1986) (distinguishing between a rulebook-based legitimacy and the legitimacy flowing from the collective appreciation that we live in a "community of principle"); Tom R. Tyler & Jonathan Jackson, *Popular Legitimacy and the Exercise of Legal Authority: Motivating Compliance, Cooperation and Engagement*, 20 Psychol. Pub. Pol'y & Law 78 (2014) (empirical support for the idea that popular engagement and support for law, rather than mere acquiescence in or compliance with law, requires that people be persuaded of the values found in legal rules).

> **Sec. 3. Definition.** "Vehicle" for purposes of this law means any mechanism for conveying a person from one place to another, including automobiles, trucks, motorcycles, and motor scooters. *Provided that*, bicycles shall be allowed in Lafayette Park, so long as they are being pushed or carried and not ridden.

Even though this is a simple statutory scheme, it helps us figure out the ordinary meaning of the statute's directive, in section 2, that "[n]o vehicles of any kind shall be allowed in Lafayette Park" and that no one may "drive[ ] a vehicle into Lafayette Park."

Recall, from chapter one, the trouble we had figuring out whether the simpler "Park Safety Act" had an ordinary meaning that included mopeds (motorized bicycles without pedals). The first sentence of section 2 seems applicable to mopeds, but the second sentence raises some doubt, because mopeds are not vehicles one normally "drives." Please revisit the complete Park Safety Act that is printed above, and consider this question: Does the whole act help you resolve the tough issue whether the statute regulates mopeds? If so, which provisions help you resolve the ambiguity, and why? Jot down your answer and read the following analysis.

Section 1 makes clear that the statutory purpose is public safety and that Congress has imposed a sweeping prophylactic remedy, namely a "ban [against] any and all vehicles." As a matter of ordinary language, mopeds are properly characterized as vehicles, and their potential speed renders them safety hazards for park users. They also fall securely within section 3's definition of vehicle, because mopeds are mechanisms for conveying a person from one place to another. Indeed, they are very similar to the mechanisms specifically listed in section 3, namely, "automobiles, trucks, motorcycles, and motor scooters." One cannot object that mopeds are not specifically named, for the list is grammatically not exclusive (the term "include[es]" the listed mechanisms).[29] Most important, mopeds (such as the vespa models pictured in the previous chapter) are very similar to motor scooters. Not only are they similar and shape and design, but both mopeds and motor scooters are motorized vehicles that can go pretty fast (forty miles per hour, sometimes faster) and so may cause serious accidents to park users. State law usually groups mopeds and motor

---

[29] 2A *Sutherland Statutes and Statutory Construction* § 47:2 (7th ed. 2015) (definitions "including" specified items are not exhaustive); National Conference of Commissioners on Uniform State Laws, *Drafting Rules: 2012 Edition*, Rule 301(d) (same).

scooters together for regulatory purposes such as registration requirements, speed limits, safety requirements (such as helmets and goggles), and so forth.[30]

The parallel between mopeds and motor scooters also helps the interpreter resolve the ambiguity suggested by the second sentence of section 2, which creates a rule that one cannot "drive[ ] a vehicle" into the park. We usually say we operate or ride (rather than drive) a moped—but the same is true for motor scooters. Motor scooters are clearly covered by the first sentence in section 2 ("[n]o vehicles of any kind shall be allowed" in the park), and it is likely that "vehicles" covered by the first sentence are also covered by the second one ("[a]ny person who drives a vehicle"), and vice-versa. As we have seen in chapter one, it is unusual but not unheard of to say that one "drives" a motor scooter, as well as a moped. If the Park Safety Act covers "driving" a motor scooter, then it very probably covers "driving" a moped.

To the extent any doubt remains, it is resolved by the bicycle proviso, which clinches the whole act argument. In a bit of erratic drafting, section 3 creates a special rule for bicycles—they can be brought into the park but not ridden. If you interpreted the Park Safety Act to be inapplicable to mopeds, you would have a very strange statute with an incoherent policy. That is, an interpretation excluding mopeds from the law would still regulate bicycles, even though bicycles are not as speedy or as heavy as mopeds and therefore do not implicate the statutory safety purpose as clearly as mopeds do.

Am I right in thinking that reading the whole act would lead most neutral and reasonable interpreters to agree that mopeds are covered by the statute? If so, this exercise illustrates the potential rule of law value of the whole act rule, namely, to create interpretive closure for isolated statutory provisions that, if read in isolation, would be susceptible of more than one plausible meaning. By revealing the coherence of the statutory plan, the whole act rule honors the legislative process and may advance the governance project as well.

An interesting ambiguity remains even if we conclude that the statute covers mopeds. Are mopeds "vehicles" barred from the park

---

[30] See, e.g., DMV.org, *The DMV Made Simple: Virginia—Mopeds and Motor Scooters*, available at http://www.dmv.org/va-virginia/other-types.php (viewed Jan. 1, 2015).

altogether (section 2), or are they "bicycles" allowed in the park but only if pushed or carried (the section 3 proviso)? Because dictionaries tell us that a moped is both a small motor scooter and a motorized version of a bicycle, it is similar to both a bicycle (regulated by the section 3 proviso) and a motor scooter (regulated by section 2). Reading the whole act, there can be little doubt that the law covers mopeds, but the interpreter might be of two minds about which statutory prohibition applies to mopeds. You might want to jot down your view: Section 2? Section 3's proviso? A complete tie?

It is here that the whole code rule might help. Assuming that there is no authoritative precedent or legislative history shedding light on this remaining Park Safety Act ambiguity, you might find decisive assistance elsewhere in the law of vehicles. Are mopeds better treated as regulated bicycles or as prohibited vehicles? Recall that the Dictionary Act of 1947 provides a general definition of "vehicle," applicable throughout the United States Code: "The word 'vehicle' includes every description of carriage or other artificial contrivance used, or capable of being used, as a means of transportation on land."[31] Although section 3 of the Park Safety Act provides this law's particularized definition, the Dictionary Act might be consulted to break the logjam; it clearly suggests that bicycles and mopeds are presumptively "vehicles" as a matter of federal law.

One might also consult codifications at the state level, as persuasive (but not binding) authority along the same lines.[32] The 2000 Uniform Vehicle Code, discussed in the previous chapter, may be instructive. The Code defines "bicycle" as "[e]very vehicle propelled solely by human power upon which any person may ride, having two tandem wheels and except scooters and similar devices." This is in contrast with the Code's definition of "motor vehicles" as "[e]very vehicle which is self-propelled, and every vehicle which is propelled by electric power obtained from overhead trolley wires but not operated upon rails, except vehicles moved solely by human power and motorized wheelchairs."[33] This evidence provides a useful

---

[31] Dictionary Act of July 30, 1947, ch. 388, § 4, 61 Stat. 633, codified at 1 U.S.C. § 4 (defining land "vehicles" for purposes of the U.S. Code); cf. id. § 3 (defining water "vehicles").

[32] 2B *Sutherland Statutes and Statutory Construction* § 51:6 (7th ed. 2015) (statutes from different states but relating to the same subject matter and reflecting a similar policy might be consulted as persuasive authority).

[33] Compare National Committee on Uniform Traffic Laws and Ordinances, 2000 Uniform Vehicles Code § 1–109 (definition of "bicycle" for purposes of the UVC), with id. § 1–156 (definition of "motor vehicle"). Both definitions are quoted in text.

regulatory principle for categorizing mopeds as (motor) vehicles rather than bicycles, if a choice must be made. The regulatory principle is that having a motor makes a decisive difference in determining what vehicular grouping one should place things like mopeds.

Additional support for that conclusion comes from a preliminary search of the U.S. Code and the Code of Federal Regulations. The primary federal "vehicles" law is the Motor Vehicle Safety Act of 1966, which does not apply to bicycles but which regulates motor vehicles quite stringently for safety purposes. The regulatory agency charged with implementing that law has determined that mopeds are "motor driven cycles," regulated by the statute in the same category as motor scooters and motorcycles.[34] While ordinary conversation does not reference the Motor Vehicle Safety Act any more than it references the Uniform Vehicle Code, the bicycle-versus-motor vehicle issue is one as to which ordinary meaning is at an impasse, because a moped is both a bicycle and a motor vehicle. To figure out precisely how the Park Safety Act regulates mopeds, one needs to choose which category is right for mopeds. From a regulatory perspective, the Uniform Vehicle Code and the Motor Vehicle Safety Act are useful sources because both are concerned with safety, and both treat mopeds as raising greater safety concerns than bicycles do, and the same kinds of safety concerns as motor scooters. Critically, the regulatory principle comports with the statutory safety purpose that is set forth in section 1 of the law: Bicycle speeds are normally five to twenty miles per hour, while mopeds (like motor scooters) can easily zip along at thirty or forty miles per hour, creating greater safety hazards for park users.

Notice how consideration of the whole act and the whole code (including the uniform act) actually clarifies the meaning of the statute and, thereby, generates rule of law benefits like greater predictability. In the previous chapter, we considered the stand-alone meaning of a rule saying that no one may "drive a vehicle of any kind" into Lafayette Park. We found plenty of ambiguity in this directive. Recall Figure 2, from that chapter.

---

[34] The Office of Chief Counsel for the regulatory agency has determined that mopeds are "motor driven cycles" subject to the regulatory requirements of the Motor Vehicle Safety Act of 1966. See Department of Transportation, National Highway Traffic Safety Administration, *Requirements for Manufacturers of Motorcycles* 1 (Feb. 2000).

FIGURE 2

Ordinary Meaning Continuum: "Driving a Vehicle" in the Park

Core Coverage	Penumbra			Outside the Statute	
Cars	Motorcycles	Mopeds	Bicycles	Tricycles	Wheelbarrows
Trucks	Motor Scooters			Skateboards	Baby Carriages

Read in light of the whole act, most of the ambiguities disappear. Section 3's definition of "vehicles" covered by the Park Safety Act brings motorcycles and motor scooters into the statutory orbit; its bicycle proviso brings bikes into a less restrictive regime. A clear implication of section 3's definition and its bicycle proviso is that the statute also covers mopeds, an implication strongly reinforced by the statutory purpose identified in section 1.

Figure 4 reveals the new plain meaning continuum, understood in light of the whole act and related laws.

FIGURE 4

Plain Meaning Continuum: "Driving a Vehicle" in the Park (§ 2), in Light of Statutory Purpose (§ 1) and Definition (§ 3)

Core Coverage		Penumbra	Outside the Statutes
Cars & Trucks	Bicycles	Adult Tricycles	Kid's Tricycles
Motorcycles			Baby Carriages
Motor Scooters			Wheelbarrows
Mopeds			

Notice that the whole act does more than expand and clarify the core coverage of the Park Safety Act. It also draws a few mechanisms into the penumbral area, where it is plausible that a mechanism one does not "drive" now falls within the statute nonetheless. Section 3's proviso draws bicycles into the statutory scheme, which expands the statute beyond the motorized vehicles listed in section 3's definition. Because section 1 identifies park safety as the statutory goal, the interpreter ought to open her mind to the argument that other nonmotorized vehicles are included in the statute, so long as they are vehicles that create safety hazards.

The foregoing analysis does not disturb our earlier conclusion that neither wheelbarrows nor baby carriages are regulated by the Park Safety Act. But how about adult tricycles, three-wheeled mechanisms that can go almost as fast as bicycles? An argument can be made for their regulation, either as section 2 vehicles or, more likely in light of the analysis above, as bicycles under the proviso of section 3. To be sure, there is a good whole act argument against including adult tricycles. Reread the entire statute: How might regulation of adult tricycles cut against the implicit *structure* of the Park Safety Act? This is a more speculative enterprise than the earlier ones in this chapter and chapter one, but see if you cannot generate an insight.

One way to understand the Park Safety Act, read as a whole, is that the statute creates three levels of regulation, grounded upon the safety concerns posed by different vehicles. The *top level* consists of motorized vehicles (the items listed in section 3, including mopeds), and the statute bans them entirely. This makes a lot of sense: The prototypical vehicle is a car; when you say "vehicle," many interlocutors immediately assume motor vehicles. Indeed, when federal law refers to "vehicles," the reference is usually to motorized vehicles.[35]

The *intermediate level* consists of "bicycles"; the statute allows them into the park but does not allow people to ride them through the park. This, too, makes policy sense: Bicycles belong in parks in ways that motorized vehicles do not, but they pose safety concerns because bicycles can race through a park faster than some motorized vehicles (such as Segways). The special characteristics of bicycles seem to explain the unusual regulation, namely, the proviso's rule allowing bicycles to be carried or pushed in Lafayette Park but not ridden through the park.

How about potential "vehicles" that are neither motorized nor bicycles? Implicit in the statutory scheme suggested by sections 1 (purpose) and 3 (definitions) may be a policy that nonmotorized vehicles other than bicycles are not regulated. This is the *lowest level*, namely, private activities that the law leaves alone. The kid with the wagon, the parents pushing the baby carriage, and the youth on the pogo stick are all unregulated: They are doing quintessential "park-

[35] For leading references to "vehicles" in federal law, see National Traffic and Motor Vehicle Safety Act of 1966, 80 Stat. 718 (1966), implemented by Department of Transportation, National Highway Traffic Safety Administration, *Federal Motor Vehicle Safety Standards*, 49 C.F.R. Part 571 (2013); Department of Labor, Mine Safety and Health Administration, *Safety and Health Standards for Underground Metal and Nonmetal Mines*, 30 C.F.R. §§ 57.6202–.6220 (1999) (maintenance of transport vehicles); Environmental Protection Agency, *Control of Emissions of Air Pollution from 2004 and Later Model Year Heavy-Duty Highway Engines and Vehicles*, 40 C.F.R. Parts 85–86 (2011).

like" things and are posing very little danger to others. Does this understanding of the statutory structure make sense to you? Even if you agree with me, please keep in mind that I am speculating here, and so my proposed structure is more of a hypothesis to be explored than a plain meaning to be insisted upon.

Under this understanding of the statutory scheme, adult tricycles do not fall within the highest regulatory level, because they are not motorized. The key question is whether adult tricycles are "bicycles" falling under section 3's proviso; if so, they may be pushed or carried through Lafayette Park but not ridden. A bicycle does not lose its name or its identity if it has four wheels, when two of those wheels are training wheels. Indeed, an adult tricycle (like the vehicle on the left below) looks a lot like a bicycle with training wheels in the rear (like the vehicle on the right). So why should we not consider adult tricycles nothing more than a bicycle with big training wheels—especially given the speed with which adult three-speed adult tricycles can zip along the park?[36]

Adult Tricycle

Bicycle with Training Wheels

These are mighty powerful arguments, but they do not establish a plain meaning that adult tricycles fall within the bicycle proviso of section 3, for one very simple reason. The anchor for statutory interpretation remains ordinary meaning. With *two* wheels, a *bi*cycle is linguistically different from a *tri*cycle, with its *three* wheels. Sure, bicycles sometimes have training wheels, but in ordinary parlance we call these vehicles "bicycles with training wheels." Admitting that I should be reluctant to apply the Park Safety Act to adult tricycles, I am inclined to say that the statute remains ambiguous as regards

---

[36] For an adult tricycle that looks like a bicycle with training wheels, see the Trifecta Twenty-Inch Three-Speed Folding Tricycle, available at http://www.walmart.com/ip/Port–O–Trike–3–Speed–Deluxe–Adult–Folding–Tricycle/2189247 (viewed Dec. 1, 2014).

this application. (Recall that the continuum approach to ordinary meaning contemplates the possibility of ambiguity even when one interpretation strikes us as somewhat more likely than the other.)

The foregoing analysis illustrates the potential utility of the whole act rule for the interpreter's investigation into a provision's meaning. The analysis here has been similar in many respects to that in the previous chapter. As before, the anchor has been ordinary meaning, understood as if we were engaged in a normative conversation. Ordinary meaning depends, critically, on the point of the conversation or the purpose of the statute. The whole act rule is often helpful precisely because the larger statute has more language that can help us better understand the statute's overall plan or purpose and the precise mechanism(s) the statute deploys to carry out that plan or purpose.

Notice that the foregoing analysis is not encumbered with various clear statement rules, presumptions, or even tiebreakers—the language often used in association with the whole act or whole code canons. As explained in the introduction to this volume, I am a fan of the canons, but do not understand them as formal rules that magically guarantee uniform, predictable application of statutes to fact situations. Even as arrayed in this volume's appendix reporting dozens of canons applied by the U.S. Supreme Court, the canons are not a step-by-step guidebook for the judge wanting to anticipate exactly how the Supreme Court would have her interpret a particular provision.

Instead, the canons are an interpretive regime that provides a vocabulary for questions, factual investigations, and tentative conclusions in the process by which a judge thinks through a statutory problem, always in light of the larger rule of law, democracy, and governance goals of statutory interpretation. Now consider some of the canons that have guided the reasoning process in this chapter, as well as others that might have been relevant under different statutory texts and structures.

Whole Act Canons

Most of the whole act canons seek relative statutory harmonization or coherence. They strive to make unified sense of the statute, with each word and each provision playing a role that advances the statutory plan. Harmonization is a classic feature of the rule of law, as implemented by interpretation. Much as the biblical interpreter seeks to read Scripture as an integrated whole, so the legal interpreter seeks to read a statutory scheme as an integrated whole. Indeed, there is an aesthetic as well as practical feature of the rule of law that makes the whole act rule most attractive: People reading a document (not just the Bible) tend to assume coherence, often unconsciously, and a document that is internally consistent is a stronger text than one filled with inconsistencies.

Consistent with traditional judicial practice, however, harmonization must remain subordinate to ordinary meaning. Citizens and even their lawyers are not as likely to read and understand the whole statute as they are to read and understand the ordinary meaning of the statutory directive immediately applicable to their conduct. Sometimes, the harmonization feature of the whole act rule helps effectuate the important public project or values Congress chose when it enacted the statute. But recall that legislative drafters themselves follow the ordinary meaning canon as best they can but do not believe that some of the whole act canons are realistic, given the dynamic nature of the legislative process for drafting, deliberation, and constant revision. Even when there is a single drafting group seeking to create an internally consistent statutory scheme, most major bills are changed and edited by multiple redrafters in the dynamic process that leads to enactment, a process that makes the harmonization canons potentially anti-democratic.[37]

With these caveats in mind, consider a number of whole act canons. The final part of the chapter will introduce, evaluate, and elaborate upon several useful whole code canons.

Title and Caption Canons. As standard drafting practice, Congress and state legislatures usually provide a long descriptive title at the beginning of the enacted bill. For our hypothetical no vehicles law, the long title is "An Act to ensure public safety in Lafayette Park." Sometimes legislators also include a short title in the text of the enacted law; other times, the short title comes through practice, as is the case with our "Park Safety Act." Within an enacted public law having more than one provision, legislatures will almost always include a caption or heading that describes the material included within each provision or cluster of provisions. Even our short little Park Safety Act has captions for its three sections.

---

[37] Nourse & Schacter, *The Politics of Legislative Drafting* (reporting findings from empirical survey of congressional staff); accord, Gluck & Bressman, *Statutory Interpretation from the Inside, Part I*, 65 Stan. L. Rev. at 930–38 (subsequent empirical study, reaching similar conclusions). But see Shobe, *Intertemporal Statutory Interpretation*, 114 Colum. L. Rev. at 831–32, 857–59 (reporting that statutes drafted in the last several decades better internalize the whole act and even whole code rules than statutes drafted earlier).

Federal and state courts, including the Supreme Court in some recent cases, have sometimes found significance in the statute's title or its relevant captions.[38] The potential utility of titles and captions is their signaling statutory purpose and coverage. Both the long and the short titles of the "Park Safety Act of 1992" reinforce the conclusion that the purpose or the focus of the statute is assuring safety in Lafayette Park. For interpreting federal statutes, the utility of titles and captions is quite limited, because they are, by their nature, short, condensed, and therefore oversimplified statements describing a statute or a provision.[39]

Unlike the U.S. Constitution, state constitutions typically limit legislation to a "single subject" and, in the same clause, require legislatures to include a title that accurately describes the contents of the law; legislative drafters take this constitutional requirement very seriously.[40] For this reason, state courts ought to be more interested in how the title frames the legislation—but that interest does not carry over to captions. Only two state codifications include the caption canon, and as many as twenty-two state codifications reject it. The West Virginia Code puts the matter well: "Chapter, article or section headings, headlines or headnotes of any act of the Legislature, whether in the act at the time of passage or inserted by the clerk * * * are hereby declared to be mere catchwords and shall not be deemed or construed to be titles of such chapters, articles or sections, or as

---

[38] E.g., *United States v. Yates*, 135 S.Ct. 1074, 1083 (2015) (Ginsburg, J., for a plurality); id. at 1090 (Alito, J., concurring in the judgment) (relevance of a provision's caption and, for the plurality, the title); *Abbott v. United States*, 562 U.S. 8, 20 (2010) (title); *Almendarez-Torres v. United States*, 523 U.S. 224, 234 (1998) (title and caption); *Church of the Holy Trinity v. United States*, 143 U.S. 457, 463 (1892) (title); *Larimore*, 2 So.3d at 112–13 (Fla.) (title and heading/caption); *Klida v. Braman*, 748 N.W.2d 244, 248 (Mich. App. 2008) (title); 2A *Sutherland Statutes and Statutory Construction* §§ 47:3 & 47:14 (7th ed. 2015) (title and headings).

[39] For cautionary statements of the title and caption canons, see *Yates*, 135 S.Ct. at 1094 (Kagan, J., dissenting); *People v. Wheeler*, 841 P.2d 938, 943–44 (Cal. 1992); *Camaj v. S.S. Kresge Co.,* 393 N.W.2d 875 (Mich. 1986); *Suffolk Regional Off-Track Betting Corp. v. New York State Racing & Wagering Bd.*, 900 N.E.2d 970, 975–76 (N.Y. 2008) (Kaye, C.J.); 2A *Sutherland Statutes and Statutory Construction* §§ 47:3 & 47.14 (7th ed. 2015); CRS Report, *Statutory Interpretation*, 33–34 (updated 2011); Scalia & Garner, *Reading Law*, 221–24.

[40] E.g., Alaska Const. art. III, § 13 (requiring a title that accurately expresses the legislative intent), applied in Legislative Affairs Agency, State of Alaska, *Manual of Legislative Drafting* 10–12 (2015); Fla. Const., art. III, § 6 (requiring legislature to include a title that accurately describes changes in the law accomplished by the statute), applied in Florida Senate, *Manual for Drafting Legislation* ch. 3, at 34–36; Md. Const., art. III, § 29 (similar), applied in Maryland Dep't of Legislative Servs., Office of Policy Analysis, *Legislative Drafting Manual 2016*, at ch. 5 (Sept. 2015) (title must describe subject matter of bill; poor title might be fatal to proposed legislation).

any part thereof, or as indicating or expressing legislative intent or purpose."[41] The U.S. Code is similarly dismissive, though not in as targeted a manner as the West Virginia Code.[42] Given the analytical objections to reliance on legislative titles and explicit statutory disapproval, federal judges should probably not rely on titles or captions (which are "junior" titles) as anything but supporting evidence when they are interpreting statutes.[43] And state judges might be more attentive to titles, but perhaps not to captions.

Purpose Canon. The primary whole act canon is that the judge ought to interpret statutory provisions in light of the statutory plan (as the Supreme Court sometimes puts it in recent Terms) or of the legislative purposes and objectives (as traditionally expressed).[44] As the Colorado legislative drafting office has directed, the first and primary duty of the statutory drafter is to find out from the sponsors and the enacting coalition what the statute is trying to accomplish—and then to organize the statutory structure and provisions accordingly.[45]

Many legislative drafting manuals discourage drafters from including clauses detailing legislative findings and the purpose(s) of the legislation; drafting offices have been concerned that general

---

[41] W.V. Code § 2–2–12 (quotation in text); see *Yates*, 135 S.Ct. at 1094–95 (Kagan, J., dissenting) (criticism of title and captions, because they are by nature short and incomplete); Scott, *Codified Canons*, 98 Geo. L.J. at 358 (Table 3) (reporting rejection of the caption canon by 22 states).

[42] See Tobias A. Dorsey, *Some Reflections on* Yates *and the Statutes We Threw Away*, 18 Green Bag 2d 377 (2015) (arguing that Congress is not keen on inferences drawn from the formal trappings of statutes, such as placement and titles).

[43] E.g., *Abbott v. United States*, 562 U.S. at 20 (briefly noting the law's title to confirm skepticism that Congress was going easy on criminals); *Oregon v. Gonzales*, 546 U.S. at 273–74 (mentioning a provision's caption to add nuance and slight confirmation for the Court's understanding of the relationship among various statutory powers).

[44] E.g., *King v. Burwell*, 135 S.Ct. at 2489; *Abramski*, 134 S.Ct. at 2269; *Abbott v. United States*, 562 U.S. at 20–21. For the classic articulation of the purposive approach to the whole act rule, see Henry M. Hart Jr. & Albert M. Sacks, *The Legal Process: Basic Problems in the Making and Application of Law* (William N. Eskridge Jr. & Philip P. Frickey eds., 1994) (tent. ed. 1958). Accord, Stephen Breyer, *Active Liberty: Interpreting Our Democratic Constitution* 85 (2006); Scalia & Garner, *Reading Law*, 63–66.

[45] Office of Legislative Legal Services, Colorado Legislature, *Colorado Legislative Drafting Manual* § 1.2.1 (on-line edition, viewed Jan. 1, 2016); accord, Ira B. Forstater, Office of Legislative Counsel, U.S. House of Representatives, *House Legislative Counsel's Manual on Drafting Style* §§ 102(f), 325(b) (Nov. 1995); Kentucky Legislative Research Comm'n, *Bill Drafting Manual* § 103; Maryland Dep't Legislative Servs., *Legislative Drafting Manual 2016*, ch. 2, p. 15–16 (detailed protocol for bill drafters to work with sponsors to make sure the bill reflects sponsor's goals).

expressions of purpose might be misleading and are better handled in committee reports or statements made on the floor of the legislature.[46] Some legislative drafting manuals are concerned that general statements of purpose will be used to expand statutes beyond legislative expectations. "Because a legislative statement generally declares broad public policy objectives, a court may use a legislative statement to infer a legislative intent that is arguably not supported by the substantive provisions of the statute. In light of this risk," the Utah drafting manual urges that "a legislative statement should be used only in limited circumstances, when the legislative statement may help a court or an implementing agency to determine the intent of the Legislature."[47]

Nonetheless, statutes often include provisions explicitly setting forth legislative findings and statutory purposes on the face of the law; findings and purposes can be in clauses denominated as such or in "whereas" clauses.[48] Federal and state courts sometimes rely on (or refer to) statutory purpose clauses, findings, whereas clauses, and the like to refine their purpose-based analysis.[49] Because purpose clauses are enacted into law as part of the statute and because they provide an authoritative normative context for reading the entire statute, my view is that judges should consider them, to guide judicial discussions of statutory purpose. Indeed, because legislative drafters presume against including purpose clauses unless statutory sponsors insist upon them, it may be the case that statutory purpose clauses take on added significance (they have been insisted upon).

---

[46] Forstater, House Office of Legislative Counsel, *Manual on Drafting Style*, § 325; cf. House Office of Legislative Counsel, *Introduction to Legislative Drafting*, 7–8 (Jan. 7, 2015) (similar statement, but omitting reference to committee reports). Some drafting manuals, however, encourage findings and purpose provisions. E.g., Colorado Office of Legislative Legal Servs., *Legislative Drafting Manual*, § 124(a)–(c).

[47] Office of Legislative Research & General Counsel, Utah Legislature, *Legislative Drafting Style Manual* ch. 2, § 1(b) (quotation in text); accord, Office of Code Revision, Legislative Serv. Agency, *Drafting Manual for the Indiana General Assembly* ch. 3, § H(2) (Dec. 19, 2012).

[48] E.g., *Crown Life Ins. Co. v. Casteel*, 22 S.W.3d 378, 383–84 (Tex. 2000) (relevance of purpose clause); see Scalia & Garner, *Reading Law*, 217–20 (surveying prefatory materials and endorsing their significance as indications of statutory purposes).

[49] E.g., *Sutton v. United Airlines, Inc.*, 527 U.S. 471, 484–86 (1999) (congressional findings); *Casteel*, 22 S.W.3d at 383–84 (Tex.) (purpose clause); 2A *Sutherland Statutes and Statutory Construction* §§ 47:4 & 47:6 (7th ed. 2015) (collecting state as well as federal cases mentioning or relying on legislative findings, preambles, and purview provisions).

Section 1 of the Park Safety Act not only confirms the statutory focus on safety that is suggested by the title, but also includes legislative findings that help the interpreter refine her understanding of the precise statutory plan. The main limitation of statutory purpose as a source of guidance in statutory interpretation is the level of generality problem, as expressed by the Utah drafting manual. If the statutory purpose is general public safety, we do not know how much a safety risk should be regulated. Even a baby carriage runs the risk of injury to park visitors, but isn't that risk *de minimis*? For that reason, general, abstract purpose analysis must always be grounded in linguistic and holistic analysis for the concrete text. But, for our vehicles in the park law, that text includes purpose and findings provisions.

In gauging the breadth of the statutory purpose, for example, the Park Safety Act's findings might be helpful in resolving the case of the adult tricycle. A key finding in section 1 is that "vehicles operating in Lafayette Park have contributed to several serious accidents requiring hospitalization in the last five years." Observe that this provision focuses on "serious accidents," namely, "those requiring hospitalization." This suggests little if any congressional concern for scraped knees and similar injuries associated with tricycle riding—but significant congressional concern for the more serious injuries that can be imposed by motorcycles, motor scooters, mopeds, and even bicycles in the park, for those vehicles are not only heavier but also much faster than a tricycle. This finding also suggests an item for further research: What kinds of vehicles caused the hospitalizations identified in the preamble? If the only hospitalizations occurred as a result of motor scooter and motorcycle traffic through Lafayette Park, that fact becomes a reason to limit the statute's application to motor vehicles, a possibility supported by the definitional list in section 3.[50]

Additionally, the statutory findings in section 1 help us address the question (raised above) whether an adult tricycle falls under the bicycle proviso. That issue requires the judge to figure out how broadly she should read the proviso. For ordinary meaning reasons, I should be reluctant to read "bicycle" broadly enough to include any kind of "tricycle," but I might reconsider my view if there had been twenty accidents requiring hospitalization in Lafayette Park and some of those "serious accidents" involved crazy persons terrorizing

---

[50] For an excellent argument for a limited statutory purpose based upon precise congressional findings, see *Sutton*, 527 U.S. at 494–95 (Ginsburg, J., concurring).

park users on their adult tricycles. Conversely, if the only "serious accidents" involved motorized vehicles, that knowledge would strengthen my reluctance to read the bicycle proviso broadly.

Consistent Use Canon. In our legal system, interpreters traditionally assume that "identical words used in different parts of the same act are intended to have the same meaning."[51] The rule of law value of predictability supports this assumption, which is of course much more powerful when the statute defines the term in question and makes that definition applicable to the entire statute. Moreover, three-fifths of the state legislatures have codified this canon, making it one of the most popular among the state codes of canons.[52] Legislative drafting manuals strongly support this idea. The Illinois drafting manual puts it well: "Although variation is often recommended to enliven standard prose, variation without purpose in statutory prose can lead to confusion. Using synonyms to express the same concept is confusing. Using the same word to refer to different concepts is confusing. Thus, consistent use of words and phrases in statutes is a great virtue."[53] Especially succinct is the advice given Delaware's legislative drafters: "Embrace monotony."[54]

Notwithstanding these drafting aspirations, the consistent use canon is sometimes at odds with the legislative process, especially for complicated statutes that involve different subjects and hence different drafting committees, as well as statutes that are repeatedly amended over the years.[55] The more drafters involved in the process,

---

[51] *Sullivan v. Stroop*, 496 U.S. 478, 484 (1990); see *Hall v. United States*, 132 S.Ct. 1882, 1891 (2012); *Milner v. Department of Navy*, 562 U.S. 562, 570 (2011); *Powerex Corp. v. Reliant Energy Servs., Inc.*, 551 U.S. 224 (2007); *Gustafson v. Alloyd Co.*, 513 U.S. 561, 570 (1995) (leading case); *Barrett v. Rosenthal*, 146 P.3d 510, 526 (Cal. 2006); *Robinson v. City of Lansing*, 782 N.W.2d 171, 181 (Mich. 2010); see CRS Report, *Statutory Interpretation*, 14–15 (updated 2011); Scalia & Garner, *Reading Law*, 170–73.

[52] Scott, *Codified Canons*, 98 Geo. L.J. at 368 (Table 3).

[53] State of Illinois, *Illinois Bill Drafting Manual* § 90–10(b)(1) (Dec. 2012) (quotation in text); accord, Office of the Legislative Counsel, U.S. Senate, *Legislative Drafting Manual*, § 1.05(a) (Feb. 1997); Forstater, House Office of Legal Counsel, *Manual on Drafting Style*, §§ 201(b)(2)(B), 325(b) (Nov. 1995); Alabama Legislative Reference Sev., *Drafting Style Manual*, Rule 5; Florida Senate, *Manual for Drafting Legislation* ch. 2, at 13 (6th ed. 2009); Kentucky Legislative Research Comm'n, *Bill Drafting Manual*, § 305 (2011); Texas Legislative Council, *Texas Legislative Council Drafting Manual* § 7.23 (Jan. 2015); Wisconsin Legislative Reference Bur., *Bill Drafting Manual 2011–2012*, § 2.01(15)(a) (2012).

[54] Delaware Legislative Council, *Legislative Drafting Manual*, pt. VI, ch. 2, Rule 3, Comment (Nov. 2013) (quotation in text).

[55] Gluck & Bressman, *Statutory Interpretation from the Inside, Part I*, Stan. L. Rev. at 936–37 (empirical finding that congressional staff believe that consistent

the more likely it is that different parts of the statute will use the same terminology in different ways, but without necessarily intending different applications or different meanings. This is one way that modern omnibus legislation, such as the Affordable Care Act of 2010 and the Clean Air Act Amendments of 1990, is very different from conventional legislation such as our Park Safety Act of 1992.[56]

For short statutes such as the Park Safety Act, the consistent use canon is particularly useful and is often taken for granted. Thus, the analysis throughout this chapter has assumed that the term "vehicle" in the Park Safety Act means the same thing every time it occurs within the statute. Section 3's definition of "vehicle" makes that clear—but even without section 3's confirmation, the canon of consistent use would support that assumption, which is most valuable for police implementing the statute and park visitors subject to the statutory rules. Thus, section 2 says: "No vehicles of any kind shall be allowed in Lafayette Park. Any person who drives a vehicle into Lafayette Park shall be guilty of a misdemeanor." The consistent use canon suggests that the term "vehicle" in the first sentence means the same thing as "vehicle" in the second sentence. Because the second sentence speaks of a person who "drives" a vehicle, the pet fish canon from chapter one limits "vehicles" to mechanisms that are "driven"—and the consistent use canon suggests that the first sentence also focuses on "vehicles" that can be "driven."

Meaningful Variation Canon. This canon is the flip side of the consistent use canon and is well expressed in the U.S. Senate's drafting manual: "Do not use different words in a single bill or statute to refer to the same thing. A court presumes that different words have different meanings."[57] Where a statute repeatedly uses one term or phrase, one expects that a materially different phraseology

---

drafting is a good goal but rarely attainable under the conditions of the modern legislative process).

[56] *King v. Burwell*, 135 S.Ct. 2480; *Robinson v. Shell Oil Co.*, 519 U.S. 337, 345–46 (1997); Shobe, *Intertemporal Statutory Interpretation and the Evolution of Legislative Drafting*, 114 Colum. L. Rev. at 858–59. For a recent debate within the Court, involving the Clean Air Act Amendments of 1990, compare *Utility Air Regulatory Group v. EPA,* 134 S Ct. 2427, 2439–42 (2014) (Scalia, J., for a plurality), with id. at 2452–56 (Breyer, J., dissenting on this issue).

[57] Senate Office of Legislative Counsel, *Legislative Drafting Manual*, § 1.05(a) (quotation in text); accord, Wisconsin Legislative Reference Bur., *Bill Drafting Manual 2011–2012*, § 2.01(15)(a).

demands a different reading.[58] Grammarians tend to be stricter about this idea than do regular people engaged in conversation, so the ordinary meaning anchor suggests that this canon be applied with some leniency—especially if a statute is a product of different drafting committees. Among the cases where judges have found the meaningful variation canon most useful have been those where the legislature uses a series of words in one provision and just one such word in a related part of the statute. Thus, if Congress enacted an omnibus park safety law barring "vehicles, bicycles, and adult tricycles" from Lafayette Park in one section but in another section barred only "vehicles" from Lincoln Park (another federal park in the District), a court would be unlikely to apply the second section to adult tricycles, and properly so.[59]

The meaningful variation canon is most useful as a trigger to further inquiry. Where a statute uses two different terms, this canon suggests inquiry into *why* the statute uses different language.[60] One interesting issue raised by the Park Safety Act is whether bicycles are regulated because they are "vehicles" (hence they would be covered by the rule in section 2 if not for the section 3 proviso) *or* only because they are covered by the proviso in section 3. Standard drafting practice would suggest that bicycles are "vehicles" as defined in section 3, with the proviso giving those particular vehicles a limited exemption from the statutory prohibition.[61]

This is probably the right answer, but the meaningful variation canon provides a modest argument suggesting consideration of the

---

[58] *Russello v. United States*, 464 U.S. 16, 23 (1983); *United States v. Fisher*, 6 U.S. (2 Cranch) 358, 388–97 (1805) (leading cases); accord, *Department of Homeland Security v. MacLean*, 135 S.Ct. 913, 919 (2015); *Loughrin v. United States*, 134 S.Ct. 2384, 2390 (2014); *Dean v. United States*, 556 U.S. 568, 572–73 (2009); *Lawrence v. Florida*, 549 U.S. 327, 333–34 (2007); *Hamdan v. Rumsfeld*, 548 U.S. 557, 577–79 (2006); *Keene Corp. v. United States*, 508 U.S. 200, 208 (1993); *Department of Treasury, IRS* v. *FLRA*, 494 U. S. 922, 931–32 (1990); *United States Fidelity Ins. & Guar. Co. v. Michigan Catastrophic Claims Ass'n*, 795 N.W.2d 101, 108 (Mich. 2009); *Byker v. Mannes*, 641 N.W.2d 210, 215 (Mich. 2002); see CRS Report, *Statutory Interpretation*, 15–17 (updated 2011); Scalia & Garner, *Reading Law*, 170.

[59] *MacLean*, 135 S.Ct. at 919; *Russello*, 464 U.S. at 23.

[60] See *Michigan v. EPA*, 135 S.Ct. at 2709; *Field v. Mans*, 516 U.S. 59, 67–76 (1995). For a remarkable textualist opinion going to great lengths to rebut the meaningful variation canon, see *Robinson v. City of Lansing*, 782 N.W.2d 171, 175–76 (Mich. 2010) (Markman, J.); cf. id. at 184–87 (Young, J., concurring) (finding the meaningful variation argument very powerful but agreeing, on balance, that its presumption has been overcome).

[61] *Abbott v. United States*, 562 U.S. 8, 25–26 (2010) (proviso or exception clause is confined to the subject matter of the provision to which it is attached); accord, *United States v. Morrow*, 266 U.S. 531, 534–35 (1925) (leading case).

contrary view, that the statute does not treat a bicycle as a "vehicle." Section 2 refers to "driv[ing]" a vehicle—in striking contrast to the verbs used in the bicycle proviso: Bicycles are allowed, so long as they are being "pushed or carried and not *ridden*." As before, this evidence secures its cogency by helping illuminate the ordinary meaning anchor. Because we are reluctant to say, in conversation, that one "drives" a bicycle, we might be reluctant to say that a bicycle is the kind of vehicle covered by section 2—an argument that is buttressed by the meaningful variation canon, which finds significance in the fact that the statute, like the ordinary speaker, says that bicycles are "ridden" and not "driven."

This clash between standard drafting practice and the meaningful variation canon helps us see that the Park Safety Act is not a well-drafted statute. But it also suggests that meaningful variation of terminology within a statute ought not be as powerful a consideration as ordinary meaning, statutory purpose and structure, and some of the other whole act canons. Put the two points together, and I agree with über-textualist Justice Stephen Markman that "the Legislature is not required to be overly repetitive in its choice of language," and interpreters ought to focus on the overall statutory plan rather than snafus that recur in statutory drafting under the pressure of cross-cutting legislative demands.[62]

Exceptions and Provisos Canon. Exceptions and provisos limit general legislative language, usually by carving out matters exempted from a general rule announced in the statute. A proviso is placed within the body of a provision (usually with the helpful lead-in, "provided that"), while an exception is a separate provision.[63] The interpretive valence is roughly the same. When a general policy is qualified by an exception or proviso, courts "usually read the exception narrowly in order to preserve the primary operation" of the policy, and do not extend a statutory exception or proviso to circumstances unless they are "plainly and unmistakably within its terms."[64] State legislatures have frequently codified this canon and

---

[62] *Robinson*, 782 N.W.2d at 181 (Markman, J.).

[63] 2A *Sutherland Statutes and Statutory Construction* § 47:11 (7th ed. 2015). Many legislative drafting manuals today discourage the use of provisos and strongly urge that drafters identify carefully drawn exceptions in a separate sentence or even provision. E.g., Kentucky Legislative Research Comm'n, *Bill Drafting Manual* § 312; see also Alaska Legislative Affairs Agency, *Manual of Legislative Drafting* 64 (exceptions should be "very specific").

[64] *Commissioner v. Clark*, 489 U.S. 726, 739–40 (1989) (first part of the quotation in text); *A.H. Phillips, Inc. v. Walling*, 324 U.S. 490, 493 (1945) (second part of the quotation). Accord, *Maracich v. Spears*, 133 S.Ct. 2191, 2200 (2013); *Abbott v.*

have never rejected it.[65] In Minnesota and Pennsylvania, states with detailed codifications of the canons, the legislatures have directed that "[p]rovisos shall be construed to limit rather than to extend the operation of the clauses to which they refer" and that "[e]xceptions expressed in a statute shall be construed to exclude all others."[66]

Recall the issue, raised above, whether the bicycle proviso covers adult tricycles, which look like bicycles with training wheels. Does the exceptions or proviso canon suggest that the bicycle proviso be read narrowly? This is actually a complicated issue. Because the Park Safety Act calls the second sentence of section 3 a "proviso," proper drafting practice suggests that bicycles are "vehicles" within the definition of section 3, but are then exempted from the broad prohibition in section 2 and given a more lenient treatment. Should the proviso be read to cover adult tricycles? To answer that question in the affirmative, we need to decide, first, that adult tricycles are "vehicles" that are the target of section 2 and, then, that they are "bicycles" subject to the special rule of section 3's proviso. Because people refer to two-wheeled vehicles as *bi*cycles (even when there are training wheels in addition to the main ones) and three wheeled vehicles as *tri*cycles, I should lean toward the view that adult tricycles are not covered by the proviso and, by implication, are not statutory vehicles either. As before, however, this is an issue as to which linguistic uncertainty would motivate me to resolve by resort to other evidence, especially statutory precedents (the next chapter in this volume) or legislative materials (chapter four).

Anti-Surplusage (-Redundancy) Canon. Because courts try to give every word and every provision of a statute a legal effect, it is a "cardinal rule of statutory interpretation that no provision should be construed to be entirely redundant" or meaningless.[67] This anti-

---

United States, 562 U.S. at 24–26; *City of Edmonds v. Oxford House, Inc.*, 514 U.S. 725, 732 (1995).

[65] See Scott, *Codified Canons*, 98 Geo. L.J. at 368 (Table 3) (reporting that 10 states have codified the exceptions canon); 3 *Sutherland Statutes and Statutory Construction* § 60:1 (7th ed. 2015) (citing state cases for the proposition that exceptions to remedial statutes must be narrowly construed).

[66] The quotations in text can be found in both Minn. Stat. § 645.19, and 1 Pa. Cons. Stat. § 1924. See Scott, *Codified Canons*, 98 Geo. L.J. at 366–67.

[67] *Kungys v. United States*, 485 U.S. 759, 778 (1988) (plurality opinion) (quotation in text); accord, *Texas Dep't of Hous. & Community Affs. v. Inclusive Communities Project, Inc.*, 135 S.Ct. 2507, 2521 (2015); *Young v. United Parcel Service, Inc.*, 135 S.Ct. 1338, 1352–53 (2015); *Circuit City Stores, Inc. v. Adams*, 532 U.S. 105, 114 (2001); *Babbitt v. Sweet Home*, 515 U.S. at 697–98.

redundancy canon is usually called the rule against surplusage.[68] Consistent with the premises of the whole act rule, this canon suggests that every provision, indeed every word, of a statute adds something to the statutory scheme, if plausible. Like the consistent use canon, state legislatures have frequently codified this canon,[69] and state as well as federal judges invoke it frequently.[70] Almost every legislative drafting manual I consulted strongly recommended brevity as a fundamental virtue in drafting statutes; some manuals warn drafters that courts will list against redundancy and advise that, "[i]f a provision would have the same meaning if a word were deleted, delete the word."[71]

Nonetheless, the premise upon which this canon rests is often unrealistic from the point of view of the operation of the legislative process outside of the drafting office. Congressional staff say that they draft bills and amendments that are sometimes purposefully redundant, because the public and private groups pushing for legislation *demand* redundancy. Thus, legislators and their staff have incentives to add duplicative language and provisions in order to reassure those groups that the statute is carrying out their program.[72] Although the anti-surplusage canon is supported by rule of law considerations and by the aspirations of proper drafting, it ought not be applied in a manner that undermines either legislative expectations or effective governance.

Recall section 1 of the vehicles in the park law: "Finding that vehicles operating in Lafayette Park have contributed to several serious accidents requiring hospitalization in the last five years, and finding further that vehicles create risks of serious injury to park

---

[68] E.g., *Agnew v. State Bd. of Equalization*, 981 P.2d 52, 65 (Cal. 1999); CRS Report, *Statutory Interpretation*, 13–14 (updated 2011) (canon that statutory language will be presumed not to be "mere surplusage"); Scalia & Garner, *Reading Law*, 174–79 (the "surplusage canon").

[69] See Scott, *Codified Canons*, 98 Geo. L.J. at 368 (Table 3) (reporting that 10 states have codified the anti-surplusage canon).

[70] 2B *Sutherland Statutes and Statutory Construction* § 46:6 (7th ed. 2015) (reporting federal and state court decisions applying the anti-surplusage canon); see, e.g., *Bennett v. St. Vincent's Med. Center, Inc.*, 71 So.3d 828, 838 (Fla. 2011); *Whitman v. City of Burton*, 831 N.W.2d 223, 229 (Mich. 2013); *Scott v. Massachusetts Life Ins. Co.*, 657 N.E.2d 769, 772 (N.Y. 1995); *Kallinen v. City of Houston*, 462 S.W.3d 25, 28 (Tex. 2015).

[71] Senate Office of Legislative Counsel, *Legislative Drafting Manual*, § 1.05(b); accord, Wisconsin Legislative Reference Bur., *Bill Drafting Manual 2011–2012*, § 2.001(2).

[72] Gluck & Bressman, *Statutory Interpretation from the Inside, Part I*, 65 Stan. L. Rev. at 934–36.

users, Congress resolves that there is an urgent public need to ban any and all vehicles from Lafayette Park." The anti-surplusage canon suggests that we ought to be open to the idea that a statute consisting of just sections 2 and 3 has a different ambit than a statute consisting of sections 1, 2, and 3. Accordingly, Figure 4 above (reflecting sections 1, 2, and 3) ought to look somewhat different in probabilistic terms than Revised Figure 4 below (reflecting just sections 2 and 3). A statute consisting of sections 1, 2, and 3 is more likely to be limited to motor vehicles and bicycles than a statute consisting of just sections 2 and 3.

REVISED FIGURE 4

Plain Meaning Continuum: "Driving a Vehicle" in the Park (§ 2), in Light of Statutory Definition (§ 3)

Core Coverage		Penumbra		Outside the Statute
Cars & Trucks	Bicycles	Adult Tricycles	Kid's Tricycles	Baby Carriages
Motorcycles		Skateboards		Wheelbarrows
Motor Scooters				
Mopeds				

Specifically, section 1's emphasis on risks of "serious injury" makes it somewhat less likely that the Park Safety Act regulates adult tricycles, skateboards, and kid's tricycles.

Note how the Park Safety Act illustrates the limitations of the anti-surplusage canon. With or without section 1, adult tricycles are in the penumbral area, where it is debatable whether the statute may apply. Section 1 simply makes it a bit *less likely* that adult tricycles are regulated. More important, the interpreter must not press the anti-surplusage canon too far; specifically, the interpreter ought not apply the canon to create significance in minor locutions. For example, section 1 would have exactly the same meaning if its ban extended to "all vehicles," instead of the current language "any and all vehicles." As Judge Kavanaugh has reminded us, "lawmakers, like Shakespeare characters, sometimes employ overlap or redundancy so as to remove any doubt and make doubly sure."[73]

Administrability Canon. The Supreme Court and other appellate courts are attentive to the effects of their interpretations on the administration of the statute going forward, especially for

[73] *Loving* v. *Internal Revenue Serv.*, 742 F.3d 1014, 1019 (D.C. Cir. 2014).

statutes essentially administered by lower courts. Hence, an interpretation that has been shown over a period of time to have been easy to administer will be preferred to one that is less time-tested and harder to administer.[74] Anita Krishnakumar calls this the *anti-messiness principle*, whereby the Supreme Court avoids the creation of legal rules that require "inelegant, complex, indeterminate, impractical, confusing, or unworkable factual inquiries" from lower court judges implementing the rules.[75] There may be a broader point here, as the Supreme Court and state high courts also avoid interpretations that would play out in ways that would undermine the statutory scheme.[76] Because of this broader application, we should consider this to be the *administrability canon,* a locution I draw from the drafting manual published by the House Legislative Counsel.[77]

Administrability has much to recommend it, especially if judges understand that such a canon should not supplant the ordinary meaning rule and should be the handmaiden of statutory purpose. In Park Safety Act cases, if the Court of Appeals for the D.C. Circuit develops a rule of law that produces unpredictable and heterogeneous rulings from lower court judges, it risks legal chaos that disserves the rule of law. Nor does it serve congressional goals to have lower courts imposing different obligations on similarly situated persons. As a matter of governance, the institutional capacity of courts is strained if minor issues produce endless litigation.

Consider a modest illustration of the administrability canon in action. Recall that Justice Scalia and Professor Garner came up with this definition of *vehicle* for purposes of a generic vehicles in the park law: "The proper colloquial meaning in our view (not all of them are to be found in dictionaries) is simply a *sizable* wheeled conveyance (as

---

[74] *United States v. Tinklenberg*, 131 S.Ct. 2007, 2014–15 (2011); *Hertz v. Friend*, 559 U.S. 77, 94–95 (2010); *Negusie v. Holder*, 555 U.S. 511, 527 (2009) (Scalia, J., concurring); *Till v. SCS Credit Corp.*, 541 U.S. 465, 479 (2004) (plurality opinion). See also *People v. Leiva*, 297 P.3d 870, 880–82 (Cal. 2013) (interpreting ambiguous statute to avoid difficulties and unfairness in its administration).

[75] Anita S. Krishnakumar, *The Anti-Messiness Principle in Statutory Interpretation*, 87 Notre Dame L. Rev. 1465, 1469 (2012).

[76] E.g., *King v. Burwell*, 135 S.Ct. 2480, 2493 (2015) (interpreting the Affordable Care Act of 2010 to avoid a "death-spiral" chain reaction that would destroy the economic premise of the law); *Hernandez v. Barrios-Paoli*, 720 N.E.2d 866, 870 (N.Y. 1999).

[77] Forstater, House Office of Legislative Counsel, *Manual on Drafting Style*, § 101(3)(A) (advising legislative drafters to create a statutory structure that is "administrable"); accord, Kentucky Legislative Research Comm'n, *Bill Drafting Manual*, § 103.

opposed to one of any size that is motorized)."[78] Their point of law—*sizable* wheeled conveyances are barred from the park—is problematic if the purpose of the statute is safety. But it might be more administrable than a rule of law that says to bar mechanisms that create safety risks. Conversely, the Scalia and Garner rule of law inquiry (Is the mechanism "sizable"?) is less administrable than a safety-based rule of law that asks, "Is the mechanism motorized?" Indeed, in the context of the Lafayette Park Safety Act as I have recast it in this chapter, an administrability canon would prefer a rule against *motorized* mechanisms as opposed to a rule against *sizable* ones—and once the safety purpose comes into sharp relief, an approach based upon size loses even more ground.

Professor Krishnakumar also identifies the Achilles heel of the anti-messiness principle, and the same weakness surely afflicts any kind of administrability canon: Such a consideration is itself not completely predictable.[79] "Administrability" is sometimes in the eye of the beholder. An affirmative action plan that liberals consider workable and just will be interpreted by critics as messy and arbitrary in operation. Like the surplusage, consistency, and meaningful variation canons, therefore, the administrability canon ought to be a modest rather than decisive consideration in all but the most extreme cases. As in the debate over size-versus-motors as the criterion for separating statutory "vehicles" from other mechanisms, administrability becomes a useful consideration after ordinary meaning and purpose have narrowed the options.

Moreover, administrability is a factor judges ought to include when thinking about the entire statute. The whole act rule requires interpreters to consider how the different provisions or parts of the statute fit together, and how each part contributes to the legislative project. Such an exercise often has great significance for figuring out how to apply particular provisions.[80] Thus, the purpose of the vehicles in the park law is to make Lafayette Park safer for visitors (sections 1–2), but not at the cost of ridding the park of all mechanisms that might be called vehicles. As suggested above, one way to conceptualize this law is to imagine three levels of regulation:

---

[78] Scalia & Garner, *Reading Law*, 37.

[79] Krishnakumar, *Anti-Messiness Principle*, 87 Notre Dame L. Rev. at 1492–95; see id. at 1495–1502 (identifying other complications or problems with an anti-messiness canon).

[80] For excellent examples of reasoning from statutory structure, see, e.g., *Perez v. Mortgage Bankers Ass'n*, 135 S.Ct. 1199 (2015); *Babbitt v. Sweet Home*, 515 U.S. at 700–04.

- **Complete Ban.** Vehicles that pose big safety risks are banned entirely. Section 3 seems to target motor vehicles, and so this category might be considered the core of the statute.
- **Regulation.** The bicycle proviso creates a special rule for the (nonmotorized) vehicle that can go very fast, and hence that poses a big risk of accidents with severe consequences, but that otherwise might belong in parks. The special rule allows these vehicles in the park, but they cannot be operated in ways that create safety hazards.
- **Allowance.** By process of statutory elimination, everything that is not a motor vehicle or a bicycle is allowed in Lafayette Park.

Without committing myself to this elegant structure as the global litmus test for applying this statute, notice that it has several mutually reinforcing virtues: This structure is fairly easy to apply by judges and (for the same reason) is pretty predictable for park visitors *and* is faithful to and makes sense of Congress's plan and the structure created by Congress.

Whole Code Canons

For the United States Supreme Court, the whole code is an increasingly important source of evidence for reading statutes and particular provisions. Some of the canons that follow from the whole act rule also have some bite in reference to the whole code. Consistent use and meaningful variation are examples, but usually with diminished cogency when the framework is broader, for reasons suggested earlier in this chapter. Other canons are distinctive to whole code analysis. The best-known example is the canon against implied repeals. As the U.S. Code expands to accommodate new and updated statutory schemes, the prospect of colliding statutes increases—and interpreters need strategies for preventing or resolving those collisions. These strategies are reflected in various whole code harmonization canons, of which the implied repeals canon is the most famous but the reconciliation canon is more useful and important. These harmonization practices exemplify the potential utility of canons if understood functionally, as we are doing in this book. Rarely does one single canon decide tough cases, but the canons may help judges see the many angles presented by tough cases.

The normative appeal of the whole code rule is legal coherence: There is a rule of law elegance to the aspiration that the entire U.S. Code or state code presumptively be read as a unified whole, just as Scripture is presumed to have a single cohering Author. And the comparative institutional competence of judges is to harmonize, to the extent possible, new statutes with the rules and duties established by existing ones. The U.S. Code and state codes are constantly evolving, and there are often governance justifications for a vigorous whole code analysis.

On the other hand, as documented above, the whole code canons represent a much greater risk of judicially overriding legislative assumptions and policies, because legislators and their staff are not aware of these canons or do not easily apply them. (Thus, virtually none of the state or federal legislative drafting manuals even mentions the whole code act or its accompanying canons, including the canon against implied repeals.) Accordingly, the whole code canons reflect a sacrifice or even a rejection of the "faithful agency" theory of judicial statutory interpretation and pose problems of democratic legitimacy. Their overall effect on governance is completely indeterminate, as far as I can gather. So it is with special caution that I introduce the main whole code canons.

Noscitur a Legibus Sociis *Canon.* Substantive statutes typically include legislative decisions about where to codify their provisions in the United States Code or in the relevant state code. Because the Lafayette Park Safety Act regulates a national park administered by the National Park Service, one would expect it to be codified in Title 54 (reserved for the "National Park System"), perhaps as a new Chapter 1035 in that title. Assume, however, that Congress codifies the new law in Title 49 ("Transportation"), Subtitle VI ("Motor Vehicles and Driver Programs"), as a new Chapter 306 in that subtitle. Does this decision affect your interpretation of the law? Specifically, does it make you more likely to limit the Lafayette Park Safety Act to "motor vehicles," which are the exclusive focus of Subtitle VI?

The answer would seem to be affirmative. The canonical precept that words should be understood in the context of their *relationship* plays out at the sentence level: Section 3's definition of "vehicle" includes mechanisms whose main similarity is that they are motorized or pose risks because they go so fast ("automobiles, trucks, motorcycles, and motor scooters"). The same precept plays out at the level of the whole act: Section 3's definition should be understood in relationship to the statutory purpose, which is aimed at speedy (typically motorized) mechanisms that can inflict serious injury. And the same precept might be relevant at the level of the whole code: The vehicles in the park law is in the "motor vehicles" regulatory portion of the Transportation Title.

In an important and much-discussed plurality opinion, Justice Ruth Bader Ginsburg has recently relied on the placement of a statute within the United States Code.[81] Justice Ginsburg did not have a short name for this canon, and I should like to suggest a name linking it to the *noscitur a sociis* canon, which at the sentence level asks the judge to consider immediately neighboring words ("*sociis*"). The whole code rule asks the judge to consider immediately neighboring and previously codified statutes, so I'd dub this canon *noscitur a legibus sociis,* Latin for "it shall be known by its neighboring statutes."

Admittedly, there is a normative concern with this canon: Is it consistent with congressional drafting practices? Might it undermine the legislative process? Because Congress and most state legislatures now rely on professional drafting staff whose job is to fit statutes into the integrated United States Code, one would expect this not to be a huge problem.[82] Indeed, the *noscitur a legibus sociis* canon is more consistent with congressional and state legislative drafting practices than some of the whole act and whole code canons, especially the anti-surplusage canon.

Surprisingly, there is evidence that federal legislators do not necessarily see things this way. Recall, from the discussion above, legislative doubt that titles and captions ought to be considered as evidence of statutory meaning. Does this dubiety extend to neighboring laws? Section 5600 of the Revised Statutes (1873) said this when Congress recodified federal laws after the Civil War:

> The arrangement and classification of the several sections of the revision have been made for the purpose of a more convenient and orderly arrangement of the same, and therefore no inference or presumption of a legislative

---

[81] *Yates,* 135 S.Ct. at 1083–84 (Ginsburg, J., for a plurality). For earlier invocations of the idea that judges should consider the surrounding U.S. Code provisions and the title in which a provision is added, see *Henderson ex rel. Henderson v. Shinseki,* 562 U.S. 428, 439–40 (2011).

[82] Shobe, *Intertemporal Statutory Interpretation*, 114 Colum. L. Rev. at 831–32 (reporting that Legislative Counsel for the House and the Senate focus on clarity and coherence, based upon their understanding of the policy underlying proposed legislation in discussions with committee and sponsor's staff).

> construction is to be drawn by reason of the Title, under which any particular section is placed.[83]

This is an old provision inapplicable to Title 49 (an entirely post-1873 creation). Moreover, section 5600 would not necessarily veto consideration of laws surrounding the new vehicles in the park law in Subtitle VI. Nonetheless, Tobias Dorsey reports that broader and more recent versions of this admonition are embedded in the Criminal Code (Title 18), the Tax Code (Title 26), and various other parts of the United States Code.[84] This information provides a note of caution but, in my view, does not entirely defeat these considerations. Because Congress usually votes for statutory language that sets forth the placement of provisions in the United States Code and because code coherence is an important governance as well as rule of law value, I propose that judges continue to consider interstatutory context (*legibus sociis*).

For a simple example supporting the utility, and perhaps the inevitability, of such a canon, ask yourself whether the Lafayette Park Safety Act applies to Lafayette Park in Houston, Texas (google "Lafayette Park" and "Houston"). Or Lafayette Park in the Westlake district of Los Angeles, California. Or New York City's Lafayette Park. Or dozens of other Lafayette Parks located all around the United States. The ordinary meaning of section 2 does not limit the statutory coverage to the Lafayette Park in Washington, D.C.—yet you would almost certainly limit the statute in this way, right? How would you justify such a limitation as a matter of purely text-based interpretation? (In chapter four, I shall argue that the interpreter ought to examine the legislative history of the 1992 law, which would solve this problem easily. But we are just considering text-based arguments in these early chapters.)

To begin with, the whole act rule might help narrow the statutory application. Section 1, for example, assumes a series of accidents that are probably distinctive to Lafayette Park in Washington, D.C. (To figure that out, of course, you would have to dip into the legislative history.) But the whole code canon of *legibus sociis* probably seals the deal on that issue. If the Lafayette Park Safety Act were codified in either Title 54 ("National Parks") or Title 5 (treating the District of Columbia), as would be likely, that codification would

---

[83] Revised Statutes of the United States, § 5600, 18 Stat. 1085 (1873).

[84] Tobias A. Dorsey, *Some Reflections on* Yates *and the Statutes We Threw Away*, 18 Green Bag 2d 377 (2015).

probably help the interpreter narrow the application of the law to the only Lafayette Park that is a national park (Title 54) or that is located in the District of Columbia (Title 5). Conversely, if the statute were codified in Title 49 (Transportation), the law would remain ambiguous, and the interpreter would have to search elsewhere for decisive evidence of statutory limitation.

In Pari Materia *and Borrowed Act Canons.* The consistent use canon discussed above as a whole act canon is often applicable when the frame of reference is the whole code. Congress's use of a term repeatedly to mean the same thing across a variety of statutes is evidence that a new federal statute containing that term carries forth the meaning it has had in the other statutes.[85] This notion is especially persuasive when the same term, phrase, or provision is found in statutes that are very similar in object, purpose, and subject matter to the one being interpreted.[86] "The correct rule of interpretation is, that if divers statutes relate to the same thing, they ought all to be taken into consideration in construing any one of them, and it is an established rule of law, that all acts *in pari materia* are to be taken together, as if they were one law."[87]

This canon is supported by the rule of law and good governance, both of which place a high value on coherent policy, as we explored in the previous chapter. Unlike the other whole code canons, this one also probably reflects legislative expectations. Most state legislatures have codified this canon, and none has rejected it. Colorado's code is typical: "If a statute is ambiguous, the court, in determining the intention of the general assembly, may consider * * * [t]he common law or former statutory provisions, including laws upon the same or

---

[85] *Pierce v. Underwood*, 487 U.S. 552, 565 (1988).

[86] See 2B *Sutherland Statutes and Statutory Construction* ch. 51 (7th ed. 2015) (examining the *in pari materia* canon, with extensive citations to federal and state case law; demonstrating that the canon has its greatest force for statutes that cover the same subject matter); see also Scalia & Garner, *Reading Law*, 252–55 (calling this the "related-statutes canon").

[87] *United States v. Freeman*, 44 U.S. 556, 564 (1845) (leading case, quotation in text); see *Texas Dep't of Hous. & Community Affs. v. Inclusive Communities Project, Inc.*, 135 S.Ct. 2507, 2516–21 (2015); *Erlenbaugh v. United States*, 409 U.S. 232, 243–44 (1972); accord, *People v. Tran*, 354 P.3d 148, 153 (Cal. 2015) (Liu, J.); *Hopkins v. State*, 105 So.3d 470 (Fla. 2012); *Duffy v. Michigan Dep't of Natural Resources*, 805 N.W.2d 399 (Mich. 2011); *Albany Law School v. New York State Office of Mental Retardation*, 968 N.E.2d 967, 975 (N.Y. 2012); see 2B *Sutherland Statutes and Statutory Construction* §§ 51:1 to 51:3 (7th ed. 2015).

similar subjects."[88] Some students of the federal legislative process say that it is quite consistent with the unified drafting practices that are increasingly followed in Congress, but other scholars point out that different committees have different drafting styles that render cross-statute comparisons much less reliable.[89] The latter point of view finds voice in some legislative drafting manuals, one of which says "[t]here is little, if any, validity to the idea that particular language, having been construed by a court, will be assigned the same meaning in another statutory context."[90]

Moreover, the *in pari materia* canon cannot be applied without close attention to context. By definition, the canon ought not apply across statutes covering different subjects, but even for statutes covering the same subjects the same words might have different meanings because "the conditions are different, or the scope of the legislative power exercised in one case is broader than that exercised in another," or because the different laws have different purposes.[91] In short, even this highly defensible whole code canon is of more limited utility than the consistent use canon associated with the whole act rule.

As with other whole code canons, the *in pari materia* canon ought to stimulate further inquiries. Thus, it motivates a judge interpreting the Park Safety Act to consider other federal statutes relating to the "same thing." Several important federal statutes regulate motor vehicles. That those statutes have been understood to apply to mopeds (as well as the prototypical motor vehicles, namely, automobiles and trucks) is evidence that a judge might consider when figuring out the ordinary meaning of the Park Safety Act. Because the judge needs to be careful to make sure the statutes regulate the "same thing" and are part of the same general plan, the *in pari*

---

[88] Colo. Rev. Stats. § 2–4–203 (quotation in text); see Scott, *Codified Canons*, 98 Geo. L.J. at 374–76 (majority of state legislatures have codified the *in pari materia* canon).

[89] Compare Shobe, *Intertemporal Statutory Interpretation*, 114 Colum. L. Rev. at 851–54, 857–59 (documenting the greater standardization of congressional drafting), with Gluck & Bressman, *Statutory Interpretation from the Inside: Part I*, 65 Stan. L. Rev. at 934–37 (different congressional committees follow very different drafting styles, making cross-statute comparisons more tricky).

[90] Texas Legislative Council, *Texas Legislative Council Drafting Manual* § 72.4 (Jan. 2015) (quotation in text). See also Senate Office of Legal Counsel, *Legislative Drafting Manual*, § 105(a) (limiting the consistent use idea to the same statute, unmindful of the *in pari materia* idea).

[91] *Yates*, 135 S.Ct. at 1082 (plurality opinion) (citing many cases and quoting *Atlantic Cleaners & Dyers, Inc. v. United States*, 286 U.S. 427, 433 (1932)).

materia canon presses us toward federal statutes that regulate park safety, especially those (if any) relating to vehicle prohibitions in federal parks and other lands.[92]

Consistency across the U.S. Code or a state's general code is particularly relevant when it is clear, from the statutory text and/or legislative history, that the similar or identical terminology is not a coincidence, because the legislature has borrowed it from a previous law. "When [a legislature] adopts a new law incorporating sections of a prior law, [legislators] normally can be presumed to have had knowledge of the interpretation given to the incorporated law, at least insofar as it affects the new statute."[93] This *borrowed statute canon* (examined in more detail in chapter three) finds support not only in rule of law values of coherence and predictability, but also in democratic legitimacy and the public purposes of law. While it is perilous to presume that Congress or state legislatures draft statutes with an omniscient eye to the entire U.S. Code or state code, it is a reasonable assumption that copying a previous statute bespeaks an awareness of the previous statute and its purposes that can legitimately inform the application of the new one.

Assume that the Lafayette Park Safety Act is not the first time Congress has adopted safety legislation for federal parks in the District of Columbia. Let us say that Congress had already enacted a statute to protect public safety in Folger Park, a small recreational national park located a few blocks south of the U.S. Capitol. If the Folger Park Safety Act had been consistently applied only to motorized vehicles and bicycles (per the proviso) but was not applied to any other conveyances, the judge ought to presume the same

---

[92] *Inclusive Communities Project*, 135 S.Ct. at 2516–21. For an instance where the Court declined to apply the *in pari materia* concept to a prior rule reflecting a somewhat different kind of policy, see *Wachovia Bank v. Schmidt*, 506 U.S. 303, 315–16 (2006).

[93] *Lorillard v. Pons*, 434 U.S. 575, 581 (1978) (quotation in text); accord, *Inclusive Communities Project*, 135 S.Ct. at 2520–21; *Shannon v. United States*, 512 U.S. 573, 581 (1994); *California State University v. Superior Court*, 108 Cal. Rptr. 2d 870, 879 (Cal. App. 2001); *In re G.G.*, 667 A.2d 1331, 1334–35 (D.C. 1995); *State v. Aiuppa*, 298 So.2d 391, 394 (Fla. 1974); *People v. Katt*, 662 N.W.2d 12 (Mich. 2003); *City of Garland v. Dallas Morning News*, 22 S.W.3d 351, 360 (Tex. 2000); see 2B *Sutherland Statutory Construction* § 52:2 (7th ed. 2015); Scalia & Garner, *Reading Law*, 322–26 (dubbing this the "prior-construction canon"). On the legislative practice of copying prior statutory language and ideas, see Frank E. Horack Jr., *The Common Law of Legislation*, 23 Iowa L. Rev. 41 (1937) (dubbing this practice "stare de statute"). For a useful contrast of the borrowed statute and *in pari materia* canons, see John L. Flynn, Note, *Mixed-Motive Causation Under the ADA: Linked Statutes, Fuzzy Thinking, and Clear Statements*, 83 Geo. L.J. 2009, 2037 & n.143 (1995).

interpretations for the newer Lafayette Park Safety Act. Various canons reinforce one another: consistency of interpretation for the same term across the U.S. Code and the deployment of that term in a statute covering the same subject area *and* forming the basis for the new statute, which Congress closely copied from the previous one. If it had been understood to regulate mopeds, the interpretive history of the Folger Park Safety Act would be very strong evidence that the new statute covers mopeds as well.

The *in pari materia* or borrowed act canon may presumptively fill in many of the details of a statutory scheme, based upon the implementation history of the earlier law. Recall that the second sentence of section 2 provides that someone driving a vehicle into Lafayette Park is subject to "a fine not exceeding $500 for each violation." Neither this nor any other provision in our short statute tells the judge exactly what process the government must follow to prosecute violations. For the most part, the statute relies on the default structure for enforcing federal offenses. One important issue is whether a person charged with a violation has a right to a jury trial. Apart from any constitutional requirement (taken up in chapter six), it is very likely that the earlier statute answers this question: Have judges been providing violators charged under the Folger Park Safety Act with jury trials? If they have not been doing so, that is strong evidence that a judge should interpret the Lafayette Park Safety Act (the statute that borrows the language from the earlier law) the same way.

Meaningful Variation Canon. Recall the meaningful variation canon, which can be applied to variations in wording across related statutes as well as within a statute. "From the general presumption that the same expression is presumed to be used in the same sense throughout an Act or a series of cognate Acts, there follows the further presumption that a change of wording denotes a change in meaning."[94] Thus, "courts presume a different intent when a legislature omits words used in a prior statute on a similar subject" or

---

[94] P. St. J. Langan, *Maxwell on the Interpretation of Statutes* 282 (12th ed. 1969) (quotation in text); *West Virginia Univ. Hosps. v. Casey*, 499 U.S. 83, 99 (1991) (leading American case); see *Arlington Cent. Sch. Dist. Bd. of Educ. v. Murphy*, 548 U.S. 291, 297–98 (2006); *Jama*, 543 U.S. at 342–43; *Meghrig v. KFC Western, Inc.*, 516 U.S. 479, 485 (1996); *Central Bank of Denver, N.A. v. First Interstate Bank of Denver, N.A.*, 511 U.S. 164, 176–77 (1994).

when a legislature "inserts a provision in only one of two statutes that deal with a closely related subject."[95]

The idea that a change in wording denotes a change in meaning is most strikingly relevant when the legislature amends a statute to add language. In everyday conversation as well as statutory interpretation, we assume that the new text adds something to the law and changes its meaning in some respects.[96] The meaningful variation canon (examined earlier in this chapter) asks the interpreter to take an additional step, to assume that when the legislature adopts different locutions in the same enactment, interpreters ought to find different meanings. When expanded to meaningful variation among the provisions in related statutes, the canon demands yet another inferential leap—and that strikes me as quite a reach, and a reach that judges ought *not* take frequently.

For example, assume that the Park Safety Act originally excluded "motor vehicles" rather than just "vehicles" from the park. If Congress amended the law to strike "motor" everywhere it appears, leaving only "vehicles" regulated, an interpreter would assume that the textual change broadened the ambit of the statute, to regulate some nonmotorized vehicles posing safety risks of the sort identified in section 1. The contrast between "motor vehicles" and "vehicles" would be significant. It is a short step from this hypothetical to the following one: If the Folger Park Safety Act, adopted a decade earlier, banned "motor vehicles," the narrower term, there would be some significance if the Lafayette Park Safety Act simply banned "vehicles." At the very least, the interpreter would want to consider, and investigate, precisely what kinds of nonmotorized vehicles might fit within the safety purpose of section 1 and the broader ambit suggested by section 2.

Quite a different case is presented by a final, and most pertinent, variation of this thought experiment. Long before Congress enacted the Lafayette Park Safety Act of 1992, it had enacted the Motor Vehicle Safety Act of 1966. By its title and consistent interpretation by the implementing agency and courts, the 1966 Act applies to automobiles, trucks, motorcycles, and mopeds, but not to bicycles, adult tricycles, skateboards, and baby carriages. Both statutes are

---

[95] 2B *Sutherland Statutes and Statutory Construction* § 51:2 (7th ed. 2015); accord, *Gause v. United States*, 6 A.3d 1247, 1253 (D.C. 2010); *Olmstead v. FTC*, 44 So. 3d 76, 82 (Fla. 2010).

[96] *Osborn v. Bank of the United States*, 22 U.S. (9 Wheat.) 738, 817–18 (1824) (Marshall, C.J.) (leading case).

safety laws and both regulate "vehicles" (albeit with different regulatory strategies). Is the variation in terminology legally "meaningful"? Probably not. Notwithstanding their similarities, the two statutes are fundamentally different regulatory regimes. The 1966 Act regulates the design and construction of motor vehicles, while the 1980 Act regulates the introduction of vehicles into a park.

This last example illustrates the relative weakness of meaningful variation as a whole code canon. Although the U.S. Supreme Court episodically salutes this canon, its fan base is limited. No state legislature has codified it; the codes that provide for consideration of "laws on the same or similar subjects," focus on similarities and not variations.[97] State courts have not made meaningful variation the prominent guidepost that the *in pari materia* canon is; indeed, the main point of variation in terms across different statutes is to render the *in pari materia* canon irrelevant. Although legislative drafting manuals focus on and illustrate the meaningful variation canon at the whole act level, they generally do not prod the statutory drafter to look beyond the four corners of the statute to make sure she is not creating a meaningful variation within the larger U.S. Code or state code.[98] Moreover, because different legislative committees (or the same committees at different points in time) create different statutes, it is highly unrealistic to impose the meaningful variation canon upon interstatutory comparisons in most cases.[99]

In short, I harbor some doubt that meaningful variation across statutes (even related statutes) ought to be a canon to start with, and do not believe that it should be given as much weight as the widely accepted *in pari materia* canon or even my new *noscitur a legibus sociis* canon. In my view, this is precisely the sort of textual canon that courts ought *not* apply without considering statutory purpose and legislative history (chapter four). For example, if the statute

---

[97] Tex. Govt. Code § 311.023(4) (typical codification of the *in pari materia* canon, not seeming to encourage meaningful variation analysis); see Scott, Codified Canons, 98 Geo. L.J. at 376.

[98] E.g., Senate Office of Legislative Counsel, *Legislative Drafting Manual*, § 105(a) (assuming that consistent use and meaningful variation only apply to the whole act); Texas Legal Council, *Drafting Manual*, §§ 7.23–7.24 (endorsing the meaningful variation idea but only for variation within the whole act, not the whole code). Compare CRS, Report, *Statutory Interpretation*, 16 (updated 2011) ("Congress knows how to say").

[99] Gluck & Bressman, *Statutory Interpretation from the Inside: Part I*, 65 Stan. L. Rev. at 934–37 (different congressional committees follow different drafting styles, making cross-statute comparisons especially problematic).

under consideration has borrowed its structure and provisions from another statute, whether from the same jurisdiction or from another one, then variation in terminology strikes me as significant (and worth further investigation). Another context where meaningful variation might be relevant is one where the legislature has adopted certain boilerplate provisions in the vast array of statutes, but departs from the boilerplate in one statute. In that event, too, I'd want to figure out why the variation—meaningful or not?

Canon Against Implied Repeals. The whole code rule has a broader significance in light of the fact that Congress and state legislatures have, over time, adopted so many laws that statutes collide more often than they did before the New Deal era. Given the proliferation of laws, an increasingly important role for courts is to reconcile potentially conflicting statutes. This is the same kind of role judges play in constitutional judicial review. That is, they decide whether or not a statute collides with the Constitution; if so, the role of the judge is to declare the statute invalid, because statutes are subordinate to the Constitution. But colliding statutes do not admit of such an easy answer. How do judges deal with colliding statutes? Several canons help judges think about this issue—the canon against implied repeals (treated here) as well as the reconciliation and specificity and last-in-time canons (treated in the sections following this one).

To illustrate the problem of colliding statutes, consider the dilemma presented for Lafayette Park regulators by motorized wheelchairs, such as the one illustrated on the next page.

Motorized Wheelchair
[Memasa, Photographer (2010)]

A wheelchair might be a "vehicle," broadly understood, and such a wheelchair is like the examples of vehicles listed in section 3 because it is motorized; for that same reason, it is unlike the mechanisms we have excluded from the ambit of the law. Recall the discussion from chapter one. One of the few bright lines for application was that even very small motorized vehicles, like the Léon Bollée Voiturette (pictured at the front of chapter one), might be covered by the statute. So there are good textual reasons for applying the statute to this mechanism. Yet, like me, most lawyers and citizens would be reluctant to apply the law to bar motorized wheelchairs from the park, partly because they don't go nearly as fast as the vehicles listed in section 3 (including bicycles, regulated in the proviso) and partly because excluding them would impose a great burden on many persons with disabilities. Why should they not be able to enjoy the park just as easily as everyone else?

There is also a really good statutory reason to allow motorized wheelchairs in Lafayette Park. In 1973, Congress enacted the Rehabilitation Act, which requires all programs and services funded by federal monies to establish rules and structures providing equal access and enjoyment by people with disabilities.[100] (The better-known Americans with Disabilities Act of 1990 does not apply to the federal government, although the National Park Service and other agencies are guided by that law in their implementation of the Rehabilitation Act.) If the Park Safety Act were a state or municipal statute, the Rehabilitation Act would preempt such a statutory prohibition it if the park in question wanted to continue to receive federal funds. If in conflict, federal statutes trump state or local statutes, just as the U.S. Constitution trumps federal statutes that conflict with its rules (see chapter six).

Because the Park Safety Act is itself a federal statute, however, it is not subject to such a trumping rule. Assume that banning motorized wheelchairs makes Lafayette Park less accessible for some visitors with physical disabilities and, hence, inconsistent with the Rehabilitation Act. The legal issue then boils down to this: Has the Rehabilitation Act been overridden by the Park Safety Act, which was enacted *after* the Rehabilitation Act, and which might be read broadly to regulate motorized wheelchairs in all national parks. To put the matter even more sharply, have National Park Service directives ensuring access to national parks been overridden, in part, by the new vehicles in the park law?[101] What do you think? Jot down your initial thoughts in the margin, please.

Notice that there is no provision in the Park Safety Act declaring that the Rehabilitation Act has been adjusted as regards the use of Lafayette Park. Motorized wheelchairs, moreover, are not quite the same as the other vehicles clearly subject to the statutory exclusion; they do not go as fast as motor scooters or even the antique Léon Bollée, for example. Most of them go a lot slower than bicycles, and so the tripartite structure of the Park Safety Act (outlined above) might support a ruling that they are not "vehicles."

Supporting a reluctance to bar motorized wheelchairs from the park is the "cardinal rule * * * that repeals by implication are not favored." The Supreme Court will find an implied repeal only where provisions in two statutes are in "irreconcilable conflict," or where the

---

[100] Rehabilitation Act of 1973, P.L. 93–112, 87 Stat. 355 (1973). The Department of the Interior has implemented the Rehabilitation Act in regulations published as *Enforcement of Nondiscrimination on the Basis of Handicap in Department of the Interior Programs*, 43 C.F R. §§ 17.501–17.570.

[101] Robert Stanton, Director, National Park Service, *Director's Order #42: Access for Visitors with Disabilities in National Park Service Programs and Services* (Nov. 4, 2000).

latter Act covers the whole subject of the earlier one and "is clearly intended as a substitute."[102] This *canon against implied repeals* is very popular among both federal and state judges. The Supreme Court is sometimes willing to rewrite statutory texts to avoid implied repeals,[103] though its recent decisions have avoided such messiness.[104]

Like other canons, this one reflects the desirability of continuity in legal duties and rights. If a statutory policy has been set and continuously implemented, our legal culture presumes against changes in that policy unless done so after legislative deliberation and the enactment of a text that clearly revokes the prior policy and announces a new rule.[105] Although most major legislation is written under some time pressure and without full exploration of the implications of proposed legislation for other statutory policies, members and staff in Congress do aspire toward some degree of coherence among related statutory policies, and the Congressional Research Service helps members, their staff, and chamber drafting offices see the larger picture. (Theoretically, state legislative drafting offices aspire to this level of service as well.[106]) Not surprisingly, the Congressional Research Service's statutory interpretation guidelines for congressional staff give significant emphasis to the canon against implied repeals. Indeed, the guidelines provide a great deal of detail for this canon, such as the admonition that repeals by implication are

---

[102] *Posadas v. National City Bank*, 296 U.S. 497, 503 (1936) (both quotations in text), quoted in *Morton v. Mancari*, 417 U.S. 535 (1974) (leading case); accord, *POM Wonderful LLC v. Coca-Cola Co.*, 134 S.Ct. 2228, 2236–37 (2014); *Hamdan v. Rumsfeld*, 548 U.S. 557, 593–94 (2006); *Schatz v. Allen Matkins Leck Gamble & Mallory LLP*, 198 P.3d 1109, 1119–21 (Cal. 2009); *United States Parole Comm'n v. Noble*, 693 A.2d 1084, 1087 (D.C. 1997); *Olmstead v. FTC*, 44 So. 3d at 83 (Fla.); *IBM Corp. v. Department of the Treasury*, 852 N.W.2d 865, 871–72 (Mich. 2014); *Local Gov't Assistance Corp. v. Sales Tax Asset Receivable Corp.*, 813 N.E.2d 587, 600–01 (N.Y. 2004); *Eppenauer v. Eppenauer*, 831 S.W.2d 30 (Tex. App. 1992); *Shumway v. Worthey*, 37 P.3d 361, 367 (Wyo.2001); see Scalia & Garner, *Reading Law*, 327–33.

[103] E.g., *Branch v. Smith*, 538 U.S. 254, 273 (2003) (plurality opinion) (completely rewriting a voting rights statute to avoid an implied repeal of an earlier, obsolescent statute); id. at 293 (dissenting opinion, noting that the Court had not found a repeal by implication since 1975).

[104] See *Credit Suisse Securities (USA) LLC v. Billing*, 551 U.S. 264 (2007) (finding an implied repeal of the nation's antitrust laws).

[105] On the importance of continuity in the law, and its relevance to statutory interpretation, see David L. Shapiro, *Continuity and Change in Statutory Interpretation*, 67 N.Y.U. L. Rev. 921 (1992).

[106] E.g., Kentucky Legislative Research Comm'n, *Bill Drafting Manual*, § 205 (admonishing legislative drafters to check for conflicts between the proposed statute and existing laws).

especially disfavored when interpreting appropriations laws and statutes adopted in the same session of Congress.[107]

The canon against implied repeals has its critics. Judge Richard Posner complains that this canon is "a mixed bag," from a governance point of view. "It protects some old statutes from * * * inadvertent destruction, but it threatens to impale new statutes on the concealed stakes planted by old ones."[108] This would be a more telling point if there were not other canons that address Posner's concern—and that reveal the canon against implied repeals to be not nearly as puissant as its fans suggest. Indeed, most federal and state legislative drafting manuals do not mention this canon, and some drafting offices ignore this precise canon when discussing statutory collisions.[109]

Reconciliation Canon. If the Park Safety Act had been enacted *before* the Rehabilitation Act, would the canon against implied repeals require a judge to find that the Rehabilitation Act does not guarantee access to Lafayette Park for users of motorized wheelchairs? This is the concern raised by Judge Posner, but this is not a fatal concern, and poses no severe problems here. To begin with, it is not clear to me that the Rehabilitation Act would be an "implied" repeal. If the Park Safety Act had barred motorized wheelchairs from Lafayette Park before 1973, the Rehabilitation Act would have explicitly required a new policy, as it forbids federally funded programs from denying reasonable access to people with disabilities. Conversely, if the Park Safety Act had never been applied to motorized wheelchairs (a much more likely scenario), the Rehabilitation Act might press interpretation away from coverage of motorized wheelchairs, given that the "meaning of one statute may be affected by other Acts."[110]

Perhaps most relevant to figuring out the relationship between the disabilities law and the vehicles in the park law is the precept

---

[107] CRS Report, *Statutory Interpretation*, 29–30 (updated 2011).

[108] *Friedrich v. City of Chicago*, 888 F.2d 511, 516 (7th Cir. 1989) (Posner, J.) (quotation in text). The canon against implied repeals also has fierce defenders. E.g., Jesse W. Markham Jr., *The Supreme Court's New Implied Repeal Doctrine: Expanding Judicial Power to Rewrite Legislation Under the Ballooning Conception of "Plain Repugnancy,"* 45 Gonzaga L. Rev. 437 (2009–01).

[109] Senate Office of Legislative Counsel, *Legislative Drafting Manual*, § 314(b)(1) (setting forth mechanisms for dealing with colliding statutes, with emphasis on the reconciliation canon, but not mentioning the canon against implied repeals). See also Kentucky Legislative Research Comm'n, *Bill Drafting Manual*, § 205 (similar).

[110] *FDA v. Brown & Williamson Corp.*, 529 U.S. 120, 133 (2000); accord, *United States v. Fausto*, 484 U.S. 439, 453 (1988).

that " '[w]hen two statutes are capable of co-existence, it is the duty of the courts * * * to regard each as effective.' "[111] Specifically, judges "must read [two allegedly conflicting] statutes to give effect to each if [it] can do so while preserving their sense and purpose."[112] While this *reconciliation* (or *harmonization*) *canon* is typically lumped together with the canon against implied repeals, it operates as a broader canon.[113] Thus, in our revised hypothetical, where the Park Safety Act precedes the Rehabilitation Act, the canon against implied repeals either does not support application of the later statute or is neutral, and so all the work is being done by the reconciliation canon. In contrast, the reconciliation canon works in tandem with the canon against implied repeals when the Rehabilitation Act precedes the Park Safety Act. Whichever statute was enacted first, the reconciliation canon will very likely assure that motorized wheelchairs can operate in Lafayette Park.

The reconciliation canon is also related to the anti-surplusage canon, for both appeal to the norm that the entire legal corpus (the entire act or the entire code, respectively) should not only be given effect, but should be harmonized, to the extent possible. Thus, the Minnesota Legislature has directed its state courts: "When a general provision in a law is in conflict with a special provision in the same or another law, the two shall be construed, if possible, so that effect may be given to both."[114] Legislators and their staffs elsewhere probably agree with the Minnesota Legislature, for this canon honors the work of both past and current legislatures. It is also a form of analysis well-suited to judges, whose bread and butter has traditionally been the reconciliation and harmonization of unruly precedents.

---

[111] *Radzanower v. Touche Ross & Co.,* 426 U.S. 148, 155 (1976) (quoting *Morton v. Mancari*, 417 U.S. at 551).

[112] *Watt v. Alaska*, 451 U.S. 259, 267 (1981) (quotation in text); accord, *POM Wonderful LLC,* 134 S.Ct. at 2237; *Ruckelshaus v. Monsanto Co.,* 467 U.S. 986, 1017–18 (1984); *Bank of America, N.A. v. District of Columbia*, 80 A.3d 650, 670–72 (D.C. 2013); *Cannella v. Auto-Owners Ins. Co.,* 801 So.2d 94, 98 (Fla. 2001); *South Metro. Fire Prot. Dist. v. City of Lee's Summit*, 278 S.W.3d 659, 666 (Mo. 2009); *In re Goodman*, 731 N.E.2d 600, 603–04 (N.Y. 2000); *Acker v. Texas Water Comm'n,* 790 S.W.2d 299, 301 (Tex. 1990).

[113] See Senate Office of Legislative Counsel, *Legislative Drafting Manual* § 314(b)(1)(A) (requiring drafters to seek reconciliation of apparently conflicting statutes). Most of the cases cited in the CRS Report, *Statutory Interpretation*, 29–30 (updated 2011) under the heading of "implied repeals," are cases where an argued repeal was negated by reconciliation of the two statutes allegedly in conflict.

[114] Minn. Stat. § 645.26 (quotation in text); see 2B *Sutherland Statutes and Statutory Construction* § 53:1 (7th ed. 2015) (principle of harmonization of statute law, to the extent consistent with statutory texts).

The reconciliation inquiry here is relatively straightforward: What is the point of each statute? Which statutory purpose would be most compromised if that statute did not apply? The Park Safety Act seeks to make Lafayette Park safe for visitors, especially young children and older adults. Interpreting the statute to allow motorized wheelchairs does not undermine that purpose much, if at all. The Rehabilitation Act seeks to open up federally funded programs and services to persons with disabilities. If disabled persons needing motorized wheelchairs were excluded from federal parks, this might create a significant hole in the Rehabilitation Act's statutory purpose, from the perspective of the statutory beneficiaries—and needlessly. Considering the twin statutory purposes, the judicious interpreter has no problem reconciling the Rehabilitation Act and the Park Safety Act by allowing motorized wheelchairs into Lafayette Park. And the reconciliation analysis does not depend in any significant way on which statute was enacted first.

The subtle analysis sometimes required by the reconciliation canon can be illustrated by the application of our vehicles in the park law to the Bock Otto SuperFour outdoor hybrid all-terrain wheelchair, with all-wheel drive, pictured on the next page. As the gentle reader can see, *this* motorized wheelchair is not only a lot larger than the ordinary motorized wheelchair pictured earlier, but it looks like a small car. Indeed, its purpose is to allow wheelchair-bound people to get out in rough terrain, somewhat like a four-wheel drive for disabled outdoorsmen and women. The Bock Otto SuperFour is much heavier than the Léon Bollée Voiturette, the small proto-automobile introduced in chapter one. Reportedly, the Bock Otto can travel a little faster than the Léon Bollée.

Bock Otto SuperFour Motorized Wheelchair

In my view, the reconciliation canon comes out the other way for the Bock Otto SuperFour than for an ordinary motorized wheelchair (such as the one pictured earlier). This degree of mechanical power and versatility seems much less necessary for disabled persons to have full access to Lafayette Park, which is level terrain. And it is a much sharper threat to park safety than the earlier wheelchair might be. Hence, I'd draw the line at motorized wheelchairs that look like and drive like little automobiles—they are "vehicles" barred from the park. Neither result, under my analysis, depends on whether the Park Safety Act was enacted after the Rehabilitation Act. Notice that there may be a modest administrability problem with such a looks-like-a-car test, but in practice this would probably come up very rarely, as it is hard to imagine many visitors demanding to drive a Bock Otto SuperFour into Lafayette Park.

Specificity and Last-in-Time Canons. Suppose the judge has a harder time reconciling the two colliding statutes than I have had. For example, would the Rehabilitation Act tolerate a rule that allowed regular wheelchairs but not motorized wheelchairs into Lafayette Park? Such a rule would allow people with mobility problems to use the park, and so the Rehabilitation Act and the Park Safety Act might be reconciled in this manner. I should be skeptical. Because Lafayette Park is pretty large and because drop-off points are far from its center, many people with mobility limitations could not take advantage of the park unless they could use a motorized wheelchair, or so it seems to me. This is an issue where the trial judge needs reliable information and might invite affidavits, briefing, or even a hearing on this question. Such a factual inquiry might make it harder to reconcile the two statutes in the manner I did above.

In that event, there are some tiebreakers. In the same provision as its reconciliation canon, the Minnesota Legislature also codified a *specificity canon*: "If the conflict between the two provisions be irreconcilable, the special provision shall prevail and shall be construed as an exception to the general provision, unless the general provision shall be enacted at a later session and it shall be the manifest intention of the legislature that such general provision shall prevail."[115] The U.S. Supreme Court has articulated a similar concept: "Where there is no clear intention otherwise, a specific statute will not be controlled or nullified by a general one, regardless of the priority of enactment."[116]

This canon might suggest that the Rehabilitation Act's more specific directive should trump the ambiguous notion that a motorized wheelchair is the kind of "vehicle" Congress excluded from Lafayette Park. Maybe, but I am dubious that the specificity canon adds anything to the reconciliation canon, because the former is so malleable. While I am inclined to say that the Rehabilitation Act is the more specific statute with regard to motorized *wheelchairs* in the park, others might reasonably conclude that the Park Safety Act is the more specific statute for wheelchairs in the *park*. Perhaps the underlying reason why I think the Rehabilitation Act is the more specific statute is that its purpose and plan are deeply invested in allowing motorized wheelchairs in all public spaces, including federal parks, while I don't see the Park Safety Act's purpose and plan

---

[115] Minn. Stat. § 645.26 (quotation in text); accord, Cal. Civ. Proc. Code § 1859; Tex. Govt. Code § 311.026(b). For state court applications of the specificity canon, see, e.g., *Duffy v. Michigan Dep't of Natural Resources*, 805 N.W.2d 399, 408–09 (Mich. 2011); *In re State ex rel. Tyler*, 2015 WL 6651948 (Tex. App. Oct. 30, 2015).

[116] *Morton v. Mancari*, 417 U.S. at 550–51 (quotation in text); accord, *Brown & Williamson Corp.*, 529 U.S. at 133; *Bock Laundry Mach. Co.*, 490 U.S. at 524–26; *Crawford Fitting Co. v. J.T. Gibbons, Inc.*, 482 U.S. 437, 444–45 (1987); cf. *RadLAX Gateway Hotel, LLC v. Amalgamated Bank*, 132 S.Ct. 2065, 2072 (2012) (applying the specific-over-the-general canon to provisions within a single statute); Scalia & Garner, *Reading Law*, 183–88 (describing a broadly applicable "general/specific canon").

disturbed by allowing these modest "vehicles" in Lafayette Park. Conversely, as regards the Bock Otto SuperFour, a proto-range rover for people with disabilities, the Park Safety Act seems to me the more specific statute. Notice that my specificity analysis for the regular motorized wheelchair and for the Bock Otto SuperFour wheelchair tracks the analysis posed earlier under the reconciliation canon.

Notwithstanding support for the specificity canon in judicial opinions and among academic treatises, I urge caution before giving this canon decisive weight, because of its malleability. Stated another way, deployment of this canon relies on the same kind of normative analysis that undergirds the reconciliation canon, which I urge as the primary canon for resolving issues arising out of colliding statutes. If the reconciliation canon cannot neutrally resolve the clash, the canon that is easier to administer is the reservation clause of the Minnesota statute—namely, the *last-in-time canon*: State and federal legislatures have virtually plenary authority to repeal, amend, or override previous enactments. If the specificity analysis is genuinely indeterminate, the judge should probably apply the most recent statute, a tiebreaker that is well-known to congressional drafters.[117]

* * *

Some gentle readers might be surprised (or annoyed) that this chapter has uncovered and applied so many whole act and whole code canons. Although my goal has not been to surprise any reader and has been to apply the canons critically, this chapter has endeavored to bring the whole act and whole code canons out of their academic closet. They are a bigger deal than ever before in American judicial practice—yet are too often ignored in theoretical debates.

For example, John Manning, the leading theorist of the new textualism, usually ignores or marginalizes the whole act and whole code canons.[118] In his books, Justice Scalia gained traction from his claim that his approach simply applies the ordinary meaning anyone

---

[117] Senate Office of Legislative Counsel, *Legislative Drafting Manual*, § 314(b)(1)(B) (where colliding statues cannot be reconciled, follow the later-enacted statute). For an example of two conflicting statutes, either of which could have been characterized as "specific," see *Young v. Haines*, 718 P.2d 909, 914 (Cal. 1986). The Court broke the tie by applying the last-in-time canon, discussed in the text. Id. at 914–15.

[118] E.g., John F. Manning, *What Divides Textualists from Purposivists?*, 106 Colum. L. Rev. 70 (2006) (describing the new textualism as all about objective meaning of statutory provisions, with little or no mention of whole act and whole code "objective" context); see id. at 81–82 (briefly recognizing that new textualists mention substantive canons but ignoring whole act and whole code canons).

can derive from "reading law," perhaps armed with *Black's Law Dictionary*—but when authoring or joining judicial opinions, Justice Scalia often created or denied ambiguity by refining the ordinary language of a statutory provision through a wide array of holistic and substantive canons.[119] Another leading textualist thinker, Adrian Vermeule, pays more attention to holistic canons, but only to reject them completely.[120] One punch line of the current chapter is that whole act and most of the whole code canons are deeply entrenched in American judicial practice—finding expression in all eras of American history and at all levels of American judging. As far as I can tell, there is not a state court today that does not pervasively rely on holistic canons, and they saturate federal court decisionmaking more than they have at any other point in American history.

Traditional legal process theorists, in turn, also tend to ignore the holistic canons—even though legal process judges, such as Justice Breyer, invoke them in judicial opinions. The silence of legal process theorists is just as puzzling as the silence of textualist thinkers. On the one hand, holistic canons are a primary mechanism by which dogmatic text-stressing judges on the U.S. Supreme Court and the Michigan Supreme Court (to take the two best examples) carry forth their project of denying ambiguity in statutory cases. As you can see in this chapter, I am with the textualists on this point. The whole act, especially, does often operate to reduce the number of penumbral cases, and sometimes the whole code can do the same. One reason the whole act rule increases the clarity of statutes is that the whole act helps the interpreter to understand the statutory purpose better. Purpose is one factor emphasized by legal process theorists, and they have unfortunately neglected the opportunities offered for understanding purpose by reference to a statutory scheme, and not just by reference to legislative history.

Like the ordinary meaning canons, the holistic canons illustrate the illusory divide between formal textualists and functional purposivists. Statutory text cannot be understood without a sense of statutory purpose—but purpose cannot be understood without diving

---

[119] For examples of ambiguities created or resolved though complicated whole act or whole code analysis in opinions authored by Justice Scalia, see, e.g., *Michigan v. EPA*, 135 S.Ct. at 2707–08 (Scalia, J., considering the statutory scheme and particular provisions to narrow the phase "appropriate and necessary" to require the agency to consider the cost of different regulatory alternatives); *Entergy Corp. v. Riverkeeper*, 556 U.S. at 233 (Scalia, J., narrowing of the Clean Air Act Amendments in light of the statutory scheme).

[120] Adrian Vermeule, *Judging Under Uncertainty* 202–04 (2006).

into and exploring the statutory scheme, often enriched with related statutes. Statutory interpretation is both elegantly formalist, taking apart and then re-assembling the statutory structure, and practically functionalist, addressing mischiefs and seeking to solve problems, but in the calibrated manner laid out by the legislature, after inputs from stakeholders and political institutions.

A theme of this chapter has been *harmonization*. Judges specialize in seeing the big legal landscape, which is overwhelmingly a statutory landscape nowadays. The ordinary meaning canons integrate statutory directives into our language practices, so that We the People can know what the law requires of us. But sometimes what the law requires becomes clear only in light of the larger landscape, and this is where the holistic canons play a key role. Harmonization is a satisfying formal, almost aesthetic, goal for judges, who like it when everything fits together. But harmonization is also functionally important. Harmonizing one part of a law with another honors the hard work of the legislative process, treating its product seriously even if perfecting it in marginal respects. Harmonizing statutes enacted at different points in time, often without a clear vision of potential conflict, helps knit the law together. Overall, harmonization has the potential to render the law better integrated in service of common themes, norms, and principles. And law that enjoys a certain level of integrity is especially worthy of our engagement as well as our obedience.

Chapter 3

STATUTORY PRECEDENTS

1946 Rex Motorized Bicycle
[Harald Bischoff, Photographer (2010)]

Any statute that generates lawsuits also generates judicial *precedents.* Precedents are judicial decisions applying law (common law, statutes and treaties, the Constitution) to new facts and justifying that application by reference to preexisting legal authority—including prior decisions, for precedents themselves have the force of law. For example, future applications of statutory law to newer facts will not only consider the plain meaning and whole act, but will also (and should) consider precedents interpreting the relevant statutory provision.[1]

[1] For classic treatments of the topic of precedent in our legal tradition, start with Benjamin N. Cardozo, *The Nature of the Judicial Process* (1921) (the Storrs Lectures); Ronald Dworkin, *Law's Empire* (1986); Neil Duxbury, *The Nature and Authority of Precedent* (2008); Michael J. Gerhardt, *The Power of Precedent* (2008); Henry Paul Monaghan, *Stare Decisis and Constitutional Adjudication*, 88 Colum. L. Rev. 723 (1988); Lewis F. Powell, Jr., Stare Decisis *and Judicial Restraint*, 47 Wash. &

In short, the relevant materials for statutory interpretation include judicial precedents. To illustrate the operation of precedent, return to the Lafayette Park Safety Act of 1992 (introduced in chapter two):

> **An Act to ensure public safety in Lafayette Park**
>
> **Sec. 1. Findings and Purpose.** Finding that vehicles operating in Lafayette Park have contributed to several serious accidents requiring hospitalization in the last five years, and finding further that vehicles create risks of serious injury to park users, Congress resolves that there is an urgent public need to ban any and all vehicles from Lafayette Park.
>
> **Sec. 2. No Vehicles in the Park.** No vehicles of any kind shall be allowed in Lafayette Park. Any person who drives a vehicle into Lafayette Park may be assessed a fine not exceeding $500 for each violation.
>
> **Sec. 3. Definition.** "Vehicle" for purposes of this law means any mechanism for conveying a person from one place to another, including automobiles, trucks, motorcycles, and motor scooters. *Provided that*, bicycles shall be allowed in Lafayette Park, so long as they are being pushed or carried and not ridden.

Recall from chapter two that there was room for debate as to which section of the law bars mopeds. Mopeds are clearly covered by the statute, but it is not clear whether they are governed by the bicycle proviso in section 3 (hence, not banned entirely) or whether they are governed only by section 2 and not by the proviso (hence, banned entirely).

However ambiguous the text and structure of Park Safety Act might be on this particular issue, legal ambiguity comes to an end when (or if) an appellate court renders a definitive interpretation. Assume, for example, that the Park Service fines Cynthia Hogan $100 because she rides her antique 1946 Rex motorized bicycle

---

Lee L. Rev. 281 (1990); and Frederick Schauer, *Precedent*, 39 Stan. L. Rev. 571 (1987), and consult the varying and thoughtful perspectives offered by Gary Lawson, *The Constitutional Case Against Precedent*, 17 Harv. J.L. & Pub. Pol'y 23 (1994); Christopher J. Peters, *Foolish Consistency: On Equality, Integrity, and Justice in Stare Decisis*, 105 Yale L.J. 2031 (1996); David L. Shapiro, *The Role of Precedent in Constitutional Adjudication: An Introspection*, 86 Tex. L. Rev. 929 (2008); Larry M. Solan, *Precedent in Statutory Interpretation* (draft 2016); David A. Strauss, *Common Law Constitutional Interpretation*, 63 U. Chi. L. Rev. 877 (1996).

(pictured at the front of this chapter) through Lafayette Park when traveling from her home to the Office of the Vice President, where she is working in the 1990s. Notice that Hogan's case involves an old-fashioned "motorized bicycle," such as the one pictured at the front of this chapter. I am not using the term "moped," which was deployed in chapter one to apply to motorized bicycles that do not have pedals and that operate solely on motor power.

Finding a violation of the statute, the District Court sustains the fine, and the U.S. Court of Appeals for the District of Columbia Circuit affirms. The panel opinion for the Court of Appeals not only resolves the issue for Hogan's case, but establishes a precedent binding in the District of Columbia.[2] Unless reversed by the Court of Appeals sitting *en banc* (all of the active judges) or reversed or abrogated by the U.S. Supreme Court, *Hogan v. National Park Service* provides the legal rule for deciding any future motorized bicycle in Lafayette Park case. (If the Supreme Court takes review in *Hogan* or any other similar case and resolves the case on the merits, its interpretation would provide the legal rule for deciding any future case of this sort.)

The gentle reader can immediately see that her interpretation of the Park Safety Act cannot stop with the materials in the U.S. Code. At the very least, she must also consider any precedents interpreting the statute, usually easy to discover by reference to the U.S. Code Annotated or Westlaw. Precedent and *stare decisis* (the rule that "decisions must stand" in future cases) are essential elements for any theory of statutory interpretation and any statutory practice. Indeed, where there is an authoritative precedent "on point," that precedent is more immediately important than the ordinary meaning that today's judge might have otherwise found. Thus, if a federal trial judge believes the Park Safety Act has an ordinary meaning that includes "motorized bicycles" as "bicycles" covered by section 3's proviso, she would nonetheless follow a Supreme Court or D.C. Circuit precedent interpreting the law to ban motorized bicycles from the park entirely because they are "vehicles" (section 2) but not "bicycles" (section 3's proviso).

This insistence on following a statutory precedent, rather than applying the current judge's understanding of the statute's ordinary

---

[2] *Stare decisis* is the rule followed not only by the Supreme Court, but also by each of the federal courts of appeals, some of which adhere to that rule more strictly than the Supreme Court does. See Joseph W. Mead, *Stare Decisis in the Inferior Courts of the United States*, 12 Nev. L.J. 787, 794 (2012).

meaning, strikes observers from all over the world and on the Michigan Supreme Court as a very odd legal regime.[3] Legislation scholars and authors of canons-based handbooks and treatises usually don't give this consideration much thought, and no general theory of statutory interpretation treats precedent as anything but peripheral. Are dozens of legal cultures, most of the Justices on the Michigan Supreme Court, and so many eminent scholars wrong? Or short-sighted? What do you think? For example, should a judge have to follow a precedent saying that motorized bicycles are "vehicles" and not "bicycles," even if she is thoroughly convinced that the plain meaning of the bicycle proviso includes "motorized bicycles"?

There are powerful rule of law reasons to follow the longstanding Anglo-American precept that all judges must follow authoritative statutory precedents when they are on point or when they otherwise resolve the legal controversy at hand. The Supreme Court has repeatedly said that *stare decisis* is "a foundation stone of the rule of law" in statutory as well as constitutional and common law cases.[4] Assuring Americans predictable legal rules handed down by judges unswayed by ideology, the rule of law not only generates economic benefits and greater efficiency, but is the foundation of freedom itself. "Liberty finds no refuge in a jurisprudence of doubt."[5] Almost everyone agrees that the rule of law is a boon to society: Do precedent and *stare decisis* contribute to this boon? Admittedly, there is no compelling empirical evidence one way or the other, so I shall suggest the strongest arguments and counterarguments. Readers can decide for themselves whether *stare decisis* properly ought to have a central role in statutory interpretation, but unless you are certain that *stare*

---

[3] Since 1999, the Michigan Supreme Court has overruled dozens of statutory precedents on the ground that they did not follow the strict plain meaning rule that the court majority believes is the only legitimate approach. E.g., *People v. Gardner*, 753 N.W.2d 78, 84–91 (Mich. 2008); Robert A. Sedler, *The Michigan Supreme Court,* Stare Decisis, *and Overruling the Overrulings*, 55 Wayne L. Rev. 1911 (2009) (reporting that, between 1999 and 2008, the Court applied the plain meaning rule to overrule at least 38 supreme court precedents, most of them statutory precedents).

[4] *Michigan* v. *Bay Mills Indian Community*, 134 S.Ct. 2024, 2036 (2014), followed and quoted in *Kimble v. Marvel Entertainment, LLC,* 135 S.Ct. 2401, 2409 (2015); see *Halliburton Co.* v. *Erica P. John Fund, Inc.*, 134 S.Ct. 2398 (2014); *Payne v. Tennessee*, 501 U.S. 808 (1991) (a leading discussion of the rule of law virtues of *stare decisis*); *People v. Jones*, 278 P.3d 821, 834–38 (Cal. 2012) (Liu, J., concurring). Cf. Thomas W. Merrill, *Originalism,* Stare Decisis, *and the Promotion of Judicial Restraint,* 22 Const. Comm. 271 (2005) (arguing that, in constitutional cases, *stare decisis* is more important to the rule of law and judicial restraint than the plain meaning rule).

[5] *Planned Parenthood of Pa. v. Casey,* 505 U.S. 833, 844 (1992) (joint opinion for a plurality); see Friedrich von Hayek, *The Constitution of Liberty* 142, 153 (1960).

decisis ought to be relaxed, you ought not throw over an interpretive principle that has been at the core of American law since the founding era. As I see it, *stare decisis* does contribute, on balance, to the rule of law.

To begin with an obvious point, *stare decisis* (if taken seriously in a legal system) ensures the continuity of *authoritative* judge-made interpretations. Statutory precedents are not only hard to overrule, but even when they are overruled, the process proceeds over a period of years and often results in a modest change in the rule. To the extent that statutory interpretation proceeds through judge-made precedent (a phenomenon that varies from statute to statute), *stare decisis* commits our legal system not only to continuity of legal rules, but also to incrementalism in modifying, narrowing, expanding, or updating them.[6]

Relatedly, *stare decisis* promises greater predictability and certainty in the application of law and probably delivers significantly greater predictability, especially in the early stages of a statute's application.[7] Typically, legislators opt for broad terminology whose application is not easily predictable—and the passage of time produces more ambiguities as new and unanticipated circumstances present themselves. Simply reading the Park Safety Act does not readily tell park visitors or police whether motorized bicycles are "vehicles" barred altogether by section 2, **or** whether they are "bicycles" allowed under restrictive circumstances pursuant to section 3's proviso. Before the Court of Appeals decides *Hogan v. National Park Service,* no one knows with certainty what the statute means with regard to motorized bicycles. After the court decision is handed down, we know exactly what the statute means, based upon the holding of the Court in *Hogan*. That is, motorized bicycles are "vehicles" barred by section 2 and are not "bicycles" subject to the special rule in section 3's proviso. As we shall see below, the *Hogan* precedent not only provides a predictable rule for motorized bicycles in the park, but may create greater predictability for application of the Park Safety Act to other putative vehicles.

---

6 Randy J. Kozel, *Precedent and Reliance*, 62 Emory L.J. 1459, 1481 (2013); Richard M. Re, *Narrowing Precedents in the Supreme Court*, 114 Colum. L. Rev. 1861 (2014).

7 See Stephanie A. Lindquist & Frank B. Cross, *Empirically Testing Dworkin's Chain Novel Theory: Studying the Path of Precedent*, 80 N.Y.U. L. Rev. 1156 (2005) (empirical study finding that precedents do appear to constrain judges in the early stages of a statute's implementation, but are not clearly constraining later on, as precedents pile up).

Precedent and *stare decisis* further contribute to the rule of law by reinforcing a culture of judicial reasoning that is objective and grounded in general, neutral principles.[8] Because all federal judges in the District of Columbia are bound by the rule of *Hogan v. National Park Service,* subsequent judges ought to have less discretion when they evaluate future motorized bicycles in the park cases. Moreover, judges considering the application of the Park Safety Act to other mechanisms will consider the reasoning as well as result of *Hogan.* This process might constrain judges, as illustrated by the discussion in the next part of this chapter.[9]

Stare decisis also promises to reduce the discretion of the appellate judges who actually decide *Hogan* (the first case arising under this statute), even if there are no relevant statutory precedents directly constraining them. How is that? The judges deciding *Hogan* know that the rule they announce will be binding on lower courts and on themselves for the foreseeable future, and so they have an incentive to be cautious when announcing the rule and suggesting its scope. *Stare decisis* thus motivates appellate judges to announce a rule that is not only grounded in general principles and legislative policy, determinable by any judge, but is also narrowly tailored to resolve the case and reach no further than needed or desirable. This is why appellate judges are, famously, interested in hypotheticals beyond the facts of the case at hand. They want to know what implications for future cases logically follow from each chain of reasoning that they might invoke to decide the case before them.

For example, an appellate judge in *Hogan* would explore the possibility that section 3 of the Park Safety Act brings all "motorized" conveyances into the prohibition created by section 2. (Then she would have to consider whether Hogan's motorized bicycle *also* falls under the section 3 proviso.) If that general principle is going to be the starting point for the judge's holding, she wants to consider the implications that principle might have for future cases. So she thinks about motorized conveyances that might be swept up in such a

---

8 Henry M. Hart Jr. & Albert M. Sacks, *The Legal Process: Basic Problems in the Making and Application of Law* 569 (William N. Eskridge Jr. & Philip P. Frickey eds. 1994) (tent. ed. 1958); Jeremy Waldron, Stare Decisis *and the Rule of Law: A Layered Approach,* 111 Mich. L. Rev. 1 (2012).

9 Cardozo, *Nature of the Judicial Process,* 149–50; Schauer, *Precedent,* 39 Stan. L. Rev. at 599–600; Waldron, Stare Decisis *and the Rule of Law,* 111 Mich. L. Rev. at 21–26. On the historical origins of *stare decisis* as a mechanism for controlling judicial discretion, see Frederick G. Kempin, Jr., *Precedent and Stare Decisis: The Critical Years, 1800 to 1850,* 3 Am. J. Legal Hist. 28 (1959).

general rule—such as Segways (pictured below). Is the judge prepared to announce a rule that would affect Washington, D.C.'s thriving Segway population? Even a judge who thinks Segways are a nuisance might still hesitate before writing a broad opinion, fearful that a decision grounded upon an anti-motor vehicles policy would be too broad. Who wants to write a decision that is used to exclude motorized wheelchairs from a national landmark?

Segways in Washington, D.C.
[Fourandsixty, Photographer (2015)]

Even if *stare decisis* were not completely constraining, statutory precedents might serve a rule of law purpose. Lawrence Solan demonstrates that the Supreme Court invokes its precedents for a wide variety of purposes—to support methodological points, to ascertain the meaning of certain words, and to bring in general principles, as well as to build upon substantive holdings particular to the statute in question.[10] For example, if the Court invokes the *ejusdem generis* canon (chapter one), the opinion will invariably cite a prior decision (and sometimes a bunch of decisions) relying on that canon. The Court does not accord formal *stare decisis* effect to its

---

[10] Solan, *Precedent in Statutory Interpretation* (draft 2016)

methodological precedents.[11] But it does cite them a lot, and those precedents have a *quasi-stare decisis* authority, not formally binding but weighty nonetheless. Professor Solan maintains, persuasively, that the Court's compulsive citation of prior decisions for factual, methodological, as well as strictly legal points reflects the value our legal culture vests in demonstrations of coherence with past practices.[12]

Thus, the rule of law provides a multifaceted case for the role of *stare decisis* in statutory interpretation. But do not overstate the rule of law virtue for precedent; as we shall see below, the predictability and neutrality promised by *stare decisis* have many shortfalls. If judges do not cooperate within the limits of a strongly professional rule-of-law culture most of the benefits will evanesce (just ask any dissident Russian businessman). Moreover, even a well-operating precedent-based rule of law will pose a range of possible costs to democratic legitimacy, the second critically important value at stake in statutory cases. Recall Figure 4, from the previous chapter:

FIGURE 4

Plain Meaning Continuum: "Driving a Vehicle" in the Park (§ 2), in Light of Statutory Purpose (§ 1) and Definition (§ 3)

Core Coverage		**Penumbra**	**Outside the Statute**
Cars & Trucks	Bicycles	Adult Tricycles	Kid's Tricycles
Motorcycles		Skateboards	Baby Carriages
Motor Scooters			Wheelbarrows
Mopeds			
Motorized Bicycles			

The legislative process has produced a statutory structure that answers most of the immediate issues in a straightforward way: The Park Safety Act clearly regulates cars, trucks, motorcycles, motor scooters, motorized bicycles, and bicycles and does not regulate kid's tricycles, baby carriages, and wheelbarrows. Most of those mechanisms will never generate a judicial precedent, because they are not worth litigating or taking an appeal. And for the ones that are

[11] Sydney Foster, *Should Courts Give Stare Decisis Effect to Statutory Interpretation Methodology?*, 96 Geo. L.J. 1863 (2008); Abbe R. Gluck, *Intersystemic Statutory Interpretation: Methodology as "Law" and the Erie Doctrine*, 120 Yale L. J. 1898 (2011); see also Jeffrey A. Pojanowski, *Statutes in Common Law Courts*, 91 Tex. L. Rev. 479 (2013).

[12] Solan, *Precedent in Statutory Interpretation* (draft 2016)

litigated and appealed, such as the case of the motorized bicycle, we can trust our judiciary to reach the result dictated by the statutory text and structure.

If there were litigation producing an appellate decision, it is likely to involve a penumbral case, such as the Park Police's citation of Cynthia Hogan for zipping through Lafayette Park on her motorized bicycle soon after the vehicles in the park statute was enacted. However the judges rule in Hogan's case, judges rather than legislators will be filling in the details of the law. Because federal judges are appointed for life, rather than elected for specific terms, they are less democratically accountable than legislators. That legal scholars call such case-by-case gapfilling "interstitial lawmaking" does not change the fact that unelected judges are making new law.[13] As judicial precedents build up over time, the focus of statutory interpretation will shift *away from* statutory text and structure and *toward* precedent,[14] unless Congress frequently amends the statute. It appears that congressional staff and, by implication, our elected representatives do not assume that judges will have such extensive lawmaking power.[15]

A potential justification for strong *stare decisis* in statutory cases is that it puts legislators on notice that they, and not judges, have primary responsibility for updating statutory law and sweeping away obsolescent statutory rules.[16] Between 1967 and 1999, each Congress overrode an average of fifteen Supreme Court statutory decisions—although that average plummeted after President Clinton's impeachment and trial in 1998 and has never recovered its pre-

---

[13] For a candid admission of the way judges "make law" in statutory cases, see Sol Wachtler, *Judicial Lawmaking*, 65 N.Y.U. L. Rev. 1 (1990).

[14] For example, Supreme Court decisions creating a standard for employer vicarious liability to employees subjected to harassment by supervisors introduced a new term ("supervisor") into Title VII law. When the Supreme Court was called upon to define exactly who is a supervisor for Title VII purposes, the Court reasoned from the statutory precedents rather than from the statutory text. See *Vance v. Ball State Univ.*, 133 S.Ct. 2434, 2443–49 (2013). For similar instances where the Court is reasoning mostly from its own statutory precedents, with little reference to statutory text, see *Bilski v. Kappos*, 561 U.S. 593 (2010) (Patent Act); *Leegin Creative Leather Prods. v. PSKS, Inc.*, 551 U.S. 877 (2007) (Sherman Act).

[15] Lisa Schultz Bressman & Abbe R. Gluck, *Statutory Interpretation from the Inside: An Empirical Study of Congressional Drafting, Delegation, and the Canons: Part II*, 66 Stan. L. Rev. 725, 770–71, 774, 776 (2014).

[16] *Burnet v. Coronado Oil & Gas Co.*, 285 U.S. 393, 406–07 (1932) (Brandeis, J., dissenting); see *Kimble*, 135 S.Ct. at 2409–12 (recent synthesis); William N. Eskridge Jr., *Overruling Statutory Precedents*, 76 Geo. L.J. 1361 (1988).

impeachment vigor.[17] Since 2011, congressional override activity has virtually dried up. For the time being, Congress is no longer capable of carrying out its responsibilities. Fortunately, most state legislatures seem capable of carrying out this function much better than Congress does.

Under current federal circumstances, where overrides are not likely, democratic accountability suffers unless judicial evolution of statutory schemes through case-by-case application and accumulation of precedent is linear and predictable. Unfortunately, a case-by-case process of applying precedents over a period of decades is not likely to be linear and predictable. Under circumstances where precedents build up and the statutory text remains unchanged, more of the content of the law is effectively constructed by judges and less by legislators. One might consider statutes to be like ships launched into the ocean.[18] The initial trajectory is determined by legislators, who set the course through the language and structure of the law. But over the years seemingly minor decisions by the captain and others interpreting the original instructions will yield a course far different from that mapped by the legislature that launched the ship in the first place.

This nautical point would be less troubling to democratic theory if judges followed a mechanical approach to *stare decisis* that yielded a predictable chain of decisions over time. But the world changes, often in response to the statute itself, and new cases offer fresh opportunities for judicial innovation. Critics sometimes assume that judges greedily grab every opportunity they can to read their own values into statutes; I do not share that view of judges. But even a scrupulous judge will be dubious about the results and reasoning of precedents she is obliged to respect (and not overrule) and will have opportunities to exercise discretion when she (1) characterizes or narrows the holdings of prior precedents, (2) chooses which precedent or string of precedents to emphasize, and (3) applies the "relevant"

---

[17] Matthew R. Christiansen & William N. Eskridge Jr., *Congressional Overrides of Supreme Court Statutory Interpretation Decisions, 1967–2011*, 92 Tex. L. Rev. 1317, 1480–1514 (2014) (appendix documenting congressional overrides of Supreme Court statutory decisions, 1967–2011); Richard L. Hasen, *End of the Dialogue? Political Polarization, the Supreme Court, and Congress*, 86 S. Cal. L. Rev. 205, 208–10, 217–19 (2013) (first noting the recent decline in overrides).

[18] Francis Bennion, *Bennion on Statutory Interpretation* 356 (1984) (originating the nautical metaphor for statutory interpretation over time); T. Alexander Aleinikoff, *Updating Statutory Interpretation,* 87 Mich. L. Rev. 20 (1988) (contrasting the "nautical" metaphor for applying statutes, with an "archaeological" approach and suggesting that the former is inevitable over time).

precedent to the new circumstances, in the process adjusting the precedent yet more.[19] This is a lot of discretion at each step in this process. When you add up all the cases over time, the discretion is enlarged. This point should not be overstated, however. A judge's discretion in applying binding precedent is often strongly constrained by the reasoning of that precedent[20] and by a consensus about how to read the precedent by lower courts and by neutral scholars.[21]

Consider our third public value for statutory interpretation, namely, the purposes of governance. As with democratic legitimacy, the story here is mixed. *Stare decisis* serves some of the purposes of governance, but at significant and variable costs. An institutional value of *stare decisis* is that it asks judges to perform duties and analyses where they are the experts. If law schools still do not teach law students enough about the legislative process and reasoning from statutory text and structure, they do a very good job introducing students to reasoning from precedents. A large majority of appellate judges not only excelled at this analysis in law school, but impressed the legal community with their precedent-based reasoning ability in handling real world problems. While judges, understandably, tend to exaggerate the coherence of precedents and the predictability of reasoning from the body of precedent, this is a system that has over the centuries delivered a rule of law that the rest of the world might envy.

If judges are skilled at filling in the details of a statute with precedent-based rules, then *stare decisis* gives the community greater security and confidence that the rules governing park use will be stable, until and unless the legal process changes them through democratic deliberation.[22] These *reliance interests* are important

---

19 See Re, *Narrowing Precedent in the Supreme Court*, 114 Colum. L. Rev. at 1875–86 (exploring the various legitimate reasons for judges to narrow precedents); Solan, *Precedent in Statutory Interpretation* (draft 2016) (arguing that the piling up of precedents over time often increases judicial discretion).

20 E.g., *Arizona v. United States,* 132 S.Ct. 2492, 2500–01 (2012) (carefully parsing the Court's immigration preemption precedents by a bipartisan majority); id. at 2524–35 (Alito, J., concurring in part and dissenting in part) (applying precedent to reach results surprising for a very conservative jurist); *Los Angeles County, California v. Humphries,* 562 U.S. 29 (2011) (closely following a § 1983 precedent's reasoning to solve a potentially divisive issue regarding municipal liability for violating federal law).

21 E.g., *CSX Transp., Inc. v. McBride,* 131 S.Ct. 2630, 2637–41 (2013) (scrupulous application of precedent in light of its reasoning as well as its reception by lower courts and scholars); *People v. Hampton,* 992 N.E.2d 1059, 1064–66 (N.Y. 2013) (similar).

22 *CSX Transp.,* 131 S.Ct. at 2640–41. On the stability and reliance values of *stare decisis,* see Edward H. Levi, *An Introduction to Legal Reasoning,* 15 U. Chi. L.

byproducts of the rule of law discussed earlier. If the courts have authoritatively ruled that Segways are not covered by the Park Safety Act, and hence are allowed in the park, tour guides and companies may invest in such mechanisms. The Park Police would internalize the Court's holding and its reasoning in its handbook for officers and would probably extrapolate from that ruling other potential "vehicles" that ought to be allowed as well, such as hoverboards. If the Court of Appeals overruled its precedent and all of a sudden announced that Segways are "vehicles" barred from Lafayette Park, that ruling would unsettle all sorts of reliance interests built upon the earlier decision. Congress, of course, can override the earlier decision, but only after a deliberative process considering the interests of relevant stakeholders. Moreover, Congress can provide a series of transition rules to make the harm to reliance interests less severe. As a general matter, congressional alteration of a rule of law is much more legitimate than a similar alteration by the courts or the executive.[23]

But faithfully following precedents also has its costs, which might dwarf the benefits of *stare decisis* if judges followed earlier rulings too strictly. Against the value of the foregoing reliance interests must be balanced possible ossification costs of legal rules that are set early on and cannot be changed when circumstances expose their dysfunction. Courts are not unresponsive to these costs, though. Recall that one value of *stare decisis* is its incentive value for judges to write cautious decisions and to address only those issues whose resolution seems clear to them. Additionally, statutory precedents themselves evolve over time, as they address unforeseen circumstances and as judges adjust those precedents to fit the practicalities of the situation and the evolving legal terrain.[24] Finally, as explained below, courts do sometimes overrule statutory precedents that have become isolated from other developments in society and the law. How to balance the stability-of-the-law value of *stare decisis* against its potential ossification costs is a delicate balance that is reflected in the judicial doctrines that allow

---

Rev. 501, 540 (1948); Powell, Stare Decisis *and Judicial Restraint,* 47 Wash. & Lee L. Rev. at 286–87.

[23] On the greater legitimacy of legislative overrides over judicial updating, see Christiansen & Eskridge, *Congressional Overrides*, 92 Tex. L. Rev. at 1415–22.

[24] Re, *Narrowing Precedent in the Supreme Court*, 114 Colum. L. Rev. at 1875–87.

overrulings under limited circumstances.[25] Whether our legal system has achieved the optimal balance of stability and adaptation is doubtful, but no institutional cost-benefit analysis has successfully demonstrated that another system would work better in the areas where Congress and state legislatures have delegated gapfilling authority to courts.[26]

In short, our legal system has long accepted the idea that judges must follow statutory precedents. As we shall see, statutory precedents enjoy super-strong *stare decisis* effect. While I am doubtful about this boost theoretically afforded statutory precedents, ordinary *stare decisis* for statutory precedents probably redounds to the benefit of the country as a whole. As a positive matter of describing our legal system, I should insist that precedent be recognized as a core source of meaning in statutory interpretation. Any theory that claims to focus exclusively on either statutory text or legislative purpose is a nonstarter in our legal system. Now, let's see how this process works.

The *Stare Decisis* Rule

Because the Supreme Court is unlikely to accept appeals involving the local park safety statute, the U.S. Court of Appeals for the District of Columbia Circuit will, in effect, be the final word on the interpretation of our hypothetical Park Safety Act of 1992. Unlike the Supreme Court, which has virtually complete discretion whether to grant a petition for review, the Court of Appeals must hear any appeal from a lower court judgment applying the Park Safety Act. Although the Court of Appeals may dispose of many appeals summarily, even summary dispositions may be cited as precedent.[27]

---

[25] On the balance between stability and evolution that courts must attempt in applying precedent, see Daniel A. Farber, *The Rule of Law and the Law of Precedents*, 90 Minn. L. Rev. 1173, 1175–76 (2006); Stephen M. Rich, *A Matter of Perspective: Textualism,* Stare Decisis, *and Federal Employment Discrimination Law,* 87 S. Cal. L. Rev. 1197, 1203–04 (2014).

[26] Compare Adrian Vermeule, *Judging Under Uncertainty* (2006) (propounding a complicated institutional cost-benefit analysis highly critical of judicial competence in statutory cases), with William N. Eskridge Jr., *No Frills Textualism*, 119 Harv. L. Rev. 2041 (2006) (criticizing Professor Vermeule's analysis as unsupported by evidence and ultimately indeterminate).

[27] Since 2005, Rule 32.1 of the Federal Rules of Appellate Procedure has allowed counsel to cite and rely on unpublished decisions. For commentary critical of appellate court efforts to prohibit citation to unreported decisions, see, e.g., Martha Dragich Pearson, *Citation of Unpublished Decisions as Precedent,* 55 Hastings L.J. 1235 (2004); Lawrence J. Fox, *Those Unpublished Opinions: An Appropriate Expedience or an Abdication of Responsibility?*, 32 Hofstra L. Rev. 1215 (2004).

Hogan v. National Park Service is the Court's initial effort to grapple with the meaning of the Act. In this hypothetical world, the Court holds that motorized bicycles are "vehicles" covered by section 2 of the Park Safety Act but are not "bicycles" regulated more gently under the section 3 proviso. Henceforth, the National Park Service, the U.S. Park Police, and federal judges know that motorized bicycles are barred from the park. Attorneys representing motorized bicycle riders cited for violating section 2 will tell their clients that they cannot, consistent with legal ethics, argue to the judge that motorized bicycles are not really "vehicles" covered by the statute—unless they can summon up arguments for overruling *Hogan* (an exercise very unlikely in the short term).

Moreover, *Hogan* will perform a settlement function for other mechanisms whose status (as "vehicles" vel non) is uncertain if we only have the statutory text as our guide. For example, does *Hogan* have implications for youthful Billy Treanor, whom the Park Police fine for riding his skateboard in Lafayette Park? At first blush, one would think not, because a motorized bicycle (illustrated at the front of this chapter) is so different from a skateboard. Yet the case of the motorized bicycle will be relevant to the subsequent case of the skateboard, because the Court's *reasoning* in *Hogan* will have bearing on, and often be decisive for, the judicial deliberation about how the Park Safety Act applies to the skateboarder.[28]

What is legally relevant about a precedent is not just the result (motorized bicycles are vehicles), but also the reasoning by which the Court justifies its result. The precise reasoning in the statutory precedent might make a big difference in the resolution of the new case. Although American courts generally do not give *stare decisis* effect to the interpretive method of prior decisions, they do treat as authoritative the conclusions of law invoked by the Court as necessary to justify its specific application, namely, the *holding* of the case.[29] To be sure, subsequent courts may recharacterize a

---

[28] For detailed analyses of the reasoning as well as holdings of statutory precedents, see, e.g., *Kimble*, 135 S.Ct. at 2407-14; *United States v. Home Concrete & Supply, LLC,* 132 S.Ct. 1836, 1839–44 (2012); *CSX Transp.,* 131 S.Ct. at 2636–41; *CBOCS West, Inc. v. Humphries,* 553 U.S. 442, 445–48, 457 (2008); *Ledbetter v. Goodyear Tire & Rubber Co.,* 550 U.S. 615, 625–28 (2007).

[29] Cf. *Seminole Tribe of Fla. v. Florida*, 517 U.S. 44, 67 (1996) (*stare decisis* requires that "it is not only the result but also those portions of the opinion necessary to that result by which we are bound"); Henry Paul Monaghan, *Stare Decisis and Constitutional Adjudication*, 88 Colum. L. Rev. 723, 764–65 (1988). See generally Rich, *Matter of Perspective,* 87 S. Cal. L. Rev. at 1206–18 (demonstrating that the Supreme

precedent's holding, often unconsciously, but they generally take it seriously. Assume that the Court of Appeals in *Hogan* justified its conclusion in the following manner:

HOGAN'S HOLDING

1. The 1992 statute completely bars "vehicles" from Lafayette Park but allows "bicycles" so long as they are being pushed and not ridden.
2. The prototypical "vehicle" is a speedy, typically motorized, mechanism used primarily to transport persons or things from one place to another.
3. The prototypical "bicycle" is a speedy, nonmotorized mechanism with two wheels, propelled by human pedaling.
4. A "motorized bicycle" is a speedy mechanism with two wheels for conveying a person from one place to another.
5. A "motorized bicycle" is a motorized mechanism and is only partially propelled by human pedaling.
6. *Therefore*, a motorized bicycle is a "vehicle" completely barred by the statute and not a "bicycle" regulated less severely by the statute.

(I am omitting the sources of interpretive guidance the Court relied on for these conclusions of law.) How would this articulation of the holding of the *Hogan* precedent affect the trial judge's deliberation about whether to apply the statutory prohibition to Treanor's most excellent skateboard adventure in Lafayette Park? Jot down your answer: Is a skateboard a "vehicle" after *Hogan*?

Although the Treanor case is easily "distinguishable" from *Hogan* (i.e., a skateboard is a very different mechanism from a motorized bicycle), the Court of Appeals' reasoning is relevant to both district and circuit judges applying that precedent in future cases. The reasoning in Hogan's case suggests a definitional principle that "vehicle" in this law means speedy, and typically motorized, mechanisms for transporting persons and things from one place to another. Because the Court in *Hogan* gave some emphasis to motorization, we don't know whether nonmotorized but speedy

---

Court does not give *stare decisis* effect to methodology, but does give *stare decisis* effect to a precedent's identification of an ordinary meaning or legislative purpose).

skateboards fall outside the statute's domain. Given its secondary focus on motorization, the statutory precedent makes it more likely that skateboards do fall outside the statutory bar than would be the case without the statutory precedent.

An important doctrinal distinction is between a precedent's *holding* (the reasoning necessary to support the conclusion of law) and its *dicta* ("words" that are not necessary to justify the legal result).[30] The reasoning chain above represents *Hogan*'s holding, but the Court's decision will of course have a much more extended discussion. Mindful of the practice that judges not "decide too much," the Court might set aside a pitch made by the government, to announce a definition of "vehicles" tied only to their speed and risk of mischief. "Because motorized bicycles are both motorized and speedy, we need not address the government's sensible suggestion that nonmotorized mechanisms ought to be considered vehicles if they are fast and dangerous." This sentence is dictum; as a matter of standard doctrine, it is not binding on the Court of Appeals or on lower courts.[31] But as a matter of practical application, attorneys and judges in future cases will take this sentence into account. Counsel who advise her skateboard client, in a future case, that this dictum is irrelevant and that the Court of Appeals would not extend *Hogan* to a nonmotorized mechanism, is committing malpractice. The language may not be binding as a matter of *stare decisis*, but it has some modest predictive value, especially in the short term.[32]

Consider a different way the Court of Appeals could have analyzed and decided Hogan's case. Because a motorized bicycle might be considered a "bicycle," the Court could have ruled that Hogan violated the bicycle proviso, without addressing the larger question whether it is also a vehicle. If that had been the basis for the Court's disposition—the *holding* of the precedent—it would probably have no effect on Billy Treanor's case, for a skateboard is certainly not a bicycle. This variation suggests an important lesson: The precise reasoning of a judicial precedent affects its relevance for future cases. If the Court lays out a broad rule as part of its holding, namely, the basis of its decision (e.g., all motorized vehicles fall

---

[30] See Michael Abramowicz & Maxwell Stearns, *Defining Dicta*, 57 Stan. L. Rev. 953 (2005).

[31] For decisions where courts declined to apply dicta from prior statutory decisions, see, e.g., *Klein v. United States,* 235 P.3d 42, 85, 87 (Cal. 2010).

[32] For caution about the holding-dictum dichotomy, see David Klein & Neal Devins, *Dicta, Schmicta: Theory Versus Practice in Lower Court Making*, 54 Wm. & Mary L. Rev. 2021, 2048 (2013).

within the law, anything without a motor does not), that reasoning ought to have a great deal of influence in subsequent cases. As we saw above, a broad holding accompanied by even broader dicta will probably have more influence among lower courts. A rule for decision tightly limited to the case at hand (e.g., a motorized "bicycle" falls within the proviso) and unaccompanied by extensive dicta is likely to be less broadly influential.

Applying the reasoning in *Hogan*, the trial court in *Treanor* rules that skateboards are not "vehicles" barred by section 2, because they have no motor and are not as speedy as cars or even bicycles. Assume other trial judges follow that holding. As reflected in Figure 5, *Hogan* and *Treanor* boost the rule of law contribution already made by the ordinary meaning and whole act rules (chapters one and two).

FIGURE 5

Plain Meaning Continuum: "Driving a Vehicle" in the Park (§ 2), in Light of Statutory Purpose (§ 1) and Definition (§ 3) and Precedent (*Hogan* + *Treanor*)

Core Coverage		Penumbra	Outside the Statute
Cars & Trucks	Bicycles	Segways	Kid's Tricycles
Motorcycles	Adult Tricycles		Wheelbarrows
Motor Scooters			Skateboards
Mopeds			Roller Blades
Motorized bicycles			Baby Carriages

On the other hand, after these precedents clarify the ambit of the Park Safety Act, making clear that motorized bicycles are within its domain and skateboards are not, the law might easily become unsettled.

Assume that the government takes an appeal in *Treanor*. Pointing to evidence that skateboards can go fast and have contributed to dozens of accidents in federal parks within the District of Columbia, the National Park Service argues that they are vehicles presenting the very safety risks that called forth the statute in 1992. As for *Hogan*, the Park Service interprets the precedent through the lens of statutory purpose: The relevance of motorization was its contribution to speed and, therefore, to heightened risk of accidents. Even without a motor, skateboards pose risks of accidents; indeed, the government might be able to show that skateboards are even more injury-producing than motorized bicycles. Because of *stare decisis*, the Court of Appeals is not going to overrule *Hogan*—but *stare decisis* does not prevent an appellate court from reading a precedent expansively or recharacterizing it. Reversing the District Court, the Court of Appeals holds in *National Park Service v. Treanor* that speed and documented safety problems justify an interpretation of *Hogan* (and the statute) to regulate some nonmotorized vehicles that go at dangerous speeds or are hard to control.

A corollary to the *stare decisis* rule is that appellate courts ought to be cautious about recharacterizing the reasoning of leading precedents.[33] Much of the rule of law value of *stare decisis* flows from the fact that officials, lawyers, and judges take the reasoning seriously and use it to figure out how the statute will apply in future cases. In the wake of the Court of Appeals' decision in *Treanor,* the statute now extends to nonmotorized vehicles that are speedy enough to create significant risks of serious injuries to park users, and so the police wonder whether they should also be applying it to roller blades or roller skates. Before *Treanor*, the police confronted with a roller-blading youth would have been more reluctant to apply the Park Safety Act than they would be after *Treanor*. The new precedent opened up new possibilities, reflected in Revised Figure 5.

REVISED FIGURE 5

Plain Meaning Continuum: "Driving a Vehicle" in the Park (§ 2), in Light of Statutory Purpose (§ 1) and Definition (§ 3) and Precedent (*Hogan* + *Treanor*)

Core Coverage		Penumbra	Outside the Statute
Cars & Trucks	Bicycles	Segways	Kid's Tricycles
Motorcycles	Adult Tricycles		Wheelbarrows
Motor Scooters		Sleighs	
			Baby Carriages
Motorized Bicycles		Roller Blades	
Skateboards		Roller Skates	

This process is a limitation on the settlement function of precedent, especially precedent that confirms a broad ambit for a statutory scheme. Courts are tempted to recharacterize precedent if it fits the

[33] Rich, *A Matter of Perspective,* 87 S. Cal. L. Rev. at 1203–04; Solan, *Precedent in Statutory Interpretation* (draft 2016); see Barry Friedman, *The Wages of Stealth Overruling (with Particular Attention to* Miranda v. Arizona), 99 Geo. L.J. 1 (2010); Christopher J. Peters, *Under-the-Table Overruling*, 54 Wayne L. Rev. 1067 (2008). But see Re, *Narrowing Precedent in the Supreme Court*, 114 Colum. L. Rev. at 1865–71 (arguing that precedential narrowing is often defensible).

new case rather poorly; the judges deciding *Hogan* probably did not even consider the possibility of skateboards wreaking havoc in the park, and the *Treanor* judges are updating the law with new information not available to either the Court of Appeals in *Hogan* or Congress when it enacted the law. But if courts engage in too much recharacterization of precedent, they squander much of the rule of law value for *stare decisis*, and may sacrifice the legitimacy of the judiciary in the process.

The foregoing thought experiment reveals the normative complexity of a legal system relying on judicial precedents as the primary mechanism for filling in the details of the statutory scheme. On the whole, *Hogan* and *Treanor* carry forth the rule of law by resolving hard cases where the statutory text is ambiguous *and* by providing justifications that will help resolve cases involving other conveyances. But there is a rule of law tradeoff insofar as the motorized bicycle and skateboard decisions create new openings for regulatory application that seemed foreclosed before those precedents. And there is a democracy tradeoff insofar as judges develop the law through case-by-case adjudication and legislators fail to amend the statute to codify or override those decisions.

Treanor also illustrates how the rule of law and the governance values of statutory interpretation may clash. The District Court's libertarian interpretation creates a more predictable legal regime, but at the expense of the statute's carrying out its safety function (if the government's statistics are true). The Court of Appeals' regulatory interpretation advances the statutory goal, but at some expense to predictability. Looking at future cases, the Court of Appeals' focus on speed and likelihood of serious injury is a more context-dependent inquiry than the mechanical one suggested by the District Court, namely, does the conveyance have a motor? A bright-line rule limiting the statute to motor vehicles would have been easier to administer as a clear rule of law, but at the risk of allowing dangerous mechanisms in the park. This is the famous problem of (bright-line) rules versus (fuzzier) standards: Neither provides the best approach in all cases, and over time the balance between rules and standards will usually change.[34] If judges believe the safety project for Lafayette Park is a matter of great complexity, they will formulate narrow rules and

---

[34] On rules versus standards, see Hart & Sacks, *The Legal Process,* 139–41 (Eskridge & Frickey eds.) (the classic articulation of rules versus standards as different strategies for legal regulation), as well as Pierre Schlag, *Rules and Standards,* 33 U.C.L.A. L. Rev. 379 (1985); Kathleen M. Sullivan, *The Supreme Court, 1991 Term—Foreword: The Justices of Rules and Standards,* 106 Harv. L. Rev. 22 (1992).

fuzzy standards—but over time a pattern of accidents may press judges to announce broader bright-line rules.

Now consider the application of the Park Safety Act to Segways, two-wheeled self-balancing conveyances powered by electric (battery-charged) motors, of the sort illustrated earlier in this chapter. Segways were first marketed around the turn of the millennium, and so they did not exist when Congress enacted the Park Safety Act in 1992. These days, Washington, D.C. is filled with Segways, many of which are used by guides giving visitors tours of the nation's capital. The Park Police decide to crack down on Segways and issue a citation to Mike Giannotto, a Segway tour guide as he leads his tourists through Lafayette Park one day.

How should a trial judge decide the new case, *National Park Service v. Giannotto*? Does the Park Safety Act bar Segways? Would you be inclined to read the text and structure of the Park Safety Act to regulate Segways? Does your answer change once you read the Court of Appeals' decisions in *Hogan* and *Treanor*? Jot down your answers in the margin.

As I read the statute, Segways can easily fall under the definition of "vehicle" as "any mechanism for conveying a person from one place to another" (section 3). Almost any dictionary definition of Segway (as well as the one in Wikipedia) calls it a "vehicle." Like the examples listed in section 3 (automobiles, motorcycles, motor scooters), Segways are motorized; that their motor is battery-driven does not make them different from electric automobiles, which are clearly included within the statute. The big difference between Segways and the listed motorized vehicles is that the former can only go ten to twelve miles per hour. Hence, their capacity for inflicting serious injuries upon park visitors is much less than is the capacity of automobiles, motorcycles, and other speedy motor vehicles.

Whether the Park Safety Act applies to Segways is a tough question, one not clearly answered by the statutory text and structure. Nor do the *Hogan* and *Treanor* precedents provide firm guidance, because those precedents are easily "distinguishable" from the case of the Segway. This is an important point about statutory precedents. They are not determinative for future cases that are distinguishable, or materially different. What does that mean? Every case is, technically, distinguishable from every other case. The case of the skateboard is different from the case of the Segway, because they evaluate different forms of conveyance. But that is not what judges mean when they say a precedent is "distinguishable." Distinguishing a precedent entails this inquiry: Given the reasoning of the previous decision (the precedent), is the new case materially different, with regard to the principle or policy invoked by the precedent?

Recall that *Hogan* and *Treanor* applied the Park Safety Act to motorized bicycles and skateboards, respectively. Segways are, of course, different forms of conveyance—but are they materially different from motorized bicycles and skateboards, *given the reasoning of the Court in those previous decisions*? The answer to this question must consider the risk of serious injury to park visitors. Motorized bicycles characteristically zip along at twenty to thirty miles per hour and can go much faster.[35] If a motorized bicycle runs into a pedestrian, the latter can suffer serious injuries. Skateboarders have been known to reach speeds of eighty miles per hour![36] Even the typical skateboarder can generate bursts of speed well in excess of the more plodding and predictable Segways.

Are Segways involved in serious accidents? The answer is, yes, sometimes they are. In Washington, D.C., emergency rooms report many serious accidents involving Segways, including facial/head injuries and broken bones—but almost all the injuries are to users of Segways.[37] That is, people fall off of Segways, run them over the sidewalk and tumble onto the road, crash their Segways into obstacles, and occasionally plunge to their death when they drive the machine off a cliff, as happened in 2011 to James Heselden, the owner of the company manufacturing Segways.[38] It is unusual, however, for a runaway Segway to injure a third party. For example, the late Mr. Heselden was actually backing his Segway to avoid running into a dog walker, when he ventured too close to a cliff and plummeted to his death. Do skateboard and motorized bicycle accidents involve a different pattern of injuries? A quick search of the Internet suggests that many but by no means all skateboard and

---

[35] *See, e.g., 100 MPH E-Bike*, Gear Junkie, http://gearjunkie.com/raht-racer-e-bike.

[36] *Mischo Erban breaks Guinness World Record for Fastest Skateboard Speed from a Standing Position*, Telegraph, June 25, 2012.

[37] See Keith Boniface et al. *Serious Injuries Related to the Segway Personal Transporter: A Case Series*, 57 Ann. Emergency Medicine 370 (2011) (studying emergency room reports at George Washington University Hospital and reporting many accidents injuring Segway operators).

[38] *Segway Company Owner Rides Scooter Off Cliff, Dies*, NBC, Sept. 27, 2010, http://www.nbcnews.com/id/39377851/ns/world_news-europe/t/segway-company-owner-rides-scooter-cliff-dies/#.VjLJBqWARUQ (viewed March 1, 2016).

motorized bicycle injuries are to the persons riding those vehicles (often slamming into automobiles) and not to third parties.[39]

Given the *Hogan* and *Treanor* decisions, a very good case can be made for regulating Segways under the statute and, therefore, excluding them from Lafayette Park. But the issue remains debatable, because Segways really do go more slowly than the other mechanisms. Notice, however, that the case of the Segway would be easier if the reasoning of the case of the motorized bicycle (the precedent established by *Hogan*) had rested upon a reading of section 3 that found controlling the policy that all motorized vehicles are statutorily excluded from Lafayette Park (the District Court view in *Treanor*). So the difficulty and perhaps even the result of the case of the Segway is a product of the Court of Appeals' interpretation of its own precedent (*Hogan*) in *Treanor*. And a Court of Appeals that can recharacterize *Hogan* when it decides *Treanor* might just as easily recharacterize *Treanor* when it decides *Giannotto*.

In short, precedent does not always settle cases that have no clear ordinary meaning, nor a plain meaning created by consulting the whole act. Moreover, notice how the order of the litigation makes a potentially big difference. If the first case to come before the Court of Appeals were not the case of the motorized bicycle, but were the case of the Segway, the string of appellate decisions might have been different. Writing on a clean slate and influenced by an *amicus* brief's argument that Segways are important to tourism, the *Giannotto* Court might well have ruled that Segways are not covered by the Park Safety Act. The Court could have emphasized the relatively slow speed of Segways and the unlikely prospect that they would cause serious harm to other park users. With *that* decision as the leading precedent, the Court would have been less likely, in the next case, to find skateboards within the statutory domain, especially if there were evidence that skateboarders were (like Segway users) causing injuries only to themselves and not to third parties.

The importance of sequence suggests yet another reason that the path of the law is not entirely predictable after Congress passes the original statute. Depending on which potential "vehicle" generates an authoritative appellate decision first, the Park Safety Act may regulate a broad array of minor vehicles (starting with skateboards

---

[39] Automobile drivers and their passengers are rarely injured when a skateboarder or motorized bicycle runs into them, because the car is so much more formidable than the smaller vehicle. And there just don't seem to be very many serious accidents where the motorized bicycle or skateboard runs over a pedestrian.

and then Segways) or may exempt them (starting with Segways and then skateboards). Combined with the capacity of appellate judges to pick and choose among precedents and to recharacterize precedent, this thought experiment also illustrates the important role both judges and process (or just dumb luck) might play in the elaboration of statutory policy.[40]

This phenomenon teaches us something about both the rule of law and democratic accountability. A polity enjoying a stable rule of law is *not* one where the law does not evolve. Evolution to meet new circumstances is inevitable; what distinguishes the rule of law polity is that the elaboration of statutory policy is reasoned and is confined by predictable markers such as ordinary meaning. Unanticipated by the enacting legislators, Segways pose a hard case because they are motorized but relatively slow. Other new conveyances do not pose such difficulties, because they fit so snugly within the statutory parameters. Thus, the enacting Congress might not have known that electric cars would someday populate the streets of the nation's capital, but the interpreter has no difficulty whatsoever concluding that electric automobiles are statutory "vehicles" just the same as those with internal combustion engines.

As a matter of democratic accountability, judge-driven statutory evolution is less problematic so long as judges are faithful agents of the language, purpose(s), and norms reflected in the Park Safety Act. Return to Cynthia Hogan's case. Although Congress was not focusing on motorized bicycles when it enacted the vehicles in the park law, there can be little doubt that a judge applying standard reasoning should rule that motorized bicycles are regulated by the statute. Conversely, a judge who ruled that motorized bicycles are entirely excluded from the statute, would be undermining the rule of law and would be betraying the trust the democratic process had placed in her and her judicial colleagues. Such a judge might be entirely well-motivated. She might adhere to a tightly "literalist" theory of law. Because section 3 of the Park Safety Act lists included vehicles and does not list motorized bicycles, and because the proviso to section 3 only covers "bicycles" and not "motorized bicycles," she rules that motorized bicycles are not within the "letter of the law," the terms of the statute read strictly and literally. She urges Congress to update the statute. As earlier chapters have argued, such literalism, even if completely honest, is *not* faithful to the interpretive process because

---

[40] See Oona A. Hathaway, *Path Dependence in the Law: The Course and Pattern of Legal Change in a Common Law System*, 86 Iowa L. Rev. 601 (2001).

it is inconsistent with the statutory purposes and with effective governance. In my view, one shared by Justices Scalia *and* Breyer among others, literalism of this sort is not consistent with the rule of law.[41]

The sins of literalism also include denigration of the democratic process and undermining effective governance.[42] If appellate judges followed such a narrowly literalist approach to the Park Safety Act in the case of the motorized bicycle (*Hogan*), the damage of the incorrect methodology might have ripple effects, as *Hogan* would be a precedent that lower court judges and the appellate court would have to respect in the future. This could unravel the advantages of *stare decisis*—but assuming subsequent judges did not cleave to a narrow literalism for long periods of time, the damage of *Hogan* would probably fade over time and might vanish altogether if Congress overrode the decision by amending the statute to include motorized bicycles in section 3's list.[43]

As we have seen, Congress no longer responds to statutory precedents. State legislatures are more likely to codify or override controversial precedents, and someday Congress will become operational again. But in the meantime, courts are interpreting away. From a governance perspective, a regime where courts fill in the details of the statutory scheme as new mechanisms arise is a regime that is responsive to new developments, integrates them into the legal terrain, and creates public policy that is acceptable to Us the People as well as our representatives. Consider a final variation. What was a hypothetical in the movie *Back to the Future*—Marty McFly's hovercraft—has now come to the American consumer. In light of the legal text, the statutory scheme, and the precedents (*Hogan*, barring motorized bicycles, and *Treanor*, barring skateboards) is there any legal doubt whether McFly could be fined if he rode his hovercraft into Lafayette Park?

---

[41] E.g., Stephen Breyer, *Active Liberty: Interpreting Our Democratic Constitution* (2006); Antonin Scalia, *A Matter of Interpretation* (1997); John F. Manning, *What Separates Textualists from Purposivists,* 106 Colum. L. Rev. 70, 78 (2006).

[42] Hart & Sacks, *The Legal Process* (Eskridge & Frickey eds.); accord, Stephen Breyer, *Making Our Democracy Work: A Judge's View* (2010).

[43] The congressional override discussed in text might be swamped with continuing bad effects of the narrow precedent if the Court of Appeals continued to follow its reasoning, a phenomenon that occurs in civil rights statutes, for example. See Deborah A. Widiss, *Undermining Congressional Overrides: The Hydra Problem in Statutory Interpretation*, 90 Tex. L. Rev. 859 (2012).

The Super-Strong Presumption of Correctness for Statutory Precedents

Not only do judges presumptively follow statutory precedents, but most of them say they are more reluctant to overrule or adjust them than they are to overrule or adjust common law or constitutional precedents.[44] Indeed, judges and commentators have often said that heightened adherence to *stare decisis* "marks an essential difference between statutory interpretation on the one hand and [common] law and constitutional interpretation on the other."[45] Like the ordinary meaning rule and the whole act rule, this *super-strong presumption of correctness for statutory precedents* purports to be a foundation for the application of federal statutes in the modern regulatory state. Like the U.S. Supreme Court, the New York Court of Appeals follows super-charged *stare decisis* in statutory cases,[46] as do other state high courts, such as the Texas Supreme Court.[47] But the doctrine is not universally accepted among state judges. The California and Florida Supreme Courts, for example, do not routinely follow a super-strong presumption of correctness and, instead, treat statutory precedents as matters of ordinary *stare decisis*, with occasionally more bite.[48] Perhaps alone among state supreme courts,

---

[44] On the super-strong importance of precedents in statutory interpretation, see, e.g., *Boys Market, Inc. v. Retail Clerk's Union*, 398 U.S. 235, 257–58 (1970) (Black, J., dissenting); Eskridge, *Overruling Statutory Precedents*, 76 Geo. L.J. at 1361–69; Levi, *Introduction to Legal Reasoning*, 15 U. Chi. L. Rev. at 540; C. Paul Rogers III, *Judicial Interpretation of Statutes: The Example of Baseball and the Antitrust Laws*, 14 Houston L. Rev. 611, 626 (1977).

[45] Levi, *Introduction to Legal Reasoning*, 15 U. Chi. L. Rev. at 540 (quotation in text); see *Patterson v. McLean Credit Union,* 491 U.S. 164, 172–73 (1989); *Flood v. Kuhn,* 407 U.S. 258, 282–84 (1972).

[46] E.g., *State Farm Mut. Auto. Ins. Co. v. Fitzgerald,* 38 N.E.3d 325, 339–40 (N.Y. 2015); *People v. Damiano,* 663 N.E.2d 607, 613–15 (N.Y. 1996) (Simons, J., concurring) (New York Court of Appeals almost never overrules its statutory precedents); *People v. Hobson,* 348 N.E.2d 894, 902 (N.Y. 1976) (Breitel, C.J.). But compare *People v. Rudolph,* 997 N.E.2d 457, 458–59 (N.Y. 2014) (majority willing to overrule a statutory precedent to protect youthful offenders), with id. at 466–68 (Read, J., dissenting) (objecting that the overrule was not consistent with the Court's *stare decisis* jurisprudence).

[47] E.g., *Southwestern Bell Tel. Co. v. Mitchell,* 276 S.W.3d 443, 447 (Tex. 2008); *Fiess v. State Farm Lloyds,* 202 S.W.3d 744, 749–50 (Tex. 2006); *Grapevine Excavation, Inc. v. Md. Lloyds,* 35 S.W.3d 1, 5 (Tex. 2000). But see *Marsh USA, Inc. v. Cook,* 354 S.W.3d 764, 788–94 (Tex. 2011) (Green, J., dissenting) (assailing the majority's implicit overruling of a statutory precedent notwithstanding legislative acquiescence).

[48] E.g., *People v. Whitmer,* 329 P.3d 154, 159–60 (Cal. 2014) (reinterpreting precedent and discounting legislature acquiescence); *People v. Jones*, 278 P.3d 821, 823–27 (Cal. 2012) (overruling one important statutory precedent and ignoring another one, without the super-strong justifications required for overruling federal statutory

the Michigan Supreme Court has, as a practical matter since 1999, afforded little or no effective presumption of correctness for statutory precedents that a current majority believe did not correctly apply their understanding of plain meaning.[49]

The precept of super-strong *stare decisis* for statutory precedents is not new to American law. Reflecting American common law's traditional devotion to *stare decisis,* nineteenth-century judges, especially in contract and property cases, treated statutory precedents as glosses on the statutory text itself—and hence formally untouchable by subsequent judges (though of course subject to future legislative amendments). "After a statute has been settled by judicial construction, the construction becomes, so far as contract rights acquired under it are concerned, as much a part of the statute as the text itself, and a change of decision is to all intents and purposes the same in its effect on contracts as an amendment of the law by means of a legislative enactment."[50]

Once the modern administrative state replaced the common law as the regulatory baseline, some judges and scholars advocated a relaxed approach to *stare decisis* for statutory precedents, along the lines now practiced by the Michigan Supreme Court. That is, a court should not be "inexorably bound by its own precedents, but, in the interest of uniformity of treatment to litigants, and of stability and certainty in the law * * * will follow the rule of law which it has

---

precedents); *Bouton v. USAA Cas. Ins. Co.,* 186 P.3d 1, 7–8 (Cal. 2008) (overruling a recent statutory precedent, without any of the drama that accompanies an overruling by federal courts); *Brown v. Nagelhout,* 84 So.3d 304, 309–10 (Fla. 2012) (overruling a statutory precedent under normal precepts of common law *stare decisis*); cf. *Coicou v. State,* 39 So.3d 237, 243 (Fla. 2010) (fairly casual approach to *stare decisis*).

[49] E.g., *People v. Gardner,* 753 N.W.2d 78, 84–91 (Mich. 2008); *Robinson v. City of Detroit,* 613 N.W.2d 307, 319–22 (Mich. 2000) (extensive discussion of considerations that might save a statutory precedent, but ultimately overruling three landmark precedents because the majority found them inconsistent with plain meaning); Marilyn Kelly & John Postulka, *The Fatal Weakness in the Michigan Supreme Court's Majority's Textualist Approach to Statutory Construction,* 10 T.M. Cooley J. Prac. & Clinical L. 287, 288–93 (2008) (arguing that the textualist majority overruled statutory precedents with insufficient regard for *stare decisis*); Sedler, *Michigan Supreme Court,* Stare Decisis, 55 Wayne L. Rev. at 1929–41 (discussing the unprecedented amount of overruling statutory precedents the Court accomplished in less than a decade). The Montana Supreme Court has also been criticized for applying *stare decisis* unevenly. Jeffrey T. Renz, Stare Decisis *in Montana,* 65 Mont. L. Rev. 41 (2004).

[50] *Douglass v. Pike County,* 101 U.S. 677, 687 (1879) (quotation in text); see *Kimble,* 135 S.Ct. at 2409–12 (emphasizing the super-importance of *stare decisis* when precedent defines people's contract or property rights); *Environmental Processing Sys., L.C. v. FPL Farming, Ltd.,* 457 S.W.3d 414, 419 (Tex. 2015) (Texas courts afford super-strong *stare decisis* effect to precedents involving property rights).

established in earlier cases unless clearly convinced that the rule was originally erroneous or is no longer sound because of changed conditions and that more good than harm would come by departing from precedent."[51] In the New Deal era and afterwards, however, almost all judges and most scholars have rejected such a relaxed version of *stare decisis.* And the U.S. Supreme Court says that it adheres to the super-strong presumption of correctness, on the ground that Congress and not the Court is more institutionally competent to override incorrect or obsolete precedents. Indeed, the New Deal Court often treated Congress's failure to override questionable judicial decisions as a reason for the Court itself to be especially reluctant to overrule them.[52]

Scholars were long dismissive of this rationale, for they believed that Congress rarely revised Supreme Court statutory decisions. Like many other academic assumptions, this belief was mistaken. Between 1968 and 1998, Congress regularly overrode Supreme Court statutory precedents; indeed, there is some evidence that government agencies and private groups brought almost half of the Court's decisions, and most of the controversial ones, to the attention of congressional committees and induced some kind of legislative deliberation during this golden age of overrides.[53] Researchers have found that when Congress overrides the Court, the process is one that is deliberative and enjoys the participation of most of the stakeholders interested in the operation of the particular statutory scheme. Precisely as the Supreme Court assumes, the override process is one that is

---

[51] J.W. Moore & R.S. Oglebay, *The Supreme Court, Stare Decisis and Law of the Case*, 21 Tex. L. Rev. 514, 539–40 (1943); accord, Justice William O. Douglas, *Stare Decisis*, 49 Colum. L. Rev. 735 (1949); *Robinson,* 613 N.W.2d at 319–22 (Michigan Supreme Court, following these sources).

[52] *Burnet v. Coronado Oil & Gas Co.*, 285 U.S. 393, 406–07 (1932) (Brandeis, J., dissenting) (leading statement of the proposition in text). For early Supreme Court decisions reaffirming questionable precedents based upon Justice Brandeis's rationale, see, e.g., *Toolson v. New York Yankees, Inc.*, 346 U.S. 356, 356–57 (1953) (per curiam); *United States v. South Buffalo Ry.*, 333 U.S. 771 (1948); *Cleveland v. United States*, 329 U.S. 14, 18 (1946); *Screws v. United States*, 325 U.S. 91, 109–13 (1945) (plurality opinion); *Helvering v. Griffiths*, 318 U.S. 371 (1943); *cf. Commissioner* v. *Estate of Church*, 335 U.S. 632, 690 (1949) (Frankfurter, J., dissenting) (listing cases from previous decade in which reenactment of statute reinforced earlier judicial decision).

[53] William N. Eskridge Jr., *Overriding Supreme Court Statutory Interpretation Decisions*, 101 Yale L.J. 331, 341–43 (1991) (examining judiciary committee review of Supreme Court statutory decisions falling within the committees' jurisdiction, 1978–88).

democratically legitimate and an engine of relatively effective governance.[54]

On the other hand, congressional responsiveness is uneven, and increasingly so. Most of the statutory arenas that generate Supreme Court decisions are ones where Congress has regularly overridden the Court—especially the law of the workplace, civil rights law, bankruptcy and tax law, environmental law, criminal law and procedure, civil procedure and federal jurisdiction, and intellectual property law. But the override process is biased in favor of state actors and agencies. Specifically, the Department of Justice and other federal agencies are the biggest winners in the politics of overrides, followed by state and local governments. Ironically, racial minorities, people with disabilities, and women are also well-represented in the politics of overrides—but distinctly underrepresented are the interests of poor people, beneficiaries of social welfare programs, consumers and debtors, and (most of all) prisoners and criminal defendants.[55] Even more troubling is that the congressional override process has slowed down considerably since President Clinton's impeachment in 1998 and has almost entirely dried up since 2011.[56] Because the override process operates in a slanted way and now quite rarely, we should be cautious about applying *stare decisis* too dogmatically in federal statutory cases. The same might not be true at the state level, where legislatures codify and override statutory interpretations much more regularly. Even the famously gridlocked New York Legislature has responded repeatedly to New York Court of Appeals statutory interpretations.[57]

Consider an example of the operation of super-strong *stare decisis*, in the context of our vehicles in the park law. Assume, for this purpose, that the case of the skateboard (*Treanor*), and not the case of the motorized bicycle (*Hogan*), generates the first appellate decision interpreting the Park Safety Act. Further assume that the Court of Appeals for the D.C. Circuit in this revised scenario rules that

---

[54] Jeb Barnes, *Overruled? Legislative Overrides, Pluralism, and Contemporary Court-Congress Relations* (2004); Christiansen & Eskridge, *Congressional Overrides, 1967–2011.*

[55] Christiansen & Eskridge, *Congressional Overrides, 1967–2010,* 92 Tex. L. Rev. at 1375–87 (detailed analysis of relative winners and losers in the congressional override process, compared with the judicial process in particular).

[56] Id. at 1331–33, 1340–53; Hasen, *End of the Dialogue?*, 86 S. Cal. L. Rev. 205, 208–10, 217–19.

[57] See *Rudolph*, 997 N.E.2d at 467–68 (Read, J., dissenting) (providing many recent examples where New York Legislature overrode the Court of Appeals' statutory decisions).

skateboards are not "vehicles" regulated by the Act. The Court's reasoning is as follows:

TREANOR'S HOLDING

1. The Park Safety Act only applies to conveyances that can cause serious injuries if involved in an accident in the park.
2. Skateboards can only go five to ten miles per hour and so pose virtually no risk of accidents causing serious injuries.
3. *Therefore*, skateboards are not "vehicles" regulated by the Park Safety Act.

Unless reversed (on direct appeal) or abrogated (in a subsequent decision) by the Supreme Court or overruled by the D.C. Circuit sitting *en banc*, this rule of law is embedded in the statute.

Twenty years after *Treanor*, the National Park Service conducts a study of accidents and injuries in federal and municipal parks in the District. The study finds that there were very few serious accidents in Lafayette Park in those two decades—but there were forty-one reported accidents involving skateboards and requiring medical attention, ten of which required hospitalization. While most of the accidents injured only persons riding their own skateboards, eleven injured third parties, three of whom were hospitalized. No other type of accident came close to the numbers generated for skateboards in Lafayette Park, now that motorized vehicles and bicycles are no longer operated there. The report also finds that skateboards are involved in a significant number of accidents in all of the city's parks. Finally, the report notes that skateboards are now sometimes operated at speeds in excess of twenty miles per hour and that skateboarders have reached speeds of eighty miles per hour. This report generates a new attitude toward skateboards by the regulatory authorities.

Under this revised scenario, assume that the U.S. Park Police then assess a fine against young Liam Treanor for riding his skateboard dangerously in Lafayette Park. Ironically, Liam is the son of William Treanor, once a skater kid but now a distinguished law professor and dean. Liam "lawyers up" (with one of his father's law buddies) and moves to dismiss the charges and to enjoin the police from enforcing the no vehicles in the park law against him and other skateboarders. His lawyer confidently invokes the twenty-year-old William Treanor precedent. The U.S. Attorney, representing the

National Park Service, argues that *Treanor* should be overruled, because it rests upon a demonstrably false premise in step two of the reasoning process depicted above. Today, no one disputes that skateboarders often travel over twenty miles per hour, and all the expert studies conclude that skateboards are involved in more serious injuries suffered by persons in parks, than are occasioned by any other cause (including firearms). If you were the district court judge, would you dismiss the citation against young Treanor? Specifically, would you follow and apply *Treanor*, the statutory precedent? Would it make a difference that you were a court of appeals judge instead? Jot down your thoughts in the margin.

To begin with, it is important to understand that the District Court, the trial court in the federal system, has no authority to overrule or ignore the Court of Appeals' precedent, namely, *Treanor*. As an authoritative appellate construction of the Park Safety Act, the precedent is binding on all federal judges in the D.C. Circuit unless it has been abrogated by the Supreme Court, overruled by the Court of Appeals, or overridden by Congress.[58] So in the ordinary case where the binding precedent is "on point" and not honestly distinguishable, the District Court must reject Liam Treanor's arguments and must refuse to dismiss charges against him. If Liam is convicted, he can appeal the judgment against him and can ask the Court of Appeals to overrule *Treanor*. The Court of Appeals has the authority to overrule its own statutory precedents—but those judges will be reluctant to overrule *Treanor*.

The punch line for ordinary *stare decisis* is that an error of fact, a logical gap, an erroneous premise, or an offbeat reason does not justify the overruling of a precedent. "Respecting *stare decisis* means sticking to some wrong decisions. The doctrine rests on the idea, as Justice Brandeis famously wrote, that it is usually 'more important that the applicable rule of law be settled than that it be settled right.' Indeed, *stare decisis* has consequence only to the extent it sustains incorrect decisions; correct judgments have no need for that principle to prop them up. Accordingly, an argument that [the Court] got something wrong—even a good argument to that effect—cannot by itself justify scrapping settled precedent."[59]

---

[58] *Auto Equity Sales, Inc. v. Superior Court of Santa Clara Cnty.*, 369 P.2d 937, 939–40 (Cal. 1962) (lower courts absolutely bound by supreme court statutory rulings).

[59] *Kimble,* 135 S.Ct. at 2409, quoting *Burnet*, 285 U.S. at 406 (Brandeis, J., dissenting); accord, *Palladino v. CNY Centro, Inc.*, 12 N.E.3d 436, 441–42 (N.Y. 2014).

Once the Court of Appeals (or the Supreme Court) has authoritatively interpreted the Park Safety Act to be inapplicable to skateboards, the responsibility for correcting erroneous reasoning or updating the statute to reflect new experience and knowledge about the dangers of skateboards is supposed to rest with Congress. By refusing to revisit statutory precedents that look wrong in retrospect, the Court dramatically confirms the continuity of established legal rules until or unless changed through the normal legislative process.[60]

Consider another possibility. The challenged precedent (*Treanor*) might be questionable for a broader reason, namely, that its decision reflected a theory of interpretation that the Court of Appeals no longer follows. A generation ago, federal courts of appeals, including the D.C. Circuit, considered the lodestar for statutory interpretation to be congressional "intent" and liberally considered legislative history. Sometimes, those courts would reject an apparent plain meaning because it was inconsistent with the legislative history. Thus, the *Treanor* precedent might have relied critically on committee report language saying that Congress did not intend to regulate purely "recreational" mechanisms such as roller skates and roller blades. By analogy, the Court of Appeals reasoned that skateboards are not "vehicles" regulated by the statute, for the same reasons roller blades are not "vehicles." Today, as a matter of statutory methodology in the federal courts, a judge needs strong justification to interpret a statute contrary to its ordinary meaning. If the William Treanor case were a matter of first impression today, the Court of Appeals for the D.C. Circuit would be very reluctant to depart from ordinary meaning because of the committee report evidence. Combined with the report on skateboard safety problems, does the problematic methodology in *Treanor* justify its overruling twenty years later by the D.C. Circuit? Jot down your answer in the margin.

The answer remains "no." If methodological disagreement allowed a subsequent Court to revisit precedents following a now-discredited statutory methodology, many statutory precedents would be vulnerable to challenge. Such an exception to *stare decisis* would be the exception that would swallow the rule.[61] On the other hand,

---

[60] *Patterson*, 491 U.S. at 172–73; see *Kimble,* 135 S.Ct. at 2410–12; *Bilski* v. *Kappos*, 561 U. S. 593, 601–602 (2010); *Watson v. United States*, 552 U.S. 74, 82–83 (2007); *Fitzgerald,* 38 N.E.3d at 339–40 (New York).

[61] For useful discussions, much of it critical, of the inapplicability of *stare decisis* to issues of methodology, see, e.g., Sydney Foster, *Should Courts Give* Stare

the methodological shift might limit the Court of Appeals' willingness to expand upon *Treanor*.[62] Thus, the Court might interpret the Park Safety Act to regulate roller blades, because of their safety hazards and notwithstanding committee report language suggesting their exclusion.

Is *stare decisis* an absolute rule? Not at all. What sounds like a relatively firm, unbending rule does have play in its joints. To begin with, *stare decisis* does not necessarily protect dicta, or statements not necessary to the legal result reached by the earlier court, nor does it always apply to reasoning in the holding that was not based upon full briefing by the parties and deliberation by the judges. Justice Felix Frankfurter explained the procedural requirements for *stare decisis* in this way: "[T]he relevant demands of *stare decisis* do not preclude considering for the first time thoroughly and in the light of the best available evidence of congressional purpose, a statutory interpretation which started as an unexamined assumption on the basis of inapplicable citations and has the claim of a dogma solely through reiteration."[63] Thus, if the only appellate interpretation of the vehicles in the park law had applied it to motorized bicycles (*Hogan*) and had stated, in dicta unnecessary to the decision, that the law does not apply to less speedy conveyances, such as skateboards, that decision would not be precedent requiring full *stare decisis* respect on the matter of skateboards. Even if later decisions assumed, without argument or deliberation, that skateboards are not covered, the procedural caveat suggests that *stare decisis* might not kick in, unless private persons or public officials had relied on that reasoning in important ways.

Additionally, appellate courts *do* sometimes overrule statutory precedents. A statutory precedent is especially vulnerable to being

---

Decisis *Effect to Statutory Interpretation Methodology?*, 96 Geo. L.J. 1863 (2008); Abbe R. Gluck, *The States as Laboratories of Statutory Interpretation: Methodological Consensus and the New Modified Textualism*, 119 Yale L.J. 1750 (2010); Jonathan R. Siegel, *The Polymorphic Principle and the Judicial Role in Statutory Interpretation*, 84 Tex. L. Rev. 339, 385 (2005).

62 E.g., *People v. Whitmer,* 329 P.3d 154, 159–60 (Cal. 2014) (reading a statutory precedent narrowly, justified by the precedent's failure to notice a relevant statute).

63 *Monroe v. Pape,* 365 U.S. 167, 220–21 (1961) (Frankfurter, J., dissenting); accord, *Johnson v. United States,* 135 S.Ct. 2551, 2561–63 (2015) (constitutional *stare decisis*); *Thompson v. North American Stainless LP,* 562 U.S. 170, 176–77 (2011); *Hohn* v. *United States*, 524 U.S. 236, 251 (1998). See generally Eskridge, *Overruling Statutory Precedents*, 76 Geo. L.J. at 1369–76 (discussing a wide array of cases where Supreme Court has invoked a proceduralist exception to overrule a statutory precedent).

overruled if (1) there has been an "intervening development of the law" that has rendered that precedent "irreconcilable with competing legal doctrines or policies," (2) the precedent has become as a "positive detriment to coherence and consistency in the law," either internally or in relation to policy objectives associated with other laws, and (3) the precedent has been proved outdated and contrary to contemporary understandings of justice and social welfare.[64] In other words, when courts overrule statutory precedents, they emphasize that they have become stranded from the current legal landscape, not that they were wrongly decided years ago. Consider how these established factors might play out in the new case of the skateboard.

Treanor settled the matter of skateboards when they might plausibly have been considered a localized issue of park safety. But recall that Lafayette Park is right across the street from the White House, and the Park Safety Act of 1992 was enacted in an era where national security concerns were much less salient than they became after terrorist attacks in Oklahoma City on April 19, 1995 and, especially, in New York City and Northern Virginia on September 11, 2001. In the wake of the Oklahoma City attack, the federal government temporarily closed off Pennsylvania Avenue between Lafayette Park and the White House; the closure was made permanent after 9/11, and security was tightened in the area. Some of the new security practices generate lawsuits.

In one (hypothetical) case, *Byrne v. National Park Service,* the D.C. Circuit upholds a new Park Service directive prohibiting people (in this case, one J. Peter Byrne) from rollerblading through the park. Although Byrne's lawyers strenuously argue that his case is covered by *Treanor*, the Court of Appeals rejects the analogy, in part because the Park Service invokes an incident where a roller-blading youth zipped across Lafayette Park, through an open White House gate, and right up to the unlocked front door of the White House itself. The newspapers had a field day with this incident, and the Secret Service, the Park Service, and the Park Police cracked down on potentially threatening behavior. What might have, before 9/11, passed as

---

[64] *Patterson,* 491 U.S. at 173–74; accord, *Kimble,* 135 S.Ct. at 2408–12 (recent survey and reaffirmation of the *Patterson* factors); *Halliburton Co.,* 134 S.Ct. at 2411–13; *John R. Sand & Gravel Co. v. United States,* 552 U.S. 130, 139 (2008); *Bell Atlantic Corp. v. Twombly,* 550 U.S. 544, 554–64 (2007). For state practice, see, e.g., *Brown v. Nagelhout,* 84 So.3d 304, 309–10 (Fla. 2012); *North Florida Women's Health & Counseling Servs., Inc. v. State,* 866 So.2d 612, 637 (Fla.2003); *People v. Rudolph,* 997 N.E.2d 457, 460–63 (N.Y. 2014) (Graffeo, J., concurring); *Marsh USA, Inc. v. Cook,* 354 S.W.3d 764, 779–80 (Tex. 2011).

innocent recreation and a minor incursion into the White House grounds now looms as a potential threat to national security.

Since 9/11, Washington, D.C. has been obsessed with national security, which has saturated statutory policies not immediately connected with anti-terrorism campaigns—like the Park Safety Act. Unfortunately, the nation's obsession with national security has coincided with the collapse of Congress as a lawmaking body, as noted above. For the time being, a gridlocked Congress is not able to override *Treanor*, the reading of the Park Safety Act that allows skateboards in Lafayette Park. Should the Court of Appeals now overrule the William Treanor precedent in order to sustain the new prosecution of Liam Treanor for skateboarding through Lafayette Park? As updated by these political and legal developments, the case for overruling *Treanor* is grounded in legal *coherence*: The precedent allowing skateboards in the park is not only based upon an erroneous factual premise, but is also at odds with a subsequent precedent (*Byrne*), as well as the nation's new post-9/11 national security meta-policy. If the Park Service pressed its case strongly, with the support of the Departments of Justice and Homeland Security, these arguments would motivate the Court of Appeals to revisit and probably overrule or dramatically narrow its statutory precedent.[65]

Consider now some important nuances relevant to the super-strong presumption of correctness of statutory precedents. As emphasized at the beginning of this chapter, the justifications for these nuances are overwhelmingly grounded in rule of law norms of legal coherence, continuity, and predictability and perhaps also in precepts of effective governance—but are not deeply or cogently grounded in realistic assumptions about how our elected representatives carry out their democratically-accountable lawmaking responsibilities.[66] The normal rule of *stare decisis* affords plenty of protection for statutory precedents, which ought to be followed and taken seriously even if judges today find their reasoning imperfect. Like all other precedents, statutory ones might be overruled when they are grievously wrong, their error is deeply inconsistent with other legal norms, and there has not been

---

[65] For the Supreme Court's willingness to overrule statutory precedents based upon similar legal coherence concerns, see, e.g., *Leegin Creative Leather Prods., Inc. v. PSKS, Inc.*, 551 U.S. 877, 901–04 (2007); *Dickerson v. United States*, 530 U.S. 428, 443 (2000); *Patterson,* 491 U.S. at 173–74; *Monell v. Department of Social Servs.*, 436 U.S. 658, 695–701 (1978). See generally *Kimble,* 135 S.Ct. at 2418–19 (Alito, J., dissenting); Eskridge, *Overruling Statutory Precedents,* 76 Geo. L.J. at 1382–85.

[66] See Bressman & Gluck, *Statutory Interpretation from the Inside: Part II.*

significant public (legislative) or private reliance on the discredited precedent.

But the super-strong presumption of correctness—the extra reluctance of courts to overrule statutory as opposed to common law precedents—is grounded in assumptions about the Court-Congress dialogue that have not been realistic for almost a generation, and have completely evaporated in the last several years.[67] Whether a statutory precedent is virtually immune to change ought to be a context-dependent inquiry and not automatic—more like the practice of the California Supreme Court than of the U.S. Supreme Court.

Rather than just declaring all statutory precedents virtually immune from overruling, the Supreme Court and state high courts should consider reliance interests. (Even the precedent-skeptical Michigan Supreme Court says that reliance might save poorly reasoned precedents, though the majority Justices almost never find the requisite reliance.[68]) Specifically, the case law supports an inquiry into reliance along the following lines:

- *Legislative reliance.* Has Congress or a state legislature relied on the questioned precedent? Has it amended or revisited the statute without adjusting a politically salient interpretation?[69] More cogently, has the legislature built upon the precedent, by amending the statute with a provision that assumes the correctness of the now-challenged precedent?[70]
- *Judicial and agency reliance.* Has the Supreme Court itself relied on the challenged precedent as a building block on which to elaborate the statutory scheme? Has

[67] For critiques of the super-strong presumption even before the congressional override process dried up, see Eskridge, *Overruling Statutory Precedents*, 76 Geo. L.J. at 1385–1409; Frank H. Easterbrook, *Stability and Reliability in Judicial Decisions*, 73 Cornell L. Rev. 422 (1988).

[68] Kelly & Postulka, *Michigan Supreme Court's Majority's Textualist Approach to Statutory Construction*, 10 T.M. Cooley J. Prac. & Clinical L. at 288–93 (highly critical analysis).

[69] For recent cases where some boost might have been appropriate, see *Kimble*, 135 S.Ct. at 2408–12; *Halliburton Co.*, 134 S.Ct. at 2411–13; *John R. Sand & Gravel Co.*, 552 U.S. at 139; *State Farm v. Fitzgerald*, 38 N.E.3d at 334–39 (New York).

[70] *People v. Williams*, 29 P.3d 197, 203–04 (Cal. 2001); cf. *Babbitt v. Sweet Home Chapter of Communities for a Great Oregon*, 515 U.S. 687, 700–01 (1995) (finding congressional reliance on an agency interpretation, which was the background assumption for 1982 amendments to the statute).

there been a lower court consensus applying and building on the precedent?[71]

- *Private reliance.* Have private persons and institutions built their lives or their businesses guided by the precedent in important ways? Outside of Michigan, even a weak precedent can be saved by longstanding industry reliance, especially when backed up by legislative and judicial reliance over a period of decades.[72]

Conversely, when a precedent is recent enough or for other reasons has not generated strong reliance interests, courts should accord normal rather than supercharged *stare decisis* to statutory precedents. In light of this general analysis, consider some canons the Supreme Court has developed for applying *stare decisis* in statutory cases.

One of the canons relaxes super-strong *stare decisis* for some statutes, while the other two canons tighten it. Overall, I urge courts not to become tied up in knots about tiers of *stare decisis.* Ordinary *stare decisis* provides strong protection for precedents, and the main variable for whether a statutory precedent ought to super-charge should be whether it has generated private or, especially, public reliance.

Canon of Relaxed* Stare Decisis *for Common Law Statutes. Congressional inertia sometimes liberates courts from super-strong *stare decisis* in statutory cases, based upon an exception the Supreme Court has recognized for "common law statutes." The Sherman Anti-Trust Act of 1890 was once the situs for some pretty remarkable Supreme Court decisions reaffirming obsolete precedents, such as the notorious precedents excluding baseball from the Sherman Act.[73] Congress rarely revisits this law, however, which has

---

[71] For a discussion of the boost a lower court consensus can provide a statutory precedent, see *CSX Transp.,* 131 S.Ct. at 2640.

[72] The classic case where law students are eager to overrule an old statutory precedent, but sound doctrine would be more reluctant, for reasons of strong private and public reliance is *Flood v. Kuhn,* 407 U.S. at 273–74, 283–84, where the Court reaffirmed professional baseball's exemption from the Sherman Act.

[73] *Flood v. Kuhn,* 407 U.S. 258, reaffirming *Federal Baseball Club v. National League*, 259 U.S. 200 (1922), as well as *Toolson v. New York Yankees, Inc.*, 346 U.S. 356 (1953); see generally Brad Snyder, *A Well Paid Slave: Curt Flood's Fight For Free Agency in Professional Sports* (2007). For a sharp critique of the Court's adherence to super-strong *stare decisis* in *Flood v. Kuhn,* see Stephen Ross, *The Story of* Flood v. Kuhn (1972): *Dynamic Statutory Interpretation, At the Time,* in *Statutory Interpretation Stories* 36–57 (Eskridge, Frickey & Garrett eds., 2011).

evolved in a common law manner through judicial decisions, richly informed by administrative guidance in the form of *amicus* briefs. Given this institutional default and the open-textured language of the statute, the Court has followed Justice John Paul Stevens's suggestion that the Sherman Act be treated as a "common law statute," with relaxed *stare decisis* for statutory precedents. Although the Court is still not eager to overrule Sherman Act precedents, it is willing to do so when old precedents do not reflect the consumer welfare economics embedded in the Court's decisions since the 1970s.[74]

The notion of a common law statute is a federal judicial invention and apparently has little if any democratic pedigree. Congress has never endorsed it, and congressional staff are not particularly comfortable with the idea.[75] State courts have not created *stare decisis* exceptions for common law statutes. What purpose does this notion serve? The rule of law could operate more predictably without this floating exception to strict *stare decisis*. The exception for common law statutes ultimately rests upon institutional practicalities needed for effective governance. If Congress enacts a statute and vests the judiciary with primary interpretational authority, and then leaves the statute to judicial development without congressional attention, then judges believe that they must assume primary responsibility for an orderly evolution of the law. And this understanding negates the primary reason for heightened *stare decisis* for statutory precedents, as explained above.

Like the Sherman Act, the Park Safety Act of 1992 is a short statute, using common law terminology in an open-textured way, and leaves gapfilling and updating duties to federal courts to carry out case by case. Thus far in our examination, Congress has neglected to amend or update the Park Safety Act. To the extent that the vehicles in the park law is a common law statute, *Treanor* might be more

---

[74] The notion that *stare decisis* ought to be more relaxed for common law statutes such as the Sherman Act originated with Justice Stevens, see *Guardians Ass'n v. Civil Serv. Comm'n*, 463 U.S. 582, 641–42 n.12 (1983) (Stevens, J., dissenting), and has been robustly applied since *State Oil Co. v. Khan*, 522 U.S. 3 (1997), overruling *Albrecht v. Herald Co.*, 390 U.S. 145 (1968). See, e.g., *Leegin Creative Leather Products v. PSKS, Inc.*, 551 U.S. 877 (2007), overruling *Dr. Miles Medical Co. v. John D. Park & Sons Co.*, 220 U.S. 373 (1911). See also *Kimble*, 135 S.Ct. at 2418 (2015) (Alito, J., dissenting) (applying the common law statute exception to a precedent interpreting the Patent Act, another generally phrased law that has been developed in a common law fashion).

[75] Bressman & Gluck, *Statutory Interpretation from the Inside: Part II*, 66 Stan. L. Rev. at 776.

vulnerable to an overruling in light of *Byrne* and new national security concerns. On the other hand, if there were evidence that Congress has relied on judicial development of a statute, that might give this supposed canon some bite, but otherwise I would urge judges to focus on the substantive objections to an obsolete precedent and not engage in diversions into tiers of *stare decisis*.[76]

Acquiescence Canon. My critique of the super-duper version of *stare decisis* for statutory precedents has assumed a do-nothing Congress, but this current phase in the nation's political history will not last forever—and Congress has certainly not been so paralyzed for most of its history. Like state legislatures, Congress has traditionally monitored the Supreme Court's statutory jurisprudence quite carefully. Where legislators have become aware of a judicial precedent, have deliberated its policy value, and have revealed a great deal of support for the precedent, that evidence strengthens the *stare decisis* effect of the precedent, even when the lawmakers' interest has not resulted in enacted legislation.

Although the U.S. Supreme Court and some state supreme courts sometimes say that "long congressional acquiescence enhance[s] even the usual precedential force we accord to our interpretations of statutes,"[77] legislative inaction, alone, ought not be enough to enhance the already powerful presumption of correctness. For *stare decisis* to supercharge, defenders of a vulnerable precedent should show that Congress or a state legislature has seriously revisited the underlying statute, especially when the precise issue has been salient yet not acted upon, and that subsequent legislation is consistent with or even builds upon the statutory precedent.[78]

Thus, if Congress fails to amend the Park Safety Act for twenty years after the D.C. Circuit's decision in *Treanor v. National Park*

---

[76] Thus, the Supreme Court has declined to extend the common law statute idea to laws that Congress has regularly updated and overridden or codified judicial decisions. E.g., *Kimble,* 135 S.Ct. at 2409–12 (patent law); *Stoneridge Investment Partners, LLC v. Scientific-Atlanta, Inc.*, 552 U.S. 148, 163 (2008) (securities law).

[77] *Watson v. United States,* 552 U. S. 74, 82–83 (2007) (quotation in text), citing *Shepard v. United States*, 544 U.S. 13, 23 (2005); *Cable v. State,* 51 So.3d 434, 443 (Fla. 2010). Cf. William N. Eskridge Jr., *Interpreting Legislative Inaction,* 87 Mich. L. Rev. 67 (1988) (skeptical analysis of "acquiescence" claims grounded on nothing more than legislative inaction).

[78] *Kimble,* 135 S.Ct. at 2410; *Halliburton Co.,* 134 S.Ct. at 2411–13; *Runyon v. McCrary,* 427 U.S. 160, 174–75 (1976); *Flood v. Kuhn,* 407 U.S. at 279; *Sara M. v. Superior Court,* 116 P.3d 550, 558–59 (Cal. 2005); *People v. Williams,* 29 P.3d at 203–04 (California); *State Farm v. Fitzgerald,* 38 N.E.3d at 334–39 (New York); *Marsh USA,* 354 S.W.3d at 788–94 (Texas) (Green, J., dissenting).

Service, that inattention, standing alone, does not suggest any kind of positive acquiescence—though such a long stretch of time suggests inquiry into reliance by private actors and other government organs. The issue of skateboarding in a single park is unlikely to reach the complicated congressional agenda, and even if it did there are too many legislative roadblocks to make it likely that a skeptical Congress would act. But if Congress revisits the Park Safety Act and fails to act on proposals to override the skateboarding decision, *stare decisis* would supercharge, at least a little. Don't forget that normal *stare decisis* protects *Treanor* from being overruled because of factual errors or oddball reasoning; any indication that the political process was okay with the exclusion of skateboards should only reinforce the *stare decisis* effect of *Treanor*.

Reenactment Canon. Legislative acquiescence in judicial precedent is more persuasive when Congress or a state legislature has not only informed itself about the utility of the precedents and considered overriding or codifying it, but has actually reenacted or revised the statute and left the precedent in place. This is consistent with the underlying institutional theory of the super-strong *stare decisis* for statutory precedents, which places primary responsibility for correcting or updating precedents with the legislature. If Congress or a state legislature reenacts or materially amends the statute, makes no material change in the provision that has been interpreted, and leaves the precedent in place, courts are, properly, more reluctant to reconsider the underlying precedent.[79] The reenactment canon does not apply, of course, if legislators revisit the statute and change the provision that has been authoritatively interpreted.[80]

The Supreme Court rests the reenactment canon, in part, on assumed knowledge within the congressional drafting and deliberation process. "Congress is presumed to be aware of an administrative or judicial interpretation of a statute and to adopt that

---

[79] *Pierce v. Underwood*, 457 U.S. 552 (1988) (leading case); accord, *Kimble*, 135 S.Ct. at 2409–12; *Helvering v. Wilshire Oil Co.*, 308 U.S. 90, 100–01 (1939); *McCaughn v. Hershey Chocolate Co.*, 283 U.S. 488, 492–93 (1931); *Heald v. District of Columbia*, 254 U.S. 20, 22–23 (1920); *United States v. Cerecedo Hermanos y Compañia*, 209 U.S. 337, 339 (1908); *Sara M. v. Superior Court*, 116 P.3d at 558–59 (California); *Essex Ins. Co. v. Zota*, 985 So.2d 1036, 1043–44 (Fla. 2008); *Remington v. City of Ocala*, 940 So.2d 1207, 1209–10 (Fla. App. 2006); *State Farm v. Fitzgerald*, 38 N.E.3d at 334–40 (New York).

[80] *Holder v. Martinez Gutierrez*, 132 S.Ct. 2011, 2018 (2012); *Jama v. Immigration and Customs Enforcement*, 543 U.S. 335, 349 (2005). See generally Eskridge, *Interpreting Legislative Inaction*, 87 Mich. L. Rev. at 78–84 (discussing the cases applying and not applying the reenactment canon).

interpretation when it re-enacts a statute without change."[81] This presumed intent justification is unusually weak in this instance, however. Although congressional hearings may touch upon interpretations of statutes in the course of amending them, legislative attention is generally laser-focused on the specific issue lobbyists and institutional counsel have secured on the congressional agenda. Indeed, even the Congressional Research Service, which periodically provides surveys of the canons of statutory interpretation to Congress, has not homed in on the reenactment canon—or on any of the other *stare decisis* canons.[82] Not surprisingly, therefore, empirical surveys of congressional staff have not turned up any evidence that laws are drafted with these canons in mind. If the reenactment canon is defensible, it is so for institutional and rule of law (continuity) reasons, and not because judges can assume that the democratic process has known about and ratified the precedent.

Thus far, we have assumed no legislative updating, recodification, or revision of the Park Safety Act of 1992. Under these conditions, the D.C. Circuit is reluctant enough to revisit the *Treanor* precedent. If Congress, however, amended section 3 to add "skateboards" to the illustrative list of "vehicles" excluded from Lafayette Park, that action would be dispositive. *Stare decisis* would not protect skateboarders at all once Congress has clearly overridden the precedent. If, instead, Congress amended section 3 to add at the end of the first sentence "but not including skateboards," that action would be dispositive the other way. The Court of Appeals would consider the amendment to have been a codification of *Treanor*. Nancy Staudt and her colleagues have demonstrated that Congress frequently codifies Supreme Court decisions, in tax statutes anyway.[83] Although there is no systematic survey, state legislatures frequently codify as well as adjust statutory interpretation decisions. In the event of a statutory codification, the Court would be likely to apply *Treanor* and its reasoning more liberally, perhaps deducing from the codification that Congress agreed that recreational

---

[81] *Lorillard v. Pons,* 434 U.S. 575, 580 (1978); accord, *Jones v. ETS of New Orleans, Inc.,* 793 So.2d 912, 917 (Fla. 2001).

[82] Larry M. Eig, American Law Division, Congressional Research Service, Report, *Statutory Interpretation: General Principles and Recent Trends* (updated Dec. 19, 2011) (hereinafter cited as CRS Report, *Statutory Interpretation*) (detailed survey of canons offered as a congressional staff resource, but not mentioning any of the *stare decisis* canons).

[83] Nancy C. Staudt et al., *Judicial Decisions as Legislation: Congressional Oversight of Supreme Court Tax Cases, 1954–2005,* 82 N.Y.U. L. Rev. 1340 (2007).

conveyances are more like "toys" than "vehicles" and are therefore appropriate for Lafayette Park.

Consider a third course for congressional amendment of the Park Safety Act, a course of action that mobilizes the reenactment canon. If Congress amends section 3 to add "motorized bicycles" to the illustrative list, legislators have neither overridden nor codified *Treanor*, but the statutory revision does have consequences for that statutory precedent. That is, the Court of Appeals would be even more unlikely to overrule *Treanor* once Congress has revised the statutory provision on point and has left untouched the skateboard-liberating precedent, especially if there were proposals before Congress that would have overridden the precedent.[84] The case for overruling becomes a closer one if Congress amended section 3 before 9/11 and if, after 9/11, there were security incidents generating the *Byrne* precedent regulating roller blades as "vehicles" and new attentiveness to Lafayette Park activity, right across the street from the vulnerable White House.

Other Precedent-Based Canons

The foregoing discussion ought to be sufficient to establish that no theory of statutory interpretation can be complete without a thorough account of the role of *stare decisis* for judicial precedents authoritatively construing the statute. Certainly, no description of how judges interpret statutes can be complete, or even minimally accurate, without a detailed understanding of the role of *stare decisis*. It is, therefore, quite surprising that leading theories of statutory interpretation give such short shrift to the role of statutory precedents, and that even the Congressional Research Service ignores this fundamental source in its guidance documents for legislative staff.[85]

Prescriptively, the matter is more complicated. Although members of Congress and their staffs are perfectly comfortable delegating a great deal of interpretive authority to courts in many statutes, they often do so without a sufficient understanding of the canons courts follow for their precedents. Today, federal courts leave

---

[84] *Kimble,* 135 S.Ct. at 2409–10.

[85] CRS Report, *Statutory Interpretation* (updated 2011) (a detailed examination of dozens of canons but with no mention of *stare decisis*); Antonin Scalia & Bryan F. Garner, *Reading Law* 42–43, 252–55, 322–26 (2012) (setting aside *stare decisis* but examining the *in pari materia* and borrowed statute canons, which are diluted versions of *stare decisis*).

statutory precedents alone under the assumption that Congress ought to have the primary responsibility to correct errors—but representatives and their staffs are not deeply aware of this responsibility and are, in any event, unable to carry it out under current conditions of gridlock. At whatever time congressional gridlock eases, there will still be a democratic deliberation problem and a governance problem with the strict *stare decisis* federal courts claim to follow in statutory cases.

On the other hand, the rule of law justifications for *stare decisis* for statutory precedents are quite powerful, as explained above. Yet those justifications can easily be overstated, for precedent is not as constraining as judges assume. Courts sometimes slight or ignore precedents whose dicta or even holdings were not the result of careful briefing, pick and choose which precedents to emphasize and how to characterize the relevant precedents, recharacterize precedents, and occasionally overrule them. Indeed, the requirements of effective governance press judges to fudge on *stare decisis* in these ways.

This is not the end of the matter, for judicial decisions are relevant to statutory interpretation in many instances where there is no authoritative, binding precedent of the sort we have been evaluating. Looking beyond strict *stare decisis,* I shall now consider the role played by non-binding judicial decisions that form critical legal background to statutes adopted by Congress or state legislatures. Unlike the super-strong presumption of correctness for binding statutory precedents, the canons that follow are gentler advisory guideposts to statutory meaning—guideposts that can be more easily offset by other sources, including the context of the whole act (chapter two) as well as legislative history (examined in the next chapter).

Common Law Canon (Terms of Art). For most of American history, the common law was the baseline for legal regulation. Reflecting that baseline, courts narrowly construed statutes "in derogation of the common law." The modern regulatory state has superseded this understanding of interpretation. In our republic of statutes, most enactments are in derogation of the common law, but that is no justification for interpreting them narrowly. Instead, all statutory language should be given its normal, ordinary meaning, in light of its purpose(s), a precept established in post-New Deal case law and codified in many state codes.[86] This sea change in governance

[86] *Isbrandtsen Co. v. Johnson*, 343 U.S. 779, 783 (1952); 3 *Sutherland Statutes and Statutory Construction* § 61:4 (7th ed. 2015) (reporting case law and state codes

has not rendered the common law irrelevant, however. (This topic will recur, more ambitiously, in chapter six.)

Recall the term of art canon from chapter one; many legal terms of art derive their meaning from the common law. "Where Congress uses terms that have accumulated settled meaning under either equity or the common law, a court must infer, unless the statute otherwise dictates, that Congress means to incorporate the established meaning of these terms."[87] Thus, if the Park Safety Act of 1992 did not define "vehicles" excluded from Lafayette Park, the common law understanding of the term would be highly relevant, subject to the anchoring ordinary meaning rule.

The term of art canon, common law style, is related to the dictionary canon discussed in chapter one, and they substantially converge in *Black's Law Dictionary,* which sets forth definitions that are typically drawn directly or indirectly from the common law.[88] Interestingly, *Black's* also draws extensively from statutory codifications of common law and other terms. As suggested in chapter one, terms of art nowadays might secure their entrenched legal meaning from a pattern of statutes and administrative regulations, in addition to or in place of the common law. Federal, state, and local legislatures and administrators all over the country use the regulatory term "vehicle" (and "driving" a "vehicle"). If there were a rough regulatory consensus that "vehicle" includes motorized bicycles, for example, the term of art canon would support a reading of the statute that excludes motorized bicycles from the park.

The Park Safety Act, of course, defines the term "vehicle" in section 3. Does that render the common law or the term of art canon irrelevant? Not necessarily. Legislated definitions themselves are subject to interpretation and typically do not specify all possible applications. Hence, common law understandings might still be useful, up to a point. Let's say that neither judicial nor administrative

---

rejecting the broad anti-derogation canon). For a thoughtful exposition of the eighteenth century view that statutes should not derogate from the common law, see David Lieberman, *The Province of Legislation Determined* 16–20, 28, 52–72 (1989).

[87] *NLRB v. Amax Coal Co.*, 453 U.S. 322, 329 (1981); accord, *Microsoft Corp. v. i4i Ltd. Partnership,* 131 S.Ct. 2238, 2245 (2011); *Scheidler v. NOW,* 537 U.S. 393, 402 (2003); *United States v. Wells*, 519 U.S. 482, 491 (1997); *Community for Creative Non-Violence v. Reid,* 490 U.S. 730, 739 (1989); *In re Bradley Est.,* 835 N.W.2d 545, 550–51 (Mich. 2013); *Ford Motor Co. v. City of Woodhaven,* 716 N.W.2d 247, 254–55 (Mich. 2006).

[88] Sarah Yates, Black's Law Dictionary: *The Making of an American Standard,* 103 Law Lib. J. 175, 182–83 (2011).

common law understandings of "vehicles" had been applied to Segways. That should not be dispositive, because Segways are too recent an innovation to have generated such quick regulatory consensus; the statutory interpreter must focus on the ordinary meaning of the text, the whole act, and precedents like *Treanor*—without much attention to the common law. On the other hand, the administrative and judicial common law of "vehicles" strongly supports our intuition that the vehicles in the park law does not include baby carriages and wheelbarrows. Even though both baby carriages and wheelbarrows fit within the broad section 3 definition, neither poses the safety problem the statute was addressing—and their omission in the common law of vehicle regulation reinforces our belief that these conveyances are not within the statute's domain.[89]

Borrowed Act Canon. Most federal and state statutes borrow terminology, specific text, concepts, and sometimes entire titles and subtitles from previously enacted statutes—a practice Frank Horack dubbed *stare de statute.*[90] Typically, there are judicial precedents interpreting the earlier statute from which language is borrowed. Those precedents have interpretive significance, not because of strict *stare decisis,* but because of our legal system's presumption of continuity and coherence. The *borrowed act canon* says that when the legislature has copied language or even concepts from another statute, courts will presume that the new statute also incorporates the authoritative interpretations in place at the time of borrowing.[91] The borrowed act canon is most persuasive when an entire statutory scheme, including its underlying policy, has been borrowed from another jurisdiction; it is least persuasive when the borrowing jurisdiction has made substantial changes in the statute or has a different public policy tradition relevant to the interpretive issue.[92]

---

[89] On the relevance of common law terminology even when there is a statutory definition, see Scalia & Garner, *Reading Law,* 228–32; *Babbitt v. Sweet Home,* 515 U.S. at 719–20 (Scalia, J., dissenting).

[90] Frank E. Horack Jr., *The Common Law of Legislation,* 23 Iowa L. Rev. 41 (1937).

[91] *Inclusive Communities Project,* 135 S.Ct. at 2520–21; *Sekhar v. United States,* 133 S.Ct. 2720, 2724 (2013); *Shannon v. United States,* 512 U.S. 573, 580–81 (1994); *Lorillard v. Pons,* 434 U.S. 575, 580–81 (1978); *Metro. R.R. Co. v. Moore,* 121 U.S. 558, 572 (1887); accord, *State v. Aiuppa,* 298 So.2d 391, 394 (Fla. 1974). See generally 2B *Sutherland Statutes and Statutory Construction* § 52:2 (7th ed. 2015) (collecting state and federal cases for the borrowed act rule); Scalia & Garner, *Reading Law,* 322–26 (dubbing this the "prior-construction canon").

[92] *Shannon,* 512 U.S. at 580–81; see 2B *Sutherland Statutes and Statutory Construction* § 52:2 (7th ed. 2015).

Judges often say that this canon has a democratic pedigree. "[W]here * * * Congress adopts a new law incorporating sections of a prior law, Congress normally can be presumed to have had knowledge of the interpretation given to the incorporated law, at least insofar as it affects the new statute."[93] This is usually a fiction. There is scant evidence that members of Congress, their advisory and drafting staffs, or groups lobbying them "normally" have significant knowledge of all the interpretations given the law that is being borrowed. Although the Congressional Research Service can and sometimes does provide this information to Congress,[94] members and their staffs do not routinely ask for it and do not deeply appreciate its role in statutory interpretation.[95] Although some state legislative drafting manuals admonish drafters to research the general subject matter of bills they are drafting, there is little evidence that state legislators vote with any more knowledge about the legal regime embedded in the borrowed act (and probably a good deal less) than Congress does.[96] The best justification for this canon, as for the *stare decisis* canon, rests upon our admiration of a predictable, largely coherent body of law and upon the convenience of a set of ready-made gapfilling rules that can be taken wholesale from the jurisdiction originating the statute. But this canon ought not be defended as a presumption about what members of Congress and their staff "know" about the interpretive history of the statutes they borrow.

On the other hand, it is plausible to think that the borrowed act canon might not be inconsistent with democratic premises, if (for example) legislators do not object to judicial harmonization and do not believe that it usually undermines legislative purposes. Perhaps

---

[93] *Lorillard v. Pons,* 434 U.S. at 581.

[94] Jarrod Shobe, *Intertemporal Statutory Interpretation and the Evolution of Legislative Drafting,* 114 Colum. L. Rev. 807 (2014).

[95] The few empirical studies of congressional drafting practice did not focus on knowledge of the borrowed statute canon and acquaintance with the interpretive history of borrowed statutes, but the leading studies suggest that this knowledge is rarely a priority during the deliberative process. See Abbe R. Gluck & Lisa Schultz Bressman, *Statutory Interpretation from the Inside—An Empirical Study of Congressional Drafting, Delegation, and the Canons: Part I,* 65 Stan. L. Rev. 901, 933, 936–37 (2013); Victoria F. Nourse & Jane S. Schacter, *The Politics of Legislative Drafting: A Congressional Case Study*, 77 N.Y.U. L. Rev. 575, 594–97 (2002). See also CRS Report, *Statutory Interpretation* (updated 2011) (comprehensive guide to the canons by the Congressional Research Service, but without any mention of the borrowed act canon).

[96] Cf. Kentucky Legislative Research Comm'n, Kentucky General Assembly, *Bill Drafting Manual* § 103 (rev. 2011) (setting forth an ambitious research agenda for bill drafters, including the substantive law of the subject area of the proposed legislation).

for this reason, a modest number of state legislatures have codified the borrowed act canon and none has rejected it.[97] Like other states, however, Wyoming has codified the canon only with particular reference to "uniform laws" drafted by national law revision bodies and adopted in that state: "Any uniform act shall be interpreted and construed to effectuate its general purpose to make uniform the law of those states which enact it."[98]

Congress might well have borrowed or adapted the language and structure of our (hypothetical) Park Safety Act of 1992 from a municipal ordinance barring vehicles from local parks. Assume that the District of Columbia's Council had enacted precisely this statute for its municipal parks in 1977, shortly after achieving home rule, and that Congress adapted the District's law to regulate Lafayette Park and borrowed sections 2 and 3 verbatim. If, between 1977 and 1992, the District of Columbia's highest local court had interpreted its Park Safety Act to include skateboards as "vehicles," that local precedent would be highly relevant when the federal appeals court later considers whether the congressional law applies to skateboards. In that event, the Court of Appeals for the D.C. Circuit (the federal appeals court for the District) would have presumed that Congress meant to incorporate the authoritative constructions of the District's law whose language was borrowed. Note that the local precedent would only have persuasive power and would not carry the force of *stare decisis*.

Does the borrowed act canon apply to interpretations of the borrowed statute rendered *after* the legislature has borrowed the operative language? Thus, if the District of Columbia courts found skateboards to be included *after* 1992, when Congress enacted the Park Safety Act, would that interpretation have any bearing on the D.C. Circuit's deliberations in William Treanor's case? Generally, the borrowed act canon has little formal bite in such circumstances.[99] The New Mexico Legislature codified this canon in a manner that reflects

---

[97] Jacob Scott, *Codified Canons and the Common Law of Interpretation*, 98 Geo. L.J. 341, 378 (2010) (Table 6) (reporting that eight states have codified the borrowed act canon, and none has rejected it).

[98] Wyo. Stat. § 8–1–103(a)(vii); accord, Tex. Govt. Code § 311.028 (similar); Scott, *Codified Canons*, 98 Geo. L.J. at 377–78 (collecting codifications of the uniform act canon).

[99] See, e.g., *Smith v. Bayer Corp.*, 131 S.Ct. 2368, 2378 (2011) (examining a state rule borrowed from the federal side, but declining to impose federal precedents upon a state law that had shown an evolution quite independent from the federal precedents); 2B *Sutherland Statutes and Statutory Construction* § 52:2 (7th ed. 2015) (citing federal and state cases for the same idea).

the traditional understanding: Courts should follow the "settled judicial construction in another jurisdiction as of the time a statute or rule is borrowed from the other jurisdiction."[100]

But, informally, the coherence norm that best justifies the borrowed act canon would augur in favor of some judicial consideration of those subsequent interpretations as persuasive authority for the borrowing jurisdiction as well. Additionally, a related canon might provide guidance—the *in pari materia* canon discussed in the previous chapter. Judges interpreting for the first time a provision in one statute will consider how courts have construed similar provisions in other statutes.

Shadow Precedents Canon. If Congress overrides a statutory precedent, does that override necessarily negate its precedential force? Surprisingly, the answer is "not necessarily." Although critical of the practice in workplace discrimination cases, Deborah Widiss has identified a "shadow precedents" practice by the Supreme Court. Depending on how broadly it is drafted, a statutory override of the precedent's result may not negate the force of the precedent's reasoning.[101] In a new empirical study, Professor Widiss and Brian Broughman demonstrate that lower courts almost immediately stop citing Supreme Court decisions that the Court itself has *overruled,* but often continue to cite and to follow Supreme Court decisions that Congress has *overridden.* Judges tend to treat the latter as correcting a particular result, while the former resets the analytical structure for a statutory provision.[102]

To understand the operation of the shadow precedents canon, return to the case of the motorized bicycle, *Hogan v. National Park Service.* Recall that the Court of Appeals holds that motorized bicycles are "vehicles" covered by section 2, but not "bicycles" subject to the more lenient rule of the section 3 proviso. As mapped out earlier, the Court's reasoning is as follows:

---

[100] N.M. Stat. § 12–2A–20(B)(1) (quotation in text).

[101] Deborah A. Widiss, *Shadow Precedents and the Separation of Powers: Statutory Interpretation of Congressional Overrides,* 84 Notre Dame L. Rev. 511 (2009); Widiss, *Hydra Problem in Statutory Interpretation.* Accord, CRS Report, *Statutory Interpretation,* 48 (updated 2011).

[102] Brian Broughman & Deborah Widiss, "After the Override: An Empirical Analysis of Shadow Precedent" (Working Paper March 2015) (empirical demonstration that lower courts continue to cite many Supreme Court precedents overridden by Congress but not precedents overruled by the Court itself).

HOGAN'S HOLDING

1. The 1992 statute completely bars "vehicles" from Lafayette Park but allows "bicycles" so long as they are being pushed and not ridden.
2. The prototypical "vehicle" is a speedy, typically motorized, mechanism used primarily to transport persons or things from one place to another.
3. The prototypical "bicycle" is a speedy, nonmotorized mechanism with two wheels, propelled by human pedaling.
4. A "motorized bicycle" is a speedy mechanism with two wheels for conveying a person from one place to another.
5. A "motorized bicycle" is a motorized mechanism and is only partially propelled by human pedaling.
6. *Therefore*, a motorized bicycle is a "vehicle" completely barred by the statute and not a "bicycle" regulated by the statute.

Now consider a hypothetical political reaction to this decision—outrage. Senator Dreama Soaper, the chair of the committee with jurisdiction over federal parks, denounces the decision. "It is ridiculous for a court to say that a *bicycle* is not a 'bicycle' simply because it has a small motor. A bicycle is a 'bicycle' is a *bicycle*!" Senator Soaper's committee condemns the court decision as "an arid formalism, focusing on irrelevant language distinctions and ignoring the recreational and tourism purposes of Lafayette Park." The senator introduces legislation to override the judicial decision.

Notwithstanding congressional gridlock on the budget, transportation and roads, the income tax code, global warming, and other topics of commanding national importance, the Soaper Amendment to the Park Safety Act sneaks through Congress and is signed by the President in 2013. As crafted by the Senate committee, the new law amends section 3 to read as follows, with the new language **in bold**:

SOAPER AMENDMENT OF 2013

Sec. 3. Definition. "Vehicle" for purposes of this law means any **thing used** for conveying a person from one place to another, including automobiles, trucks, motorcycles, and motor scooters—**but not including motorized**

> **bicycles**. *Provided that*, bicycles **of any kind shall not be considered "vehicles" and** shall be allowed in Lafayette Park, so long as they are being pushed or carried and not ridden.

The Soaper Amendment overrides the result reached in *Hogan v. National Park Service* (Step 6 in the foregoing chain of reasoning). But the amendment probably does not negate the effect of *Hogan* as a "shadow" statutory precedent, because it does not disturb *Hogan*'s core reasoning, that a prototypical "vehicle" is a speedy, typically motorized mechanism used primarily to transport persons or things (Steps 2 and 4).

The next case is Liam Treanor's skateboarding through Lafayette Park. Is a skateboard a "vehicle"? Even though Congress has overridden the result in *Hogan*, it did not override the reasoning reflected in *Hogan,* and so the Court of Appeals is likely to follow that reasoning (unless the judges have a good reason to recharacterize *Hogan*). Step 2 in the reasoning process anchors the regulatory term "vehicle" upon the notion of a "speedy, typically motorized mechanism used primarily to transport persons or things." Applying the shadow precedent to the new case involving skateboarding, the Court of Appeals is likely to rule that skateboards are not "vehicles" as that term is used in section 3. To be sure, the Court can reach that result without any reference to *Hogan*, but Professor Widiss's empirical point is that judges are *likely* to cite *Hogan* in this way, even though its result has been overridden.[103]

Moreover, if the motorized bicycle issue were to arise under a similar statute, such as the (hypothetical) Folger Park Safety Act discussed in chapter two, the Court of Appeals is likely to follow the reasoning of *Hogan* to hold motorized bicycles entirely excluded from Folger Park. Not only is the Court unlikely to extend the Soaper Amendment to the Folger Park statute, but many judges would cite the Soaper Amendment as an additional reason to include motorized bicycles within the section 3 definition of "vehicles." Those judges would cite the meaningful variation canon: When Congress wanted to regulate motorized bicycles only as "bicycles" and not as "vehicles," it knew how to do that—as illustrated by the Soaper Amendment! Professor Widiss calls this the *hydra problem* and roundly denounces

---

[103] Broughman & Widiss, "After the Override: An Empirical Analysis of Shadow Precedent" (March 2015).

it. She would presume that the Soaper Amendment carries over to statutes *in pari materia,* like the Folger Park law.[104]

But notice that Congress could have overridden the reasoning as well as the result of *Hogan*. For example, the Soaper Amendment could have rewritten section 3 in the following way (again, with the new statutory language **in bold**):

BROADENED SOAPER AMENDMENT OF 2013

> **Sec. 3. Definition.** "Vehicle" for purposes of this law means any **thing used** for conveying a person from one place to another, including automobiles, trucks, motorcycles, [ ] motor scooters, **and other forms of conveyance that pose safety hazards to park users because of their speed**. *Provided that,* bicycles **of any kind shall not be considered "vehicles" and** shall be allowed in Lafayette Park, so long as they are being pushed or carried and not ridden.

Under this revised Soaper Amendment, changes to the proviso are intended to override the result in *Hogan* (Step 6), while the changes to section 3's first sentence are expected to override the precedent's reasoning (Step 2). Also, Congress could have revised the Dictionary Act's definition of "vehicle" to exclude motorized bicycles everywhere in the U.S. Code. This would have addressed the hydra problem.

The foregoing analysis may not be a satisfactory answer to Professor Widiss's concerns, in part because Congress and its staff are unaware of the shadow precedent canon that the Court has been applying in a number of important cases. Even if staff were aware of this canon (perhaps by reading the present volume or, even better, Professor Widiss's excellent work), it is doubtful they could internalize it very effectively. It is hard for Congress to adopt laws that reach further than the immediate problem at hand. Congressional overrides are usually like the original Soaper Amendment and are not as ambitious a rethinking of the statutory rationale as reflected in my broadened Soaper Amendment. Because any ambitious rethinking of a statute brings more private interest groups and public officials into the deliberative process and risks more vetogate challenges, a broad override of the reasoning as well as result requires a great deal more political capital and energy than a targeted override. Congress almost never amends the Dictionary Act;

---

[104] Widiss, *Hydra Problem in Statutory Interpretation,* 90 Tex. L. Rev. at 860–66, 908–26 (providing many examples of the "hydra problem").

the last time it did so, in the Defense of Marriage Act of 1996, the Supreme Court invalidated the amendment in an opinion that cast Congress in a very bad light.[105]

In short, judges ought to apply the shadow precedent canon cautiously. When Congress has overridden a judicial decision interpreting a particular statute, courts should not treat the overridden precedent with the same supercharged adherence that they show for precedents that have not been overridden. The Court ought to have discretion to preserve that part of the precedent that has not been explicitly overridden, but ought not treat the matter as one where judges have no room for judgment. As the next chapter will argue, judges ought to consider the legislative deliberations surrounding the override before invoking the override, hydra-like, as a justification for extending the reach of a shadow precedent under cover of the *in pari materia* canon.

Responding to the hydra problem, Professor Widiss proposes that an overridden interpretation should not be applied to similar or related statutes.[106] For the same reason that I would urge caution in applying the shadow precedents canon, I should be cautious in response to Professor Widiss's proposed canon. As just suggested, the fate of the overridden precedent ought to depend on the precise nature of Congress's disagreement with it. And for that, the interpreter ought to consult the legislative materials, the focus of our next chapter.

* * *

If an appellate court authoritatively construes a statute, the court's holding is binding on future courts. In contrast to dicta, the holding is the specific application of statutory text to particular facts, together with the legal reasoning deemed necessary to support that application. In practice, subsequent courts may be willing to recharacterize a precedent's reasoning, within limits. Thus, the Court of Appeals for the D.C. Circuit might recharacterize *Hogan*'s reasoning with a focus on speed and danger, deemphasizing the precedent's invocation of motors as a feature of statutory "vehicles."

---

[105] *United States v. Windsor,* 133 S.Ct. 2675 (2013) (invalidating the Defense of Marriage Act provision amending the Dictionary Act to bar federal recognition of valid same-sex marriages).

[106] Widiss, *Shadow Precedents and the Separation of Powers*, 84 Notre Dame L. Rev. at 566 (proposing a presumption against applying an overridden interpretation to similar statutes); Widiss, *Hydra Problem in Statutory Interpretation.* 90 Tex. L. Rev. at 926–41 (elaborate defense of the presumption).

And the normal common law process requires judges to make judgments about how broadly or narrowly to read *Hogan*.

Stare decisis does not protect all precedents from being overruled; it is not an absolute doctrine, and in my view the supposed super-strong presumption of correctness for statutory precedents is more rhetoric than reason. Ultimately, statutory precedents are vulnerable to being overruled if (1) there has been an "intervening development of the law" that has rendered that precedent "irreconcilable with competing legal doctrines or policies," (2) the precedent has become as a "positive detriment to coherence and consistency in the law," either internally or in relation to policy objectives associated with other laws, and (3) the precedent has been proved outdated and contrary to contemporary understandings of justice and social welfare.[107] Note the similarity to the Supreme Court's criteria for overruling constitutional precedents. The Court asks whether (1) the decision's rule of law "has been found unworkable" or has generated reliance interests, (2) whether "developments in the law and society the law's growth in the intervening years" has left the precedent's rule of law "a doctrinal anachronism discounted by society," and (3) whether the decision's factual premises have been undermined so much "as to render its central holding somehow irrelevant or unjustifiable in dealing with the issue it addressed."[108]

As to both statutory and constitutional precedents (and common law precedents, for that matter), legislative and administrative feedback should play a role in a court's evaluation of precedent. If legislative deliberations and statutory developments move decisively away from a precedent for substantive reasons, those developments will and should actually affect the precedent's force and even viability. Recall that *stare decisis* demands a balance between continuity and evolution. In a republic of statutes, judges are the polity's most important institution of legal continuity—but they need to be attentive to how their corpus of precedents interact with the corpus of laws and regulations created by the political, policymaking institutions. This notion will be an important theme of the next chapter.

---

[107] *Patterson,* 491 U.S. at 173–74.

[108] *Planned Parenthood of Southeastern Pa. v. Casey,* 505 U.S. 833, 854–55 (1992) (joint opinion) (leading statement of the Court's criteria for overruling constitutional precedents).

Chapter 4

LEGISLATIVE HISTORY

The Horse Mounted Unit, U.S. Park Police

No federal or state judge and no serious scholar maintains that judges interpreting statutes should ignore ordinary meaning, the whole act and related statutes elsewhere in the code, or relevant statutory precedents. Most of the sources examined in this and the next two chapters are more controversial, and no source has generated greater debate than the status of *legislative history*, the materials recording legislative deliberations from the time a bill is introduced until the time it is signed into law (and sometimes beyond).[1]

The Lafayette Park Safety Act of 1992, as amended by the Soaper Amendment of 2013, now reads as follows:

---

[1] For contrasting perspectives on the utility of legislative history for judges interpreting statutes, compare Stephen Breyer, *Active Liberty: Interpreting Our Democratic Constitution* 85 (2006), and Robert A. Katzmann, *Judging Statutes* 35–54 (2014), with Antonin Scalia & Bryan Garner, *Reading Law: Interpretation of Legal Texts* 269–91, 344–46 (2012). Also compare William N. Eskridge Jr., *The New Textualism,* 37 U.C.L.A. L. Rev. 621 (1990), with John R. Manning, *What Divides Textualists from Purposivists?,* 106 Colum. L. Rev. 70 (2006), and both with Jonathan Molot, *The Rise and Fall of Textualism*, 106 Colum. L. Rev. 1 (2006).

An Act to ensure public safety in Lafayette Park

Sec. 1. Findings and Purpose. Finding that vehicles operating in Lafayette Park have contributed to several serious accidents requiring hospitalization in the last five years, and finding further that vehicles create risks of serious injury to park users, Congress resolves that there is an urgent public need to ban any and all vehicles from Lafayette Park.

Sec. 2. No Vehicles in the Park. No vehicles of any kind shall be allowed in Lafayette Park. Any person who drives a vehicle into Lafayette Park shall be guilty of a federal offense, and may be assessed a fine not exceeding $500 for each violation.

Sec. 3. Definition. "Vehicle" for purposes of this law means any thing used for conveying a person from one place to another, including automobiles, trucks, motorcycles, motor scooters, and other forms of conveyance that pose safety hazards to park users because of their speed. *Provided that*, bicycles of any kind shall not be considered "vehicles" and shall be allowed in Lafayette Park, so long as they are being pushed or carried and not ridden.

Figure 6 flags a few ambiguities. Can the congressional process that yielded the Soaper Amendment help resolve some of them?

FIGURE 6

Plain Meaning Continuum: "Driving a Vehicle" in the Park (§ 2), in Light of Statutory Purpose (§ 1) and the Soaper Amendment (§ 3)

Core Coverage		Penumbra	Outside the Statute
Cars & Trucks		Roller Blades	Wheelbarrows
Motorcycles		Segways	Baby Carriages
Motor Scooters		Skateboards	
Mopeds	Bicycles (§ 3 proviso)	Adult Tricycles (§ 3 proviso?)	
Motorized Bicycles			

Under Article I, Section 7 of the Constitution, no bill can become a law unless it is passed by *both* the Senate *and* the House of Representatives, in exactly the same language. Each chamber normally refers proposed legislation to one or more committees, where ninety percent of bills die each session. Consider the classic account of the congressional process for enacting statutes. Bills taken seriously are afforded hearings by the relevant committees or subcommittees; in the hearings, legislators hear from supporters and critics. If a committee votes in favor of sending a bill to the full chamber, it must submit a written report that might be studied by legislators and their staffs. For a bill to be considered by the chamber, however, it must be expedited through a special rule in the House and a unanimous consent agreement in the Senate. Before a bill is passed by either chamber, it is usually debated and amended. Each of these steps in the congressional process generates published documents—congressional hearings, committee reports, and records of floor debates, amendments, and votes. State legislatures have a similar, committee-driven process, with a wide array of vetogates that can block legislation.

In the last generation, this classic version of the federal legislative process has frequently given way to what political scientist Barbara Sinclair calls *unorthodox lawmaking*.[2] Unorthodox lawmaking is nowadays the normal path for complicated legislation and omnibus bills. Unorthodox legislation is different from the classic model in several practical respects. First, and most important, congressional committees and their chairs are not necessarily the central players for most statutes adopted in this manner. Work on complicated or omnibus legislation is usually carried out by several different committees in each chamber—and sometimes the committee process is bypassed altogether. Second, because of the hyperpartisan divisions dominating Congress (which have, for example, made filibusters routine in the Senate and have blocked majority-supported legislation from reaching the House floor), the final deals are often worked out in party or executive-congressional summits rather than in conference committees. Finally, Presidents have been more aggressive in issuing signing statements to signal executive branch views about the constitutionality and proper interpretation of statutes and in going beyond statutes through executive orders or encouraging ambitious agency rulemaking. For unorthodox lawmaking, there is usually the same kind of documentary record (committee hearings and reports, floor debate, and formal votes), but

---

[2] Barbara Sinclair, *Unorthodox Lawmaking: New Legislative Processes in the U.S. Congress* (4th ed. 2011); Gregory J. Wawro & Eric Schickler, *Filibuster: Obstruction and Lawmaking in the U.S. Senate* (2006). See also Abbe R. Gluck, Anne Joseph O'Connell & Rosa Po, *Unorthodox Lawmaking, Unorthodox Rulemaking,* 115 Colum. L. Rev. 1789 (2015), reflecting on the challenges unorthodox lawmaking poses to statutory interpreters.

the record is more sprawling and complicated. Sometimes, important deliberative moments (such as executive-congressional summits) occur entirely off the record.

Whether the statute is the product of classic or unorthodox lawmaking, the documents produced in the legislative process are potentially relevant to understanding the meaning of the language being considered by Congress. Consider our vehicles in the park law, which I shall say (for purposes of this chapter) passed through the classic process. (Chapter six will examine a broader vehicles in the park law contained in an omnibus bill enacted through the unorthodox lawmaking process.)

Thus, the Senate and House committees and/or subcommittees having jurisdiction over the National Park System would have held hearings pertaining to Lafayette Park safety in or before 1992. Section 1 of the Park Safety Act of 1992 reports a congressional finding that "vehicles operating in Lafayette Park have contributed to several serious accidents requiring hospitalization in the last five years." The hearings and committee reports probably contain or describe the range of vehicles that were involved in accidents requiring hospitalization in the five-year period. If those documents reveal that there had been fifteen serious accidents of this sort, and all had involved "automobiles, trucks, motorcycles, and motor scooters" (the vehicles identified in section 3), the statutory interpreter has useful information about how broadly (or not) to read the definition of "vehicles" in section 3. Specifically, this particular context would discourage application of the statute to roller blades and would also counsel against including adult tricycles, because these mechanisms are not only very different from the automobiles etc. listed in section 3, but also because nothing close to roller blades or tricycles had been the cause of "serious accidents," as far as anyone in Congress knew. Notice how application of the *noscitur a sociis* canon (chapter one) and the whole act rule (chapter two), in this hypothetical, depends on knowing the legislative history in order to generate clear insights into the proper interpretation of the statute.

This particular legislative history of the 1992 Act would not be highly relevant to the coverage of Segways, the tourist conveyances discussed in the previous chapter. Segways were not in use in 1992—but the legislative history of the Soaper Amendment of 2013 might be relevant. Segways have been a big hit in the new millennium; you now see them all over Washington, D.C. The next page offers a photo of some Segway users touring the nation's capital.

Segways in Washington, D.C.
[Fourandsixty, Photographer (2015)]

In the last chapter, I raised without resolving the question whether the Park Safety Act, as amended in 2013, regulates Segways. Without looking at the legislative history that follows, would you apply the statutory text to cover Segways? (Assume that the 2013 Soaper Amendment renders the statutory precedents inapplicable.)

Here is the internal legislative history of the 2013 amendment. Senator Soaper's original bill passed the Senate, after extensive hearings and debate criticizing the Court of Appeals' decision in *Hogan* and evaluating various override possibilities. The Senate bill would have amended section 3 in this way (with new proposed language in bold).

SENATE VERSION OF 2013 AMENDMENT

> **Sec. 3. Definition.** "Vehicle" for purposes of this law means any mechanism for conveying a person from one place to another, including automobiles, trucks, motorcycles, **[ ]** motor scooters, **and other forms of conveyance that pose safety hazards to park users because of their speed**. *Provided that,* bicycles **of any kind shall not be considered vehicles and** shall be allowed in Lafayette Park, so long as they are being pushed or carried and not ridden.

The *Hogan* override bill that passed the House, however, would have amended section 3 in a very different manner (again, the proposed new language is in bold):

HOUSE VERSION OF 2013 AMENDMENT

> **Sec. 3. Definition.** "Vehicle" for purposes of this law means any mechanism for conveying a person from one place to another, including automobiles, trucks, motorcycles, [ ] motor scooters, **Segways, and other forms of motorized conveyance**. *Provided that*, bicycles **of any kind** shall be allowed in Lafayette Park, so long as they are being pushed or carried and not ridden.

Because both the House and the Senate must pass the same language to satisfy the bicameralism requirement of Article I, Section 7, situations like this one have traditionally been resolved through a House-Senate conference committee, which produces a single text reconciling the different bills.

The final version of section 3 (offered by the conference committee report and voted on by both House and Senate) followed the Senate version, with one exception (in bold):

CONFERENCE VERSION OF 2013 AMENDMENT

> **Sec. 3. Definition.** "Vehicle" for purposes of this law means any **thing used** for conveying a person from one place to another, including automobiles, trucks, motorcycles, motor scooters, and other forms of conveyance that pose safety hazards to park users because of their speed. *Provided that*, bicycles of any kind shall not be considered vehicles and shall be allowed in Lafayette Park, so long as they are being pushed or carried and not ridden.

The joint explanation of the conferees reads as follows: "The House recedes and accepts the Senate version of section 3. The statute seeks to protect park users against unnecessary safety hazards. Because motorized bicycles can reach speeds of 25–30 miles per hour, they should be regulated as 'bicycles', but not prohibited entirely as 'vehicles'."

Start with this question. Reading just the statutory text, after the Soaper Amendment has revised section 3, which provision regulates motorized bicycles—section 2, completely barring them, or the section 3 proviso, allowing them but barring riding? Motorized bicycles fall under the ordinary meaning of both section 2 and the section 3 proviso. So which controls? Under standard drafting practice, provisos are supposed to be carve-outs from general rules, and so I'd start with the assumption that motorized bicycles are "vehicles" covered by section 2, but might also be "bicycles" given a special rule in section 3. Provisos are supposed to be narrowly construed (chapter one). If the section 3 proviso for "bicycles" were confined to its prototypical core meaning, it is possible that motorized bicycles would not be subject to its special rule.

Hold on? Wait a second! The gentle reader who has carefully read chapter three might be alarmed that I am even raising this question. (Those who have skimmed over chapter three should go back and read the last several pages.) The whole point of the Soaper Amendment was to override *Hogan*, where the Court of Appeals had held that motorized bicycles are section 3 "vehicles" and not "bicycles" covered by the proviso. This is true, but if you are a judge who refuses to consult legislative history how would you know that (unless you read the newspaper accounts of the 2013 amendment or peaked at the legislative history)? The Soaper Amendment broadens both the section 3 definition of "vehicle" and its "bicycle" proviso, and it can be argued that because of their speed motorized bicycles still better fit the core definition of "vehicle" than that of "bicycle," even "of any kind."

Whatever ambiguity one might discern in the new statutory text is cleared up by the legislative history. The purpose of Senator Soaper's amendment was to override *Hogan,* which regulated motorized bicycles under section 2, and the explanation of the conferees confirms that the final statutory language had that purpose. In my view, the legislative history demands that the text of the proviso include motorized bicycles, which should then be exempted from the general prohibition of section 2. And I bet that if you put 100 textualists in a conference room, required them to read chapter three of this volume, and then asked them what the statute means after 2013, all but a handful of them would say that the statute plainly overrides *Hogan* and situates motorized bicycles within the proviso. While few of the textualists would cite the legislative history, once they have read it their textual analysis would be framed by that knowledge. For most people, you cannot unring the bell. Once you know *why* Congress amended the statute, that will influence the way you read the statutory text.[3]

---

[3] For an excellent example of the way that legislative history frames even a textual reading of a statutory amendment, compare *Rumsfeld v. Forum for Academic & Inst'l Rights,* 547 U.S. 47, 54 (2006) (describing the purpose of a 2004 amendment to

That legislative history can be decisive in this way can be illustrated by flipping the history. For purposes of contrast, consider an alternative scenario. Assume the legislative history revealed that Senator Soaper and her committee colleagues thoroughly *approved* the Court of Appeals decision in *Hogan*, which regulated motorized bicycles as "vehicles" barred by section 2. That is the reason, says the committee report, why the Senate committee added at the end of the definition, "and other forms of conveyance that pose safety hazards to park users because of their speed." The committee report also explains that the new language in the proviso, covering bicycles "of any kind," was added to make sure that bicycles with training wheels, reclining bicycles, and even adult tricycles were covered by the more lenient regulation. The conference committee reports the Senate version of new section 3, with this explanation by the conferees: "The House recedes and accepts the Senate version of section 3. The statute seeks to protect park users against unnecessary safety hazards. Because motorized bicycles can reach speeds of 25–30 miles per hour, they pose safety hazards that require them to be barred under section 2, precisely as the Court of Appeals ruled in *Hogan v. National Park Service*."

With this *different* legislative history in hand but the same text that we have been analyzing, would you still read the Lafayette Park Safety Act, as amended in 2013, to regulate motorized bicycles under the section 3 proviso, and not to exclude them entirely under section 2? If our 100 textualists were required to read this legislative background, rather than the one provided at the end of chapter three, would their textual analysis not flip along precisely the lines suggested by the new history? Same text, different interpretations. The only variable, the item that has changed, is the legislative history.

For more than a century, federal judges have been willing to consider legislative history such as the explanation of the conferees

---

the Solomon Amendment as overriding a lower court interpretation and codifying the Department of Defense's view, relying entirely on an explicit discussion in a committee report), with id. at 57–58 (confidently asserting that "what Congress had in mind" when it adopted the 2004 amendment was to require universities to do exactly what the committee report said, but without further citation of the report). Justices Scalia and Thomas, the most avid textualists on the Court, joined this analysis without any quarrel. A more recent example is *DePierre v. United States*, 131 S.Ct. 2225, 2232, 2234–35 (2011) (terminology used during committee hearings helping to clear up a messy statutory text); id. at 2237–38 (Scalia, J., concurring in part) (objecting to the Court's extensive discussion of congressional hearings on pp. 2234–35 but joining the Court's framing discussion of the same hearings on p. 2232).

hypothesized here. In 1892, the Supreme Court (in the [in]famous *Holy Trinity* case) not only considered Senate and House committee reports in a statutory case, but deployed these materials to justify its refusal to follow the "literal" meaning of the statutory provision.[4] In subsequent cases, the Court considered an expanding array of legislative materials. During the New Deal and for a generation afterwards, the Court relied on legislative history in most cases and often gave these materials much greater attention than the statutory text.[5]

Most state judges have followed the federal practice, with a time lag as state legislative materials became accessible to the public (at different points in different states). Thus, the California Supreme Court, the New York Court of Appeals, the Texas Supreme Court, and (to a lesser extent) the Florida Supreme Court not only routinely consider legislative materials in statutory cases, but also frequently weave legislative materials into their whole act, purposive, and even precedent-based analysis.[6] A large majority of state supreme courts now refer to legislative materials, with impressive sophistication for the most part.[7] Almost alone is the post-1999 majority of the

---

[4] *Holy Trinity Church v. United States,* 143 U.S. 457 (1892); see Carol Chomsky, *Unlocking the Mysteries of* Holy Trinity*: Spirit, Letter, and History in Statutory Interpretation*, 100 Colum. L. Rev. 901 (2000). The Court in *Holy Trinity* ignored ordinary meaning and whole act arguments that supported the Church's position. See William N. Eskridge Jr., *Textualism: The Unknown Ideal?*, 96 Mich. L. Rev. 1509 (1998) (detailed analysis of the previously ignored original meaning arguments in *Holy Trinity*). For the revival of *Holy Trinity* style analysis by the Supreme Court's new textualists, see Richard M. Re, *The New* Holy Trinity, 18 Green Bag 2d 407 (2015).

[5] Nicholas R. Parrillo, *Leviathan and Interpretive Revolution: The Administrative State, the Judiciary, and the Rise of Legislative History, 1890–1950,* 123 Yale L.J. 266 (2013). See also William N. Eskridge Jr., *Dynamic Statutory Interpretation* 208–18 (1994).

[6] For recent, representative examples of lavish reference to legislative materials, woven throughout important statutory opinions, see, e.g., *Jones v. Lodge at Torrey Pines Partnership,* 177 P.3d 232 (Cal. 2008); *Carter v. California Dep't of Veterans Affs.*, 135 P.3d 637 (Cal. 2006); *People v. Williams,* 29 P.3d 197 (Cal. 2001); *Hall v. State,* 826 So.2d 268 (Fla. 2002); *G.G. v. Florida Dep't of Law Enforcement,* 97 So.3d 268 (Fla. App. 2012); *State Farm Mut. Auto. Ins. Co. v. Fitzgerald*, 38 N.E.3d 325, 334–40 (N.Y. 2015); *Texas Mut. Ins. Co. v. Ruttiger,* 381 S.W.3d 430 (Tex. 2012) (both majority and dissenting opinions); *Ojo v. Farmers Group, Inc.*, 356 S.W.3d 421, 430–33 (Tex. 2011) (majority opinion, over objection of concurring Justice Willett, id. at 445–49); *Helena Chem. Co. v. Wilkens*, 47 S.W.3d 486 (Tex. 2001) (majority and dissenting opinions).

[7] For sophisticated handling of legislative materials by state courts in small states, most of which have modest legislative staffing, see, e.g., *State v. Batts,* 195 P.3d 144 (Alaska 2008); *Price v. Thomas Built Buses, Inc.*, 260 S.W.3d 300, 305–06 (Ark. 2007); *Romanoff v. State Comm'n on Judicial Performance*, 126 P.3d 182 (Colo. 2006); *Tomei v. Sharp*, 902 A.2d 757, 764–65 & 769 n.41 (Del. Super. 2006); Aiken *v. United*

Michigan Supreme Court, which generally refuses to acknowledge legislative materials.[8]

As the Michigan example illustrates, legislative materials are now controversial, and the use of legislative history in U.S. Supreme Court opinions has fallen off substantially from its peak in the 1970s.[9] In its first decade, the Roberts Court was progressively more likely to cite and analyze dictionaries than legislative history in statutory cases,[10] and the Court was loathe to admit that it was relying on legislative history to justify even minor departures from the ordinary meaning of the enacted words.[11] When it is invoked by

---

States, 956 A.2d 33, 43–44 (D.C. 2008); *Gillan v. Government Employees Ins. Co.,* 194 P.3d 1071 (Haw. 2008); *Gonzalez v. Thacker,* 231 P.3d 524, 527 (Idaho 2009); *State v. Allen,* 708 N.W.2d 361, 366–67 (Iowa 2006); *State v. Skipper,* 906 So.2d 399, 404–05 (La. 2005); *Stewart Title Guar. Co. v. State Tax Assessor,* 963 A.2d 169 (Me. 2009); *Kramer v. Liberty Prop. Trust,* 968 A.2d 120 (Md. 2009); *Stockman Bank of Mont. v. Mon-Kota, Inc.,* 180 P.3d 1125 (Mont. 2008); *Shipler v. General Motors Corp.,* 710 N.W.2d 807, 831–32 (Neb. 2006); *Chanos v. Nevada Tax Comm'n,* 181 P.3d 675 (Nev. 2008); *State v. Nigou,* 937 A.2d 887, 890 (N.H. 2007); *State v. Geiser,* 763 N.W.2d 469 (N.D. 2009); *State v. Mayes,* 186 P.3d 293, 297–98 (Or. App. 2008); *Travelers Indemn. Co. v. Reker,* 100 S.W.3d 756, 763–65 (Ky. 2003); *In re Hospital Pricing Litigation v. Anmed Health,* 659 S.E.2d 131, 134–36 (S.C. 2008); *Fin-Ag, Inc. v. Cimpl's, Inc.,* 754 N.W.2d 1, 6–7 (S.D. 2008); *Lawrence Cnty. Educ. Ass'n v. Lawrence Cnty. Bd. of Educ.,* 244 S.W.3d 302, 310–14 (Tenn. 2007); *State ex rel. Z.C.,* 165 P.3d 1605 (Utah 2007); *Department of Corrections v. Human Rights Comm'n,* 917 A.2d 451, 453 (Vt. 2007).

[8] For vigorous internal debates within the Michigan Supreme Court over the relevance of legislative materials, compare majority opinions rejecting their relevance, e.g., *People v. Likine,* 823 N.W.2d 50, 75 & n.96 (Mich. 2015); *People v. Gardner,* 753 N.W.2d 78, 84–85, 88–91 (Mich. 2008), with dissenting opinions relying centrally on legislative materials. *Likine,* 823 N.W.2d at 83–84 (Kelly, J., dissenting); *Gardner,* 753 N.W.2d at 97–98 (Cavanaugh, J., dissenting). Some states appear to have little if any usable legislative history. See *Direct T.V., Inc. v. Levin,* 907 N.E.2d 1212, 1253 (Ohio App. 2009); *Such v. State,* 950 A.2d 1150, 1158–59 (R.I. 2008); *Moncrief v. Harvey,* 816 P.2d 97, 111–12 (Wyo. 1991) (Urbigkit, J., dissenting).

[9] David S. Law & David Zaring, Law *Versus Ideology: The Supreme Court and the Use of Legislative History,* 51 Wm. & Mary L. Rev. 1653 (2010); Anita S. Krishnakumar, *Statutory Interpretation in the Roberts Court's First Era: An Empirical and Doctrinal Analysis,* 62 Hastings L.J. 221 (2010).

[10] E.g., *Baker Botts L.L.P. v. ASARCO LLC,* 135 S.Ct. 2158 (2015) (interpreting the Bankruptcy Reform Act of 1978, against a common law baseline, with reliance on dictionaries and no mention of legislative history).

[11] See, e.g., *King v. Burwell,* 135 S.Ct. 2480 (2015) (interpreting the Affordable Care Act of 2010 to depart from the ordinary meaning of statutory language, first by arguing that there was some ambiguity and, then, by relying on statutory structure, with no reference to the extensive legislative history briefed by the parties). Reflecting the Roberts Court baseline understanding of legislative history canons is Larry M. Eig, American Law Division, Congressional Research Service, Report, *Statutory Interpretation: General Principles and Recent Trends* 43–46 (updated Dec. 19, 2011) (hereinafter cited as CRS Report, *Statutory Interpretation*) (drafting guidances for congressional staff, emphasizing plain meaning but if there is ambiguity legislative materials can be relevant).

the Court, legislative history was often given a back seat, confined to footnotes or tossed in at the end of the opinion—but even in those cases there was sometimes judicial pushback.[12] In recent Terms, Justices wanting to confirm ordinary meaning with legislative materials routinely prefaced their invocation with the caveat, "for those who find such materials useful." Is this a path of marginalization the Court should continue? Federal courts of appeal? Should state courts follow as well? Consider the debate among the commentators.

Some judges, public officials, and scholars maintain that statutory interpreters should *never* or *almost never* consider legislative history. The late Justice Antonin Scalia, Judge Frank Easterbrook, and Professor John Manning have been the main exponents of this point of view,[13] as has Justice Stephen Markman, who has led the Michigan Supreme Court toward the exclusionary approach since 1999.[14] A more widely held view, especially within state courts, is that judges can only consider legislative history to clear up ambiguities; if the statutory text, structure, and precedent yield a clear answer, legislative history is unnecessary or even inadmissible.[15] Under either the exclusionary approach or the

---

[12] Compare *Samantar v. Yousuf,* 560 U.S. 305, 319 n.12, 323 (2010) (majority opinion, relying on committee reports to confirm ordinary meaning and whole act arguments), with id. at 326 (Alito, J., concurring) (opining that the legislative history added nothing); id. at 326 (Thomas, J., concurring in part and in the judgment) (refusing to join any of the legislative history discussion); id. at 326–29 (Scalia, J., concurring in the judgment) (extended critique of legislative materials as wasteful expenditures of energy, worthless, malleable, and counterproductive in this case).

[13] Antonin Scalia & Bryan A. Garner, *Reading Law: Interpretation of Legal Texts* (2012); accord, Frank H. Easterbrook, *Statutes' Domains*, 50 U. Chi. L. Rev. 533 (1983); John F. Manning, *The Absurdity Doctrine*, 116 Harv. L. Rev. 2387 (2003).

[14] For a leading statement of the Michigan Supreme Court's post-1999 approach, see *In re Certified Questions from the United States Court of Appeals for the Sixth Circuit,* 659 N.W.2d 597, 600–02 (Mich. 2003) (Young, C.J.). Following the 2008 defeat of the Chief Justice, there was a brief period where the strict textualists were in the minority and legislative history was considered, e.g. *Bush v. Shabahang,* 772 N.W.2d 272, 282–83 (Mich. 2009), but after the 2010 election the strict textualists, still led by Justice Markman, are again in the majority, for the time being. E.g., *Ligonis v. Crittenden Hosp.*, 803 N.W.2d 271 (Mich. 2011).

[15] E.g., *Schwegmann Bros. v. Calvert Distillers Corp.,* 341 U.S. 384, 395 (1951) (Jackson, J., concurring); *People v. Gray,* 319 P.3d 988, 992 (Cal. 2014); *Atwater v. Kortum,* 95 So.3d 85 (Fla. 2012); *Ojo v. Farmers Group,* 356 S.W.3d at 445–49 (Texas) (Willett, J., concurring in part); *Cortez v. State,* 469 S.W.3d 593 (Tex. Crim. App. 2015); *State ex rel. Kalal v. Circuit Court for Dane Cnty.,* 681 N.W.2d 110 (Wis. 2004); 2A *Sutherland Statutes and Statutory Construction* § 48:1 (7th ed. 2015). A particularly lucid explanation of the plain meaning rule as applied to exclude legislative history unless there is ambiguity can be found in CRS Report, *Statutory Interpretation,* 41–43 (updated 2011).

resolve-ambiguities approach, if you believe that "bicycles of any kind" unambiguously and plainly brings motorized bicycles into the section 3 proviso, you would (in theory) not even read the revised legislative history that strongly cuts the other way. In my opinion, if you read the revised legislative history (where Congress codifies rather than overrides *Hogan*), you would be less likely to say there is an ordinary or plain meaning.

Perhaps for this reason, the traditional approach, still discreetly followed by most federal judges and openly championed by Justice Stephen Breyer, Chief Judge Robert Katzmann, and Chief Justice Shirley Abrahamson, is to consider relevant legislative history even if the judge believes there is or might be an ordinary or plain meaning.[16] Under this view, legislative history is usually used or cited to *confirm* ordinary or plain meaning, to make doubly certain that the judge has not missed anything.[17] The California and Texas Supreme Courts, for example, routinely examine legislative history even when the Justices believe there is a plain meaning for the text, read in light of the statutory structure and purpose.[18] Most state court systems will consider relevant legislative materials even when there is or may be a plain meaning.[19] Even the Michigan Supreme

---

[16] *Bank One Chi. N.A. v. Midwest Bank & Trust Co.*, 516 U.S. 264, 276–79 (1996) (Stevens, J., concurring); *People v. Park,* 299 P.3d 1263, 1272–73 (Cal. 2012) (finding a plain meaning but considering the legislative history and finding it consistent with the plain meaning); *Klein v. United States,* 235 P.3d 42 (Cal. 2010) (similar); *State ex rel. Kalal,* 681 N.W.2d at 128–37 (Abrahamson, C.J., dissenting); see Katzmann, *Judging Statutes,* 35–54 (strong defense of legislative history by one of the most influential federal appellate judges); Eskridge, *The New Textualism,* 37 U.C.L.A. L. Rev. at 627–40 (detailed account of the "soft plain meaning rule" traditionally followed by the U.S. Supreme Court, and the variety of legislative materials the Court has traditionally examined).

[17] E.g., *DePierre*, 131 S.Ct. at 2232, 2234–35; *Adoptive Couple v. Baby Girl,* 134 S.Ct. 2552, 2561 (2013); *Carr v. United States*, 560 U.S. 438 (2010); *Wisconsin Public Intervenor v. Mortier*, 501 U.S. 597, 610 n.4 (1991); see Katzmann, *Judging Statutes,* 29–30, 35; James J. Brudney, *Confirmatory Legislative History*, 76 Brooklyn L. Rev. 901 (2011).

[18] E.g., *People v. Albillar,* 244 P.3d 1062 (Cal. 2010); *People v. Anderson,* 235 P.3d 11 (Cal. 2010); *Ojo v. Farmers Group,* 356 S.W.3d at 430–33 (Tex.); *Helena Chem. Co. v. Wilkins,* 47 S.W.3d 486, 493 (Tex. 2001); cf. id. at 506–10 (Abbott, J., dissenting) (insisting upon strict adherence to text but also examining legislative history). See also *Cortez v. State,* 469 S.W.3d 593 (Tex. Crim. App. 2015) (plain meaning rule, but also considering legislative history).

[19] *State v. Batts,* 195 P.3d 144 (Alaska 2008); *People v. Ramirez,* 201 P.3d 466 (Cal. 2009); *Romanoff v. State Comm'n on Judicial Performance*, 126 P.3d 182, 186 (Colo. 2006); *District of Columbia v. Place*, 892 A.2d 1108, 1113–15 (D.C. 2006); *People v. Collins,* 824 N.E.2d 262, 267 (Ill. 2005); *State v. Allen,* 708 N.W.2d 361, 366–67 (Iowa 2006); *Rural Water Dist. #2 v. City of Louisburg,* 207 P.3d 1055 (Kan. 2009); *State v. Skipper,* 906 So.2d 399 (La. 2005); *Kramer v. Liberty Prop. Trust,* 968 A.2d 120 (Md.

Court, which is most adamant against reference to legislative history, sometimes relies on it to confirm plain meaning.[20]

This view suggests the possibility that legislative history can trigger a reconsideration of plain meaning, as one might do in response to the revised legislative history I have presented.[21] This does not happen a lot, because the statutory text and structure usually reflect the explanations in the legislative history; if legislators anticipated the issue, either the statutory text addresses it or, if not, the legislative history is usually silent as well. When there is a direct clash, as I have just presented it, most judges will, internally, reconsider their reading of the statute but, in their written opinion, they will "find" an ambiguity that opens up the statute to the interpretation suggested by the legislative history. Federal and most state judges today will rarely admit that they are trumping text-based meaning with legislative "intent" derived from internal legislative materials, even when they are essentially doing exactly that—a point vividly argued by Richard Re's analysis of some strongly normative opinions authored or joined by the Supreme Court's strictest textualists.[22] Additionally, many judges today set a

---

2009); *Dawson v. Townsend & Sav., Inc.*, 735 So.2d 1131, 1137–39 (Miss. App. 1999); *Stockman Bank of Mont. v. Mon-Kota, Inc.*, 180 P.3d 1125 (Mont. 2008); *State v. Nigou*, 937 A.2d 887, 890 (N.H. 2007); *State v. Smith*, 98 P.3d 1022 (N.M. 2004); *People v. Garson*, 848 N.E.2d 1264 (N.Y. 2006); *State v. Geiser*, 763 N.W.2d 469 (N.D. 2009); *Williams v. Nova Store Sys., L.L.C.*, 109 P.3d 356 (Okla. App. 2004); *State v. Gaines*, 206 P.3d 1042 (Or. 2009) (renouncing the hard plain meaning rule of earlier cases); *Fin-Ag, Inc. v. Cimpl's, Inc.*, 754 N.W.2d 1 (S.D. 2008); *Lawrence Cnty. Educ. Ass'n v. Lawrence Cnty. Bd. of Educ.*, 244 S.W.3d 302, 310–14 (Tenn. 2007); *Alex Sheshunoff Management Servs., L.P. v. Johnson*, 209 S.W.3d 644, 652–55 (Tex. 2006); *Summit Water Distribution Co. v. Summit Cnty.*, 123 P.3d 437 (Utah 2005); *Department of Corrections v. Human Rights Comm'n*, 917 A.2d 451 (Vt. 2007); *Cosmopolitan Engr'g Group, Inc. v. Ondeo Degrement, Inc.*, 149 P.3d 666, 672–73 (Wash. 2006).

[20] E.g., *National Pride at Work, Inc. v. Governor of Michigan*, 748 N.W.2d 524, 541 & nn.22–23 (Mich. 2008) (Markman, J.) (relying on advocacy materials opposing an anti-gay constitutional "marriage or similar union" initiative to strip from gay couples their collective bargaining benefits for nonmarital "domestic partners").

[21] For a classic example, see the House of Lords decision in *Pepper v. Hart*, [1993] 1 All E.R. 42, [1992] 3 W.L.R. 1032 (1992), where the Lords found a plain meaning upon first hearing but reconsidered the plain meaning when provided with cogent legislative history on rehearing. See James J. Brudney, *Below the Surface: Comparative Legislative History Usage by the House of Lords and the Supreme Court*, 85 Wash. U.L. Rev. 1 (2007).

[22] Richard M. Re, *The New* Holy Trinity, 18 Green Bag 2d 407 (2015). Compare *Zuni Pub. Sch. Dist. No. 89 v. Department of Educ.*, 550 U.S. 81 (2007) (Breyer, J., for the Court) (framing a statutory interpretation case through the lens of its legislative and administrative history, before turning to the statutory text, which the Court found ambiguous), and *id.* at 104–06 (Stevens, J., concurring) (announcing that he would apply the legislative intent even if the text were not ambiguous), with *id.* at 107–22 (Scalia, J., dissenting) (finding a plain meaning and strongly denouncing any

higher bar for legislative history in order for them to reconsider their reading of the statutory text and structure.[23]

Which approach is most defensible? To figure out whether legislative history has any value whatsoever, we need to work through the most thoughtful objections to its deployment, including its deployment in cases where there appears to be an ordinary meaning or where the whole act suggests a plain meaning. If legislative history is admissible, as it traditionally has been and as it remains in federal courts and in most state court systems, can it justify a reconsideration of ordinary or plain meaning? Finally, how can judges consider legislative history in a manner that squeezes the most value out of it, without the biggest risks or costs?

The Legislative History Rule

Before turning to the intense legislative history debate, let me start with something uncontroversial—namely, *statutory history*, or the formal changes in the Code made by the legislature when it enacts new laws and amends them over time. The statutory history of vehicles regulation in Lafayette Park would start with whatever published administrative rules or guidances the National Park Service had before 1992, would then contrast the new rules established by the Lafayette Park Safety Act of 1992, and would conclude with the changes in the U.S. Code made by the Soaper Amendment of 2013. Statutory history also includes authoritative court decisions, such as *Hogan v. National Park Service*. The characteristic feature of statutory history is that it does not include the documents and reports generated by the *internal* deliberations of Congress in or around 1992 and 2013.

No one in the academy and no federal or state judge maintains that statutory history is not admissible and potentially relevant when judges are interpreting those laws.[24] For more than a century, courts

---

derogation, as well as announcing the death of *Holy Trinity*), and with *id.* at 123 (Souter, J., dissenting) (finding that an unambiguous statutory text must trump clear congressional intent). Note that Justice Stevens has retired, and no current Justice has dared rely on *Holy Trinity* since 2007.

[23] Compare, e.g., *Hall v. United States*, 132 S.Ct. 1882, 1892 (2012) (declining to depart from plain meaning based upon legislative history the majority found less than compelling), with id. at 1895–98 (Breyer, J., dissenting) (presenting very strong legislative history and purpose arguments in support of a more flexible reading of the text).

[24] See CRS Report, *Statutory Interpretation,* 44 (updated 2011) (contrasting the formal changes made in a statute over the years, what I call "statutory history" and

in the United Kingdom would not consider legislative history but would consider statutory history, which in that polity often included the reports of law reform commissions to which Parliament responded with new statutes or amendments to old ones. In many cases, statutory history is relevant and sometimes critically persuasive to judges in this country, especially state court judges, including judges who are skeptical of internal legislative history.[25]

The simple statutory history for our Park Safety Act is surprisingly relevant (and relevant in surprising ways) to an understanding of that statute. Consider this issue: Are Segways (such as the ones pictured above) "vehicles" prohibited by the statute? The statutory history demonstrates how the process of amendment created new ambiguities in the law. Pre-1992 Park Service regulations had nothing to say about Segways, as they did not show up in the nation's capital until the new millennium. The Park Safety Act of 1992 created a new regulatory regime that might have regulated Segways as "vehicles" when they came into wide public use. After *Hogan v. National Park Service,* which held that motorized bicycles are "vehicles" because they are motorized and speedy mechanisms conveying people, Segways might have been covered by the statute (depending on how liberally a judge would interpret *Hogan*'s "speed" criterion). But the enacted version of the Soaper Amendment of 2013 overrode the regulatory test of *Hogan.* After 2013, the key inquiry for the definition of "vehicle" is no longer whether a mechanism (or thing) is motorized and speedy, but

---

which is not controversial to consult, from internal "legislative history," which is controversial now).

[25] E.g., *Kellogg Brown & Root Servs., Inc. v. United States ex rel. Carter,* 135 S.Ct. 1970 (2015) (unanimous Court) (interpreting the Wartime Suspension of Limitations Act by reference to statutory history and dictionaries, but ignoring internal legislative materials); *Astrue v. Capato,* 132 S.Ct. 2021, 2031 (2012); *Schindler Elevator Corp. v. United States ex rel. Kirk,* 563 U.S. 401 (2011); *King v. Campbell,* 988 So.2d 969 (Ala. 2007); *Price v. Thomas Built Buses, Inc.,* 260 S.W.2d 300, 305–06 (Ark. 2007); *Bautista v. State,* 863 So.2d 1180, 1186 (Fla. 2003); *Sikes v. State,* 485 S.E.2d 206, 211 (Ga. 1997); *Jacobs v. State,* 640 N.E.2d 61 (Ind. App. 1994); *State v. Crone,* 545 N.W.2d 267, 271–73 (Iowa 1996); *Fournier v. Elliott,* 966 A.2d 410 (Me. 2009); *Dawson v. Townsend & Sons, Inc.,* 735 So.2d 1131, 1137–39 (Miss. App. 1999); *State v. Premium Standard Farms, Inc.,* 100 S.W.3d 157 (Mo. App. 2003); *S.L.H. v. State Compensation Mut. Ins. Fund,* 15 P.3d 948 (Mont. 2000); *Klumb v. Board of Educ.,* 970 A.2d 354 (N.Y. 2009); *State v. Smith,* 98 P.3d 1022, 1027–29 (N.M. 2004); *In re K.L.,* 674 S.E.2d 789, 793–94 (N.C. App. 2009); *Enos v. Doe,* 669 S.E.2d 619 (S.C. 2008); *State v. Nieberger,* 128 P.3d 1223, 1228 (Vt. 2006); *American Water Co. v. Prince William Cnty. Serv. Auth.,* 436 S.E.2d 618, 622–23 (Va. 1993); *McCoy v. Van Kirk,* 500 S.E.2d 534, 541–42 (W.Va. 1997). See generally *People v. Gardner,* 753 N.W.2d 78, 89 (Mich. 2008) (endorsing the use of statutory history but not legislative history by post-1999 textualist majority).

whether it is so speedy as to pose undue safety risks. Under this statutory history, which almost any judge would carefully consider, it is even less clear that Segways fall under section 3's definition. Their maximum speed is ten to twelve miles per hour. Is this fast enough to be a safety risk?

Statutory history is always admissible but does not usually provide closure for the interpretive issue before the court—and sometimes the statutory history deepens the statutory ambiguity, as it does in our case of the Segway. How might judges resolve this potential ambiguity? Is a Segway traveling as fast as twelve miles per hour sufficiently hazardous to park users to qualify as a "vehicle" the statute bars from Lafayette Park? Given the statutory history and the current text of the entire statute, how would you answer this question? Jot down in the margin whether you think Segways are "vehicles" regulated by the law. How confident are you that this is the right answer?

Do you think you also ought to consider the internal materials generated within Congress when it amended the statute in 2013? Review the Soaper Amendment's legislative history, as laid out at the beginning of this chapter (ignore the revised history, where Congress approved *Hogan*). Do you think these materials ought to be consulted by the judge? Several powerful theoretical objections have been leveled against judicial reliance on legislative history.[26] (I reserve a few practical objections to the next part of the chapter.) No one argues that these theoretical objections apply to statutory history.

To begin with, critics of legislative history maintain that it undermines the *rule of law*, by diverting judicial attention away from the ordinary or plain meaning of statutory texts, and toward some amorphous, floating, and incoherent inquiry into "legislative intent." Under both the U.S. Constitution and state constitutions, the role of the legislature is to enact statutory texts that have the force of law, and the role of judges is to interpret these texts through an objective method. Any diversion from enacted statutory text and from the

---

[26] An early critique of legislative history is Max Radin, *Statutory Interpretation,* 43 Harv. L. Rev. 863 (1930). For more recent critiques, see Scalia & Garner, *Reading Law*, 269–91; Office of Legal Policy, Dep't of Justice, *Using and Misusing Legislative History: A Re-Evaluation of the Status of Legislative History in Statutory Interpretation* (Jan. 5, 1989) (Assistant Attorney General Stephen Markman headed the Office); Frank H. Easterbrook, *Text, History, and Structure in Statutory Interpretation,* 17 Harv. J.L. & Pub. Pol'y 61 (1994); Alex Kozinski, *Should Reading Legislative History Be an Impeachable Offense?,* 31 Suffolk U.L. Rev. 807 (1998); John F. Manning, *Textualism as a Nondelegation Doctrine*, 97 Colum. L. Rev. 673 (1997).

formal evolution of the statute (i.e., statutory history) renders law less predictable and less objective.[27] Do you think that consulting the legislative history of the Soaper Amendment makes it less predictable whether the statute regulates Segways? Less objective? Does it make a difference at all? After revisiting the legislative history I originally presented (and not the revised history)—Senator Soaper's original concerns, the Senate and House bills, the conference report and the joint explanation of the conferees—jot down your thoughts.

Thus, critics complain that legislative materials such as committee reports and explanations of conference committees lead courts toward "psychoanalysis of Congress" rather than "analysis of the statute," to quote Justice Robert Jackson's felicitous objection.[28] This might be defensible if judges could be sure that legislative history would reveal to them a unified legislative will or intent. Like state legislatures, Congress is a "We" and not an "It." It is challenging to aggregate a collective "intent" of an institution with so many members (most of whom say nothing about legislation they vote for) and with a process requiring bicameral approval and presentment to another official, the chief executive. According to some critics, the only way you can attribute a collective intent to Congress is to pay attention to the words actually voted on and passed by the House and Senate and presented to the President. Anything else is unreliable and subject to manipulation—even the explanation of conferees accompanying a conference committee report, which is neither voted on by the House and Senate nor presented to the President.[29] Notice that this critique has even greater bite for unorthodox legislation, especially laws that bypass the committee process.

These longstanding quarrels with reliance on legislative materials were supplemented with a deeper critique of their use in the 1980s. That critique can be linked with larger rethinking of the role of judges in our polity. At exactly the point in time that conservative commentators and judges (like Judge Scalia of the D.C.

---

[27] Office of Legal Policy, *Using and Misusing Legislative History*; accord, Scalia & Garner, *Reading Law;* Antonin Scalia, *A Matter of Interpretation* (1997); Easterbrook, *Statutes' Domains*, 50 U. Chi. L. Rev. at 547–49.

[28] *United States v. Public Utilities Comm'n of Calif.,* 345 U.S. 295, 319 (1953) (Jackson, J., concurring).

[29] On the difficulty of aggregating legislative statements into a collective "intent," see Radin, *Statutory Interpretation*, 43 Harv. L. Rev. at 870–71 (classic critique), as well as Kenneth Shepsle, *Congress Is a "They," Not an "It": Legislative Intent as Oxymoron,* 12 Int'l Rev. L. & Econ. 239 (1992). See also Jeremy Waldron, *Law and Disagreement* (1999).

Circuit) were abandoning "original intent" theories for interpreting the U.S. Constitution, they were criticizing "legislative intent" as a relevant inquiry in statutory interpretation. The new metric, for both kinds of interpretation, became "original meaning."[30]

Moreover, the current criticism is not just a quarrel over abstractions, i.e., psychoanalyzing Congress or finding a coherent legislative intent. By considering legislator statements—whether they be the explanations of conferees or floor speeches by bill sponsors or questions raised in committee hearings—courts may *encourage* legislators to make normative statements supplementing or supplanting statutory texts. This may corrupt the legislative process itself (as well as statutory interpretation), for legislators may understand the audience for their statements to be judges and other interpreters and not just their colleagues. At best, this process may undermine the candor needed for productive legislative deliberation. At worst, this process might produce more tricks and deceitful statements by legislators and their staffs. Such a corrupting process is therefore potentially anti-democratic.[31]

Legislative history is often deployed to flesh out a statutory purpose, which then becomes a reference point for rewriting statutory text. (Indeed, some judges and scholars conflate deployment of legislative history with "purposivist" interpretation generally, which is quite wrong, as textualists themselves invoke purpose and sometimes rely on it as their primary reason for an interpretation.) Critics maintain that this is lamentable, not only for the reasons adduced in the rule of law and democracy criticisms, but also for institutional reasons. The job of judges is to apply texts predictably, objectively, even mechanically (the rule of law objection). They are not doing their jobs when they wander into legislative materials, and they are potentially disrupting future legislative deliberations (the democracy objection). The institutional objection to legislative

---

[30] Steven G. Calabresi, *A Critical Introduction to the Originalism Debate,* 31 Harv. J.L. & Pub. Pol'y 875 (2008) (excellent survey of the origins of "original meaning" as the focus of conservative judicialism); Vasan Kesavan & Michael Stokes Paulsen, *The Interpretive Force of the Constitution's Secret Drafting History,* 91 Geo. L.J. 1113 (2003). This critique of "intent" immediately found its way into statutory interpretation, as reflected in Antonin Scalia, "Speech on Use of Legislative History" (delivered between fall, 1985, and spring, 1986, at various law schools), discussed in Daniel A. Farber & Philip P. Frickey, *Legislative Intent and Public Choice*, 74 Va. L. Rev. 423, 440–43 (1988).

[31] See William N. Eskridge Jr. & John Ferejohn, *Politics, Interpretation, and the Rule of Law*, in *The Rule of Law: Nomos XXXVI* (Ian Shapiro ed. 1993). An early version of this point was suggested in Scalia, "Speech on Use of Legislative History," 7.

materials is that they encourage judges to engage in investigations beyond their competence and to take on a role unsuited to their office, namely, implementation of statutes to carry out their purposes. Selected through an elite process focusing on their legal abilities and serving life tenures, federal judges have neither the wisdom nor the institutional capacity nor the legitimacy to implement statutory purposes in a manner that serves the long-term public interest. (State judges are often elected or subject to retention elections, so their legitimacy may have a stronger grounding, a topic explored in depth by Aaron Bruhl and Ethan Leib.[32]) Instead, that is the job of agencies, which are staffed by experts in the field and are democratically accountable to the chief executive and the legislature in ways that judges are not.[33]

These are thoughtful criticisms of judicial consideration of legislative history. At the very least, they require a reconsideration of what judges ought to be doing when they consult such materials. On the whole, do you think the critics have make out a compelling case for complete exclusion of legislative history? Or for a selective invocation of legislative history, perhaps when the textual and precedential sources are completely indeterminate? Going beyond these stances, I shall now argue in favor of a *legislative history rule* reflecting the approach traditionally followed by the U.S. Supreme Court, the New York Court of Appeals, the California Supreme Court, and the Texas Supreme Court: Reliable legislative materials ought to be a rich source of guidance when interpreters figure out the ordinary meaning of statutory language, read in light of the statutory purpose, both understood through the eyes of the legislators responsible for the statute.[34]

Rule of Law: The Meaning of Words and the Structure of the Statute. Most commentators and a large majority of judges agree that the focus of statutory interpretation must be the text enacted by Congress. Today, most federal and state judges will consult

---

[32] Aaron-Andrew P. Bruhl & Ethan J. Leib, *Elected Judges and Statutory Interpretation,* 79 U. Chi. L. Rev. 1215 (2012).

[33] Antonin Scalia, *Judicial Deference to Administrative Interpretations of Law,* 1989 Duke L.J. 511; accord, Adrian Vermeule, *Judging Under Uncertainty* (2006) (advancing a more radical institutionalist critique of both legislative history and whole act analysis).

[34] The meta-rule in text is derived from Eskridge, *Dynamic Statutory Interpretation,* ch. 4, and Henry M. Hart Jr. & Albert M. Sacks, *The Legal Process: Basic Problems in the Making and Application of Law* 1253–54 (William N. Eskridge, Jr. & Philip P. Frickey eds. 1994) (tent. ed. 1958).

dictionaries as well as their own understanding of grammar to help figure out the ordinary meanings of statutory words (chapter one). Moreover, judges are, increasingly, willing to consult the Internet and other popular sources of guidance for how words are used in our language. If judges are willing to consult all these sources for guidance about the meaning of statutory words, phrases, and sentences, why should judges not be willing to consult contemporary legislative materials to see how legislators and legislative committees were using words, phrases, and sentences when they deliberated about the very statute being interpreted?[35]

Indeed, re-read the Park Safety Act, reprinted at the beginning of this chapter. Does the Act itself not suggest inquiries into legislative history that would help the interpreter figure out the meaning of "vehicle," as used in this law? Specifically, if you were asked whether roller skates, skateboards, and adult tricycles were regulated by the statute, would you consider a dictionary more helpful than legislative history suggested by reading the statute?

A dictionary would be of little value in figuring out what "vehicle" means in the context of this particular law. Not only does the statute provide its own definition of "vehicle" in section 3, but sections 1 and 2 provide other language clues about the ambit of the statute that render dictionaries less relevant and legislative history potentially more relevant for the interpretive enterprise. For example, section 1 includes a congressional finding that there have been "serious accidents" in Lafayette Park, and some have required "hospitalization." What kinds of vehicles were the causes of these accidents? The legislative history probably provides evidence along these lines. If the legislative history revealed that only automobiles, trucks, motorcycles, and motor scooters were involved in those serious accidents, an interpreter would (and ought to be) much more reluctant to read the term "vehicle" broadly to include such minor items as roller blades, tricycles, or even skateboards. On the other hand, if one or more of the "serious accidents" in the park was caused by a skateboarder, that is powerful evidence—much more powerful than a dictionary—that a broader understanding of "vehicle" is appropriate.

---

[35] Hart & Sacks, *The Legal Process,* 1253 (Eskridge & Frickey eds.). For examples of how committee hearings and reports can be a useful legislative dictionary, revealing how legislators used the statutory terms during their deliberations, see *Mohamad v. Palestinian Auth.*, 132 S.Ct. 1702, 1709–10 (2012); id. at 1711 (Breyer, J., concurring); *DePierre*, 131 S.Ct. at 2232, 2234–35; *Gray,* 319 P.3d at 992–93 (Cal.).

Does section 3 of the Park Safety Act, as revised in 2013, define "vehicles" broadly enough to include Segways? Using the terminology of section 3, one can say that a Segway is a "thing used for conveying a person from one place to another," but is it a "form[ ] of conveyance that pose[s] safety hazards to park users because of their speed"? Clipping along at up to twelve miles per hour, a Segway is much less speedy than the specific examples listed in section 3, namely, "automobiles, motorcycles, [and] motor scooters." Indeed, a Segway is much slower than a bicycle and even slower than the 1897 Léon Bollée Voiturette described in chapter one. Because Segways have little motors, the Court's precedent in *Hogan v. National Park Service*, examined in the prior chapter, might bring them within the definition of "vehicle," but the Soaper Amendment negates "motorized" as the litmus test for "vehicles." Now, re-read the joint explanation of the conferees: Does this help you figure out whether motorized bicycles qualify as a statutory "vehicle"?

The joint explanation of the conferees suggests that the Soaper Amendment supersedes the motor-focused reasoning of *Hogan* and suggests a line of inquiry that helps clarify what might be the standard for inclusion as "vehicles." Recall the conferees' reason for excluding motorized bicycles from section 3's definition: "Because motorized bicycles can reach speeds of 25–30 miles per hour, they should be regulated, but as 'bicycles', and should not be prohibited entirely as 'vehicles'." Segways, operating at ten to twelve miles per hour, are much slower than motorized bicycles (as the conferees understood them), and this fact is a strong reason to think that Segways are not regulated "vehicles." For exactly the same reason that the conferees exempted motorized bicycles from the general prohibition of "vehicles," Segways should be exempted. Because they are not analogous to bicycles, the conferees surely expected Segways not to be subject to the section 3 proviso, either.

Why is this such a persuasive reason for excluding Segways from the statutory definition of "vehicles"? The statute defines "vehicle" in a particular way, rendering dictionaries less reliable and suggesting caution to a judge before she applies her personal intuitions onto the statutory term. The joint explanation of the conferees is like a dictionary for the entire phrase, "any thing used for conveying a person from one place to another, including automobiles, trucks, motorcycles, motor scooters, and other forms of conveyance that pose safety hazards to park users because of their speed." Indeed, it is better than a dictionary, because the authors of the joint explanation were contemporary observers close to the process by which the Soaper

Amendment was enacted. They are more knowledgeable about the linguistic as well as policy context of the terminology than a judge is going to be.[36]

Perhaps surprisingly, the biggest critics of legislative history have, indirectly, conceded that such materials can be used to show how words were used and what general principles lend coherence to the structure of a legal document. When interpreting the Constitution of 1789, Justice Scalia (like most of his colleagues) routinely relied on the Constitution's "legislative history," namely documents from the ratification debates, especially *The Federalist Papers*.[37] The Framers of the Constitution were a "We" and not an "It," and of course the ultimate ratifiers were "*We* the People." Hence, almost all of the criticisms of statutory legislative history are equally applicable to constitutional legislative history. The famous essays by James Madison and Alexander Hamilton were not vetted or voted upon by the other Framers, were published after most states had already ratified the Constitution, and could not have influenced more than a handful (if that many) of delegates to the New York ratifying convention.[38]

When asked to justify his repeated citation and reliance on these background documents, never voted upon by the states and not a part of the Constitution's text, Justice Scalia offered this explanation:

> I rely on [*The Federalist Papers*] because it sets forth the views of intelligent, well-informed persons of the time, which are entitled to great weight on the basis of their experience and their closeness to the process. For similar reasons, I'll consider what Thomas Jefferson says, though he also was not present at the Constitutional Convention and though his words were most unlikely to have been before the ratifying conventions. His words won't be conclusive, but they may supply a persuasive indication of what the

---

[36] Katzmann, *Judging Statutes,* 35–39.

[37] E.g., *Printz v. United States*, 521 U.S. 898, 910–15 (1997) (Scalia, J.) (exhaustive analysis of a few of the *Federalist Papers,* to refute the suggestion made by the Government and the dissenters that a nontextual constitutional anti-commandeering principle is not applicable to state executive officials); *id.* at 919–22 (extensive reliance on *Federalist Papers* to establish an anti-commandeering principle from the federalist structure of the Constitution).

[38] For realistic appraisals of how little authority *The Federalist Papers* can be said to possess, see Arthur Furtwangler, *The Authority of Publius: A Reading of* The Federalist Papers (1984); Larry D. Kramer, *Madison's Audience,* 112 Harv. L. Rev. 611 (1999).

> Constitution meant to the people at the time. That's quite different from legislative history.[39]

Like *The Federalist Papers,* legislative materials "are entitled to great weight" as the interpreter tries to figure out what the words of the law mean. To help us understand what the Park Safety Act, as amended, "meant to the people at the time," the joint explanation of the conferees is "entitled to great weight" for exactly the same reason Justice Scalia gave for considering *The Federalist Papers.*

By the way, Justice Scalia had a much better answer to the question, How can you rely on *The Federalist Papers* to interpret the Constitution, while ignoring legislative history to interpret statutes? Because federal judges have been relying on legislative materials for so long, there is a danger that members of Congress or their staff may insert statements into the legislative record in order to influence judges and not to honestly explain what their proposed legislation means and how it will solve problems.[40] There was much less danger of such strategic use of legislative history by the authors of *The Federalist Papers,* who famously opined that their writings ought to have no value for future interpreters of the Constitution. To be sure, congressional staff deny that they manufacture legislative history for these purposes, and any manipulative deployment of the legislative record in this way would hurt or even sink the career of a member of Congress or staff counsel.[41]

Another concern about the use of legislative materials is that, for complicated legislation, they tend to be sprawling and full of potential contradictions. Thus, committee hearings and floor debates on the Soaper Amendment might point in several different directions. While the conferees may have agreed that motorized bicycles having speeds

---

[39] Antonin Scalia & John F. Manning, *A Dialogue on Statutory and Constitutional Interpretation,* 80 Geo. Wash. L. Rev. 1610, 1618 (2012).

[40] William N. Eskridge Jr., *Should the Supreme Court Read the* Federalist *But Not Statutory Legislative History?,* 66 Geo. Wash. L. Rev. 1301 (1998); see also *Blanchard v. Bergeron,* 489 U.S. 87, 98–99 (1989) (Scalia, J., concurring in part); Scalia, "Speech on Legislative History," 7.

[41] James J. Brudney, *Congressional Commentary on Judicial Interpretation of Statutes: Idle Chatter or Telling Response?,* 93 Mich. L. Rev. 1, 41–56 (1994) (reporting that Members of Congress would lose credibility if they lied to their colleagues about bills for which they are floor managers or committee chairs); Abbe R. Gluck & Lisa Schultz Bressman, *Statutory Interpretation from the Inside: An Empirical Study of Congressional Drafting, Delegation, and Statutory Interpretation: Part I,* 65 Stan. L. Rev. 901 (2013) (reporting that congressional staff, from both political parties, believe that legislative history serves important congressional process purposes and is reliable for that reason).

of twenty-five miles per hour were not "vehicles" as they were using the term, other parts of the congressional record might reveal a broader use of the term. Recall that the House bill specifically included Segways in its proposed rewrite of section 3's definition. That is a fair concern. Just as dictionaries will offer a rich array of definitions for popular terms, so legislative history will often offer variety. Does this undermine its utility in resolving ambiguities? Not necessarily.

Don't forget that Justice Scalia opined that *The Federalist Papers* "are entitled to great weight on the basis of their experience and their closeness to the process." In figuring out the public meaning of "vehicles" in the Park Safety Act, as amended in 2013, interpreters ought to give special attention to the views of the conferees, because they were the closest legislators to the process that produced the *final statutory language*. That they were the authors of the final text does not render their views dispositive, but surely their role is relevant in resolving textual ambiguities. Specifically, the conferees *rejected* the House version of section 3, which targeted Segways and conceptualized vehicles as motorized, and *adopted* the Senate version of section 3, which ignored Segways and conceptualized vehicles as safety hazards because of their great speed. Like the Senate, the House then voted for the Soaper Amendment as rewritten in the conference report; the revised bill, Senator Soaper's version, is what the President signed into law. This legislative history makes me much more reluctant to read the plain text of the Park Safety Act, as amended, to include Segways.

Governance: Applying Statutory Text in Light of Legislative Principle, Plan, or Purpose. Some interpreters would read the Park Safety Act and its statutory history to regulate Segways as "vehicles" under section 3 and would bar them entirely from Lafayette Park. Because such mechanisms are motorized, they are similar to the items listed in the section 3 definition of "vehicle." Although I believe this conclusion is debatable as a textual matter, some judges might say there is a statutory plain meaning. However, if those judges considered the rejection of the House bill in conference and if they read the joint explanation of the conferees, some of them (and I should hope most of them) would change their minds about whether section 3 has a plain meaning that regulates Segways as vehicles.[42]

---

[42] For a dramatic example where judges found a statutory plain meaning but then changed their minds after consulting legislative materials, see *Pepper v. Hart,*

Such judges *ought* to change their minds, partly for rule of law reasons. As discussed earlier in this volume, it is bad manners and poor interpretive skills for an interlocutor to ignore the point of a conversation. It is even more wrong for a statutory interpreter to ignore the point of a statutory text—its purpose, the legislature's underlying plan or policy, even the principle it represents. The joint explanation of the conferees suggests that the *purpose* or *principle* of revised section 3 is to exclude really speedy vehicles entirely, to provide a modest regulation for bicycles of all sorts, and implicitly to allow other, less speedy, mechanisms into Lafayette Park. Interestingly, Justice Scalia made exactly this point for *The Federalist Papers*, which he said are especially relevant in figuring out the general principles that give coherence to the Constitution.[43]

Good governance is another reason judges should reconsider an apparent plain meaning that is at odds with the plan of the legislation. Following the Supreme Court's use, I am using the term "plan of the legislation" to discuss how the different parts of the statute fit together and create public policy.[44] Whether Segways are banned from the park entirely (as "vehicles") represents a normative judgment not just about words, but about public safety and what kind of stuff the state is willing to allow in Lafayette Park. Judges usually have little or no comparative advantage in deciding these issues; even the most brilliant judge cannot read the four corners of the Park Safety Act, as amended, and figure out what is the precise policy or purpose of revised section 3. Legislative materials tend to be particularly helpful here, for the reporting committees and floor managers generally explain the proposed legislation in terms of the

---

[1993] 1 All E.R. 42, [1992] 3 W.L.R. 1032 (House of Lords 1992). See also James J. Brudney, *Below the Surface: Comparative Legislative History Usage by the House of Lords and the Supreme Court*, 85 Wash. U.L. Rev. 1 (2007). For an example where powerfully persuasive deliberative materials supporting a voter initiative left Justice Markman and his textualist colleagues on the Michigan Supreme Court *unpersuaded*, see *National Pride at Work*, 748 N.W.2d 524 (holding that collective bargaining "domestic partnership" benefits amount to government "recognition" of a "marriage or other similar union," notwithstanding strong evidence that supporters of the initiative repeatedly denied that it would affect domestic partnership benefits).

43 Scalia & Manning, *Dialogue on Statutory and Constitutional Interpretation*, 80 Geo. Wash. L. Rev. at 1618.

44 See Abbe R. Gluck, *Imperfect Statutes, Imperfect Courts: Understanding Congress's Plan in the Era of Unorthodox Lawmaking*, 129 Harv. L. Rev. 62 (2015) (analyzing the majority opinion in *King v. Burwell*, which ironed out odd consequences of specific statutory language by interpreting it in light of the overall "plan" for the Affordable Care Act of 2010).

problems it will solve or ameliorate, the overall purpose of the law, and the policies and principles that undergird it.[45]

Finally, there is a reliance feature supporting judicial consideration of legislative history. Between the 1930s and the 1990s, the U.S. Supreme Court pervasively relied on legislative history to discern and refine statutory purpose(s) as well as specific understandings of language and policy compromises. Congressional drafters relied on that practice, specifically to downplay provisions in federal statutes setting forth congressional findings and purpose(s). The House of Representatives' drafting manual, created in 1995 (three years after the enactment of the Lafayette Safety Act), says this: "Discourage clients [House sponsors and committees] from including findings and purposes. Both are matters that are more appropriately and safely dealt with in the committee report than in the bill."[46] As a matter of legislative supremacy as well as carrying out the deliberated goals of Congress, legislative history might even be required reading, even for textualist judges, when federal statutes were enacted during the heyday of legislative history.[47]

As before, there are legitimate concerns about the use of legislative history to illuminate statutory purposes, principles, or plans. There is a level of generality problem and a plurality of purposes problem. The statutory plan often entails a number of purposes, all of which are discussed with excessive optimism and none of which should be pursued at all costs. Discussion among legislators, whether in committee hearings or reports or in floor debates, tends to operate at a high level of generality, to ignore the variety of purposes animating statutes, and to bury possible competing purposes.

Hence, when statutory text supports a particular interpretation, judges should not reject that interpretation simply because it is inconsistent with their reading of the statutory purpose or plan. Instead, the judges should ask themselves whether they are reading

---

[45] Hart & Sacks, *The Legal Process*, 1228–33, 1253–54 (Eskridge & Frickey eds.).

[46] Ira B. Forstater, Office of Legislative Counsel, U.S. House of Representatives, *House Legislative Counsel's Manual on Drafting Style* § 325(a) (Nov. 1995); cf. House Office of Legislative Counsel, *Introduction to Legislative Drafting* 7–8 (Jan. 7, 2015) (similar statement, but omitting reference to committee reports).

[47] Eskridge, *The New Textualism*, 37 U.C.L.A. L. Rev. at 683–84 (raising a constitutional "bait and switch" problem with a court's refusing to consider legislative history generated in the period where Congress was relying on judicial consultation of such materials).

the purpose too broadly or the text too narrowly. Recall, from the introduction, that text and purpose have a dialectical "both/and" rather than oppositional "either/or" relationship. To ground her inner dialogue between text and purpose in proper statutory policy, it behooves the judge to inform herself of the legislative deliberations and compromises that accompanied the enactment of the statute.

Democracy: Viewing Statutes Through the Eyes of Legislators Responsible for Those Statutes. Almost all judges and scholars agree that legislative expectations are important in statutory interpretation. For decades, it was boilerplate language in statutory interpretation decisions that the relevant inquiry was "legislative intent." The U.S. Supreme Court has stepped away from this language in the last generation, but few state legislators and judges have followed the Justices in this regard. "In interpreting a statute, a court shall diligently attempt to ascertain legislative intent," prescribed the Texas Legislature in 1985.[48] Even the über-textualist Michigan Supreme Court continues to say that "[t]he cardinal rule of statutory construction is to discern and give effect to the intent of the Legislature."[49]

The primary disagreement is whether "legislative intent" is exclusively or predominantly known by examining the text enacted by the legislators—or whether judges gain greater understanding of that intent through reading the materials created during the legislative process. Ignored in the legislative history debate is the fact that every legislature to have addressed the issue has passed statutes inviting judicial reliance on legislative history.[50] Typical is North Dakota's codification: "If a statute is ambiguous, the court, in determining the intention of the legislation, may consider among other matters * * * [t]he legislative history."[51] When Oregon's judiciary moved toward a modified textualist approach that excluded legislative history in the large majority of cases, the Oregon Legislature responded with this mild rebuke that the Oregon Supreme Court interpreted to direct it to consider legislative history: "A court shall give the weight to the

---

[48] Texas Code Construction Act of 1985, Acts 1985, 69th Leg., ch. 479, Tex. Govt. Code § 312.005.

[49] *People v. Williams,* 814 N.W.2d 270, 274 (Mich. 2012), quoting *People v. Dowdy,* 802 N.W.2d 239 (Mich. 2011) (itself quoting a 1995 decision).

[50] Jacob Scott, *Codified Canons and the Common Law of Interpretation,* 98 Geo. L.J. 341, 378–82 (2010) (providing a comprehensive survey of state codified canons and reporting that every state that has addressed the issue has invited reliance on legislative history).

[51] N.D. Cent. Code § 1–02–39(3).

legislative history that the court considers to be appropriate."[52] The Texas statute is more liberal: "In construing a statute, whether or not the statute is considered ambiguous, a court may consider among other matters the * * * legislative history."[53]

At the federal level, Congress has never enacted a statute generally authorizing or inviting courts to consider legislative history, but the 1995 drafting manual used by the Legislative Counsel of the House of Representatives explicitly assumes that courts are reading committee reports, at the very least.[54] This is not always the case in written opinions, and leading legislators from both parties have expressed concern that relevant congressional materials are sometimes being ignored by federal judges.[55] In their empirical examination of the congressional drafting and dealmaking process, Abbe Gluck and Lisa Schultz Bressman report that "legislative history was emphatically viewed by almost all of our respondents—Republicans and Democrats, majority and minority—as the most important drafting and interpretive tool apart from text. * * * Nor is it the case that members of Congress—or even their staffs—are more engaged with textual drafting than with legislative history drafting. In fact, many of our respondents said precisely the opposite: members and their staffs focus more on legislative history, while the nonpartisan professional drafters in the Offices of Legislative Counsel focus on text."[56]

The foregoing evidence is preliminary, but it is significant that no one familiar with the congressional process has published a disagreement with Professors Gluck and Bressman on this score, and knowledgeable scholars of the legislative process credit their findings.[57] If the statutory evidence from state codified canons and

---

[52] Ore. Rev. Stat. § 174.020(3), expansively applied in *State v. Gaines*, 206 P.3d 1042 (Or. 2009). See Abbe R. Gluck, *The States as Laboratories of Statutory Interpretation: Methodological Consensus and the New Modified Textualism,* 119 Yale L.J. 1750, 1775–85 (2010) (examining the Oregon experiment in substantial exclusion of legislative materials, the mild legislative pushback, and the judicial retreat from the exclusion).

[53] Tex. Govt. Code § 311.023(3).

[54] See Forstater, Office of Legislative Counsel, House of Representatives, *Manual on Drafting Style* § 325(a) (discouraging statutory purpose provisions, because purpose is better handled in committee reports).

[55] See Katzmann, *Judging Statutes,* 36–37.

[56] Gluck & Bressman, *Statutory Interpretation from the Inside: Part I,* 65 Stan. L. Rev. at 965–66; accord, Victoria F. Nourse & Jane S. Schacter, *The Politics of Legislative Drafting: A Congressional Case Study*, 77 N.Y.U. L. Rev. 575 (2002).

[57] Katzmann, *Judging Statutes,* 37–39, 43 (endorsing the Gluck and Bressman findings about the importance and reliability of internal legislative history); cf. CRS

the survey evidence of congressional staff are taken seriously, the new textualist rejection of legislative materials is strongly inconsistent with legislative supremacy in the statutory arena and with the faithful agency theory of statutory judging. That is, judges refusing to consult legislative materials are being recalcitrant rather than faithful agents of the legislature; they are not implementing statutes in the way legislators expected and thought they had directed. Are the rule of law and cost-benefit objections to legislative history so compelling as to upbend legislative expectations in this way? The burden on the critics is higher than we thought earlier, based upon the long history of reliance on legislative history at the federal level and the increasing reliance at the state level (as more legislative history becomes available on-line).

Although he was not aware of the rich empirical work on this issue, Justice Scalia would have responded that legislators ought to be more alarmed than they are about legislative history, because (in his view) it increases the discretion of judges, by giving them a wide array of materials from which to choose and, hence, to liberate them to interpret statutes to reflect their own subjective preferences and not the objective policies required by the statutory language. As Judge Harold Leventhal famously quipped, "using legislative history is like looking out over the crowd and picking out your friends."[58] From this remark, and without any citation to political science scholars or empirical studies, Justice Scalia argued that legislative history offers result-oriented judges many options to escape from textual plain meanings and to read their own values into statutes. If true, this crowd-shopping feature of using legislative history not only undermines the rule of law, but is undemocratic as well.

Apart from the fact that argument from quip is an unreliable form of reasoning, an important problem with the crowd-shopping objection is that it can be made about most sources of guidance in statutory interpretation. The most stringent textualist approaches to

---

Report, *Statutory Interpretation*, 41–47 (updated 2011) (providing statutory interpretation guidance to congressional drafters, with a lengthy discussion of legislative history as a relevant source of guidance for ambiguous statutory provisions).

58 Judge Patricia Wald, *Some Observations on the Use of Legislative History in the 1981 Supreme Court Term*, 68 Iowa L. Rev. 195, 214 (1983) (quoting Judge Leventhal). Justice Scalia's initial version of the now-legendary quip was this: "Judge Harold Leventhal used to describe the use of legislative history as the equivalent of entering a crowded cocktail party and looking over the heads of the guests for one's friends." *Conroy v. Aniskoff*, 507 U.S. 511, 519 (1993) (Scalia, J., concurring in the judgment). Justice Scalia varied the precise "text" of the Leventhal quip when he has discussed it subsequently. E.g., Scalia & Garner, *Reading Law*.

statutory interpretation will consider (1) statutory language addressing the legal issue, (2) surrounding statutory context, (3) judicial canons of textual and holistic interpretation, (4) judicial precedents, and (5) statutory history. (These "new textualists" either will not consider (6) legislative history or will examine it only under tightly limited circumstances.) Even for the simple park safety law we have been examining, a result-oriented textualist has plenty of "friends" to pick out under an approach to statutory interpretation that excludes legislative history.[59] There are, literally, hundreds of dictionaries from which to shop definitions for words or phrases, the Internet offers more options for researching or shopping word use, and precedents are subject to selective invocation and recharacterization (as we saw in chapter three). More generally, there are dozens of judicial canons relevant to the ordinary meaning rule, the whole act rule, the whole code rule, and the *stare decisis* rule, all of which are essential to statutory interpretation under any theory.[60] And chapter six, introducing substantive canons accepted and aggressively deployed by the new textualists, will add yet more layers of judicial discretion to statutory interpretation.

Not least important, there is a bait-and-switch feature to the new textualism's unwillingness to examine legislative history.[61] For most of the twentieth century, Congress enacted legislation against the background knowledge that the Supreme Court would examine the legislative record as it applied those laws, even to unanticipated circumstances. If the Court were to exclude these materials altogether, the assumptions of the democratic process would be shattered, for pre-1986 statutes at the very least. Bait-and-switch is a pretty nasty gambit in general, and when the victim of the gambit is Congress it might be unconstitutional as well. Judges ought to be mighty sure that legislative history is misleading or corrupting before they throw over a century's worth of statutory practice.

---

[59] Eskridge, *The New Textualism,* 37 U.C.L.A. L. Rev. at 670–76 (textualist sources, like the whole act and the canons, offer just as many shopping opportunities as legislative history); accord, William W. Buzbee, *The One Congress Fiction in Statutory Interpretation*, 149 U. Pa. L. Rev. 171 (2000).

[60] For an excellent textualist debate, where each side has a dozen or so textualist canons, each cutting in different ways, compare the majority and dissenting opinions in *Babbitt v. Sweet Home Chap. of Communities for a Great Oregon,* 515 U.S. 687 (1995). See William N. Eskridge Jr., *The New Textualism and Normative Canons,* 113 Colum. L. Rev. 531 (2013). A recent example is the debate between the majority and dissenting opinions in *King v. Burwell*, 135 S.Ct. 2480 (2015).

[61] Eskridge, *The New Textualism,* 37 U.C.L.A. L. Rev. at 683–84.

To the contrary, judicial shopping appears to be more associated with cherry-picking textualists than legislative history-citing purposivists. Thus, there is preliminary empirical evidence that textual canons are *more* closely correlated with result-oriented (ideological) voting than legislative history is. James Brudney and Corey Ditslear have conducted a series of empirical examinations of the 578 labor and tax cases decided by the Supreme Court between 1969 and 2006. These scholars found that when "liberal" (presumptively pro-employee) Justices meaningfully relied on legislative history, their votes tended to be more pro-employer—against their ideological preferences—than when they relied on textual or precedent-based sources.[62] During the Burger Court (1969–1986), "conservative" (presumptively pro-business) Justices were more likely to vote in favor of worker interests—against their ideological preferences—when they relied on legislative history. After 1986, conservative, largely textualist Justices ratcheted up their pro-employer results, relying increasingly on canons of statutory construction and typically ignoring legislative history entirely.[63] In a number of high-profile cases, conservative Supreme Court majorities have invoked textual canons to press pro-employer results that seem clearly to trump the expectations of the enacting Congresses.[64] In his survey of the Michigan Supreme Court's *stare decisis* legisprudence between 1999 and 2008, Robert Sedler reports that the steady textualist majority, appointed by a pro-business, tough-on-crime governor, overruled dozens of statutory precedents with an even more astounding ideological regularity—(almost) always to restrict the rights of criminal defendants, consumers, and workers and (almost) never to burden prosecutors or businesses.[65]

---

[62] James J. Brudney & Corey Ditslear, *Liberal Justices' Reliance on Legislative History: Principle, Strategy, and the Scalia Effect*, 29 Berkeley J. Emp. & Lab. L. 117, 121 (2008).

[63] *Id.* at 144–46; see James J. Brudney & Corey Ditslear, *The Decline and Fall of Legislative History?: Patterns of Supreme Court Reliance in the Burger and Rehnquist Eras*, 89 Judicature 220, 229 (2006) (arguing accepted canons of construction do not constrain judges from imposing ideology in decisions).

[64] For an exhaustive analysis of cases where canons-wielding textualist opinions reached pro-employer results in the face of strong evidence that legislators expected employee protections, see James J. Brudney & Corey Ditslear, *Canons of Construction and the Elusive Quest for Neutral Reasoning*, 58 Vand. L. Rev. 1 (2005).

[65] Robert A. Sedler, *The Michigan Supreme Court,* Stare Decisis, *and Overruling the Overrulings*, 55 Wayne L. Rev. 1911 (2009) (between 1999 and 2008, the Court applied the plain meaning rule to overrule 38 supreme court precedents, all of them for the benefit of business in private law cases and the government in criminal cases).

The evidence assembled by Professors Brudney, Ditslear, and Sedler is consistent with evidence from the analysis Lauren Baer I performed for more than 1000 Supreme Court decisions handed down between 1984 and 2006 where the Justices considered an agency interpretation of a federal statute. The most textualist Justices on the Court revealed a consistent pattern of ideological voting, with Justice Thomas favoring "conservative" agency interpretations almost all the time and "liberal" interpretations less than half the time; Justice Scalia's voting record revealed a less dramatic but also significant pattern of ideological voting. Although several less textualist Justices also revealed patterns of ideological voting, it is notable that Justices Scalia and Thomas (the most textualist Justices) had significantly higher levels of ideological voting than most other Justices and that the lowest levels of ideological voting were found for Chief Justice Roberts and Justices Alito, Kennedy, and Breyer, the last three of whom are avid readers and citers of legislative history.[66]

In short, not only is there is no rigorously empirical evidence that a strict textualist methodology, excluding legislative history, exercises any constraint on judges' tendency to lean toward interpretations consistent with their policy preferences in close cases, but there is preliminary evidence that statutory language and textualist canons (chapter one) are *less* constraining than legislative history. How is this possible? Can you think of a reason why judges consulting legislative history as well as dictionaries, textual canons, and precedent might be *more* constrained than judges consulting just dictionaries, textual canons, and precedent?

An important value of legislative history is *hermeneutic*. Hermeneutics is the philosophy of interpretation, but I am using the term more colloquially to mean any thought process that connects today's interpreter to yesterday's text. Especially if a law were adopted decades earlier, the judicial interpreter is a stranger to the statute. The challenge of interpretation is for the judge to understand the statutory language, structure, and purpose deeply—from the perspective of the original project, brought forward to the facts of the current case. A judge who supplements the bare text with her favorite dictionaries, canons, and precedents is less likely to understand the statute from the statute's point of view than the judge who also

---

[66] William N. Eskridge Jr. & Lauren E. Baer, *The Continuum of Deference: Supreme Court Treatment of Agency Statutory Interpretations from* Chevron *to* Hamdan, 96 Geo. L.J. 1083, 1153–56 (2008) (ideological voting for seven of the nine current Justices, through 2006).

consults the underlying committee reports, subcommittee hearings, and floor debates. Empirical studies of cognitive decisionmaking suggest that extrinsic legislative materials provide a broader focus that frees judges from hyper-focused, biased readings of text.[67]

If a judge is bound and determined to wrench a specific politically pleasing result from a statute, making her read and respond to legislative history will not stop her—but neither will forcing her to focus on the text, the whole act, dictionaries, textual canons, precedents, and so forth. More fundamentally, there is no empirical or systematically anecdotal evidence that appellate judges are result-oriented in this way. The reason that researchers consistently find some evidence of ideological voting among Supreme Court Justices is that the process operates subconsciously. Social psychologists tell us that the mind often anchors itself on a preferred view and then filters subsequent information through the prism of that view. The challenge of judging is to minimize this process of "cognitive dissonance" and to seek an interpretation that best reflects the anchor Congress secured in the statute, as refracted through subsequent legal and other developments in the larger polity.

Under this realistic decisionmaking framework, legislative history actually works together with textual analysis in ways that might advance both the rule of law and respect for democratic deliberation. Textual and precedent-based analysis forces the interpreter to evaluate her anchoring view against hard evidence, and that process will weed out many idiosyncratic or blatantly biased interpretations. Often, the biased judge will not be able to write a judicial opinion providing law-based reasons for her interpretation, nor will she be able to defend her interpretation against questions from her appellate colleagues. But often statutory language itself is open-textured, the statutory structure confusing, and the precedents cross-cutting. Under these circumstances, even the most scrupulous judge will tend to pick out her friends among a wide and tempting array of dictionaries and precedents. Might legislative history, in addition to these other sources, not channel the judge's interpretation

---

[67] Victoria F. Nourse, "Petty Textualism" (draft Feb. 2016); accord, Katzmann, *Judging Statutes,* 35–54; Patricia M. Wald, *The Sizzling Sleeper: The Use of Legislative History in Construing Statutes in the 1988–1989 Term of the United States Supreme Court,* 39 Am. U.L. Rev. 277, 285 (1990). Indeed, legislative history in federal statutory interpretation was viewed as an antidote to the tendency of federal judges in the *Lochner* era to read their own pro-employer views into labor laws. See James Landis, *A Note on "Statutory Interpretation,"* 43 Harv. L. Rev. 886 (1930).

toward applications that better reflect the country's, and not just the judge's, normative commitments?

What is especially useful about legislative history is that reading and taking it seriously forces the interpreter to read about the statutory project in the words chosen by those close to it. Like *The Federalist Papers*, which transport us back into the framing era and its aspirations, legislative history transports us back to the period of a statute's framing (or amendment). It helps the honest but anchored judge to see things from the perspective of legislators, and that will loosen the anchoring effect in many cases—including the case of the Segway. Whatever the judge's views might be about Segways, when she consults the legislative as well as statutory history of the Park Safety Act, she will be inclined to say that these pesky tourist conveyances are not statutory "vehicles" barred from Lafayette Park.

Go back to the beginning of this section of the chapter, where you wrote in the margin how you would apply the Park Safety Act to Segways, considering only the statutory text and its formal history. In retrospect, do you think your reading of the statutory text was completely driven by its ordinary meaning and uninfluenced by your own views about Segways? Did the legislative history change your mind? If not, did the legislative history make you more confident you are not just reading your own preferences into the statute? (Because of my fear of falling off and breaking some bones, I am leary of Segways and consider them kind of hazardous, but I would be inclined to exclude them from the statutory prohibition, based mainly on the joint explanation of the conferees.)

How Judges Ought to Use Legislative History

The theoretical objections, discussed above, make a far from compelling case against the use of legislative history in statutory interpretation, and the foregoing analysis of those objections suggests some positive values for considering legislative materials. Thus, legislative materials might be useful for judges seeking illumination about the meaning of particular words and phrases, about the purpose(s) or plan of the statute, and about deals and compromises that were made to enable the statute to traverse the vetogates of the legislative process. At every point, the judge should tie legislative materials to the statutory text, structure, and plan. Often the hard textual evidence will suggest inquiries that the legislative materials can help answer. "The interpreter, in other words, should go to the legislative history not with a blank mind waiting to be instructed but with an inquiring mind searching for answers to questions which have been soundly thought out ahead of time."[68]

Although the theoretical objections are far from dispositive, some institutional governance objections to legislative history use are much weightier. The best institutional objection is one that then-Judge Scalia made thirty years ago in a series of speeches at various law schools. Because federal judges rely on legislative history, lawyers have to research it. For landmark statutes, there might be volumes of legislative history to research. Scalia recalled that when he was the head of the Office of Legal Counsel, sixty percent of the attorneys' time was spent researching legislative history. Even if legislative history does no harm, is its value so great as to justify this level of human effort?[69]

Although most legislative history is on-line and therefore easier to research today, this is still an excellent point and ought to be a matter of great concern. No one has ever done a comprehensive cost-benefit analysis of the value added (or subtracted) by our legal system's deployment of legislative materials. Unfortunately, such an analysis would be hard to accomplish, both because the tangible costs would be hard to calculate and because the intangible rule of law costs (if any) and democracy benefits (if any) would resist uncontroversial statement or evaluation. Moreover, a cost-benefit analysis would also have to include the costs of shifting from a legal system that considers legislative history to one that does not, as well as the steep transition costs. Nonetheless, this objection is the strongest reason to abandon legislative history. Ironically, at the same time Judge Scalia was raising this objection, the United Kingdom and the Commonwealth nations were in the process to moving in exactly the other direction—abandoning the famous exclusionary rule for parliamentary materials and allowing legislative history to be admissible in statutory cases.[70]

---

[68] Hart & Sacks, *The Legal Process,* 1254 (Eskridge & Frickey eds.).

[69] Scalia, "Speech on Use of Legislative History," 14–15.

[70] *Pepper v. Hart,* [1993] 1 All E.R. 42, [1992] 3 W.L.R. 1032 (House of Lords 1992) (House of Lords overrules its exclusionary rule and allows legislative materials under specified circumstances); James J. Brudney, *The Story of* Pepper v. Hart (1992): *Examining Legislative History Across the Pond,* in *Statutory Interpretation Stories* 258–93 (Eskridge, Frickey & Garrett eds. 2011) (reporting that the *Pepper* restrictions have been relaxed in practice and that legislative materials remain somewhat controversial). For parallel developments in other Commonwealth countries, see Lord Lester of Herne Hill, Pepper v. Hart *Revisited,* 15 Statute L. Rev. 10 (1994).

Another institutionalist objection is that judges are incompetent to handle legislative materials; handing over tasks to judges that they are incompetent to carry forth is a recipe for bad governance. Because law schools have traditionally done nothing (and still do not do enough) to educate law students and practicing lawyers about the operation of Congress and state legislatures, judges and their law clerks do not know how to research legislative history, might be easily tricked by strategic statements inserted into the legislative record, and can be misled more than guided by adversarial briefing of those materials.[71]

At the federal appellate level, this criticism is not as strong as it once might have been, both because legislative history is electronically accessible (and searchable) and because there is every reason to believe that judges and their law clerks can handle these materials competently. Indeed, most federal judges enjoyed thriving careers and well-earned respect for their own work with legislative materials (as advocates, dealmakers, government officials).[72] Many circuit court judges are world-renowned experts on Congress or are former participants in the legislative process, including Judges Cornelia Pillard, Thomas Griffith, Bret Kavanaugh, David Barron, Robert Katzmann, Richard Posner, Frank Easterbrook, Marsha Berzon, Alex Kozinski, Scott Matheson, and William Pryor Jr. On the Supreme Court, Justices Stephen Breyer and Clarence Thomas were important legislative counsel in the Senate before their appointments to the bench. Likewise, many state court judges, such as Justices Mariano-Florentina Cuéllar and Goodwin Liu of the California Supreme Court, are experts on the legislative process. Chief Justice Shirley Abrahamson of the Wisconsin Supreme Court and the late Chief Judge Judith Kaye of the New York Court of Appeals have been two of the most eminent scholars of statutory interpretation in the last half century. One must not understate the ability of judges to understand legislative history, and their law clerks these days have typically taken a legislation or statutory interpretation course in law school, a big change from a generation ago.

---

[71] For a trenchant indictment of legal education's sad neglect of Congress, and the ignorance this neglect foments among law clerks and judges, see Dakota S. Rudesill, *Closing the Legislative Experience Gap: How a Legislative Law Clerk Program Will Benefit the Legal Profession and Congress,* 87 Wash. U.L. Rev. 699, 706–08 (2010).

[72] The leading source for the argument that federal judges are incompetent to use legislative history is Adrian Vermeule, *Judging Under Uncertainty* (2006), whose main example of incompetence is an 1892 Supreme Court decision handed down without the benefit of briefing by the government (the losing party) and decades before legislative history became a common source of guidance in statutory cases.

Not least important, when judges do reveal gaps in their knowledge about how Congress operates, it affects their textual and structural analysis and not just their use of legislative history. In the recent Supreme Court dust-ups over the Affordable Care Act of 2010, for example, controlling opinions by Chief Justice John Roberts did reveal some confusion about the complicated legislative process that resulted in this putative super-statute. Interpreting the Affordable Care Act as a tax measure (so that it might be constitutional) was judicial strong-arming or wishful thinking rather than neutral interpretation of the statutory plan, and the Chief Justice's recent opinion preserving federal subsidies for low-income health insureds in all states tossed off in one paragraph an erroneous caricature of a bumbling Congress delivering a health care law with scant public deliberation and debate.[73] These unsophisticated analyses reflect the fact that federal judges do not know as much as they should about Congress's procedures, but it is notable that in neither case did the Chief Justice rely on legislative history. Instead, he relied on statutory text and a structural understanding of the legislative plan, as well as some judicial canons of construction.[74]

For the lawyer or judge concerned with these practical objections to legislative history, I recommend the work of Victoria Nourse, who was an important Senate staffer before turning to legal academe. A master of the congressional process as well as a leading theoretician in the field of legislation, Professor Nourse has laid out a methodology for researching and using legislative history "by the Rules" (of Congress). Her work suggests no fewer than three important canons for using legislative materials, set forth below.[75]

The Nourse code for using legislative materials by the Rules can be illustrated by another variation in our application of the Park Safety Act. Does the statute bar from Lafayette Park horses carrying mounted police, such as the officers pictured at the front of this chapter? A word of context is in order. Enforcement of rules

---

[73] See *National Federation of Independent Business v. Sebelius,* 132 S.Ct. 2566, 2593–94 (2012) (Roberts, C.J.) (interpreting the Affordable Care Act [ACA] to rest upon Congress's taxing authority, even though it is not clear there was any support in the ACA Congress for a new tax statute), hotly criticized in id. at 2650–55 (joint dissent); *King v. Burwell,* 135 S.Ct. 2480, 2492 (2015) (Roberts, C.J., for the Court) (setting forth an inaccurate understanding of the ACA as written in a secret, nondeliberative, and bumbling process).

[74] See Gluck, *Imperfect Statutes, Imperfect Courts* (detailed analysis of the Chief Justice's opinion in *King v. Burwell*).

[75] Victoria F. Nourse, *A Decision Theory of Statutory Interpretation: Legislative History by the Rules,* 122 Yale L. J. 70 (2012).

administered by the National Park Service is carried out by the United States Park Police. Established in 1934, the Horse Mounted Unit of the Park Police patrols federal parks to assure safety, obedience to the law, and crowd control on certain occasions. The photo at the front of the chapter depicts the Horse Mounted Unit on patrol between Lafayette Park and the White House. The question is whether the Lafayette Park Safety Act, as expanded in 2013, covers these equestrian pairings of horse and officer. (Mounted police would still be allowed around the White House, just outside the park, as depicted in the illustration above.)

The gentle reader may find this new application far-fetched, but please bear with me. The amended text of the statute defines "vehicles" as "any thing used for conveying a person from one place to another, including automobiles, trucks, motorcycles, motor scooters, and other forms of conveyance that pose safety hazards to park users because of their speed." A police horse is a "thing," usually "convey[s] a person from one place to another," and it is a "form[ ] of conveyance that pose[s] safety hazards to park users because of [its] speed" (horses can go a lot faster than Segways, for example). Many an honest textualist would be hard put to escape the implication that section 3 covers horses. Could a textualist depart from the plain meaning by invoking the absurdity canon (itself controversial among textualists)?

Congress itself has suggested that it is not absurd to consider a horse to be a regulated vehicle. As amended in 1926, the Traffic Act of 1925 that Congress passed for the District of Columbia (and still in force for the District) defines "vehicles" to include "any appliance moved over a highway on wheels or traction tread, including street cars, draft animals, and beasts of burden."[76] Although there is no consensus approach, some state vehicle codes regulate horses for purposes of laws prohibiting operation of "vehicles" while under the influence of alcohol. The North Carolina Court of Appeals, for example, recently held that the state's vehicular drunk driving law covered an inebriated gentleman riding a horse down the street.[77]

---

[76] Act of July 3, 1926, To Amend the Traffic Act of 1925, ch. 739, § 1, 44 Stat. 812, adding a definition of "vehicle," currently codified without change at D.C. Code § 50–2201.02(17).

[77] *State v. Dellinger,* 73 N.C. App. 685, 327 S.E.2d 609 (1985) (holding that a horse is a vehicle for purposes of the state driving while under the influence [DWI] of alcohol law); accord, *Conrad v. Dillinger,* 270 P.2d 216 (Kan. 1954) (finding horses to be "devices" for conveying people, therefore upholding a DWI conviction for a drunk horse rider). Contra, *State v. Euton,* 665 N.E.2d 775 (Ohio Mun. 1996) (finding horses not to

Although police horses might fall within the four corners of section 3's definition, as the North Carolina court recognized, that ought not be the end of inquiry—indeed, I think this analysis is only the starting point for serious understanding. Section 3 seems prototypically focused on inanimate mechanisms, not animals. For some of the same reasons the Supreme Court recently held that a red grouper is not a "tangible object" subject to a federal destruction-of-evidence law, one might hesitate to say that horses and other animals are "things" for purposes of section 3.[78]

Finally, the fact that the horse in question is in the service of law enforcement might provide a narrow basis for resolving this issue. Judges ought not strain a statute's language to interfere with the operation of the federal and local law enforcement officials. At the very least, the case of the mounted police is a hard case, where the statutory history, text, and structure raise more questions than they answer. Can legislative history help resolve this issue? Yes, it can. Many appellate decisions start with a law's statutory and legislative history, the step-by-step progress of the relevant bill through the congressional process, before commencing the relevant statutory analysis. Then, the decision ties the history to various analytical points, such as the ordinary meaning of the enacted text, the statutory plan or purpose, and the legislative stance toward pre-enactment judicial precedents and agency practice.[79] This approach is usually a useful one, grounding a judge's analysis in the discourse of the democratically accountable process. Within this framework, Professor Nourse suggests several canons for applying legislative history.

Backwards Induction Canon. The first Noursian rule for using legislative history is to focus on the last legislative decision

---

be "vehicles" for purposes of state DWI law); *Utah v. Blowers,* 717 P.2d 1321 (Utah 1986) (finding horses not to be "devices" for conveying people from one place to another for purposes of the state drunk driving law). See generally David P. Chapus, Annotation, *Horseback riding or operation of horse-drawn vehicle as within drunk driving statute,* 71 A.L.R.4th 1129 (1989).

[78] *Yates v. United States,* 135 S.Ct. 1074 (2015) (ruling that the federal statute criminalizing the destruction of any "record, document, or tangible object" relevant to a federal law enforcement investigation does not include a red grouper as an "object" whose destruction could trigger the statute).

[79] For classic analyses, consider *United Steelworkers v. Weber,* 443 U.S. 193 (1979) (majority and dissenting opinions), and *Green v. Bock Laundry Mach. Co.,* 490 U.S. 504 (1990), both subjected to critique in Nourse, *Legislative History by the Rules.* An increasing number of state court decisions engage in this illuminating analysis. E.g., *People v. Leiva,* 297 P.3d 870, 878–80 (Cal. 2013).

creating the final version of the relevant statutory text and then to work backwards.[80] What is the relevant statutory language the interpreter is trying to understand and apply? When was it added to the bill that ultimately became a statute? Start with the end-game legislative materials and work backwards if need be. The logic behind this backwards induction canon for using legislative history is that the legislative discussions and explanations are most useful when they are focusing on the text that was actually enacted into current law. Current section 3, containing the statutory definition of "vehicle," came into its current form only with the Soaper Amendment—"any thing used for conveying a person from one place to another, including automobiles, trucks, motorcycles, motor scooters, and other forms of conveyance that pose safety hazards to park users because of their speed." This is a different definition of "vehicle" than that enacted by the Park Safety Act of 1992 and than that contained in the House bill whose definition was rejected in the conference committee. Hearings, committee reports, and floor debates that pertain to the 1992 definition or to the House bill are not as relevant as those pertaining to the explanation and debates pertaining to the Senate bill and, especially, to the final version of the Soaper Amendment that passed in 2013.

Consider the application of that text to the case of the mounted police. Can a horse be a vehicle regulated by the Park Safety Act, as amended? As noted above, the vehicle codes of the District of Columbia and a number of states do regulate horses as vehicles for some purposes. This fact is most interesting but is no more dispositive than is the fact that a few dictionaries or thesauruses might list horses as examples of "vehicles." Both dictionaries and precedents from other jurisdictions reveal that a horse *might* be a vehicle—but they do little to persuade me that a horse is a vehicle as that term is being used in the Park Safety Act. The actual text of the Soaper Amendment gets me closer to such a conclusion, though. A horse is a "thing," it conveys people from one place to another, and a person can ride a horse at significant speeds (up to thirty miles per hour, faster than a Segway but not as fast as a car), posing the safety risks that were the focus of the original statute and that are encoded into section 3's definition by the Soaper Amendment.

---

[80] Although Professor Nourse makes the backwards induction canon her second "principle," see Nourse, *Legislative History by the Rules,* 122 Yale L.J. at 76–77, 98–109, I think it is her most striking and practically useful idea, so I should place it first and foremost.

Case closed? Hardly. The prototypical (and most ordinary) meaning of "vehicle" is a mechanism, not a living animal. With that in mind, I'd be interested in reading the Senate and House debates on the conference bill, if any, as well as the Senate committee report and the Senate debates on the Senate bill, which was virtually the same as the conference bill that became law. Although I'd be most impressed if Senator Soaper herself included "horses, mules, donkeys, and jackasses" in a list of "things" that she considered vehicles, legislative history research usually does not turn up that kind of smoking gun; often, the legislative history is as vague as the statutory language. But the discussions still might be useful for resolving the case of the mounted police. What kinds of things did the members of Congress uncontroversially accept as "vehicles" for purposes of the Soaper Amendment? If the committee report and floor debates contained an extensive discussion of things now barred from Lafayette Park by the new definition, it would be most informative to see what was widely included and what was never mentioned. For example, if there were 150 separate notations of things considered vehicles, it would be significant to me if all 150 of them were references to motorized vehicles that can reach speeds in excess of fifty miles per hour (faster than a horse).

At this point, the reader should pause and reflect. Given the statutory language, and the analytical points made about such language above, would you find a plain meaning absolutely excluding horses from the statutory definition of "vehicle"? Or a plain meaning absolutely including horses? Are you so sure of your interpretation that you would refuse to examine exactly what Senator Soaper and the conference committee had to say, in public utterances, about the definition in new section 3? Now, here is a key question: Even if you were open to reading other materials, how clear would they have to be in order to dislodge you from your initial impression?

We need to be candid about our pre-understandings (a nice word for our preexisting biases). My biases are as follows. Horses are not, in my view, prototypical "vehicles," partly because their function today is not necessarily to convey us from one place to another. When I taught at the University of Virginia, I lived on a horse farm and had equestrian training—yet I never rode a horse simply to get from one place to another, the way I drive my car, ride a bicycle, or would operate a Segway (if I were not afraid of falling off). I rode horses for exercise, for fun, for social interaction, and for love of horses. So it is a bit of an uphill climb for me to read a vehicles in the park law to bar horses because they are "vehicles." Horses are not prototypical vehicles the way automobiles, motorcycles, mopeds, and even bicycles would be (or the way horses would have been in 1800). On the other hand, I cheerfully admit that a mounted police officer is riding a horse for precisely the reasons identified by the statute—to convey her/himself from one place to another, often in pursuit of purse-snatchers, suspected terrorists, rogue White House staffers, etc. But knowing that the only horses affected by being considered statutory vehicles are going to be horses conveying mounted police protecting the White House makes me more dubious about the enterprise of reading "vehicle" broadly enough to include horses.

Could legislative history make a difference to me? Sometimes you do discover a smoking gun. Assume that Senator Soaper explained the conference bill to her colleagues in the Senate and, in response to a question from an opponent, engaged in this colloquy:

> **SENATOR HUSHPUPPY.** With due respect, this bill is a mess. No one knows exactly what is going to be a "vehicle" and what is not.
>
> **SENATOR SOAPER.** I should be happy to address the confusion of the Senator from Arkansas. The new definition is pretty clear: any thing conveying people or things that goes fast—say more than 20 miles per hour—is going to be regulated by the revised statute. The statute lists some popular motor vehicles, but it also covers other things that go fast.
>
> **SENATOR HUSHPUPPY.** The esteemed Senator from West Virginia cannot mean what she says. Horses convey people, and they can go more than 20 miles per hour. How about the mounted police? Are they excluded from Lafayette Park?
>
> **SENATOR SOAPER.** Yes, Senator, they would be. We considered and accepted the National Park Service's suggestion that mounted police be excluded from Lafayette Park. The Service reported that the horses had been involved in three serious and five minor park accidents in the last decade. A representative of the United States Park Police told us that its officers can police the area around the White House without the equestrian unit's operating in Lafayette Park.

Exchanges like this are often "planned," and critics scoff at them, but so long as this exchange is part of the public record and was made on the floor of the Senate (a fact that can be checked through C-SPAN), I would credit this exchange, for what it is worth—as do political scientists and congressional staffers.[81]

The Soaper-Hushpuppy colloquy would impel me to read the Senate committee hearings, to see what I could learn from the National Park Service and Park Police testimony, and any reaction from the senators. If confirmed by the earlier materials, the congressional exchange on the floor would change my mind, for the same reasons Justice Scalia said his mind was open to education about the Constitution's principles and language based upon reading *The Federalist Papers*. Yes, if all this evidence checks out, I'd say that the mounted police are excluded from Lafayette Park. You learn something new every day.

The Rules of Proceedings Canon. Article I, Section 5 of the Constitution requires the House and the Senate each to "keep a Journal of its Proceedings, and from time to time publish the same," and authorizes each chamber to "determine the Rules of its Proceedings." (State constitutions have similar requirements and authorizations but impose many more restrictions on state legislatures.[82]) Section 5 provides a constitutional foundation for public legislative history, accessible to We the People, who might want legislators to provide explanations and justifications for the statutes that they adopt. As James Brudney has argued, the Journal Clause rejected British traditions of parliamentary secrecy and, according to some of the founding generation, sought a public record that would "aid the Executive in administering the Government [and] the Judiciary in expounding the laws."[83] The Journal Clause is constitutional support for the idea that the legislative history of a

---

[81] Gluck & Bressman, *Statutory Interpretation from the Inside: Part I,* 65 Stan. L. Rev. at 987 (exhaustive survey of congressional drafting staff, who report that even planned colloquies are especially reliable legislative history, because they reflect public announcements about how the enacting coalition represents the effect of statutory language); McNollgast, *Positive Canons: The Role of Legislative Bargains in Statutory Interpretation,* 80 Geo. L.J. 705 (1992) (political science account of legislative bargaining, valorizing public statements made by bill sponsors, for they are not the kind of "cheap talk" opponents like Senator Hushpuppy engage in to sink proposals).

[82] Michael E. Libonati, *State Constitutions and Legislative Process: The Road Not Taken*, 89 B.U.L. Rev. 863 (2009).

[83] James J. Brudney, *Canon Shortfalls and the Virtues of Political Branch Interpretive Assets*, 98 Cal. L. Rev. 1199, 1120 (2010) (quoting from Eldridge Gerry's proposal for the House to appoint official stenographers who would transcribe and publish its debates).

statute ought to be public and its corollary that the public record might legitimately inform statutory interpretation.[84]

The Rules of Proceedings Clause then provides the constitutional foundation for the second Noursian canon for using legislative history. Each chamber has adopted Rules of Proceedings, the Senate through a permanent body of Standing Rules that are amended from time to time, and the House through House Rules adopted each Congress, but with significant continuity with prior House Rules. Those Senate and House Rules structure the deliberations of each chamber and provide the framework for legislative history. For example, House Rule XIII and Senate Rule XVII require committees reporting bills to their chambers to include a committee report and direct that such report (as well as the record of committee hearings) be available to members of the chamber before vote on the proposed legislation. Do these Rules mean that legislation is always voted on with a printed committee report on each member's desk? No. But the Rules do make it reasonable for courts to assume that committee reports are presumptively available to all members of the chamber before they vote and that the committee reports form a common background to congressional consideration of proposed legislation.[85]

The Nourse code suggests that courts read legislative history "by the Rules," that is, with an assumption that Congress is following the Rules established by its respective chambers. For example, House Rule XXI and Senate Rule XVI direct that it is out of order for an appropriations bill to include additions or changes to "general" substantive law. The Supreme Court has relied on these rules to strongly presume that appropriations measures do not implicitly repeal or amend substantive law. To be sure, the appropriations process can determine whether a substantive statute has any effect (and how much), but the Court's inference is that the terms of the substantive statute are presumptively unaffected by appropriations laws.[86]

---

[84] Professor Brudney argues that Article I, § 5, including its original meaning and early operation, "confers upon legislative history an element *Id.* at 1224.

[85] Nourse, *Legislative History by the Rules,* 122 Yale L.J. at 76, 91–98 (describing and applying her "first principle" for interpreting legislative history by the Rules).

[86] *Tennessee Valley Auth. v. Hill,* 437 U.S. 153 (1978) (leading case), analyzed and criticized in Nourse, *Legislative History by the Rules,* 122 Yale L.J. at 130–34. Professor Nourse points out that appropriations measures have the power to fulfill or undermine substantive statutes and argues that the Court in *Hill* was wrong to say

Now consider a way in which legislative history by the Rules helps us resolve a minor issue in the case of the mounted police. Assume that the only relevant legislative history of the Soaper Amendment is the conference committee's reconciliation of the House and Senate bills, as well as the joint explanation of the conferees. Even if this were the only pertinent legislative history, it would help the interpreter clear up an ambiguity relevant to the case of the mounted police. Section 3 in the original Park Safety Act said a vehicle means "any mechanism" for conveying people from one place to another; revised section 3 provides that a vehicle means "any thing used" for conveying people from one place to another. The new definition helps open up the Act to regulating horses as vehicles, because an ordinary speaker of the English language is much more likely to say that a horse is a "thing" than that a horse is a "mechanism."[87]

Why did Congress change the noun from "mechanism" to "thing"? Ought this to be treated as a significant change? The answer to that question, "by the Rules," is not at all. Recall that *both* the original Senate (Soaper) bill *and* the House bill retained "mechanism" in the statutory definition; the conference substituted "thing" for "mechanism." The joint explanation of the conferees does not explain why, but interpreting "by the Rules" suggests an excellent reason why the substitution should not be considered a substantive change at all. Senate Rule XVIII 2(a) says this: "Conferees shall not insert in their report matter not committed to them by either House, nor shall they strike from the bill matter agreed to by both Houses." House Rule XXII is to similar effect. Both bills used the term "mechanism" and not "thing." Unless the change was just a stylistic one, which is permitted "by the Rules," this change would violate Senate Rule XVIII 2(a) and House Rule XXII. That no one raised a point of order against the conference report creates an inference that no substantive change was made when the conference report made this substitution.[88] Because it is really odd to say that a horse is a "mechanism for conveying people from one place to another," this

---

that the Endangered Species Act was unaffected by Congress's continuing appropriations for the Tellico Dam.

[87] But note that some judges have found a horse to be a "device" for conveying people or things. Compare *Conrad v. Dillinger,* 270 P.2d 216 (Kan. 1954) (finding horses to be "devices" for conveying people), with *Utah v. Blowers,* 717 P.2d 1321 (Utah 1986) (finding horses not to be "devices" for conveying people).

[88] For a resolution similar to the one in text (i.e., presume that the conference committee makes no substantive changes), see *Bankamerica Corp. v. United States,* 462 U.S. 122, 138–39 (1983).

presumption makes it less likely that the judge will find that the police horse is a vehicle barred from the park.

The Sore Losers Canon. Reflecting both federal and state case law, a third Noursian canon is that interpreters ought to discount or ignore the legislative history written or spoken by the losers, namely, the legislators who unsuccessfully opposed the legislation.[89] Recall the colloquy excerpted above, between Senator Hushpuppy, an opponent of the Soaper Amendment, and Senator Soaper herself. Although the Hushpuppy view that the amendment would regulate horses is interesting, it is not weighty evidence that horses are section 3 "vehicles." The reason is that an opponent has strong incentives to exaggerate the effects and distort the ambit of proposed legislation. The mocking tone of the colloquy suggests that Senator Hushpuppy is playing with language and is engaged in what political scientists call *cheap talk*. Cheap talk by opponents is of little value in figuring out the meaning of statutory text and structure adopted by Congress over their objections.[90]

In contrast, Senator Soaper's agreement with Senator Hushpuppy is quite significant. Not only is Soaper knowledgeable about her own bill, but she has strong incentives to make accurate representations about its effects and its regulatory ambit. Her statement is especially creditworthy, because she is not giving the easy answer. Quite the opposite of cheap talk, Soaper's agreement with Hushpuppy comes at a potential cost of making her bill harder to pass.[91] Last of all, Soaper's response explains why she agrees with Hushpuppy that her bill would bar mounted police from Lafayette Park. And her explanation is subject to easy verification or falsification: Did the Park Service provide the testimony she mentioned?

---

[89] Nourse, *Legislative History by the Rules,* 122 Yale L.J. at 118–28. Like the others, Professor Nourse's sore losers canon finds support in the case law. E.g., *Bankamerica Corp.,* 462 U.S. at 138–39; *NLRB v. Fruit & Vegetable Packers,* 377 U.S. 58, 66 (1964) (leading case); *National Pride at Work,* 748 N.W.2d at 546–49, 552 (Michigan) (Kelly, J., dissenting) (critiquing majority for accepting an interpretation advanced by the losers in a ballot initiative).

[90] McNollgast, *Positive Canons,* 80 Geo. L.J. at 741; Daniel B. Rodriguez & Barry R. Weingast, *The Positive Political Theory of Legislative History: New Perspectives on the 1964 Civil Rights Act and Its Interpretation,* 151 U. Pa. L. Rev. 1417, 1442–48 (2003); Rodriguez & Weingast, *The Paradox of Expansionist Statutory Interpretations,* 101 Nw. U.L. Rev. 1207, 1219–22 (2007).

[91] For a discussion sharply contrasting the cheap talk of opponents and the costly concessions made by the floor managers of legislation, see Nourse, *Legislative History by the Rules*, 122 Yale L.J. at 122–25; Rodriguez & Weingast, *Positive Political Theory of Legislative History*, 151 U. Pa. L. Rev. at 1442–48.

Accordingly, statements by opponents might be useful to know, insofar as they call forth responses from the legislators speaking for the enacting coalition. Again, consider the parallel to constitutional interpretation. Almost no one relies on representations about the Constitution's meaning by the Anti-Federalists, the articulate opponents to ratification. Eager to play on fears of the uncertainties posed by a new governing document, they acted on incentives to exaggerate the changes made by the proposed Constitution. So their views are far from reliable—though they are often worth reading, because *The Federalist Papers* were written in response to their percipient arguments. *The Federalist Papers* are entitled to "great weight," but *The Anti-Federalist Papers* are not.

Hierarchy of Legislative History Sources

The gentle reader following the foregoing discussion may be persuaded that a statutory interpreter ought to consider legislative history as part of the process by which she tries to figure out the meaning of statutory text. Such history can help her understand the meaning of statutory words and phrases, the purpose and plan of the law, and the deals legislators had to make to secure bicameral approval and presidential support or acquiescence. Consideration of legislative history must be closely tied to relevant statutory text and structure—while at the same time responsive to the state legislative and judicial consensus (one shared by Congress and by the U.S. Supreme Court before the 1980s) that "legislative intent" is the lodestar for statutory interpretation.

In addition to the guidance provided by the Nourse code are more traditional admonitions about what legislative materials the judge ought to consult. An examination of these materials helps us understand how the interpreter can link her analysis to a "legislative intent" that is not devastated by the legal realist critique explained above. Since the New Deal, judges, scholars, and sometimes legislators have evaluated the utility or cogency of legislative materials based upon their relevance, reliability, and utility.[92]

- **Relevance:** Do the statements, explanations, and reports provide interpreters with information that is

[92] Hart & Sacks, *The Legal Process,* 1253–54 (Eskridge & Frickey, eds.); see 1 Pa. Cons. Stat. § 1939 (urging consideration of legislative history that is reliable and available to the public); Stephen Breyer, *On the Uses of Legislative History in Interpreting Statutes,* 65 S. Cal. L. Rev. 845 (1992); CRS Report, *Statutory Interpretation,* 43–47 (updated 2011).

relevant to a statutory issue that is presented to the court?

- **Reliability:** Are they generated under conditions that give us reason to believe that the word use, the phraseology, and the explication of purpose are not idiosyncratic and, instead, reflect the views that can reasonably be attributed to the enacting coalition?
- **Utility:** Do the reliable and relevant materials provide useful information about how statutory words and phrases were being used, about statutory purpose(s), and about deals and compromises needed to move proposed legislation to completion?

This inquiry is not necessarily vulnerable to the aggregation problems with figuring out the actual legislative intent of a majority of the House and a (super)majority of the Senate. Recall that a demonstrable *subjective* legislative intent is difficult to prove for a large, complicated institution such as Congress—but this inquiry focuses on objective meaning of words, phrases, sentences, and provisions and on an intent that might fairly be "attributed" to the legislature.

Thus, a judge interpreting a statute "by the Rules" is interested in a *conventional* legislative intent, one that is presumed or inferred from the rules that structure the legislative process.[93] Conventional intent is a familiar concept to lawyers and most other Americans. Thus, the law routinely attributes intent to corporations and other institutions, based upon rules structuring those institutions and responsibilities attributed to them.[94] As a constitutional actor, Congress is more broadly purposive than private corporations, so some kind of intent-based metaphor ought to be theoretically possible for understanding Congress.

---

[93] Lawrence M. Solan, *The Language of Statutes: Laws and Their Interpretation* 82–119 (2010); Victoria F. Nourse, *Elementary Statutory Interpretation: Rethinking Legislative Intent and History,* 55 B.C.L. Rev. 1613 (2014), drawing from Christian List & Philip Pettit, *Group Agency* (2011). For discussions of an "institutionalist" approach to legislative history along similar lines as those developed by Professors Solan and Nourse, see Breyer, *Uses of Legislative History in Interpreting Statutes*; Charles Tiefer, *The Reconceptualization of Legislative History in the Supreme Court*, 2000 Wis. L. Rev. 205 (2000).

[94] Lawrence M. Solan, *Private Language, Public Laws: The Central Role of Legislative Intent in Statutory Interpretation*, 93 Geo. L.J. 427, 437–49 (2005).

Professor Nourse, in particular, has laid out a path forward. Like the new textualists, she rejects a "meeting of the minds" approach to legislative intent as both impractical and normatively troubling. But Congress does work through proposed plans, adjusts them in the process of give-and-take required by the vetogates, and votes on those plans through a majority-wins (or a supermajority-wins) process. The decisions committees and chambers of Congress make are democratically structured and often generate documents that are highly illuminating for the statutory interpreter. "If it is true that government by 'unexpressed intent' is decidedly tyrannical, government by constitutionally supported procedures is decidedly democratic."[95]

Given the Rules of Proceedings adopted by the House and the Senate and the process by which each chamber makes collective decisions that reveal intentional, purposive behavior, all legislative materials are not created equal. Like the funnel of sources for statutory interpretation (ordinary meaning, whole act, etc.) presented in the introduction to this volume, there is a rough reliability-based hierarchy of legislative materials.[96] Explanations accompanying conference and committee reports are the most reliable, because they represent the public statements of those who crafted and defended the final statutory text, while post-enactment statements by legislators and chief executives are the least reliable. Other materials, such as committee hearings and reports of legislative study commissions, are sometimes going to be relevant as well.[97]

---

[95] Nourse, *Rethinking Legislative Intent and History,* 55 B.C.L. Rev. at 1616; accord, Solan, *Language of Statutes*, 82–119.

[96] Eskridge, *The New Textualism*, 37 U.C.L.A. L. Rev. at 636–40 (setting forth a hierarchy of legislative materials, similar to the canons discussed in text); accord, Frank B. Cross, *Theory and Practice of Statutory Interpretation* 64–67 (2009); George A. Costello, *Average Voting Members and Other "Benign Fictions": The Relative Reliability of Committee Reports, Floor Debates, and Other Forms of Legislative History,* 1990 Duke L.J. 39, 41–60. For a similar hierarchy suggested to congressional staff, see CRS Report, *Statutory Interpretation*, 43–52 (updated 2011).

[97] For an illuminating survey of legislative materials examined by the Wisconsin Supreme Court, see *Kalal*, 681 N.W.2d at 130–37 (Abrahamson, C.J., dissenting).

Least Reliable **Subsequent History**

Legislative Silence

Reports by Agencies Etc.

Rejected Proposals

Sponsor Explanations

Committee Reports

Most Reliable Materials **Explanations of the Conferees**

LEGISLATIVE HISTORY FUNNEL

Committee Report Canon. Traditionally, the most cited congressional materials have been House and Senate committee reports,[98] as well as the explanation of conferees accompanying conference reports (conference reports themselves are just the finalized statutory texts).[99] As state legislatures have become more professionalized, with permanent staff (for example), committee reports or analogous documents have become more prominent in state court legisprudence.[100]

Although the U.S. Supreme Court still explicitly relies on committee reports in some of its statutory cases,[101] dictionaries have

---

[98] *Thornburg v. Gingles*, 478 U.S. 30, 43 n.7 (1986); 2A *Sutherland Statutes and Statutory Construction* § 48:6 (7th ed. 2015) (collecting state and federal cases). For statistical demonstrations of committee report predominance, see Jorge Carro & Andrew Brann, *The U.S. Supreme Court and the Use of Legislative Histories: A Statistical Analysis*, 22 Jurimetrics J. 294, 304 (1982), updated by James J. Brudney & Corey Ditslear, *The Warp and Woof of Statutory Interpretation: Comparing Supreme Court Approaches in Tax Law and Workplace Law*, 58 Duke L.J. 1231, 1262 (2009).

[99] *Public Citizen v. Department of Justice,* 491 U.S. 440, 461–63 (1989); id. at 470–74 (Kennedy, J., concurring in the judgment); *Green v. Bock Laundry Mach. Co.,* 490 U.S. 504, 519–24 (1989) (leading case); 2A *Sutherland Statutes and Statutory Construction* § 48:8 (7th ed. 2015); see Costello, *Relative Reliability of Committee Reports, Floor Debates, and Other Forms of Legislative History,* 1990 Duke L.J. at 57–60 (collecting cases demonstrating high value traditionally given explanations of the conferees).

[100] The California Supreme Court, for example, routinely cites committee reports, especially to discern statutory purpose. E.g., *Apple, Inc. v. Superior Court*, 292 P.3d 883, 888–89, 892–94 (Cal. 2013); *People v. Leiva*, 297 P.3d at 878–80 (Cal.); *In re M.M.*, 278 P.3d 1221 (Cal. 2012); *People v. Manzo,* 270 P.3d 711, 715 (Cal. 2012). For a collection of recent state cases relying on committee reports, see William N. Eskridge Jr., Philip P. Frickey, Elizabeth Garrett & James J. Brudney, *Cases and Materials on Legislation and Regulation: Statutes and the Creation of Public Policy* 609–13, 811–13 (5th ed. 2014).

[101] For recent examples of Roberts Court reliance on committee reports, see *Texas Dep't of Hous. & Community Affs. v. Inclusive Communities Project, Inc.,* 135

replaced committee reports as the Court's go-to source for how to justify its interpretation of particular statutory language and phrases. From the perspective of democratic accountability, this is a lamentable trend—though one to which the increasing complexity of the legislative process has contributed. Thus, Congress increasingly supplements or supersedes the normal committee process with "unorthodox" procedures when it adopts complex legislation, as it did for the Affordable Care Act of 2010, which the Court criticized for its "inapt" drafting and organization.[102]

Committee reports are particularly *relevant* when committees have deliberated upon and reported the text that is ultimately enacted into law. The backwards induction canon will help the interpreter see how relevant the committee report is, because the interpreter will see its exact connection (or not) to the language enacted into law. In our case of the mounted police, the Senate committee report is most relevant, because the Soaper bill it reported contained the language for section 3 that the conference committee selected (together with the unexplained substitution of "thing" for "mechanism"). Scholars generally believe that committee reports are usually the most valuable legislative history, with conference committee explanations particularly valuable.[103] Even many critics of judicial reliance on legislative history, such as Justice Jackson, believed that committee reports are permissible sources for statutory interpreters.[104]

S.Ct. 2507, 2519–20 (2015); *Young v. United Parcel Service, Inc.,* 135 S.Ct. 1338 (2015); *Yates v. United States,* 135 S.Ct. 1074 (2015) (plurality and dissenting opinions); *Integrity Staffing Solutions, Inc. v. Busk,* 135 S.Ct. 513 (2015); *American Broadcasting Companies, Inc. v. Aereo, Inc.,* 134 S.Ct. 2498, 2505–06 (2014). In several cases citing legislative history in recent Terms, the Court's opinions have relied on legislative history only as evidence confirming the ordinary meaning of statutory text *and* have introduced the legislative history with the caveat, "for those who consider such evidence." E.g., *T-Mobile South, LLC v. City of Roswell,* 135 S.Ct. 808, 815 (2015).

[102] *King v. Burwell,* 135 S.Ct. at 2492, lamenting that the statute was inaptly drafted and noting that it did not go through the regular committee process. See John Cannan, *A Legislative History of the Affordable Care Act: How Legislative Procedure Shapes Legislative History*, 105 L. Lib. J. 131, 163 (2013).

[103] On the great reliability and utility of committee reports and conference committee explanations, see, e.g., Eskridge, *Dynamic Statutory Interpretation,* 221–22; Katzmann, *Judging Statutes,* 35–54; Costello, *Relative Reliability of Committee Reports, Floor Debates, and Other Forms of Legislative History,* 1990 Duke L.J. at 43–50.

[104] See *Schwegmann Bros. v. Calvert Distillers Corp.,* 341 U.S. 384, 396 (1951) (Jackson, J., concurring) (criticizing the Court's increasing reliance on legislative history but exempting committee reports from the strongest critique).

When relevant as adjudged by the backwards induction canon, committee reports are frequently *useful,* because the reports reflect both subject matter expertise and political knowledge by the representatives usually closest to the legislation. Most congressional reports contain a great deal of policy narrative, setting forth the problem addressed by the legislation, as well as its purpose and its policy context. The Senate committee report for the Soaper Amendment would have explained the amendment as a response to the D.C. Circuit's decision in *Hogan,* which had categorized motorized bicycles as prohibited vehicles (and not as bicycles) because of their motors. From reading the report, judges could readily confirm what is suggested by the ordinary meaning of new section 3: The Soaper Amendment overrode not only the *Hogan* result, by relocating motorized bicycles into the section 3 proviso, but also the *Hogan* reasoning, by announcing speed and safety risks as the key regulatory variable in the new language for the definitional sentence of section 3.

While one might figure this out from reading the statutory text, the committee report serves a useful function of strongly confirming such a reading—and heading off a judge's tendency to follow the *Hogan* reasoning (though not its result) under the shadow precedent canon discussed in the previous chapter. Committee reports' narratives also use the statutory words and phrases and might illuminate how the legislators were using those words and phrases. Committee reports normally have section-by-section analyses. Those analyses typically do no more than repeat the statutory language (perhaps in simplified form), but sometimes they explain legislative deals in a way that renders the text more comprehensible.

Finally, committee reports producing the final text that is enacted into law are generally *reliable* sources of statutory guidance. Although committees are not always perfectly representative of the chamber as a whole, they are, for the most part, agents of the chamber majority and take that responsibility seriously, as political scientists have demonstrated.[105] Lawyers who have actually worked in Congress overwhelmingly testify that committee staff faithfully serve the elected representatives they work for and do not subvert their bosses' agendas and bargains reached in the committee

---

[105] See Keith Krehbiel, *Information and Legislative Organization* (1992) (demonstrating empirically that congressional committees serve chamber majorities and not just the "special interests" that cluster around their jurisdictions). For an empirical test providing significant support for information theory, see Tim Groseclose & David C. King, *Committee Theory Reconsidered* (Aug. 2000).

process.[106] If a committee chair and her staff do try to slip tricky language into a committee report, congressional fire alarms and whistleblowers almost invariably reveal the subterfuge.[107] Critically important is the fact that the most knowledgeable officials in the federal government—agency officials and congressional staffers—overwhelmingly endorse the proposition that committee reports are the most reliable indication of congressional intent.[108]

The flip side of the foregoing analysis suggests circumstances when committee reports are not relevant, useful, or reliable sources of guidance for the statutory interpreter. Where the committee report's draft of the proposed legislation is superseded by amendments and changes, its relevance is greatly diminished. This was the fate of the House committee report for the Soaper Amendment, because the House version of the bill was rejected in conference committee, in favor of the Senate version. Because the House committee report is not as relevant to the final language of the bill as the Senate committee report, the former is also less reliable and useful than the latter. The House report, however, might still be useful background for the policy debate within Congress and might help the interpreter hone her understanding of the statutory purpose.[109]

Complex legislation that is the product of several committees in each chamber and of party or interbranch summits is likely to generate committee reports that discuss the legal issue in discordant or even contradictory ways. Or the committee reports will be relevant for some issues but not all of them, because a great deal of the final statutory language will have been negotiated outside the committee process. Committee reports might be useful background documents to help the interpreter understand the internal congressional evolution of the final law, but they will be less relevant and useful for purposes

---

[106] E.g., James J. Brudney, *Congressional Commentary on Judicial Interpretation of Statutes: Idle Chatter or Telling Response?*, 93 Mich. L. Rev. 1, 41–56 (1994).

[107] E.g., Nathan Persily, *The Promise and Pitfalls of the New Voting Rights Act*, 117 Yale L.J. 174 (2007) (identifying partisan manipulation of the committee report process, and its immediate exposure by congressional whistleblowers).

[108] For empirical support for the proposition that legislators and agencies find committee reports the most reliable form of legislative history, see Gluck & Bressman, *Statutory Interpretation from the Inside: Part I,* 65 Stan. L. Rev. at 976–78; Christopher J. Walker, *Inside Agency Statutory Interpretation*, 67 Stan. L. Rev. 999, 1043–44 (2015).

[109] *Carr v. United States,* 560 U.S. 438 (2010) (relying on a superseded committee report to help evaluate the government's purpose argument).

of word meaning and even purpose, it they are not talking about exactly the same language that is enacted into law.

Sometimes, committee report language is at odds with the enacted text of the statute and/or explanations by the sponsor or the floor manager.[110] The conventional wisdom, to which I subscribe, is that when there is a direct clash between a committee report explanation and statutory text, judges should focus on the latter, which controls statutory meaning if there is a clear conflict. Such dissonance can easily occur, because the committee report language is drafted or approved by different congressional staff than the language of the text voted on by the chamber: Legislative Counsel dominate the latter process, while committee staff dominate the former.[111] Because the House and Senate only vote on the statutory text, and not the committee report, the former should take primacy. *But* when a committee report contains a discussion that cuts against the ordinary meaning a judge draws from a statutory text, the better approach is for the judge to reconsider her reading of the text. Is it really so clear? Sometimes the committee report will point to other statutory text or context that the judge has missed.[112]

Most state legislatures generate documents that explain committee action on proposed legislation. The Florida, Michigan, and Texas Legislatures, for examples, create staff analyses of legislation deliberated and reported by committees. Such analyses will often be relevant and useful, and the key question is whether they are reliable: Do they accurately reflect the views of the legislators and the enacting coalition? Or are they just post-hoc documents that legislators do not read or rely on? The Florida, Michigan, and Texas Supreme Courts have answered these questions in opposite ways, sometimes yes for Florida and Texas, while almost always no for

---

[110] Compare *Hall v. United States*, 132 S.Ct. 1882, 1888 nn. 3–4 (2013) (majority relying on committee reports), with id. at 1895–96 (Breyer, J., dissenting) (dissenters relying on more targeted statement by Senate sponsor); see Costello, *Relative Reliability of Committee Reports, Floor Debates, and Other Forms of Legislative History*, 1990 Duke L.J. at 43–46.

[111] Jarrod Shobe, *Intertemporal Statutory Interpretation and the Evolution of Legislative Drafting*, 114 Colum. L. Rev. 807 (2014).

[112] For an example of a too-quick textual finding of plain meaning, see *In re Sinclair*, 870 F.2d 1340 (7th Cir. 1989), where Judge Easterbrook dismissed the conferees' explanation because it clashed with a clear text. P.L. 99–554, § 302(c)(1). What the judge (and apparently counsel) did not see was that the conference committee discussion was focused on a different text, id. § 256(1), which arguably conflicted with the text analyzed by Judge Easterbrook. For analysis of *Sinclair* and the additional and highly relevant statutory text, see Eskridge, Frickey, Garrett & Brudney, *Statutes and the Creation of Public Policy*, 801–03 (5th ed.).

Michigan.[113] The Pennsylvania Legislature has endorsed consultation of the "comments or report of the commission, committee, association or other entity which drafted a statute, so long as they are generally available and not inconsistent with the statutory text."[114]

New York and California follow a distinctive approach: When both chambers of the Legislature have passed a bill, the Governor's counsel prepares a "bill jacket" to help the Governor decide whether to sign or veto the law; bill jackets are publicly available.[115] The New York Court of Appeals and the California Supreme Court frequently rely on the memoranda and letters in the bill jacket, including those from sponsors and committees responsible for the legislation.[116] Like the staff analyses, this kind of legislative history has reliability problems, because the materials are post-hoc and are assembled by the executive branch, which will have incentives to cherry pick. The California Supreme Court also relies on traditional committee reports and floor debates,[117] but the New York Court of Appeals usually just has the bill jacket, making its use of legislative history more questionable.[118]

Sponsor's Statement Canon. Proposed laws (bills) invariably have floor managers, or primary sponsors who ordinarily speak for the enacting coalition; often the sponsor or floor manager is the chair of the reporting committee. Legislative drafters work closely with the

---

113 Compare *Diamond Aircraft Indus., Inc. v. Horowitch*, 107 So.3d 362, 368 (Fla. 2013) (relying on committee staff analysis), and *Kasischke v. State*, 991 So.2d 803, 818–19 (Fla. 2008) (discussing committee staff analysis but expressing ambivalence about its value), and *City of Dallas v. Abbott,* 304 S.W.3d 380, 384–85 (Tex. 2010) (relying on committee report), and *Brown v. De La Cruz,* 156 S.W.3d 560, 565 (Tex. 2004) (relying on staff bill analysis), with *Gardner*, 753 N.W.2d at 88–89 (Markman, J., rejecting staff analyses as unreliable).

114 1 Pa. Cons. Stat. § 1939.

115 New York State Library, Bill, Veto and Recall Jackets (describing New York's practice), available at http://www.nysl.nysed.gov/billjack.htm (visited Jan. 1, 2016).

116 For California and New York statutory decisions relying on the materials in bill reports, see, e.g., *People v. Manzo,* 270 P.3d at 715 (Cal.); *Elsner v. Uveges*, 102 P.3d at 924–25 (Cal.); *Lolley v. Campbell*, 48 P.3d 1128 (Cal. 2002); *State Farm Mut. Auto Ins. Co. v. Fitzgerald,* 38 N.E.3d 325, 328, 335–36 (N.Y. 2015); *Myers v. Bartholomew*, 697 N.E.2d 160 (N.Y. 1998). See generally *Majewski v. Broadalbin-Perth Cent. Sch. Dist.*, 696 N.E.2d 978, 981–84 (N.Y. 1998) (extensive discussion of materials in a bill jacket).

117 E.g. *Larkin v. Workers' Comp. Appeals Bd.*, 358 P.3d 552, 560–61 (Cal. 2015); *Cassel v. Superior Court,* 244 P.3d 1080 (Cal. 2011); *Committee for Green Foothills v. Santa Clara County Bd. of Supervisors,* 224 P.3d 920 (Cal. 2010); *Elsner v. Uveges*, 102 P.3d 915, 934 n.19 (Cal. 2004).

118 Eric Lane, *How to Read a Statute in New York: A Response to Judge Kaye and Some More*, 28 Hofstra L. Rev. 85, 110–19 (1999).

sponsor to draft the legislation based upon her explanations of its purpose and design. Legislative drafting offices usually consider the sponsor to be their "client." "The first and most important step in preparing legislation is to comprehend the sponsor's objectives and gain a thorough understanding of what the measure is intended to accomplish."[119] The prime directive for both congressional and state legislative drafters is to understand the client's (sponsor's) goals, the problem she is trying to solve, and the compromises she has to make to secure needed support.[120]

These drafting conventions reflect the universally accepted political understanding that the primary sponsor or floor manager represents the legislative coalition supporting the legislation. Undecided as well as friendly legislators will attend closely to the sponsor's answers to opponents' objections or assertions about how the proposed legislation would actually be interpreted and implemented. Thus, when Senator Soaper responded affirmatively to Senator Hushpuppy's mounted police query, she was presumptively speaking for the enacting coalition and was speaking from strength, because she was willing to concede that her amendment would expand the statute in a surprising way. This is relevant and useful evidence—and it is reliable for the same kinds of reasons committee reports are reliable, though judges will generally prefer on-point committee report discussion in the event the sponsor's comments push in a different direction.[121]

Traditionally, the Supreme Court and other federal courts have routinely considered statements by sponsors when relevant to an issue of statutory interpretation. For statutes where the final text could not be linked easily to a committee report, the Court's legislative history discussion has often focused on sponsor's

---

[119] Kentucky Legislative Research Comm'n, *Bill Drafting Manual, Kentucky General Assembly* § 103 (rev. 2011).

[120] For a classic explication, see Forstater, House Office of Legislative Counsel, *Manual on Drafting Style* §§ 101(1), 102(f) & 325(a). For a similar statement at the state level, see Office of Legislative Legal Services, Colorado Legislature, *Colorado Legislative Drafting Manual* § 1.2.1, at pp. 1–4 (on-line, viewed Jan. 1, 2016).

[121] *Zuber v. Allen,* 396 U.S. 169, 186 (1969) (preferring deliberated written committee report language over a sponsor's floor speech); see Costello, *Relative Reliability of Committee Reports, Floor Debates, and Other Forms of Legislative History,* 1990 Duke L.J. at 50–53. For a defense of the primacy of committee reports and sponsor statements in judicial consideration of legislative history, see Nathan Oman, *Statutory Interpretation in Econotopia*, 25 Pace L. Rev. 49 (2004).

statements.[122] Most state courts will consider statements by the floor manager or sponsor, so long as those statements are available to the public in a reliable format.[123] Floor debates are publicly available in a large majority of states and available on the internet in many. An increasing number of legislatures post videos of the floor debates for recent legislation and often have audio recordings for committee hearings.

In recent terms, the Supreme Court curtailed its reference to sponsor's statements.[124] During the 2014 Term, for instance, the Court mentioned a sponsor's explanation in only one statutory interpretation case, and the mention was part of a string cite in that case.[125] While a large majority of the opinions for the Court in statutory cases centrally relied on and discussed dictionaries, that solitary opinion cited a speech by a legislative sponsor who was most intimately familiar with the proposed legislation. This is even more remarkable in light of the close analogy to constitutional materials, where the Roberts Court cites and debates *The Federalist Papers* as though they were barnacles attached to the Constitution.[126] Those

---

[122] E.g., *North Haven Bd. of Educ. v. Bell,* 456 U.S. 512, 526–27 (1982); *United Steelworkers of America v. Weber,* 443 U.S. 193 (1979) (both majority and dissenting opinions relying overwhelmingly on representations by congressional sponsors); 2A *Sutherland Statutes and Statutory Construction* §§ 48:14–48:15 (7th ed. 2015) (citing federal as well as state cases crediting statements of bill sponsors and floor managers); Stephen F. Ross, *Where Have You Gone, Karl Llewellyn? Should Congress Turn Its Lonely Eyes to You?,* 45 Vand. L. Rev. 561, 576 (1992) (reliance on sponsor's statements when legislators are relying on their explanations).

[123] See Eskridge, Frickey, Garrett & Brudney, *Cases and Materials on Legislation and Regulation,* 814, 826–27 (5th ed.) (listing state supreme court decisions relying on sponsor's statements); 2A *Sutherland Statutes and Statutory Construction* §§ 48:14–48.15 (7th ed. 2015) (endorsing reliance on explanations by sponsors and floor managers, with reference to state and federal cases and with the caveat that the sponsor may be the puppet of groups outside the legislature).

[124] E.g., *Lawson v. FMR LLC,* 134 S.Ct. 1158, 1169–71 & n.13 (2014) (plurality opinion eschewing sponsor's statement); id. at 1176–77 (concurring opinion noting that sponsor's statement has been rejected). In addition to the diminished number of references to sponsor's statements by the Roberts Court, it is instructive to compare Rehnquist Court and Roberts Court interpretations of the same statute. Compare *Landgraf v. USI Film Prods.*, 511 U.S. 244 (1994) (extensive discussion and reference to statements by floor managers and supporters of the Civil Rights Act Amendments of 1991), with *Ricci v. DeStefano,* 557 U.S. 557 (2009) (no reference to any legislator statements when interpreting the same legislation).

[125] *Inclusive Communities,* 135 S.Ct. at 2519–20 (relying on Senate sponsor as support for a committee report analysis). In one case, the Court relied on a previous decision that quoted and relied on a sponsor's explanation. *Mach Mining, LLC v. EEOC,* 135 S.Ct. 1645, 1655 (2015).

[126] E.g., *Zivotofsky v. Kerry,* 135 S.Ct. 2076 (2015); *United States v. Noel Canning,* 134 S.Ct. 2550 (2014).

essays by Madison and Hamilton are for the U.S. Constitution pretty much what Soaper's statements are for the 2013 Amendment to the Park Safety Act—intelligent, well-informed, and widely read explanations of legal text and structure by persons acknowledged to be leading representatives of enacting coalitions. In future cases, the Court ought to give these relevant materials more attention.

Rejected Proposal Canon. Recall that the House bill explicitly named Segways as "vehicles" subject to regulation under the vehicles-have-motors precept, also expressed in that bill. The conference committee rejected the House bill in favor of the Senate bill. For the statutory interpreter, it ought to be highly relevant that the conference committee rejected a serious proposal not only seeking to codify the vehicles-have-motors policy, but also naming Segways as regulated "vehicles." The Senate bill chosen by the conferees not only codified vehicles-are-too-fast-for-public-safety as the governing policy, but dropped any reference to Segways. This history ought to trigger an investigation to determine why the conference committee rejected the House bill and, even standing alone, ought to be evidence that Segways are probably not covered by the revised statute. "Few principles of statutory construction are more compelling than the proposition that Congress does not intend sub silentio to enact statutory language that it has earlier discarded in favor of other language."[127] A related idea is that when a legislative committee or

---

[127] *Immigration & Naturalization Serv. v. Cardoza-Fonseca*, 480 U.S. 421, 442–43 (1987); accord, *Inclusive Communities Project,* 135 S.Ct. at 2519–20; *Jerman v. Carlisle, McNellie, Rini, Kramer & Ulrich LPA*, 559 U.S. 573, 588–89 (2010); *Hamdan v. Rumsfeld,* 548 U.S. 557, 579–80 (2006); *FDA v. Brown & Williamson Tobacco Corp.*, 529 U.S. 120 (2000); *United States v. Riverside Bayview Homes, Inc.*, 474 U.S. 121, 137 (1985); *Blau v. Lehman*, 368 U.S. 403, 411–12 (1962); William N. Eskridge Jr., *Interpreting Legislative Inaction,* 87 Mich. L. Rev. 67, 134–37 (1988) (collecting earlier Supreme Court decisions).

The rejected proposal canon is also popular among state courts. E.g., *McWilliams,* 300 P.3d at 891–92 (Cal.) (expressing reluctance to interpret a statute to track language rejected by the legislature); *Apple, Inc.*, 292 P.3d at 888–89 (Cal.) (similar for language rejected in committee); *Ex parte Emerald Mountain Expressway Bridge*, 856 So.2d 834, 840 (Ala. 2003); *People v.* Summers, 208 P.3d 251 (Colo. 2009); *In re Greenspan,* 910 A.2d 324, 341–43 (D.C. 2006); *Tomei v. Sharp,* 901 A.2d 757, 764–65 (Del. Super. 2006); *Travelers Indemn. Co. v. Reker,* 100 S.W.3d 756, 763–65 (Ky. 2003); *Reier v. State Dep't of Assessments & Taxation,* 915 A.2d 970, 985–86 (Md. 2007); *Theriot v. Midland Risk Ins. Co.*, 694 So.2d 184, 191–92 (La. 1997); *State v. Nieberger,* 128 P.3d 1223, 1228 (Vt. 2006); *Commonwealth v. Fairfax Cnty. Sch. Bd.*, 645 S.E.2d 337 (Va. App. 2007); 2A *Sutherland Statutes and Statutory Construction* § 48:18 (7th ed. 2015) (citing state statutory interpretation cases relying on rejected proposals). Even the Michigan Supreme Court has relied on rejected proposals. See *Bush v. Shabahang,* 772 N.W.2d 272, 282–83 (Mich. 2009).

chamber edits proposed legislation to make it clearer that a certain meaning is expected, that process ought to be probative as well.[128]

The utility and reliability of rejected proposals are substantially dependent on the particular circumstances, specifically, whether the record reveals why legislators rejected the proposed language. The case of the Segway exemplifies the best case scenario. Where there is a formal vote rejecting proposed statutory language and the circumstances suggest that the language was rejected on its merits (as the House bill was in favor of the Senate version), courts should be very reluctant to read that rejected policy into the statute. Not only does the Supreme Court, both now and in years gone by, embrace the rejected proposal canon under those circumstances—but even Judge Scalia gave it a friendly nod in his speech assailing committee reports in 1985–86, and Justice Markman followed suit in an opinion for the Michigan Supreme Court in 2008.[129]

A rejected proposal might be considered to be modest or no probative support for an interpretation under other circumstances. Legislative proposals by their nature are suggestions to change the legal status quo. If the legislature is aware of those proposals and ignores them or votes them down, judges frequently take that as evidence supporting the status quo. Specifically, when judges or agencies have long interpreted a statute one way, the fact that the legislature has considered and not acted on specific proposals to override those interpretations may be modest support for a court's disinclination to overrule its own precedents, disturb a consensus among lower court decisions, or reject a longstanding agency interpretation.[130] On the other hand, when legislators fail to act upon

---

[128] E.g., *Mohamad v. Palestinian Auth.*, 132 S.Ct. 1702, 1710 (2012) (relying on a committee mark-up as confirmatory evidence of ordinary meaning); id. at 1711 (Breyer, J., concurring) (relying on same evidence to resolve what the Justice considered ambiguity).

[129] See Scalia, "Speech on Legislative History," 10–11 (open to reliance on rejected proposals, so long as the rejection was apparently on the merits); *Gardner*, 753 N.W.2d at 89 (Markman, J.) (similar).

[130] See, e.g., *Inclusive Communities Project,* 135 S.Ct. at 2519–20 (rejected proposal confirms Court's disinclination to disturb a lower court consensus); *Kimble v. Marvel Entertainment, LLC,* 135 S.Ct. 2401 (2015) (rejected proposals confirm Court's disinclination to overrule its own precedent); *Brown & Williamson* (rejected proposals confirm Court's disinclination to allow agency to change its longstanding interpretation). See generally Eskridge, *Interpreting Legislative Inaction,* 87 Mich. L. Rev. at 134–37 (appendix of Supreme Court decisions relying on or refusing to rely on rejected proposals); CRS Report, *Statutory Interpretation,* 46 (updated 2011) (announcing that there is "no general rejected proposal rule" but conceding that federal courts sometimes consider rejected proposals decisive).

proposed statutory language or provision, without discernible explanation, courts generally pay no heed to that evidence.[131] Recall our discussion of the (weak) acquiescence canon in chapter three.

Dog Didn't Bark Canon. Continuity is a prominent feature in the rule of law. Society assumes that longstanding rules remain in force unless there is public notice that Congress or an agency is considering a change in the rule and there is a process for change that invites input from We the People (and Our Lobbyists). As noted in the introduction to this volume, *continuity* in the law is a prominent feature of the canons in general.[132]

An important continuity-based canon is inspired by the Sherlock Holmes story "The Silver Blaze." The detective solved the case by deduction from the fact that the dog in the barn did not bark—meaning that the death of the victim was not caused by an intruding stranger, who would have caused the dog to bark. The *dog didn't bark canon* posits that Congress does not make a significant change in the legal status quo without some legislative "barking"—namely, discussion, deliberation, or at least mention.[133] On the whole, this canon (like most of them) reflects common sense. Because there are so many vetogates in the congressional process and because most of them generate detailed records, one would expect some mention (and objection) if proposed legislation would effect major changes in existing policy. Given the more slender documentary records available for the legislative process in most states, it is harder to determine whether the dog barked, and so this canon has not been prominent in state court legisprudence.[134] Where statutes have been

---

[131] E.g., *Milner v. Department of Navy,* 562 U.S. 562, 572 (2011); *Mead Corp. v. Tilley*, 490 U.S. 714, 723 (1989).

[132] David Shapiro, *Continuity and Change in Statutory Interpretation*, 67 N.Y.U. L. Rev. 921 (1992); Amanda Tyler, *Continuity, Coherence, and the Canons*, 99 Nw. U.L. Rev. 1389 (2005).

[133] E.g., *Zuni Pub. Sch. Dist. No. 89 v. Dep't of Educ.*, 550 U.S. 81, 88 (2007); *Scheidler v. N.O.W.*, 547 U.S. 9, 20 (2006); *Chisom v. Roemer*, 501 U.S. 380, 396 & n.23 (1991) (compare id. at 406, where the dissenting opinion argues that sleeping dogs often don't bark); *Elsner v. Uveges*, 102 P.3d at 924 & n.18 (Cal.) (explicitly invoking *Silver Blaze* to make the dog doesn't bark point); see John Paul Stevens, *The Shakespeare Canon*, 140 U. Pa. L. Rev. 1373 (1992) (explaining and justifying the dog doesn't bark canon), as well as Rebecca Kysar, *Penalty Default Interpretive Canons,* 76 Brooklyn L. Rev. 953, 962–64 (2011) (examining this canon in connection with the no-elephants-in-mouseholes canon examined in chapter five of this volume).

[134] The California Legislature offers detailed records of its deliberations, and so the dog-doesn't-bark canon has surfaced in that state. See *Elsner v. Uveges*, 102 P.3d at 933 (Cal.). But elsewhere this is a canon that doesn't bark often. E.g., *Kasischke*, 991 So.2d at 818–19 (Fla.) (Lewis, J., dissenting).

enacted through a shortened, mostly off-the-record process (as is sometimes the case for unorthodox lawmaking), the dog-doesn't-bark canon ought to have even less weight, because there is less opportunity for legislative "barking."

After Congress enacted the Park Safety Act in 1992, there was no formal regulation of the mounted police in Lafayette Park. The Soaper Amendment of 2013 expanded the statute in some respects and might be interpreted to include horses as vehicles because of their speed and the risk of serious injury to park visitors. As argued above, there are good reasons to be skeptical of such an interpretation, but the skepticism might inspire the assiduous judge to consult the Senate committee hearings and report, the Senate debate on the original Soaper bill, and the House and Senate debate on the conference report (adopting the Soaper bill with one change). Perhaps to her surprise, the judge would find a lot of discussion—the National Park Service's committee testimony, the Soaper-Hushpuppy colloquy, and perhaps other evidence. From that record of deliberation, it becomes apparent that Senator Soaper herself believed mounted police should be barred from Lafayette Park, the Park Service opposed the idea but conceded that the exclusion was administrable, and Senator Hushpuppy pressed Senator Soaper to discuss that record on the floor of the Senate. All this evidence suggests that the dog *barked*, and the canon is satisfied. Given this legislative history, even a skeptic such as I ought to say that horses are barred from Lafayette Park.

Subsequent Legislative History Canon. After a statute has become the law of the land, legislators often continue to deliberate about what the statute meant. In the course of considering the Soaper Amendment of 2013, congressional committees may continue to deliberate about whether the D.C. Circuit's decision in *Hogan v. National Park Service* correctly interpreted the original Park Safety Act of 1992. If the Senate and House committees had both published pre-2013 committee reports opining that *Hogan* was wrongly decided, this "subsequent" (to the 1992 statute) legislative history would not have been a persuasive basis for the D.C. Circuit to reconsider its *Hogan* precedent. Apart from the strong pull of *stare decisis*, the Court would have been reluctant to credit subsequent legislative history untethered to an actual statute adopted by Congress.[135] Those

[135] E.g., *Bruesewitz v. Wyeth LLC,* 562 U.S. 223, 240–43 (2011); *Jones v. United States*, 526 U.S. 227, 238 (1999); *Sullivan v. Finkelstein*, 496 U.S. 617, 628 n.8 (1990); *United States v. Mine Workers*, 330 U.S. 258, 281–82 (1947).

pre-2013 committee reports would, of course, *not* be "subsequent" legislative history with regard to the Soaper Amendment of 2013, and so they ought to be considered if they contain analysis relevant to interpreting the Park Safety Act, once that statute was amended in 2013.

The current federal judicial understanding is that subsequent legislative history is generally not a reliable source for statutory meaning.[136] Recall that the whole code rule teaches that a *subsequent statute* might affect the meaning of the earlier statute, but this canon says that *subsequent legislative history* should not. Is that a defensible canon? Just as pre-enactment legislative deliberations may help the interpreter understand the potential meaning of statutory words and phrases, especially when used in particular combinations, so might post-enactment legislative deliberations. Indeed, in constitutional interpretation, original meaning Justices are happy to examine post-enactment materials to confirm or elaborate on what they believe was the original public meaning of a constitutional provision when it was adopted.[137]

For the same reasons that jurists consider post-enactment public deliberations relevant to the "original meaning" of the Constitution of 1789 or the Bill of Rights, judges ought to consider similar deliberations following statutory enactments—not because they are "authoritative," but because they might help the interpreter understand language use, the structure of the statute, and its plan or purpose (or because Congress has relied on that understanding in a significant way, discussed below). So if Senator Soaper had in the early millennium wondered whether the Park Safety Act regulated horses and had learned that mounted horses were causing serious injuries to park users from time to time, those committee deliberations ought sometimes to be relevant to the statutory interpreter. To be sure, they are not sufficient to override the D.C. Circuit's precedent in *Hogan v. National Park Service*, but if a judge

---

[136] *Bruesewitz*, 562 U.S. at 240–43; *Mine Workers*, 330 U.S. at 281–82 (leading case); 2A *Sutherland Statutes and Statutory Construction* § 48:20 (7th ed. 2015) (citing federal and state cases opposing reference to "post-enactment" history).

[137] *Noel Canning*, 134 S.Ct. at 2592, 2607–10 (Scalia, J., concurring in the judgment) (finding relevant to the "original meaning" of the Recess Appointments Clause [1789] the discussion of that clause in the early post-1789 Congresses and in the cabinets of George Washington, John Adams, and John Quincy Adams); *District of Columbia v. Heller*, 554 U.S. 570, 605–10 (2008) (finding relevant to "original meaning" the "postenactment" discussions of the right to bear arms and extensively relying on such evidence to "confirm" the Court's conclusions about the Second Amendment's "public meaning" in 1791).

were working from a clean slate (without that precedent on the books) the judge ought to consider these deliberations. To be clear, the current U.S. Supreme Court and the highest courts of many states do not currently follow this version of the canon, but it has been followed by the Supreme Court in previous decades[138] and is still followed by many state courts.[139]

The best argument against judicial consideration of post-enactment legislative history is one grounded in democratic accountability and respect for the vetogate-laced lawmaking process. If courts routinely considered committee reports and legislator floor statements made *after* a statute is enacted, then such statements would proliferate, with a big risk of strategic manipulation by legislators and their staffs. While strategic manipulation is a concern with pre-enactment legislative history as well, that concern is ameliorated by the close monitoring of committee hearings, reports, and floor debates before a statute is enacted. This system of whistleblowers and fire alarms does not operate for post-enactment statements nearly as well, because there is so little political attention.

The most compelling case for considering subsequent legislative materials would be a circumstance where they were persuasive evidence that legislators were *relying* on a particular interpretation of an existing statute when they enacted a new law.[140] For example, assume that right after Congress passed the Soaper Amendment to the Lafayette Park Safety Act in 2013, it passes a new Folger Park Safety Act of 2014. Section 3 of the new statute is patterned on the Lafayette Park law, as amended, but with one change: In the Folger Park law, Congress reinserts "mechanism" and drops "thing." The

---

[138] Compare *Seatrain Shipbuilding Corp. v. Shell Oil Co.,* 444 U.S. 572, 596 (1980) (holding that "the views of subsequent Congresses" expressed in committee reports "are entitled to significant weight," and "particularly so when the precise intent of the enacting Congress is obscure"), with *Finkelstein*, 496 U.S. at 631–32 (Scalia, J., concurring in part) (arguing that subsequent legislative history ought never be considered), and *Bruesewitz,* 562 U.S. at 242 (ruling that "[p]ost-enactment legislative history (a contradiction in terms) is not a legitimate tool of statutory interpretation").

[139] For state court decisions giving significant weight to subsequent legislative deliberations, see, e.g., *Elsner v. Uveges*, 102 P.3d at 934 (Cal.); *Rural Water Dist. #2 v. County of Louisburg*, 207 P.3d 1055 (Kan. 2009); *Reier v. State Dep't of Assessments & Taxation*, 915 A.2d 970 (Md. 2007); *State v. Nigou*, 937 A.2d 887, 890 (N.H. 2007); *State ex rel. Z.C.*, 165 P.3d 1605, 1612 (Utah 2007).

[140] E.g., *Inclusive Communities Project,* 135 S.Ct. at 2519–21 (interpreting 1988 amendments to the Fair Housing Act of 1968 to have ratified the court of appeals consensus that the original law had a disparate impact claim for relief, based upon changes made by the 1988 amendments that relied on that consensus and made little sense otherwise).

committee reports for both chambers explain that the earlier law barred mounted police from Lafayette Park, and the National Park Service was fine with that—but the District of Columbia police have strongly objected to barring their equestrian unit from Folger Park, which has more drug-related crimes. So the committee reports say that horses should be allowed in Folger Park and that the new language ("mechanism") is expected to limit the statutory prohibition to mechanical vehicles and, hence, to allow vehicular critters such as horses.

This committee report is strong evidence that the Folger Park Safety Act of 2013 ought not be interpreted to regulate horses as "vehicles," and it is *also* persuasive evidence that the Soaper Amendment of 2013 ought to be interpreted to regulate horses as "vehicles."[141] As to the Folger Park law, the committee report is pre-enactment history; as to the Lafayette Park amendment, the committee report is, technically, post-enactment history. Yet a judge really ought to consider the report for understanding *both* statutes and regulating *both* parks. When the enacting coalition for a statute relies on a particular interpretation for an earlier statute and builds upon that earlier interpretation, this ought to be very powerful evidence for how words and phrases are being used by Congress. Indeed, I'd consider a judicial practice that ignored such evidence to be anti-democratic.[142]

Executive Statements Canon. Assume that Congress passes the Soaper Amendment, with the foregoing legislative history, and President Barack Obama signs it, with the following statement:

> Some have opined that this legislation will bar the District's mounted police from Lafayette Park, because horses are now "vehicles" under the amended statute. Nothing could be further from the intent of Congress. It is absurd to say that a horse is a vehicle, and the safety of the White House

[141] For a very close analogue to the hypothetical example in text, see *Montana Wilderness Ass'n v. United States Forest Serv.*, 655 F.2d 951 (9th Cir. 1981) (vacating a prior statutory decision based upon subsequent legislative history demonstrating that a conference committee had relied on a different interpretation when enacting a new statute).

[142] *Bruesewitz,* 562 U.S. at 259–61 (Sotomayor, J., dissenting) (arguing for congressional reliance based upon a subsequent appropriations measure); *Seatrain Shipbuilding Corp.*, 444 U.S. at 595–96 (establishing congressional reliance on a particular interpretation of a 1936 statute by reference to committee reports for a statute adopted in 1972).

perimeter needs the flexibility of mounted police in Lafayette Park.

The National Park Service and the United States Park Police will pay careful attention to this signing statement, and it might trigger a reconsideration of their previous memorandum of understanding (discussed above), which agreed to leave the mounted police clear of the park.[143] But should the President's signing statement be considered if *judges* have occasion to apply the Soaper Amendment to the case of the mounted police? As always, the statement might be cited as evidence of language use ("vehicles" are rarely used to include horses), but does the President's statement carry any further weight?

The American Bar Association and most scholars are skeptical. The Article I, Section 7 concern is the chief reason not to credit presidential signing statements in statutory interpretation. The signing statement might, technically, be pre-enactment "legislative history," if uttered by the President before he or she actually signs the bill into law, but it is uttered or promulgated after Congress has completed its work and cannot change the bill and, more important, offers the executive branch a strategic opportunity that renders this kind of statement less reliable than committee reports, sponsor's statements, and rejected proposals.[144]

Contrast another form of state executive department inputs often rendered after the state legislatures have passed a bill. Recall that the Governors of New York and California have traditionally made their decisions to veto or sign legislation based upon a "bill report" or "bill jacket" prepared for the Governor. In addition to statements or letters from legislators, these bill reports and bill jackets usually include statements or letters from private groups supporting or opposing the legislation, relevant agencies and government groups, and law revision commissions and the like. The plurality of sources vests these materials with greater persuasive

---

[143] Walker, *Inside Agency Statutory Interpretation*, 67 Stan. L. Rev. at 1044–45 (agencies take presidential signing statements seriously even when courts would not).

[144] American Bar Ass'n, Task Force on Presidential Signing Statements and the Separation of Powers Doctrine, Report with Recommendations (2006); Marc N. Graber & Kurt A. Wimmer, *Presidential Signing Statements as Interpretations of Legislative Intent: An Executive Aggrandizement of Power,* 24 Harv. J. Legis. 363 (1987); accord, CRS Report, *Statutory Interpretation,* 51–53 (updated 2011). For a spirited defense of signing statements as contributing to good government, see Curtis Bradley & Eric Posner, *Presidential Signing Statements and Executive Power,* 23 Const. Comm. 307 (2006).

authority than the chief executive's statement. If judges examining a bill jacket or bill report believe it represents a genuine variety of political views and of institutions supporting or implementing the bill ready to be signed into law, then any consensus or assumed point of law could be reliable evidence of statutory meaning.

Stepping further back into the legislative process, moreover, presidential or gubernatorial statements are admissible and potentially valuable legislative history. Before the 1980s, most presidential statements were made in the course of the legislative process, and not at the end. Because Article I, Section 7 renders the President always relevant to the legislative process and a likely participant in any deal that might be reached in Congress, the President's public statements during the deliberative process are potentially relevant, and the same is true for statements by a state governor.[145]

Thus, if President Obama had denounced Senator Soaper's view that her amendment brought mounted police into the vehicles in the park prohibition, his denunciation would have been relevant legislative history—but relevant in a way that would not please the President, because it might become evidence for a rejected proposal. That is, if Senator Soaper says that her bill will regulate horses as vehicles, the President denounces that during active congressional deliberations, Senator Soaper's committee makes no change, and the conference committee also rejects the President's position and adopts the Soaper version of the bill, *then* the President's statement is a relevant link in the chain of legislative history under the backwards induction canon. And the chain supports an interpretation of the Act that bars mounted police from Lafayette Park.

As we shall see in the next chapter, the President and state governors have a much more effective means of influencing statutory interpretation than issuing contrarian signing statements or engaging in congressional debates.

* * *

---

[145] E.g., *Kasten v. Saint-Gobain Performance Plastics Corp.*, 563 U.S. 1, 12 (2011); *BankAmerica Corp.*, 462 U.S. at 126–127, 134–35 (relying on presidential statements as well as congressional testimony of presidential adviser); see 2A *Sutherland Statutes and Statutory Construction* § 48:5 (7th ed. 2015) (suggesting that presidential/gubernatorial statements are most useful in identifying the purposes of statutes the President or the Governor sponsored); McNollgast, *Legislative Bargains in Statutory Interpretation,* 80 Geo. L.J. at 718–20 (insisting that statutory interpreters consider the President's public participation in congressional deliberations and dealmaking, where relevant to an interpretive issue).

The potential value that a statute's internal legislative history might have for the statutory interpreter tracks the overall purposes underwriting the project of statutory interpretation in the first place.

First, legislative history is potentially useful for figuring out the public meaning of language enacted into law by Congress or a state legislature, in coordination with the President or governor. Whether the speaker is a legislative sponsor or the chief executive, the use of language by participants in the legislative process is worth considering by the most ardent textualist. Indeed, read critically, legislative history is often more useful for *textual analysis* than either dictionaries or a judge's independent understanding of grammar and word meaning. Dictionaries do a poor job of telling us what combinations of words mean, and might be misleading in helping us understand language within its inevitably normative context. Legislative discussion of the words, clusters of words, and sentences in their final enacted form helps the reader (i.e., the judge) form a more reliable understanding of the public meaning of those words, clusters, and sentences.

Second, legislative history is useful for linking a statutory application to the democratic deliberation that produced the legislation being interpreted. At the federal level, committee reports and sponsor's statements are intelligent representations that are the conventional basis for congressional chamber voting and for presidential signatures. The legislative process rests upon and runs on these conventions. To credit them, you don't have to claim to have discerned some abstract congressional "intent." Instead, you credit them for the same kinds of reasons everyone credits *The Federalist Papers:* "They set[ ] forth the views of intelligent, well-informed persons of the time, which are entitled to great weight on the basis of their experience and their closeness to the process," as Justice Scalia put the matter above.

It is high time to discard the textualist objections that judges cherry-pick the legislative history to read their own values into statutes, that judges are incompetent to handle legislative materials, and that judges will be confused by too much legislative evidence. These objections have never been substantiated, and actual evidence suggests that they understate the capacity of federal and state appellate judges. In truth, the only valid objections to the use of legislative history are practical ones of a different sort: It takes a lot of time to research legislative history (though much less now that so much legislative history is on-line), and one might wonder whether it is time well-spent. This is a valid question, but not susceptible to a strictly economic analysis, because the main value of legislative history is democratic accountability and legitimacy, which are not easily valued.

Third, legislative history is useful for helping the judge understand the statutory purpose, the congressional plan, and the overall governance norms for the subject matter under consideration. Sometimes, the statutory preamble and purpose provisions address these matters, but rarely with the nuance that legislative history still might contribute, as the House Legislative Counsel recognized in its 1995 drafting manual.[146] This third, underappreciated, value of legislative history links up with a broader concept, that of a *regulatory history* for a statute, that shall be the subject of the next chapter. To whet the appetite of the gentle reader whose attention might be flagging after the exhaustive discussion of legislative history here, the next chapter will return to and resolve the riddle of what to do about the Park Police's equestrian unit—while at the same time tackling the even more dramatic issue whether the statute authorizes the detention of American citizens for violating its vehicular prohibitions.

---

[146] Forstater, House Office of Legislative Counsel, *Manual on Drafting Style* § 325(a).

Chapter 5

AGENCY INTERPRETATION AND REGULATORY HISTORY

Guantánamo Bay Detention Camp

When lawyers talk about statutory interpretation, they usually assume that judges are the interpreters. Yet the overwhelming weight of official statutory interpretation is by administrators and agencies, not by judges.[1] Judges remain important because they can trump agency interpretations with authoritative opinions, though it

[1] William N. Eskridge Jr. & John Ferejohn, *A Republic of Statutes: The New American Constitution* (2010); Peter L. Strauss, *When the Judge Is Not the Primary Official with Responsibility To Read: Agency Interpretation and the Problem of Legislative History*, 66 Chi.-Kent L. Rev. 321 (1990).

is also true that few agency interpretations end up in court and most judicial opinions agree or go along with agency views.[2]

We have already seen that process at work in our exploration of the Lafayette Park Safety Act of 1992 (as amended). In our earlier examination of the ordinary meaning and the whole act rules as applied to particular mechanisms, there were judicial opinions *only* when federal officials issued citations to Cynthia Hogan, William and Liam Treanor, and J. Peter Byrne—and of course those "perps" only generated litigation because they objected to the citations and pursued their views through an appellate process which more often yields written opinions and citable precedents. If the National Park Service and its police did not believe a mechanism is a statutory "vehicle," there would normally have been no opportunity for judges to weigh in. Thus, even if the Court of Appeals would have ruled that skateboards are regulated vehicles under the Park Safety Act, the legal status of skateboards would remain uncertain if the Park Service did not consider them vehicles or ignored them as minor risks.

Even when statutory regimes do not depend upon government citation and prosecution the way our vehicles in the park law does, administrative views and practices are critically important to statutory interpretation by judges, for the same kinds of rule of law, democracy, and governance reasons that ordinary meaning is relevant. To begin with, administrative interpretation typically serves the rule of law values of transparency and predictability, because the most relevant applications of a statute are those announced or practiced by the officials administering it, and not those issued by judges.[3] If the Park Police have never issued citations for baby carriages, tricycles, skateboards, and other non-motorized mechanisms, most park users will consider this laissez-faire approach to be the relevant legal regime—even if some of the lawyerly park users believe that a court would find a few non-motorized

---

[2] E.g., William N. Eskridge Jr. & Lauren E. Baer, *The Continuum of Deference: Supreme Court Treatment of Agency Statutory Interpretations from* Chevron to Hamdan, 96 Geo. L.J. 1083 (2008) (over 22 years and more than 1000 statutory cases, the Supreme Court agreed with agency interpretations 67% of the time); Cass R. Sunstein, *Beyond* Marbury: *The Executive's Power to Say What the Law Is*, 115 Yale L.J. 2580 (2006).

[3] Peter L. Strauss, *One Hundred and Fifty Cases Per Year: Some Implications of the Supreme Court's Limited Resources for Judicial Review of Agency Action*, 87 Colum. L. Rev. 1093, 1118–29 (1987); accord, Jerry Mashaw, Richard Merrill, Peter Shane & Nicholas Parrillo, *Administrative Law, The American Public Law System: Cases and Materials* 35–36 (7th ed. 2014).

mechanisms to be statutory "vehicles." For "vehicles" the Park Service believes are worth regulating, the agency is likely to issue detailed guidances or website links listing prohibited vehicles and perhaps laying out its enforcement scheme—and the moment the agency does so there is a predictable legal regime that answers most of the issues that might arise.

Indeed, agency guidances and regulations have added rule of law value for very practical reasons: Agencies publish almost all regulations and most guidances and also make them available on websites and other fora, agencies usually organize the materials topically which makes them easier to research, and administrators make an effort to render the rules and allowances in plain English.[4] Put another way, it is impossible for most ordinary citizens to read a complicated statute and understand exactly what her rights and duties are, under the law—and it is usually much easier for the citizen to understand her rights and duties by calling agency officials or reading administrative guidebooks and websites. To be sure, these administrative materials may also be hard for the lay person to understand, and many agencies do not maintain their websites as efficiently as private companies do.[5] Nonetheless, agency guidances and so forth are likely to be much more comprehensible than the statute itself. This is true even for the very short statute we have been working with; the Park Safety Act is hard to apply, not because it is long and technical, but because it is short and vague (the key regulatory term, "vehicle").

Agency practice and publication provide notice and predictability to citizens (a core rule of law value)—indeed, most citizens know the law and understand its application only through agency guidance, and not by reading the statute itself. On the other hand, agency interpretation is not as strong as judicial interpretation in advancing other rule of law values, especially consistency over time and coherence with the larger legal landscape. Because of the many vetogates, statutes tend to be moderate departures from the status quo and, of course, are hard to amend. Agency guidances, in contrast,

---

[4] Office of Management & Budget, *Guidelines for Ensuring and Maximizing the Quality, Objectivity, Utility, and Integrity of Information Disseminated by Federal Agencies*, 67 Fed. Reg. 8452, 8458–59 (Feb. 22, 2002) (establishing an array of agency publishing requirements to ensure that accurate information is effectively conveyed to the public).

[5] David Robinson et al., *Government Data and the Invisible Hand*, 11 Yale J.L. & Tech. 160, 161 (2009) (documenting the widening gap between the quality of private search websites and government databases).

can change without a lot of prior notice. Unlike judges, administrators do not follow strict rules of *stare decisis*; administrators do have to follow binding judicial precedents, but are not strongly bound by their own.[6] Thus, the Park Service and the Park Police may allow skateboards in Lafayette Park for years—and then, after an "incident," such as a skateboarder's invasion of the White House grounds described in the previous chapter, the Park Service might decide to regulate skateboards, usually after some public notice. This is a comparative institutional point: Agencies do not routinely disrupt people's expectations by readily throwing over their own precedents, but they are more prone to do so than courts (because of *stare decisis*) or legislatures (because of vetogates).[7]

The comparative institutional point has even greater bite when considering the democratic legitimacy of agency interpretations. Like federal judges, federal administrators, enforcement officers, and even agency heads are not elected by We the People and are, therefore, not as democratically accountable as legislators. (Many state administrators, especially attorneys general, are elected just as governors are; judges in most states are either elected or subject to retention votes.) Unlike judges, however, most policy-level administrators do not have life tenure, and agency heads are usually appointed by and accountable to high-ranking elected officials (like the chief executive).[8] Thus, the Director of the National Park Service is nominated by the President and must be confirmed by the Senate. The President can ask the director for his or her resignation, and changes in presidential administrations have since 1985 always triggered new directorial appointments. Because a director who creates trouble for the White House or the Interior Department is going to lose her or his job, the National Park Service is unlikely to make controversial pronouncements about what people can do in Lafayette Park.[9] The media would have a field day with a director

---

[6] E. H. Schopler, Comment, *Applicability of* Stare Decisis *Doctrine to Decisions of Administrative Agencies*, 79 A.L.R.2d 1126 § 6 (1961).

[7] Indeed, courts not only stick to their traditional interpretations, but make it harder for agencies to change theirs. See Jerry L. Mashaw & David L. Harfst, *Regulation and Legal Culture: The Case of Motor Vehicle Safety*, 4 Yale J. Reg. 257, 294 (1987).

[8] *Chevron U.S.A., Inc. v. Natural Resources Defense Council, Inc.*, 467 U.S. 837 (1984) (observing that, relatively speaking, agencies are more democratically accountable than federal judges because they are appointed by the elected chief executive).

[9] Mashaw et al., *Administrative Law, The American Public Law System*, 29–30 (7th ed.); Kevin M. Stack, *Agency Statutory Interpretation and Policymaking Form*, 2009 Mich. St. L. Rev. 225.

who allowed the Park Police to harass parents pushing baby carriages, kids roller skating, and disabled persons in motorized wheelchairs—and hence you are not going to see those mechanisms regulated under the statute, given this quasi-democratic accountability. Because officials are being responsive to popular opinion, this is a form of democracy in action.

Moreover, the Park Service Director is going to be more responsive to Congress than the Court of Appeals for the D.C. Circuit or the Supreme Court would be. Agency rules are richly informed by legislative deliberations underlying statutes and their amendments. Christopher Walker's empirical survey of agency rule drafters found that more than three-quarters of them relied on legislative history when writing rules.[10] And administrators are relatively skilled at navigating their way through even complicated legislative histories, because they or their predecessors are usually actors as well as observers in the legislative process. Agency officials have long provided both technical and substantive input into congressional drafting.[11]

Agencies are also responsive to the current Congress. "In communicating with agencies about legislation, Congress has a variety of tools at its disposal, such as confirmation hearings, appropriation hearings, authorization hearings, oversight hearings and investigations, committee reports, floor debates at the time of legislative consideration of a bill, and other non-statutory controls."[12] Both congressional research services and political scientists, for

---

[10] Christopher J. Walker, *Inside Agency Statutory Interpretation*, 67 Stan. L. Rev. 999, 1020 (2015) (Figure 2).

[11] Nicholas R. Parrillo, *Leviathan and Interpretive Revolution: The Administrative State, the Judiciary, and the Rise of Legislative History, 1890–1950*, 123 Yale L.J. 266 (2013) (New Deal agencies drafted statutes that Congress then enacted); Walker, *Inside Agency Statutory Interpretation*, 67 Stan. L. Rev. at 1036–38 (empirical report finding that almost 80% of agencies were involved in drafting statutes, with most drafters reporting a substantive and not just technical role in the process); Ganesh Sitaraman, *The Origins of Legislation*, 91 Notre Dame L. Rev. 79, 103–06 (2015) (similar); cf. Matthew R. Christiansen & William N. Eskridge Jr., *Congressional Overrides of Supreme Court Statutory Interpretation Decisions, 1967–2011*, 92 Tex. L. Rev. 1317 (2014) (agencies almost always involved in congressional override legislation, usually as supporters testifying in favor of such legislation).

[12] Robert A. Katzmann, *Judging Statutes* 24 (2014). For an overview of mechanisms for congressional influence on agencies, see Joel Auerbach, *Keeping a Watchful Eye: The Politics of Congressional Oversight* (1990); Lawrence C. Dodd & Richard L. Schott, *Congress and the Administrative State* (2d ed. 1986); Paul C. Light, *Government by Investigation: Congress, President, and the Search for Answers, 1945–2012* (2013); David H. Rosenbloom, *Building a Legislative-Centered Public Administration: Congress and the Administrative State, 1946–1999* (2000).

example, have documented the significant effect legislative budgetary and appropriations measures have on agency policy.[13] Knowledgeable scholars have also found a significant effect for oversight hearings and substantive riders to appropriations laws.[14]

An official, like the Director of the National Park Service, who is soliciting funds from Congress, who is testifying at oversight and other committee hearings, and who is fielding telephone calls from congressional staff, is not an official who is going to irritate influential legislators by bothersome statutory interpretations. Even if the Interior Department were willing to support a director who insists upon excluding tricycles from Lafayette Park, the Park Service would hesitate before regulating such tiny "vehicles" if the director and staff expected objections from members of Congress—especially members who were serving on the committees handling public land management matters, including budget and appropriations. In this way, agencies mediate the tension between broad legislation seeking to solve a problem, with the messy details of applying statutes to unthought-of circumstances. On the other hand, these examples illustrate the tension between the rule of law and original statutory meaning and the process of applying statutes dynamically in light of new political circumstances. Current democratic pressures will sometimes work against the rule of law in our republic of statutes.[15]

A mechanism that agencies can deploy to enhance the democratic legitimacy of their interpretations is notice-and-comment rulemaking.[16] If Congress in the Park Safety Act granted legislative

---

[13] Curtis W. Copeland, Cong. Research Serv., *Congressional Influence on Rulemaking and Regulation Through Appropriations Restrictions* (2008); Daniel P. Carpenter, *Adaptive Signal Processing, Hierarchy, and Budgetary Control in Federal Regulation*, 90 Am. Pol. Sci. Rev. 283, 299 (1996) (effect of appropriations pressure on FDA); Barry R. Weingast & Mark J. Moran, *Bureaucratic Discretion or Congressional Control? Regulatory Policymaking by the Federal Trade Commission*, 91 J. of Pol. Econ. 765, 787, 792 (1983) (same, FTC).

[14] Neal E. Devins, *Regulation of Government Agencies Through Limitation Riders*, 1987 Duke L. J. 456 (1987); Mary K. Olson, *Agency Rulemaking, Political Influences, Regulation, and Industry Compliance*, 15 J.L. Econ. & Org. 573, 598 (1999).

[15] For a classic examination of how congressional pressure works against the rule of law, see Robert Klonoff, *The Congressman as Mediator Between Citizens and Government Agencies: Problems and Prospects*, 16 Harv. J. Legis. 701 (1979) (empirical analysis of congressional case-handling and its tension with the neutral application of law by agencies).

[16] Henry S. Richardson, *Democratic Autonomy: Public Reasoning About the Ends of Policy* (2002). See also Lisa Schultz Bressman, *Beyond Accountability: Arbitrariness and Legitimacy in the Administrative State*, 78 N.Y.U. L. Rev. 461, 541–544 (2003); Mark Seidenfeld, *A Civic Republican Justification for the Bureaucratic*

rulemaking authority to the Park Service, there is a democratic authorization for the agency to make substantive law, so long as it advances the legislative purposes. If the agency wants to take advantage of this rulemaking power, however, the Administrative Procedure Act requires the agency to give public notice of its proposed rules in the *Federal Register*, to afford interested citizens and institutions a chance to submit comments, and to reconsider its proposed rules in light of the comments.[17] Additionally, final rules are subject to judicial review, which will reject agency rules that don't have good answers to important objections raised by commenters.[18] These procedural requirements encourage agencies to avoid rulemaking for some policy pronouncements,[19] but when they do follow this process their interpretations are more democratically legitimate than those of unelected federal judges.[20] New technology potentially enhances the legitimacy of notice-and-comment "e-rulemaking," as it opens up the process to wider public inputs.[21]

The foregoing analysis also suggests the variety of ways agency interpretations might advance effective governance. Effective governance is the biggest comparative advantage that agencies have in policymaking. The primary governance advantage of agency interpretations comes when administrators are applying their "expertise," which is what agency officials believe themselves to be doing when they draft rules and guidances.[22] What is expertise? First, expertise is specialized, often technical knowledge that allows government officials to perform ends-means, "instrumental" analysis:

State, 105 Harv. L. Rev. 1511 (1992); Jody Freeman, *Collaborative Governance in the Administrative State*, 45 U.C.L.A. L. Rev. 1 (1997).

[17] 5 U.S.C. § 553 (procedures for notice-and-comment rulemaking). See generally Cornelius Kerwin, *Rulemaking: How Government Agencies Write Law and Policy* (4th ed. 2010); Peter L. Strauss, *The Rulemaking Continuum*, 41 Duke L.J. 1463 (1992).

[18] *Motor Vehicle Manufacturers Ass'n v. State Farm Mut. Automobile Ins. Co.*, 463 U.S. 29 (1983) (interpreting arbitrariness review of notice-and-comment rulemaking).

[19] Connor Raso, *Agency Avoidance of Rulemaking Procedures*, 67 Admin. L. Rev. 65 (2015).

[20] *Chevron, U.S.A.*, 467 U.S. at 865–66.

[21] Comm. on the Status & Future of Fed. E-Rulemaking, *Achieving the Potential: The Future of Federal E-Rulemaking: A Report to Congress and the President* (2008); Cynthia R. Farina et al., *Rulemaking 2.0*, 65 Miami L. Rev. 395 (2011).

[22] Walker, *Inside Agency Statutory Interpretation*, 67 Stan. L. Rev. at 1053 (Figure 10) (empirical survey reporting that agency rule drafters view their job as applying the agency's "expertise" to fill in the details and address omissions in the statutory scheme).

If the country's goal is thus-and-so, will regulating such-and-such be useful at a reasonable cost?[23] Technical expertise is characteristic of but not limited to agencies such as the Patent Office, the Federal Energy Regulatory Commission, and the Federal Reserve Board. The National Park Service has or can acquire technical expertise in addressing fundamental issues of safety. Recall our quandary, explored by the last couple of chapters, in determining whether motorized but plodding Segways are "vehicles" regulated under the Park Safety Act. It does not require an expert to tell us how fast Segways can go, but administrators dedicated to studying park safety are more likely to know, or find out, how likely Segways are to cause accidents that injure park users. Unlike judges, park service administrators can compile survey evidence and even carry out their own studies about Segway safety.

A second form of agency expertise is institutional, namely, how to deploy limited resources to carry out public goals. Agencies operate in a world of limitations; they have budgetary constraints, face discipline and backlash for unpopular decisions, work under the sometimes watchful eye of the White House, and coordinate their work with that of other agencies. Thus, the National Park Service and the U.S. Park Police might decline to enforce the Park Safety Act to exclude Segways in the first few years of the new millennium, in large part because the Park Police might have just one officer on site during the day, and she says that her hands are full with keeping bicycles from being ridden through the park, and other tasks. (And in her view Segways are much less of a hazard than bicycles.) If, after 9/11, the White House puts pressure on the Park Service to "tighten up" its regulation of potentially threatening vehicles, the Service will find the resources to clear the park of Segways.

A third form of expertise is openly normative, that is, an understanding of how public goals evolve with experience and how they interact with other, often emerging, public goals.[24] We have already seen this at work in the history of the Lafayette Park Safety

---

[23] James Landis, *The Administrative Process*, 23–24 (1938); Emily Hammond Meazell, *Super Deference, the Science Obsession, and Judicial Review as Translation of Agency Science*, 109 Mich. L. Rev. 733, 743–50, 756–59 (2011); James T. O'Reilly, *Losing Deference in the FDA's Second Century: Judicial Review, Politics, and a Diminished Legacy of Expertise*, 93 Cornell L. Rev. 939, 948 (2008); Cass R. Sunstein, *Law and Administration after* Chevron, 90 Colum. L. Rev. 2071, 2088 (1990).

[24] On the exercise of practical reasoning, see Henry S. Richardson, *Practical Reasoning about Final Ends* (1994), as well as Richardson, *Democratic Autonomy* (applying the insights of the earlier book to administrative application of statutes).

Act of 1992. Its original purpose was to protect tourists and other park users from being injured by speedy "vehicles," but after 9/11 the Park Service and the Park Police would be more attentive to the security of the White House as an important public goal. Cooperating with other institutions, such as the Secret Service, the Park Service and Park Police today would consider White House security concerns as well as regular safety concerns when it determines whether a mechanism is a regulated "vehicle" for purposes of the statute. Agencies not only know more about Congress's statutory scheme and how to implement it effectively than judges do, but they understand how this statutory scheme fits (or is in tension with) other important national policies, such as anti-terrorism policies.

On the other hand, agency interpretations do not always carry forth effective governance. There are many pitfalls that might impede an agency's ability or willingness to carry forth effective governance. The overarching problem is potential agency bias. Administrators might be biased because of *tunnel vision*; they overgeneralize from limited information and take regulation too far or ignore critical features of the problem legislators have tasked them with addressing.[25] Thus, the Park Service might well implement the vehicles in the park law with a simple rule of thumb: If it has a motor, we keep it out of the park (bicycles can come into the park but cannot be ridden). That rule of thumb might be a low-cost means for making the park safer, but a literal-minded officer might apply it to prevent a disabled person from operating her motorized wheelchair in the park. The humiliation suffered by the person, together with the ends-means irrationality of the application, is inconsistent with the policy of the Rehabilitation Act of 1973 (chapter two) and with far-sighted administration of the Park Safety Act of 1992.

Agencies also might be biased because of *capture by special interests*. A generation ago, academics as well as citizens believed that agencies are routinely captured by the interests they are supposed to regulate, and judges viewed agency initiatives with skepticism that they represented the public interest.[26] Although learned commentators no longer consider capture to be the norm, it

---

[25] Stephen Breyer, *Breaking the Vicious Cycle: Toward Effective Risk Regulation* 11–19 (1993) (tendency of agencies to take regulation too far); cf. Morell E. Mullins, *Tools, not Rules: The Heuristic Nature of Statutory Interpretation*, 30 J. Legis. 1, 51–53 (2004) (tendency of agencies to overgeneralize from limited evidence).

[26] E.g., Thomas W. Merrill, *Capture Theory and the Courts: 1967–1983*, 72 Chi.-Kent L. Rev. 1039, 1050–52 (1997); Richard B. Stewart, *The Reformation of American Administrative Law*, 88 Harv. L. Rev. 1667 (1975).

remains a troubling feature of the administrative state.[27] For example, if the National Park Service Director were appointed by the President as a political payoff for tourist industry support for the President's reelection, the agency would be much less likely to keep Segways and other tourism-facilitating mechanisms out of Lafayette Park. Administrative law scholars have suggested a number of institutional design features, such as White House review and revolving door prohibitions, to minimize agency capture.[28] Like tunnel vision, capture does occur and undermines an agency's ability to carry out its statutory mission in an appropriate manner.

Let me summarize the foregoing discussion. For most issues of statutory interpretation in the modern state, including issues arising under our vehicles in the park law, the rule of law consists mostly of rules announced or practically enforced (or not) by administrators, and not of precedents announced by judges. The methodology followed by agencies is similar to that laid out in the first four chapters of this volume, but with some different emphases. Agencies are more likely than courts to read statutory text broadly in light of purpose, to change their interpretations over time, and to consider the statute's legislative history, including subsequent legislative history and informal signals from legislators.[29] As applied to our case study, what this means is that the National Park Service is much more likely than a court to give a practical reading to the Park Safety Act, ignoring some mechanisms that might be regulated under the statute, while dynamically adding others to the regulatory ambit. Administrators would narrow or expand the letter of the law, based on the statutory safety purpose and overall public policy, as dynamically understood by the agency in light of its regulatory

---

[27] For balanced accounts of the possibility of agency capture and mechanisms to prevent it, see, e.g., Daniel A. Farber & Philip P. Frickey, *Law and Public Choice: A Critical Introduction* (1991); Jerry L. Mashaw, *Greed, Chaos, and Governance: Using Public Choice To Improve Public Law* (1997); Einer Elhauge, *Does Interest Group Theory Justify More Intensive Judicial Review?*, 101 Yale L.J. 31 (1991); Thomas W. Merrill, *Does Public Choice Justify Judicial Activism After All?*, 21 Harv. J. L. & Pub. Pol. 219 (1997); *Symposium: Getting Beyond Cynicism: New Theories of the Regulatory State*, 87 Cornell L. Rev. 267 (2002).

[28] Rachel E. Barkow, *Insulating Agencies: Avoiding Capture Through Institutional Design*, 89 Tex. L. Rev. 15 (2011); Michael A. Livermore & Richard L. Revesz, *Regulatory Review, Capture, and Agency Inaction*, 101 Geo. L. J. 1337 (2013).

[29] Jerry L. Mashaw, *Norms, Practices and the Paradox of Deference: A Preliminary Inquiry into Agency Statutory Interpretation*, 57 Admin. L. Rev. 501 (2005); Kevin M. Stack *Purposivism in the Executive Branch: How Agencies Interpret Statutes*, 109 Nw. U. L. Rev. 871 (2015); Walker, *Inside Agency Statutory Interpretation*, 67 Stan. L. Rev. at 1020, 1034–48.

experience, new federal priorities (e.g., anti-terrorist policies), and ever-changing congressional and presidential pressures.

Typically, even when a court weighs in with its interpretation of the statute (which for most laws will be exceptional), it will do so against the backdrop of agency practice and interpretation, perhaps subject to changes over time. Should the court ignore the agency's experience? I hardly see how that is a responsible course of action. Surely, the court ought to consider the agency interpretation and the reasons advanced for its view of the statute. Should the court then consider an agency's reasons with the same dispassionate eye it would give the reasons of any other interested institution? Again, the answer is "no." This might be surprising. Let me now explain why courts ought to consider agency interpretations and why those interpretations will usually provide relevant information not provided by other sources of statutory meaning.

The *Skidmore* Canon
The Interpretive Value of Regulatory History

Recall the Lafayette Park Safety Act of 1992, as amended in 2013, that has been the basis for our examination in the last several chapters:

> **An Act to ensure public safety in Lafayette Park**
>
> **Sec. 1. Findings and Purpose.** Finding that vehicles operating in Lafayette Park have contributed to several serious accidents requiring hospitalization in the last five years, and finding further that vehicles create risks of serious injury to park users, Congress resolves that there is an urgent public need to ban any and all vehicles from Lafayette Park.
>
> **Sec. 2. No Vehicles in the Park.** No vehicles of any kind shall be allowed in Lafayette Park. Any person who drives a vehicle into Lafayette Park shall be guilty of a civil offense, which may be punished by a fine not exceeding $100 and confiscation of the offending vehicle, or both.
>
> **Sec. 3. Definition.** "Vehicle" for purposes of this law means any thing used for conveying a person from one place to another, including automobiles, trucks, motorcycles, motor scooters, and other forms of conveyance that pose safety hazards to park users because of their speed. *Provided that,* bicycles of any kind shall not be considered

"vehicles" and shall be allowed in Lafayette Park, so long as they are being pushed or carried and not ridden.

Now, apply this statute, as amended, to the issue raised and illustrated in the previous chapter: Does the law bar mounted police from Lafayette Park?

Assume that the federal judge has available to her the barebones statutory history (but not the legislative history) laid out in the previous chapter: the text of the Park Safety Act as it was enacted in 1992, the Court of Appeals' decision in *Hogan v. National Park Service*, and the 2013 congressional override (the Soaper Amendment), which revised the language of section 3 to read as it does above. Does the Park Police horse qualify as a section 3 "vehicle," namely, "any thing used for conveying a person from one place to another, including automobiles, trucks, motorcycles, motor scooters, and other forms of conveyance that pose safety hazards to park users because of their speed." How does your reasoning incorporate section 2, which bars people from "driv[ing]" vehicles in the park? Jot down your interpretation of the statute in the margin. Now consider how the regulatory background might make a difference in your interpretation.

For those readers who scoff at the notion of regulating horses as statutory "vehicles," imagine the following regulatory background, to supplement the textual and precedential materials. Assume that the National Park Service allowed mounted police officers to trot through Lafayette Park after the enactment of the Park Safety Act in 1992, just as those officers had done before 1992. In other words, the agency did not view the 1992 law as changing the United States Park Police's traditional practice of deploying its Horse Mounted Unit in Lafayette Park. An internal 1995 memorandum of understanding among the National Park Service, United States Park Police, and the Secret Service reasoned that horses are not "mechanisms" for transporting people from one place to another, and so mounted police were simply beyond the statute's domain.

Unfortunately, the Park Service faced new regulatory challenges, as mounted police actually did create safety problems in the park: Some tourists sustained minor injuries when they fell down trying to keep from being bumped by police horses trotting through the park, and a few park users sustained serious injuries when horses bumped into them or, in one case, kicked a southern congressman "upside the head" (as he colorfully put it in the congressional oversight hearing that followed his release from the hospital). Based upon this experience with the statute and the ire of the House member and his subcommittee, the National Park Service changed its mind about whether the mounted police *ought* to be excluded from Lafayette Park. Although the agency's counsel still believed that the Park Safety Act did not regulate horses because they are not "mechanisms" (section 3) or vehicles that one "drives" (section 2), the Park Service in 2001 entered into a new memorandum of understanding with the Park Police and the Secret Service, whereby the former agreed to keep mounted police out of Lafayette Park. When Senator Soaper's committee held hearings for her proposed amendment to the vehicles in the park law, the Park Service Director testified that horses and the mounted police should be excluded. The director reported no serious injuries in Lafayette Park since the 2001 memorandum covering mounted police. Representatives of the Park Police and the Secret Service said their departments had no objection to the Park Service's position.

Although mainly aimed at overriding *Hogan*, the Soaper Amendment also aimed to regulate mounted police. Recall, from the last chapter, Senator Soaper's colloquy with a skeptical legislator:

> **SENATOR SOAPER.** * * * The new definition is pretty clear: any "thing" conveying people or things that goes fast—say more than 25 miles per hour—is going to be regulated by the revised statute. The statute lists some popular motor vehicles, but it also covers other things that go fast.
>
> **SENATOR HUSHPUPPY.** The esteemed Senator from West Virginia cannot mean what she says. Horses convey people, and they can go more than 25 miles per hour. How about the mounted police? Are they excluded from Lafayette Park?
>
> **SENATOR SOAPER.** Yes, Senator, they would be. We considered and accepted the National Park Service's suggestion that mounted police be excluded from Lafayette Park. The Service reported that the horses had been involved in three serious and five minor park accidents in the last decade. A representative of the United States Park Police told us that its officers can police the area around the White House without the equestrian unit's operating in Lafayette Park.

The park amendments went to conference, which opted for Senator Soaper's bill plus a substitution of "thing" for "mechanism" in revised section 3. Explaining the conference report language to her colleagues, Senator Soaper said that the substitution was accomplished so that horses could be considered vehicles and so that mounted police would be included in the statute's domain.

In light of this evidence, are you sure the Park Safety Act, as amended, does not regulate the horse-mounted unit? Those readers who announced themselves eager to regulate mounted police under the Park Safety Act, as amended, will surely feel vindicated by the foregoing account. I now invite the regulate-the-horses readers to consider a different (and equally hypothetical) history of agency interpretation and application.

As before, assume that the National Park Service continued to allow mounted police officers to ride through Lafayette Park after the enactment of the Park Safety Act in 1992. A 1995 internal memorandum of understanding among the Park Service, the Park Police, and the Secret Service reasoned that a horse is probably not a "vehicle" under section 3 and certainly is not a "vehicle" one might "drive" under section 2; hence, mounted police are simply beyond the statute's domain. Contrary to the scenario above, however, assume that this arrangement worked really well in the 1990s and the new millennium: Carefully trained by the Park Police, officers of its Horse Mounted Unit patrolled Lafayette Park regularly but never galloped through the park at great speeds. As a result, there were no reported injuries, serious or minor, caused by mounted police horses after 1992. In the wake of 9/11, more law enforcement personnel (and more officers riding horses) guarded the area around the White House, including more mounted police, still without causing injuries to park users.

When Senator Soaper's committee held hearings for her proposed amendment to the vehicles in the park law, the National Park Service Director explained to the committee the foregoing history of (non)enforcement, the dearth of reported injuries, and the more urgent need for access by equestrian units to the park in case of an attack on or threat to the White House. Representatives of the Secret Service and the Park Police strongly supported this last point, with detailed analyses. Every other sentence in these officials' testimony used the words "national security" (as in "national security requires this"). The director urged the committee to leave horses out of the vehicle-regulatory statute—while also accepting Soaper's effort to override *Hogan*.

With this testimony as background, Senator Soaper's colloquy with a skeptical legislator took a very different turn than it did in my earlier hypothetical. Here is the revised version of her response to Senator Hushpuppy:

> **SENATOR HUSHPUPPY.** * * * Horses convey people, and they can go more than 25 miles per hour. How about the mounted police? Are they excluded from Lafayette Park?
>
> **SENATOR SOAPER.** No, Senator, they would not be. The National Park Service has been allowing mounted police in the park for decades; its director testified that the horses never gallop through the park and that there have been neither serious nor minor injuries caused by horses bumping against park users. Given the national security concerns for the White House, emphasized by the United States Park Police and the Secret Service as well as by the National Park Service, the committee emphatically does not intend to change the current pattern of nonenforcement. Besides which, who calls a horse a "vehicle"? In West Virginia, we call a horse a "horse" or, if we are in an ornery mood, a "nag."

The park amendments went to conference, which opted for Senator Soaper's bill plus a substitution of "thing" for "mechanism" in revised section 3. Explaining the conference report language to her colleagues, Senator Soaper said that the substitution was accomplished so that "skateboards and the like" might be covered by the statute. Because some conferees worried that "mechanisms" was too narrow a term, the conference committee changed the Senate bill to define "vehicles" as "things" rather than "mechanisms."

Given *this* version of the agency's regulatory experience with the vehicles in the park law, are those readers who found a plain meaning that includes horses as "vehicles" really so certain about your interpretation of the statute? Or is there room for the agency's views?

Notice how the *same* statutory text and structure and the *same* statutory history might be read in diametrically opposite ways, depending on the law's evolving regulatory history. My first account of the agency's regulatory history makes it obvious that the amended statute must consider horses to be excluded "vehicles" and therefore affects the Horse Mounted Unit of the Park Police. But my second account makes the opposite result even more painfully clear: If this were the real regulatory history, the amended statute certainly does *not* exclude horses on the ground that they are statutory "vehicles."

These dueling accounts suggest that agency interpretations and their history are sometimes going to be most valuable for the judicial interpreter's understanding of statutory terms ("vehicle"), the whole act, and the statutory history, as well as the legislative history. The Supreme Court has recognized this general idea in what I should call the "*Skidmore* canon," after a leading case where the always-quotable Justice Robert Jackson said that the "weight" of an agency interpretation in a particular case will depend upon "the thoroughness evident in its consideration, the validity of its reasoning, its consistency with earlier and later pronouncements, and all those factors which give it power to persuade, if lacking power to control."[30] Many state supreme courts follow Justice Jackson's expression of the weight to be accorded ordinary agency interpretations of the statutes they are charged with implementing.[31]

My version of the *Skidmore* canon tweaks Justice Jackson's sensible formulation in an important way (but consistent with the Court's actual application in *Skidmore* and other cases).[32] Before delivering an authoritative interpretation of a statute, judges will consider not just the agency's interpretation of the statute, including its reasoning, longevity, and consistency (the Jackson factors), but also the entire regulatory history, including feedback from Congress, the White House, the states, and the public. In the larger normative framework suggested by the current volume, I should say that the *regulatory history* of a statute is relevant and often dispositive even when judges are interpreting a statute as to which they have primary authority. By "regulatory history," I mean the history of an agency's practice before the statute was enacted; its role in the deliberations leading up to the new statute; the agency's implementation of the statute, including feedback from the citizenry and legislators, as well as agency adjustments, refinements, and new directions; the agency's

---

[30] *Skidmore v. Swift & Co.*, 323 U.S. 134 (1944). On the current relevance of the *Skidmore* canon, see Eskridge & Baer, *The Continuum of Deference*, 96 Geo. L.J. at 1100, 1109–11; Thomas W. Merrill & Kristin E. Hickman, Chevron's *Domain*, 89 Geo. L.J. 833 (2001); Peter L. Strauss, *"Deference" is too Confusing—Let's Call them* "Chevron *Space" and* "Skidmore *Weight*," 112 Colum. L. Rev. 1143 (2012).

[31] E.g., *Yamaha Corp. of America v. State Bd. of Equalization*, 960 P.2d 1031, 1037–38 (Cal. 1998) (sharply distinguishing, for deference purposes, between agency "quasi-legislative" rules and "interpretive" rules, the latter meriting weaker *Skidmore* deference), applied in *Sara M. v. Superior Court*, 116 P.3d 550 (Cal. 2005). *Yamaha* relied and drew from Michael Asimow, *The Scope of Judicial Review of Decisions of California Administrative Agencies*, 42 U.C.L.A. L. Rev. 1157 (1995).

[32] The New Deal Court in Justice Jackson's era found administrative practice, rather than just an isolated agency interpretation, richly informative. See Parrillo, *Administrative State, the Judiciary, and the Rise of Legislative History, 1890–1950.*

role in subsequent amendments to the statute and its practice and interpretations after any new amendments. Using the dueling accounts of the Park Safety Act's regulatory history, let me elaborate on the utility of regulatory history.

To begin with, a statute's regulatory history is very useful for judges attentive to the classic rule of law values of objectivity, predictability, and continuity. Thus, the National Park Service's practice in my thought experiment is highly relevant for a judge who is interested in the ordinary meaning of the words of the law and in the statutory structure. If the Park Service and the Park Police, for example, were in agreement that horses do not fit within the section 3 definition of "vehicle" either before or after the 2013 Soaper Amendment, that is relevant, even if not dispositive, evidence of ordinary meaning. On the other hand, recall that the statutory focus is mechanisms (or, after 2013, things) that pose risks of serious injury to park visitors. Given that focus, if the Park Service understood mounted police as not posing safety threats and its understanding is borne out by experience under the statute (my first scenario), that is powerful evidence of plain meaning as well (namely, ordinary meaning considered in light of the statutory structure).

The rule of law is valuable, in part, because citizens and institutions can rely on predictable rules in planning their activities and enterprises. If the Park Service has maintained a consistent practice of excluding mounted police from the statutory bar, the Park Police and the Secret Service will rely on that consistent understanding of the law to work around this limitation in order to protect the White House and visitors to the area. Indeed, Congress itself will probably rely on that stable understanding when it revisits the statute. Under the second regulatory scenario detailed above, a Congress wanting to override the Court of Appeals decision in *Hogan* but not inclined to override the National Park Service's allowance of mounted police will ignore the latter issue, with the assurance that this allowance will probably continue indefinitely.

The last point suggests a second potential value for regulatory history, namely, its value in linking the democratic process to the implementation of the statute. Under either account set forth above, the regulatory history of the Park Safety Act is essential to understanding the legislative history of the statute and its amendment. Most important statutes enacted by Congress involve administrative inputs, and many laws are drafted or developed within the executive branch.[33] Congressional overrides, such as the Soaper Amendment, are usually suggested to Congress by agencies and almost always involve executive branch organs as important players during Congress's deliberative process.[34]

Does the Soaper Amendment expand the Park Safety Act to give mounted police the boot from Lafayette Park? The amendment involved some degree of bargaining between the House and Senate, and you usually cannot understand the statutory compromise and its implications for the mounted police without knowing the regulatory history. Notice that the dueling accounts above reveal several linkages between agency policy implementation and congressional deliberations. A caveat is in order, however. Agencies know the regulatory history (including its link to legislative history) better than any other institution and can be expected to exploit that knowledge to support their favored statutory interpretations. This practice raises concerns that agency viewpoints, which may be quite biased, will sometimes prevail when they should not—a concern that is somewhat ameliorated by the fact that agency positions in appellate courts must clear the Office of the Solicitor General, which scrupulously hews to thoughtful and usually nonideological interpretations of federal statutes.[35]

A third potential value for regulatory history relates to effective governance. A statute's regulatory history reveals how the expert administrators sought to carry forth the statutory purpose—and often reveals how successful (or not) those administrators are in carrying out their mission. Judges serious about understanding the Park Safety Act ought to be very interested in the Park Service's experience with mounted police: Did they cause accidents with serious injuries to park users? (This is the key point of divergence in the dueling accounts of the regulatory history set forth above.) If so, under what circumstances?

---

[33] Executive Order 12,988, *Civil Justice Reform*, 61 Fed. Reg. 4729, 4731–32 (Feb. 5, 1996), reprinted 28 U.S.C. § 519 (guidelines for executive branch agencies drafting and commenting on legislation for Congress); Parrillo, *Leviathan and Interpretive Revolution* (describing intimate involvement of New Deal agencies in legislative drafting); Walker, *Inside Agency Statutory Interpretation*, 67 Stan. L. Rev. at 1036–38 (extensive involvement of agencies in statute-drafting today).

[34] Christiansen & Eskridge, *Congressional Overrides, 1967–2011*, 92 Tex. L. Rev. at 1375–80.

[35] Lincoln Caplan, *The Tenth Justice: The Solicitor General and the Rule of Law* (1990); Margaret H. Lemos, *The Solicitor General as Mediator Between Court and Agency*, 2009 Mich. St. L. Rev. 185 (reporting that the Solicitor General often rejects or modifies agency interpretations in Supreme Court briefs).

If statutory interpretation is usually a governance moment with consequences for public policy, then agency implementation, experience, and experiments offer lessons and insights that judges cannot easily find anywhere else. Often the agency's most useful contribution is a deeper understanding of the evolution of statutory goals and how they fit into other public policy priorities. When the Park Safety Act was enacted in 1992, protecting the White House was not the central concern of lawmakers and administrators. By the time Congress amended the law in 2013, protecting the nation's iconic buildings against terrorist attack had become a national obsession. That meta-policy weighs heavily in favor of allowing mounted police in Lafayette Park, but reasonable judges might have different views about this. Administrative experience would be very important for judges making this delicate judgment. For example, even a judge who initially thinks that the Park Safety Act, as expanded in 2013, plainly precludes riding horses through the park would reconsider her views if the National Park Service, the United States Park Police, and the Secret Service could document episodes where mounted police were able to head off calamities, especially if there were an episode where the White House itself was under threat.

Pause to reflect upon what we have learned up to this point about the application of the Park Safety Act in light of the ordinary meaning of its relevant text, the statutory structure, judicial precedent and the congressional override, and the regulatory history (including the legislative history) of the statute to date. Figure 7 below provides a summary of the statute's range of applications along the familiar continuum.

FIGURE 7

Plain Meaning Continuum: "Driving a Vehicle" in the Park (§ 2), in Light of Statutory Purpose (§ 1) and the Soaper Amendment (§ 3), as well as the Statute's Regulatory History

Core Coverage	Penumbra	Outside the Statute
Cars & Trucks	Roller Blades	Wheelbarrows
Motorcycles	Skateboards	Baby Carriages
Motor Scooters		Motorized Wheelchairs
Mopeds Bicycles (§ 3 proviso)		Adult Tricycles (§ 3 proviso)
Motorized Bicycles (§ 3 proviso)		Mounted Police Horses
		Segways

The ordinary meaning of the definition of "vehicle" in section 3, understood in light of the statutory structure, provides a plain meaning applicable to most mechanisms that might appear in a park (wheelbarrows are not vehicles, mopeds are). Given the protections of the Rehabilitation Act, the whole code rule establishes that motorized wheelchairs are not covered by the Park Safety Act. Judicial precedents such as *National Park Service v. Hogan* are probably no longer centrally relevant, because they have been supplanted by the Soaper Amendment of 2013—but the legislative history of the Soaper Amendment makes it likely that Segways, for example, are outside the statute's domain. The regulatory history of the treatment of mounted police makes it likely that they, too, are outside the statute's coverage. Recall that we are still operating within the continuum idea: The statutory interpreter can be certain that baby carriages are not statutory "vehicles," but is not as certain that Segways are not and is substantially undecided about skateboards.

The *Chevron* Rule
Judicial Deference to Agency Lawmaking

The National Park Service's interpretation of the Lafayette Park Safety Act of 1992, as amended, might be something more than just a regulatory history or a practical application of the law. The agency's interpretation might actually be the law of the land. Assume, for illustrative purposes, that the Soaper Amendment of 2013 adds a new section 4 as well as its already-discussed revision of section 3.

> **An Act to ensure public safety in Lafayette Park**
>
> **Sec. 1. Findings and Purpose.** Finding that vehicles operating in Lafayette Park have contributed to several serious accidents requiring hospitalization in the last five years, and finding further that vehicles create risks of serious injury to park users, Congress resolves that there is an urgent public need to ban any and all vehicles from Lafayette Park.
>
> **Sec. 2. No Vehicles in the Park.** No vehicles of any kind shall be allowed in Lafayette Park. Any person who drives a vehicle into Lafayette Park shall be guilty of a civil offense, which may be punished by a fine not exceeding $100 and confiscation of the offending vehicle, or both.
>
> **Sec. 3. Definition.** "Vehicle" for purposes of this law means any thing used for conveying a person from one place to another, including automobiles, trucks, motorcycles, motor scooters, and other forms of conveyance that pose safety hazards to park users because of their speed.

> *Provided that*, bicycles of any kind shall not be considered "vehicles" and shall be allowed in Lafayette Park, so long as they are being pushed or carried and not ridden.
>
> **Sec. 4. Enforcement and Implementation.** The National Park Service shall have authority to establish rules implementing the provisions of this Act. The Service will follow the rulemaking procedures specified in 5 U.S.C. § 553, and the rules thus promulgated will be immediately enforceable.

According to federal court practice in the last half century, section 4's general authorization for substantive rulemaking is treated as a delegation of lawmaking authority to the agency.[36] Congress could also have given the Park Service lawmaking authority with a provision giving the agency authority to adjudicate violations of the statute and apply penalties to rulebreakers (with judicial review).

The procedures for legislative rulemaking (section 553) require the agency to publish notice and an explanation of proposed rules in the *Federal Register*, to consider comments on those proposed rules that are submitted by interested persons or institutions, and to promulgate final rules in the *Federal Register*, together with responses to important comments.[37] The final rules are subject to judicial review, to ensure that the agency considered serious comments and had plausible responses to them and to override rules that are inconsistent with the authorizing statute.[38] This is a rather arduous process, one that agencies circumvent much of the time, through loopholes and exceptions in the APA and other statutes.[39]

Connor Raso reports that federal agencies do not follow APA notice-and-comment procedures for approximately one-third of their "major rules" (having an impact of $100 million or more), but that

---

[36] *United States v. Mead Corp.*, 533 U.S. 218, 227–30 (2001); accord, Gluck & Bressman, *Statutory Interpretation from the Inside: Part I*, 65 Stan. L. Rev. at 999 (congressional drafting staff believe that authorization for notice-and-comment rulemaking constitutes a delegation of lawmaking authority to fill in statutory gaps); cf. Thomas W. Merrill & Kathryn Tongue Watts, *Agency Rules with the Force of Law: The Original Convention*, 116 Harv. L. Rev. 467 (2002) (reporting that early congressional delegations of lawmaking authority entailed authorization of sanctions by the agency, a limitation that vanished in the 1970s).

[37] 5 U.S.C. § 553 (procedures for informal legislative rulemaking); see generally Peter L. Strauss, *The Rulemaking Continuum*, 41 Duke L.J. 1463 (1992).

[38] 5 U.S.C. § 706(2)(A) & (C) (judicial review of final agency action).

[39] Connor N. Raso, *Agency Avoidance of Rulemaking Procedures*, 67 Admin. L. Rev. 65 (2015).

means two-thirds of those rules do follow the standard APA procedures.[40] For rules that might generate controversy, notice-and-comment rulemaking has the systemic advantage of requiring the agency to justify its rules in light of public criticisms and suggestions. The process is also quasi-democratic, for it involves We the People in lawmaking. From the agency's point of view, notice-and-comment rulemaking is usually pretty expensive and often quite bothersome, but if successful it does open the door to considerable deference under what we should call the "*Chevron* rule," after the Supreme Court's leading case.[41]

The National Park Service can use its legislative rulemaking authority to fill in the details of the statutory scheme established by the Park Safety Act of 1992, as amended in 2013. The proposed rules would probably open with a sophisticated statement of regulatory purpose, focusing on safety for park visitors. The Park Service would then articulate, in as much detail as it believes prudent, mechanisms that are within the statute, as *vehicles*, and a list of mechanisms that some might consider "vehicles" but that the agency finds outside the statutory definition. And the agency would have to explain why it was including the specified "vehicles" while excluding others. Until successfully challenged or stayed by court order, the agency rules would have the force of law.

So the National Park Service's "Final Rules on Vehicles Covered by the Lafayette Park Safety Act" would explain why automobiles, trucks, motorcycles, mopeds, bicycles, and motorized bicycles, etc. are within the statutory definition and would probably specify exactly what mechanisms should be considered "automobiles" and "trucks" and so forth. The agency, for example, would have the authority to define "automobiles" to include even small, slow cars, such as the 1897 Léon Bollée Voiturette (the antique proto-automobile featured in chapter one), thereby barring them from Lafayette Park. In these ways, the agency rules would serve the notice, predictability, and other functions of the rule of law with greater specificity than a judge-created regime could easily do.

Filling in the details of the statutory scheme, the National Park Service might also address penumbral applications (though it has the discretion not to do so). Knowing that skateboards are not so clearly

---

[40] See id. at 83–84 & n.76, 92.

[41] *Chevron*, 467 U.S. 837, as interpreted in *Mead Corp.*, 533 U.S. 218. For an early expression of the *Chevron* idea, see *United States v. Vowell & M'Clean*, 9 U.S. (5 Cranch) 368, 372 (1810).

covered as automobiles nor so clearly excluded as baby carriages, the Park Service Director and her staff could dedicate more regulatory attention to skateboards. If the agency decides to include skateboards as statutory vehicles, its explanation would emphasize the documented safety risks such mechanisms pose to park visitors as well as to skateboarders themselves.

Recall Liam Treanor, the youthful skateboarder from chapter three. If he were cited for violating the Park Safety Act, as amended in 2013, he would invoke his father's case, *Treanor v. National Park Service* (following *Hogan* to exclude skateboards because they are not motorized), as a shadow precedent. The government would respond that the Soaper Amendment overrode the reasoning undergirding both *Hogan* and *Treanor*, and so the judge in 2016 must apply the revised statutory text and not the superseded precedent. Prosecutors would then defend the citation of young Treanor on the ground that the District Court should "defer" to the Park Service's interpretation of the statute: Even if the judge would not read the Park Safety Act to regulate skateboards, she should go along with the agency's interpretation, delivered after notice-and-comment rulemaking.

This is the difference between the *Skidmore* canon and the *Chevron* rule: The former asks the judge to consider administrative experience with the statute as the judge decides what its proper interpretation might be, while the latter asks the judge not to override the law established by the agency rule unless the rule clashes with the statute itself.[42] As the Supreme Court said in *Chevron*, "[s]uch legislative regulations are given controlling weight unless they are arbitrary, capricious, or manifestly contrary to the statute."[43] Because manifestly contrary to the statute, the agency has no authority to consider baby carriages, wheelbarrows, and motorized wheelchairs as statutory "vehicles" excluded from the park, nor does it have the authority to say that automobiles, motorcycles, motor scooters, and even mopeds are not covered by the statute (see Figure 7 above). To be sure, the Park Service might announce that it does not intend to cite people for driving mopeds through Lafayette Park, but such a move would properly be announced as a refusal to exercise

---

[42] For useful treatments distinguishing judicial deference to agency lawmaking (*Chevron*) and judicial consideration of agency views (*Skidmore*), see John F. Duffy, *Administrative Common Law in Judicial Review*, 77 Tex. L. Rev. 113, 202 (1998); Michael E. Herz, *Deference Running Riot: Separating Interpretation and Lawmaking under* Chevron, 6 Admin. L.J. Am. U. 187, 199 (1992); Strauss, "Chevron *Space" and* "Skidmore *Weight.*"

[43] *Chevron*, 437 U.S. at 843–44.

enforcement discretion rather than an understanding that the statute does not exclude those vehicles.

Generally, mechanisms that fall within the penumbral region, where there are good arguments for and against regulation based upon the ordinary meaning, are those where *Chevron* deference has bite. After the Soaper Amendment adds new text overriding the *Hogan* precedent and establishing speed and safety as the linchpins for understanding statutory vehicles, the National Park Service might have to decide whether skateboards pose significant public safety problems. Not only does the Park Service have expertise to evaluate skateboard safety risks in the context of this park, but the Park Service's settlement of this issue is more democratically legitimate than a court's settlement. It is more legitimate for three reasons, two of which were emphasized in *Chevron*. First, because Congress has delegated its lawmaking authority to the agency, and not to the courts, the Park Service acts under a legitimacy-enhancing authorization from Congress itself, an authorization that reflects an actual congressional consensus.[44] Second, the Park Service Director is appointed by and can be discharged by the President, a nationally elected official, and so is democratically accountable in a way that life-tenured federal judges are not.[45] Third, Congress monitors the agency just as the President does, and so the agency remains accountable to the current as well as enacting Congress. (Recall the discussion in the introduction to this chapter.)

Democratic legitimacy and expertise dovetail very nicely in the case of the youthful skateboarder. That is, the governmental organ that is more legitimate is also the organ best situated to develop a statutory scheme that fulfills the congressional safety purpose, and with due regard to the public's enjoyment of Lafayette Park. (Hence, the kid on a tricycle is welcome to pedal around the park, and the parents don't have to worry that a motorcycle will run over her.) From a governance perspective, the Park Service is also better at filling in the details of the statutory scheme than the D.C. Circuit, for institutional as well as expertise reasons. Thus, the agency is in a

---

[44] *Chevron*, 467 U.S. at 865, as interpreted by *Mead Corp.,* 533 U.S. 218; see Gluck & Bressman, *Statutory Interpretation from the Inside: Part I*, 65 Stan. L. Rev. at 995–1000 (reporting that the *Chevron* regime, as clarified by *Mead*, is most consistent with the assumptions of statutory drafting and deliberation). For a thoughtful critique, see Mark Seidenfeld, Chevron's *Foundation*, 86 Notre Dame L. Rev. 273 (2011).

[45] *Chevron*, 467 U.S. at 865–66; see Frederick Liu, Chevron *as a Doctrine of Hard Cases*, 66 Admin. L. Rev. 285, 317–20 (2014) (providing a jurisprudential defense of agency rather than judicial gapfilling in hard statutory cases).

better position than courts are to benefit from the experience of other agencies (such as the Secret Service) and to coordinate its policy with that of other agencies (such as the Department of Homeland Security).

Sometimes, the most important power an agency has is the discretion not to enforce. If the National Park Service were to overenforce the vehicles in the park law, against tricycles for example, the cited person (or her parents) would be able to persuade a judge to throw out the charges because they are not authorized by the statute. In contrast, if the Park Service were to underenforce the law, there would usually be no one who has standing to complain through a lawsuit. The power to underenforce can be abused, but responsible agencies can make good use of it, from a governance perspective. Recall that the proviso to section 3 of the Park Safety Act bars people from riding bicycles through the park. The Park Service allows Park Police officials riding horses—so why not allow Park Police officials riding bicycles?

Even though the latter fall within the statute's ordinary meaning, the agency may allow bicycle-riding police in the park as a matter of its discretion. Neither the executive nor legislative branches will object, and judges will probably never have the opportunity to evaluate this nonapplication. If a civilian bike rider objected that the law was being applied in a discriminatory manner, a judge would probably override the objection, deferring to the Park Service's prosecutorial discretion on this matter.

The *Chevron* regime, strongly deferring to agency rules issued pursuant to a legislative delegation of lawmaking authority, is followed by federal courts and an increasing number of state courts interpreting state statutes (listed in the margin).[46] Without exactly

---

[46] See generally Michael Pappas, *No-Two Stepping in the Laboratories: State Deference Standards and Their Implications for Improving the* Chevron *Doctrine*, 37 McGeorge L. Rev. 977 (2008) (state-by-state survey of deference regimes). An increasing number of state supreme courts either cite *Chevron* as the model they are following or as consistent with their practice. See, e.g., *QCC, Inc. v. Hall*, 757 So.2d 1115 (Ala. 2000); *Ariz. Water Co. v. Ariz. Dep't of Water Res.*, 91 P.3d 990 (Ariz. 2004); *North Colorado Medical Center, Inc. v. Committee on Anticompetitive Conduct*, 914 P.2d 902, 907 (Colo. 1996); *Mallof v. District of Columbia Bd. of Elections*, 1 A.3d 383, 392 & n. 39 (D.C. 2010); *Donato v. AT & T*, 767 So.2d 1146, 1153 (Fla. 2000); *Honda v. Bd. of Trs. of the Emps.' Ret. Sys.*, 118 P.3d 1155 (Haw. 2005); *J.R. Simplot Co. v. Idaho Tax Comm'n*, 820 P.2d 1206, 1218–20 (Idaho 1991); *Shaffer v. State*, 795 N.E.2d 1077 (Ind. App. 2003); *Board of Trustees of Judicial Form Retirement System v. Attorney General of the Commonwealth*, 132 S.W.3d 770, 786–87 (Ky. 2003); *Protective Life Ins. Co. v. Sullivan*, 682 N.E.2d 624, 627–28 (Mass. 1997); *Goldberg v. Board of Health of Granby*, 830 N.E.2d 207 (Mass. 2012); *Guilford Transp. Indus. v. Public Utility*

adopting *Chevron*, the California Supreme Court and a few other state systems follow its general approach, more strongly deferring to agency rules that are "quasi-legislative," than to those that are "interpretive."[47] That so many state courts have adopted *Chevron*'s regime or a similar regime (grounded upon the special status of agency rules issued pursuant to legislative delegations) is remarkable, because state courts have traditionally assumed that agency interpretations are reviewed de novo, with *Skidmore*-like bows to specialized agency knowledge.

On the other hand, many state courts have not adopted the *Chevron* regime and make a point of preserving the *Marbury* role of judges as the primary or sole expositors of the law. Thus, the New York Court of Appeals, the Michigan Supreme Court, and the Texas Supreme Court appear (as of 2016) to follow a less deferential regime than *Chevron*, namely, a regime where agency rules and adjudications receive "respectful consideration," more along the lines of *Skidmore* than *Chevron*.[48] Other states are hard to classify.

Comm'n, 746 A.2d 910, 913 (Me. 2000); *Mississippi Gaming Comm'n v. Imperial Palace of Miss., Inc.*, 751 So.2d 1025 (Miss. 1999); *Util. Serv. Co. v. Dep't of Labor and Indus. Relations*, 331 S.W.3d 654 (Mo. 2011); *Thompson v. J.C. Billion, Inc.*, 294 P.3d 397 (Mont. 2013); *In re Distribution of Liquid Assets*, 773 A.2d 6 (N.J. 2001); *City of Albuquerque v. New Mexico Pub. Reg. Comm'n*, 79 P.3d 297, 305–06 (N.M. 2003); *W.W. Wallwork, Inc. v. Duchschereer*, 501 N.W.2d 751 (N.D. 1993); *State ex rel. Turner v. Eberlin*, 884 N.E.2d 39, 42 (Ohio 2008); *Seeton v. Pennsylvania Game Comm'n*, 937 A.2d 1038 (Pa. 2007); *Alba v. Cranston Sch. Comm.*, 90 A.3d 174, 180 (R.I. 2014); *Shroyer v. Harrison County Bd. of Educ.*, 564 S.E.2d 425 (W.Va. 2002); *Qwest Corp. v. State ex rel. Wyoming Dep't of Revenue*, 130 P.3d 507, 511 (Wyo. 2006).

[47] *In re Cabrera*, 287 P.3d 72, 74–75 (Cal. 2012) (highly deferential review of a quasi-legislative rule, but without citing *Chevron*). See generally *Yamaha Corp. of America v. State Bd. of Equalization*, 960 P.2d 1031 (Cal. 1998) (establishing a firm division between quasi-legislative agency rules and those that are merely interpretive). For other examples of state court deference regimes that echo *Chevron*'s rule that agency regulations pursuant to a delegation of lawmaking (or broad implementing) authority receive heightened deference, but without citing *Chevron*, see *Center for a Sustainable Coast v. Coastal Marshlands Protection Committee*, 670 S.E.2d 429, 433–34 (Ga. 2008); *In re New Hampshire Dep't Transp.*, 883 A.2d 272, 280–81 (N.H. 2005); *People ex rel. Madigan v. Illinois Commerce Comm'n*, 25 N.E.3d 587, 594–95 (Ill. 2015); *Affiliated Foods Co-op, Inc. v. State*, 611 N.W.2d 105, 110 (Neb. 2000); *Consumer Advocate Div'n v. Greer*, 967 S.W.2d 759, 761–62 (Tenn. 1998); *R.O.A. General, Inc. v. Utah Dep't Transp.*, 966 P.2d 840, 843 (Utah 1998).

[48] *In re Complaint of Rovas Against SBC Michigan*, 754 N.W.2d 259, 270–72 (Mich. 2008) (rejecting *Chevron*); *Suffolk Regional Off-Track Betting Corp. v. New York State Racing & Wagering Bd.*, 900 N.E.2d 970, 973 (N.Y. 2008) (Kaye, C.J.) (giving no special deference to agency views); *First Auto Title Ins. Co. v. Combs*, 258 S.W.3d 627, 644–46 (Tex. 2008) (declining to adopt *Chevron*). But see *TGS-NOPEC Geophysical Co. v. Combs*, 340 S.W.2d 432, 438 (Tex. 2011) (giving considerable deference, but not citing *Chevron* or the federal deference cases). For other states declining to adopt *Chevron* and affording agencies little or no "special" deference, see *Southern New England Tel. Co. v. Cashman*, 931 A.2d 142 (Ct. 2007); *Public Water Supply Co. v.*

Oregon's Supreme Court, for example, tailors deference to whether statutory terms are "exact" (some deference) or "inexact" (little or no deference) or "delegative" (a great deal of deference, *Chevron*-like).[49] Wisconsin tailors deference in a functional continuum, with "great weight" to longstanding and consistent agency views about a law legislators charged it with implementing, "due weight" where there has been some delegated authority, and "no deference" for issues where the agency has been inconsistent.[50]

As Figure 8 reveals, agency lawmaking, with judicial deference along *Chevron* lines or something similar, can swiftly create a comprehensive rule of law that not only tells citizens what statutes require of them in particular circumstances but also can be updated in light of new developments in technology or society.

FIGURE 8

Statutory Applications After National Park Service Rulemaking, to Which Federal Courts *Chevron*-Defer

Core Coverage	Penumbra	Outside the Statute
Cars & Trucks		Wheelbarrows
Motorcycles		Baby Carriages
Motor Scooters		Motorized Wheelchairs
Mopeds	Bicycles* (§ 3 proviso)	Adult Tricycles
	Motorized Bicycles* (§ 3 proviso)	Mounted Police Horses
Segways		Roller Blades
Skateboards		

* Inapplicable to police officers on bicycles, as a matter of agency discretion not to enforce

Thus, *Chevron* promises enormous rule of law advantages over a system of case-by-case judicial precedent. Early critics of *Chevron* feared that this degree of judicial deference would unbalance government, allowing the executive branch to bleed lawmaking authority even more rapidly from the legislative branch and

DePasquale, 735 A.2d 378, 383 (Del. 1999); *Higgins v. Abilene Mach., Inc.*, 204 P.3d 1156, 1158 (Kan. 2009); *Bowers v. Firefighters Ret. Sys.*, 6 So.3d 173, 176 (La. 2009); *Hranicka v. Chesapeake Surgical Ltd.*, 116 A.3d 507, 512 (Md. 2015).

[49] *Coast Security Mortgage Corp. v. Real Estate Agency*, 15 P.3d 29 (Ore. 2000), followed and applied in *Oregon Occupational Safety & Health Div. v. CBI Servs., Inc.*, 341 P.3d 701, 706 (Ore. 2014); *Bergerson v. Salem-Keizer Sch. Dist.*, 144 P.3d 918, 924 (Ore. 2006).

[50] *County of Dane v. Labor & Indus. Rev. Comm'n*, 759 N.W.2d 571 (Wis. 2009), followed in *DeBoer Transp. Co. v. Swenson*, 804 N.W.2d 658, 666–68 (Wis. 2011).

sacrificing the role of federal courts as monitors of agency lawmaking.[51] To the contrary, however, the *Chevron* structure, as applied by the Supreme Court, leaves plenty of room for judicial monitoring of agency mistakes. This monitoring role for the judiciary may be robust, even though scholars have found that the Supreme Court and lower courts do not apply *Chevron* in a predictable manner.[52]

Think about it: What kinds of mistakes is an agency likely to make? For the most part, there are three major kinds of mistakes:

- *Turf-Grabbing.* Federal agencies have a tendency to expand the reach of their authority, perhaps overreaching at times. Federal courts are independent monitors to protect against agency usurpation of policy issues properly left to elected officials.
- *Evading the Limits of the Law.* Agencies tend to interpret statutes purposively, applying statutory text aggressively to solve problems. Federal courts are well-positioned to reign in agencies that flaunt statutory limits and disrupt reasonable reliance interests.
- *Undermining Statutory Purpose.* Either because they are captured by the interests they are supposed to regulate or because they are incompetent, agencies sometimes implement rules or practices that undermine rather than advance the legislative purpose. Federal courts are not well-positioned to make this kind of judgment but may stand as potential monitors to discourage (even if not eliminate) this kind of agency slacking.[53]

---

[51] Stephen Breyer, *Judicial Review of Questions of Law and Policy*, 38 Admin. L. Rev. 363, 370 (1986); Cynthia R. Farina, *Statutory Interpretation and the Balance of Power in the Administrative State*, 89 Colum. L. Rev. 452 (1989).

[52] For empirical evidence of the unpredictable application of *Chevron*, see Lisa Schultz Bressman, *How Mead Has Muddled Judicial Review of Agency Action*, 58 Vand. L. Rev. 1443 (2005) (lower courts, after the Supreme Court's 2001 decision in *Mead*); Eskridge & Baer, *The Continuum of Deference* (Supreme Court, 1984–2006); Jason J. Czarnezki, *An Empirical Investigation of Judicial Decisionmaking, Statutory Interpretation, and the Chevron Doctrine in Environmental Law*, 79 U. Colo. L. Rev. 767, 770–71 (2008) (lower courts). For an argument that such a "deference lottery" still allows effective monitoring of agencies, see Jud Mathews, *Deference Lotteries*, 91 Tex. L. Rev. 1349 (2013).

[53] Mark Seidenfeld, *Cognitive Loafing, Social Conformity, and Judicial Review of Agency Rulemaking*, 87 Cornell L. Rev. 486 (2002).

Interestingly, the *Chevron* framework articulated by the Supreme Court leaves ample room for federal judges to perform each of these roles. As Thomas Merrill and Kristin Hickman first articulated, the Court's *Chevron* framework entails three "Steps"—Zero, One, and Two.[54] I now explain how each *Chevron* Step addresses each kind of agency mistake identified above.

Major Questions Canon (**Chevron** ***Step Zero).*** *Chevron* Step Zero (the term originated by Professors Merrill and Hickman) represents the triggering inquiry: Is the agency rule or interpretation issued pursuant to a congressional grant of lawmaking authority? If so, then the *Chevron* framework applies; if not, then the *Skidmore* canon is applicable. Although *Chevron* itself suggested that such a delegation existed whenever Congress "has explicitly left a gap for the agency to fill," the Supreme Court has subsequently held that gapfilling is not sufficient and that Congress must explicitly or implicitly delegate lawmaking authority to the agency for *Chevron* to apply to an administrative interpretation.[55]

What constitutes a congressional delegation of lawmaking authority? Most commonly, a statutory grant of general rulemaking authority triggers *Chevron* deference.[56] Thus, the National Park Service's rulemaking pursuant to section 4 of the Park Safety Act, as amended in 2013, can trigger the *Chevron* regime. If Congress had authorized the National Park Service to adjudicate alleged violations of the statute, that, too, would have been a lawmaking delegation.[57] On occasion, the Supreme Court has found an implicit delegation of lawmaking authority based upon the pervasive regulatory power given an agency over a segment of the economy.[58]

---

[54] Merrill & Hickman, Chevron's *Domain*, 89 Geo. L.J. at 873 (identifying a *Chevron* "Step Zero" to go with the already canonized *Chevron* Steps One and Two, all discussed in text).

[55] *Mead Corp.*, 533 U. S. at 229–31. For critique of the Court's Step Zero reliance on delegation, see id. at 239–50 (Scalia, J., dissenting) (doctrinal and practical critique); Liu, Chevron *as a Doctrine of Hard Cases*, 66 Admin. L. Rev. at 328–35 (jurisprudential critique).

[56] *Mead Corp.*, 533 U.S. at 229–31 & n.12; e.g., *Mayo Foundation v. United States*, 562 U.S. 44 (2011) (overruling an earlier precedent following a less deferential regime for the IRS's revenue rulings issued under a general rulemaking authorization).

[57] *Mead Corp.*, 533 U. S. at 230–31 & n.12 (listing cases where the Court has *Chevron*-deferred to agency adjudications).

[58] *NationsBank of North Carolina v. Variable Annuity Life Ins. Co.*, 513 U.S. 251, 256 (1995), followed in *Smiley v. Citibank (South Dakota)*, 517 U.S. 735, 740 (1996).

So the National Park Service's rulemaking is entitled to *Chevron* deference. Is that true when the Service is opining as to its own jurisdiction, namely, the limits of its own authority? The Supreme Court has explicitly ruled, and many state supreme courts have implicitly ruled, that deference applies to jurisdictional issues, in part because it is impossible to separate questions of an agency's jurisdiction and applications of the statute.[59] For example, the Park Service's "jurisdiction" is limited to identifying and excluding "vehicles" from Lafayette Park—which overlaps completely with the agency's substantive application of the statute. In other words, procedure (jurisdiction) and substance (what mechanisms must be barred from the park) pervasively overlap—and so *Chevron* deference applies however the issue is characterized.

Instead of an exception for jurisdictional questions, the Supreme Court has carved out a potentially important exception to delegation, the *major questions canon*. Even if Congress has delegated an agency general rulemaking or adjudicatory power, judges presume that Congress does not delegate its authority to settle or amend major social and economic policy decisions. "We expect Congress to speak clearly if it wishes to assign to an agency decisions of vast 'economic and political significance.' "[60] For example, assume that the National Park Service engaged in rulemaking to determine that human beings are "vehicles" because we carry babies and other small persons from one place to another; as a result of that finding, the agency bars human beings from all the national parks under its jurisdiction. Judges would not presume that Congress gave the Park Service lawmaking authority that would purge national forests of all human visitors, because such a policy would be a major move best left to Congress.

The major questions canon is a potentially elastic loophole to *Chevron*'s broad commitment of judicial deference to agency interpretations pursuant to congressional delegations of lawmaking authority, because many issues can be understood as either "major

---

[59] *City of Arlington, Texas v. FCC*, 133 S.Ct. 1863 (2013).

[60] *Utility Air Regulatory Group v. EPA*, 134 S.Ct. 2427, 2444 (2014) (plurality opinion), quoting *FDA v. Brown & Williamson Tobacco Corp.*, 529 U.S. 120 (2000); accord, *King v. Burwell*, 135 S.Ct. 2480, 2489 (2015); *Gonzales v. Oregon*, 546 U.S. 243, 266–67 (2006); cf. *MCI Telecomm. Corp. v. AT&T Co.*, 512 U.S. 218 (1994) (refusing to accord the FCC authority to make major changes in the statutory scheme, through a modest interpretation). See generally Theodore W. Ruger, *The Story of* FDA v. Brown & Williamson: *The Norm of Agency Continuity*, in *Statutory Interpretation Stories* 334 (William N. Eskridge Jr., Philip P. Frickey & Elizabeth Garrett eds., 2011).

questions" or "routine applications."[61] For example, if the National Park Service interpreted the statute to allow mounted police to ride around in Lafayette Park, I should think this to be a routine application of the statute—but some Americans would view this as a "major question" addressing matters of "vast political significance," if they understood the agency action to have implications for White House security. (Say they are right about that. A judge would still probably follow the agency's view under the *Skidmore* canon, essentially bowing to the expertise of the agency.)

Notwithstanding these fuzzy edges, the major questions canon strikes me as defensible along precisely the same lines as *Chevron* itself. The key reason is the strong presumption of continuity for major policies unless and until Congress has deliberated about and enacted a change in those major policies; recall David Shapiro's thesis, discussed in the introduction to this volume, that continuity and coherence are the normative linchpins of the canons.[62] Because a major policy change would disrupt reliance interests, continuity is consistent with rule of law values. Because a major policy change should be made by the most democratically accountable process—Article I, Section 7 legislation—this kind of continuity is consistent with democratic values. Although Congress is sometimes criticized for booting controversial issues to agencies to avoid political accountability, congressional drafting staff overwhelmingly support the premise of the major questions canon, because they do not view lawmaking delegations as reaching policy shifts not explicitly made by statute.[63]

The presumption of continuity is consistent with both the rule of law and democratic accountability—albeit often inconsistent with effective governance. As *Chevron* recognized, a central role of agencies is to update statutory policy to take account of new

---

[61] Abigail R. Moncrieff, *Reincarnating the "Major Questions" Exception to Chevron Deference as a Doctrine of Non-Interference (Or Why* Massachusetts v. EPA *Got it Wrong)*, 60 Admin. L. Rev. 593 (2008) (arguing that the Court applies the major questions exception erratically); Cass R. Sunstein, Chevron *Step Zero*, 92 Va. L. Rev. 187, 193–95, 231–47 (2006) (opposing a major questions exception to what Merrill and Hickman call *Chevron* Step Zero).

[62] David Shapiro, *Continuity and Change in Statutory Interpretation*, 67 N.Y.U. L. Rev. 921 (1992); accord, John F. Manning, *Continuity and the Legislative Design*, 79 Notre Dame L. Rev. 1863 (2004).

[63] Gluck & Bressman, *Statutory Interpretation from the Inside: Part I*, 65 Stan. L. Rev. at 994, 1003–04.

circumstances.[64] The major questions doctrine ought not disturb the ability of agencies to carry out this important mission (within the limits imposed by *Chevron*), but for the most important statutory issues the modern regulatory state usually profits from an interaction among Congress, which sets policy; agencies, which apply congressional policy to new circumstances; and the judges, who integrate statutes and agency rules into the broader fabric of the law.

Plain Meaning Rule (**Chevron** ***Step One).*** That an agency engages in lawmaking activity authorized by Congress does not mean that the agency's lawmaking is insulated from judicial review. The authorizing statute dominates the agency's rule if there is a conflict, and the role of judges in that case is to give effect to the statute—just as judges will enforce the Constitution against a statute that is inconsistent with its mega-rule of law.[65] What has made *Chevron* the most-cited statutory interpretation case of all time is that the Court laid out a two-step approach for judges to take in balancing their duties toward the statute and the allowance needed for agency flexibility when elaborating on the statute over time.[66]

Once triggered at Step Zero, the *Chevron* regime itself purports to be simple: "First, always, is the question whether Congress has directly spoken to the precise question at issue. If the intent of Congress is clear, that is the end of the matter; for the court, as well as the agency, must give effect to the unambiguously expressed intent of Congress."[67] If Congress has "directly addressed" the issue, its answer is the one the judge should enforce, and the court's inquiry is completed at this Step One. "[I]f the statute is silent or ambiguous with respect to the specific issue, the question for the court is whether

---

[64] *Chevron*, 467 U.S. at 843; accord, Antonin Scalia, *Judicial Deference to Administrative Interpretations of Law*, 1989 Duke L. J. 511, 517–18 (1989).

[65] See *The Federalist* No. 78 (Hamilton) (analyzing judicial review as a choice of law exercise).

[66] The *Chevron* two-step has been the subject of hundreds of law review articles. The ones that have been most influential for my account have been Merrill & Hickman, Chevron's *Domain*, which anticipated and was followed in *Mead Corp.*, as well as Michael E. Herz, *Deference Running Riot: Separating Interpretation and Lawmaking under* Chevron, 6 Admin. L.J. Am. U. 187 (1992); Thomas W. Merrill, *Textualism and the Future of the* Chevron *Doctrine*, 72 Wash. U.L.Q. 351 (1994); Antonin Scalia, *Judicial Deference to Administrative Interpretation of Law*, 1989 Duke L.J. 511; Strauss, "Chevron *Space" and* "Skidmore *Weight*." My own empirical work was published as Eskridge & Baer, *The Continuum of Deference*.

[67] *Chevron*, 467 U.S. at 842–43.

the agency's answer is based on a permissible construction of the statute," that is, the inquiry in Step Two.[68]

Although judicial practice has been fairly diverse, the Supreme Court and most state high courts applying *Chevron* pose the Step One question this way: Does the statute have a plain meaning as applied to these facts? Recall, from the first three chapters, that the plain meaning inquiry involves consideration of the ordinary (prototypical) meaning of the statutory text on point, understood and often clarified in light of the whole act, binding statutory precedents, relevant parts of the entire code, and the textual and precedential canons explored in those chapters. Recall the plain meaning continuum developed in the earlier chapters. After the Soaper Amendment erased the leading statutory precedents, most issues were resolved by Congress one way or the other: As a matter of statutory plain meaning, mopeds, motor scooters, and motorcycles are not allowed in the park because they are statutory "vehicles," while wheelbarrows, baby carriages, and toy cars are allowed in the park, because they are not statutory "vehicles." For mechanisms falling in the penumbral area of the continuum, such as Segways and skateboards, there is no statutory plain meaning, and so a court would evaluate the agency's interpretation under the highly deferential criteria of *Chevron* Step Two.

Here is an interesting issue: At Step One, should the judge consider the statute's legislative and regulatory history? For the reasons advanced in chapter four and the first part of this chapter, judges should consider legislative and administrative materials if they help the interpreter see whether the statutory text and structure "directly address" the issue in the case. Indeed, *Chevron* itself devoted more pages to a discussion of legislative materials than to anything else before the Court concluded, only after a thorough examination of the regulatory and legislative history, that Congress had not "directly addressed" the issue resolved by the agency.[69] As suggested by Figure

---

[68] Id. at 843.

[69] Id. at 851–53 (detailed examination of legislative history to make sure that Congress had not foreclosed the "bubble concept" in the Clean Air Act Amendments of 1977). For other examples of examination of legislative materials as part of Step One, see *EPA v. EME Homer City Generation, L.P.*, 134 S.Ct. 1584 (2014); *Zuni Pub. Sch. Dist. No. 89 v. Department of Education*, 550 U.S. 81, 89–93 (2007); *Gonzales v. Oregon*, 546 U.S. at 269–73. The Supreme Court in the last decade has been more reluctant to discuss legislative history in *Chevron* cases than it was twenty years ago. In *Zuni*, for example, Justice Breyer's elaborate examination of the regulatory and legislative history materials before addressing statutory text brought a concurring caution from Justices Kennedy and Alito. 550 U.S. at 107 (Kennedy, J., concurring). Since *Zuni*, no

7, assume that the Park Service rulemaking includes Segways as statutory "vehicles" and therefore bars them from Lafayette Park. Does *Chevron* Step One prevent the agency from making this move?

Recall, from chapter four, the legislative history of the Soaper Amendment. The House bill explicitly included Segways as regulated "vehicles," but the Senate bill more generally focused on conveyances that posed safety hazards because of their speed. The conference committee chose the Senate version, with this explanation from the conferees: "The House recedes and accepts the Senate version of section 3. The statute seeks to protect park users against unnecessary safety hazards. Because motorized bicycles can reach speeds of twenty-five to thirty miles per hour, they should be regulated as 'bicycles', but not prohibited entirely as 'vehicles'." The maximum speed of the Segway i-2 series (as of 2016) is twelve and one-half miles per hour—well under the speed that the conferees relied on to say that motorized bicycles are not "vehicles" targeted by the statute.

By rejecting the House bill and its inclusion of Segways and explaining its acceptance of the Senate bill in these precise terms, has the conference committee not given the judge a sufficient reason to find that the Park Safety Act directly addresses the question whether conveyances snailing along at twelve miles per hour (i.e., Segways) are included within the statutory park bar? Each chamber of Congress voted for the statutory text explicated by the conferees, and this is the text signed by the President. A judge insisting that "Congress" has not directly addressed the Segway issue is a judge who is inattentive to the legislative process.

To be sure, this is unusually specific legislative history, delivered at the end of the process, when the final text was ironed out and presented for up-and-down votes. If the only relevant legislative history were the conference committee's choice of the Senate bill over the House bill, with no explanation, then it cannot be said that Congress has "directly addressed" Segways. But with the explanation provided above, Congress has done so.

Brand X *Canon* (Chevron *Step Two*). Recall the Supreme Court's articulation of Step Two: "[I]f the statute is silent or ambiguous with respect to the specific issue, the question for the court is whether the agency's answer is based on a permissible

---

majority opinion has followed Justice Breyer's approach of starting with the legislative and regulatory history and then analyzing the statutory text.

construction of the statute."[70] What is a "permissible construction of the statute" in our case of the Segway? If Congress has not directly addressed the issue, the agency's exercise of delegated lawmaking authority ought to be upheld by the court so long as it is a reasonable effort to advance the statutory purpose(s). This is a forgiving standard, as it should be. *Chevron* Step Two is satisfied if an agency rule advances the statutory purpose even if based upon the agency's speculation and even if the benefit of the rule is ease of administration.[71]

As has been the practice in the Court of Appeals for the Seventh Circuit, judges who refuse to consider legislative history and purpose at *Chevron* Step One ought to consider these materials in *Chevron* Step Two.[72] Thus, if a judge reviewing our agency rule barring Segways from Lafayette Park found that the statute delegated lawmaking authority (section 4) and did not directly address the issue of Segways (sections 2–3), she ought to consider the legislative history to determine whether the rule is "reasonable." In light of the conference report (rejecting the House bill, which had included Segways) and the explanation of the conferees (explaining why a mechanism going twenty miles per hour is not a "vehicle" for purposes of that statute), I'd consider the agency's rule to be unreasonable under *Chevron* Step Two.

Consider another and more important feature of *Chevron* Step Two jurisprudence, namely, its relation to *stare decisis*. If the Court of Appeals for the D.C. Circuit rules in *Giannotto v. National Park Service* (2015) that the Park Safety Act, as amended in 2013, does *not* regulate Segways as "vehicles" because they are too slow to raise the safety risks targeted by the statute, the agency is bound by that ruling unless the decision is overridden by Congress, abrogated by the Supreme Court, or overruled by the D.C. Circuit.[73] Even if the agency

---

[70] *Chevron*, 467 U.S. at 843.

[71] For an excellent debate about what is a reasonable agency rule, compare *Scialabba v. Cuellar de Osorio*, 134 S.Ct. 2191 (2014) (Kagan, J., for a plurality) (deferring to the immigration agency because the statute contained conflicting directives, and reasoning that the agency rather than a court should make this policy choice), with id. at 2214–16 (Roberts, C.J., concurring in the judgment) (finding the statute ambiguous and deferring to the agency to resolve the ambiguity and fill in details).

[72] *Coyomani-Cielo v. Holder*, 758 F.3d 908, 914–15 (7th Cir. 2014); *Bankers Life & Cas. Co. v. United States*, 142 F.3d 973, 983, 987–88 (7th Cir. 1998).

[73] Sometimes, federal agencies decline to acquiesce in an intermediate appellate court decision, in hopes of persuading the Supreme Court to rule differently in an appropriate future case. But the nonacquiescence doctrine (controversial to start with)

discovers in 2020 that a new generation of Segways can zip along the nation's capital at thirty miles per hour and that these speedier Segways are actually injuring people in Lafayette Park and its environs, the agency is still bound by *Giannotto* and would probably not be able to persuade the Court of Appeals to overrule that statutory precedent.

Consider a variation on *Giannotto*. Under this alternative scenario, the Park Service itself has decided that it does *not* have the authority to regulate Segways, because their unimpressive speed does not, in the agency's view, pose undue risks to park users. Nonetheless, a Giannotto Segway runs into and kills a pedestrian in Lafayette Park—and the estate of the unlucky pedestrian sues not only the judgment-proof Mike Giannotto but also the Park Service. In *Kaplan v. Giannotto*, the Park Service will likely prevail in a motion to dismiss it from the case. One argument made by the Park Service is that it was acting validly when it adopted a rule excluding Segways from the statute. Agreeing with this argument, the Court of Appeals adopts the following chain of reasoning:

COURT OF APPEALS HOLDING IN *GIANNOTTO*

> Step Zero. The Park Service rule allowing Segways in Lafayette Park falls within its delegated lawmaking authority and thereby triggers the *Chevron* regime.
>
> Step One. Congress did not directly address this issue in the broadly worded Park Safety Act.
>
> Step Two. The agency's rule is reasonable in light of the legislative history and purpose.

In 2020, the agency learns that Segways are speedier and are causing more accidents. The Giannotto incident was the beginning of a new trend. May the Park Service reopen the issue, through new notice-and-comment rulemaking, and adopt a new rule classifying Segways as statutory "vehicles" excluded from Lafayette Park? Itself upholding the EPA's volte-face on an air pollutant-emissions issue, *Chevron* explained that "[a]n initial agency interpretation is not carved in stone. On the contrary, the agency, to engage in informal rulemaking, must consider varying interpretations and the wisdom of

---

has no place for an issue that cannot easily recur in other federal courts of appeals. See Samuel Estreicher & Richard Revesz, *Nonacquiescence by Federal Administrative Agencies*, 98 Yale L.J. 679 (1989).

its policy on a continuing basis."[74] But is the agency's new interpretation, that Segways are "vehicles" regulated by the Park Safety Act, inconsistent with the binding *Giannotto* precedent? If so, does the *stare decisis* rule trump the *Chevron* rule?

Chapter three suggested that the limitations imposed by *stare decisis* depend on the precedent's precise reasoning and how broadly subsequent courts are inclined to interpret it. As re-presented in the two previous paragraphs, the holding of *Giannotto* is that the Park Service acted within its zone of discretion when its rulemaking put Segways outside the category of regulated "vehicles"—but if that is the holding, why can the agency not make a new determination, so long as this new determination, too, is within the zone of agency discretion? As Peter Strauss has suggested, the best way to understand *Chevron* is to view it as recognizing that an agency delegated with lawmaking power enjoys a zone of discretion within which it may set policy.[75] For issues Congress has directly addressed in the statute, the agency has little or no lawmaking discretion; where Congress has not provided an answer in the statute, the agency has a lot of discretion to set and change policy. Figure 9 illustrates this Straussian understanding. Notice its similarity to the ordinary or plain meaning continuum figures in earlier chapters.

FIGURE 9

Zone of *Chevron* Discretion for National Park Service

Directly Addressed: Vehicles	**Not Directly Addressed: Zone of Discretion**	**Directly Addressed: Not Vehicles**
Cars & Trucks etc.	Segways	Wheelbarrows etc.

The Supreme Court has recognized this structure in its 2005 *Brand X* decision.[76] Under the *Brand X* canon, a judicial precedent holding that the court must defer to the agency interpretation within its zone of discretion (i.e., exactly as I reframed *Giannotto*) does not

---

[74] *Chevron*, 467 U.S. at 863–64; see William N. Eskridge Jr., *Dynamic Statutory Interpretation* 161–73 (1994) (positing that the primary engine of dynamic statutory interpretation is agencies).

[75] Strauss, "Chevron *Space" and* "Skidmore *Weight,*" 112 Colum. L. Rev. at 1163–64 (diagramming the article's basic insight).

[76] *National Cable & Telecommunications Ass'n v. Brand X Internet Services*, 545 U.S. 967, 980–83 (2005). For analysis and critique, see, Kathryn T. Watts, *Adapting to Administrative Law's* Erie *Doctrine*, 101 Nw. U. L. Rev. 997 (2007), as well as Claire R. Kelly, *The* Brand X *Liberation: Doing Away with* Chevron's *Second Step as Well as Other Doctrines of Deference*, 44 U.C. Davis L. Rev. 151 (2011).

stand in the way of the agency's adoption of a new interpretation, so long as it is also within its zone of discretion (i.e., is not unreasonable). In short, the *Brand X* canon permits an agency latitude sometimes to abandon one interpretation of its governing statute and to adopt a completely different interpretation, so long as it, too, falls within the agency's zone of (*Chevron*) discretion.

The *Brand X* canon depends upon the reasoning of the precedent at issue. An interesting question is posed by pre-*Chevron* precedents, and not a few post-*Chevron* precedents as well: How can the current agency and court tell whether the earlier court was deferring to an agency's interpretation or simply interpreting the statute? Because most pre-*Chevron* appellate court decisions simply interpreted the statute, they are typically binding on the agency. Thus, if the statutory precedent were premised on a finding of statutory plain meaning, without citation to one of the dozens of pre-*Chevron* deference precedents, it is likely that the agency remains bound by the statutory precedent; even if the previous court recognized some ambiguity in the *ordinary meaning* of the statutory language, the *Brand X* canon is inapplicable if the court resolved the ambiguity sufficiently to find a *plain meaning*.[77] On the other hand, if the statutory precedent finds no unambiguous ordinary meaning and fails to find a likely plain meaning based upon the whole act or other aids, and especially if it cites one of the dozens of pre-*Chevron* deference precedents, the agency can probably alter or throw over its previous rule.[78]

Other Deference Canons

The Supreme Court's "deferprudence" does not stop with the *Chevron* rule and the *Skidmore* canon, for the Court has recognized a number of other deference regimes—most of which are being absorbed by *Chevron*, as they should be.[79] In this concluding part of the chapter, I shall examine the main regimes that remain, one of

---

77 *United States v. Home Concrete & Supply, LLC,* 132 S.Ct. 1836, 1844 (2012); *Fernandez v. Keisler*, 502 F.3d 337, 347–48 (4th Cir. 2007).

78 *Brand X,* discussed in text; *Levy v. Sterling Holding Co. LLC*, 544 F.3d 493, 502–03 (3d Cir. 2008).

79 Eskridge & Baer, *Continuum of Deference*, 96 Geo. L.J. at 1098–1120, 1183–90 (elaborating the Court's complicated "continuum of deference" and urging that the various regimes be boiled down to *Chevron* and *Skidmore*); Mathews, *Deference Lotteries*, 91 Tex. L. Rev. 1349 (suggesting a managerial advantage of a variety of deference regimes). See, e.g., *Mayo Foundation*, 562 U.S. 44 (overruling a tax-specific deference regime and requiring *Chevron*-deference to IRS revenue rulings).

which may disappear or be reconceptualized at the federal level. So I shall start with that one.

Seminole Rock/Auer *Canon.* Since the New Deal, the Supreme Court has sometimes announced special deference to an agency's interpretation of its own regulations. Such interpretations are "controlling unless plainly erroneous or inconsistent with the regulation."[80] We may call this the *Seminole Rock/Auer* canon, after its two leading cases; the previous quotation is from *Seminole Rock*, the older case. Thus, if after notice-and-comment rulemaking the National Park Service had issued a residual regulation barring from Lafayette Park "all transport mechanisms, including recreational ones, that pose safety problems for pedestrians," the agency's interpretation of its own regulation would, theoretically, be entitled to special deference, as quoted above. So if the Park Service interpreted the residual regulation to include skateboards, would that interpretation be entitled to some kind of super-deference? *Should* it enjoy super-deference?

For starters, it is far from clear what the *Seminole Rock* statement of the canon adds to the *Chevron* deference rule. If the Park Service is interpreting a guidance, and not a legislative rule, the canon is inapplicable: Like the guidance itself, the agency interpretation receives only *Skidmore* deference. If the Park Service is interpreting a legislative regulation, then the *Chevron* rule applies: The agency prevails if its interpretation is *either* consistent with the statute's plain meaning *or* is a reasonable interpretation of a statutory ambiguity. What does *Seminole Rock* add to that level of deference? If the statute's plain meaning is inconsistent with the regulation of skateboards (*Chevron*), then the agency's view is "plainly erroneous" (*Seminole Rock*), yes? Indeed, *Seminole Rock* could be read to add an extra level of scrutiny to the agency's interpretation by suggesting that a directive the agency could have adopted, consistent with the statute, is not allowed if it is "inconsistent with the regulation." (So the Park Service might adopt the directive by notice-and-comment rulemaking, but not by interpreting this particular legislative rule.)

---

[80] *Bowles v. Seminole Rock & Sand Co.*, 325 U.S. 410, 414 (1945). The *Seminole Rock* rule survives *Chevron*, as illustrated by *Auer v. Robbins*, 519 U.S. 452 (1997); *Geier v. American Honda Motor Co.*, 529 U.S. 861, 883–84 (2000); *Coeur Alaska, Inc. v. Southeast Alaska Conserv. Coun.*, 557 U.S. 261 (2009); *Talk America, Inc. v. Michigan Bell Telephone Co.*, 131 S.Ct. 2254, 2260–61 (2011) (*Auer*-deferring to an agency interpretation posed in an *amicus* brief filed on the agency's behalf by the Solicitor General).

In fact, the Supreme Court's pattern of statutory decisions seems to marginalize *Seminole Rock* along these lines. Lauren Baer and I examined more than 1000 Supreme Court decisions (1984–2006) involving an agency interpretation of a federal statute. We found that 155 of those decisions involved an agency interpretation of its own legislative rule—yet the Court invoked *Seminole Rock* deference in only eleven cases.[81] In short, the Court applied *Seminole Rock* (or a subsequent case reflecting its deference regime, such as *Auer*) in only 7.1 percent of the cases where it was, by its terms, applicable. In one-fifth of the 155 cases, the Court applied the *Chevron* rule, and in one-third it suggested *Skidmore* deference or something similar.[82] Although the Court has continued to cite the *Seminole Rock* canon, sometimes to decisive effect in important cases, the Court has ignored or marginalized the canon when the majority chooses.[83] While no one has systematically examined state practice, state courts do often afford "substantial deference" to an agency's interpretation of its own regulations, but it is far from clear that this doctrine impels judges to be more accommodating to agency views than they would be under *Chevron* or even *Skidmore*.[84]

If *Seminole Rock* actually did add something to the *Chevron* rule, it would sometimes be a questionable addition. As Justice Thomas recognized more than twenty years ago, agencies could use *Seminole Rock* to bootstrap vague rules into ever-expanding assertions of jurisdiction.[85] By essentially parroting the statutory language (section

---

[81] Eskridge & Baer, *The Continuum of Deference*, 96 Geo. L.J. at 1103–05.

[82] Id. at 1105 (Table 2).

[83] Compare *Coeur Alaska*, 557 U.S. at 275, 278 (conservative majority applying *Seminole Rock/Auer* to sustain a major environmental compromise by the Bush-Cheney Administration), with *Christopher v. SmithKline Beecham Corp.*, 132 S.Ct. 2156, 2170 (2012) (same conservative majority declining to apply *Seminole Rock/Auer* to a case applying detailed administrative regulations developed under the Fair Labor Standards Act).

[84] Most state court decisions evaluating agency interpretations of their own regulation, just apply *Chevron* or another regime, see, e.g., *Seeton v. Pennsylvania Game Comm'n,* 937 A.2d 1028 (Pa. 2007), and when state courts announce "substantial" deference for agency interpretation of its own regulations, it is not clear whether this adds anything to the agency's advantage. For a sampling of cases, see *Tibbs v. Bunnell,* 448 S.W.3d 796 (Ky. 2014); *Biogen IDEC MA, Inc. v. Treasurer & Receiver General*, 908 N.E.2d 740 (Mass. 2009); *Inner Harbor Hosps. v. State Dep't Soc. Servs.,* 559 N.W.2d 487, 491 (Neb. 1997); *Friends of the Columbia Gorge, Inc. v. Columbia River Gorge Comm'n,* 212 P.3d 1243, 1251 & n.14 (Or. 2009).

[85] *Thomas Jefferson Univ. v. Shalala,* 512 U.S. 504, 525 (1994) (Thomas, J., dissenting); John F. Manning, *Constitutional Structure and Judicial Deference to Agency Interpretations of Agency Rules*, 96 Colum. L. Rev. 612 (1996), endorsed by *Talk America,* 131 S.Ct. at 2265–66 (Scalia, J., concurring and suggesting that he would reconsider *Seminole Park/Auer* deference).

3), the Park Service's hypothetical regulation noted above could be a funnel through which the agency could launder all sorts of aggressive interpretations. Concerns about agency bootstrapping may explain why the Court almost never relies on *Seminole Rock*; in a few cases, the Court has explicitly rejected its application for this kind of reason.[86]

In the last few years, other Justices have joined Justice Thomas in urging reconsideration or abrogation of *Seminole Rock* as a separate deference canon.[87] I am inclined to think that *Skidmore* and *Chevron* are sufficient. If the Court were to leave *Seminole Rock* in place as a separate regime, it should be limited to cases like *Auer*, where the Court deferred to an agency "elaboration" of a concept the agency itself had created to implement the statute. Under *Auer*, the Court would first determine whether the agency regulation enjoys *Chevron* deference and therefore falls within the agency's zone of discretion.[88] Turning to the agency's interpretation of its own valid regulation, the Court would then apply the *Seminole Rock* test (quoted above) and determine whether the interpretation is reasonable, as will usually be the case when an agency is applying its own regulatory concept.[89] Notably, some state supreme courts that have rejected *Chevron* deference for legislative rulemaking have announced *Auer*-like deference for agency interpretations of their own rules.[90] In short, a narrowly-circumscribed *Auer* canon might be a reasonable successor to *Seminole Rock*. Such a canon might also apply to administrative resolution of inter-agency jurisdictional questions.[91]

Curtiss-Wright *Super-Deference Canon.* The Supreme Court has said that "congressional legislation * * * within the international field must often accord to the President a degree of discretion and freedom from statutory restriction which would not be admissible

---

[86] E.g., *Gonzales v. Oregon*, 546 U.S. at 256–58 (rejecting the application of *Auer* deference because the vague agency rule just "parroted" the statute).

[87] In a recent decision applying the Administrative Procedure Act to allow agencies to amend interpretive rules without going through notice-and-comment rulemaking, three Justices went out of their way to question *Seminole Rock*'s deference regime. See *Perez v. Mortgage Bankers Ass'n*, 135 S.Ct. 1199, 1210 (2015) (Alito, J., concurring in part); id. at 1211–13 (Scalia, J., concurring in the judgment); id. at 2013 (Thomas, J., concurring in the judgment).

[88] *Auer*, 519 U.S. at 457–58.

[89] Id. at 461.

[90] See, e.g., *Bowers v. Firefighters' Ret. Sys.*, 6 So.3d at 176 (Louisiana); *Hranicka*, 116 A.3d at 512 (Maryland).

[91] *Coeur Alaska*, 557 U.S. at 276–78.

were domestic affairs alone involved."[92] *Curtiss-Wright* deference (after the leading case, just quoted) is theoretically different from *Chevron* deference. Because it rests upon the President's Article II authority, rather than Congress's Article I authority, *Curtiss-Wright* deference does not necessarily depend upon a statutory delegation of lawmaking responsibilities, although the power of its presumption would be greatly strengthened by such delegation.[93] Moreover, the *Curtiss-Wright* canon is considered to be a more deferential standard than *Chevron*: The executive department interpretation prevails not only in cases of statutory ambiguity, but also in cases where Congress has not clearly and specifically trumped the agency or presidential construction.[94] Although the Supreme Court itself does not always cite the canon, it is highly deferential to presidential and executive directives bearing on foreign affairs, the armed forces, and diplomacy.[95]

Consider the potential power of this canon as applied to the Lafayette Park Safety Act of 1992, as amended in 2013. Assume that White House security is breached repeatedly in the 2010s, including two incidents where a skateboarder and a person on roller skates zip past the "H" Street gate and up to the front door of the White House. The President directs the Secretary of the Interior and, through her, the Director of the National Park Service to tighten up security in Lafayette Park, through which the skateboarder and roller skater, respectively, had sped to reach the "H" Street gate. After notice-and-comment rulemaking, the Park Service dutifully amends its safety regulations to bar roller skates as well as skateboards. While skateboards would probably fall within the agency's zone of discretion

---

[92] *United States v. Curtiss-Wright Export Co.*, 299 U.S. 304, 320 (1936).

[93] It is black-letter constitutional law that the President's power is at its zenith (and a high point at that) when he is acting pursuant to a congressional delegation of its Article I powers as well as pursuant to his own Article II powers. See *Youngstown Sheet & Tube Corp. v. Sawyer (the Steel Seizure Case)*, 343 U.S. 579 (1952) (Jackson, J., concurring).

[94] For cases where the Court is highly deferential to executive department interpretations in matters of foreign affairs, see, e.g., *Jama v. Immigration and Customs Enforcement*, 543 U.S. 335, 348 (2005); *Hamdi v. Rumsfeld*, 542 U.S. 507 (2004); *Department of Navy v. Egan*, 484 U.S. 518 (1988); *Dames & Moore v. Regan*, 453 U.S. 654 (1981). For an intense debate, where the *Curtiss-Wright* canon had much less punch, compare the majority and dissenting opinions in *Hamdan v. Rumsfeld*, 548 U.S. 557 (2006).

[95] Eskridge & Baer, *Continuum of Deference*, 96 Geo. L.J. at 1100–02 (finding that the Supreme Court between 1984 and 2006 almost always went along with executive department interpretations of treaties and statutes touching upon national security, foreign affairs, and military matters).

in an ordinary *Chevron* case, roller skates probably would not; in ordinary cases, many judges (and I) would likely say that the Park Safety Act directly addresses and excludes roller skates from the statutory scheme.

Does the national security context of the new regulation make a difference? Most assuredly. If the agency makes the proper showing of danger, the Court of Appeals would probably *Curtiss-Wright* defer to its new interpretation that brings roller skates as well as skateboards into the statutory scheme. Rather than asking whether the statute directly addresses the issue (*Chevron*), the court would ask whether the statute specifically bars or channels national security initiatives taken by the executive branch.[96] Although it is a stretch to consider roller skates to be "vehicles" under the statute, the precise language of section 3 permits such a reading—especially if "safety hazards" were understood to include national security threats as well as the more pedestrian safety concerns that were Congress's focus in 1992 and 2013.

To be sure, the simpler approach for the President to take would be an executive order, pursuant to his Article II powers, regulating Lafayette Park directly rather than the indirect Park Service rulemaking approach suggested above. Such an executive order would presumably be constitutional, and that fact surely informs the powerful *Curtiss-Wright* super-deference canon. Are there no limits on the President's authority? There certainly are, as illustrated by the last set of canons discussed in this chapter.

Anti-Deference Canons. Assume the President, either on his own authority or through the National Park Service's rulemaking, not only bars roller skates, skateboards, Segways, and the like from Lafayette Park, but also announces that anyone violating this new regime will be arrested and may be detained indefinitely in the United States prison camp at Guantánamo Bay, Cuba (illustrated at the front of this chapter). The first person arrested under this new regime is Mike Giannotto, for operating his Segway tour in Lafayette Park. Military officers transfer the hapless Segway operator to the Guantánamo Bay prison camp for interrogation, while his devoted family objects to his arrest and detention.

Many gentle readers will be alarmed by this new rule and by the Giannotto arrest: Is this lawful for the President to do? Will federal

---

[96] *Department of the Navy v. Egan*, 484 U.S. 518, 530 (1988); Eskridge, *Dynamic Statutory Interpretation*, 325.

judges go along with this presidential initiative? Well, probably not. The federal criminal code prohibits the precautionary detention of U.S. citizens "except pursuant to an Act of Congress," and the Lafayette Park Safety Act does not seem to be such a statute. Recall that section 2 makes violation only a "civil offense" and explicitly limits punishment to a monetary fine. Unless there were another statute, better targeted at Giannotto's transgression, the whole code rule and the reconciliation canon ensure that the President cannot unlawfully detain the "vehicular" entrepreneur.[97]

Set aside the anti-detention statute (just quoted) and consider the Giannotto arrest and detention in a broader public law framework. Judges are not always deferential to executive initiatives even in the foreign affairs arena, and they tend to be positively *un*deferential when the executive branch is acting contrary to libertarian principles that saturate the Constitution and animate much America's history. Mike Giannotto's family can help him seek a writ of habeas corpus to challenge his detention,[98] and the Giannottos stand a good chance of success in securing his release.

The next chapter will examine, in greater detail, some substantive canons that operate in the Giannotto situation. For example, the rule of lenity says that judges will not impose criminal sanctions (especially imprisonment) unless Congress has clearly criminalized the defendant's conduct. The best justification for the rule of lenity is that Congress, not prosecutors and judges, must make the normative judgments about what conduct merits the condemnation of the criminal law and (potentially) the loss of liberty for adjudicated criminals.[99] If the Department of Justice sought to apply the Lafayette Park Safety Act as a criminal statute, the rule of lenity would operate as an *anti-deference* canon: Not only will a court refuse to bend over backwards to accommodate the executive branch interpretation, but the court will demand that prosecutors affirmatively demonstrate a precise and persuasive legal basis for

---

[97] 18 U.S.C. § 4001(a) (quotation in text). In *Hamdi*, a Supreme Court majority agreed that a congressional Authorization of Military Force implicitly authorized the President to detain terrorist citizens—a far cry from the vehicles in the park law we have been examining, which is not even a criminal statute. *Hamdi*, 542 U.S. at 517–19 (O'Connor, J., for four Justices); id. at 587 (Thomas, J., concurring on this point).

[98] For a recent example of judicial resistance to the Bush-Cheney Administration's efforts to suspend habeas corpus, through a liberty-based statutory and constitutional analysis, see *Boumediene v. Bush*, 553 U.S. 723, 739–46, 789–93, 798 (2008).

[99] *United States v. Wiltberger*, 18 U.S. 76, 92 (1820) (Marshall, C.J.); Daniel M. Kahan, *Lenity and Federal Common Law Crimes*, 1994 Sup. Ct. Rev. 345.

their interpretation. Given the text, structure, and history of the Park Safety Act, that is not possible here, for the reasons mentioned in the previous paragraph.

Even if the executive branch does not claim criminal law authority, any statutory argument for detention of Mike Giannotto would run up against the avoidance canon (also examined in the next chapter), which urges judges to construe statutes to avoid "serious constitutional problems."[100] Admittedly, this is an unusually elastic canon, one that can plausibly be raised on both sides of many statutory cases. The President would argue that an interpretation of relevant statutes that denied him authority to protect the White House and national security would raise serious Article II problems.[101] In the hands of judges, however, the avoidance canon usually creates a background norm of anti-deference when the executive branch seeks to deprive a citizen of liberty—not just freedom from detention, but also freedom to speak, to associate, to raise a family, and so forth.

* * *

At this point in the volume, the gentle reader has surely noticed how dynamic statutory interpretation is, as a practical matter. Earlier chapters have demonstrated how even the simplest statutory scheme (our vehicles in the park law) plays out dynamically over time.[102] One reason for dynamic statutory interpretation is that statutes are applied to circumstances unanticipated by legislators and essentially unaddressed by the statute, such as the emergence of Segways as vehicles populating the parks of the nation's capital. Changed circumstances sometimes also upbend assumptions underwriting the statutory scheme. Thus, skateboards have emerged, through improved technology as well as heightened skill levels, as a more threatening form of conveyance in 2016 than they would have appeared in 1992 (when the statute was adopted). As the last three chapters have illustrated, sometimes the changed circumstance will

---

[100] *NLRB v. Catholic Bishop of Chicago*, 440 U.S. 490 (1979); *United States ex rel. Attorney General v. Delaware & Hudson Co.*, 213 U.S. 366 (1909); see John Copeland Nagle, Delaware & Hudson *Revisited*, 72 Notre Dame L. Rev. 1495 (1997); Adrian Vermeule, *Saving Constructions*, 85 Geo. L.J. 1945 (1997).

[101] Trevor W. Morrison, *Constitutional Avoidance in the Executive Branch*, 106 Colum. L. Rev. 1189 (2006).

[102] On the inevitability of dynamic statutory interpretation over time because of changed circumstances, effective delegation of gapfilling and interpretive authority to agencies and judges, and evolving constitutional culture, see Eskridge, *Dynamic Statutory Interpretation*, 48–80.

be the law itself. The Soaper Amendment not only overrode a court decision, but changed the structure of the Lafayette Park law and introduced new elements of dynamism into the statutory scheme.

Another reason that statutes evolve beyond and sometimes against the expectations of their framers is that different officials—judges and administrators—are interpreting the laws that legislators enact. Chapters one through three have vividly demonstrated how a pattern of judicial interpretations of the Park Safety Act transformed that law in ways legislators would not have predicted. This chapter demonstrates the dynamic features of agency interpretation. Because administrators tend to focus on statutory purpose and apply purpose in light of their learning curve regarding the statutory scheme, agency interpretation is especially dynamic. When you recall that most official interpretation comes from agencies and not courts, this agency dynamism has a considerable effect on the evolution of a statutory scheme.

Let me close this chapter with the deep tension that destabilizes the judicial deference doctrines. When agencies interpret statutes, they pay close attention to the statutory text and plan, but not to the whole code, and they emphasize both purpose and legislative history (broadly understood to include subsequent history).[103] As we have seen in chapters one through four, judicial opinions in statutory cases focus more closely on statutory text and plan, give greater emphasis to the whole code and statutory precedents, and give less attention to legislative history (at the federal level and in most states). In short, agencies and courts apply significantly different methodologies when they interpret statutes. I do not celebrate the differences quite so much as Jerry Mashaw, for example,[104] as I think courts ought to follow the agency emphasis on statutory purpose and attention to legislative history, with less dogmatic application of the whole code rule. This is only a matter of degree, however, as I embrace the traditional view that judges' comparative advantage lies in their focus on text and structure and their ability to integrate statutory text into the larger corpus of the law.

---

[103] Walker, *Inside Agency Statutory Interpretation*, 67 Stan. L. Rev. at 1029–31 (agencies follow the ordinary meaning and whole act rules, but pay little attention to the whole code); id. at 1042–47 (agencies pay close attention to legislative history).

[104] Jerry L. Mashaw, *Norms, Practices and the Paradox of Deference: A Preliminary Inquiry into Agency Statutory Interpretation,* 57 Admin. L. Rev. 501 (2005).

Accordingly, judicial deference law, the focus of this chapter, ought to be understood as the doctrinal structure within which judges mediate the tension between dynamic, democratically responsive agency interpretations and the relatively text-based, holistic judicial stance. Because agencies do pay close attention to statutory text and because judges are mindful that administrators carry the load for applying statutes coherently over time, courts normally go along or ratify agency interpretations. In my view, judges ought never trump an agency interpretation without being sure that it is significantly inconsistent with the statutory plan, informed by consulting legislative history as a way to ground text-based judicial construction in the project *legislators* were launching and not the project judges would prefer. In short, federal and state court deference doctrine allows most purposive interpretation to proceed, but with occasional checks to make sure the agency is not creating arbitrary rules and is not making major policy moves properly left to the legislative and democratic process.

The next chapter and the conclusion will explore a larger and more aggressive (hence, more controversial) judicial role in statutory interpretation, reflecting yet another force pressing statutes in dynamic direction: the evolving public values and constitutional norms of our society. Contrary to the deferential stance toward the legislature and agencies we have been emphasizing in this and the previous chapter, the concluding portions of this volume will explore occasions when judges openly play a more aggressive role, through constitutional review and, more pervasively, through clear statement canons that reflect deep normative commitments that judges enforce upon a sometimes reluctant political system.

Chapter 6

CONSTITUTIONAL PRINCIPLES AND BACKGROUND NORMS

Central Park, New York City

Throughout this volume, normative context has been critical for applying the vehicles in the park law. Social norms, legislative purposes, and public plans have taken center stage from the beginning, when I criticized Justice Scalia and Professor Garner for announcing that a bicycle cannot, as a matter of ordinary meaning, be a "vehicle" regulated by such a law. If the legislative purpose were safety of children and older persons, if the park plan entailed special bike paths limited to the perimeter, if the legislature had created a broad code-wide definition for the term "vehicle," or if there were a longstanding social consensus that bicycles were not allowed in the park, any of these background norms would require judges to include bicycles as "vehicles," no matter that textualist judges or even professional linguists might say in the abstract.

What has not been emphasized, thus far, is the background role played by constitutional and other norms widely accepted as fundamental. To illustrate these meta-norms in statutory interpretation, we need to update and expand the vehicles in the park law once more. Let us say that a terrorist incident in Washington, D.C. triggers the 2020 election of a President and Congress determined to ramp up the national security state. The first statute enacted after the election is the Never on Our Nation's Soil: Efforts Needed to Suppress Enemies Act of 2021. The "Nation's Soil Act" includes thirty-three titles, each of which addresses a different security concern, from the Internet to air travel. Title 27 ("Public Spaces"), subtitle 43 repeals the old Lafayette Park law (among others) and enacts the following:

An Act to ensure safety in public parks

Sec. 1. Findings and Purpose. Finding that vehicles operating in public parks pose potential dangers to public safety and national security, Congress resolves that there is an urgent need to ban vehicles from public parks.

Sec. 2. No Vehicles in Public Parks. No vehicles shall be allowed in any public park. Any person who brings a vehicle into a public park shall be guilty of a criminal misdemeanor. Each violation may be punished by a fine not exceeding $10,000 or confinement in jail for up to two months or both.

Sec. 3. Definition. "Vehicle" for purposes of this law means any thing that is used for conveying a person or object from one place to another and that poses unacceptable safety risks.

Sec. 4. Enforcement and Implementation. (a) Implementation. The National Park Service shall have authority to establish rules implementing this Act. Persons injured because of conduct violating this Act shall have a claim for relief against the government if its agents have not properly enforced this Act.

(b) Sentencing. No more than two weeks after a judge has tried and convicted a defendant for violating this Act, the judge will sentence the defendant.

(c) Attorney's Fees. If a person is prosecuted and acquitted of violating this statute, that person will have a claim against the federal government for payment of any and all attorney's fees incurred in the defense.

The primary congressional sponsor of the new law is Senator Casius Hushpuppy, from Pine Bluff, Arkansas. In 2021, he is the Chair of the Senate Homeland Security Committee.

The President, Senator Hushpuppy, and other supporters expect this omnibus homeland security law to be a super-statute, creating a pervasively influential legal framework for protecting the country against dangers of all sorts. One linchpin of this landmark legislation is its vesting broad authority in the executive branch to make and enforce prophylactic rules that will head off future attacks on American soil. Although the Lafayette Park Safety Act has been superseded, the National Park Service will make this park the situs for an especially vigorous application of the new law.

But judges will still have an important role to play. Applying the new law, judges will be attentive to the values entrenched in the U.S. Constitution and American law more generally. Recall Mike Giannotto's case in the previous chapter. For bringing a Segway into Lafayette Park, the plucky entrepreneur was not only charged with a violation of the vehicles in the park law but was detained abroad without trial. I insisted that the vehicles in the park law must be interpreted in light of the anti-detention value that pervades American public law (including the Constitution, the common law, and international law) and that is encoded in a particular statute. If an executive action is clearly contrary to that statute and America's public law tradition, most judges would interpret the statute narrowly.

In my view, indefinite detention of Mike Giannotto for violating the civil rule against vehicles in Lafayette Park would violate the Due Process Clause of the Fifth Amendment—but most judges would not reach this question and would instead interpret the statute to avoid such an unconstitutional application. This is the *classic avoidance canon*:[1]

---

[1] On the "classic" version of the avoidance canon, distinguishing it from "modern" avoidance discussed below, see John Copeland Nagle, Delaware & Hudson *Revisited,* 72 Notre Dame L. Rev. 1495 (1997); Adrian Vermeule, *Saving Constructions,* 85 Geo. L.J. 1945, 1949 (1997). An important application of classic avoidance is *National Federation of Indep. Bus. v. Sebelius,* 132 S.Ct. 2566, 2593–94 (2012) (opinion of Roberts, C.J., writing only for himself but delivering the judgment of the Court which saved the Affordable Care Act from invalidation). An early statement of classic avoidance is *Mossman v. Higginson,* 4 U.S. 12, 14 (1800). See Amy Coney Barrett, *Substantive Canons and Faithful Agency,* 90 B.U.L. Rev. 109, 138–43 (2010) (discussing other early nineteenth-century statements of this canon).

CLASSIC AVOIDANCE CANON

1. Statute is ambiguous: it can mean either A or B.
2. Interpretation A would violate the Constitution, but Interpretation B would not.
3. *Therefore,* Court should choose Interpretation B.

Classic avoidance is a longstanding, fundamental rule for statutory interpretation. The rule of law in this country rests upon and respects the Constitution as the foundation of the law and of the limits of legal authority. A statute inconsistent with the Constitution is void and unenforceable, but the first step is to determine what the statute itself means. If there are two plausible interpretations of a statute, and one is unconstitutional but the other constitutional, a straightforward understanding of the rule of law suggests that the judge should choose the second interpretation. For the same reasons judges must choose the Constitution over statutes if there is a direct conflict, they must choose the narrower interpretation of an ambiguous law if the broader one would be unconstitutional.[2]

Some commentators worry that the avoidance doctrine and other constitutional canons invite "stealth constitutionalism," whereby judges invent new constitutional doctrines in a low-stakes manner that insulates them from intense public scrutiny.[3] That is, judges announce the new doctrine (Step 2) but do not generate controversy and public debate, because they do not actually strike down the statute (Step 3), and then later on treat the new doctrine as "settled" when they actually do strike down legislation. This line of critique

---

[2] *The Federalist* No. 78 (Hamilton) (arguing that courts will apply the Constitution over an inconsistent statute *and* that courts ought to narrowly construe "unjust and partial laws," including those at odds with constitutional norms); William N. Eskridge Jr., *All About Words: Early Understandings of the "Judicial Power" in Statutory Interpretation,* 101 Colum. L. Rev. 990, 1025–30, 1046–55 (2001) (wide acceptance in the framing period for the practice of judicial narrowing statutes inconsistent with "fundamental law"). Ironically, the leading case for judicial review, *Marbury v. Madison,* engaged in "reverse-avoidance," as the Court construed the Judiciary Act of 1789 broadly rather than narrowly and chose an interpretation that was at odds with both the plain meaning of the statute and (assertedly) with Article III of the Constitution. See William van Alstyne, *A Critical Guide to* Marbury v. Madison, 1969 Duke L.J. 1.

[3] William N. Eskridge Jr. & Philip P. Frickey, *The Supreme Court, 1993 Term—Foreword: Law as Equilibrium,* 108 Harv. L. Rev. 26, 81–87 (1994) (articulating the idea in text). For a recent application of the idea to the avoidance doctrine, see Neal Kumar Katyal & Thomas P. Schmidt, *Active Avoidance: The Modern Supreme Court and Legal Change,* 128 Harv. L. Rev. 2109 (2015), criticizing (inter alia) *Shelby County, Alabama v. Holder,* 133 S.Ct. 2612 (2013).

would also wonder whether constitutional avoidance can be countermajoritarian and potentially inconsistent with democratic premises.[4] As Frederick Schauer says, "it is by no means clear that a strained interpretation of a federal statute that avoids a constitutional question is any less a judicial intrusion than the judicial invalidation on constitutional grounds of a less strained interpretation of the same statute."[5]

A further concern is that judges confronted with a statute that seems to traverse a constitutional line sometimes bend over backwards to find a saving construction for the statute, while on other occasions they will refuse to bend at all when faced with equally compelling constitutional concerns.[6] This frustrates the rule of law aspirations that constitutional principles should be applied in a predictable manner and that judges should generally follow a statute's ordinary meaning.[7] For example, the Due Process Clause of the Fifth and Fourteenth Amendments requires federal and state governments (respectively) to give clear notice of precisely what conduct a criminal law sanctions. A statute that says, "It is a criminal offense for anyone to bring into a public park any mechanism that the park police consider to be inconsistent with the public interest," is too "vague" to satisfy the Due Process Clause.[8] Under cover of classic avoidance, however, it is not entirely predictable what a judge would actually do with such a statute. Although the most obvious course of action would be to invalidate the law and render it entirely unenforceable, judges will often impose a narrowing construction they believe consistent with Congress's core concerns; when they do so, that narrowing construction will be a judge-crafted rule that may require considerable elaboration over time.[9]

---

4 William N. Eskridge Jr. & Philip P. Frickey, *Quasi-Constitutional Law: Clear Statement Rules as Constitutional Lawmaking*, 45 Vand. L. Rev. 593, 636–40 (1992).

5 Frederick Schauer, Ashwander *Revisited,* 1995 Sup. Ct. Rev. 71, 74; accord, John F. Manning, *Nondelegation as a Canon of Avoidance,* 2000 Sup. Ct. Rev. 223, 253–56.

6 E.g., Lisa A. Kloppenberg, *Avoiding Serious Constitutional Doubts: The Supreme Court's Construction of Statutes Raising Free Speech Concerns*, 30 U.C. Davis L. Rev. 1 (1996) (criticizing the Supreme Court's unpredictable application of the avoidance canon).

7 Barrett, *Substantive Canons and Faithful Agency,* 90 B.U.L. Rev. at 121–25; Schauer, Ashwander *Revisited,* 1995 Sup. Ct. Rev. at 74; accord, Manning, *Nondelegation Doctrine as a Canon of Avoidance.*

8 See *Kolender v. Lawson*, 461 U.S. 352, 357 (1982).

9 Compare *Skilling v. United States*, 561 U.S. 358, 409–13 (2010) (finding a federal law making it a crime to engage in a "scheme or artifice to deprive another of the intangible right of honest services" was too vague and had to be narrowed to

The simple answer to this line of critique would be for courts to apply the classic avoidance canon *only* when there is genuine statutory ambiguity and *only* when the constitutional violation is clear. But a judge's views about the Constitution will often be tentative, and her honest interest in exploring a constitutional idea may influence her understanding of a statute's ordinary meaning. If some gentle readers find it incredible that a judge would be swayed by her political philosophy in this way, please read the Supreme Court opinions finding (as well as the opinions refusing to find) that a two-line authorization for the use of military force against terrorists implicitly authorized the Bush-Cheney Administration to detain American citizens without charges and without an immediate opportunity to challenge the terms of their detentions.[10]

Even classic avoidance, arguably the most defensible of the substantive canons discussed here, is controversial among academics and (to a lesser extent) judges. The canon puts pressure on the ordinary meaning rule which grounds statutory interpretation in the rule of law, and therefore this canon and others discussed in this chapter are a particularly big problem for textualism, as Amy Coney Barrett has argued.[11] Professor Barrett's point also applies to theories committed to implementing popular and legislative will, as the avoidance and other constitutional canons lure judges into results that are anti-democratic much of the time.

Notwithstanding these concerns, the classic avoidance canon is deeply entrenched in doctrine and would affect judicial practice even

---

schemes involving bribes or kickbacks), with id. at 415, 422–24 (Scalia, J., concurring in part and dissenting in part) (agreeing with the Court that the statute was unconstitutionally vague and urging that it simply be invalidated rather than rewritten).

[10] *Hamdi v. Rumsfeld,* 542 U.S. 507, 517–24 (2004) (O'Connor, J., for a plurality) (finding presidential authority to respond to emergencies, a constitutional notion that bled into her reading of the two-line authorization for use of military force in response to terrorist attack). Compare id. at 583–87 (Thomas, J., dissenting) (reading Article II more liberally than the plurality, a liberality that bled over into his reading of the authorization), with id. at 542–54 (Souter, J., concurring in part and dissenting in part) (reading Article II more restrictively, a constitutional understanding that bled over into his reading of the authorization), and id. at 555–79 (Scalia, J., dissenting) (reading the habeas corpus and criminal procedure provisions of the Constitution more strictly, a constitutional understanding that drove his dismissal of the authorization as irrelevant).

[11] Barrett, *Substantive Canons and Faithful Agency,* 90 B.U.L. Rev. at 163–77 (demonstrating that the avoidance and other constitutional canons lead textualists away from the ordinary meaning of statutory texts and, therefore, pose a problem for Justice Scalia's new textualism).

if it were doctrinally renounced.[12] Thus, constitutional principles and fundamental norms pervasively seep into statutory interpretation through cognitive osmosis. This process is reflected in a variety of quasi-constitutional canons of statutory construction. Although many scholars object to these quasi-constitutional canons, some rather strenuously, they are widely deployed by judges at all levels of our system and from all different political backgrounds (in other words, conservative judges appointed by Republican Presidents as well as liberal judges appointed by Democratic Presidents).

It is easy to see why. The rule of law in a constitutional democracy requires attention to the Constitution itself. For the same reasons courts, populated by life-tenured experts in the interpretation of law, are accepted as the best institution to enforce the Constitution directly, they are also best situated to enforce constitutional values less directly, through narrowing interpretations that integrate new statutes into the ongoing traditions of American constitutionalism. Life tenure allows judges to take the long view of an issue and sometimes to resist temporary political expediency in service of larger national commitments. The collegial nature of judging and the requirement that decisions be justified by neutral reasons do not prevent a judge's values from affecting her legal reasoning but do rein it in. And there are institutional pressures preventing truly outlying judgments; the judiciary is known as "the least dangerous branch" for good reason.[13]

Moreover, it appears that the avoidance doctrine is not inconsistent with the conventions and expectations of the legislative process. The Constitution requires both state and federal legislators to take an oath to obey the Constitution, and there is no reason to believe that most legislators do not take that oath seriously.[14] Like

---

[12] Compare *Brown v. Plata,* 131 S.Ct. 1910, 1939–42 (2011) (interpreting the Prison Litigation Reform Act [PLRA] in light of the Court's Eighth Amendment jurisprudence), with id. at 1950–51, 1952–55 (Scalia, J., dissenting) (demanding that the Court avoid "travesty" and "outrageous" results and hew to a more narrow understanding of both the Eighth Amendment and of the PLRA).

[13] *The Federalist* No. 78 (Hamilton) (explaining why the judiciary is "the least dangerous branch" and why that makes judges well-suited to declare constitutional and statutory meaning). On the disciplining value of the institutional weakness of the judiciary, see Alexander H. Bickel, *The Least Dangerous Branch: The Supreme Court at the Bar of Politics* (1962); Stephen Breyer, *Making Our Democracy Work: A Judge's View* 110–18 (2010); Neal K. Komesar, *Imperfect Alternatives: Choosing Institutions in Law, Economics, and Public Policy* (1994); Andrew B. Coan, *Judicial Capacity and the Substance of Constitutional Law*, 122 Yale L.J. 422 (2012).

[14] U.S. Const., art. VI, cl. 3 (all legislators, state as well as federal, required by oath to support the Constitution).

legislatures in other states, the Texas Legislature has directed courts in this manner: "In enacting a statute, it is presumed that * * * compliance with the constitutions of this state and of the United States is intended."[15] No state legislature has rejected such a canon. Also, legislative support offices urge drafting staff to research constitutional questions and, implicitly and sometimes explicitly, suggest that they work with legislative sponsors to avoid potential violations.[16] Abbe Gluck and Lisa Schultz Bressman's survey of congressional staff suggests that the state legislative consensus (presuming consistency with constitutional rules) enjoys similar support within Congress.[17]

But would state and federal legislators be happy with the classic avoidance canon if they believed that courts routinely twist statutory language to avoid speculative constitutional rules? I suspect not, but no one has shown that this happens very often. Consider an example that is more typical. The new 2021 vehicles in the park law says very little about the process that must be followed to prosecute people accused of bringing vehicles into a public park. If the federal government prosecutes Mike Giannotto for operating a Segway in Lafayette Park and if the government seeks a prison sentence, is defendant Giannotto entitled to a jury trial? Section 4(b) of the Act might be read to contemplate that trials will be to the judge, but unless they waive their rights, criminal defendants like Giannotto enjoy a right to a jury trial under the Sixth Amendment. Should the judge invalidate section 4(b)? Or interpret it narrowly? Jot down your answer in the margin.

---

[15] Tex. Govt. Code § 311.021(1); accord, Colo. Rev. Stat. § 2–4–201; Iowa Code § 4.4; Minn. Stat. § 645.17; 1 Pa. Cons. Stat. § 1922. See generally Jacob Scott, *Codified Canons and the Common Law of Interpretation*, 98 Geo. L.J. 341, 388 (2010) (Table 8, reporting that several state legislatures have codified the avoidance canon and none has rejected it).

[16] Legislative drafting manuals focus on technical matters, but many of them also urge drafters to research constitutional law and educate legislators about constitutional limits. E.g., Delaware Legislative Council, Division of Research, *Delaware Legislative Drafting Manual* pt. II, chs. 2–3 (2015); Office of Code Revision, Legislative Serv. Agency, *Drafting Manual for the Indiana General Assembly* ch. 2, § B(1) (Dec. 19, 2012); Kentucky Legislative Research Comm'n, Kentucky General Assembly, *Bill Drafting Manual* §§ 103 & 205 (rev. 2011); Office of Policy Analysis, Maryland Dep't of Legislative Servs., *Legislative Drafting Manual 2016,* ch. 4 (Sept. 2015).

[17] Abbe R. Gluck & Lisa Schultz Bressman, *Statutory Interpretation from the Inside: An Empirical Study of Congressional Drafting, Delegation, and Statutory Interpretation: Part I,* 65 Stan. L. Rev. 901, 947–49 (2013).

Why should the judge interpret section 4(b) to say anything definitive about the right to a jury trial? The text is ambiguous to say the least. Though the sentence seems to assume judge trials, it does not explicitly require them in all cases, nor does it explicitly deny defendants their Sixth Amendment rights. The sentence may even be a mistake that often occurs when Congress enacts large omnibus legislation. The more complicated the legislation and the more time pressure faced by Congress and its drafting offices, the more likely there will be mistakes such as this one.[18] Complexity and time pressure assure drafting errors, partly because the bill has many interconnected parts that are drafted and put together under strong time pressure, but also because complex bills usually evolve. New sections and titles are tacked on, inter-party deals and summits create compromises that require revisions, and controversial sections and entire titles are dropped or narrowed. This process of constant revision inevitably produces errors, as we saw with the Affordable Care Act of 2010.[19]

Does the legislative history suggest that the congressional process focused on judge trials as the only way to address violations of the new vehicles in the park law? That the enacting coalition considered this an important feature of the statutory enforcement scheme? If not, it seems unnecessarily confrontational and scolding for a court to invalidate a provision that can be read more narrowly and that does not reflect a considered, and democratically accountable, legislative judgment that trials must be before a judge. In other words, the Constitution's norm of interbranch comity and the axioms of good governance (not to mention the institutional needs of the judicial branch) demand that courts show the coordinate branches respect and a cooperative attitude toward their work product—even as they resist or edit that work product to sustain consistency with our constitutional traditions.[20]

---

[18] For an excellent analysis of drafting errors that inevitably creep into complicated omnibus legislation, see Jesse Cross, *The Staffer's Error Doctrine:* King v. Burwell *and the Congressional Division of Labor* (draft July 2015).

[19] *King v. Burwell,* 135 S.Ct. 2480, 2493 (2015) (correcting a likely drafting error introduced during the complicated deliberative process that produced the Affordable Care Act).

[20] For classic statements of the constitutional and institutional reasons why courts ought to and must display a cooperative attitude toward the political branches, see Breyer, *Making Our Democracy Work*; Robert A. Katzmann, *Courts and Congress* (1997).

Constitution-Based Canons

The influence of the Constitution on statutory interpretation is hardly exhausted by the classic avoidance canon. Indeed, you don't need a canon to be influenced by the osmosis of fundamental norms or constitutional principles into statutory interpretation. Fundamental norms and constitutional principles affect the way judges read the words of a statute, its structure and plan, statutory precedents, and its legislative as well as regulatory history. In cases where constitutional norms loom large, judges mold statutes to accommodate those norms—or (more accurately) their understanding of those norms.[21]

Section 3 of the Public Park Safety Act of 2021 defines "vehicles" as "any thing that is used for conveying a person or object from one place to another and that poses unacceptable safety risks." If the police applied the law to arrest and detain a six year-old riding her tricycle erratically in a covered park, judges would be quick to reverse for any of several reasons. Some judges would say that a tricycle is not a mechanism typically posing significant "safety risks"; others would find it absurd to apply the safety and security law to a kid essentially using the park for its core purpose; some judges might be so bold to invoke the avoidance canon, on the ground that applying a criminal statute to a six year-old child would be unconstitutional or would, at least, raise serious constitutional difficulties. Whatever reason and whatever canon the judge chose (from this list or a longer one), the judge would read the statute through the lens of shared normative commitments—including the constitutional notion that a criminal statute must give adequate notice of illegal conduct and cannot be applied to people who are not mature enough to have the mental state needed for culpability.[22]

---

[21] For just a handful of dramatic examples, see *Brown v. Plata,* 131 S.Ct. 1910 (majority and dissenting opinions) (interpreting the Prison Litigation Reform Act by reference to different judicial understandings of the Eighth Amendment); *Ricci v. DeStefano*, 557 U.S. 557 (2009) (interpreting the Civil Rights Act of 1991 in light of the Court's equal protection jurisprudence); *Solid Waste Agency of Northern Cook County v. U.S. Army Corps of Engineers*, 531 U.S. 159, 168 (2001) (interpreting the Clean Water Act of 1972 in light of the Court's Commerce Clause jurisprudence); *Bob Jones Univ. v. United States*, 461 U.S. 574 (1983) (interpreting the Internal Revenue Code in light of fundamental anti-segregation norms).

[22] On the limited culpability of minors in our criminal justice system, see *Roper v. Simmons*, 543 U.S. 551, 570 (2005) (minors cannot receive the death penalty for culpability reasons); *Graham v. Florida*, 560 U.S. 48, 74 (2010) (applying *Roper* to hold that minors cannot receive mandatory life sentences); *Miller v. Alabama*, 132 S.Ct.

The Supreme Court has formalized these intuitions in the last half century, through the articulation of an array of "clear statement rules" or even "super-strong clear statement rules": Such-and-such Constitution-based norm applies unless Congress negates it by a (very) clear statement on the face of the statute.[23] As a general matter, these constitutional clear statement rules are justified by the notion that courts should resist legislative intrusion into constitutional demilitarized zones and should raise the costs of legislation touching upon sensitive areas.[24] The constitutional clear statement rules are also subject to all the objections raised against the classic avoidance canon, especially the objections that judges are diluting rather than protecting the Constitution when they slip its penumbral protections into statutory schemes and that they are doing so at the expense of the statutory scheme crafted by the legislative process.[25] Let us start with a more liberal version of the avoidance canon and then examine some canons inspired by constitutional federalism. This part will conclude with the severability canon, which has all the virtues and none of the vices of the constitutional clear statement rules. Unlike those other rules, the severability canon reflects legislative assumptions, protects reliance interests, and is relatively easy to apply.

Modern Avoidance Canon. Section 2 of the Public Park Safety Act of 2021 says that "[n]o vehicles shall be allowed in any public park." Although section 3 defines "vehicles," the statute has no definition of "public park." Does this criminal prohibition extend to Central Park in New York City (romantically pictured in the front of this chapter)? Central Park is a municipal "park" open to the "public," so it would appear to fit within the terms of the statute. The law is broadly phrased (*any* public park), in contrast to statutes specifically

---

2455, 2464–69 (2012) (applying *Roper* and *Graham* to hold that minors cannot receive life without parole for robbery).

[23] Eskridge & Frickey, *Quasi-Constitutional Law*, 45 Vand. L. Rev. at 611–29 (cataloguing a variety of super-strong clear statement rules and contrasting them with regular clear statement rules and presumptions).

[24] Ernest A. Young, *Constitutional Avoidance, Resistance Norms, and the Preservation of Judicial Review*, 78 Tex. L. Rev. 1549 (2000); Matthew C. Stephenson, *The Price of Public Action: Constitutional Doctrine and the Judicial Manipulation of Legislative Enactment Costs*, 118 Yale L.J. 2, 11–16 (2008).

[25] John F. Manning, Comment, *Clear Statement Rules and the Constitution*, 110 Colum. L. Rev. 399 (2010) (some constitutional clear statement rules dilute or distort constitutional law); Gluck & Bressman, *Statutory Interpretation from the Inside: Part I*, 65 Stan. L. Rev. at 1016 (congressional drafters do not know about the new constitutional clear statement rules and do not intuitively consider those rules when they craft statutes).

regulating *national* parks in Title 54 of the United States Code. The security purposes of the omnibus Nation's Soil Act of 2021 would plausibly be served by such a sweeping application. The plain meaning of "public park" seems to include Central Park.

On the other hand, it is unusual for a federal statute to regulate municipal parks. If the law extends to Central Park, does it also include state parks and private parks that are open to the public? How about amusement parks? A moment's reflection suggests need for further research. The term "any public park" should be understood in light of the statutory structure as well as the legislative history. If the remainder of Title 27 ("Public Spaces") of the omnibus 2021 law were clearly limited to national parks and other federal lands, for example, the whole act rule would suggest that "any public park" should be read narrowly, applicable only to national parks.[26]

Assume that the contextual evidence from the whole act and from the legislative history leaves section 2 as open-ended as it appears upon initial reading. The provision might well be read to regulate private, municipal, and state "public parks" as well as national parks—but such a reading will seem immediately odd to federal legislative drafters as well as to constitutional lawyers, in part because there are no congressional findings that national security or interstate commerce is affected by vehicular accidents in Central Park and other local venues.[27] Without congressional findings, judges must figure out for themselves what constitutional authority Congress was relying on to reach private, municipal, and state parks open to the public. (Elsewhere in Title 27 of the Nation's Soil Act, there might be textual evidence suggesting Congress's constitutional basis for regulating local and not just national parks, but assume that Title 27, too, is unhelpful.)

Does the regulation rest upon the Commerce Clause of Article I, Section 8? That is the basis for most congressional regulation

---

[26] Cf. *Small v. United States*, 544 U.S. 385 (2005) (adopting a narrowing interpretation of "any court" in a sentence-enhancement law); see *United States v. Gayle*, 342 F.3d 89 (2d Cir. 2003) (Katzmann, J.) (same issue); Robert A. Katzmann, *Judging Statutes* 70–81 (2014) (providing a detailed and balanced analysis of the issue presented in *Small* and *Gayle*).

[27] See Ira B. Forstater, Office of Legislative Counsel, U.S. House of Representatives, *Manual on Drafting Style* § 325 (Nov. 1995) (discouraging drafters from including congressional findings on the face of the statute, except where necessary to establish congressional authority under the Commerce Clause, for example); Office of the Legislative Counsel, U.S. Senate, *Legislative Drafting Manual* § 124(a), (c) (Feb. 1997) (same).

(including many civil rights laws)—but broad regulation of local noneconomic activities without congressional findings raises "serious constitutional questions" under the Supreme Court's precedents. The Supreme Court, for example, has ruled that a federal statute making gun possession close to local schools a crime did not fall within Congress's Commerce Clause authority, because gun possession is not an "economic" activity and because Congress did not include a commerce-linked jurisdictional requirement.[28] On the other hand, the national security features of the Public Park Safety Act of 2021 suggest counterarguments supporting congressional authority to adopt prophylactic measures to prevent or discourage terrorist attacks. If a court were persuaded that the law was necessary and proper to disrupt networks of terrorists and criminals through micromanaging local as well as national parks, the law might pass constitutional muster.[29] Or it might not. At the very least, the constitutionality of such a law is seriously debatable, and a broad reading of section 2, therefore, raises serious constitutional questions.

Because section 2 might be read broadly or narrowly, it should be limited to federal parks, even if one were uncertain whether the broad reading would actually be unconstitutional. Under the *modern version of the avoidance canon*, "it is incumbent on [the court] to determine whether the [agency's] exercise of its jurisdiction here would give rise to serious constitutional questions. If so, we must first identify 'the affirmative intention of the Congress clearly expressed' before concluding that the Act grants jurisdiction" over Central Park as well as private, municipal, and state parks more generally.[30]

MODERN AVOIDANCE CANON

1. Statute is ambiguous: it can mean either A or B.
2. Interpretation A would raise serious constitutional difficulties, while Interpretation B would not.
3. *Therefore,* Court should choose Interpretation B.

---

[28] *United States v. Lopez,* 514 U.S. 549, 561 (1995) (striking down a federal law targeting persons who have a gun in proximity to local schools, in part because there was no factual record or congressional findings linking this activity to interstate commerce, and in part because gun possession is not an "economic" activity).

[29] For cases allowing congressional regulation to disrupt patterns of illegality, see *Gonzales v. Raich*, 545 U.S. 1 (2005); *United States v. Haney*, 264 F.3d 1161 (10th Cir. 2001).

[30] *NLRB v. Catholic Bishop of Chicago*, 440 U.S. 490, 501 (1979) (leading recent case); *Delaware & Hudson Co. v. United States*, 213 U.S. 366 (1909) (leading case).

Although the line is not unwavering, modern avoidance allows more flexibility than classic avoidance, because the court does not commit itself to the precept that the broader interpretation is actually unconstitutional. Modern avoidance is much more often cited than classic avoidance and is a popular canon among both Supreme Court Justices[31] and state court judges all over the country.[32]

Among commentators and judges, however, modern avoidance is much more controversial than classic avoidance.[33] The stealth constitutionalism objection is more powerful as an objection to modern avoidance, because the court not only avoids striking down a statute but also avoids a firm statement of the constitutional rule. This opens up a space for more aggressive judicial narrowing of otherwise clear statutory texts and for sneaking half-formed, often untenable ideas into constitutional doctrine.[34] But the question recurs: How significant a problem is this? In the example offered here, there is a genuine ambiguity, and the avoidance canon suggests a narrow interpretation that is also supported by the practicalities of the situation. If the 2021 vehicles in the park law were read broadly, to regulate not only Central Park but also every other public park in

---

[31] E.g., *Descamps v. United States*, 133 S.Ct. 2276, 2288–89 (2013); *Brown v. Plata*, 131 S.Ct. at 1928–29, 1937; *Northwest Austin Mun. Utility Dist. No. One v. Holder*, 557 U.S. 193 (2009); *Rapanos v. United States*, 547 U.S. 715 (2006) (plurality opinion); *Zadvydas v. Davis*, 533 U.S. 678, 696–99 (2001); *Public Citizen v. United States Dep't of Justice*, 491 U.S. 440, 465–66 (1989); *Edward J. DeBartolo Corp. v. Florida Gulf Coast Building & Constr. Trades Council*, 485 U.S. 568, 575 (1988).

[32] For a variety of state court deployments of modern avoidance, see *People v. Chandler*, 332 P.3d 538, 560 (Cal. 2014); *People v. Leiva*, 297 P.3d 870, 876–77 (Cal. 2013); *Le Francois v. Goel*, 112 P.3d 636 (Cal. 2005); *Gay Rights Coalition v. Georgetown University*, 536 A.2d 1 (D.C. en banc 1987) (opinion of Mack, J.); *Palm Beach County Canvassing Bd. v. Harris*, 772 So.2d 1220 (Fla. 2000), vacated sub nom. *Bush v. Palm Beach County Canvassing Bd.*, 531 U.S. 70 (2000); *People v. McKinley*, 852 N.W.2d 770 (Mich. 2014); *Overstock.com, Inc. v. New York State Dept. of Taxation & Fin.*, 987 N.E.2d 621 (N.Y. 2013); *People v. Baker*, 984 N.E.2d 902 (N.Y. 2013); *In re Jacob*, 660 N.E.2d 397 (N.Y. 1995) (Kaye, C.J.); *Marcus Cable Assocs., L.P. v. Krohn*, 90 S.W.3d 697, 706–07 (Tex. 2002). By my reading, the Florida Supreme Court has relied on classic avoidance more often than modern avoidance, a practice that is very unusual these days. E.g., *License Acquisitions, LLC v. Debary Real Estate Holdings, LLC*, 155 So.3d 1137, 1146–47 (Fla. 2014); *McNeil v. Canty*, 12 So.3d 215 (Fla. 2009).

[33] Nagle, Delaware & Hudson *Revisited*, 72 Notre Dame L. Rev. at 1497–98 (identifying a 1909 Supreme Court decision as inaugurating the heyday of aggressive Supreme Court avoidance legisprudence). For other critiques of modern avoidance, see Henry J. Friendly, *Benchmarks* 210 (1967); Kloppenberg, *Avoiding Serious Constitutional Doubts*, 30 U.C. Davis L. Rev. 1; Harry H. Wellington, Machinists v. Street: *Statutory Interpretation and the Avoidance of Constitutional Issues*, 1961 Sup. Ct. Rev. 49, 67–71.

[34] Richard A. Posner, *The Federal Courts Crisis and Reform* 284–85 (1985); Eskridge & Frickey, *Law as Equilibrium*, 108 Harv. L. Rev. at 81–87.

the United States, a whole host of questions must also be considered: What counts as a "public park"? Many private spaces are called "parks" but might not be appropriate for federal regulation. Ought the National Park Service make special rules for amusement parks, which require vehicles on site? Other kinds of private parks? Municipal parks, generally? Or only those municipal parks that are not large and sprawling the way Central Park is?

Who would enforce the statute and rules for the different kinds of parks? The United States Park Police would presumably enforce the rules for national parks—but would they also enforce them for state and municipal parks? Privately owned parks, including amusement parks? Does the Park Police have the resources to do so? If not, would there not be constitutional difficulties with federal commandeering local police to enforce the federal rules?[35] These questions, and others, remind us of the administrability canon (chapter two), which reinforces the suggestion that the 2021 statute should be interpreted cautiously, to avoid a thorny thicket of implementation issues.

With this example in mind, one might say that the modern avoidance canon is most defensible when (1) the statute is deeply and not just conveniently ambiguous as to how extensive a change Congress is making in the legal status quo, (2) there is a genuinely serious constitutional doubt about one plausible interpretation and (3) the constitutional issue is not "ripe" for judicial determination, for prudential and practical reasons. As the late Philip Frickey argued in support of the second and third conditions, many of the Supreme Court's applications of modern avoidance have been in cases where the Court had insufficient information or too little political cover to make a confident constitutional judgment one way or the other.[36] Very often, the Supreme Court *ought* to withhold firm judgment on whether a statute is unconstitutional. If the Justices are not certain that the statute violates the Constitution, they certainly ought not

---

[35] Cf. *Printz v. United States*, 521 U.S. 898 (1997) (striking down federal statutory commandeering of local sheriffs to do background checks for national gun regulation).

[36] Philip P. Frickey, *Getting from Joe to Gene (McCarthy): The Avoidance Canon, Legal Process Theory, and Narrowing Statutory Interpretation in the Early Warren Court,* 93 Calif. L. Rev. 397 (2005). For another example, *Catholic Bishop of Chicago* involved the NLRB's assertion of jurisdiction over teachers at religious schools; the Court was not prepared to say, on the record before it, that the Free Exercise Clause prohibited that, but the majority wanted a clearer directive from Congress before getting the NLRB involved in negotiations that might trench on the schools' religious missions. See *Catholic Bishop of Chicago,* 440 U.S. at 502–04.

strike it down—but neither should they legitimate the statute when they are not sure it meets the requirements of the Constitution. This is the point of the passive virtues, and one such virtue is the modern avoidance canon.[37]

Conversely, the modern avoidance canon is least defensible when (1) the statute is not really ambiguous and the narrowing construction is a stretch, in order to (2) provide a low-stakes preview of a possible constitutional rule that (3) really cannot be justified as constitutional doctrine, even when political conditions would permit judicial announcement. How often is modern avoidance deployed along these lines? Supporters assume that modern avoidance reflects an appropriate judicial deference to constitutional norms.[38] Critics maintain that application of modern avoidance is about as arbitrary as being struck by lightning; it is a transformative event but happens rarely and often without warning.[39] The struck-by-lightning metaphor is telling, as it suggests (correctly) that judges do not routinely deploy the modern avoidance canon to engage in major statutory invalidation or revision.

Federalism Canons (Anti-Preemption, Federal-State Balance, and Eleventh Amendment Canons). Let's continue to focus on the possibility that section 2 of the Public Park Safety Act of 2021 might apply to Central Park as well as other private, municipal, and state parks. Even if the avoidance canon were set to one side, other constitutionally inspired canons would press federal courts against interpreting the statute expansively. To begin with, a broad interpretation of section 2 would have the effect of preempting a great deal of state law. State and local law allows a lot of vehicular traffic within the confines of Central Park, including automobile traffic on public highways cutting through the park and horse-drawn carriages on roads internal to the park. A broad reading of section 2 to reach

---

[37] On the application of the passive virtues to support avoidance, and thereby effecting a "remand" to the political process for more deliberation in light of constitutional values, see Alexander M. Bickel & Harry H. Wellington, *Legislative Purpose and the Judicial Process: The Lincoln Mills Case*, 71 Harv. L. Rev. 1, 34–35 (1957); Frickey, *Avoidance Canon, Legal Process*, 93 Calif. L. Rev. at 455–59; Lawrence Gene Sager, *Fair Measure: The Legal Status of Underenforced Constitutional Norms*, 91 Harv. L. Rev. 1212 (1978).

[38] For academic support of the modern avoidance canon, see William N. Eskridge Jr., *Dynamic Statutory Interpretation* ch. 6 (1994); Antonin Scalia & Bryan A. Garner, *Reading Law: The Interpretation of Legal Texts* 247–51 (2012); Frickey, *Avoidance Canon, Legal Process*, 93 Calif. L. Rev. at 455–59.

[39] Richard L. Hasen, *Constitutional Avoidance and Anti-Avoidance by the Roberts Court*, 2009 Sup. Ct. Rev. 181, 189, 195–213 (2009).

municipal and other local parks would nullify at least some of those state and local law allowances under the Supremacy Clause. As above, this radical change would generate a host of practical and legal questions: Would New York City have to close all the roads running through Central Park, connecting the East Side and West Side of Manhattan? Would the federal statute bar horse-drawn carriages? Small vehicles used for park maintenance? Bicycles? Why did Congress not create transition rules and an administrative structure to implement such a preemptive measure?

The *anti-preemption canon* cautions against such an interpretation. Where Congress has legislated in a field which "the States have traditionally occupied," such as property, contract, and tort rules, federal courts "start with the assumption that the historic police powers of the States were not to be superseded by the Federal Act unless that was the clear and manifest purpose of Congress."[40] An expansive interpretation of "public park" in the new federal statute would unsettle both state property law and local law applicable to Central Park and other municipal and private parks. These are areas of distinctively non-national regulation where reliance interests and continuity are especially important, and so federal courts have recognized an additional federalism consideration that we might call the *federal-state balance canon*: "[I]t is incumbent upon the federal courts to be certain of Congress' intent before finding that federal law overrides" the "usual constitutional balance of federal and state powers," especially for rules pertaining to state governance, property rights, and criminal law.[41]

The federal-state-balance canon and other new federalism canons have proliferated in the last generation; the appendix to this volume lists them, together with Supreme Court decisions applying

---

[40] *Rice v. Santa Fe Elevator Co.,* 331 U.S. 218, 230 (1947) (leading case), followed in *CTS Corp. v. Waldburger*, 134 S.Ct. 2175, 2188–89 (2014); *Wyeth v. Levine*, 555 U.S. 555, 561 (2009); *Altria Group, Inc. v. Good*, 555 U.S. 70, 77 (2008); *Cipollone v. Liggett Group, Inc.*, 505 U.S. 504 (1992); see Nina A. Mendelson, Chevron *and Preemption,* 102 Mich. L. Rev. 737 (2004); President Barack Obama, Memorandum on Preemption, 2009 Daily Comp. Pres. Doc. 384 (May 20, 2009) (admonishing agencies not to interpret federal law to preempt state law without a compelling statutory purpose as the foundation); cf. *Cohens v. Virginia*, 19 U.S. 264, 443, 447 (1821) (early statement of the anti-preemption precept). But see *PLIVA, Inc. v. Mensing*, 131 S.Ct. 2567, 2579–80 (2011) (Thomas, J., for a plurality) (invoking the Supremacy Clause to argue against judicial efforts to reconcile apparently conflicting federal and state laws, even in areas traditionally dominated by state law, such as tort liability).

[41] *Gregory v. Ashcroft*, 501 U.S. 452, 460 (1991) (state governance); accord, *Bond v. United States*, 134 S.Ct. 2077, 2088 (2014) (criminal law); *BFP v. Resolution Trust Corporation*, 511 U.S. 531, 544 (1994) (property rights).

them. Like modern avoidance, the federalism canons have generated more than their share of criticism. For example, they seem malleable and not entirely predictable in application. At the Supreme Court level, Justices in federalism cases tend to vote their political preferences more than the nation's federalism principles. Liberal Justices tend to embrace federalism when state law is pro-consumer or environmentally friendly, while conservative Justices tend to embrace it when state law protects business interests.[42] It seems to be the case that appellate judges much too often invoke the constitutional canons selectively in order to advance their own views about the correct resolution of public law controversies. Because constitutional canons are more likely to be relevant in normatively charged cases, their selective deployment is more apparent than is the deployment of textual, precedential, legislative history, and agency deference canons, which are potentially relevant to the broad range of cases.

On the other hand, the public values reflected in these federalism canons are widely admired and enjoy popularity among We the People as well as those in government. Federalism is a central feature of the Constitution, perhaps the greatest constitutional innovation we have offered world history. Political scientists and law professors believe that federalism is an unusually efficient form of governance, as the local governments are in competition with one another and thus have incentives to govern effectively.[43] In light of this relative consensus, it is ironic that federalism guarantees are what Larry Sager calls "underenforced constitutional norms": courts are loathe to invalidate federal statutes on federalism grounds but are much more willing to narrow ambiguous statutes to protect state regulatory primacy, especially in areas such as property and contract.[44]

---

[42] Compare Frank B. Cross & Emerson H. Tiller, *The Three Faces of Federalism: An Empirical Assessment of Supreme Court Federalism Jurisprudence*, 73 S. Cal. L. Rev. 741, 753–54, 757 n.81, 761–62 (2000) (showing that liberal Justices are likely to invoke federalism to defeat business plaintiffs and support consumers), with Richard H. Fallon, Jr., *The "Conservative" Paths of the Rehnquist Court's Federalism,* 69 U. Chi. L. Rev. 429, 471–72 (2002) (showing that conservative Justices are likely to invoke federalism to support business and state interests and less likely when consumers would benefit from federalism canons).

[43] Roderick M. Hills, Jr., *Against Preemption: How Federalism Can Improve the National Legislative Process*, 82 N.Y.U. L. Rev. 1 (2007).

[44] Lawrence Gene Sager, *Fair Measure: The Legal Status of Underenforced Constitutional Norms*, 91 Harv. L. Rev. 1212 (1978), applied to the federalism canons by Eskridge & Frickey, *Quasi-Constitutional Law*, 45 Vand. L. Rev. at 630–36.

Additionally, the federalism canons probably match reasonably well with federal as well as state legislative expectations. In their comprehensive survey, Abbe Gluck and Lisa Schultz Bressman report that congressional drafting staff are usually aware of the federalism canons and draft statutes with those presumptions in mind.[45] There is good reason to believe, therefore, that if Congress in 2021 wants to sweep private, municipal, and state parks within the new vehicles in the park law, legislators would have addressed the issue specifically. (Indeed, the law would almost certainly have been considerably more complicated, as drafters would have carved out a complicated array of compromises to accommodate state regulatory interests.) These federalism canons, therefore, fit better with the notion of a Congress-Court dialogue than many others—though Professors Gluck and Bressman caution that congressional staff do not quite understand the operation of federalism canons as clear statement rules, especially when applied with super-strong bite.[46]

The democratic accountability risks of the federalism canons are most alarmingly reflected in the Supreme Court's *Eleventh Amendment canon*. Assume that federal judges interpret the Public Park Safety Act of 2021 to apply to state parks. Iowa fails to implement the new law, with terrible consequences. Mia and Jack Cudahy are young people taking a family vacation in Iowa with their learned parents; they are enjoying a summer day in a state park, until an insane dirt biker runs into them. The injuries are minor, but the young Cudahys and their lawyer parents are outraged that Iowa had posted no signs and made no effort to bar motor vehicles from a state park that attracted nature-lovers such as them. Through their parents as their representatives, Mia and Jack Cudahy file a federal damages lawsuit against the State of Iowa, the Iowa Department of Natural Resources, and Mike Giannotto, once a Segway operator but now, after his disastrous experience in Lafayette Park, an Iowa tour guide leading people through state parks on dirt bikes.

Iowa and its Department of Natural Resources will have many defenses on the merits of the lawsuit, which asserts both state law tort claims and section 1983 damage claims for violating a federal statute. But their easiest defense, and the one that will secure a swift dismissal of the lawsuit against them, would be sovereign immunity. As interpreted by the Supreme Court, the Eleventh Amendment

---

[45] Gluck & Bressman, *Statutory Interpretation from the Inside, Part I,* 65 Stan. L. Rev. at 942–44.

[46] See id. at 945–46.

guarantees the state and state organs immunity from damages suits in state or federal court.[47] Congress may abrogate that immunity under its Fourteenth Amendment and its Bankruptcy Clause powers, but not under its Commerce Clause powers.[48] Assume that the Supreme Court would recognize a congressional abrogation authority for the kind of statutory advance made in the Nation's Soil Act. Has Congress abrogated that constitutional immunity in the Public Park Safety Act of 2021?

Section 4(a) provides that "[p]ersons injured because of conduct violating this Act shall have a claim for relief against the government if its agents have not implemented this Act." Iowa and the Department might be "the government" the statute says may be sued, but a federal judge might hold that section 4(a) is not a congressional abrogation of Eleventh Amendment immunity.[49] This suggestion will strike the gentle reader as quite odd: Doesn't the statute explicitly create a cause of action against "the government"? Wouldn't this provision be superfluous, without effect, if state governments retained their sovereign immunity? The constitutional rule is that "Congress may abrogate the States' constitutionally secured immunity from suit in federal court only by making its intention *unmistakably clear* in the language of the statute."[50] This is an example of a super-strong clear statement rule. A big drawback of such a rule is that Congress and its staff are not aware that statutes need to be super-clear; sometimes, it has taken Congress three statutes to accomplish what the enacting coalition expected to have

---

[47] *Alden v. Maine*, 527 U.S. 706, 713 (1999) (broad interpretation of Eleventh Amendment protections, extending them to state court proceedings).

[48] Congress may only abrogate state Eleventh Amendment immunity when it enacts statutes pursuant to its powers to enforce the Bankruptcy Clause, see *Central Virginia Community College v. Katz*, 546 U.S. 356, 377–78 (2006), or the Reconstruction Amendments, see *Fitzpatrick v. Bitzer*, 427 U.S. 445, 456 (1976).

[49] Cf. *Sossamon v. Texas*, 563 U.S. 277, 284 (2011) (holding that states do not waive Eleventh Amendment immunity if they take federal funds pursuant to statute imposing duties upon state prisons and offering damages remedies against "government").

[50] *Atascadero State Hosp. v. Scanlon,* 473 U.S. 234, 242 (1985) (emphasis added); accord, *Nevada Dep't of Human Resources v. Hibbs*, 538 U.S. 721 (2003) (finding abrogation); *Raygor v. Regents of the Univ. of Minn.*, 534 U.S. 533 (2002); *Blatchford v. Native Village of Noatak*, 501 U.S. 775, 779 (1991); *Hoffman v. Connecticut Dep't of Income Maintenance*, 492 U.S. 96 (1989); *Dellmuth v. Muth*, 491 U.S. 223 (1989); *Will v. Michigan Dep't of State Police*, 491 U.S. 58 (1989). For an early statement of this canon, see *Chisholm v. Georgia*, 2 U.S. 419, 450 (1793) (Iredell, J., dissenting from the Court's reading of Article III, a dissent that was vindicated by the Eleventh Amendment).

been effected in the original law.[51] Now that Congress rarely passes controversial statutes and almost never overrides the Court anymore, the super-strong clear statement rules will reflect a stronger judicial influence on statutory implementation. The Eleventh Amendment canon is a valid rule of statutory interpretation, but its requirement of a super-strong statement from Congress is not supportable.

Severability Canon. Avoidance notwithstanding, assume that the 2021 Congress intended to regulate state parks and to render states themselves liable to lawsuit—and that the new vehicles in the park law violates the Constitution in doing so. If there is a constitutional violation, what should be the remedy? Should the entire subtitle—the Public Park Safety Act of 2021—be invalidated? Or Title 27, covering public spaces? Or the whole statute, namely, the Nation's Soil Act of 2021? The last two courses of action seem wildly disproportionate, and would probably be headed off if Congress included at least one "severability clause" in the omnibus statute. Such a clause would provide that, if one provision or cluster of provisions were constitutionally invalidated, Congress intends that the rest of the law would remain in effect. Generally, courts will give effect to severability clauses, so long as the unconstitutional provision(s) can be disentangled from the remainder of the law without fundamentally destroying the legislative design.[52]

Ironically, congressional drafting practice mildly discourages severability clauses—because the issue is covered by a canon![53] Since the 1930s, the Supreme Court has usually posed the severability issue as a determination whether Congress would have wanted the statute to remain in effect, without the benefit of its unconstitutional provision(s).[54] Like other counterfactual inquiries, this one eludes

---

[51] Eskridge & Frickey, *Quasi-Constitutional Law,* 45 Vand. L. Rev. at 636–40.

[52] E.g., *California Redevelopment Ass'n v. Matosantos,* 267 P.3d 580, 608–10 (Cal. 2011). Most commentators favor enforcement of severability clauses at least as strongly as suggested in text. E.g., Mark L. Movsesian, *Severability in Statutes and Contracts,* 30 Ga. L. Rev. 41 (1995); Emily Sherwin, *Rules and Judicial Review,* 6 Legal Theory 299 (2000); Michael D. Shumsky, *Severability, Inseverability, and the Rule of Law,* 41 Harv. J. Legis. 227 (2004); Robert L. Stern, *Separability and Separability Clauses in the Supreme Court,* 51 Harv. L. Rev. 76 (1937).

[53] Forstater, House Office of the Legislative Counsel, *Manual on Drafting Style,* § 328 (suggesting that severability clauses are typically not needed because of the Supreme Court's canon presuming severability).

[54] *Alaska Airlines, Inc. v. Brock,* 480 U.S. 678, 680–81 (1987) (leading recent case); *Champlin Refining Co. v. Corporation Comm'n of Okla.,* 286 U.S. 210, 234 (1932) (leading New Deal era case); accord, *People v. On Sight Mobile Opticians,* 26 N.E.3d 234 (N.Y. 2014) (mem.); *Horizon/CMS Healthcare Corp. v. Auld,* 34 S.W.3d 887, 902 (Tex. 2000).

consistent application—except that the Court has, increasingly, applied it with a canonical thumb on the scale. Thus, an unconstitutional provision is "presumed severable if what remains after severance 'is fully operative as a law.'"[55] As statutes have proliferated and have grown longer and more complex, and as federal judges have invalidated ever more provisions as constitutional violations, the stakes of nonseverability have escalated, and the Court presumptively refuses to throw out major statutes based upon the invalidity of one provision. "Generally speaking, when confronting a constitutional flaw in a statute, we try to limit the solution to the problem," severing any "problematic portions while leaving the remainder intact."[56]

This severability canon has the virtues of predictability and practicality: It almost always results in severance of the unconstitutional provision(s), and it allows important legislative schemes to continue to operate, usually pretty much as planned. Additionally, there is strong evidence that the severability canon is consistent with overall legislative expectations. In his survey of state legislative codified canons, Jacob Scott reports that "[l]egislatures are wildly enthusiastic about severability: it is codified in thirty-five jurisdictions; none have rejected it. Severability generally reinforces legislative power because it permits as much of a questionable act to survive as possible"[57] Typical of the thirty-five codifications is the Alabama one, which says that, if a provision or portion of a law is found to be invalid, "such invalidity shall not affect the provisions or application of this code or such amendment or statute that can be given effect without the invalid provisions or application, and to this end, the provisions of this code and such amendments and statutes are declared to be severable."[58]

---

[55] *Immigration & Naturalization Service v. Chadha,* 462 U.S. 919, 934 (1983); see John Copeland Nagle, *Severability,* 72 N.C.L. Rev. 203, 232–34 (1993) (proposing that courts strictly enforce severability or nonseverability clauses and, if there is no provision, require severability).

[56] *Ayotte v. Planned Parenthood of Northern New Eng.*, 546 U.S. 320, 328–29 (2006), followed and quoted in *Free Enterprise Fund v. Public Co. Accounting Oversight Bd.,* 561 U.S. 477, 508 (2010); accord, *National Federation of Independent Business v. Sebelius*, 132 S.Ct. 2566, 2607–08 (2012); *United States v. Booker*, 543 U.S. 220, 258–59, 265 (2005); *State v. Catalano,* 104 So.3d 1069 (Fla. 2012); *Hynes v. Tomei,* 706 N.E.2d 1201 (N.Y. 1998).

[57] Scott, *Codified Canons and the Common Law of Interpretation*, 98 Geo. L.J. at 385–86.

[58] Ala. Code § 1–1–16; see Scott, *Codified Canons and the Common Law of Interpretation*, 98 Geo. L.J. at 386–88 (discussing variation in state legislative codifications of the severability canon).

Notwithstanding these considerable virtues, the canon has been subject to critical comment. One criticism is that judicial invalidation of one portion of a statute, leaving the remainder of the statute intact, is judicial lawmaking; the statute has, in effect, been amended without the benefit of the Article I, Section 7 process that ought to be the only way to change statutory text.[59] Tom Campbell (a former member of the House of Representatives) proposes complete abolition of the severability canon and would substitute an anti-severability canon for this reason.[60] Dean Campbell's proposal strikes me as off base. Starting with *Marbury v. Madison* (where the Court invalidated a provision of the Judiciary Act of 1789 without tossing out the entire statute), the Supreme Court has for two centuries invalidated statutory provisions without serious claims that the Court was "amending" the statute.[61]

Dean Campbell's argument is a highly formalist exercise—but as a purely formal matter, judicial review leaves the statutory text completely alone and unamended. Congress may later repeal or revise the unconstitutional provision(s), but until it does so the statute remains in the United States Code—just unenforceable in those circumstances where it would violate the Constitution. Indeed, if a federal court ruled that section 2 of our Public Park Safety Act could not constitutionally be applied to private, municipal, or state parks, the U.S. Code would not only remain unchanged, but there really would be no need for Congress even to rewrite the law. Notice that this is the same result that would be reached by the avoidance canon or the federalism canons. In short, both the rule of law and democratic premises recoil at the notion that judges should not minimize the effects of judicial review when only one or a few provisions of a long statute traverse constitutional boundaries. Needless to say, considerations of governance weigh even more strongly against Dean Campbell's proposal, especially now that Congress is chronically unable to fund basic services in an orderly manner. How does this affect your vote in the case of the delinquent cyclist?

A more cogent criticism is that the legislative intent test theoretically followed by the Supreme Court cannot be applied predictably and ought to be replaced by a harder default rule. Sharply

---

59 *National Federation of Independent Business*, 132 S.Ct. at 2676 (joint dissenting opinion).

60 Tom Campbell, *Severability of Statutes*, 62 Hastings L.J. 1495 (2011).

61 Tobias A. Dorsey, *Sense and Severability*, 46 U. Rich. L. Rev. 877 (2012).

criticizing the Court's erratic case law, John Copeland Nagle urges that courts follow a text-based, rather than counterfactual intent-based, approach. Accordingly, judges should enforce severability or nonseverability clauses and, if there is no statutory provision, sever unconstitutional provisions from the remainder of the statute.[62] I agree with Professor Nagle, except that severability ought to be abandoned when the statutory design is fundamentally weakened or transformed.[63]

Nondelegation Canons

The Constitution allows Congress to delegate lawmaking authority to agencies and courts, but only if the delegation is accompanied by congressional principles and purposes that guide the exercise of the delegated authority and link it back to policy decisions made by our elected representatives.[64] In the last century, the U.S. Supreme Court and most state courts have declined to enforce the "nondelegation doctrine" directly, by striking down legislative delegations that are too broad or that do not carry with them the requisite limitations—but the same courts often have enforced the nondelegation doctrine indirectly, through substantive canons narrowing the scope of delegated authority.[65]

This odd juxtaposition—judicial refusal to strike down laws because of excessive delegation while at the same time narrowing some of the broad delegations—might be justified on grounds of

---

[62] Nagle, *Severability,* 72 N.C.L. Rev. at 232–34.

[63] *National Federation of Independent Business*, 132 S.Ct. at 2668–76 (joint dissenting opinion) (making a strong case for nonseverability and therefore invalidation of the entire Affordable Care Act if its individual mandate and Medicaid provisions were invalidated); David H. Gans, *Severability as Judicial Lawmaking*, 76 Geo. Wash. L. Rev. 639, 687–94 (2008) (viewing severability as a matter of remedies and favoring severability except where invalidation fundamentally alters the statutory scheme).

[64] *J.W. Hampton, Jr. & Co. v. United States*, 276 U.S. 394, 406–09 (1928) (leading case); see Thomas W. Merrill, *Rethinking Article I, Section 1: From Nondelegation to Exclusive Delegation*, 104 Colum. L. Rev. 2097 (2004).

[65] On the decline of the nondelegation doctrine as a matter of constitutional law, to be replaced with nondelegation canons, see *Mistretta v. United States*, 488 US 361, 373 & n.7 (1989) (observing that the Court has almost never struck down statutes for violating the nondelegation doctrine but has often construed them narrowly), elaborated in Eskridge & Frickey, *Quasi-Constitutional Law,* 45 Vand. L. Rev. at 607; William N. Eskridge Jr. & John Ferejohn, *The Article I, Section 7 Game,* 80 Geo. L.J. 523, 561–62 (1992); Cass R. Sunstein, *Nondelegation Canons*, 67 U. Chi. L. Rev. 315 (2000).

democracy and governance.[66] To begin with, legislatures cannot address the many social and economic problems facing the country without massive delegations to agencies, the courts, and the chief executive. Because judicial invalidation of even a fraction of these delegations would threaten the ongoing process of governance, and because judges have never devised workable standards for enforcing the doctrine in the first place, this is not a constitutional doctrine courts ought to vigorously enforce by striking down statutory delegations.[67]

Trimming back broad delegations through narrowing constructions of statutes is a less intrusive way for courts to give effect to the constitutional principle underlying the nondelegation doctrine, namely, that the big policy decisions in our republic of statutes should be made by the most democratically accountable and legitimate institution (Congress). Such a canonical approach is a workable and lower-stakes way for respecting and giving effect to an underenforced constitutional norm.[68]

Notwithstanding these virtues, nondelegation canons, like the other constitutional canons discussed above, have been the object of criticism. As with the avoidance canon, critics object that judges do not apply nondelegation canons consistently and often use those canons to narrow or even trim back statutes unnecessarily.[69] As before, the critics have never documented the extent of this problem: How often do judges deploy nondelegation canons to trim back statutes without justification? How often are judges disserving the democratic process? No one has even attempted to answer this question, but the empirical survey by Professors Gluck and Bressman has documented a strong consensus among congressional drafters

---

[66] See Jerry Mashaw, *Pro-Delegation: Why Administrators Should Make Political Decisions*, 1 J.L. Econ. & Org. 81, 91–93 (1985); Richard B. Stewart, *Beyond Delegation Doctrine*, 36 Am. U.L. Rev. 323, 324–28 (1987), responding to David Schoenbrod, *The Delegation Doctrine: Could the Court Give It Substance?*, 83 Mich. L. Rev. 1223 (1985). For the best defense of the nondelegation doctrine, see David Schoenbrod, *Power Without Responsibility: How Congress Abuses the People Through Delegation* (1993).

[67] *Mistretta,* 488 U.S. at 415–16 (Scalia, J., dissenting from the Court's judgment but agreeing that the Sentencing Commission's rulemaking authority did not violate the nondelegation doctrine).

[68] See Sager, *Legal Status of Underenforced Constitutional Norms*, 91 Harv. L. Rev. 1212, applied to the nondelegation idea by Eskridge & Frickey, *Quasi-Constitutional Law*, 45 Vand. L. Rev. at 630–32 & nn. 182, 185 & 191.

[69] Jacob Loshin & Aaron Nielson, *Hiding Nondelegation in Mouseholes,* 62 Admin. L. Rev. 19 (2010); John F. Manning, *The Nondelegation Doctrine as a Canon of Avoidance*, 2000 Sup. Ct. Rev. 223.

that Congress does not intend to delegate major questions to agencies.[70]

The deeper debate that the nondelegation canons ought to call forth is what role judges should play in the modern regulatory state. Given their institutional limitations and professional backgrounds, judges tend to be regulatory foot-draggers—and nowhere is their institutional caution better illustrated than in the nondelegation canons. The larger governance question is whether foot-dragging is productive. In our legal culture, the regulatory-restrictive effect of the nondelegation canons is most dramatic when the state is charging people with crimes that might subject them to imprisonment. For this reason, the rule of lenity is the oldest and most entrenched example of a nondelegation canon. Hence, I shall start with the rule of lenity and follow with two less well-known but very important nondelegation canons. These canons are entrenched in American legisprudence, but it is an open question whether they actually affect American governance and, if so, whether that effect has been salutary.

Rule of Lenity. In earlier chapters, the vehicles in the park law created a civil rule enforceable through fines alone. The more ambitious vehicles in the park law introduced in this chapter creates a criminal offense punishable by imprisonment or fines or both. Does this fact affect judicial interpretation of the law? The rule of lenity suggests that it does. The rule of lenity says that punitive or criminal laws cannot penalize acts that are not clearly targeted by the statute; if the judge believes that such a law is ambiguous as regards the defendant's activities, the government is supposed to lose.[71] Some judges express the rule of lenity as "a tie-breaking principle, of relevance when 'two reasonable interpretations of the same provision stand in relative equipoise.' "[72]

---

[70] Gluck & Bressman, *Statutory Interpretation from the Inside: Part I,* 65 Stan. L. Rev. at 994, 1003–04.

[71] *Yates v. United States*, 135 S.Ct. 1074, 1088–89 (2015) (plurality opinion); *Cleveland v. United States*, 531 U.S. 12, 25 (2000); *Crandon v. United States*, 494 U.S. 152, 158–60 (1990); *Liparota v. United States*, 471 U.S. 419, 427 (1980); *Bifulco v. United States*, 447 U.S. 381, 387, 400 (1986); *Rewis v. United States*, 401 U.S. 808, 812 (1971); *United States v. Shackford,* 27 F. Cas. 1038, 1039 (C.C.D. Me. 1830) (No. 16,262) (Story, J.); *Keeler v. Superior Court,* 470 P.2d 617 (Cal. 1970) (a leading state lenity case); *People v. Montes*, 73 P.3d 489 (Cal. 2003); *People v. Golb,* 15 N.E.3d 805, 814 (N.Y. 2014); *Brown v. De La Cruz,* 156 S.W.3d 560, 565 (Tex. 2004).

[72] *Lexin v. Superior Court,* 222 P.3d 214, 249 n.30 (Cal. 2010); cf. *Muscarello v. United States,* 524 U.S. 125, 138–39 (1998) (the rule of lenity only carries weight where "grievous ambiguity or uncertainty" exists in the statute).

The rule of lenity varies widely across the states, in part because many state legislatures have sought to abrogate this special rule for penal statutes. Enacted in 1872, the California renunciation is typical: "The rule of the common law, that penal statutes are to be strictly construed, has no application to this Code. All its provisions are to be construed according to the fair import of their terms, with a view to effect its objects and to promote justice."[73] Notwithstanding this statute, the California Supreme Court regularly mentions the rule of lenity but (consistent with the spirit of the statute) usually eliminates ambiguity through clarification provided by the whole act and/or legislative history.[74] In contrast, the Florida Legislature has largely codified the rule of lenity,[75] and the Florida Supreme Court enforces it rather vigorously.[76] In short, the rule of lenity is uneven and on the whole rather anemic at the state level, possibly due to its lack of political support and to the fact that most state appellate judges are subject to electoral checks, through retention or other elections.[77]

But at the U.S. Supreme Court, the rule of lenity appears to have some bite, as the government loses so many criminal law cases where the statutory text is broad and open-textured—precisely the cases where courts usually go along with agency interpretations, for the reasons developed in chapter five.[78] While criminal statutes are the most obvious and common type of penal law, many civil statutes

---

[73] Cal. Penal Code § 4 (1872 statute), copied by Ariz. Rev. Stats. § 1–211(C); N.Y. Penal Law § 5 (1965 statute); S.D. Cod. Laws § 22–1–1 (1939 statute); accord, La. Stats. § 14:3 (1950 statute); Minn. Stat. § 609.01(1) (1963 statute); Mont. Code § 45–1–102(2) (1973 statute); Ore. Rev. Stat. § 161.025 (1971 statute); Tex. Govt. Code § 311.035 (2015 statute).

[74] For recent examples of weak application of the rule of lenity, where judges strained to avoid ambiguity, see, e.g., *People v. Cornett*, 274 P.3d 456 (Cal. 2012); *People v. Manzo*, 270 P.3d 711, 718 (Cal. 2012); *Lexin*, 222 P.3d 214 (California).

[75] Fla. Stats. § 775.021(1) (1974 statute, subsequently amended to narrow application of the rule of lenity in abortion and other cases).

[76] *Kasischke v. State*, 991 So.2d 803 (Fla. 2008); *Liner v. Workers Temp Staffing, Inc.*, 990 So.2d 473 (Fla. 2008); *Griffis v. Florida Fish & Wildlife Conserv. Comm'n*, 57 So.3d 929 (Fla. App. 2011).

[77] Zachary Price, *The Rule of Lenity as a Rule of Structure*, 72 Fordham L. Rev. 885, 899–906 (2004) (highly uneven application of the rule of lenity by both federal and state appellate courts); William J. Stuntz, *Pathological Politics of Criminal Law*, 100 Mich. L. Rev. 505, 559–65 (2001).

[78] See William N. Eskridge Jr. & Lauren E. Baer, *The Continuum of Deference: Supreme Court Treatment of Agency Statutory Interpretations from* Chevron *to* Hamdan, 96 Geo. L.J. 1083, 1115–17, 1144–45 (2008) (demonstrating that the Supreme Court fails to mention the rule of lenity in most cases where it is relevant, but that the federal government's win rate is lower for criminal appeals than for all but a handful of case categories).

(especially environmental laws) have criminal penalties as well, and judicial application of the rule of lenity has been more episodic for these hybrid statutes.[79]

Judges' uneven or lethargic deployment of the rule of lenity is lamentable, given the strong rule of law and governance justifications for this canon (not to mention its antiquity). One justification for the rule of lenity is that the citizenry must have super-clear notice of what conduct is subject to punitive sanctions, so that they might conform their activities to the dictates of the criminal law.[80] While few criminals study the U.S. Code before hatching their plans, this due process value is important for the operation of a fair criminal justice system. For example, clear notice usefully limits prosecutorial discretion as a practical matter.[81]

On balance, the best justification for the rule of lenity is derived from the nondelegation doctrine.[82] As the Supreme Court has said since 1811, judges in our tradition are not empowered to create common law crimes, nor can Congress delegate to judges and prosecutors power to make common law crimes, because the moral condemnation inherent in crimes ought only to be delivered by the popularly elected legislature.[83] If the legislature alone has the authority to define crimes, it is inappropriate for judges to elaborate on criminal statutes so as to expand them beyond the clear words adopted by the legislature. There is also a separation of powers concern that judicial expansion of criminal statutes, common-law style, threatens to expand prosecutorial discretion beyond that contemplated by the legislature.[84] To be sure, the nondelegation

---

[79] E.g., *Babbitt v. Sweet Home Chap. of Communities for a Great Oregon,* 515 U.S. 687, 696–97 & n.9 (1995) (environmental statute); Bruce A. Markell, *Bankruptcy, Lenity, and the Statutory Interpretation of Cognate Civil and Criminal Statutes*, 69 Ind. L.J. 335 (1994).

[80] *McBoyle v. United States*, 283 U.S. 25, 27 (1931) (leading case); see *United States v. Lanier*, 520 U.S. 259, 265–66 (1997); *Keeler,* 470 P.2d at 624 (California); 3 *Sutherland Statutes and Statutory Construction* § 59:3 (7th ed. 2015); Lawrence M. Solan, *Law, Language, and Lenity*, 40 Wm. & Mary L. Rev. 57, 134–41 (1998).

[81] *United States v. Standard Oil Co.,* 384 U.S. 224, 236 (1966) (Harlan, J., dissenting); accord, *Evans v. United States*, 504 U.S. 255, 289, 296 (1992) (Thomas, J., dissenting); *United States v. Bass*, 404 U.S. 336 (1971).

[82] Daniel M. Kahan, *Lenity and Federal Common Law Crimes*, 1994 Sup. Ct. Rev. 345; cf. Price, *Rule of Lenity as a Rule of Structure* (lenity limits criminal statutes to the meanings for which voters might reasonably hold legislators accountable).

[83] *United States v. Wiltberger*, 18 U.S. 76, 92 (1820) (Marshall, C.J.) (dictum); accord, *Schall v. Martin*, 467 U.S. 253, 268 n.18 (1984); *Whalen v. United States,* 445 U.S. 684, 689 (1980); *Keeler,* 470 P.2d at 625–26 (California).

[84] See Herbert L. Packer, *The Limits of the Criminal Sanction* 79–96 (1968).

dimension of the rule of lenity has this odd feature: Unlike most other nondelegation canons, the rule of lenity is almost completely unknown to legislators and their staffs and apparently plays little if any role in the drafting and deliberation for federal or state criminal laws.[85]

Notwithstanding all these cavils and complaints, the rule of lenity has bite in American law, as illustrated by the 2021 version of the vehicles in the park law. Recall that section 3 defines excluded "vehicles" to include "any thing that is used for conveying a person or object from one place to another and that poses unacceptable safety risks." The ordinary meaning of this provision might be mapped onto the continuum this volume has been deploying. In my view, swift motorized vehicles such as cars, trucks, motorcycles, mopeds, and the like are at the core of the statute: Everyone calls these mechanisms "vehicles," and their speed assures risks to public safety that most of us would consider "unacceptable" in the context of a park. Conversely, most people would place slow-moving wheelbarrows, baby carriages, motorized wheelchairs, and children's tricycles as core examples of mechanisms outside the statute: They are conveyances but are not speedy enough to pose "safety risks," much less those that are "unacceptable" in the context of a park. In the penumbral region are mechanisms that convey persons or objects at speeds that create safety risks, but not necessarily risks that are "unacceptable"; these include bicycles, roller blades, and skateboards, all of which kids enjoy in park settings but also pose some risks for other park users. Figure 10 expresses my views, with the caveat that other interpreters would place some mechanisms in different spots along the continuum.

FIGURE 10

Ordinary Meaning Continuum: Mechanisms Used for Conveying Persons/Objects *and* Posing Unacceptable Safety Risks (2021)

Core Coverage		Penumbra	Outside the Statute
Cars & Trucks		Roller Blades	Wheelbarrows
Motorcycles		Skateboards	Baby Carriages
Motor Scooters		Segways	Motorized Wheelchairs
Mopeds	Bicycles		Tricycles

---

[85] Gluck & Bressman, *Statutory Interpretation from the Inside: Part I,* 65 Stan. L. Rev. at 956–57, 1016 (Table 3) (congressional drafters do not know about the rule of lenity and do not draft criminal laws with anything like that concept in mind).

If the 2021 vehicles in the park law imposed only civil penalties, Giannotto the Segway entrepreneur and Treanor the skateboarder (from chapter three) might well fall within the statute. If the National Park Service had legislative rulemaking authority, the *Chevron* rule would defer to directives including these penumbral applications in the coverage of the statute, as we saw in chapter five.

In theory, the difference the rule of lenity makes is that it would require the judge to rule against the Park Service in these penumbral cases (or for prosecutors to refrain from bringing charges, fearing that judges would rebuff them). So Giannotto the Segway entrepreneur, whom the agency could regulate under *Chevron* and perhaps under the *Skidmore* canon as well (where the agency presents expert evidence of the dangers posed by Segways), ought to be acquitted and might not even be charged if the rule of lenity applies instead. Segways fall in the statutory penumbra, but notice that bicycles fall closer to the statutory core and would require further reflection.

That is not quite the end of inquiry, even for Segways. The responsible judge needs to examine the entire statute and code, which might provide greater closure than the ordinary meaning of section 3 does. Recall that the new vehicles in the park law is embedded within a comprehensive security statute, the Nation's Soil Act of 2021. What are the overall plan and the regulatory history of this law and especially Title 27 ("Public Spaces"), within which the vehicles in the park subtitle is located? If the overall plan of this omnibus legislation were an integrated set of criminal prohibitions, civil obligations, and institutional arrangements aimed at making the nation safe from new forms of risk and attack, the responsible judge would want to examine precisely what those new forms of risk and attack might be and how much power and discretion Congress vested in the enforcement agencies.

In such an examination, should the judge consider legislative history? If the only justification of the rule of lenity were notice, the judge should probably be reluctant to do so; indeed, the judge should not readily find clarity through reference to the whole act, either. But if the rule of lenity is centrally justified by nondelegation concerns, legislative history illuminating the meaning of "vehicle" would be highly relevant if it reflected the kind of congressional deliberation and principle-setting that the nondelegation doctrine demands of the legislature—and judges who regularly consult legislative history in civil cases usually do the same in criminal cases.[86] Recall that the 2021 omnibus statute was triggered by another terrorist attack on American soil. The details of that attack, presidential and law enforcement evaluations, and congressional deliberations responding to the attack might be highly relevant to the meaning of "vehicle" in Title 27 of the new law. For example, if bicycles were involved in delivering bombs or triggering devices to the site of the attack, if the National Park Service testified before congressional committees that it needed broad authority to regulate bicycles and skateboards, and if the committees endorsed and relied on those concerns, that regulatory history would persuade me to include bicycles and skateboards (and probably Segways as well) in the new vehicles in the park law.

If the legislative history demonstrates that a fair reading of a statute that imposes criminal liability is in fact the meaning deliberated and voted by Congress, then such history may provide the clarity required by the rule of lenity. If federal enforcement agencies ask Congress for broad criminal law authority to police parks and Congress after deliberation grants that authority, courts ought not deny it. As Lawrence Solan has argued, the rule of lenity ought to confine criminal prosecutions to cases where the activity falls within the prototypical meaning of the statutory language, read in light of the statutory structure/plan and the legislative history.[87]

Once law enforcement officials have this authority, of course, they retain considerable discretion as to its exercise. If Liam Treanor brought his skateboard into Lafayette Park, it is doubtful that the Park Police would arrest him, and if they did arrest him it is doubtful he would be imprisoned if it were apparent that he was traversing the line because of youthful exuberance and not because of a conspiracy to invade or attack the White House.

No Elephants in Mouseholes Canon. Continue with the lenity theme for the newest version of the vehicles in the park law: Can Congress delegate to the Department of Justice the authority to issue legislative rules for criminal statutes such as the 2021 prohibition of vehicles in the park? Such regulations would have immediate effect as law and would trigger the *Chevron* rule—with

---

[86] E.g., *Manzo,* 270 P.3d at 715–16 (California) (legislative history clearing up ambiguities, thereby satisfying rule of lenity).

[87] Lawrence M. Solan, *Law, Language, and Lenity*, 40 Wm. & Mary L. Rev. 57, 102–15 (1998) (crediting the current understanding of the rule of lenity to Justice Frankfurter).

precisely the opposite effect for the penumbral cases than the rule of lenity. Thus, the penumbral cases in Figure 10 might all be decided *against* the government under the rule of lenity, unless statutory structure and legislative history revealed greater clarity. Under *Chevron*, those cases would all be decided *in favor of* the government, unless statutory structure and legislative history revealed greater clarity. Is this a constitutional regime for administering a criminal law?

My colleague Dan Kahan has answered this question in the affirmative and urges Congress to make such a delegation. Most other scholars do not believe this is a good idea,[88] but I doubt it is unconstitutional. It is hard to see the Supreme Court striking it down under the long-unenforced nondelegation doctrine—so long as the delegation were accompanied by principles the Department is expected to follow in its rulemaking. And the Due Process Clause's requirement of notice would actually be better served by detailed agency rules: Not only would the citizenry have a better specification of what is criminal conduct, but the specification would come more quickly and efficiently than it does through the lumbering common law process of judicial case-by-case adjudication.[89]

The critical question is not whether Congress has the constitutional power to delegate rulemaking authority to the Department of Justice, but instead whether it has done so in a particular statute and what limits the statute imposes on the Department. Consider the 2021 version of the vehicles in the park law. Section 4(a) is a delegation of authority to the National Park Service to "establish rules implementing this Act." Does this authorize the Service to issue guidelines having the force of law and triggering *Chevron* deference? Or does the rule of lenity still apply? What do you think? Reflect on what you have already learned in this volume, and then jot down your answer in the margin.

---

[88] Compare Daniel M. Kahan, *Is* Chevron *Relevant to Federal Criminal Law?*, 110 Harv. L. Rev. 469 (1996) (arguing in favor of congressional delegation of rulemaking authority in criminal cases), with Elliot Greenfield, *A Lenity Exception to* Chevron *Deference?*, 58 Baylor L. Rev. 1 (2006) (skeptical), and Solan, *Law, Language, and Lenity*, 40 Wm. & Mary L. Rev. at 128–34 (skeptical). See also Daniel C. Richman, *Federal Criminal Law, Congressional Delegation, and Enforcement Discretion,* 46 U.C.L.A. L. Rev. 757 (2000) (arguing that Kahan's proposal too quickly shifts criminal law rulemaking away from Congress, which makes nuanced institutional judgments when it enacts criminal statutes).

[89] Kahan, *Is* Chevron *Relevant to Federal Criminal Law?*, 110 Harv. L. Rev. at 488–89, 495–96.

The answer hinges upon a half-sibling to the major questions canon introduced in the preceding chapter. "Congress * * * does not alter the fundamental details of a regulatory scheme in vague terms or ancillary provisions—it does not, one might say, hide elephants in mouseholes."[90] Because legislative rulemaking having the force of law, displacing prosecution under the eye of skeptical judges, would be a major reallocation of authority in the arena of criminal law, the expansive reading of section 4(a) might be the sort of "elephant" that Congress would not put in the "mousehole" of a routine housekeeping section of the statute.[91] Like the major questions canon (which of course is also applicable here), the no elephants-in-mouseholes canon reflects concerns about the democratic legitimacy of courts and agencies making important policy decisions; such big moves are best left to Congress, whose members are directly accountable to We the People and whose structure assures that most stakeholding groups and institutions will have a voice in the deliberations.[92] As Professors Gluck and Bressman report, congressional drafters overwhelmingly see matters this way.[93]

The major questions and no elephants in mouseholes canons are ones that courts do not brandish often, in part because they reflect such an important norm that it is often invisible. Like most of the canons, but more dramatically, these canons represent a strong baseline of continuity. Interpreters assume that Congress does not depart from longstanding public law traditions without a clear statement on the face of a statute and/or public deliberation. A court applying section 4(a) might not even mention the no elephants in mouseholes canon, for the judge might find that the ordinary meaning of "rules implementing this Act" does not authorize legislative rulemaking in the criminal context, even though similar

---

[90] *Whitman v. American Trucking Assns.*, Inc., 531 U.S. 457, 468 (2001); accord, *King v. Burwell,* 135 S.Ct. 2480, 2495 (2015); *FDA v. Brown & Williamson Tobacco Corp.*, 529 U.S. 120, 160 (2000); Lisa Schultz Bressman, *Deference and Democracy*, 75 Geo. Wash. L. Rev. 761 (2007); Abigail R. Moncrieff, *Reincarnating the "Major Questions" Exception to* Chevron *Deference as a Doctrine of Noninterference (Or Why* Massachusetts v. EPA *Got It Wrong*), 60 Admin. L. Rev. 593 (2008). For the evolution of this canon, differentiating it from the major questions canon (and criticizing both), see Jacob Loshin & Aaron Nielson, *Hiding Nondelegation in Mouseholes,* 62 Admin. L. Rev. 19 (2010).

[91] *Gonzales v. Oregon,* 546 U.S. 243, 267 (2006) (very close parallel to the analysis in text).

[92] Lisa Schultz Bressman, *Deference and Democracy*, 75 Geo. Wash. L. Rev. 761 (2007).

[93] Gluck & Bressman, *Statutory Interpretation from the Inside: Part I,* 65 Stan. L. Rev. at 994, 1003–04.

language has been read to authorize legislative lawmaking in the civil context.[94]

Fee-Shifting Canon. Another kind of nondelegation canon strongly limits the authority of judges to shift litigation expenses from one party to another. Assume that the government prosecutes Mike Giannotto for riding his Segway across Lafayette Park and that the jury acquits the winsome entrepreneur. It is black letter procedure law that his acquittal does not entitle Giannotto to demand that the government pay his lawyers' fees. In contrast to the fee-shifting rule followed in other countries, the "American rule" is that each side bears its own costs and fees, unless a party behaves in bad faith.[95] Unlike the rule of lenity or the no elephants in mouseholes canon, the canon against fee-shifting is not obviously grounded in the Constitution, for its main referent is the longstanding pattern of common law decisions and statutes regulating and usually declining fee-shifting in federal courts.[96]

I consider the rule against fee-shifting to be a nondelegation canon because it, and the pattern of statutes and cases upon which it relies, reflect the Constitution's separation of powers and its grant (in Article III) of the "judicial Power" to the Supreme Court and "inferior" federal courts. Although courts can apply fee-shifting as a remedy for procedural violations and as a mechanism for controlling litigation misbehavior, the "judicial Power" does not authorize courts to redistribute substantive entitlements from one person or group of persons to others; redistribution is the province of the "legislative Power" vested in Congress by Article I.[97]

---

[94] The analysis in text is not to deny that Congress may delegate lawmaking authority through general rulemaking grants. E.g., *Mayo Foundation for Med. Educ. & Research v. United States*, 562 U.S. 44, 56 (2011), applying *Chevron* and finding that the IRS has legislative rulemaking authority under 26 U.S.C. § 7805(a), which authorizes the IRS to "prescribe all needful rules and regulations for the enforcement" of the Internal Revenue Code.

[95] *Alyeska Pipeline Serv. Co. v. Wilderness Society,* 421 U.S. 240, 249–71 (1975) (leading case for the American rule against fee-shifting). For recent reaffirmations, see *Baker Botts L.L.P. v. ASARCO LLC,* 135 S.Ct. 2158, 2163–64 (2015); *Hardt* v. *Reliance Standard Life Ins. Co.*, 560 U. S. 242, 252–53 (2010).

[96] See *Alyeska,* 421 U.S. at 249–71 (providing an exhaustive statutory and common law history, all premised upon and reinforcing the American rule against fee-shifting). See also *Baker Botts,* 135 S.Ct. at 2163–64 (grounding the American rule in the common law); Fed. R. Civ. P. 54(d)(1) (providing that the prevailing litigant should ordinary recover her litigation "costs," but not "attorney's fees").

[97] Cf. *Hanna v. Plumer,* 380 U.S. 460, 474–78 (1965) (Harlan, J., concurring) (federal courts must follow state substantive law regulating the ordinary affairs of citizens but may adopt their own transsubstantive rules for process); 28 U.S.C.

The baseline for criminal prosecutions is somewhat different than it is for civil cases. If the federal criminal defendant cannot afford an attorney, the Criminal Justice Act of 1964 guarantees the defendant counsel paid by the government.[98] Otherwise, however, the criminal defendant bears the costs of her or his counsel. In civil actions involving the United States, the Judicial Code provides that the United States may be liable in civil cases for counsel fees and other expenses if it loses and its legal arguments were not "substantially justified."[99] None of these foregoing general fee-shifting statutes applies to Giannotto's case, as he is a criminal defendant able to pay his counsel of choice. Section 4(c) of the 2021 vehicles in the park law, however, does explicitly provide for fee-shifting. If exonerated, Giannotto "will have a claim against the federal government for payment of any and all attorney's fees incurred in the defense." This provision satisfies the fee-shifting canon, and the federal government will have to pay for Giannotto's attorneys for their reasonable fees and expenses.

Now consider this issue: Does section 4(c) require the government to pay the expenses incurred when Giannotto's counsel retained an expert witness deemed essential for his defense? Jot down your answer in the margin. Does it make a difference to your analysis that the attorney's bill to Giannotto included, as part of its "administrative and clerical costs," the fee and the expenses incurred by the expert witness? Alter your answer if this information changes your view.

In light of the background norm, courts will give effect to fee-shifting statutes but will interpret them strictly. Thus, a federal court and most state courts would find that section 4(c) only allows fee-shifting for attorney's fees and not for other costs, including the monies paid to expert witnesses (even if those costs are billed by the attorney). "[W]hen a prevailing party seeks reimbursement for fees paid to its own expert witnesses, a federal court is bound by the limits of [existing statutes], absent contract or explicit statutory authority

---

§ 2074(a) (authorizing the Court to promulgate rules regulating procedure, but not to affect substantive rights). For a skeptical view whether nondelegation canons apply to the judiciary, see Margaret H. Lemos, *The Other Delegate: Judicially Administered Statutes and the Nondelegation Doctrine,* 81 So. Cal. L. Rev. 405, 455–61 (2008).

[98] Criminal Justice Reform Act of 1964, P.L. 88–455, § 2, 78 Stat. 552 (1964), codified as amended at 18 U.S.C. § 3006A.

[99] 28 U.S.C. § 2412(d)(1) (quotation in text). See generally Gregory C. Sisk, *The Essentials of the Equal Access to Justice Act: Court Awards of Attorney Fees for Unreasonable Government Conduct (Part Two),* 56 La. L. Rev. 1 (1995).

to the contrary."[100] Most commentators and some judges are critical of the stinginess of the fee-shifting canon, on the ground that its clear statement rule takes insufficient account of statutory purposes and legislative history.[101]

My sympathies are with the critics (such as Chief Judge Katzmann) who object that the fee-shifting canon is sometimes applied without appropriate attention to congressional deliberations. The standard response, that Congress and its staff are presumed to be aware of the canons and to legislate in light of their directives, lacks empirical support. The Gluck and Bressman survey of congressional staff did not ask about this canon, and the Congressional Research Service's statutory interpretation guide for legislative drafters omits it as well, even though it provides detailed analysis for no fewer than fifteen substantive canons.[102] Courts should consider legislative deliberations before interpreting fee-shifting statutes narrowly.

On the other hand, as a matter of overall coherence of the canons and constitutional principle, this canon is relatively entrenched as a strong clear statement rule, at least as regards expert witness fees. Recall the shadow precedents canon discussed at the end of chapter three. The Supreme Court has repeatedly held that statutes granting "attorney's fees" to prevailing parties do *not* shift expert witness fees, and so "attorney's fees" has now become a term of art. It is too late to disturb the entrenchment of that meaning—and its entrenchment is consistent with our country's common law traditions and with the constitutional principle apportioning distributional authority to Congress. Not least important, the fee-shifting canon is relatively easy for courts to administer.

---

[100] *Crawford Fitting Co. v. J.T. Gibbons, Inc.*, 482 U.S. 437, 439 (1987), followed and quoted in *West Virginia University Hospitals, Inc. v. Casey,* 499 U.S. 83, 86 (1991); accord, *Arlington Cent. Sch. Dist. Bd. of Educ. v. Murphy,* 548 U.S. 291 (2006) (following *Crawford Fitting* and *Casey*); *Olson v. Automobile Club of Southern California,* 179 P.3d 882, 884–90 (Cal. 2008) (same); *Pawling Cent. Sch. Dist. v. Munoz,* 788 N.Y.S.2d 267 (N.Y. App. 2005). See also *Baker Botts*, 135 S.Ct. at 2164–66 (stingy interpretation of bankruptcy compensation provision, requiring a clearer statement from Congress for shifting obligations to pay counsel fees).

[101] E.g., *Casey*, 499 U.S. at 102–03 (Marshall, J., dissenting); id. at 103–15 (Stevens, J., dissenting). See also Robert A. Katzmann, *Judging Statutes* 81–90 (2014) (gently criticizing the Supreme Court for pressing this canon in *Murphy,* where the legislative history made it clear that Congress voted for expert witness as well as counsel fee shifting).

[102] CRS Report, *Statutory Interpretation,* 18–33 (updated 2011) (detailed examination of 15 substantive canons but no mention of the fee-shifting canon).

Other Substantive Canons

The Constitution is the referent for the best known and most puissant substantive canons. The avoidance, rule of lenity, and federalism canons are only the most commonly discussed constitutional canons. There are other constitutionally-inspired canons that frame statutory interpretation in important ways but will not be analyzed in depth by this volume. For example, the *canon against retroactivity* reflects the constitutional presumption that legislation is prospective and does not apply to conduct and activities preceding the statute.[103] Although Congress and state legislatures often have the discretion to enact (noncriminal) legislation that applies retroactively, judges require a clear statement of retroactivity before they will so find.[104] Inspired by Article III, the *judicial review canon* presumes that Congress does not intend to cut off judicial review of final agency action without an affirmative indication of that intent in the statute.[105]

Nonetheless, most of the substantive canons have nonconstitutional reference points. The appendix to this volume reports more than a hundred substantive canons applied by the Supreme Court in the last thirty years, and there are surely a lot more that I have not noticed. Most of the substantive canons reflect norms applicable to particular subject areas; these background norms are grounded either in a pattern of statutory enactments or in a judicial or administrative meta-policy with which Congress might reasonably be thought to have acquiesced. Thus, federal and state

---

[103] *Landgraf v. USI Film Products*, 511 U.S. 244, 263–64 (1994) (leading case); see *Carr v. United States,* 560 U.S. 438 (2010); *Hamdan v. Rumsfeld,* 548 U.S. 557 (2006); *Bowen v. Georgetown Univ. Hospital*, 488 U.S. 204 (1988); accord, *Strauss v. Horton,* 207 P.3d 48, 119–22 (Cal. 2009) (ruling that California's Proposition 8, revoking marriage equality for same-sex couples, did not nullify marriages formalized before its adoption); *Evangelatos v. Superior Court,* 753 P.2d 585 (Cal.1988); *Florida Ins. Guar. Ass'n, Inc. v. Devon Neighborhood Ass'n, Inc.,* 67 So.3d 187, 194–96 (Fla. 2011).

[104] For the complicated operation of the canon against retroactivity, see Jill E. Fisch, *Retroactivity and Legal Change: An Equilibrium Approach*, 110 Harv. L. Rev. 1055 (1997).

[105] *Abbott Laboratories v. Gardner,* 387 U.S. 136, 140 (1967) (leading case); see *Mach Mining, LLC v. EEOC*, 135 S.Ct. 1645, 1651 (2015); *Utah v. Evans,* 536 U.S. 452, 463 (2002); *Bowen v. Michigan Academy for Family Physicians,* 476 U.S. 667 (1986) (detailed defense of the canon). But see Nicholas Bagley, *The Puzzling Presumption of Reviewability,* 127 Harv. L. Rev. 1285 (2014) (challenging the entrenched judicial review canon).

courts follow canons narrowly construing public grants[106] and tax exemptions,[107] to take a couple of well-defined examples. The Sutherland treatise sets forth dozens of substantive canons assertedly followed by state courts in the arenas of procedure,[108] domestic relations,[109] debtor-creditor law,[110] fraud and deceit,[111] social safety net legislation,[112] employment,[113] civil rights,[114] and environmental law.[115]

Jonathan Siegel maintains that different areas of law are informed by different normative baselines, and that scholars ought to develop and defend a roadmap of the background norms informing statutory interpretation in each area of law.[116] This is an exciting project; although well beyond the purview of this volume, Professor Siegel's insight ought to generate detailed studies of the background norms for each major area of law. (My appendix of canons might offer a starting point for several substantive arenas.) For example, freedom of information law—statutory requirements that governments disclose public documents upon request—operates under the general norm that, in our democracy, the public ought to have as much access to government information and data as is congenial with proper governance. The Supreme Court has derived this norm from the legislative history of the Freedom of Information Act of 1966, and from Congress's subsequent amendments rebuking the Court for

---

[106] 3A *Sutherland Statutes and Statutory Construction* ch. 63 (7th ed. 2015) (collecting federal and state cases applying the canon that public grants should be narrowly construed). The canon has not generally been applied when the grant is for a great public purpose, such as the land grants to railroads in return for their building the transcontinental railroad in the 1860s. E.g., *Leo Sheep v. United States*, 440 U.S. 668, 682 (1979); *Platt v. Union Pac. R.*, 99 U.S. (9 Otto) 48 (1878).

[107] *United States v. Burke*, 504 U.S. 229 (1992) (Souter, J., concurring in the judgment); *United States v. Wells Fargo Bank*, 485 U.S. 351, 357 (1988); cf. 3A *Sutherland Statutory Construction* § 66:3 (7th ed. 2015) (collecting state and federal cases construing tax exemptions narrowly). Some older treatises say that revenue statutes should be liberally construed in favor of the taxpayer, a canon that probably has little or no current vitality.

[108] 3A *Sutherland Statutes and Statutory Construction* ch. 67 (7th ed. 2015).

[109] Id., ch. 69 (domestic relations canons).

[110] Id., ch. 70 (debtor-creditor canons).

[111] Id., ch. 72 (fraud canons).

[112] Id., ch. 73 (social safety net canons).

[113] Id., ch. 75 (employment law canons).

[114] Id., ch. 76 (civil rights law canons).

[115] Id., ch. 77 (environmental law canons).

[116] Jonathan R. Siegel, *Textualism and Contextualism in Administrative Law*, 78 B.U.L. Rev. 1023 (1998), and *Guardians of the Background Principles,* 2009 Mich. St. L. Rev. 123.

stingy application of the original law.[117] In California, to take an interesting variation, the norm was explicitly added to the California Constitution by a voter initiative, and that state's courts follow an especially liberal approach.[118]

In the spirit of Professor Siegel's area-specific project, this chapter suggests some important meta-principles for the law of crimes—the rule of lenity, discussed above, and several canons discussed below. All of these criminal law canons are inspired by the norm that crimes represent society's moral condemnation of bad conduct carried out by a culpable state of mind. Such a condemnation must be delivered by the legislature after due deliberation and carefully confined to the targeted conduct. Following those criminal law canons are three canons relevant to transnational activities. In addition to filling in some of the details of the canonical regime for construing criminal laws and statutes touching upon transnational matters, the substantive canons discussed below have in common reference points that are both older and broader than the Constitution—the common law and the law of nations.

Common Law Canon. Earlier in this chapter, we considered whether the Public Park Safety Act of 2021 applies to New York's Central Park, and I suggested that federal judges would not apply the law to Central Park without strong whole act or legislative history evidence to that effect. Assume that Congress drafted section 2 more broadly: "No vehicles shall be allowed in any public park, including any municipal park." Assume, further, that this is a constitutional exercise of Congress's authority under Article I; there are congressional findings, amply supported by the record, that terrorist activity in municipal parks poses a threat to national security and that a prophylactic no-vehicles rule gives law enforcement officials a needed mechanism to monitor and arrest suspected terrorists and other malefactors.

As revised, the Public Park Safety Act of 2021 applies to Central Park. Soon after the statute takes effect, the American Ambassador to Spain, Columba Garnica de Gallo, has a serious medical episode in the southwest perimeter of the park close to Columbus Circle. Her

---

[117] On the liberal interpretation of the Freedom of Information Act, see *Milner v. Department of Navy*, 562 U.S. 562, 570 (2011); *United States Department of Justice v. Tax Analysts*, 492 U. S. 136, 150–51 (1989).

[118] See *Sierra Club v. Superior Court of Orange County,* 302 P.3d 1026 (Cal. 2013) (discussing the state constitutional requirement that statutes be read to give the public free access to government operations).

aide calls 911, and an ambulance (pictured below) speeds to her rescue. Notwithstanding the vehicles in the park law, the police officer allows the ambulance to rescue Ambassador Garnica de Gallo, who receives needed medical assistance in short order. Once the Ambassador has been rescued, however, the officer cites the ambulance driver, Kim Hom, for violating the statute.

Kim Hom's Life-Saving Ambulance
[EyOne, Photographer (2007)]

The United States Attorney decides to press the government's case against Hom. Assuring the defendant that she will only be fined, the prosecutor urges her to plead guilty and promises to use the episode to seek congressional amendment of the Nation's Soil Act to exempt emergency vehicles under certain circumstances.

The life-saving ambulance driver does not think this is right. Not only was she "just doing her job," and serving important public safety interests, but she thinks it's "crazy" to apply the park safety law to an emergency vehicle. "Congress was surely not focused on *ambulances* when it passed this law," Hom calmly explains in talk show interviews. Hundreds of thousands of blog posts support her view; a video of Kim Hom saving Columba Garnica de Gallo's life goes viral on the internet. The prosecutor responds with sympathy, calling Hom "a national hero" and a "safe-driving role model for everyone" in a press conference, but insists that "the law is the law, as written." So the statute applies to the ambulance, but police and prosecutors announce that they will use their discretion not to stop emergency vehicles and will penalize them only with small, largely symbolic, fines after the fact. Does the defendant have a *legal* response to the prosecutor's argument? As before, please jot down your thoughts in the margin.

For those gentle readers who were impressed by the absurdity canon from chapter one, you might consider its application here. It is not absurd to say that an ambulance is a "vehicle," in the abstract. Of course it is a "vehicle." But the apt question is whether it is absurd—beyond any reasonable inference—to say that the directive "public safety requires us to ban all vehicles from the park" includes ambulances in the ban. This is a close case for the absurdity canon. On the one hand, it is absurd (Hom called it "crazy") to say that a safety statute bars from the park a vehicle that is completely dedicated to public safety. Would the statute also ban fire engines if a building or tree were on fire in Central Park? To be sure, a speeding ambulance might run over park users, but ambulance drivers like Kim Hom have been speeding through streets of New York City for generations, with few pedestrian injuries. Pedestrians know to get out of the way, because these vehicles make a lot of noise and have flashing lights as well.

On the other hand, the police and prosecutors are making this case harder for application of the absurdity canon. They are not throwing the book at the valorous ambulance driver. Prosecutorial discretion takes the edge off of broadly written criminal statutes. (Kate Shaw pressed this point upon me.) Our legal and social culture is quite comfortable acknowledging that such-and-such socially desirable conduct technically violates the letter of the law, but that police or prosecutors or juries can show lenity to public-spirited people who violate the law in order to prevent much greater harm. While the statutory interpretation rule of lenity does not save Hom, because the statute is not ambiguous, the lenity undergirding prosecutorial discretion does save her from serious penalty. You can have your cake (the rule of law) and eat it too (Hom does not go to jail, the police are not seen as "going after" the honorable citizen). Do you agree with the foregoing analysis? How would you now decide the case of the virtuous ambulance driver? Jot down your response in the margin.

If you are knowledgeable about Anglo-American criminal law, you might have another answer to the puzzle presented by this case. The common law of crimes has recognized several defenses to prosecutions that do not fit the model of a willful lawbreaker who wantonly endangers or harms other people. One common law defense is *necessity* or *choice of evils*: Even though an accused person has done something that constitutes criminal behavior, she is exonerated if she acted to prevent imminent harm significantly greater than the harm caused by her violation of the law.[119] If I intentionally push you into the grass, I have committed a criminal as well as tortious battery—but if I push you so that a speeding bicycle will not run into you, the law will say I have a defense to the criminal charge, assuming I can persuade the finder of fact that I was preventing imminent peril and that pushing you was the only practical means for me to save you from injury. Even if the criminal battery statute contains no language suggesting a necessity defense, state courts might read that defense into the statute, as a widely accepted common law defense.[120]

Recall the term of art canon in chapter one and the common law version of that canon in chapter three. The term of art canon says that when the legislature uses common law terminology and does not otherwise define the term, courts presumptively follow the common law meaning. Consider, now, a related but broader precept. Under the *common law canon,* courts will assume that legislatures act against the background of the common law and that relevant common law doctrines will be incorporated into the statute, to the extent consistent with the statutory purpose.[121] Nineteenth-century judges often said they should narrowly construe all statutes in derogation of the common law, but in the wake of the modern regulatory state judges are more likely to treat the common law as gapfilling rules that are applicable only if not inconsistent with the statute's text, structure, and plan.[122] Both the older and the current version of the

---

[119] There are several ways that the necessity defense might be formulated, but almost all of them are similar to the statement in text. E.g., Model Penal Code, § 3.02(1) ("choice of evils" defense).

[120] Edward B. Arnolds & Norman F. Garland, *The Defense of Necessity in Criminal Law: The Right To Choose the Lesser Evil*, 65 J. Crim. Law & Criminology 289 (1974) (influential article urging widespread adoption of the necessity defense); Sanford H. Kadish, *Fifty Years of Criminal Law: An Opinionated Review*, 87 Calif. L. Rev. 943, 966–68 (1999) (cautious analysis of the necessity defense, limited mostly to emergency situations).

[121] E.g., *Baker Botts,* 135 S.Ct. at 2161–64; *Kirtsaeng v. John Wiley & Sons, Inc.,* 133 S.Ct. 1351 (2013); *Pacific Operators Offshore, LLP v. Valladolid,* 132 S.Ct. 680 (2012) (Scalia, J., concurring in the judgment); *Wal-Mart Stores, Inc. v. Dukes,* 131 S.Ct. 2541, 2557–58 (2011) (equity practice); *Staub v. Proctor Hosp.,* 562 U.S. 411 (2011); *Dura Pharmaceuticals, Inc. v. Broudo,* 544 U.S. 336, 341–42 (2005); *In re Bradley Estate,* 835 N.W.2d 545 (Mich. 2013). See 3 *Sutherland Statutes and Statutory Construction* §§ 61:1–61:2 (7th ed. 2015) (collecting dozens of federal and state cases); Geoffrey Miller, *Pragmatics and the Maxims of Interpretation,* 1990 Wis. L. Rev. 1179, 1196–98 (analysis of the common law canon under a Gricean framework).

[122] *American Electric Power Co. v. Connecticut,* 131 S.Ct. 2527, 2537 (2011) (finding federal common law displaced once Congress enacted a statute covering the subject area). Compare *Shaw v. Railroad Co.,* 101 U.S. (11 Otto) 557, 565 (1879)

common law canon rest upon the norm that "changes in the existing order of things are generally effected on a piecemeal rather than a wholesale basis," the same precept of continuity and coherence that underwrites most of the canons.[123]

The common law of crimes forms a rich set of norms against which the Supreme Court sometimes interprets federal criminal statutes.[124] Ironically, however, the Court has not recognized necessity as a defense to federal crimes generally, because the defense is often at odds with legislative policy judgments made in particular criminal statutes.[125] The case of the intrepid ambulance driver, presented here, is an attractive one for recognizing a necessity (or choice-of-evils) defense. Ambulances are barred from entering Central Park by the ordinary meaning of the 2021 law, but if the ambulance driver can demonstrate that she was on a mission to rescue a park user in distress, then she ought to have a statutory defense for the infraction, so long as she is observant of park safety. Admittedly, this defense undermines the predictability of the statute's application—but that is an acceptable price, given the injustice of penalizing heroic people like Kim Hom and the strong public policy encouraging life-saving emergency personnel and their vehicles.

The common law defense that federal courts ought to read into the Public Park Safety Act of 2021 should probably, therefore, be a strictly limited defense, consistent with the replacement of the old canon against any derogation in the common law with the current

---

(statutes in derogation of the common law ought to be narrowly construed), with *Isbrandtsen Co. v. Johnson*, 343 U.S. 779, 783 (1952) (interpreting maritime statute to reflect admiralty common law unless inconsistent with statutory purpose). Some state supreme courts remain rhetorically tied to the old canon, requiring a super-strong clear statement to abrogate the common law. E.g., *People v. Moreno,* 814 N.W.2d 624, 625, 627–28, 629, 634 (Mich. 2012) (legislative intent to abrogate common law must be expressed in "no uncertain terms," quoting *Hoerstman Gen. Contracting, Inc. v. Hahn,* 711 N.W.2d 340 (Mich. 2006)).

[123] 3 *Sutherland Statutes and Statutory Construction* § 61:1 (7th ed. 2105); cf. id. §§ 61:4–61:5 (citing case law and state codes that curtail the traditional canon against derogation of the common law and defending a more limited common law canon such as the one explained in text).

[124] *Baender v. Barnett,* 255 U.S. 224, 225–26 (1921) (suggesting that federal criminal statutes should be read to include common law defenses).

[125] See *United States v. Oakland Cannabis Buyers' Coop.*, 532 U.S. 483, 490–95 (2001) (rejecting a necessity defense where Congress has premised the statute upon a decision balancing the "evils" in a way inconsistent with the defense); Stephen S. Schwartz, Comment, *Is There a Common Law Necessity Defense in Federal Criminal Law?,* 75 U. Chi. L. Rev. 1259 (2008) (surveying the federal case law and suggesting a narrow version of the necessity defense in federal criminal law).

form of the canon, which bows deeply to statutory purpose. Thus, if Ambassador Garnica de Gallo had merely twisted her ankle or suffered another kind of minor injury, it is doubtful that the common law defense should apply, on its facts. That is, the dangers arising from driving a vehicle into Central Park outweigh the need for the speediest possible assistance to the injured diplomat.

Scienter Canon. Assume that the Court of Appeals for the Second Circuit (the federal appellate court for New York) decides that ambulances are statutory "vehicles" and declines to read a necessity defense into the Public Park Safety Act of 2021. That is not the end of inquiry, as Kim Hom has an additional statutory defense to the criminal charge—that she did not "know" that she was driving into the fringe of Central Park when she rescued Ambassador Garnica de Gallo from her heart attack. She knew that she was driving an ambulance, that an ambulance is a vehicle, and that vehicles are not allowed in Central Park—but she did not know that she was driving into Central Park. Because the Ambassador and her aide had been able to make their way toward Columbus Circle (abutting the southwest corner of the park), Hom drove only into the fringe of the park. Although she had, technically, driven into Central Park, there were no signs alerting her to that fact, and of course she was focused on saving the Ambassador's life. Assume that Hom has a plausible factual basis for this claim: Is this defense available under the 2021 statute?

Although section 2 does not contain a "scienter" (knowledge) requirement, courts have held that "mere omission from a criminal enactment of any mention of criminal intent" should not be read "as dispensing with it."[126] Federal and many state courts will "interpret[ ] criminal statutes to include broadly applicable scienter requirements, even where the statute by its terms does not contain them."[127] Applying this canon, which is akin to the common law defense canon previously discussed, the District Court will probably allow Hom to argue her defense to the jury. Note that the scienter canon normally does not permit the criminal defendant to rely on the defense that she was not aware of the statutory bar to vehicles in the park. Although

---

[126] *Morissette* v. *United States*, 342 U. S. 246, 252 (1952) (Jackson, J.) (quotations in text); see *Elonis v. United States,* 135 S.Ct. 2001, 2009–13 (2015); *Ratzlaf v. United States,* 510 U.S. 135 (1994); *United States* v. *Balint*, 258 U. S. 250, 251 (1922).

[127] *United States* v. *X-Citement Video, Inc.*, 513 U. S. 64, 70 (1994); accord, *Elonis*, 135 S.Ct. at 2009–10; *Carter v. United States*, 530 U.S. 255, 269 (2000); *Posters 'N' Things, Ltd. v. United States,* 511 U.S. 513, 524 (1994).

courts usually do not allow accused persons to argue that they were mistaken about a clear legal rule, they do typically allow accused persons to argue that they were reasonably mistaken about the factual bases for their commission of the crime.[128]

The scienter canon is often more anti-democratic than other substantive canons, including the common law canon. Although it is a well-established canon, to which congressional staff have been alerted,[129] lawmakers apparently do not always take account of it when they draft criminal statutes. (My guess is that legislators would be less surprised by the strictly limited necessity defense than by this scienter defense.) By creating a potentially significant defense against criminal liability, the scienter canon undermines the governance functions of the criminal law, and without the obvious social benefit of the necessity defense. These costs of the scienter canon are substantially indeterminate but probably large—but, perhaps, so are the systemic rule of law and governance benefits. The benefits flow from the liberal norm that "wrongdoing must be conscious to be criminal," a norm that is "as universal and persistent in mature systems of law as belief in freedom of the human will and a consequent ability and duty of the normal individual to choose between good and evil."[130]

Like the other substantive canons, the scienter canon probably has some effect on public policy—but it is hard to figure out exactly what those effects are and whether they are generally positive rather than negative. Because of its connection with liberal notions of personal responsibility, the scienter canon is as old as liberalism and for that reason remains entrenched in American public law.

Extraterritoriality Canon. As revised in this part, section 2 now reads: "No vehicles shall be allowed in any public park, including any municipal park." Under this language, the United States Attorney might prosecute a motorcyclist who speeds through Central Park in New York City. Can the U.S. Attorney also prosecute a motorcyclist who drives his vehicle through the Wellington Monument (pictured below), located in Hyde Park, London, England? The reason is that police believe the motorcyclist to be a terrorist who

---

[128] *Elonis,* 135 S.Ct. at 2009–12; *Staples v. United States*, 511 U.S. 600, 607 & n.3 (1994).

[129] CRS Report, *Statutory Interpretation*, 30–31 (updated 2011) (detailed discussion of the scienter canon).

[130] *Morissette,* 342 U.S. at 250; accord, 1 W. LaFave, *Substantive Criminal Law* § 5.1 (2d ed. 2003).

is planning an attack on the United States. They want to detain him before he gets further in his plans. The Central Intelligence Agency apprehends the alleged scoundrel in Hyde Park and spirits him back to Washington D.C. to stand trial for violating the Public Park Safety Act of 2021.

Wellington Monument, Hyde Park
[Rasmus 28, Photographer (2010)]

Although the defendant, one Frankly Unctuous, concedes that Hyde Park is a "municipal public park," the precise terminology in the statute, he contends that this law does not apply to municipal public parks outside the United States. In making this argument, he would invoke an important substantive canon. It is a "longstanding principle of American law 'that legislation of Congress, unless a contrary intent appears, is meant to apply only within the territorial jurisdiction of the United States.' "[131] It is not enough that this 2021

---

[131] *EEOC v. Arabian American Oil Co.*, 499 U.S. 244, 248 (1991), quoting *Foley Bros. v. Filardo,* 336 U.S. 281, 285 (1949); accord, *Kiobel v. Royal Dutch Petroleum Co.,* 133 S.Ct. 1659 (2013); *Morrison v. National Australia Bank Ltd.,* 561 U.S. 247 (2010); CRS Report, *Statutory Interpretation,* 24 (updated 2011); Scalia & Garner, *Reading Law*, 268–72. For an early statement of the extraterritoriality canon, see *United States v. Schooner Peggy*, 5 U.S. 103, 110 (1801) (dictum).

law is broadly written to regulate vehicles in "*any* * * * municipal public park," for the *extraterritoriality canon* requires an explicit statutory statement of coverage outside the United States.[132] "The word 'any' considered alone cannot answer this question. In ordinary life, a speaker who says, 'I'll see any film,' may or may not mean to include films shown in another city. In law, a legislature that uses the statutory phrase 'any person' may or may not mean to include 'persons' outside 'the jurisdiction of the state.' "[133]

The extraterritoriality canon makes a great deal of sense, as illustrated by the case of the London motorcyclist. As a clear statement rule, the canon is fairly predictable; few judges would disagree with my observation that it prevents application of the no vehicles law to parks in Europe. Moreover, the canon seems consistent with likely congressional expectations. Justice Breyer, a well-regarded congressional staffer before his appointment to the bench, puts it this way: "In determining the scope of the statutory phrase we find help in the 'commonsense notion that Congress generally legislates with domestic concerns in mind.' "[134] In my view, practical governance concerns also support the canon. Especially in cases such as that of Frankly Unctuous, the canon "serves to protect against unintended clashes between our laws and those of other nations which could result in international discord."[135]

Practical institutional concerns, of the sort that also inform the *Curtiss-Wright* canon discussed in the last chapter, not only support the extraterritoriality canon but also motivate judges to enforce the canon even more stringently than they did half a century ago. Unschooled in foreign law and fearful that judgments supplanting or (worse) disrespecting foreign law would lead to repercussions, American judges are especially cautious before they apply statutes to conduct outside the United States, even when the accused is the aptly named Frankly Unctuous.

---

[132] *Morrison,* 561 U.S. at 255. On the extraterritoriality canon, see William S. Dodge, *Understanding the Presumption Against Extraterritoriality*, 16 Berkeley J. Int'l L. 85, 90–91 (1998).

[133] *Small v. United States*, 544 U.S. 385, 388 (2005); Katzmann, *Judging Statutes,* 70–81 (extensive discussion of *Small* and a related case decided by the Second Circuit); see *Kiobel,* 133 S.Ct. at 1665 (similarly concluding that a statute providing for "any" civil action did not satisfy the clear statement requirement of the extraterritoriality canon).

[134] *Small*, 544 U.S. at 389, quoting *Smith v. United States,* 507 U.S. 197, 204 n.5 (1993). Accord, Zachary D. Clopton, *Replacing the Presumption against Extraterritoriality*, 94 B.U.L. Rev. 1, 23 (2014).

[135] *Arabian American Oil Co.,* 499 U.S. at 248.

International Law* (Charming Betsy*) Canon. There is another, related, rule of law consideration that may have a role in the case of the London motorcyclist. If American courts took jurisdiction over a criminal prosecution of a non-American person for driving his motorcycle in a foreign country, the United States might stand accused of violating the law of nations. Customary international law is binding on the United States.[136] Although customary international law is not usually enforceable by private parties, they may invoke it to interpret ambiguous statutes touching on matters implicating the law of nations. Throughout American history, the Supreme Court has said that "an act of Congress ought never to be construed to violate the law of nations if any other possible construction remains."[137] This canon has provided a detailed set of "phantom norms" for judges applying immigration and asylum statutes, for example.[138] Sometimes this *international law canon* (also known as the *Charming Betsy* canon, after the leading case) comes into play when the government or another litigant seeks to apply an American statute to activities that occur abroad, the same kind of case where the extraterritoriality canon might apply.[139]

As understood by American authorities, international law allows a country to prescribe law with respect to

> (1)(a) conduct that, wholly or in substantial part, takes place within its territory;

---

[136] *Sosa v. Alvarez-Machain*, 542 U.S. 692, 729 (2004) (reaffirming the principle that "the domestic law of the United States recognizes the law of nations").

[137] *Murray v. The Schooner Charming Betsy*, 6 U.S. (2 Cranch) 64, 118 (1804) (Marshall, C.J.) (leading case); accord, *Permanent Mission of India to the United Nations v. City of New York*, 551 U.S. 193, 199–200 (2007); *Chandris, Inc. v. Latsis*, 515 U.S. 347, 358 (1995); *Weinberger v. Rossi*, 456 U.S. 25, 32 (1982); Restatement (Third) of Foreign Relations Law of the United States § 118 (1987); Harry A. Blackmun, *The Supreme Court and the Law of Nations,* 104 Yale L.J. 39 (1994); Curtis A. Bradley, *The* Charming Betsy *Canon and Separation of Powers: Rethinking the Interpretive Role of International Law,* 86 Geo. L.J. 479, 524–33 (1998); Ralph G. Steinhardt, *The Role of International Law as a Canon of Domestic Statutory Interpretation,* 43 Vand. L. Rev. 1103, 1130–31 (1990). See also Roger P. Alford, *Foreign Relations as a Matter of Interpretation: The Use and Abuse of* Charming Betsy, 67 Ohio St. L.J. 1339 (2006) (supporting international law as a canon for interpreting statutes, but not the Constitution).

[138] Hiroshi Motomura, *Immigration Law After a Century of Plenary Power: Phantom Constitutional Norms and Statutory Interpretation*, 100 Yale L.J. 545, 560–64 (1990).

[139] E.g., *McCulloch v. Sociedad Nacional de Marineros de Honduras*, 372 U.S. 10 (1963) (invoking the international law canon to deny NLRB jurisdiction over a foreign controversy).

(b) the status of persons, or interests in things, present within its territory;

(c) conduct outside its territory that has or is intended to have substantial effect within its territory;

(2) the activities, interests, status, or relations of its nationals outside as well as within its territory; and

(3) certain conduct outside its territory by persons not its nationals that is directed against the security of the state or against a limited class of other state interests.[140]

Given the description above, Unctuous's activities probably fall under none of the accepted heads of prescriptive jurisdiction. Perhaps the government could persuade a judge that the third head might be applicable, based upon a nexus between the London travel and the defendant's alleged plans to attack the United States.[141] But the law of nations also says that a country cannot exercise jurisdiction that would be "unreasonable," given (for example) "the character of the activity to be regulated, the importance of regulation to the regulating state, the extent to which other states regulate such activities, and the degree to which the desirability of such regulation is generally accepted."[142]

Most academics consider the international law canon an important principle for statutory as well as constitutional interpretation, but the treatises and many judicial opinions take a passive-aggressive stance, either ignoring this canon or seeking to give it a narrow ambit.[143] Curtis Bradley, for example, persuasively argues that a broad application of the international law canon tends to be anti-democratic, because Congress frequently legislates in order

---

[140] Restatement (Third) of Foreign Relations Law § 402. See generally Gary B. Born, *International Civil Litigation in United States Courts* 493 (3d ed. 1996); Curtis A. Bradley, *Territorial Intellectual Property Rights in an Age of Globalism*, 37 Va. J. Int'l L. 505, 513–16 (1997) (justifying the extraterritoriality canon in part by reference to customary international law's restriction of a nation's prescriptive jurisdiction).

[141] Kenneth C. Randall, *Universal Jurisdiction Under International Law*, 66 Tex. L. Rev. 785 (1988) (explaining "universal jurisdiction" for aggressive prosecution of terrorism, torture, genocide, and the like).

[142] Restatement (Third) of Foreign Relations Law § 403(2)(c).

[143] Both the recent Congressional Research Service report on the canons to Congress and Justice Scalia's recent treatise on the canons give due emphasis to the canon against extraterritoriality, see CRS Report, *Statutory Interpretation,* 24 (updated 2011); Scalia & Garner, *Reading Law*, 268–72, but say nothing about the international law canon. See also Steinhardt, *International Law as a Canon of Domestic Statutory Interpretation,* 43 Vand. L. Rev. at 1111 (making this point with reference to earlier treatises and articles on statutory interpretation).

to avoid rather than comply with international law.[144] Professor Bradley and other critics would endorse international law as a gapfilling mechanism, much as the common law is today, and as a meta-avoidance canon, which (like the constitutional avoidance canon) acts as a restraint on hasty or overbroad congressional forays into foreign affairs matters better left to the executive branch.[145] It is in this mode that the international law canon has bite in the case of the London motorcyclist.

Borrowed Treaty Canon. Consider yet another variation on Frankly Unctuous's prosecution. In the wake of increased terrorist activity in the 2010s, assume that the United States enters into a Treaty on the Policing of Public Spaces, signed and ratified by the United Kingdom, Canada, Mexico, Columbia, Venezuela, and the United States. The treaty obliges these six nations, and others who join its regime, to adopt rules limiting "vehicles" in public parks and other venues where terrorists might concentrate their planning and pre-execution staging. Title 27 of the Nation's Soil Act (the title in which the new Public Park Safety Act is situated) is our nation's implementation of this treaty. Another part of the Public Spaces Treaty creates a transnational commission, with representatives from each of the six nations, to coordinate enforcement of the public spaces prophylaxis. The CIA apprehends Frankly Unctuous *only* after securing approval from the commission and cooperation from the British authorities. The negotiating materials and the executive branch presentation to the Senate confirm that the new vehicles in the park law allows each nation to prosecute suspected terrorists who use public spaces in any of the other countries. Does this change your thinking about whether the Public Park Safety Act of 2021 applies to the case of the London motorcyclist?

Even when they are not self-executing as domestic law, treaties create international law binding on the ratifying countries and so ought to have some traction under the *Charming Betsy* canon.[146] But the 2021 statute I have created is not an ordinary statute—it is a law implementing a binding treaty and, indeed, is copied from that treaty. Hence, the treaty is like a "borrowed statute" and ought to have interpretive weight along the same lines as borrowed statutes,

---

[144] Bradley, *Rethinking the Interpretive Role of International Law,* 86 Geo. L.J. at 495–97, 517–20.

[145] See id. at 525–29.

[146] Rebecca Crootof, Note, *Judicious Influence: Non-Self-Executing Treaties and the* Charming Betsy *Canon,* 120 Yale L.J. 1784 (2011).

analyzed in chapters two and three. Indeed, John Coyle has argued for recognition of a *borrowed treaty canon*, whereby domestic implementing legislation is presumed to be consistent with the treaty it is incorporating.[147] A number of Supreme Court decisions have followed a version of this precept, as they have interpreted domestic implementing legislation with extensive reference to the treaty and its background materials.[148] It is noteworthy that the leading decisions are not decisions handed down in the new millennium, however. One reason for the reluctance of the current Court to acknowledge this canon is heightened concern with popular backlash to consulting international materials to construe domestic law. Also relevant is that treaty interpretation is more purposive and dynamic than domestic statutory interpretation.[149]

Whether a judge recognizes Professor Coyle's borrowed treaty canon or not, the judge would surely consider the prosecution of Frankly Unctuous to be in a very different legal posture in light of the new treaty-based evidence. If the 2021 statute is implementing an earlier treaty, then the international law canon supports its application to Unctuous, so long as American officials have followed the treaty-based procedures. A tougher question is whether the treaty background provides the needed context to overcome the extraterritoriality canon, which the Court now treats as a rather puissant clear statement rule. The borrowed treaty canon as formulated by Professor Coyle would definitely say that it does, and I should agree, even for judges not prepared to add another canon to the list. The statute is broadly phrased ("any public park"), and so application of the borrowed treaty canon is completely consistent with

---

[147] John F. Coyle, *Incorporative Statutes and the Borrowed Treaty Rule,* 50 Va. J. Int'l L. 655 (2010). For scholarship making similar claims, see John M. Rogers, *International Law and United States Law* 106–27 (1999), as well as Jordan J. Paust, *International Law as Law of the United States* 13–15 (2003); Michael F. Sturley, *International Uniform Laws in National Courts: The Influence of Domestic Law in Conflicts of Interpretation*, 27 Va. J. Int'l L. 729 (1987).

[148] The best example of the borrowed treaty canon as the foundation for interpreting treaty-implementing legislation is *INS v. Cardoza-Fonseca*, 480 U.S. 421, 436–41 (1987) (interpreting Congress's implementing statute for an asylum convention). For other examples, see, e.g., *Vimar Seguros y Reaseguros, S.A. v. M/V Sky Reefer*, 515 U.S. 528 (1995); *Sale v. Haitian Ctrs. Council, Inc.*, 509 U.S. 155, 178–87 (1993); *INS v. Stevic,* 467 U.S. 407, 426 n.20 (1984). See also Coyle, *Borrowed Treaty Rule,* 50 Va. J. Int'l L. at 682–85 (discussing these cases); James C. Hathaway & Anne K. Cusick, *Refugee Rights Are Not Negotiable*, 14 Geo. Immigr. L.J. 481, 523 (2000).

[149] David J. Bederman, *Revivalist Canons and Treaty Interpretation*, 41 U.C.L.A. L. Rev. 953, 963–64 (1994); Michael P. Van Alstine, *The Death of Good Faith in Treaty Jurisprudence and a Call for Resurrection,* 93 Geo. L.J. 1885, 1903–04 (2005); Michael P. Van Alstine, *Dynamic Treaty Interpretation,* 146 U. Pa. L. Rev. 687, 700–01 (1998).

textualism and the rule of law, as well as respect for Congress, which ratified the treaty and then enacted this legislation specifically to implement the treaty. As to governance considerations, courts ought to defer to the executive and legislative branches about the details of the war against terrorism.

* * *

Pause to reflect upon what you have learned in the course of this volume about the practice of statutory interpretation. Most of the recent legal academic debate has been about the supposed clash between textualist and purposivist approaches to statutory interpretation. Posing the debate this way is either wrong or (at best) incomplete. Properly understood, textualism and purposivism are complements rather than competitors, two blades of a scissors cutting through legal complexities rather than two swords in a duel. It is incorrect to say that a vehicles in the park law cannot regulate bicycles; whether such a barebones law bars bicycles from the park depends very much on the statutory purpose. The nature and contours of that purpose, in turn, depend on a consideration of a good many other factors—including the whole act, (perhaps) the whole code, statutory precedents, legislative history, regulatory history, and background norms such as those developed in common law, constitutional law, and international law.

In the abstract, this all sounds quite complicated—but when you examine particular applications it's not complicated at all. Most applications of a vehicles in the park law will follow from a naïve reading of the statute, because the ordinary meaning of the language Congress enacted is going to be consistent with the rest of the statute and the rest of the code, with statutory precedents (if any), with the legislative and regulatory history of the law, and with the background norms framed by the common law, the Constitution, and the law of nations. For example, all of the relevant sources would press the interpreter toward including a small automobile in the statute and excluding a baby carriage. Most cases are easy cases under the pragmatic approach that Philip Frickey and I proposed a quarter century ago and that is the basis for the current volume.

What about the hard cases? The hard cases are not rendered easier simply because a judge says there is an answer demanded by one source, such as the ordinary meaning of a word or the holding of a binding precedent. The hard cases are "hard" precisely because the relevant sources for determining statutory meaning press in different directions, usually because the legislature did not think through all the possible applications of the statute (or could not have done so in light of unanticipated future developments). Thus, when section 2 of the Public Park Safety Act of 2021 says that "[n]o vehicles shall be allowed in any public park," Congress did not nail down the applicability of the statute to municipal parks such as Central Park in New York City. There may have been an assumption made by legislators, but they did not clearly state that assumption on the face of the statute.

It is statutory *abdication* and not statutory *interpretation* to insist that the law applies to Central Park simply because the ordinary American would say, "yes this is a *public park*." The law might well apply to Central Park, but the judge simply must investigate further. She ought to consider the statutory structure and legislative history, not only of the Public Park Safety Act, but also of Title 27 of the Nation's Soil Act, and of the omnibus 2021 law itself. Because I have not supplied further details for the Nation's Soil Act, we cannot reach complete closure on this issue—but I hope that most readers will agree, by now, that the anti-preemption canon, the federal-state balance canon, and the avoidance canon make it an uphill climb to say that Congress has regulated municipal parks in this law. That section 4(a) vests implementation of the law with the National Park Service, without any expansion of its personnel or its administrative apparatus, renders it even more doubtful that the law extends so deeply into local regulation.

On the other hand, a judge must resist the temptation to dismiss the possibility of Central Park regulation, without a more thorough examination of the entire statute and its legislative and regulatory history. Section 1 reminds us that the congressional plan is to protect not just public safety (like the Lafayette Park Safety Act of 1992), but also national security. The judge must keep her mind open to the possibility that Congress's plan was to bring all public parks, at every level, into the new regulatory network. If the 2021 omnibus law (especially Title 27) included other provisions expanding the administrative apparatus of the National Park Service and the United States Park Police, so that those organs could monitor compliance in local and state as well as national parks, then the expansive view of "public park" might be well-justified. But the judge does not know about that possibility unless she examines the entire statute and consults its legislative history.

I hope this gives you, the gentle reader, a better idea about how to deal with hard cases. You don't solve them by pretending they are easy. You make progress only by dedicating your intellect to an exploration of a variety of sources. Once you have considered ordinary meaning, the statutory plan, other relevant statutes and binding precedents, legislative and regulatory history, as well as pertinent common law, constitutional, and international law, only then, can you say you have *interpreted* the statute. And then you have graduated from this primer.

Conclusion

CANONS AND NORMS IN CONSTITUTIONAL INTERPRETATION

[Agnostic Preachers Kid, Photographer (2008)]

[Dan Vera, Photographer (2007)]

Baron Von Steuben Statue and Monument
Lafayette Park

Does the methodology for statutory interpretation outlined in the foregoing pages have any bearing on the proper method for interpreting the United States Constitution? Most of the leading theories for interpreting the Constitution find a direct parallel in the analysis posed in each of the chapters of this volume:

- *Ordinary [original] meaning* of constitutional language as it would have been understood by the typical American at the time of its adoption;[1]

---

[1] E.g., Robert H. Bork, *The Tempting of America: The Political Seduction of the Law* 74–84, 143–45, 154–55 (1990); Antonin Scalia & Bryan A. Garner, *Reading Law:*

- *Structure of the Constitution* as a presumptively coherent plan for the Union, unified by fundamental principles and policies that, in turn, provide a context for applying the Constitution;[2]
- *Precedents* decided by the Supreme Court, binding on the Court and on the nation as constitutional common law;[3]
- *Legislative history* of the Constitution and its amendments, especially state ratification debates but also (by some accounts) the drafting deliberations at Philadelphia (1787) and in Congress (for the amendments);[4]

The Interpretation of Legal Texts 78–92 (2012); Randy E. Barnett, *An Originalism for Nonoriginalists*, 45 Loyola L. Rev. 611, 620–22 (1999); Steven G. Calabresi, *A Critical Introduction to the Originalism Debate,* 31 Harv. J.L. & Pub. Pol'y 875, 883 (2008); Steven G. Calabresi & Andrea Matthews, *Originalism and* Loving v. Virginia, 2012 BYU L. Rev. 1393 (2012); Saikrishna *B. Prakash, Unoriginalism's Law Without Meaning*, 15 Const. Comm. 529 (1998).

[2] E.g., Charles L. Black Jr., *Structure and Relationship in Constitutional Law* (1969); John Hart Ely, *Democracy and Distrust: A Theory of Judicial Review* (1980); Akhil Reed Amar, *Intratextualism*, 112 Harv. L. Rev. 747 (1999); Akhil Reed Amar, *The Supreme Court, 1999 Term—Foreword: The Document and the Doctrine*, 114 Harv. L. Rev. 26, 29–30 (2000); Michael C. Dorf, *Interpretive Holism and the Structural Method, or How Charles Black Might Have Thought About Campaign Finance Reform and Congressional Timidity*, 92 Geo. L.J. 833 (2004); Vicki C. Jackson, *Holistic Interpretation:* Fitzpatrick v. Bitzer *and Our Bifurcated Constitution*, 53 Stan. L. Rev. 1259, 1279–81 (2001); John F. Manning, *Federalism and the Generality Problem in Constitutional Interpretation,* 122 Harv. L. Rev. 2003 (2009); Nicholas Quinn Rozenkranz, *The Subjects of the Constitution,* 62 Stan. L. Rev. 1209 (2010).

[3] E.g., Henry Monaghan, Stare Decisis *and Constitutional Adjudication*, 88 Colum. L. Rev. 723 (1988); Thomas W. Merrill, *Originalism,* Stare Decisis, *and the Promotion of Judicial Restraint,* 22 Const. Comm. 271 (2005); David A. Strauss, *Common Law Constitutional Interpretation,* 63 U. Chi. L. Rev. 877 (1996); David A. Strauss, *The Irrelevance of Constitutional Amendments,* 114 Harv. L. Rev. 1457 (2001); Ernest Young, *Rediscovering Conservatism: Burkean Political Theory and Constitutional Interpretation*, 72 N.C.L. Rev. 619 (1994).

[4] E.g., Akhil Reed Amar, *America's Constitution: A Biography* (2005); Raoul Berger, *Government by Judiciary: The Transformation of the Fourteenth Amendment* (2d ed. 1997); Alexander M. Bickel, *The Original Understanding and the Segregation Decision*, 69 Harv. L. Rev. 1 (1955); Vasan Kesavan & Michael Stokes Paulsen, *The Interpretive Force of the Constitution's Secret Drafting History*, 91 Geo. L.J. 1113 (2003); Ronald D. Rotunda, *Original Intent, the View of the Framers, and the Role of the Ratifiers*, 41 Vand. L. Rev. 507 (1988); William Michael Treanor, *Taking Text Too Seriously: Modern Textualism, Original Meaning, and the Case of Amar's* Bill of Rights, 106 Mich. L. Rev. 487 (2007).

- *Executive department interpretation*, especially relevant when there has been legislative deliberation and acceptance or acquiescence;[5] and
- *Background meta-norms* reflected in the common law tradition[6] and the law of nations.[7]

Many of the commentators cited in the footnotes maintain that the source they emphasize is the foundation for discerning constitutional meaning, but some have stressed, as I have in this volume, that proper interpretation must consider a variety of legal sources. The latter commentators include Daniel Farber, Philip Frickey, Philip Bobbitt, and Richard Fallon, all of whom have posed multi-factored, pragmatic theories of judicial review that are similar to the approach elaborated here.[8]

This is not to say that constitutional interpretation proceeds in exactly the same way as statutory interpretation. Quite the contrary, the Constitution and statutes are different kinds of legal documents, and their functional differences generate different approaches to interpretation. Most obviously, the Constitution is a very old and relatively short legal document, populated with open-textured terms such as "speech," "due process," and "equal protection." These

---

[5] E.g., *The Steel Seizure Case,* 343 U.S. 579, 610–15, 634–40, 659, 662, 683–702, 710 (1952) (concurring and dissenting opinions); Bruce Ackerman, *We the People, Volume 1: Foundations* (1991); William N. Eskridge Jr. & John Ferejohn, *A Republic of Statutes: The New American Constitution* (2010); John C. Yoo, *The Powers of War and Peace: The Constitution and Foreign Affairs After 9/11* (2005); Robin L. West, *Toward the Study of the Legislated Constitution,* 72 Ohio St. L.J. 1343 (2011).

[6] E.g., Ralph A. Rossum, *Antonin Scalia's Jurisprudence: Text and Tradition* 27–51 (2006).

[7] E.g., Stephen Breyer, *The Court and the World: American Law and the New Global Realities* (2015); Vicki C. Jackson, *Constitutional Law and Transnational Comparisons: The* Youngstown *Decision and American Exceptionalism*, 30 Harv. J.L. & Pub. Pol'y 191 (2006); Gerald L. Neuman, *International Law as a Resource in Constitutional Interpretation*, 30 Harv. J.L. & Pub. Pol'y 177 (2006); G. Edward White, *The Marshall Court and International Law: The Piracy Cases*, 83 Am. J. Int'l L. 727 (1989).

[8] See Philip Bobbitt, *Constitutional Interpretation* (1991) (developing "modalities" of constitutional analysis, namely, [1] textual, [2] structural, [3] ethical, [4] prudential, [5] historical, and [6] doctrinal); Richard H. Fallon Jr., *A Constructivist Coherence Theory of Constitutional Interpretation,* 100 Harv. L. Rev. 1189 (1987) (developing a pragmatic theory of constitutional sources, namely, constitutional text, intent, theory, precedent, and morality); Daniel A. Farber & Philip P. Frickey, *Practical Reasoning and the First Amendment,* 34 UCLA L. Rev. 1615 (1987) (developing a multi-factored approach to reading the First Amendment, which was a precursor to Professor Frickey's work with me on statutory interpretation, e.g., William N. Eskridge Jr. & Philip P. Frickey, *Statutory Interpretation as Practical Reasoning*, 42 Stan. L. Rev. 321 (1990)).

documentary features propel the conclusion that arguments from ordinary meaning and structure are not often going to be as decisive in the typical constitutional case as they are in the typical statutory case. The open texture of these terms invites a plurality of readings, and the antiquity of the document makes inevitable that those vague terms will be applied by a variety of different interpreters over generations, often in binding precedents that are themselves legal authorities. These features of the Constitution (and the difficulty of amending it) make it likely that evolutive sources—judicial precedent, legislative feedback, executive practice, and the law of nations—will play a larger role in constitutional than statutory interpretation, whether they are acknowledged or not.[9]

Two other big differences between the Constitution and statutes involve the policy and institutional context in which each is usually applied. Constitutional interpretation typically involves high normative stakes and is delivered primarily by "the least dangerous" and most vulnerable branch, the judiciary. Because they routinely involve big issues of governance and human rights, constitutional cases involve higher stakes than statutory cases—they affect Americans at a constitutive as well as policy level. Whether it is constitutional for Congress to enact legislation requiring everyone's participation in the marketplace for health insurance affects public policy in a really big way, but it also helps define who we are as a body politic. It is true that, in our republic of super-statutes, these high-stakes controversies are often played out through statutory rather than constitutional interpretation—and in those cases statutory interpretation operates in ways that are more like constitutional interpretation.[10]

While most official interpretation is carried out by executive branch officials, the high-stakes issues disproportionately end up at the United States Supreme Court. As Alexander Hamilton argued during the founding era, the Article III judiciary is the branch of government least able to deprive Americans of our liberties and least

---

[9] E.g., Jack Balkin, *Living Originalism* (2011).

[10] Compare *King v. Burwell*, 135 S.Ct. 2480 (2015) (high-stakes debate on whether the Affordable Care Act subsidies are limited to states where the state governments themselves establish health insurance exchanges), with *National Federation of Independent Business v. Sebelius*, 132 S.Ct. 2566 (2012) (high-stakes debate on whether the Affordable Care Act was a constitutional exercise of Congress's Article I powers).

capable of fixing important social and economic problems.[11] Lacking the power to tax or even enforce their judgments and lacking the democratic legitimacy of the accountable and elected political branches, courts cannot effectuate change on their own and may generate considerable backlash if they push too hard.[12] On the other hand, courts may wield considerable power to elevate the salience of public law issues and to reverse the burden of political inertia (so that groups excluded from public institutions are flipped into a posture defending their rights against political override rather than having to overcome the many vetogates needed to effectuate legislative change). We have recently seen this power operate in the marriage equality debate.[13]

These features of constitutional interpretation make it very risky for courts to decide constitutional issues prematurely. The risks of a definitive court decision before the body politic is at rest on an issue include popular backlash, loss of legitimacy for the judiciary, and frustration by lower courts trying to enforce the decision amidst popular resistance and conflicted views even within the government. As Alexander Bickel observed, these institutional vulnerabilities have motivated courts to exercise "passive virtues," doctrines and methods to avoid decision of combustible constitutional issues before they are ripe for adjudication.[14] Professor Bickel's passive virtues focused on justiciability doctrines (such as standing, political question, ripeness) allowing appellate courts to dismiss appeals without addressing the merits, but the passive virtues also include deference by courts to legislative and executive branch deliberations when they do address high-stakes constitutional issues.[15] Because agencies are usually the (expansive) first movers and because Congress is theoretically

---

[11] *The Federalist* No, 78 (Hamilton) (discussing the Article III courts, or what Hamilton termed "the least dangerous branch"). For updates of Hamilton's point about the institutional limitations of the judiciary, see Carl A. Auerbach et al., *The Legal Process: An Introduction to Decision-Making by Judicial, Legislative, Executive, and Administrative Agencies* (1961); Neil K. Komesar, *Imperfect Alternatives: Choosing Institutions in Law, Economics, and Public Policy* (1994).

[12] Gerald N. Rosenberg, *The Hollow Hope: Can Courts Bring About Social Change*? 339–419 (2d ed. 2008), applying the author's controversial "backlash" hypothesis to the marriage equality issue.

[13] William N. Eskridge Jr., *Backlash Politics: How Constitutional Litigation Has Advanced Marriage Equality in the United States*, 93 B.U.L. Rev. 275 (2013), responding to Rosenberg, *The Hollow Hope*.

[14] Alexander M. Bickel, *The Least Dangerous Branch: The Supreme Court at the Bar of Politics* (1962).

[15] William N. Eskridge Jr. & John Ferejohn, *A Republic of Statutes: The New American Constitution* 380 (2010).

available to correct egregious errors, courts do not have to shoulder nearly as much of the legitimacy burden of aggressive statutory interpretations.

To illustrate the foregoing points, I shall revise the hypothetical Lafayette Park Safety Act one more time, replacing the prohibited category we have been considering with another one that has recurred in American public law. To situate this final version, we need to explore some little-known features of Lafayette Park and its history. The park is dotted with statues of American military leaders, most of whom (like the Marquis Gilbert de Lafayette) were Europeans who helped the colonists prevail in the American Revolution. Less well-known, but no less important, than Lafayette was Baron Friedrich Wilhelm von Steuben, the Prussian drillmaster who whipped the Continental Army into good military order in 1778. His contributions are memorialized in an imposing Lafayette Park monument (pictured in the front of this conclusion).

Von Steuben's relationship with the birth of America is an interesting story. That the baron was even available to work with the Continental Army owes something to his affection for younger soldiers; his sexual advances were apparently a key reason for complaints against him within the Prussian army in 1776–77, at the very moment when the American revolutionaries needed expertise in military discipline and administration. Ambassador Benjamin Franklin met with Baron von Steuben in Paris and, notwithstanding his scandalous reputation, recommended him to General George Washington, who assigned von Steuben to introduce discipline, order, and morale in the troops. The Prussian exile did that to brilliant effect; historians credit the baron as a critical reason for the Americans' victory in the War for Independence and cite his influence on American military organization and practices for generations after his retirement.[16]

The von Steuben monument is topped by a tall, dark, and handsome statue of the drillmaster, below which is a written tribute to the baron and his two close aides and intimate advisers, Colonel William North and Major Benjamin Walker, who were also his

---

[16] On von Steuben's sexual notoriety in Prussian circles and his success in America, see Paul Lockhart, *The Drillmaster of Valley Forge: The Baron de Steuben and the Making of the American Military* (2008); Randy Shilts, *Conduct Unbecoming: Gays and Lesbians in the U.S. Military* 7–10 (2005). The "Drunk History" video of Baron von Steuben presents a largely accurate account in a more amusing format, https://www.youtube.com/watch?v=n8zGCcDbq18 (viewed Nov. 1, 2015).

translators. (The Prussian did not speak much English when he arrived in America.) As you face the front of the monument, the lower left side displays statues of two nude men interacting in what might be interpreted as a homoerotic posture (also pictured at the front of this conclusion). Its caption is "Military Instruction." While the sexual overtures of this moment of instruction may not have been the intent of its creator, the sculptor Albert Jaegers, they were appreciated by a good many gay Washingtonians in the decades after the monument was erected in 1910. Indeed, Lafayette Park was in the 1940s and 1950s a well-known cruising area for men seeking male sexual partners. The men solicited in this manner, however, often turned out to be undercover police officers, a practice reflecting the campaign the federal government launched after World War II to expose and persecute "homosexuals" in the nation's capital. For a dramatic example, an undercover Lafayette Park arrest for homosexual solicitation led to the suicide of a senator that flipped the partisan balance in the United States Senate in June 1954 (from 48–47 Democrat to 48–47 Republican, with one Independent).[17]

The foregoing are the historical facts, but now let me complement the historical von Steuben statue with a hypothetical statute. Near the apex of the anti-homosexual terror, Congress in 1956 would have been willing to enact almost any proposal that law enforcement officials might have suggested to suppress homosexuality in the nation's capital. Police had plenty of broad criminal laws to work with, but assume that law enforcement officials proposed and Congress passed the following statute in 1956:

> **An Act to ensure public safety in Lafayette Park**
>
> **Sec. 1. Findings and Purpose.** Finding that homosexuals loitering in Lafayette Park constitute a nuisance and are a threat to public safety, Congress resolves that there is an urgent public need to ban any and all homosexuals from this park.

---

[17] For the tragic suicide of a senator arising out of an undercover sting aimed at "homosexuals" in Lafayette Park and alleged extortion by several senators, see Rodger McDaniel, *Dying for Joe McCarthy's Sins: The Suicide of Wyoming Senator Lester Hunt* (2013). On the anti-homosexual terror and purges by the federal government and the government of the District of Columbia after World War II, see David Johnson, *The Lavender Scare: The Cold War Persecution of Gays and Lesbians in the Federal Government* (2004). For an important synthetic history, see Estelle Freedman, *"Uncontrolled Desires": The Response to the Sexual Psychopath, 1920–1960,* 74 J. Am. Hist. 83–107 (June 1986).

Sec. 2. No Homosexuals in the Park. No homosexuals shall be allowed into Lafayette Park.

Sec. 3. Penalty. Any homosexual who is found in Lafayette Park shall be guilty of a misdemeanor, punishable by imprisonment up to ten days and a fine not exceeding $500 for each violation.

Some gentle readers might consider this statute too naked a display of discrimination to be realistic, but this 1956 version of the Lafayette Park Safety Act is comparable to the array of aggressive anti-homosexual statutes sponsored and signed by Governor Earl Warren in California (1943–54) and to executive orders issued by Presidents Harry Truman and Dwight Eisenhower (1945–61).[18]

What is more, this "homosexuals" in the park law would have been considered perfectly constitutional in 1956 and might have been sustained as late as 1986. Today, this would be an easy case the other way—clearly a violation of the Constitution. How constitutional meaning has evolved with regard to this kind of law can illustrate the operation of legal interpretation that considers several sources of legal meaning, and not just one foundational source of meaning. Although the constitutional language and structure remained substantially the same in 1956 and 1986 and 2016, the legal context changed in that period. These legal developments and the evolving social norms underlying them drove changes in the Constitution's textual meaning and the application of its grand libertarian and egalitarian meta-principles. That the application of the Constitution has changed, however, does not mean that its interpretation has not been consistent with the rule of law as well as the premises of our pluralistic democracy, our primary normative templates for evaluating statutory interpretation. To see how this might be the case, I shall now apply what we have learned from the earlier chapters on statutory interpretation to this matter of constitutional interpretation. In turn, this exercise in constitutional interpretation may help us see how different interpretive sources and canons interact in the hands of judges to produce legal meaning.

---

[18] For a survey of sweeping anti-homosexual measures enacted in Governor Warren's California and propounded by the White House in the 1940s and 1950s, see William N. Eskridge Jr., *Dishonorable Passions: Sodomy Law in America, 1861–2003,* at 88–105 (2008). The culmination of White House-led anti-homosexual discrimination came in Executive Order 10,450, § 8(a)(1)(iii), 18 Fed. Reg. 1489, 2491 (April 29, 1953), where President Eisenhower excluded "sex perverts" (understood to target "homosexuals") from federal employment. As many as 5000 suspected "homosexuals" were run out of the federal civil service in the 1950s. Johnson, *Lavender Scare*, 166.

The Constitution in 1956: Democracy

Assume that, in 1956, the Park Police arrest John Doe for violating the new "homosexuals" in the park law. Doe is walking through Lafayette Park late one night, and an officer recognizes him as a character he suspects to be a "sexual pervert." Unlike the thousands of other "John Does" arrested for violating this and other anti-homosexual statutes and policies in the 1950s, this John Doe retains a lawyer and contests the charges. One challenge is a constitutional argument, that the statute violates the Due Process Clause of the Fifth Amendment.

In 1956 (as today), the Fifth Amendment says that the federal government cannot deprive any "person" of "life, liberty, or property without due process of law." If convicted and penalized, John Doe would suffer a deprivation of either "liberty" (if he goes to jail) or "property" (if he is fined) or both. But if Doe incurs these losses only after being duly charged and convicted of a crime established by the legitimate legal process, has the federal government denied him these things "without due process of law"? The ordinary reader of this language might not see how Doe has been denied due process of law under these circumstances.

So a judge should start with skepticism about this claim. Pause, however, to consider the following ordinary meaning argument. Assume that the government properly charges John Doe with a crime and gives him every opportunity to present evidence to a jury of his peers, but assume, further, that the judge then tells the jurors that they are supposed to convict Doe if they find him "offensive." The jury convicts. Has Doe been penalized "without due process of law"? I think so. Why? Although he received every opportunity to defend himself, the substantive jury charge was so arbitrary that it effectively denied him "due process," or so it seems to me. Why was the charge arbitrary? "Offensive" is such a vague term that it allows the jury to convict someone for subjective reasons unrelated to the substantive crime of being a "homosexual" in the park.

What if the judge tells the jury that they can consider the fact that John Doe is a person of color when they decide his criminality? (Reflecting a nationwide pattern, the District of Columbia police in the 1950s enforced anti-homosexual laws disproportionately against black and latino men.[19]) Is that not a denial of due process of law, as

---

[19] Eskridge, *Dishonorable Passions,* 80–82.

well? Why? Such a charge is also arbitrary, because it invites the jury to treat one class of citizens (people of color) differently than another class of citizens (people not of color). In one sense, this second charge is more arbitrary than the first. Both charges invite jurors to penalize someone for reasons unrelated to the substantive crime of disturbing public safety, but the second charge more clearly than the first entrenches a division among citizens that seems inconsistent with the neutral law of the land that might also be instinct in the phrase "due process of law." I present these as questions relating to the ordinary meaning of this constitutional language, and without insisting upon the correctness of these thoughts. But they suggest that the judge ought to investigate Doe's due process challenge more deeply.

The term of art canon asks the judge to consider whether "due process of law" had an accepted legal meaning in 1791 (when the Fifth Amendment was added to the Constitution) or during the founding era more generally. Not surprisingly, this constitutional term did have a rich legal history in 1791. The "due process of law" language found its first classic articulation in the 1354 reissue of the Magna Carta. Earlier versions of the Great Charter of 1215 contained assurances that some liberties could not be taken away except *per legem terrae* ("by the law of the land"), and apparently the 1354 reissuance, substituting "due process of law" for *per legem terrae,* was accepted as effecting no change. According to historians, both *per legem terrae* and due process of law were protections against action by the monarchy that deprived Englishmen of liberties contrary to the common law and custom.[20]

In the seventeenth and eighteenth centuries, American colonists applied the due process of law/law of the land concept somewhat more broadly, as an objection to legislative as well as executive action they considered arbitrary and contrary to common law liberties. Adopting a more expansive view, the colonists were not only influenced by their local grievances (against Parliament as well as colonial legislatures), but also by seventeenth-century social contract thinking that assured all citizens, the beneficiaries of the social contract, generality of legal treatment and that militated against special legal preferences or exclusions. Thus, the Massachusetts Body of Liberties (1641) not only protected specific liberties "by the law of the country" but also

[20] Charles A. Miller, *The Forest of Due Process of Law: The American Constitutional Tradition*, in *Due Process: Nomos XVIII* 3–68 (J. Ronald Pennock & John W. Chapman, eds., 1997). See also Geoffrey Marshall, *Due Process in England*, in id. at 69–91.

directed that "[e]very person within this Jurisdiction, whether Inhabitant or forreiner shall enjoy the same justice and law, that is generall for the plantation, which we constitute and execute one towards another without partialitie or delay."[21] This notion was widely accepted in the colonies.[22]

One of the overarching background assumptions for founding era constitutional thought was that the rule of law carries with it a presumption of generality and, thereby, equal treatment.[23] Authored by Thomas Jefferson, the Virginia Declaration of Rights (1776) was a detailed and influential statement of this understanding of the social contract. Because all people are born "equally free," and because government exists to assure each and every citizen of the protections of life, liberty, and property, all laws must be aimed at the "common benefit" and must be presumptively general in application, with no privileges carved out for only a portion of the population.[24] The Virginia Declaration endorses a social contractarian equal treatment idea and seems to combine it with the medieval libertarian anti-tyranny provision. Is the Declaration an expansive interpretation of the English concept of *per legem terrae*/due process of law? *Or* is it a mixing of two separate legal doctrines or terms—namely, the medieval concept of "due process of law" and the early modern concept of "common benefit" or equal treatment? The matter is open to debate, but my discussion of the hypothetical jury instructions in John Doe's case suggests an ordinary meaning argument in favor of

---

[21] Massachusetts Body of Liberties, art. 2 (1641).

[22] Miller, *Forest of Due Process of Law,* 7–9; see also Steven G. Calabresi & Hannah M. Begley, *Originalism and Same-Sex Marriage* (draft 2015) (surveying state constitutional guarantees of equal treatment in the founding and colonial eras).

[23] See generally Rebecca L. Brown, *Liberty, The New Equality,* 77 N.Y.U. L. Rev. 1491, 1512–20 (2002); William N. Eskridge Jr., *Original Meaning and Marriage Equality,* 52 Hous. L. Rev. 1067 (2016).

[24] Va. Declaration of Rights, §§ 1, 3 (1776). The Virginia Declaration started with the proposition that "all men are by nature equally free and independent and have certain inherent rights, of which, when they enter into a state of society, they cannot, by any compact, deprive or divest their posterity; namely, the enjoyment of life and liberty, with the means of acquiring and possessing property, and pursuing and obtaining happiness and safety." *Id.* § 1. As dictated by social contract theory, "government is, or ought to be, instituted for the common benefit, protection, and security of the people, nation, or community" *Id.* § 3. Thus, "when any government shall be found inadequate or contrary to these purposes, a majority of the community hath an indubitable, inalienable, and indefeasible right to reform, alter, or abolish it, in such manner as shall be judged most conducive to the public weal." *Id.* Finally, "no man, or set of men, is entitled to exclusive or separate emoluments or privileges from the community, but in consideration of public services; which, nor being descendible, neither ought the offices of magistrate, legislator, or judge to be hereditary." *Id.* § 4.

the view that *per legem terrae*/due process of law entails a commitment to law that does not make arbitrary distinctions, either as a matter of evidence or as a matter of how classes of people are treated by the law.

Whatever its precise terminological situs, the equal treatment concept was widely accepted in the founding era. Like the Virginia Declaration, Jefferson's Declaration of Independence says that America's constitutional democracy is premised upon the notion that "all Men are created equal." Other state constitutions implemented during and soon after the American Revolution encoded this precept explicitly in their foundational texts. As the Pennsylvania Constitution of 1776 expressed it, "government ought to be instituted * * * for the security and protection of the community as such, and to enable the individuals who compose it to enjoy their natural rights * * * without partiality for, or prejudice against any particular class, sect, or denomination of men."[25] The Massachusetts Constitution of 1780 put it this way: "Government is instituted for the common good, for the protection, safety, prosperity, and happiness of the people, and not for the profit, honor, or private interest of any one man, family, or class of men * * *."[26]

The baseline reflected in these state constitutions saturated the thinking of the framers and supporters of the Constitution of 1789. Summing up the principles that were already reflected in most of the state constitutions and that would undergird the Constitution, James Madison in 1785 maintained that "equality * * * ought to be the basis of every law," and the law should not subject some persons to "peculiar burdens" or grant others "peculiar exemptions."[27] The Constitution drafted at Philadelphia did not have the same clauses and articles found in state constitutions, though the Preamble announced that "We the People" entered into the Constitution "to promote the general Welfare," a phrase with some affinity to the "common benefit"/"common good" language in state constitutions.

---

[25] Pa. Const. of 1776, pmbl.; see id. art. V (similar to the 1776 Virginia Declaration). For a survey and analysis of these revolutionary and early state constitutions, see Melissa Lamb Saunders, *Equal Protection, Class Legislation, and Colorblindness*, 96 Mich. L. Rev. 245, 253–54 & n.34 (1997).

[26] Mass. Const. of 1780, art. VII. For other common benefits articles and clauses, see Del. Decl. Rights § 3 (1776); N.H. Const. of 1784, art. X; Pa. Const. of 1776, art. V.

[27] James Madison, A Memorial and Remonstrance, on the Religious Rights of Man ¶ 6 (1785), *reprinted in* Everson v. Bd. of Educ., 330 U.S. 1, app. 63–72 (1947) (Rutledge, J., dissenting) (reprinted as *Memorial and Remonstrance Against Religious Assessments*).

Instead, the Constitution guaranteed liberty protection and generality or equal treatment through the structures of lawmaking and implementation. Thus, the independent judiciary created in Article III (and further empowered to conduct judicial review by Article VI) protected "particular classes of citizens" against "unjust and partial laws."[28] A national system with parallel state authority was a good way to minimize the costs imposed by temporary "faction[s]" on property owners and religious minorities in particular.[29]

Important to the ratification of the Constitution was the assurance by its supporters that important individual rights would be explicitly protected as well. True to his word, Madison drafted and engineered the addition of the Bill of Rights in 1791. Following the approach and the political philosophy of the Virginia Declaration, the Constitution's Bill of Rights implemented the libertarian protections and equal treatment assurances directly, through specific protections for property owners in the Takings Clause of the Fifth Amendment and religious minorities in the First Amendment's Religion Clauses. The Due Process Clause of the Fifth Amendment clearly reflected the anti-arbitrariness protections of the *per legem terrae* concept and may also have reflected the equal treatment baseline of the state common benefits clauses.[30]

Whether you read it narrowly (*per legem terrae*) or more broadly (to include generality of law and equal treatment precepts), the Due Process Clause has a substantive fairness or nonarbitrariness component. Does that fairness feature of the clause provide a basis for striking down legislation that denies liberty or property arbitrarily to a despised class of citizens, without sound justification in the needs of the people as a whole? In my view, the Due Process Clause can be read this broadly—but it can also be read more narrowly, as Justice Thomas has maintained in a scholarly exegesis of the common law background and the framers' understanding of

---

28 *The Federalist* No. 78 (Hamilton).

29 *The Federalist* No. 10 (Madison) (avoiding oppression by "faction[s]" justified the large national governance); cf. *The Federalist* No. 51 (Madison) (arguing that federalism also protects against oppression by "faction").

30 See *United States v. Windsor*, 133 S.Ct. 2675, 2693–96 (2013) (reading the Fifth Amendment's Due Process Clause to protect family liberties and to assure equal treatment of lesbian and gay families); Saunders, *Equal Protection, Class Legislation*, 96 Mich. L. Rev. 245.

"due process of law."[31] As this volume has argued with regard to statutes, the interpreter needs to engage with several different kinds of legal materials before settling on an answer, even a tentative one, to a tough constitutional question like this one.

Consider, then, the legislative history of the Bill of Rights. When Madison introduced the Bill of Rights in Congress, he also proposed adding language to the Preamble declaring that "Government is instituted and ought to be exercised for the benefit of the people; which consists in the enjoyment of life and liberty, with the right of acquiring and using property, and generally pursuing and obtaining happiness and safety." This language would more clearly have linked the Constitution with state constitutional guarantees that government must serve the common benefit and not the interests of privileged groups. The House of Representatives, however, rejected this language. Did the House reject the language because the existing Preamble to the Constitution was already sufficiently linked to the common benefit concept? Or did the representatives reject it because they found it inappropriate for Congress to be encumbered by the equal treatment concept? Or did the founding legislators believe that the Due Process Clause of the Fifth Amendment fully integrated this precept? I do not know. Given our uncertainty, the rejected proposals canon ought not carry great weight in our deliberations.

A narrow reading of the Due Process Clause finds support in the structure of the Constitution as it read in 1956. As a matter of ordinary meaning, it might violate the Equal Protection Clause of the Fourteenth Amendment for a state or city to adopt laws arbitrarily discriminating against a class of persons, as such measures might, literally, deny them "the equal protection of the laws." But the Fifth Amendment, applicable to the federal government, has no equal protection guarantee; it just has the Due Process Clause. The canon against surplusage suggests that the Equal Protection Clause adds something to the guarantees of the Due Process Clause in the Fourteenth Amendment (which has both clauses). The meaningful variation canon suggests that the Fifth Amendment's due process protections are less than those of the Fourteenth Amendment's due process *plus* equal protection assurances. Given these different protections, it may be the case that states and cities are on shakier

---

[31] For a more narrow interpretation of the Magna Carta's *per legem terrae* assurance and its implications for due process of law, see *Obergefell v. Hodges*, 135 S.Ct. 2584, 2631–34 (2015) (Thomas, J., dissenting).

ground passing laws against "homosexuals" in the park than the federal government would be.[32]

The foregoing legal materials make it an uphill climb for a court to find anything *constitutionally* wrong in Congress's exclusion of "homosexuals" from Lafayette Park in 1956. But there is more to consider. One point of history may be relevant. The Fourteenth Amendment's "equal protection" language was a term of art that had been developed by judges, advocates, and political leaders consciously relying on *per legem terrae* and the rule of law to argue against slavery and discriminatory treatment of freed men of color.[33] Why, then, did the Fourteenth Amendment use both due process and equal protection language? Should the constitutional interpreter "read back" the Fourteenth Amendment's concepts into the Fifth Amendment, as Akhil Reed Amar and Vicki Jackson have argued based upon the structure of the Constitution and the legislative history of the Reconstruction Amendments?[34] In thinking about these vexing questions, the serious constitutional judge in 1956 has more legal sources to consult.

In *Brown v. Board of Education* (1954), the Supreme Court ruled that state-required racial segregation in public schools violates the Fourteenth Amendment's Equal Protection Clause—and on the same day also held, in *Bolling v. Sharpe,* that Congress's racial segregation of schools in the District of Columbia violates the Fifth Amendment's Due Process Clause.[35] Confronting the meaningful variation argument directly, *Bolling* reasoned, consistent with the broad social contract understanding of due process, that "the concepts of equal protection and due process, both stemming from our American ideal

---

[32] *LaBelle Iron Works v. United States,* 256 U.S. 377, 392 (1921) (flatly rejecting an equal protection challenge to a federal statute, because the Fifth Amendment has no equal protection clause), followed in *Hirabayashi v. United States,* 320 U.S. 81 (1943) (upholding a federal law creating a curfew only for citizens of Japanese ancestry).

[33] See Eskridge, *Original Meaning and Marriage Equality,* 52 Hous. L. Rev. at 1075–87 (tracing the "equal protection" language to the opposition to "class legislation" that Jacksonian Democrats and anti-slavery Free Soilers and Republicans derived from due process/*legem terrae*).

[34] Amar, *Intratextualism,* 112 Harv. L. Rev. at 766–73; Vicki Jackson, *Holistic Interpretation:* Fitzpatrick v. Bitzer *and Our Bifurcated Constitution,* 53 Stan. L. Rev. 1259, 1279–81 (2001). See also Akhil Reed Amar, *The Bill of Rights and the Fourteenth Amendment,* 101 Yale L.J. 1193, 1277–82 (1992) (Fourteenth Amendment had a "feedback effect" on First Amendment, not only pressing it against the states, but also transforming its application to the federal government).

[35] *Bolling v. Sharpe,* 347 U.S. 497 (1954), extending *Brown v. Board of Education,* 347 U.S. 483 (1954), to require desegregation in the District of Columbia's public schools.

of fairness, are not mutually exclusive. The 'equal protection of the laws' is a more explicit safeguard of prohibited unfairness than 'due process of law,' and, therefore, we do not imply that the two are always interchangeable phrases. But * * * discrimination may be so unjustifiable as to be violative of due process."[36] *Bolling* read the Fifth Amendment against the meta-norm, undergirding state and national constitutionalism at the founding, that the rule of law requires generality and is skeptical of legislation that sets a class of citizens apart for special privileges or burdens.

As a precedent binding on all federal courts, *Bolling* takes some of the edge off of the meaningful variation feature of the structural contrast between the Fifth and Fourteenth Amendments. (In chapter one of this volume, I cautioned against an aggressive use of the surplusage and meaningful variation canons, especially when law has been amended over time.) And *Bolling* supports a substantive reading of the Fifth Amendment's Due Process Clause that is consistent with the social contractarian concept of equal treatment required by the generality meta-norm.

Does *Bolling* then require a federal judge to strike down the "homosexuals" in the park law as a violation of the Fifth Amendment? While *Bolling* is not on its face limited to race discrimination, and the thoughtful judge would want to consider extending it in light of the original meaning and the constitutional background of the Due Process Clause, was there in 1956 a *legal* basis for saying that exclusion of "homosexuals" from public spaces was "so unjustifiable as to be violative of due process" in the way that school race-based segregation was in that era? In thinking about *that* issue, another constitutional meta-norm is highly relevant.

The Constitution's separation of the legislative, executive, and judicial powers vests political decisions in the legislative and, to some extent, the executive branches of government. Not coincidentally, those branches are led by officials elected by We the People and accountable to popular opinion.[37] Assured life tenure by Article III, federal judges are supposed to exercise the "judgment" associated with tradition and written laws, in contrast to the "will" exercised by the voters and their elected representatives. A meta-norm suggested

---

[36] *Bolling,* 347 U.S. at 499.

[37] The popular election of House members is required by Article I, § 2; popular election of members of the Senate is required by the Seventeenth Amendment. The President is elected by the Electoral College under Article II, whose electors are chosen by popular vote.

by this structure is that judges ought to be reluctant to overturn entrenched rules and policies that the political process has ratified with the apparent approval of the electorate.[38] There is a powerful governance feature undergirding this meta-norm: The operation of a democracy demands judicial restraint. In 1956, political scientist Robert Dahl cogently argued that deep, primordial issues as to which our pluralist democracy is evenly and intensely divided are ones that should not be decided one way or the other, until the stakes have been lowered.[39] For judicial review, the punch line for Professor Dahl's understanding of our pluralist democracy is that the Supreme Court should avoid broad pronouncements that purport to resolve high-stakes issues that divide the body politic.[40] The democracy meta-norm counsels against a broad reading of the Due Process Clause and of *Bolling* that would upbend an entrenched public policy that understood "homosexuals" *not* as a class of citizens, but instead as a category of criminals.

In 1956, every state in the country made consensual sodomy (the characteristic conduct of male "homosexuals") a crime, and every state but one made it a felony.[41] Ten state sodomy laws allowed the state to imprison violators for more than twenty years for activities between consenting adults in private places, and another fifteen states had a maximum penalty of ten to twenty years.[42] In most states, the "homosexual" brought to justice for consensual sexual activities or (more often) for soliciting other men for homosexual activities in parks and other quasi-public places, could also be committed to a mental institution as a "sexual psychopath."[43] To the extent that "homosexuals" were defined by their characteristic sexual activities (anal or oral sex, and not penile-vaginal sex), they were presumptive criminals. Given the perceived proclivity of some male "homosexuals" to furtively solicit sex in dark areas, such as secluded

---

38 E.g., John Hart Ely, *Democracy and Distrust: A Theory of Judicial Review* 88–100 (1980); James Bradley Thayer, *The Origin and Scope of the American Doctrine of Constitutional Law*, 7 Harv. L. Rev. 129, 144 (1893).

39 Robert A. Dahl, *A Preface to Democratic Theory* 93–99 (1956).

40 The point in text is developed in William N. Eskridge Jr., *Pluralism and Distrust: How Courts Can Support Democracy by Lowering the Stakes of Politics*, 114 Yale L.J. 1279 (2005).

41 Eskridge, *Dishonorable Passions*, 387–406 (appendix providing mini-histories of the sodomy laws of all 50 states and the District of Columbia).

42 Id. at 93 (Figure 3.4) (map for potential prison time for violating sodomy laws in each of the states).

43 William N. Eskridge Jr., *Gaylaw: Challenging the Apartheid of the Closet* 42–43 (1999); see id. at 354–55 (appendix of state sexual psychopath statutes, most of which were enacted or expanded in the 1950s).

spots in Lafayette Park, "homosexuals" were considered predatory as well, and nuisances at the very least.

In 1956, both federal and state governments treated gay people as outlaws. "Homosexuals and other sex perverts" (the characteristic terminology of the era) were per se disqualified from service in the armed forces, from the federal civil service, from having a license to be a school teacher or practicing law or medicine, and even from entry into the United States (if they were not citizens).[44] In the 1950s, federal and state governments censored literature, plays, and movies depicting or even suggesting same-sex intimacy. State governments barred licensed establishments from serving liquor to "homosexuals" or, in some states, even allowing them to congregate. There was no Supreme Court decision in 1956 recognizing gay people as a class of citizens, much less as a class deserving equal protection.

As we have seen above, democracy is not the only meta-norm reflected in the Constitution. The Lafayette Park law restrained the liberty of and imposed unequal burdens on the disparaged class—but one person's liberty ends where another's begins, and equal treatment requires that the two things be comparable. The legal regime in place for "homosexuals" in 1956 rested, pervasively, on an understanding of gay people that required the state to deny them the same liberties as "normal" Americans. Led by a bipartisan array of prominent legislators and executive branch officials, ranging from Senators Clyde Hoey and Kenneth Wherry to Governors Earl Warren and Charlie Johns to the FBI's J. Edgar Hoover, state and federal governments engaged in systematic legal campaigns to imprison and institutionalize "homosexuals" because they were considered prone to predation, lawbreaking, and disorder.[45] Thus, prosecutors defending the 1956 Lafayette Park law against constitutional claims that it is denying liberties to people because of their status, would reply that this prophylactic law is aimed at people with a proclivity to engage in unlawful acts and so cannot be a denial of equal treatment or of liberty. Rooted in democratic deliberation and decisionmaking at all levels of government, such arguments justifying discrimination against "homosexuals" were widely accepted by judges on the toniest

---

[44] Eskridge, *Apartheid of the Closet, 1946–1961*, 24 Fla. St. U.L. Rev. 733–53 (1997) (summarizing the disabilities imposed by the law on gay people in the 1950s).

[45] Eskridge, *Dishonorable Passions*, 83–84, 88–99 (identifying the leading anti-homosexual crusaders of the post-World War II period and setting forth the detailed legal regime constructed to flush out, imprison, and treat "homosexuals and other sex perverts").

tribunals in the country (including the Court of Appeals for the D.C. Circuit) well into the 1990s.[46]

We ought to be alarmed at the implications of this analysis: Did the democracy meta-norm mean that the Constitution tolerated racial segregation? Southern states vigorously resisted *Brown* and *Bolling*: Were those cases wrongly decided? During the Gilded Age (1890s–1910s), the Wilsonian New Freedom (1913–21), and the Return to Normalcy (1921–33), the entrenched democratic support for segregation (all over the country and, after 1912, in the federal civil service) rendered the Constitution unavailable to overturn the apartheid regime, though it was available to enforce fundamental liberties like the right to vote. Only after the civil rights movement, the negative example of nazi racism, and World War II moved public opinion away from apartheid were *Brown* and *Bolling* even possible as enforceable constitutional directives.[47] Although the Supreme Court never should have sanctioned apartheid (that was a constitutional as well as moral blunder), the Court should not have declared war on that regime until there was significant support from the democratically elected branches of government, as there was in *Brown* and *Bolling*.[48]

Thus, the democracy meta-norm has a practical as well as theoretical valence (of course the two are related). If a federal judge were so bold as to say, in 1956, that it was a violation of the Due Process Clause for the federal government to exclude "homosexuals" from a park, the judge would not only need a powerful constitutional case to overcome the strong pull of the democracy meta-norm, but

---

[46] E.g., *Steffan v. Perry,* 41 F.3d 677, 685–93 (D.C. Cir., en banc, 1994) (upholding a blanket exclusion of "homosexuals" from the armed forces, based upon their proclivity to engage in criminal behaviors, i.e., consensual sodomy, even though the gay plaintiff claimed to be celibate).

[47] See Richard Kluger, *The History of* Brown v. Board of Education *and Black America's Struggle for Equality* (1975, 2004). On the constitutional triangulation between the adoption of the Fourteenth Amendment (1868), the Supreme Court's endorsement of apartheid (1893), and the Court's renunciation (1954), compare the very different yet complementary accounts in Bruce Ackerman, *Constitutional Politics/Constitutional Law,* 99 Yale L.J. 453, 531–36 (1989), Alexander M. Bickel, *The Original Understanding and the Segregation Decision*, 69 Harv. L. Rev. 1 (1955), and Bork, *Tempting of America*, 74–77.

[48] Empirically, the Supreme Court rarely strays far from public opinion. See Nathan Persily, Jack Citrin & Patrick Egan, *Public Opinion and Constitutional Controversy* (2008); William Mishler & Reginald S. Sheehan, *The Supreme Court as a Countermajoritarian Institution? The Impact of Public Opinion on Supreme Court Opinions,* 87 Am. Pol. Sci. Rev. 87 (1993). See also Barry Friedman, *The Will of the People: How Public Opinion Has Influenced the Supreme Court and Shaped the Meaning of the Constitution* (2009).

would be opening up a politically combustible Pandora's box. If the Supreme Court insisted upon such a holding, then a great swath of municipal, state, and federal laws would have been immediately suspect. The political reaction would have been swift and possibly brutal.[49] Were judges so certain that this kind of law violates the Due Process Clause that they would be willing to call into question the nation's pervasive anti-homosexual regime, created in its most aggressive form by the man who was then the Chief Justice of the United States (i.e., former California Governor Earl Warren)? And to risk not only a more sweeping statutory terror against "homosexuals," but also a reaction against the Court's fragile constitutional moves in *Brown* and *Bolling*? Even if judges themselves could have understood gay men more realistically (not likely), no one would have dared such a move in 1956.

Many gentle readers will be shocked to read about such cruel treatment of this minority, and some may consider judges of that era to be moral cowards. Perhaps, but one must also keep in mind that these discriminatory measures were expressions of a constitutional culture constructed around fear of sexual minorities.[50] Few Americans knew that they had gay or lesbian relatives or coworkers, and most Americans only heard about "homosexuals" in connection with child molestation and other forms of predatory behavior.[51] The government and the media reports on "homosexuals and sex perverts" alternated between lurid depictions of sexual predation or mental derangement and pathetic depictions of lonely men lurking in bathrooms or behind bushes hungry for an anonymous sexual encounter. Municipalities all over the country considered

---

[49] Even mild and cautious judicial amelioration of anti-homosexual statutes was met with rebuke. See, e.g., Act of Oct. 3, 1965, Pub. L. No. 89–236, § 15(b), 79 Stat. 911, 919 (1965), a Great Society statute amending the Immigration and Nationality Act of 1952, § 212(a)(4), 66 Stat. 163, 182, codified at 8 U.S.C. § 1182(a)(4), in order to abrogate a lower court opinion finding that "psychopathic personality" was too vague to bar "homosexuals" from entry into the United States. See William N. Eskridge Jr., *Gadamer/Statutory Interpretation*, 90 Colum. L. Rev. 609, 609–11, 639–44 (1990) (tracing the statutory history of this exclusion, updated in 1965 to bar people afflicted with "sexual deviation").

[50] On the predation-based fear of "homosexuals" during the post-1945 panic, see, e.g., Robert Corber, *Homosexuality in Cold War America: Resistance and the Crisis of Masculinity* (1997); Johnson, *Lavender Scare*; George Chauncey Jr., *The Postwar Sex Crime Panic*, in William Graebner, editor, *True Stories from the American Past* 160–78 (1993).

[51] Eskridge, *Dishonorable Passions*, 82–88 (explaining how a general fear of sexual predation against children was mobilized to arrest thousands of men seeking consensual relations with other adult men); James T. Sears, *The Lonely Hunters: An Oral History of Lesbian and Gay Southern Life, 1948–1968* (1997) (similar).

"homosexual" cruising spaces (parks, beaches, restrooms, the von Steuben monument) to be public nuisances. Within such a culture and against such a legal background, it was most unlikely that a federal judge could accept a claim that the "homosexuals" in the park law violated the Constitution.

But that is not the end of the story. Although the 1950s were a bleak era for "homophile" rights (to stick with terms of that period), a prescient cadre of biologists (such as Dr. Alfred Kinsey), psychologists (such as Dr. Evelyn Hooker), and social scientists (such as Dr. Ruth Benedict and Dr. Margaret Mead) objected to prevailing social myths about sexual and gender minorities.[52] Their idea was that the human population enjoys a great deal of natural sexual and gender variation and that minorities such as "homosexuals" are not materially different from the rest of the population. This idea had little traction in popular culture during the 1950s, but it did attract allies among criminal law professors, attorneys, and police who believed that persecuting "homosexuals" was stupid, wasteful, and corrupt public policy.[53]

Do these attitudes have any relevance for the judge asked to apply the Lafayette Park Safety Act of 1956 to John Doe? If you were a judge who vaguely believed that "homosexuals" were often no threats to other people but who was committed to the democracy meta-norm, would you see any alternative to upholding the "homosexuals" in the park law and sending John Doe to jail? Jot down any thoughts you might have about this sad question.

Although it would have been hard to find an American judge willing to strike down this kind of statute as unconstitutional in 1956, a fair number of judges would have been skeptical if the police applied such a statute to a fellow walking through the park and bothering no one else—no matter what the fellow's sexual or gender orientation.[54] (If John Doe approached a teenage boy or an unwilling gentleman with lewd advances, that would be a different case.)

---

[52] Eskridge, *Dishonorable Passions,* 109–17.

[53] Id. at 118–27.

[54] One example of such a jurist was Morris Ploscowe, a magistrate in New York City who helped persuade Governor Dewey to veto a harsh law penalizing consenting "homosexuals" and who later participated in the Model Penal Code's decriminalization proposals. Eskridge, *Dishonorable Passions,* 118–19. For other examples of judges in the 1950s who put prosecutors through harsh inquiries and dismissed prosecutions reflecting "homosexual" status-based animus, see id. at 118–21, 128, 257.

Often a misconceived but popular law can be questioned more effectively by imposing upon the authorities a burden of proof rather than by declaring it unconstitutional. Thus, a judge skeptical of statutes demonizing people for their status but mindful of the national consensus stigmatizing sexual minorities, might require the prosecutor to prove to the jury, beyond a reasonable doubt, that John Doe was actually a "homosexual." Such a judge would be irreproachable: He is respecting the judgment of Congress and the President, as well as the National Park Service and the U.S. Park Police, charged with implementing this statute—but the judge is also enforcing this statute within the larger structure of due process that was itself entrenched in American constitutional culture in 1956.

What would have been the effect of such an elementary application of the rule of law in 1956? Doe's lawyer would produce character witnesses vouching for his probity and his friendship with women. Prosecutors would have a tough time presenting evidence of a category elusive at best and hard to prove without a confession from the defendant. (Because of the social stigma, few defendants in that era would admit to being "homosexual.") If the police have no evidence other than the defendant's friendly conversations with other men or the officer's evaluation of the fellow's appearance or gestures, the judge should certainly dismiss the charges upon grounds of due process or lack of evidence or something of both.[55] (If the police evidence of "homosexuality" were that Doe displayed "deviant" gestures or facial expressions, convicting him would come close to my earlier hypothetical charge supporting conviction if the jury found the defendant "offensive.") Notice how constitutional text, precedent, and structure interact to yield a judicious approach to this statute.

Notice also how statutory and constitutional interpretation interact. In the last chapter, we saw how constitutional values motivate statutory interpreters to back away from applications that threaten to violate the Constitution. Here, we see how statutory interpretation and procedure can save a judge from addressing a constitutional issue that seems premature. Even though I do not believe any judge would have flatly invalidated such a statute in 1956, some judges would have applied such a law strictly and would have required strong proof (beyond a reasonable doubt) for each of the

---

[55] *Cavazos v. Smith,* 132 S.Ct. 2, 6 (2011) (per curiam) (summarizing the standard for a judge to take a case away from a jury or overturn its verdict).

elements of the crime.[56] Such judges might have acted out of concerns that they, like the legislators who enacted the law, were not well-informed about homosexuality and that decisionmaking in the shadow of such ignorance disserves the judicial office and the polity.

The Constitution in 1986: Liberty?

The Lafayette Park Safety Act of 1956 would very probably have survived constitutional review at the beginning of the Warren Court (1953–69). Would it survive such review at the end of the Burger Court (1969–86)? Assume that John Doe Jr., the openly gay son of the John Doe arrested in 1956, is arrested for walking through Lafayette Park in 1986. A police officer correctly believes that John Jr. is gay and erroneously believes that he is afflicted with AIDS, which was a major health concern in the mid-1980s and one associated with gay men. The officer wonders whether John Jr. might not spread the HIV virus that causes AIDS to other park visitors. (This fear was unfounded in 1986 and is known to be false today, but it was widely believed then.) Does the arrest of John Doe Jr. violate the Constitution? This is a harder constitutional question in 1986 than it had been in 1956.

The relevant constitutional text and structure are the same in 1986 as they were in 1956. Between 1956 and 1986, there were constitutional amendments granting citizens of the District of Columbia the right to vote in presidential elections, abolishing the poll tax in federal elections, creating a new process of succession if the Vice-President leaves office, and granting eighteen year-olds the right to vote.[57] Although expanding the franchise in a modestly democratic manner, these amendments are not relevant to the constitutional issue we are examining. More pertinent might be the amendment that was not added to the Constitution: The Equal Rights Amendment (ERA), passed by overwhelming congressional majorities in 1972, failed to secure the needed thirty-eight states to justify its addition to the Constitution. The failure of the ERA owed something to Americans' concerns with open homosexuality, for a significant argument against the ERA was that its bar to state sex

---

[56] For cases where judges in the District and in New York tossed out sodomy solicitation prosecutions or convictions on statutory rather than constitutional grounds, see the analysis in Eskridge, *Gaylaw*, 85–86.

[57] U.S. Const. XIII–XXVI Ams.

discrimination would have required states to recognize same-*sex* (i.e., "homosexual") marriages.[58]

For statutory interpretation, the stability of a law's text and structure would be more likely to assure the same interpretation in 1986 as in 1956, subject to dynamic agency readings—but this is not the case for applying the Constitution to the Lafayette Park Safety Act of 1956. Several of the relevant legal sources for understanding the Constitution's vague language ("due process" and "equal protection") and its capacious structure changed between 1956 and 1986. The biggest law-based change is that the Supreme Court handed down important constitutional precedents that are relevant to judicial review of this "homosexuals" in the park law. The Court's precedents reflected a weakening of the support such a law derived from the democracy meta-norm and greater concern within our constitutional culture for the law's effect on competing meta-norms protecting liberty and suspicious of class legislation.[59]

Recall that *Bolling* had recognized an equal treatment feature of the Fifth Amendment's Due Process Clause but had left its contours open-ended. By 1986, the Supreme Court had made clear that the guarantees of the Fourteenth Amendment's Equal Protection Clause not only apply to the federal government, but apply with much the same force as if the Fifth Amendment itself had such a provision.[60] In 1956, a wartime Supreme Court precedent upholding a curfew for

---

[58] E.g., Church of Jesus Christ of the Latter-day Saints, First Presidency, *The Church and the Proposed Equal Rights Amendment: A Moral Issue,* Item 11, Ensign, March 1980 (explaining why the Mormons were opposed to the ERA and provided critical political support for its opponents), citing Senate Report No. 92–689, at 47 (1972) (ERA committee report, discussing Paul Freund's testimony linking the ERA with constitutionally required gay marriage based upon an analogy to *Loving v. Virginia,* 388 U.S. 1 [1967]).

[59] See Rhonda R. Rivera, *Our Straight-Laced Judges: The Legal Position of Homosexual Persons in the United States,* 30 Hastings L.J. 799 (1979). A neat barometer of softening attitudes was the internal position of the Church of Jesus Christ of the Latter-day Saints. In 1984, leaders in the Church were no longer prepared to defend homosexual sodomy laws, were inclined to remain neutral for laws barring sexual orientation discrimination in the workplace, and focused only on protecting discriminations against gay people in youth organizations and civil marriage law. See Dallin H. Oaks, Quorum of the Twelve Apostles, Church of Jesus Christ of the Latter-day Saints, *Principles to Govern Possible Public Statement on Legislation Affecting Rights of Homosexuals* 7–19 (Aug. 7, 1984).

[60] See generally *Adarand Constructors, Inc. v. Pena,* 515 U.S. 200, 213–18 (1995) (discussing the post-*Bolling* precedents and concluding that the Court had applied the same equal protection guarantees to the federal government under the Fifth Amendment that it applied to state governments under the Fourteenth Amendment), citing and following Kenneth L. Karst, *The Fifth Amendment's Guarantee of Equal Protection,* 55 N.C.L. Rev. 541, 554 (1977).

Japanese Americans could have been cited to allow the federal government to bar a suspect ethnic or racial group from Lafayette Park for security reasons—but not in 1986. By then, the wartime precedent had been discredited as a departure from the Equal Protection Clause decisions subjecting race- or ethnicity-based classifications to heightened scrutiny.[61] Would such a level of scrutiny apply to classifications targeting sexual minorities under either the Fifth or Fourteenth Amendment? In 1956, this proposition would have been inconceivable to sitting Justices of the most liberal Court in American history—but in 1986 it enjoyed support within one of the more conservative Courts in our history.

Specifically, two Justices in 1985 suggested that a case could be made for the proposition that laws targeting sexual minorities should be subject to heightened judicial scrutiny for the same reasons judges were skeptical of laws targeting racial minorities.[62] Such a view was a testament to social and legal changes in the status of sexual minorities, who by the 1980s were often referred to as lesbian and gay persons, terms more congenial than the hated nineteenth-century term "homosexuals." Reflecting a medical consensus that homosexuality is neither a disease nor a mental or emotional defect, a majority of states had repealed their consensual sodomy laws and virtually all states had abandoned enforcement of them when sexual activities occurred between consenting adults in the home.[63]

Notwithstanding a tremendous change in the legal and social status of gay people, American law had not embraced the Alfred Kinsey/Evelyn Hooker notion that sexual variation is benign, the way racial variation is considered benign as a matter of public policy (and hence an illegitimate basis for state classifications). Almost half the states still considered consensual sodomy a crime—and when the District of Columbia tried to decriminalize consensual sodomy in 1981 the House of Representatives vetoed that action by a whopping bipartisan 281–119 vote. Representatives who spoke in favor of

---

[61] In *Hirabayashi v. United States,* 320 U.S. 81 (1943), the Court upheld a wartime measure creating a curfew only for citizens of Japanese ancestry. The *Bolling* Court favorably cited *Hirabayashi,* see *Bolling,* 347 U.S. 499 n.3, but by the 1980s *Hirabayashi* was a toxic precedent, and it was disapproved in 1995. See *Adarand*, 515 U.S. at 213–14.

[62] *Rowland v. Mad River Local Sch. Dist.*, 470 U.S. 1009, 1014–17 (1985) (Brennan, J., joined by Marshall, J., dissenting from the denial of certiorari) (making a case for the proposition that sexual orientation, like race, sex, and illegitimacy, is a suspect classification triggering heightened judicial review).

[63] Eskridge, *Dishonorable Passions,* 166–228 (describing the complicated state-by-state politics of sodomy reform, 1969–86).

vetoing the District's law reform effort emphasized that "homosexuals" were threats to public order.[64] (Not a single representative mentioned that the overwhelming point of the District's sex crime reform law was to focus attention on sexual assault and rape, where coverage and penalties were increased.)

Congress's veto of local sodomy reform by the jurisdiction in which Lafayette Park is located was no public law aberration. In 1986, at the height of the AIDS epidemic that added a crimson letter to the social stigmata imposed upon gay and bisexual men in particular, a fiercely divided Supreme Court sweepingly upheld a consensual sodomy law in *Bowers v. Hardwick*.[65] The majority Justices emphasized that they were only addressing "homosexual sodomy," and reaffirmed the lesson from "millennia of moral teaching" that this behavior is abhorrent to civilized society.[66] In a low bow to the democracy meta-norm, the Court held that "majority sentiments on the morality of homosexuality" could be a rational basis justifying a law that carried with it a mandatory minimum prison sentence of one year and a possible maximum sentence of twenty years for consensual activities in the home.[67] Baron von Steuben would have been appalled (and quite alarmed) by this decision, which was subjected to scathing criticism from scholars because of its factual errors and faulty legal analysis.[68] On the Supreme Court itself, the fifth Justice signing the majority opinion not only publicly regretted his vote but also was reported to have said that he had never even met a "homosexual" in 1986 (even though one of his law clerks that year was openly gay).[69]

Notwithstanding these criticisms, *Bowers* is in 1986 a highly relevant constitutional precedent for evaluating the application of the

---

[64] Id. at 213–18 (detailed account of the District's decriminalization legislation and the House debate and veto of that effort).

[65] 478 U.S. 186 (1986).

[66] Id. at 190–91 (majority opinion); id. at 197–98 (Burger, C.J., concurring) ("millennia of moral teachings").

[67] Id. at 196 (majority opinion).

[68] Eskridge, *Gaylaw*; Charles Fried, *Order and Law—Arguing the Reagan Revolution* 81–84 (1991), 81–84; Richard A. Posner, *Sex and Reason* 341–50 (1992); Earl M. Maltz, *The Prospects for a Revival of Conservative Activism in Constitutional Jurisprudence*, 24 Ga. L. Rev. 629, 645 n. 95 (1990) (citing numerous law review articles and notes intensely critical of *Bowers*).

[69] John C. Jeffries Jr., *Justice Lewis F. Powell Jr.* (1994) (account of Justice Powell's agonizing over whether consensual sodomy laws were unconstitutional, a process affected by his belief that he had never met a "homosexual," notwithstanding many law clerks who were gay or lesbian).

1956 park security law to a "homosexual" walking through Lafayette Park. It would seem to discourage if not foreclose a broad equal protection attack on the "homosexuals" in the park law, obsolete as it may have been in 1986. But *Bowers* itself must be read against the background of the constitutional meta-norm protecting personal liberty. The Constitution as a document is saturated with the assumption that Americans ought to enjoy as much freedom as possible, within the limitations of a well-ordered and increasingly regulatory society.[70] Although *Bowers* held that gay people could be criminally responsible for their consensual activities, four dissenters made a powerful case that this holding went against the libertarian guarantees of the Constitution, and the fifth majority Justice casually suggested that the state could not imprison them on that basis.[71]

Consistent with the liberty meta-norm, another constitutional precedent is relevant to analysis of the 1956 statute—namely, the Supreme Court's 1972 decision in *Papachristou v. City of Jacksonville*.[72] The case involved an ordinance making it a crime to be "vagabonds," "habitual loafers," and so forth. The police arrested two interracial couples for driving around town, "loafing" under this statute. A unanimous Court ruled that the "archaic" law violated the Due Process Clause, because it "makes criminal actions which by modern standards are normally innocent," and was therefore mainly enforced mainly against "nonconformists."[73] Although *Papachristou* involved an apparently racist enforcement of the ordinance, the Court's reasoning did not depend on that feature of the case—and the reasoning creates some due process doubts about the Park Safety Act of 1956, which penalizes "innocent conduct" and is by 1986 "archaic."

That the 1956 statute only targets "homosexuals" also raises red flags in light of the Constitution's larger animosity to "class legislation" (discussed earlier). The generality requirement of the rule of law and the equal protection requirement of the Fourteenth and (by 1986) Fifth Amendments admonish policymakers to avoid laws that target minorities and treat them with special disapprobation. The constitutional meta-norm against class legislation would not

---

[70] For exegeses on the libertarian foundations of the Constitution, see Friedrich Hayek, *The Constitution of Liberty* (1959), as well as Randy Barnett, *Restoring the Lost Constitution: The Presumption of Liberty* (2004).

[71] *Bowers,* 478 U.S. at 197–98 (Powell, J., concurring) (reserving issue whether someone could go to jail for consensual sodomy); id. at 203–08 (Blackmun, J., dissenting).

[72] 405 U.S. 156 (1972).

[73] Id. at 163–64, 170.

have been easily mobilized in 1956, when Americans of all ideologies considered "homosexuals and other sex perverts" no more a social class than burglars, pickpockets, or prostitutes. Social perception had dramatically changed by 1986. Notwithstanding *Bowers,* many more Americans could understand that gay people were a social group and not just a category of sex predator. Also, by 1986, even poorly informed judges would have perceived (perhaps with aid of counsel) that the "homosexuals" in the park law applies to lesbians, who have not been associated with the public cruising activities that might justify a nuisance statute.[74] If the 1986 prosecution were against a lesbian couple taking a daytime stroll in the park, rather than John Doe Jr., the rule of law might be hard put to sustain a criminal charge against them.

By 1986, a judge would have been well-justified in finding that the Lafayette Park Safety Act of 1956 sweeps too broadly by excluding a whole class of citizens from a public landmark, based upon stale beliefs that those citizens are public nuisances. The rule of law would suggest that the Court of Appeals for the District of Columbia Circuit (bound by the controlling authority of *Bowers*) ought to rest any invalidation upon *Papachristou.* Judges willing to bury this outdated law would be well-advised to emphasize the nation's larger commitment to personal liberty, including the right to walk around in public spaces of the nation's capital. While *Bowers* allowed a shocking degree of state regulation of gay people's personal liberties, no one read *Bowers* to say that the state can deny "homosexuals" the right to enter into contracts, to own and inherit property, to vote, to get married (to someone of the "opposite" sex), and to travel. It is not a big step for such a judge to hold that the "homosexual," like everyone else, enjoys the freedom to take walks in public places.

Whether even a *Papachristou* argument prevails, however, depends in part upon the information and views of the relevant agencies and upon the receptiveness of appellate judges to fact-based accounts of gay people and their behavior. It is quite likely that, by 1986, the United States Park Police are not ordinarily enforcing the old "homosexuals" in the park law and that the arrest of John Doe Jr. is a complete aberration, maybe even the result of a sharp attack of

---

[74] An ordinary meaning analysis of "homosexuals" might even read the statutory term narrowly, to be limited to gay men—but such a reading would then create a sex discrimination in the law. The Supreme Court by 1986 recognized that sex discriminations must be subjected to heightened scrutiny. E.g., *Mississippi University for Women v. Hogan*, 458 U.S. 718, 723–24 (1982).

AIDS-phobia on the part of the arresting officer. It is also doubtful that the National Park Service is keen on the law either. Park Service Director William Penn Mott Jr. (1985–89), one of the most distinguished conservationists of the twentieth century, was famous for bringing more women and racial minorities into official positions.[75] It is likely that such an inclusive and conservation-focused director would not have been a fan of my hypothetical 1956 law; if he were to go on record criticizing the law as unnecessary and wasteful of park resources, one can imagine a wider variety of judges willing to strike down the law.

On the other hand, the National Park Service is under the direct control of the Secretary of the Interior and the White House; Mott's own tenure ended with the Reagan Presidency. During the Reagan Administration, the executive department's policy was to avoid public controversy of any sort with regard to homosexuality. Thus, a director rousting dozens of suspected "homosexuals" from Lafayette Park and raising a stir with the media would not last long—but neither would a director publicly criticizing a longstanding anti-homosexual statute like our 1956 law. During the Reagan era, the odds are that the relevant agencies would have bit their tongues or even lent mild support to the law.

Even if one or both agencies were to support the validity of the law, what do they or the Department of Justice (prosecuting Doe Jr.) believe is its public justification? Is there any reason to believe that "homosexuals" are public nuisances nowadays? If the law enforcement agencies are no longer enforcing the law and have no evidence that it is still needed, these are red flags that ought to trigger judicial skepticism. On the other hand, if the agencies or their attorneys have evidence suggesting that gay people are behaving too aggressively in Lafayette Park and that this is having a demonstrable effect on families or others visiting the park, that is relevant for the reviewing court as well. In the constitutional world of *Bowers v. Hardwick*, a vigorous, fact-based argument by the enforcement agencies that this law is needed to maintain the safety of families visiting the park would very likely affect the constitutional judgment of at least some judges.

For the foregoing reasons, some federal judges would be willing to strike down the "homosexuals" in the park law in 1986, but others

---

[75] Mary Ellen Butler, *Prophet of the Parks: The Story of William Penn Mott Jr.* (1999).

would not. As it turns out, many of the latter were important judges serving on the U.S. Court of Appeals for the District of Columbia Circuit. In a famous 1984 decision, Judge Robert Bork, the intellectual star of the Court and a celebrated law professor and Solicitor General before that, had anticipated the holding and reasoning of *Bowers v. Hardwick* and had applied that reasoning to justify broad discrimination against "homosexuals" by the armed forces and elsewhere.[76] Bound by circuit precedent as well as *Bowers*, a trial or appellate judge in the D.C. Circuit would be constrained not to invalidate the 1956 statute under an equal protection analysis and might be discouraged from striking it down under *Papachristou* as well (this approach would not be barred by the precedents but might be discouraged by their broadly anti-homosexual reasoning).

Nevertheless, such a judge might construe the law narrowly, in light of the libertarian meta-norm reflected in our Constitution and its common law background. Because John Doe Jr. is openly gay, he does not have the defense offered by his father in 1956, that he is not a "homosexual" regulated by the law. But Doe Jr. might invoke the avoidance canon and the common law canon to suggest a narrowing construction of the law. On its face, the 1956 statute is a nuisance law, protecting visitors against people who might disturb their peaceful enjoyment of the park. If John Doe Jr. were just walking through Lafayette Park, bothering no one, he is not a nuisance as the common law would have understood the term. And he is engaging in conduct (walking around) that *Papachristou* protects against criminal sanctions, unless there is strong justification. To avoid a broad even if literal construction of the 1956 statute that would "make[ ] criminal actions which by modern standards are normally innocent," a judge could head off a serious constitutional issue by narrowing the law.[77]

Thus, a conscientious judge who is interested in the neutral application of the criminal law, but is not so adventurous as to strike down the Lafayette Park Safety Act, ought to read into the law a condition that the offending "homosexual" must be *doing* something bothersome to other park visitors. In our constitutional tradition,

---

[76] *Dronenburg v. Zech*, 741 F.2d 1388 (D.C. Cir. 1984) (Bork, J., joined by Scalia, J.), rehearing denied, 746 F.2d 1579 (D.C. Cir., en banc, 1984) (justifying the discharge of a gay man from the armed forces in a broadly argued opinion, precisely anticipating the reasoning of *Bowers* and applying such reasoning to justify discrimination by the federal government against "homosexuals").

[77] Compare *People v. Baker,* 984 N.E.2d 902, 905–08 (N.Y. 2013) (interpreting a disorderly conduct law narrowly to require a public harm element, thereby avoiding First Amendment problems with the law).

people cannot be arrested just for being themselves—this would strike deeply at the libertarian meta-norm and would no longer (in 1986) receive support from the democracy meta-norm. This interpellation would have the virtue of avoiding the serious constitutional question posed by this statute and is a strategy the Supreme Court has sometimes followed for other vague criminal laws that deploy common law concepts.[78]

The Constitution in 2016: Equality

If the Lafayette Park Safety Act of 1956 were still in force this year, 2016, there is little doubt that federal judges would find it unconstitutional if the issue were presented in a justiciable controversy. In the sixty years since enactment of this (hypothetical) statute, the text and structure of the Constitution have not materially changed, as explained at the beginning of the last part. As before, what was not added to the Constitution may be significant. That is, a majority of the Republican-controlled Senate in 2004 and 2006 voted down a constitutional amendment to limit civil marriage to different-sex couples, a tribute to the growing political repudiation of the politics of the 1950s anti-homosexual terror. Since 2006, moreover, most Americans have come to accept marriage equality for sexual and gender minorities, who can now get married in the District of Columbia and all fifty states.[79] In short, between 1956 and 2016, the nation's constitutional culture has witnessed a sea change as regards the legal and constitutional rights of lesbian, gay, bisexual, and transgender (LGBT) persons.

Indeed, today, the biggest obstacle to judicial review of the 1956 law would be the lack of a lawsuit. The arrest and prosecution of John Doe Jr. in 1986 are unlikely enough—but it would be almost inconceivable that John Doe III (the openly gay grandson of the original John Doe defendant) would be arrested for nothing more offensive than being in Lafayette Park. Without an arrest, there would be no lawsuit subject to review by federal trial or appellate judges. But assume that the Court of Appeals for the District of

---

[78] *Skilling v. United States*, 561 U.S. 358, 409–13 (2010) (finding that a federal law making it a crime to engage in a "scheme or artifice to deprive another of the intangible right of honest services" was too vague and had to be narrowed to schemes involving bribes or kickbacks); cf. id. at 415, 422–24 (Scalia, J., concurring in part and dissenting in part) (agreeing with the Court that the statute was unconstitutionally vague and urging that it simply be invalidated rather than rewritten).

[79] *Obergefell v. Hodges*, 135 S.Ct. 2584 (2015) (recognizing a Fourteenth Amendment right to marriage equality for same-sex couples).

Columbia Circuit interpreted the law in 1986 to be limited to situations where the "homosexual" created a nuisance by making lewd advances to others in Lafayette Park (the narrowing construction suggested at the end of the last part). If Doe III did something like that, the Park Police might arrest him, and we might have a potential case or controversy. Is the Lafayette Park Safety Act of 1956, as narrowed by the Court of Appeals, unconstitutional? (By the way, the decisionmaker for this constitutional question might well be the Attorney General or the Solicitor General, and not a federal appellate court, as the discussion below will suggest.)

As narrowed, it is doubtful that the statute is inconsistent with the due process rights recognized in *Papachristou*. The government can probably regulate park visitors who are making unwanted advances to other visitors, without violating the constitutional liberty meta-norm. The key question would be whether such an anti-nuisance rule can be limited to "homosexuals." A federal judge is almost certain to say that the 1956 law, even as narrowly construed, violates the Fifth Amendment. Because an offensive "heterosexual" would not be subject to arrest, even if bothering people with the same or even more offensive lewd advances, the law subjecting offensive "homosexuals" to arrest violates the equal treatment feature of the Due Process Clause.

The court's process of reasoning would reflect the different sources that this volume has been examining in the context of statutory interpretation. Overall, the judge would find more bite in the constitutional text than judges or administrators would have found in 1956 or even in 1986—largely because LGBT Americans are more socially accepted, an acceptance that has been reflected in our national constitutional culture.[80] The constitutional case against the Lafayette Park Safety Act of 1956 would be overwhelming in 2016, such that any judge doubting its violation of the Constitution would be widely criticized throughout the legal community. Indeed, it is doubtful that Attorney General Loretta Lynch would allow the U.S.

---

[80] On the critical role that constitutional culture, educated by social movements, drives the Supreme Court's interpretation of the Constitution's individual rights protections (especially), see Robert C. Post, *The Supreme Court, 2002 Term—Foreword: Fashioning the Legal Constitution: Culture, Courts, and Law,* 117 Harv. L. Rev. 4 (2003); Reva B. Siegel, *Constitutional Culture, Social Movement Conflict, and Constitutional Change: The Case of the De Facto ERA*, 94 Calif. L. Rev. 1323 (2006). See also William N. Eskridge Jr. & John Ferejohn, *A Republic of Statutes: The New American Constitution* 431–68 (2010).

Attorney to pursue the prosecution; the U.S. Attorney is likely to concede the unconstitutionality of the 1956 law.

Although the wording of the Due Process Clause has not changed since 1956, its meaning with regard to LGBT persons has changed significantly, in part because binding precedents have recognized the deep unfairness of federal as well as state discrimination against sexual and gender minorities. Three Supreme Court precedents are fatal to the 1956 law, because it is inconsistent with their holdings, either individually or collectively. Reflecting a sea change in American constitutional culture, the precedents also reflect the collapse of democratic support for anti-gay caste legislation and near consensus for guaranteeing LGBT persons all the same liberties that everyone else enjoys.

In 1996, the Supreme Court held in *Romer v. Evans* that a state constitutional amendment preempting ordinances, executive orders, laws, or other legal measures protecting lesbian, gay, and bisexual people from discrimination violated the Equal Protection Clause.[81] "One century ago, the first Justice Harlan admonished this Court that the Constitution 'neither knows nor tolerates classes among citizens.' Unheeded then, those words now are understood to state a commitment to the law's neutrality where the rights of persons are at stake."[82] Finding the blanket exclusion, unprecedented in our public law, too little connected to legitimate public goals (such as conservation of scarce enforcement resources for civil rights measures), the Court held that the state could not treat LGBT citizens so dismissively. With its emphasis on "class legislation," *Romer* invoked the historical background and due process origins of the Equal Protection Clause.

In 1995, the Supreme Court had explicitly ruled that the equal treatment assurances in the Fifth and Fourteenth Amendments were "congruent,"[83] so *Romer* would create serious constitutional doubts about the validity of the Lafayette Park Safety Act of 1956 under the Fifth Amendment. As the *Romer* dissent reminded the Court, however, *Bowers v. Hardwick* was still good law, so a government lawyer defending the 1956 law could still maintain that if the federal government could put John Doe III in jail for consensual homosexual

---

[81] *Romer v. Evans*, 517 U.S. 620, 626–27, 635–36 (1996); see Jane S. Schacter, Romer v. Evans *and Democracy's Domain*, 50 Vand. L. Rev. 361 (1997).

[82] *Romer*, 517 U.S. at 623 (citation omitted) (quoting *Plessy v. Ferguson,* 163 U.S. 537, 559 (1896) (Harlan, J., dissenting)).

[83] *Adarand Constructors,* 515 U.S. at 213–18.

activities in the home, then the government could bar him from homosexual solicitation or lewd advances in the public shadow of Baron von Steuben's monument.

In 2003, however, the Supreme Court overruled *Bowers* in *Lawrence v. Texas*.[84] There are several relevant features of the Court's reasoning in *Lawrence* that bear on the Lafayette Park law. To begin with, *Lawrence* reinterpreted the common law background against which lesbian and gay people had been understood in *Bowers*. Resting upon a Blackstonian view of the "crime against nature" as reprehensible and creatively reading that crime to include consensual homosexual intimacy in private places, *Bowers* could be interpreted as recognizing an ancient common law tradition whereby gay people are "unnatural" criminals (consistent with Judge Bork's jurisprudence on the D.C. Circuit). *Lawrence* renounced the mischaracterization of the common law and tradition found in *Bowers*. Drawing from *amicus* briefs, the Court found that American common law had virtually nothing to say about homosexuality, limited the crime against nature to anal sex with unconsenting persons or animals, and trained upon third-party harms in public spaces and not the intimacy of lesbian or gay lovers.[85] *Lawrence* is significant not only because it overruled *Bowers,* but also because its overruling reconceptualized the deep background of the Due Process Clause in a way that did not exclude gay persons from the generality requirements of the rule of law. Not incidentally, *Lawrence* corrected glaring mistakes in *Bowers'* reading of the common law and presented an historically more accurate reading.[86]

Additionally, *Lawrence* recognized the connection between the liberty protected by the Due Process Clause and the equal treatment demanded by the Equal Protection Clause of the Fourteenth Amendment:

---

[84] *Lawrence v. Texas*, 539 U.S. 558, 574, 578–79 (2003). See generally Dale Carpenter, *Flagrant Conduct: The Story of* Lawrence v. Texas (2012); Nan D. Hunter, *Living with* Lawrence, 88 Minn. L. Rev. 1103 (2004); Jane S. Schacter, Lawrence v. Texas *and the Fourteenth Amendment's Democratic Aspirations*, 13 Temp. Pol. & Civ. Rts. L. Rev. 733 (2004) (exploring the role of *Lawrence* in creating a respectful democratic culture).

[85] *Lawrence,* 539 U.S. at 568–70, drawing (sometimes verbatim) from the Brief of the Cato Institute as *Amicus Curiae* in Support of Petitioners, *Lawrence v. Texas* (No. 02–102).

[86] See William N. Eskridge Jr., Hardwick *and Historiography,* 1999 U. Ill. L. Rev. 631 (sharply criticizing *Hardwick* for its misrepresentation of the common law of sodomy), cited and relied on by *Lawrence*, 539 U.S. at 571.

> Equality of treatment and the due process right to demand respect for conduct protected by the substantive guarantee of liberty are linked in important respects, and a decision on the latter point advances both interests. If protected conduct is made criminal and the law which does so remains unexamined for its substantive validity, its stigma might remain even if it were not enforceable as drawn for equal protection reasons. When homosexual conduct is made criminal by the law of the State, that declaration in and of itself is an invitation to subject homosexual persons to discrimination both in the public and in the private spheres. The central holding of *Bowers* has been brought in question by this case, and it should be addressed. Its continuance as precedent demeans the lives of homosexual persons.[87]

If this reasoning is to be taken seriously, the Lafayette Park Safety Act of 1956 is probably unconstitutional, for it openly discriminates against "homosexuals" because of their presumed sexual activities, perhaps even more "demean[ing]" than the Texas "homosexual sodomy law" invalidated in *Lawrence*.

Finally, as a matter of constitutional interpretation, it is significant that *Lawrence*'s criticism of *Bowers* went beyond the constitutional text, the historical understanding of due process and equal protection, the constitutional precedents, and the common law. The Court explicitly considered the constitutional deliberations engaged in by state judges and legislators and by commissions and judges in other countries.[88] To be sure, the Court's reference to "foreign" sources, in particular, has been controversial.[89] In its defense, the Court deployed these deliberations as part of a deep reconsideration of *Bowers*' understanding of constitutional liberty. That *Bowers* mischaracterized the common law and treated sexual minorities disrespectfully, does not mean that a gay rights reading of liberty is the right one. Justices might usefully consider how other

---

[87] *Lawrence,* 539 U.S. at 575; see also id. at 581 (O'Connor, J., concurring in the Court's judgment, based solely on the equal protection analysis).

[88] Id. at 570–73 (citing, as evidence that *Bowers* represented a poor understanding of constitutional liberty, state legislative judgments, state court interpretations of state constitutions, the Wolfenden Report in Great Britain, the deliberations of the American Law Institute, and constitutional decisions in Europe).

[89] E.g., id. at 598 (Scalia, J., dissenting) (sharply criticizing the majority for invoking "foreign" sources); *Foster v. Florida,* 537 U.S. 990 n.* (2002) (Thomas, J., concurring in denial of certiorari) (similar critique of American interest in "foreign moods, fads, or fashions"); *Atkins v. Virginia,* 536 U.S. 304, 324–25 (2002) (Rehnquist, C.J., dissenting) (similar).

courts, commissions, and even countries have understood liberty once LGBT people became a salient social group in those societies.[90]

Lawrence also cited and drew from an *amicus* brief by Mary Robinson, former Prime Minister of Ireland, who maintained that *Bowers* was inconsistent with international law norms.[91] Recall the international law canon discussed in chapter six; that canon is relevant to constitutional decisionmaking as well, albeit much more controversially.[92] If public international law, binding upon the United States, supports a particular norm, that is often relevant to domestic constitutional decisionmaking. Even if internal American sources point toward one interpretation of due process and equal protection, as *Lawrence* held, it is useful to see whether that interpretation is consistent with international law. If it is, the interpreter is more confident of her assessment of the domestic sources.[93] If it is not, the interpreter might want to have a second look at the domestic sources.[94] The Justices in *Bowers*, for example, would have profited from a second look, given the many inaccuracies and baseless conclusions found in that unfortunate opinion.

In 2016, international law lends considerable support to the conclusion that the modern state acts illegitimately if it criminalizes or targets sexual and gender minorities for uniquely demeaning treatment. The United Nations Charter of 1945, a source of international law, encourages "respect for human rights and fundamental freedoms for all without distinction."[95] The Universal

---

[90] For thoughtful defenses of American engagement with transnational and international law in constitutional cases, see, e.g., Breyer, *The Court and the World*; Vicki C. Jackson, *Constitutional Engagement in a Transnational Era* (2010); Melissa A. Waters, *Mediating Norms and Identity: The Role of Transnational Judicial Dialogue in Creating and Enforcing International Law*, 93 Geo. L.J. 487, 505–29 (2005).

[91] *Lawrence,* 539 U.S. at 576–77, citing and relying on Brief for Mary Robinson et al. as *Amici Curiae* in Support of Petitioners, at 11–12, *Lawrence v. Texas* (No. 02–102).

[92] See Roger P. Alford, *Foreign Relations as a Matter of Interpretation: The Use and Abuse of* Charming Betsy, 67 Ohio St. L.J. 1339 (2006) (supporting international law as a canon for interpreting statutes, but not for interpreting the Constitution); Ernest A. Young, *Foreign Law and the Denominator Problem*, 119 Harv. L. Rev. 148 (2005) (raising concerns that judges sometimes use international sources to buttress weak domestic law cases).

[93] E.g., *Washington v. Glucksberg*, 521 U.S. 702, 710, 718 (1997) (Rehnquist, C.J., for the Court); id. at 785–87 (Souter, J., concurring in the judgment).

[94] E.g., *Poe v. Ullman,* 367 U.S. 497, 548 (1961) (Harlan, J., dissenting) (urging the Court to reconsider its dismissal of privacy claims, based upon the understanding "throughout the English-speaking world" that such claims concerned "a most fundamental aspect of 'liberty' ").

[95] Charter of the United Nations ch. 1, art. 1 (1945).

Declaration of Human Rights of 1948 says that all human beings are "equal before the law" and ought not be subject to state discrimination based upon "status."[96] Led by Secretary General Ban Ki-moon and the Office of the High Commissioner for Human Rights, the United Nations has interpreted the Declaration to admonish member states against open discrimination based on sexual or gender identity.[97]

Additionally, the United States has signed the International Covenant of Civil and Political Rights (ICCPR), and the Senate ratified the convention in 1992 (with a reservation barring a private cause of action). Article 2(1) of the ICCPR requires signatory counties "to respect and to ensure to all individuals within its territory and subject to its jurisdiction the rights recognized in the present Covenant, without distinction of any kind, such as race, colour, sex, language, religion, political or other opinion, national or social origin, property, birth or other status." For more than twenty years, the Human Rights Committee has admonished signatory states that discriminatory treatment based on sexual orientation is a "distinction" based on "other status," barred by the ICCPR.[98] The United Nations treats this convention as a source of international law. Apart from that, the convention is binding domestic law in the United States because it has been ratified. In 2016, the 1956 "homosexuals" in the park law would be an international embarrassment for American law in the world community—even more than *Bowers* had been in 2003, when it was overruled in *Lawrence*.

If there were any doubt, after *Romer* and *Lawrence*, that the exclusion of "homosexuals" from Lafayette Park is a violation of the equal treatment feature of the Fifth Amendment, it should be resolved in favor of this country's adherence to international conventions which we have signed and ratified. These international sources also reinforce the Supreme Court's admonition that the

---

96 Universal Declaration of Human Rights art. 7 (1948); see also id. art. 2 (general nondiscrimination state duty).

97 United Nations, Office of the High Commissioner for Human Rights, *Born Free and Equal: Sexual Orientation and Gender Identity in International Human Rights Law* 38–53 (2012).

98 The leading statement is *Toonen* v. *Australia*, Human Rights Committee Communication No. 488/1992, CCPR/C/50/D/488/1992 (1994), which has been followed and expanded in *Young* v. *Australia*, Human Rights Committee Communication No. 941/2000 (CCPR/C/78/D/941/2000) (2003); *X* v. *Colombia*, Human Rights Committee Communication No. 1361/2005(CCPR/C/89/D/1361/2005) (2007). See generally Office of the High Commissioner, *Born Free and Equal*, 40–42 (surveying the cases).

guarantees of the Equal Protection Clause (in the Fourteenth Amendment) apply with full force to Congress by means of the Fifth Amendment. If further legal citation were required, it could be provided by *United States v. Windsor*, where the Supreme Court struck down the anti-gay Defense of Marriage Act of 1996 as a violation of the Fifth Amendment.[99] Drawing from *Romer* and *Lawrence* (Fourteenth Amendment precedents), *Windsor* ruled that the federal government's failure to recognize legitimate lesbian and gay marriages for more than 1100 national statutory and regulatory provisions was fundamentally unfair and therefore a violation of the Due Process Clause.

Even *Bowers*-nostalgic judges would recognize, in 2016, that the rule of law would require invalidation of the "homosexuals" in the park law. Our current understanding of the ordinary meaning of "due process of law," the libertarian as well as egalitarian structure of the Constitution, a host of binding Supreme Court constitutional precedents, executive department admonitions and interpretations, and treaty commitments as well as customary international law, would amount to a crushing case against the Lafayette Park Safety Act of 1956.

* * *

Reflect upon some lessons that this constitutional exercise might have for statutory interpretation, which is the primary project of this volume. Start with an important difference. Text and structure tend to be more important in statutory interpretation cases than in constitutional cases, where the primary source of reasoning is from precedent and evolving constitutional principle. What drives this difference, however, is mainly the documentary rather than normative differences between the Constitution, which is short, old, and hard to amend, and statutes, which tend to be new, detailed, and easier to amend. The Sherman Act of 1890 makes this point. It is a statute formally very similar to the Constitution in its brevity, its deployment of open-textured common law terms, and its age. So what legal sources dominate its jurisprudence? You guessed it: precedents and evolving statutory purpose.[100]

---

[99] *United States v. Windsor,* 133 S.Ct. 2675 (2013), followed and expanded in *Obergefell v. Hodges,* 135 S.Ct. 2584 (2015) (striking down state exclusions of same-sex couples from civil marriage law).

[100] Eskridge & Ferejohn, *Republic of Statutes,* 119–64 (detailed account of the evolution of the Sherman Act's legisprudence).

Similarities outweigh the differences between statutory and constitutional interpretation, however. A fundamental similarity is their shared methodological pluralism. Neither constitutional nor statutory interpreters can ignore the ordinary meaning of the legal text, how that text relates to the larger document, and how the Supreme Court (or the relevant appellate court) has authoritatively interpreted it or an analogous provision. This can hardly be controversial, but neither do these three classic rule of law factors exhaust the reasoning and justification for either statutory or constitutional decisions. Some judges are nervous about admitting that legislative history and executive department inputs influence their reading of statutory or constitutional provisions—but there can be no doubt that they do play an important role and scarcely less doubt that they should do so (or so I have argued in chapters four and five). Judges are even more hesitant to admit larger normative influences on their reading of statutes or the Constitution, but the judicially announced canons bring them out of the closet on this score as well. Notice how changing factual and normative understandings about homosexuality drive the dynamic constitutional and statutory interpretation of the Lafayette Park Safety Act of 1956 that we have been examining.

This conclusion's extended examination of the constitutional case of "homosexuals" in Lafayette Park illustrates the abstract assertion made in the introduction to this volume, that a non-foundational, multi-factor approach to interpretation does not operate mechanically. The judge does not figure out the ordinary meaning and then turn to the statutory structure and then see if precedents are relevant. The judge is thinking about all these sources of legal guidance holistically and synergistically rather than categorically and sequentially. Whether the "homosexuals" in the park law violates the Fifth Amendment requires the judge to interpret "due process of law," the relevant constitutional language. But interpreting this language means something more than applying the ordinary meaning rule or the term of art canon—it requires the judge to relate different possible interpretations to the structure of the Constitution and to the precedents declaring the meaning or purpose of that language. What gives authority to the judicial office is her willingness to keep an open mind as she evaluates the different arguments, against the template of the different legal authorities.

One canard I want to single out is the notion that, once the judge finds a statutory or constitutional "plain meaning" in the text and structure, she simply stops thinking and delivers her answer.

Ordinary meaning is an empirical inquiry (how do people actually understand this statement, in context), while plain meaning is a cumulative legal conclusion. It is cumulative in that there is no plain meaning until the judge has examined all the relevant legal sources of meaning—purpose and preamble provisions affording a policy context for the language, committee reports explaining the precise statement Congress ultimately adopted, agency implementation and experience with the law, and substantive norms that dominate the area of law. The cumulative nature of plain meaning also enriches the concept with normativity, through different normative inputs from different sources. Statements of purpose are usually written at a higher level of generality and of authority than legislator or committee declarations about the meaning of specific terms and clauses. Agency experience brings pragmatic wisdom to bear on the statute's capacity for fulfilling the advertised purposes. And meta-norms drawn from the common law and the Constitution require judges to think about application of text to specific facts in light of the larger canvass of the law and the norms that bind us into a constitutional community.

In short, plain meaning is the product of the entire interpretative process, and not some independently existing filter that prevents relevant legal sources from being considered by judges. The godfather of the new textualism, Justice Oliver Wendell Holmes Jr. put it this way: "It is said that when the meaning of language is plain we are not to resort to [extrinsic] evidence in order to raise doubts. That is rather an axiom of experience than a rule of law and does not preclude consideration of persuasive evidence if it exists."[101] Although this understanding of plain meaning is not one that most judges concede openly anymore, it does reflect the operation of judicial reasoning and does come out of the judicial closet more often than scholars have appreciated.[102]

---

[101] *Boston Sand & Gravel Co. v. United States,* 278 U.S. 41, 48 (1928) (Holmes, J.); accord, Tex. Govt. Code § 311.023; *Poole v. Orange Cnty. Fire Auth.*, 354 P.3d 346, 354–56 (Cal. 2015) (Cuéllar, J., concurring).

[102] For examples of appellate decisions revealing a process whereby an initial "plain meaning" was not just reconsidered but abandoned in light of strong contextual evidence, see *Pepper v. Hart,* [1993] 1 All E.R. 42, [1992] 3 W.L.R. 1032 (House of Lords 1992) (legislative history); *King v. Burwell,* 135 S.Ct. 2480, 2492–96 (2015) (statutory plan); *Brown v. Plata,* 131 S.Ct. 1910, 1950–51 (2011) (Scalia, J., dissenting) (absurd results); *Zuni Pub. Sch. Dist. No. 89 v. Department of Education,* 550 U.S. 81, 89–93 (2007) (statutory policy); *Gonzales v. Oregon,* 546 U.S. 243, 269–73 (2006) (constitutional norms); *People v. Leiva*, 297 P.3d 870, 876–80 (Cal. 2013) (constitutional norms and legislative history); *In re Jacob,* 660 N.E.2d 397, 399–405 (N.Y. 1995) (Kaye, C.J.) (statutory plan and constitutional norms).

Plain meaning ought to be considered dialectical, a real-time conversation among advocates vying for the judge's ruling in their favor, as well as an intertemporal conversation among a bygone Congress, an agency with a history and a mission, and a judge looking both backward to established law and ahead to skeptical scrutiny of her reasoning. Lest this kind of thinking be mistaken for an endless foray into indeterminacy, please review the materials in this volume and notice that I was able to reach interpretive closure for pretty much all the hypothetical cases examined. Critics are invited to improve upon my conclusions or, even better, pursue them in novel directions by expanding the factual horizon of the hypothetical statutes.

Another lesson from this conclusion is that the interpreter's perspective makes a difference in both statutory and constitutional interpretation. The judge, such as the late Robert Bork, who views "homosexuals" with suspicion *and* who is skeptical of equal protection claims, will not read either the Park Safety Act or the Constitution the same way as the judge, such as Ruth Bader Ginsburg (Judge Bork's colleague on the D.C. Circuit and now a Supreme Court Justice), who has many lesbian and gay friends and who celebrates a broad understanding of the Equal Protection Clause. Specifically, Judge Bork in 1986 would not have read the Constitution to provide any relief to John Doe Jr., and it is almost as certain that he would not have been willing to interpret the Park Safety Act to be limited to true "nuisance" situations, where the "homosexual" was bothering other park users. In contrast, Judge Ginsburg (as she was in 1986 still sitting on the D.C. Circuit) would have been friendlier to constitutional protection and would probably have supported a narrowing interpretation if a court majority did not accept the constitutional argument.

That different judges would have emphasized different features of the statutory and constitutional issues posed by the "homosexuals" in the park law, does not greatly undermine the rule of law. It only means that there are hard cases where the legal criteria allow a variety of answers *and* that the answer delivered by a judicial tribunal will be influenced by the judge's particular understanding of the normative context of the case and of her institutional role. Even for issues as contentious as "homosexuals" in Lafayette Park, however, the law has a learning curve. Our nation's constitutional culture not only reflects that learning curve, but constrains judges as well. In 1956, our constitutional culture understood "homosexuals" as sexual predators and even as Trojan Horses or Fifth Columns, and so even a Ruth Bader Ginsburg would not have been willing to press as far in that year than she would have pushed in 1986 or 2016. Today's constitutional culture has taken such tropes off the table and generally insists upon equal treatment. Thus, I believe that if Judge Bork were sitting on the D.C. Circuit in 2016, he would vote to strike down the Park Safety Act of 1956, based upon Supreme Court precedent if nothing else.

Although the difference that new perspectives and an evolving constitutional culture make is most dramatic in my concluding thought experiment evaluating the 1956 statute, the same phenomenon is at work in the earlier chapters as well. Thus, a national park administrator alarmed at rising levels of injury because of post-2001 Segways filling up Lafayette Park is much more likely to ban them as "vehicles" than either Judge Bork or Judge Ginsburg would have been if they were still sitting together on the D.C. Circuit. To extend my parallel, the administrator would have harbored a fear of Segways that the judges would not necessarily have shared, and the judges would have been more attentive to the precise language and structure of the statute, as a limit on what the administrator could do. More dramatic, of course, is the sea change in the nation's regulatory climate and constitutional culture after 9/11. Administrators would have strongly insisted on more security in Lafayette Park, because it is right across the street from the White House, and they would have driven the Park Safety Act of 1992 through as many barriers as needed to secure a broad understanding of prohibited "vehicles." For their parts, both a Bork and a Ginsburg would have been much more willing to accommodate the agency after 9/11 than before that date.

The foregoing point suggests a final lesson from this extended thought experiment. Statutory and constitutional interpretation are intertwined. This is dramatically evident in the normative saga of gay people in America, where the meaning of the "homosexuals" in the park law evolved as more gay people came out of the closet, first as brave individuals, then as dying men nursed by their caregivers, and more recently as couples with families. The constitutional protections available to LGBT Americans increased at roughly the same time.

The synergy between statutory and constitutional interpretation that is so obvious in the identity-politics drama of the "homosexuals" in the park law can now be seen more clearly in the playing out of the lower-stakes vehicles in the park law. When the Lafayette Park Safety Act of 1992 is applied to Cynthia Hogan, the motorized bicyclist, or to skateboarder William Treanor, or to Mike Giannotto, the Segway operator, the statute is interpreted against the background of legal traditions and social norms that influence the judge's (or the prosecutor's or the police officer's) application of the statute to this factual situation. The Constitution is explicitly relevant to statutory interpretation through all the doctrines discussed in chapter six—but it is also implicitly relevant when judges consider whether a literal application of the statutory words would be absurd (chapter one) or contrary to the statutory plan (chapter two), whether it is fair to treat a proposed "vehicle" differently from one that has been so classified by a statutory precedent (chapter three), and whether the judge's view of the statutory language and plan is consistent with the understanding of the democratically accountable branches that launched the statute (chapter four) and have implemented it (chapter five). Due process fairness, equal treatment of similar cases, and the nature of the judicial, legislative, and executive powers are the province of the Constitution—but are always at least generally relevant when the judge engages with a statute.

Conversely, as we have seen in this conclusion, constitutional interpretation itself cannot proceed until the statute has been properly interpreted. And statutory interpretation plays a more critical role in constitutional law than has been recognized by the great theorists. Most constitutional precepts are underenforced through judicial review invalidating laws and policies, and some like the nondelegation doctrine are not enforced that way at all anymore. But those same underenforced or unenforced rules find life in statutory interpretation, under cover of the avoidance, federalism, nondelegation, and other constitutional canons. Likewise, statutory interpretation to avoid constitutional conflict is the greatest of the passive virtues that enable judges to postpone decision of issues for which the nation is not at rest.

Finally, constitutional and statutory interpretation are dialectical at the normative doctrinal level as well, and this punch line is the most interesting of all. Recall the tripartite criteria laid out in the introduction and chapter one for justifying and evaluating the canons: Do they contribute to an objective (general), coherent, and predictable rule of law? Do they help judges faithfully carry forth the plan adopted by our elected representatives? Do they apportion institutional responsibilities and substantive rights in a manner consistent with good government? The gentle reader may have asked: Where did these criteria come from? What justifies each criterion, i.e., rule of law, democratic accountability, and governance? What motivated the author to subject the dry and dusty canons to such lofty analysis? The answer, of course, is the Constitution itself. Its great meta-principles are the source of and justification for my three criteria.

Thus, Article III (the "judicial Power") and the Supremacy Clause of Article VI of the Constitution underwrite the rule of law in this country, and these great constitutional provisions have been understood to require predictability, generality, and coherence in the application of law here. Articles I (the "legislative Power") and II (the "executive Power") vest policymaking with the political branches of government, whose legitimacy is enhanced by the accountability of those officials to We the People through democratic elections by a variety of constituencies as outlined by Articles I and II and by the Twelfth and Seventeenth Amendments to the Constitution. The Preamble itself lays out the criteria for good governance: We the People have formed our "more perfect Union" in order to "establish Justice, insure domestic Tranquility, provide for the common defence, promote the general Welfare, and secure the Blessings of Liberty."

The canons of statutory construction are accountable to these constitutional criteria. With them in mind, I have urged recognition of the pet fish canon (chapter one), the administrability canon and *noscitur a legibus sociis* (chapter two), the shadow precedents canon (chapter three), the Noursian legislative history canons (chapter four), the regulatory history canon (chapter five), and the borrowed treaty canon (chapter six). Conversely, I have applied these criteria, as well as empirical and other studies, to urge caution or skepticism with regard to the dictionary canon (chapter one), the title/caption canon and most of the whole code canons (chapter two), the super-strong presumption of correctness for statutory precedents (chapter four), the *Semimole Rock/Auer* canon (chapter five), and the super-strong clear statement approach to the Eleventh Amendment and the fee-shifting canons (chapter six). I have simply omitted other canons, such as the rule that ambiguities in tax statutes should be construed in favor of the taxpayer, because those canons are not normatively supportable and/or they have been honored mainly in the breech during the last several generations.

These constitutional criteria have also motivated the primary analyses announced in each chapter of this volume. Thus, I have defended the primacy of the ordinary meaning rule as understood in chapter one through the lens of prototype theory, focused on coherent statutory plans rather than mechanical consistency of terminology in chapter two, urged a flexible rather than dogmatic reading of statutory *stare decisis* in chapter three, advocated astute consultation of legislative materials in chapter four, expanded that consultation in chapter five to include the regulatory history of a statute, and linked statutes to great norms in chapter six.

There is no one-size-fits-all approach to statutory interpretation. Although focusing on a homely set of everyday examples, this volume has, I hope, illuminated its complexity while illustrating its practical wisdom.

Appendix

THE SUPREME COURT'S CANONS OF STATUTORY INTERPRETATION (1986–2016)

TEXTUAL CANONS

- *Ordinary meaning rule.* Follow the ordinary (also, "everyday" or "commonsense") meaning of the statutory text,[1] but not when that meaning requires an absurd result[2] or suggests a scrivener's error.[3] A statute has an ordinary meaning if you'd use its terminology in normal conversation "without having other people look at you funny."[4]

---

[1] Michigan v. EPA, 135 S.Ct. 2699 (2015); Octane Fitness, LLC v. ICON Health & Fitness, Inc., 134 S.Ct. 1749 (2014); Adoptive Couple v. Baby Girl, 133 S.Ct. 2552, 2560–61 (2013); Taniguchi v. Kan Pacific Saipan, Ltd., 132 S.Ct. 1997, 2002 (2012); Bilski v. Kappos, 561 U.S. 593 (2010); Massachusetts v. EPA, 549 U.S. 497, 528–29 (2007); BP America Production Co. v. Burton, 549 U.S. 84, 91 (2006); Arlington Cent. Sch. Dist. Bd. of Educ. v. Murphy, 548 U.S. 291 (2006); Pasquantino v. United States, 544 U.S. 349, 355 (2005); West Virginia Univ. Hosps. v. Casey, 499 U.S. 83, 97–98 (1991); Moskal v. United States, 498 U.S. 103, 108 (1990); United States v. Providence Journal Co., 485 U.S. 693, 700–01 (1988). See also Mohamad v. Palestinian Auth., 132 S.Ct. 1702, 1707 (2012) ("everyday parlance"); Lopez v. Gonzales, 549 U.S. 47, 53–54 (2006) (invoking "everyday understanding" and "commonsense conception" of statutory language as synonyms for "ordinary meaning"), followed in Moncrieffe v. Holder, 133 S.Ct. 1678, 1693 (2013), and Carachuri-Rosendo v. Holder, 560 U.S. 563, 574–75 (2010).

[2] Utility Air Regulatory Group v. EPA, 134 S.Ct. 2427 (2014) (plurality and concurring opinions); Brown v. Plata, 131 S.Ct. 1910, 1950–51 (2011) (dissenting opinion) (avoid "outrageous" and "absurd" results); Republic of Iraq v. Beaty, 556 U.S. 848, 861 (2009); Zuni Pub. Sch. Dist. No. 89 v. Department of Educ., 550 U.S. 81 (2007) (majority and concurring opinions); United States v. Wilson, 503 U.S. 329, 334 (1992); Green v. Bock Laundry Mach. Co., 490 U.S. 504, 509–11, 527, 530 (1989) (majority, concurring, and dissenting opinions in agreement on this point).

[3] King v. Burwell, 135 S.Ct. 2480, 2483, 2491–92 (2015); United States Nat'l Bank of Oregon v. Independent Ins. Agents, Inc., 508 U.S. 439, 462 (1993); Green v. Bock Laundry Mach. Co., 490 U.S. 504 (1989).

[4] Johnson v. United States, 529 U.S. 694, 718 (2000) (Scalia, J., dissenting).

LANGUAGE AND GRAMMAR

- *Expressio* (or *inclusio*) *unius.* Expression of one thing suggests the exclusion of others.[5] Inapplicable if statutory purpose or context suggests listing is not comprehensive.[6]
- *Noscitur a sociis.* Interpret a general term to be similar to more specific terms in a series.[7] *Noscitur* is often not helpful when applied to a technical statute whose details were hammered out through a complex process, or to a statutory list that is too short or disparate to permit generalization.[8] *Noscitur* is not dispositive if other statutory context suggests a broader reading.[9]
- *Ejusdem generis.* Interpret a general term to reflect the class of objects reflected in more specific terms accompanying it ("and other things").[10] *Ejusdem* might be trumped by other canons, such as the rule against surplusage.[11]
- *Term of art.* Where Congress uses a term that has a settled meaning as a legal or scientific term of art, interpreters should apply that specialized meaning.[12]

---

[5] POM Wonderful LLC v. Coca-Cola Co., 134 S.Ct. 2228, 2237–38 (2014); Hinck v. United States, 550 U.S. 501 (2007); TRW, Inc. v. Andrews, 534 U.S. 19 (2001); City of Chicago v. Environmental Def. Fund, 511 U.S. 328 (1994); United States v. Smith, 499 U.S. 160 (1991); Chan v. Korean Air Lines, Ltd., 490 U.S. 122, 133–34 (1989).

[6] Setser v. United States, 132 S.Ct. 1463, 1469–70 (2012); Marrama v. Citizens Bank of Mass., 549 U.S. 365 (2007); Christensen v. Harris County, 529 U.S. 576, 583–84 (2000); Burns v. United States, 501 U.S. 129, 136 (1991); Sullivan v. Hudson, 490 U.S. 877, 891–92 (1989).

[7] Yates v. United States, 135 S.Ct. 1074, 1085–86 (2015) (plurality opinion); Bullock v. BankChampaign, N.A., 133 S.Ct. 1754, 1760 (2013); Freeman v. Quicken Loans, Inc., 132 S.Ct. 2034, 2042 (2012); Samantar v. Yousuf, 560 U.S. 305, 317 (2010); Entergy Corp. v. Riverkeeper, Inc., 556 U.S. 208, 222 (2009); Gustafson v. Alloyd Co., Inc., 513 U.S. 561, 575 (1995); Beecham v. United States, 511 U.S. 368, 371 (1994); Dole v. United Steelworkers of Am., 494 U.S. 26, 36 (1990); Massachusetts v. Morash, 490 U.S. 107, 114–15 (1989).

[8] Graham County Soil & Water Conserv. Dist. v. United States ex rel. Wilson, 559 U.S. 280, 288 (2010); S.D. Warren Co. v. Maine Bd. of Environmental Prot., 547 U.S. 370 (2006).

[9] Schindler Elevator Corp. v. United States ex rel. Kirk, 536 U.S. 401, 409 (2011); Ali v. Federal Bureau of Prisons, 552 U.S. 214 (2008); Babbitt v. Sweet Home Chap. of Communities for a Great Oregon, 515 U.S. 687, 697–702 (1995).

[10] Yates v. United States, 135 S.Ct. 1074, 1086–87 (2015) (plurality opinion); Circuit City Stores, Inc. v. Adams, 532 U.S. 105 (2001); Hughey v. United States, 495 U.S. 411, 419 (1990); Norfolk & Western Ry. Co. v. American Train Dispatchers' Ass'n, 499 U.S. 117, 129 (1991).

[11] James v. United States, 550 U.S. 192, 199–200 (2007).

[12] CTS Corp. v. Waldburger, 134 S.Ct. 2175, 2186 (2014); FAA v. Cooper, 132 S.Ct. 1441, 1449 (2012); Merck & Co. v. Reynolds, 559 U.S. 633, 644 (2010); Stewart v. Dutra Constr. Co., 543 U.S. 481, 487 (2005); Scheidler v. NOW, Inc., 537 U.S. 393, 402

- Defer to experts, including agencies, regarding the meaning of technical terminology.[13]
- *Dictionaries.* Follow consensus dictionary definitions of terms,[14] unless Congress has provided a specific definition.[15] By revealing variety in word use, dictionaries can suggest ambiguity.[16] Consider dictionaries of the era in which the statute was enacted.[17] For technical terms, consult specialized dictionaries.[18] Do not credit nonstandard, idiosyncratic dictionary definitions.[19]
- *Pet fish.* Phrases and word clusters might have an ordinary meaning different from the aggregation of the separate words.[20]

(2003); United States v. Wells, 519 U.S. 482, 491 (1997); Molzof v. United States, 502 U.S. 301, 307 (1992); Community for Creative Non-Violence v. Reid, 490 U.S. 730, 739 (1989).

[13] Zuni Pub. Sch. Dist. No. 89 v. Department of Educ., 550 U.S. 81, 99–100 (2007).

[14] Kellogg Brown & Root Servs., Inc. v. United States ex rel. Carter, 135 S.Ct. 1970, 1976 (2015) (*Black's, Webster's Third, American Heritage*); CTS Corp. v. Waldburger, 134 S.Ct. 2175, 2182–83 (2014) (*Black's*); Taniguchi v. Kan Pacific Saipan Ltd., 132 S.Ct. 1997, 2002–04 (2012) (many dictionaries); Mohamad v. Palestinian Auth., 132 S.Ct. 1702, 1706–07 (2012) (*Oxford, Random House, Webster's Third*); Kawashima v. Holder, 132 S.Ct. 1166, 1172 (2012) (*Webster's Third*); Limtiaco v. Comacho, 549 U.S. 483, 489 (2007) (*Black's*); Rapanos v. United States, 547 U.S. 715, 732 (2006) (plurality opinion) (*Webster's Second*); Muscarello v. United States, 524 U.S. 125, 128, 130 (1998) (*Oxford English*); Pittston Coal Group v. Sebben, 488 U.S. 105, 113 (1988) (*Webster's*).

[15] Babbitt v. Sweet Home Chap. of Communities for a Great Oregon, 515 U.S. 687 (1995).

[16] Arizona v. Inter Tribal Coun. of Arizona, 133 S.Ct. 2247, 2254 (2013).

[17] Kellogg Brown & Root Servs., Inc. v. United States ex rel. Carter, 135 S.Ct. 1970, 1976 (2015); Taniguchi v. Kan Pacific Saipan Ltd., 132 S.Ct. 1997, 2002–04 (2012); Bilski v. Kappos, 561 U.S. 593 (2010); Permanent Mission of India to the United Nations v. City of New York, 551 U.S. 193 (2007); Cook County v. United States ex rel. Chandler, 538 U.S. 119, 125–27 (2003); St. Francis College v. Al-Khazraji, 481 U.S. 604 (1987). But see New Process Steel L.P. v. NLRB, 130 S.Ct. 2635, 2642 (2010) (relying on dictionaries from era in which controversy arose); Metropolitan Life Ins. Co. v. Glenn, 554 U.S. 105, 112 (2008) (same).

[18] Zuni Pub. Sch. Dist. No. 89 v. Department of Educ., 550 U.S. 81 (2007).

[19] MCI Telecomm. Corp. v. AT&T Co., 512 U.S. 218, 227–28 (1994) (disrespecting *Webster's Third* for including colloquial as well as standard definitions).

[20] United States v. Castleman, 134 S.Ct. 1405, 1411–12 (2014); FAA v. Cooper, 132 S.Ct. 1441, 1449 (2012); FCC v. AT&T, Inc., 462 U.S. 397, 406 (2011); Muscarello v. United States, 524 U.S. 125, 143 (1998) (dissenting opinion) ("carries a firearm" as a phrase means "packing heat").

- *Punctuation.* Congress is presumed to follow accepted punctuation standards, so that placements of commas and other punctuation are assumed to be meaningful.[21]
- *Grammar.* Congress is presumed to follow accepted standards of grammar.[22]
- *Last antecedent.* Referential and qualifying words or phrases refer only to the last antecedent, unless contrary to the apparent legislative intent derived from the sense of the entire enactment.[23] Do not apply this rule if not practical or if contrary to the statutory scheme.[24]
- "Catch-all" clauses following a specific list might be read to modify the specific items.[25]
- *May/Shall.* "May" is usually precatory and connotes decisionmaking discretion,[26] while "shall" is usually mandatory and suggests less discretion.[27]
- "Or" means in the alternative.[28]
- *Drafting manuals.* Understand the grammatical structure of complicated provisions in light of drafting practices of House and Senate Legislative Counsel.[29]

---

[21] Jama v. Immigration & Customs Enf., 543 U.S. 335, 344 (2005) (significance of periods); United States v. Ron Pair Enters., 489 U.S. 235, 241–42 (1989) (comma placement); San Francisco Arts & Athletics, Inc. v. United States Olympic Comm'n, 483 U.S. 522, 528–29 (1987).

[22] Board of Trustees, Leland Stanford Junior University v. Roche Molecular Sys., Inc., 563 U.S. 776 (2011); Fowler v. United States, 131 S.Ct. 2045, 2053 (2011) (concurring opinion); Carr v. United States, 560 U.S. 438, 449 (2010); Limtiaco v. Camacho, 549 U.S. 483 (2007); Rapanos v. United States, 547 U.S. 715 (2006) (plurality opinion); Jama v. Immigration & Customs Enf., 543 U.S. 335 (2005).

[23] Lockhart v. United States, 136 S.Ct. 958 (2016); Jama v. Immigration & Customs Enf., 543 U.S. 335 (2005); Barnhart v. Thomas, 540 U.S. 20, 26 (2003); Nobelman v. American Savs. Bank, 508 U.S. 324, 330 (1993).

[24] Paroline v. United States, 134 S.Ct. 1710, 1720–21 (2014); United States v. Hayes, 555 U.S. 415, 425 (2009); Nobelman v. American Savs. Bank, 508 U.S. 324, 330–31 (1993).

[25] Paroline v. United States, 134 S.Ct. 1710, 1721 (2014).

[26] Jama v. Immigration & Customs Enf., 543 U.S. 335 (2005); Lopez v. Davis, 531 U.S. 230, 241 (2001) ("may" vests wide discretion in agency).

[27] Shapiro v. McManus, 136 S.Ct. 450 (2015); Mach Mining, LLC v. EEOC, 135 S.Ct. 1645, 1651 (2015); National R.R. Passenger Corp. v. Morgan, 536 U.S. 101, 109 (2002); Mallard v. United States Dist. Ct., 490 U.S. 296, 302 (1989).

[28] Loughrin v. United States, 134 S.Ct. 2384, 2389–90 (2014); Hawaiian Airlines, Inc. v. Norris, 512 U.S. 246, 253–54 (1994).

[29] United States v. O'Brien, 560 U.S. 231, 233–34 (2010); Carr v. United States, 560 U.S. 438, 463–64 (2010) (dissenting opinion).

WHOLE ACT

- *Whole act rule.* Each statutory provision should be read by reference to the whole act and the statutory scheme.[30] Statutory interpretation is a "holistic" endeavor.[31] Whole act analysis can consider uncodified provisions of an enacted statute.[32]
- Read in light of the whole act, a vague or ambiguous statutory provision may acquire a plain meaning.[33] Broad, indeterminate words (such as "in connection with" or "relates to") demand judicial narrowing in light of the statutory scheme.[34]
- Read in light of the whole act, a statutory provision that seems to have a plain meaning can be rendered ambiguous.[35]
- *Statutory history.* The formal evolution of a statute, as Congress amends it over the years, is potentially relevant.[36]

---

[30] King v. Burwell, 135 S.Ct. 2480, 2495 (2015); Utility Air Regulatory Group v. EPA, 134 S.Ct. 2427, 2441 (2014); Caraco Pharmaceutical Labs., Ltd. v. Novo Nordisk A/S, 132 S.Ct. 1670, 1680 (2012); Samantar v. Yousuf, 560 U.S. 305 (2010); Ricci v. DeStefano, 557 U.S. 557, 580 (2009); Ledbetter v. Goodyear Tire & Rubber Co., 550 U.S. 618 (2007); Gonzales v. Oregon, 546 U.S. 243, 273–74 (2006); Clark v. Martinez, 543 U.S. 371 (2005); FDA v. Brown & Williamson Tobacco Co., 529 U.S. 120, 133 (2000); Babbitt v. Sweet Home Chap. of Communities for a Great Oregon, 515 U.S. 687 (1995); Pavelic & Leflore v. Marvel Entm't Group, 493 U.S. 120, 123–24 (1989); Massachusetts v. Morash, 490 U.S. 107, 114–15 (1989).

[31] Texas Dep't of Housing & Community Affs. v. Inclusive Communities Project, Inc., 135 S.Ct. 2507, 2525 (2015); King v. Burwell, 135 S.Ct. 2480, 2489 (2015); Burwell v. Hobby Lobby Stores, Inc., 134 S.Ct. 2751 (2014); Robinson v. Shell Oil Co., 519 U.S. 337, 341 (1997); United Sav. Ass'n of Texas v. Timbers of Inwood Forest Assocs., Ltd., 484 U.S. 365, 371 (1988).

[32] FAA v. Cooper, 132 S.Ct. 1441, 1452 (2012); Doe v. Chao, 540 U.S. 614 (2004).

[33] Bruce v. Samuels, 136 S.Ct. 627 (2016); Michigan v. EPA, 135 S.Ct. 2699 (2015); Arizona v. Inter Tribal Coun. of Arizona, 133 S.Ct. 2247 (2013); Caraco Pharmaceutical Labs., Ltd. v. Novo Nordisk A/S, 132 S.Ct. 1670, 1680–83 (2012); Whitman v. American Trucking Ass'ns, Inc., 531 U.S. 457, 466 (2001); Babbitt v. Sweet Home Chap. of Communities for a Great Oregon, 515 U.S. 687 (1995) (dissenting opinion).

[34] Mellouli v. Lynch, 135 S.Ct. 1980, 1990–91 (2015); Maracich v. Spears, 133 S.Ct. 2191, 2199–2200 (2013); California Div. of Labor Standards Enforcement v. Dillingham Constr., N.A., 519 U.S. 316, 335 (1997).

[35] King v. Burwell, 135 S.Ct. 2480, 2489–90 (2015); Department of Transportation v. Association of American Railroads, 135 S.Ct. 1225 (2015); Entergy Corp. v. Riverkeeper, Inc., 556 U.S. 208 (2009).

[36] Kellogg Brown & Root Servs., Inc. v. United States ex rel. Carter, 135 S.Ct. 1970, 1977 (2015); Burwell v. Hobby Lobby Stores, Inc., 134 S.Ct. 2751, 2760–62, 2772 (2014); United States v. Quality Stores, Inc., 134 S.Ct. 1395, 1401 (2014); Kawasaki Kisen Kaisha, Ltd. v. Regal Beloit Corp., 561 U.S. 89, 106–08 (2010); Powerex Corp. v. Reliant Energy Servs., Inc., 551 U.S. 224 (2007); Ballard v. Commissioner, 544 U.S. 40 (2005).

- *Purpose/Plan.* Statutes should be interpreted to advance the statutory plan and the legislative purpose(s).[37] Statutory provisions setting forth Congress's purposes should be given great weight in understanding the legislative purpose(s).[38]
- *Preambles, titles & captions.* The statute's preamble may provide clues to statutory meaning,[39] as may the title.[40] Statutory captions or headings might be supporting evidence, but are usually too short to be of assistance.[41]
- *Interpretive directives.* Statutory directives for liberal or strict construction should be respected.[42]
- *Definitions.* Statutory definitions should be applied according to their own ordinary meaning, sometimes supplanting the everyday meaning of words with a specialized meaning chosen by Congress.[43]
- *Surplusage/Redundancy.* Avoid interpreting a provision in a way that would render other provisions of the statute superfluous or redundant.[44] Avoid an interpretation that would

---

[37] Texas Dep't of Housing & Community Affs. v. Inclusive Communities Project, Inc., 135 S.Ct. 2507, 2521–22 (2015); King v. Burwell, 135 S.Ct. 2480, 2491 (2015); Utility Air Regulatory Group v. EPA, 134 S.Ct. 2427, 2442–44 (2014); Abramski v. United States, 134 S.Ct. 2259, 2267–70 (2014); Adoptive Couple v. Baby Girl, 133 S.Ct. 2552, 2572–83 (2013) (dissenting opinion).

[38] POM Wonderful LLC v. Coca-Cola Co., 134 S.Ct. 2228, 2233–34 (2014).

[39] Sutton v. United Airlines, Inc., 527 U.S. 471 (1999) (majority and concurring opinions).

[40] Yates v. United States, 135 S.Ct. 1074, 1083, 1090 (2015) (plurality and concurring opinions); Almendarez-Torres v. United States, 523 U.S. 224, 234 (1998).

[41] Compare Yates v. United States, 135 S.Ct. 1074 (2015) (plurality opinion) (relying on caption for provision added by the Sarbanes-Oxley Act), with Lawson v. FMR LLC, 134 S.Ct. 1158, 1169 (2014) (rejecting reliance on captions in same statute because they are clearly "under-inclusive"). See also Freeman v. Quicken Loans, Inc., 132 S.Ct. 2034, 2043 (2012) (refusing to find meaning in a caption).

[42] Burwell v. Hobby Lobby Stores, Inc. 134 S.Ct. 2751, 2762 & n.5 (2014); Abbott v. Abbott, 560 U.S. 1, 8–9 (2010).

[43] Samantar v. Yousuf, 560 U.S. 305, 315 (2010); Babbitt v. Sweet Home Chapter of Communities for a Great Oregon, 515 U.S. 687 (1995).

[44] Fifth Third Bancorp v. Dudenhoeffer, 134 S.Ct. 2459 (2014); RadLAX Gateway Hotel, LLC v. Amalgamated Bank, 132 S.Ct. 2065, 2070–71 (2012); Roberts v. Sea-Land Servs., Inc., 132 S.Ct. 1350, 1358 (2012); Ricci v. DeStefano, 557 U.S. 557, 580 (2009); TRW, Inc. v. Andrews, 534 U.S. 19, 29 (2001); Circuit City Stores, Inc. v. Adams, 532 U.S. 105 (2001); United States v. Alaska, 521 U.S. 1 (1997); Walters v. Metropolitan Educ. Enters., Inc., 519 U.S. 202 (1997); Rake v. Wade, 508 U.S. 464 (1993); Kungys v. United States, 485 U.S. 759, 778 (1988) (plurality opinion). The leading case is D. Ginsburg & Sons, Inc. v. Popkin, 285 U.S. 204, 208 (1932).

render a provision duplicative of a common law rule.[45] This presumption must give way when offset by other evidence of statutory meaning, however.[46]

- *Consistency*. Interpret the same or similar terms in a statute the same way.[47] Presumption rebutted when other evidence suggests Congress was using the same term for different purposes.[48]
- *Meaningful variation*. Presume against reading a specific idea into general words when precise language elsewhere in the statute reveals that Congress knew how to identify that specific idea.[49] Presumption is stronger if Congress considered and rejected the alternate wording.[50] Presumption inapplicable when the variation is a matter of detail or reasonable drafting choice, in light of statutory scheme.[51]

---

[45] Octane Fitness, LLC v. ICON Health & Fitness, Inc., 134 S.Ct. 1749, 1758 (2014).

[46] Texas Dep't of Housing & Community Affs. v. Inclusive Communities Project, Inc., 135 S.Ct. 2507 (2015); King v. Burwell, 135 S.Ct. 2480, 2492 (2015); United States v. Home Concrete & Supply, LLC, 132 S.Ct. 1836 (2012); Gutierrez v. Ada, 528 U.S. 250 (2000); Landgraf v. USI Film Prods., 511 U.S. 244, 259–60 (1994).

[47] King v. Burwell, 135 S.Ct. 2480, 2493–95 (2015); Robers v. United States, 134 S.Ct. 1854 (2014); Taniguchi v. Kan Pacific Saipan Ltd., 132 S.Ct. 1997, 2004–05 (2012); Powerex Corp. v. Reliant Energy Servs., Inc., 551 U.S. 224 (2007); IBP, Inc. v. Alvarez, 546 U.S. 21, 34 (2005); Commissioner v. Lundy, 516 U.S. 235, 249–50 (1996); Gustafson v. Alloyd Co., 513 U.S. 561, 570 (1995); Sullivan v. Stroop, 496 U.S. 478, 484 (1990); United Sav. Ass'n of Texas v. Timbers of Inwood Forest Assocs., Ltd., 484 U.S. 365, 371 (1988).

[48] Utility Air Regulatory Group v. EPA, 134 S.Ct. 2427 (2014); Roberts v. Sea-Land Servs., Inc., 132 S.Ct. 1350, 1360–62 (2012); Environmental Defense v. Duke Energy Corp., 549 U.S. 561 (2007); General Dynamics Land Sys., Inc. v. Cline, 540 U.S. 581, 595 (2004); Robinson v. Shell Oil Co., 519 U.S. 337, 343–44 (1997); Dewsnup v. Timm, 502 U.S. 410, 417 & n.3 (1992).

[49] Baker Botts L.L.P. v. ASARCO LLC, 135 S.Ct. 2158 (2015); Burwell v. Hobby Lobby Stores, Inc., 134 S.Ct. 2751, 2772–74 (2014); Loughrin v. United States, 134 S.Ct. 2384, 2390–92 (2014); Lawson v. FMR LLC, 134 S.Ct. 1158, 1165–66 (2014); University of Texas Southwestern Med. Center v. Nassar, 133 S.Ct. 2517, 2529 (2013); Sebelius v. Cloer, 133 S.Ct. 1886, 1894 (2013); Pacific Operators Offshore, LLP v. Valladolid, 132 S.Ct. 680 (2012); Tapia v. United States, 131 S.Ct. 2382, 2390 (2011); Hamilton v. Lanning, 560 U.S. 505, 514–15 (2010); Samantar v. Yousuf, 560 U.S. 305, 317 (2010); Gross v. FBL Financial Services, Inc., 557 U.S. 167 (2009); Lawrence v. Florida, 549 U.S. 327 (2007); Lopez v. Gonzales, 549 U.S. 47 (2006); Lindh v. Murphy, 521 U.S. 320 (1997); Keene Corp. v. United States, 508 U.S. 200, 208 (1993); Gozlon-Peretz v. United States, 498 U.S. 395, 404–05 (1991). The leading case is Russello v. United States, 464 U.S. 16, 23 (1983).

[50] Hamdan v. Rumsfeld, 548 U.S. 557, 579–80 (2006).

[51] Michigan v. EPA, 135 S.Ct. 2699, 2708–09 (2015); Gutierrez v. Ada, 528 U.S. 250 (2000); Field v. Mans, 516 U.S. 59, 67–69 (1995).

- *Statutory structure.* Avoid interpreting a provision in a way that is inconsistent with the overall structure of the statute[52] *or* with the assumptions of another provision[53] *or* with the assumptions embedded in a subsequent amendment to the statute.[54]
- *Amendments.* Statutory amendments are meant to have real and substantial effect.[55]
- *Elephants in mouseholes.* Congress usually does not alter the fundamental details of a regulatory scheme in vague or ancillary provisions—it does not hide elephants in mouseholes![56]
- *Specificity.* Specific provisions targeting a particular issue apply instead of provisions more generally covering the issue.[57]
- *Provisos/Exceptions.* Statutory provisos and exceptions should be read narrowly.[58] Do not create exceptions in addition to those specified by Congress.[59]

---

[52] Abramski v. United States, 134 S.Ct. 2259 (2014); University of Texas Southwestern Med. Center v. Nassar, 133 S.Ct. 2517, 2529 (2013); Samantar v. Yousuf, 560 U.S. 305 (2010); Ledbetter v. Goodyear Tire & Rubber Co., 550 U.S. 618 (2007); Beck v. PACE Int'l Union, 551 U.S. 96 (2007).

[53] Petrella v. MGM, Inc., 134 S.Ct. 1962 (2014); Lawson v. FMR LLC, 134 S.Ct. 1158, 1166–67 (2014); Ricci v. DeStefano, 557 U.S. 557 (2009); Babbitt v. Sweet Home Chap. of Communities for a Great Oregon, 515 U.S. 687 (1995); Gade v. National Solid Wastes Management Ass'n, 505 U.S. 88, 100–01 (1992); United Sav. Ass'n of Texas v. Timbers of Inwood Forest Assocs., Ltd., 484 U.S. 365, 371 (1988).

[54] Texas Dep't of Housing & Community Affs. v. Inclusive Communities Project, Inc., 135 S.Ct. 2507, 2520–21 (2015); Burwell v. Hobby Lobby Stores, Inc., 134 S.Ct. 2751, 2761–62, 2772 (2014); Gonzales v. Oregon, 546 U.S. 243, 257–58 (2006).

[55] Burwell v. Hobby Lobby Stores, Inc., 134 S.Ct. 2751, 2772 (2014); Rumsfeld v. Forum for Academic & Institutional Rights, Inc., 547 U.S. 47 (2006); Babbitt v. Sweet Home Chap. of Communities for a Great Oregon, 515 U.S. 687 (1995).

[56] FERC v. Electric Power Supply Ass'n, 136 S.Ct. 760, 773–74 (2016); King v. Burwell, 135 S.Ct. 2480, 2492–93 (2015); Gonzales v. Oregon, 546 U.S. 243, 267 (2006); Whitman v. American Trucking Ass'ns, Inc., 531 U.S. 457, 468 (2001); FDA v. Brown & Williamson Tobacco Corp., 529 U.S. 120, 160 (2000).

[57] Law v. Siegel, 134 S.Ct. 1188, 1194 (2014); RadLAX Gateway Hotel, LLC v. Amalgamated Bank, 132 S.Ct. 2065, 2070–71 (2012); Green v. Bock Laundry Mach. Co., 490 U.S. 504, 524–26 (1989); HCSC-Laundry v. United States, 450 U.S. 1, 6 (1971) (per curiam). The leading case is United States v. Chase, 135 U.S. 255, 260 (1890).

[58] Maracich v. Spears, 133 S.Ct. 2191, 2200 (2013); Cherokee Nation of Oklahoma v. Leavitt, 543 U.S. 631 (2005); City of Edmonds v. Oxford House, Inc., 514 U.S. 725, 732 (1995). The leading case is Commissioner v. Clark, 489 U.S. 726, 739 (1989). But see Republic of Iraq v. Beaty, 556 U.S. 848, 857–58 (2009) (acknowledging this general rule but applying proviso more liberally where Congress was granting the President needed foreign affairs flexibility).

[59] United States v. Smith, 499 U.S. 160, 166–67 (1991).

WHOLE CODE

- *Noscitur a legibus sociis.* The placement of a provision within a statute or within the U.S. Code may provide a clue to its meaning.[60]
- *Default definitions.* Dictionary Act, 1 U.S.C. § 1 *et seq.*, contains default definitions that apply if Congress fails to define a particular term.[61]
- *In pari materia* (consistent use across statutes). When similar statutory provisions are found in comparable statutory schemes with similar purpose, interpreters should presumptively apply them the same way,[62] especially when Congress has borrowed language from the other statute.[63] Presumption inapplicable where comparable statutes have materially different texts or purposes.[64]
- *Meaningful variation* (across statutes). Presume against reading a specific concept into general words when precise language in other statutes reveals that Congress knew how to identify that concept.[65] Broad term is presumptively ambiguous if Congress has elsewhere used more targeted terminology.[66]

---

[60] Kellogg Brown & Root Servs., Inc. v. United States ex rel. Carter, 135 S.Ct. 1970, 1976–77 (2015); Yates v. United States, 135 S.Ct. 1074, 1079, 1090 (2015) (plurality and concurring opinions); Kansas v. Hendricks, 521 U.S. 346, 361 (1997).

[61] Burwell v. Hobby Lobby Stores, Inc., 134 S.Ct. 2751, 2768–69 (2014); Mohamad v. Palestinian Auth., 132 S.Ct. 1702 (2012); Carr v. United States, 560 U.S. 438 (2010); Stewart v. Dutra Constr. Co., 543 U.S. 481 (2005).

[62] Texas Dep't of Housing & Community Affs. v. Inclusive Communities Project, Inc., 135 S.Ct. 2507, 2516–18 (2015); United States v. Castleman, 134 S.Ct. 1405, 1417 (2014) (concurring opinion); Hardt v. Reliance Standard Life Ins. Co., 560 U.S. 242 (2010); Ledbetter v. Goodyear Tire & Rubber Co., 550 U.S. 618 (2007); Smith v. City of Jackson, Mississippi, 544 U.S. 228, 233 (2005); Hawaiian Airlines, Inc. v. Norris, 512 U.S. 246, 254 (1994); Smith v. United States, 508 U.S. 223, 234–35 (1993); Pierce v. Underwood, 487 U.S. 552 (1988).

[63] Texas Dep't of Housing & Community Affs. v. Inclusive Communities Project, Inc., 135 S.Ct. 2507, 2516–18 (2015); Lawson v. FMR LLC, 134 S.Ct. 1158, 1175–76 (2014).

[64] FAA v. Cooper, 132 S.Ct. 1441, 1454–55 (2012); Ledbetter v. Goodyear Tire & Rubber Co., 550 U.S. 618 (2007); Fogerty v. Fantasy, Inc., 510 U.S. 517 (1994).

[65] University of Texas Southwestern Med. Center v. Nassar, 133 S.Ct. 2517, 2531 (2013); Arlington Cent. Sch. Dist. Bd. of Educ. v. Murphy, 548 U.S. 291 (2006); Jama v. Immigration & Customs Enforcement, 543 U.S. 335 (2005); Custis v. United States, 511 U.S. 485, 491 (1994); West Virginia Univ. Hosps., Inc. v. Casey, 499 U.S. 83, 99 (1991).

[66] Burwell v. Hobby Lobby Stores, Inc., 134 S.Ct. 2751, 2772 (2014); Zuni Pub. Sch. Dist. No. 89 v. Department of Educ., 550 U.S. 81 (2007).

- *Repeals by implication.* Strong presumption against repeals by implication.[67] But where there is a clear repugnancy between a more recent statutory scheme and an earlier one, (partial) repeal may be inferred.[68]
- *Reconciliation.* Avoid interpreting statutes to conflict with one another, unless required by clear statutory texts and deeply conflicting purposes.[69]
- *Specificity* (across statutes). If conflicting statutes cannot be reconciled, apply the more specific rule.[70]
- *International law.* Presumption that statutes be interpreted consistent with international law and treaties.[71] But international agreements do not trump the plain meaning of federal statutes.[72]
- *Borrowed treaty.* Statutes implementing, and especially those copying, a treaty the United States has ratified, should be interpreted to be consistent with the treaty.[73]

---

[67] POM Wonderful LLC v. Coca-Cola Co., 134 S.Ct. 2228 (2014); Powerex Corp. v. Reliant Energy Servs., Inc., 551 U.S. 224 (2007); Ledbetter v. Goodyear Tire & Rubber Co., 550 U.S. 618 (2007); Hamdan v. Rumsfeld, 548 U.S. 557 (2006); Granholm v. Heald, 544 U.S. 460 (2005); Branch v. Smith, 538 U.S. 254, 273 (2003); John Hancock Mut. Life Ins. Co. v. Harris Trust & Sav. Bank, 510 U.S. 86, 101–06 (1993); Morales v. TWA, Inc., 504 U.S. 374 (1992); Pittsburgh & Lake Erie R.R. v. Railway Labor Executives' Ass'n, 491 U.S. 490, 509 (1989); Communications Workers of Am. v. Beck, 487 U.S. 735, 750–52 (1988); Traynor v. Turnage, 485 U.S. 535, 547–48 (1988); Wimberly v. Labor & Indus. Relations Comm'n of Missouri, 479 U.S. 511, 517 (1987). The leading case is Morton v. Mancari, 417 U.S. 535 (1974).

[68] Dorsey v. United States, 132 S.Ct. 2321, 2330–33 (2012) (probably allowing a repeal by implication, as dissenters charged, id. at 2339–42); Credit Suisse Securities (USA) LLC v. Billing, 551 U.S. 264 (2007).

[69] POM Wonderful LLC v. Coca-Cola Co., 134 S.Ct. 2228, 2236–42 (2014); FTC v. Actavis, Inc., 133 S.Ct. 2223 (2013); Kawasaki Kisen Kaisha Ltd. v. Regal Beloit Corp., 561 U.S. 89, 108–10 (2010); FDA v. Brown & Williamson Tobacco Corp., 529 U.S. 120, 144 (2000).

[70] FDA v. Brown & Williamson Tobacco Corp., 529 U.S. 120, 133 (2000); Crawford Fitting Co. v. J.T. Gibbons, Inc., 482 U.S. 437, 444–45 (1987).

[71] Permanent Mission of India to the United Nations v. City of New York, 551 U.S. 193, 199–200 (2007); Spector v. Norwegian Cruise Line Ltd., 545 U.S. 119 (2005); id. at 142 (concurring opinion); Sosa v. Alvarez-Machain, 542 U.S. 692 (2004); Hamdi v. Rumsfeld, 542 U.S. 507 (2004) (plurality opinion); INS v. Cardoza-Fonseca, 480 U.S. 421 (1987).

[72] Société Nationale Industrielle Aérospatiale v. U.S. Dist. Ct. for the So. Dist. of Iowa, 482 U.S. 522, 538–39 (1987).

[73] Bond v. United States, 134 S.Ct. 2077, 2087 (2014) (dictum); Abbott v. Abbott, 560 U.S. 1, 8–9 (2010) (noting that implementing legislation directed that it be interpreted the same as the treaty); Vimar Seguros y Reaseguros v. M/V Sky Reefer, 515 U.S. 528 (1995); Sale v. Haitian Ctrs. Council, Inc., 509 U.S. 155, 178–87 (1993). The leading case is INS v. Cardoza-Fonseca, 480 U.S. 421, 436–41 (1987).

EXTRINSIC SOURCE CANONS

AGENCY INTERPRETATIONS

- Skidmore *deference.* Agency interpretations are entitled to respect to the extent that they have "power to persuade" based upon consistency, factual basis, and expertise.[74] Agency views that are unstable, trumped up, vague, or insufficiently developed have little or no persuasive value.[75]
- Even informal and unsettled agency interpretations (such as those embodied in handbooks or litigation briefs) may be useful confirmations for the interpreter's interpretation of statutory language.[76]
- Chevron *deference.* Reasonable agency interpretations pursuant to congressional delegation of lawmaking authority are binding on courts unless Congress has directly addressed the issue,[77] or the Court has authoritatively resolved the issue in a binding precedent.[78] Conversely, "unreasonable" agency interpretations

---

[74] Adoptive Couple v. Baby Girl, 133 S.Ct. 2552, 2561–62 (2013); Kasten v. Saint-Gobain Performance Plastics Corp., 563 U.S. 1, 14–16 (2011); Federal Express Corp. v. Holowecki, 552 U.S. 389, 401–02 (2008); Beck v. PACE Int'l Union, 551 U.S. 96 (2007); United States v. Mead Corp., 533 U.S. 218, 226–27 (2001); Burlington Indus., Inc. v. Ellerth, 524 U.S. 742, 764 (1998); Meritor Sav. Bank FSB v. Vinson, 477 U.S. 57 (1986). The leading case is Skidmore v. Swift & Co., 323 U.S. 134, 140 (1944).

[75] Vance v. Ball State Univ., 133 S.Ct. 2434, 2449–52 (2013); University of Texas Southwestern Med. Center v. Nassar, 133 S.Ct. 2517, 2533–34 (2013); Gonzales v. Oregon, 546 U.S. 243, 255–56 (2006); Burlington Northern & Santa Fe Ry. v. White, 548 U.S. 53 (2006).

[76] S.D. Warren Co. v. Maine Bd. of Envtl. Prot., 547 U.S. 370 (2006).

[77] Michigan v. EPA, 135 S.Ct. 2699, 2706–07, 2726 (2015) (majority and dissenting opinions); Utility Air Regulatory Group v. EPA, 134 S.Ct. 2427 (2014) (plurality and concurring opinions); Scialabba v. Cuellar de Osorio, 134 S.Ct. 2191 (2014) (plurality and concurring opinions); Astrue v. Capato ex rel. B.N.C., 132 S.Ct. 2021, 2033–34 (2012); Mayo Found. for Med. Educ. & Research v. United States, 562 U.S. 44, 54–55 (2011) (overruling prior precedent in favor of *Chevron* deference for tax regulations); Zuni Pub. Sch. Dist. No. 89 v. Department of Educ., 550 U.S. 291 (2007) (majority and concurring opinions); National Cable & Telecomm. Ass'n v. Brand X Internet Servs., 545 U.S. 967 (2005); ABF Freight Sys., Inc. v. NLRB, 510 U.S. 317, 324 (1994); Sullivan v. Everhart, 494 U.S. 83, 88–89 (1990); K Mart Corp. v. Cartier, Inc., 486 U.S. 281, 291–92 (1988) The leading case is Chevron U.S.A., Inc. v. Natural Resources Defense Council, Inc., 467 U.S. 837 (1984), recently questioned in *Michigan*, 135 S.Ct. at 2712–14 (Thomas, J., concurring).

[78] United States v. Home Concrete & Supply, LLC, 132 S.Ct. 1836 (2012). Cf. National Cable & Telecomm. Ass'n v. Brand X Internet Servs., 545 U.S. 967, 980 (2005) (overruling a lower court's insistence that its own construction of a statute trumps that of an agency acting within its *Chevron* zone of discretion).

are not binding on courts, even if there has been delegation of lawmaking authority.[79]

- An agency's discretion is at its height when the agency decides not to enforce a statute.[80]
- For *Chevron* purposes, whether Congress has delegated the agency lawmaking authority is itself a matter of statutory interpretation.[81] But agencies enjoy *Chevron* deference for their interpretations of the jurisdictional limits of their delegated authority.[82]
- *Major questions* (no deference). Presumption against congressional delegation of authority for agency to make fundamental changes to society or the market.[83] The Court often demands a clear statement authorizing agency constructions that press the envelope of constitutional validity or preempt state law.[84]
- Avoid the implication of broad congressional delegation of agency authority when statute carefully limits agency authority in particular matters.[85]
- Seminole Rock/Auer *deference*. Agency interpretation of its own regulations is controlling unless "plainly erroneous or inconsistent with the regulation."[86] Rule does not apply when

---

[79] Michigan v. EPA, 135 S.Ct. 2699, 2707 (2015).

[80] Massachusetts v. EPA, 549 U.S. 497 (2007).

[81] Gonzales v. Oregon, 546 U.S. 243 (2006).

[82] City of Arlington, Texas v. FCC, 133 S.Ct. 1863 (2013).

[83] FERC v. Electric Power Supply Ass'n, 136 S.Ct. 760, 773–74 (2016); King v. Burwell, 135 S.Ct. 2480, 2489 (2015); Utility Air Regulatory Group v. EPA, 134 S.Ct. 2427 (2104) (plurality and concurring opinions); Gonzales v. Oregon, 546 U.S. 243 (2006); FDA v. Brown & Williamson Tobacco Corp., 529 U.S. 120 (2000); MCI Telecomm. Corp. v. AT&T Co., 512 U.S. 218 (1994).

[84] Bond v. United States, 134 S.Ct. 2077 (2014); Wyeth v. Levine, 555 U.S. 555, 576 (2009); Rapanos v. United States, 547 U.S. 715 (2006) (plurality opinion); Edward J. DeBartolo Corp. v. Florida Gulf Coast Building & Constr. Trades Council, 485 U.S. 568, 575 (1988).

[85] Texas Dep't of Housing & Community Affs. v. Inclusive Communities Project, Inc., 135 S.Ct. 2507 (2015); Gonzales v. Oregon, 546 U.S. 243, 262–63 (2006).

[86] PLIVA, Inc. v. Mensing, 131 S.Ct. 2567, 2575–76 (2011); Talk America, Inc. v. Michigan Bell Tel. Co., 131 S.Ct. 2254 (2011); Coeur Alaska, Inc. v. Southeast Alaska Conserv. Coun., 557 U.S. 261, 283–86 (2009) (deferring to an internal EPA memorandum); Auer v. Robbins, 519 U.S. 452, 461–63 (1997); Thomas Jefferson Univ. v. Shalala, 512 U.S. 504, 512 (1994). The leading case is Bowles v. Seminole Rock & Sand Co., 325 U.S. 410, 414 (1945). This canon is controversial within the Court. Perez v. Mortgage Bankers Ass'n, 135 S.Ct. 1199, 1210–25 (2015) (concurring opinions).

agency rule merely "parrots" the statute,[87] or where agency interpretation has been unstable over time.[88]

- Curtiss-Wright *deference.* In matters of foreign affairs and national security, presidential or executive statutory interpretations enjoy a super-strong presumption of correctness.[89] (The executive is still bound by statutory and treaty directives.[90]) Similar deference for executive branch views of federal jurisdiction over foreign states.[91]
- Courts accord especially great weight to executive department interpretation of treaties.[92]

STATUTORY PRECEDENTS

- Stare decisis *rule.* Statutes should be interpreted in light of binding precedents, including the reasoning of those precedents.[93] Precedent is especially important when key statutory concepts are nontextual or beyond the text.[94]

---

[87] Gonzales v. Oregon, 546 U.S. 243, 257 (2006).

[88] Commissioner v. Schleier, 515 U.S. 323 (1995); Bowen v. Georgetown Univ. Hosp., 488 U.S. 204 (1988).

[89] Scialabba v. Cuellar de Osorio, 134 S.Ct. 2191, 2203 (2014) (plurality); Republic of Iraq v. Beaty, 556 U.S. 848, 856–57, 860 (2009); Hamdi v. Rumsfeld, 542 U.S. 507, 518 (2004) (plurality opinion of O'Connor, J.); id. at 580–81 (Thomas, J., concurring in part, with a stronger statement); Cheney v. U.S. Dist. Court for the Dist. of Columbia, 542 U.S. 367 (2004); Crosby v. National Foreign Trade Council, 530 U.S. 363 (2000); Department of Navy v. Egan, 484 U.S. 518 (1988). The leading case is United States v. Curtiss-Wright Export Corp., 299 U.S. 304 (1936).

[90] Hamdan v. Rumsfeld, 548 U.S. 557 (2006).

[91] Republic of Austria v. Altmann, 541 U.S. 677, 689–90 (2004).

[92] Sanchez-Llamas v. Oregon, 548 U.S. 331 (2006); El Al Israel Airlines, Ltd. v. Tsui Yuan Tseng, 525 U.S. 155 (1999).

[93] OBB Personenverkehr AG v. Sachs, 136 S.Ct. 390 (2015); Kimble v. Marvel Entertainment, LLC, 135 S.Ct. 2401 (2015); Bank of America, N.A. v. Caulkett, 135 S.Ct. 1995 (2015); United States v. Castleman, 134 S.Ct. 1405 (2014); Marvin M. Brandt Revocable Trust v. United States, 134 S.Ct. 1257 (2014); United States v. Home Concrete & Supply, LLC, 132 S.Ct. 1836 (2012); Kappos v. Hyatt, 132 S.Ct. 1690 (2012); Wal-Mart Stores, Inc. v. Dukes, 131 S.Ct. 2541 (2011); Global-Tech Appliances, Inc. v. SEB SA, 131 S.Ct. 2060 (2011); American Needle, Inc. v. National Football League, 560 U.S. 183 (2010); AT&T Corp. v. Hulteen, 556 U.S. 701 (2009).

[94] Vance v. Ball State Univ., 133 S.Ct. 2434, 2449–52 (2013) ("supervisor" for purposes of court-made sexual harassment doctrine); Salazar v. Ramah Navajo Chap., 132 S.Ct. 2181, 2188–95 (2012); Rehberg v. Paulk, 132 S.Ct. 1497 (2012) (§ 1983 immunity); CSX Transp., Inc. v. McBride, 131 S.Ct. 2630, 2636–41 (2011) (FELA proximate cause); Janus Capital Group, Inc. v. First Derivative Traders, 131 S.Ct. 2296, 2302–04 (2011) (§ 10(b)); Patterson v. McLean Credit Union, 491 U.S. 164 (1989) (§ 1981 liability).

- *Super-strong presumption of correctness.* Statutory precedents should rarely be overruled, as they enjoy a super-strong presumption of correctness,[95] a presumption that is enhanced if Congress has revised the statute without disturbing the precedent,[96] or if courts have relied on the precedent to create stable doctrine.[97]
- *Stare decisis* is at its "acme" when the statutory precedent regulates contract or property rights,[98] especially where there is evidence that the private sector has strongly relied on that precedent.[99]
- The super-strong rule against overruling statutory precedents is inapplicable to the Sherman Act, which is a common law statute.[100]
- The best case for overruling a statutory precedent is that it has been overtaken by significant legal developments and has become an isolated "last man standing" in the relevant legal arena.[101] Precedents that create unworkable rules of law are also vulnerable to overruling.[102]

---

95 Halliburton Co. v. Erica P. John Fund, Inc., 134 S.Ct. 2398 (2014); Michigan v. Bay Mills Indian Community, 134 S.Ct. 2024 (2014); CSX Transp., Inc. v. McBride, 131 S.Ct. 2630, 2641 (2011); John R. Sand & Gravel Co. v. United States, 552 U.S. 130, 139 (2008); Hohn v. United States, 524 U.S. 236, 251 (1998); Neal v. United States, 516 U.S. 284 (1996); California v. FERC, 495 U.S. 490, 498–99 (1990); Patterson v. McLean Credit Union, 491 U.S. 164 (1989).

96 Kimble v. Marvel Entertainment, LLC, 135 S.Ct. 2401 (2015); Michigan v. Bay Mills Indian Community, 134 S.Ct. 2024, 2036–39 (2014).

97 CSX Transp., Inc. v. McBride, 131 S.Ct. 2630, 2641 (2011).

98 Kimble v. Marvel Entertainment, LLC, 135 S.Ct. 2401 (2015); Marvin M. Brandt Revocable Trust v. United States, 134 S.Ct. 1257, 1268 (2014).

99 Flood v. Kuhn, 407 U.S. 258 (1972) (declining to overrule a series of Sherman Act precedents that had generated mega-reliance by professional baseball).

100 Leegin Creative Leather Prods., Inc. v. PSKS, Inc., 551 U.S. 877 (2007); State Oil Co. v. Khan, 522 U.S. 3 (1997); cf. Kimble v. Marvel Entertainment, LLC, 135 S.Ct. 2401, 2412–13 (2015) (declining to expand the common law statute exception to cover patent law precedents).

101 Leegin Creative Leather Prods., Inc. v. PSKS, Inc., 551 U.S. 877 (2007); Bowles v. Russell, 551 U.S. 205 (2007); Rodriguez de Quijas v. Shearson/American Express, Inc., 490 U.S. 477, 480–81 (1989). The leading case is Patterson v. McLean Credit Union, 491 U.S. 164, 173 (1989), followed and applied in Kimble v. Marvel Entertainment, LLC, 135 S.Ct. 2401 (2015).

102 Johnson v. United States, 135 S.Ct. 2551, 2557–58, 2561 (2015) (overruling precedents rejecting void-for-vagueness challenges to a criminal provision, after the failure of the Court's interpretation of the provision to provide a predictable rule of law); cf. id. at 2573–84 (dissenting opinion) (strong defense of *stare decisis*, objecting that the Court was simply "tired" of dealing with the provision).

- *Overridden precedents.* Where Congress overrides a statutory precedent, judges should apply the override with the breadth its language demands, often abrogating the reasoning as well as the result of the overridden precedent.[103]
- *Shadow precedents.* Where Congress has only overridden the narrow result of a precedent, but not its underlying doctrinal structure, that decision is still citable as a shadow precedent.[104]
- Brand X *deference.* Where a Supreme Court decision follows an agency interpretation filling a gap in the law left by Congress (*Chevron*), a revised agency interpretation through rulemaking is not barred by *stare decisis*.[105]
- *Lower court consensus.* Unanimity or consensus among federal courts of appeals about the meaning of a statute is of great practical importance, especially when the consensus has persisted over a long period of time.[106]
- *Borrowed statute.* When Congress borrows a statute, it adopts by implication interpretations authoritatively attached to that statute,[107] absent indication to the contrary.[108]
- *Reenactment.* When Congress reenacts a statute, it incorporates settled interpretations of the reenacted statute.[109] The rule is

---

[103] Young v. United Parcel Serv., Inc., 135 S.Ct. 1338, 1350, 1353, 1355 (2015).

[104] Ledbetter v. Goodyear Tire & Rubber Co., 550 U.S. 618 (2007); Arlington Cent. Sch. Dist. Bd. of Educ. v. Murphy, 548 U.S. 291 (2006).

[105] National Cable & Telecomm. Serv. v. Brand X Internet Servs., 545 U.S. 967 (2005); Christensen v. Harris County, 529 U.S. 576, 589 (2000) (concurring opinion); United States v. Watts, 519 U.S. 148, 158–59 (1997) (concurring opinion). This canon does not apply when it appears that a court has closed off agency discretion. United States v. Home Concrete & Supply, LLC, 132 S.Ct. 1836 (2012).

[106] United States v. Tinklenberg, 131 S.Ct. 2007, 2014 (2011); Holland v. Florida, 560 U.S. 631, 645 (2010); General Dynamics Land Sys., Inc. v. Cline, 540 U.S. 581, 593–94 (2004); McNally v. United States, 483 U.S. 350, 376–77 (1987) (dissenting opinion).

[107] Texas Dep't of Housing & Community Affs. v. Inclusive Communities Project, Inc., 135 S.Ct. 2507, 2518–19 (2015); Molzof v. United States, 502 U.S. 301, 307 (1992); Metropolitan Life Ins. Co. v. Taylor, 481 U.S. 58, 65–66 (1987). See also Lawson v. FMR LLC, 134 S.Ct. 1158, 1175–76 (2014) (plurality opinion) (borrowed statute rule applies to settled agency interpretations of borrowed statute as well as judicial interpretations); Jerman v. Carlisle, McNellie, Rini, Kramer & Ulrich LPA, 559 U.S. 573, 588–89 (2010) (borrowed statute had been interpreted by three courts of appeals).

[108] Smith v. Bayer Corp., 131 S.Ct. 2368 (2011); Shannon v. United States, 512 U.S. 573, 581 (1994). See also Jerman v. Carlisle, McNellie, Rini, Kramer & Ulrich LPA, 559 U.S. 573 (2010) (concurring opinion) (objecting that three court of appeals decisions did not create a settled meaning in the borrowed statute).

[109] Texas Dep't of Housing & Community Affs. v. Inclusive Communities Project, Inc., 135 S.Ct. 2507, 2519–20 (2015); Merck & Co. v. Reynolds, 559 U.S. 633, 1794–96

inapplicable when there is no settled standard Congress could have known or the re-enactment makes a material change in the text.[110]

- *Acquiescence.* Consistent agency or Supreme Court interpretation known to Congress is presumed correct.[111] Also, consider unbroken line of lower court decisions interpreting statute, but do not give them decisive weight.[112]

EXTRINSIC LEGISLATIVE SOURCES

- *Legislative history rule.* Consider legislative history (the internal evolution of a statute before enactment) if the statute is ambiguous.[113] Additionally, legislative history (especially committee reports) can be useful confirmation of a perceived ordinary meaning of statutory language.[114]

(2010); Forest Grove Sch. Dist. v. T.A., 557 U.S. 230, 244 n.11 (2009); Davis v. United States, 495 U.S. 472, 482 (1990); Pierce v. Underwood, 487 U.S. 552 (1988).

110 Holder v. Martinez Gutierrez, 132 S.Ct. 2011, 2018–19 (2012); Jama v. Immigration & Customs Enforcement, 543 U.S. 335 (2005).

111 Michigan v. Bay Mills Indian Community, 134 S.Ct. 2024 (2014); CSX Transp., Inc. v. McBride, 131 S.Ct. 2630, 2641 (2011); Zuni Pub. Sch. Dist. No. 89 v. Department of Educ., 550 U.S. 81 (2007) (agency interpretation); FDA v. Brown & Williamson Tobacco Corp., 529 U.S. 120 (2000) (agency).

112 Texas Dep't of Housing & Community Affs. v. Inclusive Communities Project, Inc., 135 S.Ct. 2507, 2519 (2015); CSX Transp., Inc. v. McBride, 131 S.Ct. 2630, 2641 (2011); Gonzalez v. Crosby, 545 U.S. 524 (2005); General Dynamics Land Sys., Inc. v. Cline, 540 U.S. 581 (2004); National Archives & Records Admin. v. Favish, 541 U.S. 157 (2004); Monessen Sw. Ry. Co. v. Morgan, 486 U.S. 330, 338–39 (1988).

113 Bond v. United States, 134 S.Ct. 2077 (2014); Mohamad v. Palestinian Auth., 132 S.Ct. 1702, 1711 (2012) (concurring opinion); United States v. Tinklenberg, 131 S.Ct. 2007, 2015–16 (2011); Safeco Ins. Co. of Am. v. Burr, 551 U.S. 47 (2007); Zuni Pub. Sch. Dist. No. 89 v. Department of Educ., 550 U.S. 81 (2007); Gonzales v. Oregon, 546 U.S. 243, 257–58 (2006); Rumsfeld v. Forum for Academic & Institutional Rights, Inc., 547 U.S. 47 (2006); Koons Buick Pontiac GMC, Inc. v. Nigh, 543 U.S. 50, 62–64 (2004); id. at 65–66 (concurring opinion); FDA v. Brown & Williamson Tobacco Corp., 529 U.S. 120 (2000); Babbitt v. Sweet Home Chap. of Communities for a Great Oregon, 515 U.S. 687 (1995) (majority and dissenting opinions); Wisconsin Pub. Intervenor v. Mortier, 501 U.S. 597, 610 n.4 (1991). But see Samantar v. Yousuf, 560 U.S. 305, 326–29 (2010) (concurring opinion) (arguing that legislative history is never useful and should not be invoked); James v. United States, 550 U.S. 192 (2007) (ignoring legislative history of a provision that was obsolete).

114 Loughrin v. United States, 134 S.Ct. 2384 (2014); Lawson v. FMR LLC, 134 S.Ct. 1158, 1165–66 (2014); Sebelius v. Cloer, 133 S.Ct. 1886, 1895 (2013); Hall v. United States, 132 S.Ct. 1882, 1888 nn. 3–4 (2012); Mohamad v. Palestinian Auth., 132 S.Ct. 1702, 1710 (2012); Tapia v. United States, 131 S.Ct. 2382, 2391 (2011); Samantar v. Yousuf, 560 U.S. 305, 316 & n.9 (2010); Carr v. United States, 560 U.S. 438, 456 (2010); Shinseki v. Sanders, 556 U.S. 396, 406–07 (2009); United States v. Ressam, 553 U.S. 272, 275–77 (2008); Zedner v. United States, 547 U.S. 489, 500–01 (2006).

- Legislative history enables the interpreter to understand the statutory scheme and purpose, and how particular provisions fit into the congressional plan.[115]
- When Congress overrides a Supreme Court interpretation, the reasons for the override ought to be consulted, as should congressional approval of the views of the original dissenting Justices.[116]
- *Conference committee explanations.* Joint or consistent statements of House-Senate conferees, explaining the deal reached in conference committee reports, are the most authoritative legislative history.[117]
- *Committee reports.* Committee reports are especially relevant to understand congressional purpose and the statutory scheme,[118] but cannot trump a textual plain meaning,[119] and should not be relied on if they are themselves ambiguous or imprecise.[120]

---

[115] Texas Dep't of Housing & Community Affs. v. Inclusive Communities Project, Inc., 135 S.Ct. 2507 (2015); American Broadcasting Cos. v. Aereo, Inc., 134 S.Ct. 2498 (2014); Petrella v. MGM, Inc., 134 S.Ct. 1962 (2014); Lawson v. FMR LLC, 134 S.Ct. 1158 (2014) (plurality opinion); Arizona v. United States, 132 S.Ct. 2492, 2503–05 (2012).

[116] Young v. United Parcel Serv., Inc., 135 S.Ct. 1338, 1350, 1353 (2015); American Broadcasting Cos. v. Aereo, Inc., 134 S.Ct. 2498 (2014); Alabama Legislative Black Caucus v. Alabama, 135 S.Ct. 1257, 1273 (2015).

[117] T-Mobile South, LLC v. City of Roswell, Georgia, 135 S.Ct. 808, 815 (2015); Green v. Bock Laundry Mach. Co., 490 U.S. 504, 519–24 (1989).

[118] Texas Dep't of Housing & Community Affs. v. Inclusive Communities Project, Inc., 135 S.Ct. 2507, 2519–20 (2015); American Broadcasting Cos. v. Aereo, Inc., 134 S.Ct. 2498 (2014); Lawson v. FMR LLC, 134 S.Ct. 1158, 1169–71 (2014) (plurality opinion); Hall v. United States, 132 S.Ct. 1882, 1888 nn. 3–4 (2012); Tapia v. United States, 131 S.Ct. 2382, 2391 (2011); United States v. Tinklenberg, 131 S.Ct. 2007, 2015–16 (2011); Brown v. Plata, 131 S.Ct. 1910, 1937 (2011); Tellabs, Inc. v. Makor Issues & Rights, Ltd., 551 U.S. 308 (2007); Rumsfeld v. Forum for Academic & Institutional Rights, Inc., 547 U.S. 47 (2006); Cherokee Nation of Oklahoma v. Leavitt, 543 U.S. 631 (2005); Intel Corp. v. Advanced Micro Devices, Inc., 542 U.S. 241 (2004); Jones v. R.R. Donnelley & Sons Co., 541 U.S. 369 (2004); Boeing Co. v. United States, 537 U.S. 437 (2003); Johnson v. DeGrandy, 512 U.S. 997, 1010–11 & n.9 (1994). But see *Lawson,* 134 S.Ct. at 1176–77 (concurring opinion objecting to legislative history as unreliable).

[119] Arlington Cent. Sch. Dist. Bd. of Educ. v. Murphy, 548 U.S. 291 (2006) (majority and concurring opinions); City of Chicago v. Environmental Def. Fund, 511 U.S. 328, 337 (1994); American Hosp. Ass'n v. NLRB, 499 U.S. 606, 613 (1991). This canon is controversial within the Court. See *Murphy*, 548 U.S. at 308–24 (dissenting opinion).

[120] Marrama v. Citizens Bank of Mass., 549 U.S. 365 (2007); Small v. United States, 544 U.S. 385 (2005).

- Committee report language that cannot be tied to a specific statutory provision cannot be credited.[121] House and Senate reports inconsistent with one another should be discounted.[122]
- *Rejected proposals.* Caution against interpretation considered and rejected by floor vote of a chamber of Congress or within committee.[123] Cautionary principle inapplicable when it is not clear why Congress rejected the proposal.[124]
- *Sponsor's statements.* Floor statements, especially by statutory sponsors, can be used to understand what Congress meant by statutory language,[125] but are generally not as reliable as committee reports.[126]
- *Legislative deliberations.* Public give-and-take between Members of Congress and executive department drafters or sponsors during committee hearings and mark-ups are relevant if they illuminate a shared meaning of statutory language by the participants closest to the process.[127]

---

[121] Shannon v. United States, 512 U.S. 573, 583 (1994).

[122] Moreau v. Klevenhagen, 508 U.S. 22, 26 (1993).

[123] Texas Dep't of Housing & Community Affs. v. Inclusive Communities Project, Inc., 135 S.Ct. 2507, 2520 (2015); Arizona v. United States, 132 S.Ct. 2492, 2504 (2012); Mohamad v. Palestinian Auth., 132 S.Ct. 1702 (2012) (committee mark-up); Jerman v. Carlisle, McNellie, Rini, Kramer & Ulrich LPA, 559 U.S. 573, 596 n.14 (2010) (committee mark-up); Hamdan v. Rumsfeld, 548 U.S. 557 (2006); Doe v. Chao, 540 U.S. 614 (2004); F. Hoffmann-LaRoche Ltd. v. Empagran S.A., 542 U.S. 155 (2004); FDA v. Brown & Williamson Tobacco Corp., 529 U.S. 120, 144 (2000); Department of Revenue v. ACF Indus. of Oregon, Inc., 510 U.S. 332, 345–36 (1994).

[124] Caraco Pharmaceutical Labs., Ltd. v. Novo Nordisk A/S, 132 S.Ct. 1670, 1685–86 (2012); Safeco Ins. Co. of Am. v. Burr, 551 U.S. 47 (2007); Rapanos v. United States, 547 U.S. 715 (2006) (plurality opinion); Solid Waste Agency of Northern Cook County v. U.S. Army Corps of Eng'rs, 531 U.S. 159, 169–70 (2001).

[125] Texas Dep't of Housing & Community Affs. v. Inclusive Communities Project, Inc., 135 S.Ct. 2507, 2520 (2015); FTC v. Actavis, Inc., 133 S.Ct. 2223, 2234 (2013) (relying on sponsor's statement for "[t]hose interested in legislative history"); Arizona v. United States, 132 S.Ct. 2492, 2504 (2012); Entergy Corp. v. Riverkeeper, Inc., 556 U.S. 208, 230–35 (2009) (concurring opinion); Hamdan v. Rumsfeld, 548 U.S. 557 (2006); Department of Revenue v. ACF Indus. of Oregon, Inc., 510 U.S. 332, 345–46 (1994). But see Graham County Soil & Water Conserv. Dist. v. United States ex rel. Wilson, 130 S.Ct. 1396, 1408–09 (2010) (rejecting sponsor's statement as too generalized).

[126] Lawson v. FMR LLC, 134 S.Ct. 1158, 1169–71 & n.13 (2014).

[127] Lockhart v. United States, 136 S.Ct. 958, 973–75 (2016) (dissenting opinion); Arizona v. United States, 132 S.Ct. 2492, 2504 (2012); Mohamad v. Palestinian Auth., 132 S.Ct. 1702, 1710 (2012); DePierre v. United States, 131 S.Ct. 2225, 2232, 2234–35 (2011); General Dynamics Land Sys., Inc. v. Cline, 540 U.S. 581 (2004); FDA v. Brown & Williamson Tobacco Corp., 529 U.S. 120 (2000); Hagen v. Utah, 510 U.S. 399, 418 (1994); Darby v. Cisneros, 509 U.S. 137, 147–51 (1993).

- *Dog didn't bark.* Presume that prior legal rule should be retained if no one during legislative deliberations even mentioned the rule or discussed any changes in the rule.[128]
- *Subsequent legislation.* Views of a subsequent Congress are a hazardous basis for inferring the intent of an earlier one,[129] but are sometimes relevant.[130] Subsequent legislation clearly incorporating these views is relevant and persuasive.[131]
- *Subsequent legislative history.* The post-enactment of a commission report, requested by Congress, might be considered to understand the enacted text.[132] But post-hoc statements by legislators, uttered after enactment of the law, are not worthy of consideration.[133]

SUBSTANTIVE POLICY CANONS

CONSTITUTION-BASED CANONS

- *Constitutional avoidance rule.* Avoid interpretations that would render a statute unconstitutional (classic avoidance)[134] *or* that would raise serious constitutional difficulties (modern avoidance).[135] Inapplicable if statute would clearly survive

---

[128] Zuni Pub. Sch. Dist. No. 89 v. Department of Educ., 550 U.S. 81 (2007); Chisom v. Roemer, 501 U.S. 380, 396 & n.23 (1991).

[129] Bruesewitz v. Wyeth LLC, 131 S.Ct. 1068, 1081–82 (2011); Graham County Soil & Water Conserv. Dist. v. United States ex rel. Wilson, 559 U.S. 280, 296 (2010); Massachusetts v. EPA, 549 U.S. 497 (2007); Doe v. Chao, 540 U.S. 614 (2004); Solid Waste Agency of Northern Cook County v. U.S. Army Corps of Eng'rs, 531 U.S. 159, 170 (2001); Sullivan v. Finkelstein, 496 U.S. 617, 628 n.8 (1990).

[130] Musick, Peeler & Garrett v. Employers Ins. of Wausau, 508 U.S. 286, 293 (1993). This canon is controversial within the Court. Sullivan v. Finkelstein, 496 U.S. 617, 631–32 (1990) (concurring opinion).

[131] FDA v. Brown & Williamson Tobacco Corp., 529 U.S. 120, 144 (2000); Babbitt v. Sweet Home Chap. of Communities for a Great Oregon, 515 U.S. 687 (1995); Franklin v. Gwinnett County Pub. Schs., 503 U.S. 60 (1992); id. at 77–78 (concurring opinion); Bowen v. Yuckert, 482 U.S. 137, 149–51 (1987).

[132] FAA v. Cooper, 132 S.Ct. 1441, 1452–53 (2012).

[133] Barber v. Thomas, 560 U.S. 474, 485–86 (2010); Heintz v. Jenkins, 514 U.S. 291, 298 (1995).

[134] National Federation of Indep. Business v. Sebelius, 132 S.Ct. 2566, 2593–94 (2012) (opinion delivering the judgment of the Court); Adoptive Couple v. Baby Girl, 133 S.Ct. 2552, 2565–71 (2013) (concurring opinion).

[135] Bond v. United States, 134 S.Ct. 2077 (2014); Descamps v. United States, 133 S.Ct. 2276, 2288–89 (2013); Brown v. Plata, 131 S.Ct. 1910, 1928–29, 1937 (2011); Northwest Austin Mun. Utility Dist. No. 1 v. Holder, 557 U.S. 193, 205–06 (2009); Rapanos v. United States, 547 U.S. 715 (2006) (plurality opinion); Cherokee Nation of Oklahoma v. Leavitt, 543 U.S. 631 (2005); Zadvydas v. Davis, 533 U.S. 678, 696–99 (2001); Public Citizen v. United States Dep't of Justice, 491 U.S. 440, 465–66 (1989);

constitutional attack or if statutory text is clear.[136]

1. Separation of Powers

- *Presidential power.* Super-strong rule against congressional interference with President's inherent powers, his/her executive authority.[137] Avoid interpretations whereby judges would interfere with foreign affairs.[138]
- Rule against review of President's core executive actions for "abuse of discretion."[139]
- Where Congress appropriates money without specific textual restrictions, the executive has leeway as to its expenditure, unlimited by more informal signals.[140]
- Rule of special treatment of President and Vice-President as litigants, affording them special privileges so as not to interfere with their official duties.[141]
- *Judicial power.* Rule against congressional curtailment of the judiciary's "inherent powers" or its "equity" powers.[142]
- Rule against congressional expansion of Article III injury in fact to include intangible and procedural injuries.[143]
- Presumption that Congress does not delegate authority without sufficient guidelines.[144]

Edward J. DeBartolo Corp. v. Florida Gulf Coast Building & Constr. Trades Council, 485 U.S. 568, 575 (1988).

[136] Arizona v. Inter Tribal Coun. of Arizona, Inc., 133 S.Ct. 2247 (2013); Astrue v. Capato ex rel. B.N.C., 132 S.Ct. 2021, 2033 (2012); Stern v. Marshall, 131 S.Ct. 2594, 2605–08 (2011); Peretz v. United States, 501 U.S. 923, 932 (1991); Rust v. Sullivan, 500 U.S. 173, 182 (1991).

[137] Department of Navy v. Egan, 484 U.S. 518, 527 (1988); Morrison v. Olson, 487 U.S. 654, 682–83 (1988); Carlucci v. Doe, 488 U.S. 93, 99 (1988); United States v. Johnson, 481 U.S. 681, 690–91 (1987).

[138] Sosa v. Alvarez-Machain, 542 U.S. 692, 725–28 (2004).

[139] Franklin v. Massachusetts, 505 U.S. 788, 800–01 (1992).

[140] Cherokee Nation of Oklahoma v. Leavitt, 543 U.S. 631 (2005); Lincoln v. Vigil, 508 U.S. 182, 191 (1993).

[141] Cheney v. U.S. Dist. Court for Dist. of Columbia, 542 U.S. 367 (2004).

[142] Brown v. Plata, 131 S.Ct. 1910, 1928–29, 1936–37 (2011); Holland v. Florida, 560 U.S. 631, 646 (2010); Chambers v. NASCO, Inc., 501 U.S. 32, 43–44 (1991).

[143] Lujan v. Defenders of Wildlife, 504 U.S. 555, 557–61 (1992); id. at 579–80 (concurring opinion).

[144] Mistretta v. United States, 488 U.S. 361, 373 n.7 (1989).

- *Implied causes of action.* Presumption against "implying" causes of action into federal statutes.[145]
- Presumption that U.S. law conforms to U.S. international obligations.[146] Presumption that Congress takes account of the legitimate sovereign interests of other nations when it writes American laws.[147]
- *Indian treaty rights.* Rule against congressional abrogation of Indian treaty rights.[148]
- *Severability.* Strong presumption favoring severability of unconstitutional provisions.[149]

2. *Federalism*

- *Core state functions.* Super-strong rule against federal invasion of "core state functions."[150]
- *Federal-State balance.* Strong presumption against statutory interpretations that would alter the federal-state balance.[151]
- *Eleventh Amendment immunity.* Super-strong rule against federal abrogation of states' Eleventh Amendment immunity from lawsuits in federal courts.[152] Eleventh Amendment rule

---

[145] Armstrong v. Exceptional Child Center, Inc., 135 S.Ct. 1378 (2015); Virginia Bankshares, Inc. v. Sandberg, 501 U.S. 1083, 1102–05 (1991); Thompson v. Thompson, 484 U.S. 174, 179 (1988).

[146] Hamdan v. Rumsfeld, 548 U.S. 557 (2006) (majority and concurring opinions); Sale v. Haitian Centers Council, Inc., 509 U.S. 155, 173–74 (1993).

[147] Samantar v. Yousuf, 560 U.S. 305 (2010); Microsoft Corp. v. AT&T Corp., 550 U.S. 437 (2007); F. Hoffmann-LaRoche Ltd. v. Empagran S.A., 542 U.S. 155, 164 (2004).

[148] South Dakota v. Bourland, 508 U.S. 679, 687 (1993).

[149] Executive Benefits Ins. Agency v. Arkison, 134 S.Ct. 2165 (2014); National Fed. Indep. Business v. Sebelius, 132 S.Ct. 2566, 2607–08 (2012) (opinion delivering the judgment of the Court); Free Enterprise Fund v. Public Co. Accounting Oversight Bd., 561 U.S. 477, 508 (2010); United States v. Booker, 543 U.S. 220, 258–59, 265 (2005). The leading case is Alaska Airlines, Inc. v. Brock, 480 U.S. 678, 684 (1987).

[150] Rapanos v. United States, 547 U.S. 715 (2006) (plurality opinion); Nixon v. Missouri Municipal League, 541 U.S. 125 (2004); BFP v. Resolution Trust Corp., 511 U.S. 531, 544 (1994); Gregory v. Ashcroft, 501 U.S. 452, 461–64 (1991).

[151] Bond v. United States, 134 S.Ct. 2077 (2014); Gonzales v. Oregon, 546 U.S. 243 (2006); Owasso Indep. Sch. Dist. No. I–011 v. Falvo, 534 U.S. 426 (2002); Raygor v. Regents of the Univ. of Minn., 534 U.S. 533 (2002); BFP v. Resolution Trust Corp., 511 U.S. 531, 544 (1994); Gregory v. Ashcroft, 501 U.S. 452, 461–64 (1991); Will v. Michigan Dep't of State Police, 491 U.S. 58, 65 (1989).

[152] Nevada Dep't of Human Resources v. Hibbs, 538 U.S. 721 (2003) (finding abrogation); Raygor v. Regents of the Univ. of Minn., 534 U.S. 533 (2001); Blatchford v. Native Village of Noatak, 501 U.S. 775, 779 (1991); Dellmuth v. Muth, 491 U.S. 223, 227–28 (1989); Pennsylvania v. Union Gas, 491 U.S. 1, 7 (1989) (finding abrogation). The leading case is Atascadero State Hosp. v. Scanlon, 473 U.S. 234, 241 (1985).

does not apply to municipalities and counties.[153]

- *Spending clause grants.* Super-strong rule against inferring conditions on federal grants to the states under the Spending Clause; conditions must be expressed clearly and unambiguously.[154] Sometimes the Court will require less than targeted statutory language, so long as states are reasonably on notice of conditions, as through agency guidances to that effect.[155]
- *Preemption.* Presumption against federal preemption of traditional state regulation and narrow interpretation of preemption provisions.[156] Presumption trumped if statutory language or statutory scheme requires preemption.[157] Presumption inapplicable or less weighty when Congress regulates under the Elections Clause, Naturalization Clause, and perhaps other nationalist parts of the Constitution.[158]
- *Intergovernmental taxation.* Presumption against federal regulation of intergovernmental taxation by the states.[159]

---

[153] Jinks v. Richland County, 538 U.S. 456 (2003).

[154] Arlington Cent. Sch. Dist. Bd. of Educ. v. Murphy, 548 U.S. 291 (2006); Barnes v. Gorman, 536 U.S. 181 (2002); Gonzaga Univ. v. Doe, 536 U.S. 273 (2002); Blessing v. Freestone, 520 U.S. 329 (1997); Suter v. Artist M., 503 U.S. 347 (1992). The leading case is Pennhurst State Sch. & Hosp. v. Halderman, 451 U.S. 1 (1981).

[155] Davis v. Monroe County Bd. of Educ., 526 U.S. 629 (1999); Franklin v. Gwinnett County Pub. Sch., 503 U.S. 60 (1992).

[156] Oneok, Inc. v. Learjet, Inc., 135 S.Ct. 1591 (2015) (regulation of natural gas); CTS Corp. v. Waldburger, 134 S.Ct. 2175, 2188–89 (2014) (statutes of repose); Wyeth v. Levine, 555 U.S. 555 (2008) (drugs); Altria Group, Inc. v. Good, 555 U.S. 70, 77 (2008); Bates v. Dow Agrosciences LLC, 544 U.S. 431 (2005); Rush Prudential HMO, Inc. v. Moran, 536 U.S. 355 (2002); Medtronic, Inc. v. Lohr, 518 U.S. 470 (1996) (drugs); Hawaiian Airlines, Inc. v. Norris, 512 U.S. 246, 252 (1994); BFP v. Resolution Trust Corp., 511 U.S. 531, 544 (1994) (bankruptcy); Cipollone v. Liggett Group, Inc., 505 U.S. 504, 518 (1992) (tobacco); California v. ARC Am. Corp., 490 U.S. 93, 100–01 (1989); Rose v. Rose, 481 U.S. 619, 635–36 (1987) (concurring opinion). But see PLIVA, Inc. v. Mensing, 131 S.Ct. 2567, 2579–80 (2011) (plurality opinion criticizing efforts to reconcile apparently conflicting federal and state regulation).

[157] FTC v. Phoebe Putney Health Sys., Inc., 133 S.Ct. 1003 (2013); National Meat Ass'n v. Harris, 132 S.Ct. 965 (2012); PLIVA, Inc. v. Mensing, 131 S.Ct. 2567 (2011); Riegel v. Medtronic, Inc., 552 U.S. 312 (2008); Geier v. American Honda Motor Co., 529 U.S. 861, 874–75 (2000).

[158] Arizona v. Inter Tribal Coun. of Arizona, Inc., 133 S.Ct. 2247, 2256–57 (2013) (elections); Arizona v. United States, 132 S.Ct. 2492, 2498–99 (2012) (inherently national focus of immigration law renders state regulations more vulnerable in this area).

[159] Davis v. Michigan Dep't of Treasury, 489 U.S. 803, 810 (1989).

- *Political process.* Presumption against application of federal statutes to state and local political processes,[160] except when statutory plain meaning or other factors counsel in favor of such application.[161]
- *State equality.* Fundamental principle of equal sovereignty among the states; presumption of equal treatment.[162]
- Presumption against congressional derogation from state's land claims based upon its entry into Union on an "equal footing" with all other states.[163]
- *State courts.* Narrow construction of federal laws to avoid any kind of interference with state court jurisdiction and judgments.[164]
- *Dormant Commerce Clause.* Rule against reading an ambiguous federal statute to authorize states to engage in activities that would violate the Dormant Commerce Clause.[165]
- *Concurrent jurisdiction.* Rule favoring concurrent state and federal court jurisdiction over federal claims.[166]
- Principle that federal equitable remedies must consider interests of state and local authorities.[167]
- *Statutes of limitations.* Presumption that Congress borrows state statutes of limitations for federal statutory schemes.[168]

---

[160] City of Columbia v. Omni Outdoor Advertising, Inc., 499 U.S. 365, 373 (1991); McCormick v. United States, 500 U.S. 257, 269 n.6 (1991); McNally v. United States, 483 U.S. 350, 361 n.9 (1987).

[161] National Meat Ass'n v. Harris, 132 S.Ct. 965 (2012) (explicit and broad preemption clause); Evans v. United States, 504 U.S. 255, 270–71 (1992).

[162] Shelby County, Ala. v. Holder, 133 S.Ct. 2612, 2622–24 (2013); Northwest Austin Municipal Util. Dist. No. One v. Holder, 557 U.S. 193, 203–04 (2009).

[163] Idaho v. United States, 533 U.S. 262 (2001); Utah Div'n of State Lands v. United States, 482 U.S. 193, 196 (1987).

[164] Smith v. Bayer Corp., 131 S.Ct. 2368 (2011) (stingy interpretation of exceptions to Anti-Injunction Act); Kokkonen v. Guardian Life Ins. Co. of Am., 511 U.S. 375, 377 (1994) (narrow construction of jurisdictional grants); Finley v. United States, 490 U.S. 545, 552–54 (1989) (similar).

[165] Granholm v. Heald, 544 U.S. 460, 484–85 (2005); Wyoming v. Oklahoma, 502 U.S. 437, 458 (1992).

[166] Mims v. Arrow Financial Servs., LLC, 132 S.Ct. 740 (2012); Tafflin v. Levitt, 493 U.S. 455, 458 (1990); Yellow Freight Sys., Inc. v. Donnelly, 494 U.S. 820, 823 (1990).

[167] Raygor v. Regents of the Univ. of Minn., 534 U.S. 533 (2002); Spallone v. United States, 493 U.S. 265, 276 (1990).

[168] Wallace v. Kato, 549 U.S. 384 (2007); Lampf, Pleva, Lipkind, Prupis & Petigrow v. Gilbertson, 501 U.S. 350, 355–56 (1991).

3. *Due Process*

- *Rule of lenity*. No punitive sanctions if there is ambiguity as to underlying criminal liability or criminal penalty.[169] Rule is trumped when Congress clearly intended to criminalize the conduct in question.[170]
- Rule of lenity may apply to civil sanction that is punitive or when underlying liability is criminal.[171]
- *Mens rea*. Presumption against criminal penalties imposed without showing of specific intent.[172] But willfulness requirement in civil sanction cases typically includes reckless conduct as well.[173]
- *Retroactivity*. Rule against interpreting statutes to be retroactive,[174] even if statute is curative or restorative.[175]
- *Jury trials*. Rule against interpreting statutes to deny a right to jury trial.[176]
- *Judicial review*. Presumption in favor of judicial review,[177] especially for constitutional questions,[178] but not for agency

---

[169] Yates v. United States, 135 S.Ct. 1074, 1088 (2015) (plurality opinion); Burrage v. United States, 134 S.Ct. 881 (2014) (majority and concurring opinions); Skilling v. United States, 561 U.S. 358 (2010); Arthur Andersen LLP v. United States, 544 U.S. 696 (2005); Cleveland v. United States, 531 U.S. 12 (2000); United States v. Aguilar, 515 U.S. 593 (1995); United States v. Granderson, 511 U.S. 39 (1994); United States v. Kozminski, 487 U.S. 931, 939 (1988).

[170] Lockhart v. United States, 136 S.Ct. 958 (2016); Abramski v. United States, 134 S.Ct. 2259 (2014); Robers v. United States, 134 S.Ct. 1854 (2014); United States v. Castleman, 134 S.Ct. 1405, 1416 (2014); Muscarello v. United States, 524 U.S. 125 (1998); Chapman v. United States, 500 U.S. 453, 463–64 (1991).

[171] Crandon v. United States, 494 U.S. 152, 158 (1990). The Court applies this canon very unevenly. E.g., Babbitt v. Sweet Home Chap. of Communities for a Great Oregon, 515 U.S. 687 (1995).

[172] Elonis v. United States, 135 S.Ct. 2001, 2009–10 (2015); Arthur Andersen LLP v. United States, 544 U.S. 696 (2005); Bryan v. United States, 524 U.S. 184, 191–92 (1998); Ratzlaf v. United States, 510 U.S. 135, 137 (1994); Cheek v. United States, 498 U.S. 192, 200–01 (1991).

[173] Safeco Ins. Co. of Am. v. Burr, 551 U.S. 47 (2007); McLaughlin v. Richland Shoe Co., 486 U.S. 128, 132–33 (1988).

[174] Vartelas v. Holder, 132 S.Ct. 1479 (2012); Fernandez-Vargas v. Gonzales, 548 U.S. 30 (2006); Landgraf v. USI Film Prods., 511 U.S. 244 (1994). See also Microsoft Corp. v. AT&T Corp., 550 U.S. 437, 454–55 (2007) (rule against retroactivity especially strong in patent law).

[175] Rivers v. Roadway Express, Inc., 511 U.S. 298 (1994).

[176] Gomez v. United States, 490 U.S. 858, 863 (1989).

[177] Mach Mining, LLC v. EEOC, 135 S.Ct. 1645, 1651 (2015); Sackett v. EPA, 132 S.Ct. 1367 (2012); Demore v. Kim, 538 U.S. 510 (2003).

[178] Webster v. Doe, 486 U.S. 592, 603 (1988).

decisions not to prosecute. Review can be channeled to particular courts if "fairly discernible" from the statute.[179]

- *Preenforcement.* Presumption against preenforcement challenges to implementation.[180]
- *Exhaustion.* Presumption against exhaustion of remedies requirement for lawsuit to enforce constitutional rights.[181]
- *Res judicata.* Presumption that judgments will not be binding upon persons not party to adjudication.[182]
- *Service of process.* Presumption against national service of process unless authorized by Congress.[183]
- *Proof.* Presumption that preponderance of the evidence standard applies in civil cases.[184]

COMMON LAW-BASED CANONS

- *Common law terms.* Presumption in favor of following common law usage where Congress has employed words or phrases with well-settled common law traditions.[185]
- *Common law as background.* When Congress enacts legislation regulating common law areas (such as torts and contracts), courts presume that Congress incorporates common law concepts and doctrine,[186] but not when common law doctrine is

---

[179] Elgin v. Department of the Treasury, 132 S.Ct. 2126, 2132–33 (2012); Thunder Basin Coal Co. v. Reich, 510 U.S. 200, 208–10 (1994).

[180] Thunder Basin Coal Co. v. Reich, 510 U.S. 200, 207 (1994).

[181] McCarthy v. Madigan, 503 U.S. 140, 146–49 (1992).

[182] Martin v. Wilks, 490 U.S. 755, 761–62 (1989).

[183] Omni Capital Int'l, Ltd. v. Rudolf Wolff & Co., 484 U.S. 97, 107–08 (1987).

[184] Grogan v. Garner, 498 U.S. 279, 286 (1991).

[185] United States v. Castleman, 134 S.Ct. 1405, 1410 (2014); University of Texas Southwestern Med. Center v. Nassar, 133 S.Ct. 2517, 2524–25 (2013); Wal-Mart Stores, Inc. v. Dukes, 131 S.Ct. 2541, 2557–58 (2011); Permanent Mission of India to the United Nations v. City of New York, 551 U.S. 193 (2007); Hamdan v. Rumsfeld, 548 U.S. 557 (2006); Dura Pharmaceuticals, Inc. v. Broudo, 544 U.S. 336 (2005); Stewart v. Dutra Constr. Co., 543 U.S. 481, 487 (2005); United States v. Texas, 507 U.S. 529, 534 (1993); Nationwide Mut. Ins. Co. v. Darden, 503 U.S. 318 (1992); Kamen v. Kemper Fin. Servs., Inc., 500 U.S. 90, 98–99 (1991); Community for Creative Nonviolence v. Reid, 490 U.S. 730, 739–40 (1989).

[186] CTS Corp. v. Waldburger, 134 S.Ct. 2175 (2014) (statutes of limitations and repose); Paroline v. United States, 134 S.Ct. 1710 (2014) (torts); United States v. Castleman, 134 S.Ct. 1405 (2014) (tort and criminal liability); Rosemond v. United States, 134 S.Ct. 1240 (2014) (accomplice culpability); Kirtsaeng v. John Wiley & Sons, Inc., 133 S.Ct. 1351 (2013) (copyright); Filarsky v. Delia, 132 S.Ct. 1657 (2012), and Rehberg v. Paulk, 132 S.Ct. 1497 (2012) (constitutional torts); Dura Pharmaceuticals, Inc. v. Broudo, 544 U.S. 336, 341–42 (2005) (fraud); Nationwide Mut. Ins. Co. v. Darden, 503 U.S. 318 (1992) (trusts). See also Pacific Operators Offshore, LLP v.

inconsistent with the specific text or the overall statutory scheme.[187]

- *Extraterritoriality.* Rule against extraterritorial application of U.S. law.[188] Presumption that Congress legislates with domestic concerns in mind.[189]
- *Foreign ships.* American laws apply to foreign-flag ships in U.S. territory and affecting Americans, but will not apply to the "internal affairs" of a foreign-flag ship unless there is a clear statutory statement.[190]
- *U.S. immunity.* Super-strong rule against waivers of United States sovereign immunity. Waivers must be "unmistakably expressed" by Congress.[191] Even if there is a waiver of immunity from suit, the scope of the immunity will often be narrowly read.[192]
- *State immunity.* Super-strong rule against congressional abrogation of state immunity from suit.[193] Common law rule does

---

Valladolid, 132 S.Ct. 680 (2012) (concurring opinion) (presuming that Congress intended an easy-to-apply common law standard rather than a novel standard that would be harder to administer).

[187] CSX Transp., Inc. v. McBride, 131 S.Ct. 2630 (2011); AT&T Mobility LLC v. Concepcion, 131 S.Ct. 1740, 1748 (2011); Pasquantino v. United States, 544 U.S. 349, 356 (2005); Taylor v. United States, 495 U.S. 575, 593–95 (1990).

[188] Kiobel v. Royal Dutch Petroleum Co., 133 S.Ct. 1659, 1664 (2013) (but see id. at 1672–73 [concurring opinion]); Morrison v. National Australia Bank Ltd., 561 U.S. 247 (2010); Microsoft Corp. v. AT&T Corp., 550 U.S. 437, 454 (2007); F. Hoffman-LaRoche Ltd. v. Empagran S.A., 542 U.S. 155 (2004); Sale v. Haitian Centers Council, Inc., 509 U.S. 155 (1993); EEOC v. Arabian Am. Oil Co., 499 U.S. 244, 248 (1991); Argentine Republic v. Amerada Hess Shipping Corp., 488 U.S. 428, 440 (1989).

[189] Morrison v. National Australia Bank Ltd., 561 U.S. 247 (2010); Small v. United States, 544 U.S. 385 (2005); Smith v. United States, 507 U.S. 197, 204 n.5 (1993).

[190] Spector v. Norwegian Cruise Line Ltd., 545 U.S. 119 (2005).

[191] FAA v. Cooper, 132 S.Ct. 1441 (2012); Richlin Security Service Co. v. Chertoff, 553 U. S. 571, 589 (2008); United States v. White Mt. Apache Tribe, 537 U.S. 465, 472–73 (2003); Lane v. Peña, 518 U.S. 187, 192 (1996); United States v. Nordic Village, Inc., 503 U.S. 30 (1992); Ardestani v. INS, 502 U.S. 129 (1991); United States v. Dalm, 494 U.S. 596, 608 (1990). For an objection to the super-strong hurdles posed by this canon, see *Cooper*, 132 S.Ct. at 1456–57 (dissenting opinion).

[192] FAA v. Cooper, 132 S.Ct. 1441 (2012); United States v. Williams, 514 U.S. 527, 531 (1995). But see United States v. Kwai Fun Wong, 135 S.Ct. 1625 (2015) (refusing to read Federal Tort Claims Act statute of limitations narrowly).

[193] Alden v. Maine, 527 U.S. 706, 713 (1999) (announcing that state immunity from suit was based on common law, not just Eleventh Amendment).

not apply to counties and other subdivisions created by the states.[194]

- *Public debts.* Rule that debts to the United States shall bear interest.[195]
- *Public lands.* Presumption against conveyance of U.S. public lands to private parties.[196]
- *Fee shifting.* Clear statement rule against attorney fee-shifting in federal courts and federal statutes.[197] Narrow construction of fee-shifting statutes to exclude costs and other items that are not explicitly identified.[198]
- *Effective date.* Rule presuming that law takes effect on date of enactment.[199]
- *Respondeat superior.* Presumption that public (government) interest not be prejudiced by negligence of federal officials.[200]
- *Public companies.* Presumption that federal agencies launched into commercial world with power to "sue and be sued" are not entitled to sovereign immunity.[201]
- *Forum selection.* Presumption favoring enforcement of forum selection clauses.[202]
- *Preclusion.* Presumption that federal judgment has preclusive effect in state administrative proceedings.[203]
- *Common law immunities.* Presumption importing common law immunities into federal civil rights statutes.[204]

---

[194] Northern Ins. Co. of New York v. Chatham County, Georgia, 547 U.S. 189 (2006).

[195] United States v. Texas, 507 U.S. 529 (1993).

[196] Utah Div. of State Lands v. United States, 482 U.S. 193, 197–98 (1987).

[197] Baker Botts L.L.P. v. ASARCO LLC, 135 S.Ct. 2158 (2015); Hardt v. Reliance Standard Life Ins. Co., 560 U.S. 242 (2010); Buckhannon Bd. & Care Home, Inc. v. West Virginia Dept. of Health & Human Resources, 532 U.S. 598, 602 (2001); Key Tronic Corp. v. United States, 511 U.S. 809 (1994). The leading case is Alyeska Pipeline Serv. Co. v. Wilderness Soc'y, 421 U.S. 240 (1975).

[198] Arlington Cent. Sch. Dist. Bd. of Educ. v. Murphy, 548 U.S. 291 (2006); West Virginia Univ. Hosps., Inc. v. Casey, 499 U.S. 83 (1991).

[199] Gozlon-Peretz v. United States, 498 U.S. 395 (1991).

[200] United States v. Montalvo-Murillo, 495 U.S. 711, 717–18 (1990).

[201] Loeffler v. Frank, 486 U.S. 549, 554–55 (1988).

[202] Carnival Cruise Lines v. Shute, 499 U.S. 585, 589 (1991); Stewart Org., Inc. v. Ricoh Corp., 487 U.S. 22, 33 (1988) (concurring opinion).

[203] Astoria Fed. Sav. & Loan Ass'n v. Solimino, 501 U.S. 104, 108 (1991).

[204] Rehberg v. Paulk, 132 S.Ct. 1497 (2012); Burns v. Reed, 500 U.S. 478, 484–85 (1991); Forrester v. White, 484 U.S. 219, 225–26 (1988).

- *Equitable tolling.* Presumption that nonjurisdictional statutes of limitations may be equitably tolled.[205] But no equitable tolling unless the plaintiff pursued rights vigorously and was prevented from suit by some "extraordinary" circumstance.[206]

STATUTE-BASED CANONS

- *Purpose rule.* Interpret ambiguous statutes so as best to carry out their statutory purposes.[207] Avoid "incongruous results."[208] Caution: no law pursues its purpose at all costs, and text-based limits on a law's scope are part of its purpose.[209]

1. General Canons

- *Administrability.* Interpret statutes with an eye to creating a rule that can be administered efficiently and predictably by agencies and courts.[210]

---

[205] United States v. Kwai Fun Wong, 135 S.Ct. 1625 (2015); Holland v. Florida, 560 U.S. 631, 645–46 (2010); Irwin v. Department of Veterans Affs., 498 U.S. 89 (1990) (leading case for tolling statute of limitations against the government).

[206] Menominee Indian Tribe of Wisconsin v. United States, 136 S.Ct. 750, 755–56 (2016); Holland v. Florida, 560 U.S. 631, 649 (2010).

[207] Texas Dep't of Housing & Community Affs. v. Inclusive Communities Project, Inc., 135 S.Ct. 2507, 2521 (2015); King v. Burwell, 135 S.Ct. 2480, 2492–93 (2015); Young v. United Parcel Serv., Inc., 135 S.Ct. 1338 (2015); American Broadcasting Cos. v. Aereo, Inc., 134 S.Ct. 2498 (2014); Clark v. Rameker, 134 S.Ct. 2242 (2014); Abramski, v. United States, 134 S.Ct. 2259 (2014); CSX Transp., Inc. v. McBride, 131 S.Ct. 2630 (2011); Wal-Mart Stores, Inc. v. Dukes, 131 S.Ct. 2541, 2557–58 (2011); AT&T Mobility (LLC) v. Concepcion, 131 S.Ct. 1740 (2011); Republic of Iraq v. Beaty, 556 U.S. 848, 864 (2009); Zuni Pub. Sch. Dist. No. 89 v. Department of Educ., 550 U.S. 81 (2007); Massachusetts v. EPA, 549 U.S. 497 (2007); Burlington Northern & Santa Fe Ry. v. White, 548 U.S. 53 (2006); Jones v. R.R. Donnelley & Sons Co., 541 U.S. 369 (2004); PGA Tour, Inc. v. Martin, 532 U.S. 661 (2001); Reves v. Ernst & Young, 494 U.S. 56, 60–61 (1990).

[208] Utility Air Regulatory Group v. EPA, 134 S.Ct. 2427 (2014) (plurality opinion); Ricci v. DeStefano, 557 U.S. 557, 579–84 (2009); Winkelman v. Parma City Sch. Dist., 550 U.S. 516 (2007); Nixon v. Missouri Municipal League, 541 U.S. 125 (2004).

[209] Limelight Networks Inc. v. Akamai Technologies, Inc., 134 S.Ct. 2111 (2014); Rapanos v. United States, 547 U.S. 715 (2006) (plurality opinion).

[210] Mellouili v. Lynch, 135 S.Ct. 1980, 1986–87 (2015); Utility Air Regulatory Group v. EPA, 134 S.Ct. 2427, 2443–44 (2014); Nautilus, Inc. v. Biosig Instruments, Inc., 134 S.Ct. 2120 (2014); United States v. Quality Stores, Inc., 134 S.Ct. 1395, 1404–05 (2014); Vance v. Ball State Univ., 133 S.Ct. 2434, 2449–52 (2013); Bullock v. BankChampaign, N.A., 133 S.Ct. 1754, 1761 (2013); United States v. Tinklenberg, 131 S.Ct. 2007, 2014–15 (2011); Till v. SCS Credit Corp., 541 U.S. 465 (2004) (plurality opinion).

- *Continuity.* Presumption that Congress does not create discontinuities in legal rights and obligations without some clear statement.[211]
- *Private enforcement.* Presumption *against* private right of action unless statute expressly provides one,[212] but once recognized a private right of action carries with it all traditional remedies.[213] Regulations cannot create a private cause of action not authorized by the statute.[214]
- *Specificity.* A precisely drawn, detailed statute preempts or governs a more general statute or remedies.[215]
- *Exclusive remedy.* When Congress enacts a specific remedy when no remedy was clearly recognized previously, the new remedy is regarded as exclusive.[216]
- *Exemptions.* Presumption against creating exemptions in a statute that has none.[217] Narrow interpretation of explicit exemptions.[218]
- De minimis *exceptions.* Allow *de minimis* exceptions to statutory rules, so long as they do not undermine statutory policy.[219]

---

[211] POM Wonderful LLC v. Coca-Cola Co., 134 S.Ct. 2228 (2014); United States v. O'Brien, 560 U.S. 218, 231 (2010); Director of Revenue of Mo. v. CoBank ACB, 531 U.S. 316, 323 (2001); Green v. Bock Laundry Mach. Co., 490 U.S. 504, 521–22 (1989); Finley v. United States, 490 U.S. 545, 554 (1989). See also Pacific Operators Offshore, LLP v. Valladolid, 132 S.Ct. 680, 691–93 (2012) (concurring opinion) (presuming that Congress intended an easy-to-apply common law standard rather than a novel standard that would be harder to administer).

[212] Armstrong v. Exceptional Child Care Center, Inc., 135 S.Ct. 1378 (2015); Gonzaga Univ. v. Doe, 536 U.S. 273 (2002); Blessing v. Freestone, 520 U.S. 329 (1997); Suter v. Artist M., 503 U.S. 347 (1992).

[213] Franklin v. Gwinnett County Pub. Sch., 503 U.S. 60 (1992).

[214] Alexander v. Sandoval, 532 U.S. 275 (2001).

[215] Credit Suisse Securities (USA) LLC v. Billing, 551 U.S. 264 (2007); EC Term of Years Trust v. United States, 550 U.S. 429 (2007). The leading case is Brown v. General Serv. Admin., 425 U.S. 820, 834 (1976).

[216] Armstrong v. Exceptional Child Care Center, Inc., 135 S.Ct. 1378, 1385 (2015); Hinck v. United States, 550 U.S. 501 (2007).

[217] Burwell v. Hobby Lobby Stores, Inc., 134 S.Ct. 2751 (2014); City of Chicago v. Environmental Def. Fund, 511 U.S. 328, 337 (1994).

[218] John Hancock Mut. Life Ins. Co. v. Harris Trust & Sav. Bank, 510 U.S. 86, 96–97 (1994); United States Dep't of Justice v. Landano, 508 U.S. 165 (1993); Citicorp Indus. Credit, Inc. v. Brock, 483 U.S. 27, 33–35 (1987).

[219] Wisconsin Dep't of Revenue v. William Wrigley, Jr., Co., 505 U.S. 214 (1992).

2. Process Canons

- *Sanctioning power.* Presumption that adjudicative bodies are vested with inherent authority to sanction abusive litigation practices.[220] Judges presumptively have discretion to raise procedural errors *sua sponte.*[221]
- *Exhaustion.* Presumption that statutory exhaustion requirements entail implicit requirements that the petitioner follow the proper procedures.[222]
- *Sue and be sued clauses.* Rule that "sue and be sued" clauses waive sovereign immunity and should be liberally construed.[223] Presumption that statute creating agency and authorizing it to "sue and be sued" also creates federal subject matter jurisdiction for lawsuits by and against the agency.[224]
- *Process "costs."* Strong presumption that each side bears its own costs in adjudications.[225] Rule against finding statutory authorization of witness fees as costs unless the statute refers explicitly to witness fees.[226]
- *Burden of proof.* Rule that the burden of proof is on the party requesting benefits or entitlements from the state.[227]
- *Waiver.* Rule that nonjurisdictional process objections (e.g., venue) are waived if not timely raised.[228]

3. Specific Statutory Subject Areas

- ***Antitrust.*** Sherman Act of 1891 should be applied in light of its overall purpose of benefitting consumers.[229]

---

[220] Marrama v. Citizens Bank of Mass., 549 U.S. 365 (2007).

[221] Day v. McDonough, 547 U.S. 198 (2006).

[222] Woodford v. Ngo, 548 U.S. 81 (2006); see also O'Sullivan v. Boerckel, 526 U.S. 838, 845 (1999) (similar rule in habeas corpus law).

[223] FDIC v. Meyer, 510 U.S. 471 (1994).

[224] American Nat'l Red Cross v. S.G., 505 U.S. 247 (1992).

[225] Buckhannon Bd. & Care Home, Inc. v. West Virginia Dep't Health & Human Resources, 532 U.S. 598 (2001). The leading case is Alyeska Pipeline Serv. Co. v. Wilderness Soc'y, 421 U.S. 240 (1975).

[226] Arlington Cent. Sch. Dist. Bd. of Educ. v. Murphy, 548 U.S. 291 (2006); West Virginia Univ. Hosps., Inc. v. Casey, 499 U.S. 83 (1991); Crawford Fitting Co. v. J.T. Gibbons, Inc., 482 U.S. 437, 445 (1987).

[227] NLRB v. Kentucky River Community Care, Inc., 532 U.S. 706 (2001).

[228] Kontrick v. Ryan, 540 U.S. 443 (2004).

[229] Weyerhaeuser Co. v. Ross-Simmons Hardwood Lumber Co., 549 U.S. 312 (2007).

- Presumption against application of Sherman Act to activities authorized by states.[230]
- Exemption from antitrust liability should not be lightly inferred.[231]
- Statutes should not be interpreted to create anti-competitive effects.[232]
- ***Arbitration.*** Liberal application of Federal Arbitration Act of 1926 (FAA). Overarching principle is respect for contract, i.e., the agreement of the parties.[233]
- Strong rule favoring arbitration of federal statutory claims unless Congress has clearly supplanted FAA.[234]
- Presumption that the FAA preempts state law failing to treat arbitration contracts on an "equal footing" with other contracts.[235]
- Federal court deference to arbitral awards; narrow construction of statutory provisions allowing judicial review.[236]
- Strong presumption in favor of arbitration and of enforcing labor arbitration agreements.[237]
- ***Banking.*** National Bank Act (NBA) policy shielding national banks from "burdensome" state regulation.[238] But national banks are subject to state laws not conflicting with the NBA's purposes.[239]

---

230 City of Columbia v. Omni Outdoor Advertising, Inc., 499 U.S. 365, 370 (1991).

231 Credit Suisse Securities (USA) LLC v. Billing, 551 U.S. 264 (2007).

232 Nautilus, Inc. v. Biosig Instruments, Inc., 134 S.Ct. 2120 (2014); Two Pesos, Inc. v. Taco Cabana, Inc., 505 U.S. 763 (1992).

233 American Express Co. v. Italian Colors Restaurant, 133 S.Ct. 2304, 2308–09 (2013); AT&T Mobility LLC v. Concepcion, 563 U.S. 333 (2011); Dean Witter Reynolds, Inc. v. Byrd, 470 U.S. 213, 220 (1985).

234 American Express Co. v. Italian Colors Restaurant, 133 S.Ct. 2304, 2308–10 (2013); CompuCredit Corp. v. Greenwood, 132 S.Ct. 665 (2012); Circuit City Stores, Inc. v. Adams, 532 U.S. 105 (2001); Gilmer v. Interstate/Johnson Lane Corp., 500 U.S. 20, 26 (1991); Shearson/American Express, Inc. v. McMahon, 482 U.S. 220, 226–27 (1987).

235 DIRECTV, Inc. v. Imburgia, 136 S.Ct. 463 (2015).

236 Oxford Health Plans LLC v. Sutter, 133 S.Ct. 2064 (2013); Hall Street Assocs., LLC v. Mattel, Inc., 552 U.S. 576, 588 (2008); United Paperworkers Int'l Union, AFL-CIO v. Misco, Inc., 484 U.S. 29, 36–37 (1987).

237 Howsam v. Dean Witter Reynolds, Inc., 537 U.S. 79, 83 (2002); Groves v. Ring Screw Works, Ferndale Fastener Div'n, 498 U.S. 168, 173 (1990).

238 Watters v. Wachovia Bank, N.A., 550 U.S. 1 (2007); Beneficial Nat'l Bank v. Anderson, 539 U.S. 1, 10 (2003); Barnett Bank of Marion County, N.A. v. Nelson, 517 U.S. 25, 32–34 (1996).

239 Atherton v. FDIC, 519 U.S. 213, 221–22 (1997).

- ***Bankruptcy.*** Bankruptcy Act of 1978 (BRA) should be construed in light of its overall purpose, to give a fresh start to the class of "honest but unfortunate debtors."[240]
- Presumption that the BRA and its amendments preserve prior bankruptcy doctrines.[241]
- Exceptions to bankruptcy discharge should be confined to those plainly expressed.[242] Exemptions should be interpreted to reflect a balance between making assets available to creditors and protecting the debtor's "essential needs."[243]
- Where BRA is ambiguous, courts should create gapfilling rules that are familiar, objective, and less expensive to administer.[244]
- Ameliorated version of final order doctrine for appeals of bankruptcy decisions that resolve "discrete disputes."[245]
- ***Civil Procedure and Jurisdiction.*** Subject-matter jurisdictional rules will be strictly enforced and applied,[246] but jurisdictional bars will not be lightly inferred and require a clear statement by Congress.[247]
- For full faith and credit purposes, only a clearly stated jurisdictional requirement will be admissible to question subject-matter jurisdiction of the court issuing a judgment relevant to a sister state's proceedings.[248]

---

[240] Marrama v. Citizens Bank of Mass., 549 U.S. 365, 374 (2007).

[241] Hamilton v. Lanning, 560 U.S. 505, 515–17 (2010); Travelers Casualty & Surety Co. of America v. Pacific Gas & Elec. Co., 549 U.S. 443, 454 (2007); Lamie v. United States Trustee, 540 U.S. 526, 539 (2004); Dewsnup v. Timm, 502 U.S. 410 (1992).

[242] Bullock v. BankChampaign, N.A., 133 S.Ct. 1754, 1760–61 (2013); Kawaauhau v. Geiger, 523 U.S. 57, 62 (1998).

[243] Clark v. Rameker, 134 S.Ct. 2242, 2247 (2014).

[244] Till v. SCS Credit Corp., 541 U.S. 465 (2004) (plurality opinion).

[245] Bullard v. Blue Hills Bank, 135 S.Ct. 1686, 1692 (2015); Howard Delivery Serv., Inc. v. Zurich Am. Ins. Co., 547 U.S. 651, 657 & n.3 (2006).

[246] Musacchio v. United States, 136 S.Ct. 709 (2016); Bowles v. Russell, 551 U.S. 205 (2007). Relatedly, courts will interpret even long-established jurisdictional exceptions narrowly. Marshall v. Marshall, 547 U.S. 293 (2006) (narrow interpretation of "probate exception"); Ankenbrandt v. Richards, 504 U.S. 689 (1992) (narrow interpretation of "domestic relations exception").

[247] United States v. Kwai Fun Wong, 135 S.Ct. 1625, 1631–32 (2015); Sebelius v. Auburn Regional Med. Center, 133 S.Ct. 817, 824 (2013); Stern v. Marshall, 131 S.Ct. 2594, 2606–07 (2011); Henderson ex rel. Henderson v. Shinseki, 562 U.S. 428, 435 (2011); Arbaugh v. Y & H Corp., 546 U.S. 500, 516 (2006).

[248] V.L. v. E.L., 2016 WL 854160 (March 7, 2016).

- Baseline in civil cases is that litigation involves claims by individuals (not groups) aggrieved by defendant's actions and presenting facts warranting plausible claim for legal relief.[249]
- Presumption that time-limitation periods, venue, and other nonjurisdictional requirements are waivable.[250]
- Federal civil procedure statutes are interpreted to be presumptively consistent with the "ordinary rules of civil procedure," such as the rule that a judgment takes effect immediately unless a court grants a stay.[251]
- Presumption that discovery and other Federal Rules of Civil Procedure apply in all kinds of federal cases, subject to a clear statutory statement to the contrary.[252]
- Federal rules of procedure and evidence must be interpreted to avoid abridging, enlarging, or modifying substantive rights.[253]
- Strict construction of statutes authorizing appeals.[254] Rule that Court of Claims is proper forum for Tucker Act claims against federal government.[255]
- ***Civil Rights.*** Aspects of section 1983, the Civil Rights Act of 1871, are governed by common law tort principles, with special relevance to the common law as it existed in 1871.[256]
- Title VII of the Civil Rights Act of 1964 should be interpreted to effectuate its goal of a workplace where individuals are not discriminated against because of their racial, ethnic, religious, or

---

[249] Wal-Mart Stores, Inc. v. Dukes, 131 S.Ct. 2541, 2550, 2561 (2011); Ashcroft v. Iqbal, 556 U.S. 662 (2009). Compare the majority and dissenting opinions in Brown v. Plata, 131 S.Ct. 1910 (2011).

[250] Stern v. Marshall, 131 S.Ct. 2594 (2011); Eberhart v. United States, 546 U.S. 12, 17–18 (2005) (per curiam).

[251] Coleman v. Tollefson, 135 S.Ct. 1759, 1764 (2015).

[252] Republic of Argentina v. NML Capital, Ltd., 134 S.Ct. 2250, 2256–57 (2014) (FSIA); Woodford v. Garceau, 538 U.S. 202, 208 (2003) (habeas); Société Nationale Industrielle Aérospatiale v. United States Dist. Ct. for Southern Dist. of Iowa, 482 U.S. 522, 539 (1987).

[253] 28 U.S.C. § 2072(b); Wal-Mart Stores, Inc. v. Dukes, 131 S.Ct. 2541, 2561 (2011); Ortiz v. Fireboard Corp., 527 U.S. 815, 845 (1999).

[254] Bowles v. Russell, 551 U.S. 205 (2007); Hohn v. United States, 524 U.S. 236, 247 (1998); California Coastal Comm'n v. Granite Rock Co., 480 U.S. 572, 579 (1987).

[255] Preseault v. ICC, 494 U.S. 1, 11–12 (1990).

[256] Filarsky v. Delia, 132 S.Ct. 1657 (2012); Wallace v. Kato, 549 U.S. 381, 384 (2007). The leading common law immunity case is Imbler v. Pachtman, 424 U.S. 409 (1976).

gender-based status.[257] But Title VII does not set forth a general code of workplace civility.[258]

- Voting Rights Act of 1965 should be interpreted in light of its core purpose of preventing race discrimination in voting and fostering a transformation of America into a society no longer fixated on race.[259]
- ***Criminal Law and Sentencing.*** Ambiguities in criminal statutes shall be decided in favor of the accused.[260] Likewise, ambiguous sentencing provisions or enhancements should be interpreted against the government.[261]
- Presumption that Congress does not intend to impose serious criminal liability without a requirement that the defendant engaged in willful conduct.[262]
- Failure of U.S. Attorneys to initiate criminal prosecutions in the past is evidence that the Attorney General's current reading of the statute is too broad.[263]
- Presumption that criminals convicted of pre-amendment activities receive the benefit of statutory amendments that reduce those penalties if they are sentenced after the new statute takes effect.[264]
- Presumption that courts retain traditional discretion to select whether the sentences they impose will run consecutively or concurrently with sentences for other crimes before the sentencing court or other courts.[265]

---

[257] Burlington Northern & Santa Fe Ry. v. White, 548 U.S. 53 (2006).

[258] Oncale v. Sundowner Offshore Servs., Inc., 523 U.S. 75, 80 (1998); Faragher v. City of Boca Raton, 524 U.S. 775, 788 (1998).

[259] League of United Latin Am. Citizens v. Perry, 548 U.S. 399, 433–34 (2006); Georgia v. Ashcroft, 539 U.S. 461, 490 (2003).

[260] See sources in note 169 *supra*.

[261] United States v. R.L.C., 503 U.S. 291 (1992).

[262] Elonis v. United States, 135 S.Ct. 2001, 2009–13 (2015); Carter v. United States, 530 U.S. 255, 269 (2000); United States v. X-Citement Video, Inc., 513 U. S. 64, 70 (1994); Ratzlaf v. United States, 510 U.S. 135 (1994). The leading case is Morissette v. United States, 342 U.S. 246, 252 (1952).

[263] Lopez v. Gonzales, 549 U.S. 47 (2006).

[264] Dorsey v. United States, 132 S.Ct. 2321, 2330–33 (2012), suggesting that the Act of Feb. 25, 1871, 1 U.S.C. § 109, has been supplanted by the Sentencing Reform Act of 1984.

[265] Setser v. United States, 132 S.Ct. 1463, 1468 (2012); Oregon v. Ice, 555 U.S. 160, 168–69 (2009).

- Even when courts are not bound by Sentencing Commission interpretations, such interpretations may be considered.[266]
- ***Environmental Law.*** Environmental laws should be applied in light of their overall purpose of cleaning up the environment at a reasonable cost.[267]
- Because Congress has vested the Environmental Protection Agency with broad lawmaking authority, courts should defer to the agency's choice among various policymaking options, so long as the choice is not barred by the statute[268] and is not unreasonable.[269]
- National Environmental Policy Act contains an implicit "rule of reason," relieving agencies of filing environmental impact statements that would serve no statutory purpose.[270]
- ***Free Exercise of Religion.*** The Religious Freedom Restoration Act bars statutory interpretations that impose substantial burdens on religious free exercise, unless they are narrowly tailored to serve a compelling governmental interest.[271]
- ***Freedom of Information.*** The Freedom of Information Act of 1966 should be liberally construed, and its exemptions from disclosure narrowly construed.[272]
- ***Habeas Corpus.*** Super-strong rule against implied congressional abrogation or repeal of habeas corpus.[273]
- Strong presumption of correctness of state criminal convictions for purposes of federal habeas corpus review.[274]

---

[266] James v. United States, 550 U.S. 192 (2007).

[267] Michigan v. EPA, 135 S.Ct. 2699, 2707–08 (2015); Utility Air Regulatory Group v. EPA, 134 S.Ct. 2427 (2014); Massachusetts v. EPA, 549 U.S. 497 (2007).

[268] Utility Air Regulatory Group v. EPA, 134 S.Ct. 2427 (2014) (plurality and concurring opinions); EPA v. EME Homer City Generation, L.P., 134 S.Ct. 1584, 1603–04 (2014).

[269] Michigan v. EPA, 135 S.Ct. 2699, 2707–08 (2015).

[270] Department of Transportation v. Public Citizen, 541 U.S. 752 (2004); Marsh v. Oregon Natural Resources Council, 490 U.S. 360, 373–74 (1989).

[271] Burwell v. Hobby Lobby Stores, Inc., 134 S.Ct. 2751 (2014).

[272] Milner v. Department of Navy, 562 U.S. 562, 570 (2011); Department of Interior v. Klamath Water Users Protective Assn., 532 U. S. 1, 7–8 (2001); U.S. Department of Justice v. Tax Analysts, 492 U. S. 136, 151 (1989).

[273] Demore v. Kim, 538 U.S. 510 (2003); INS v. St. Cyr, 533 U.S. 289, 298–99 (2001).

[274] Hardy v. Cross, 132 S.Ct. 490 (2011) (per curiam); Felkner v. Jackson, 562 U.S. 594 (2011) (per curiam); Brecht v. Abrahamson, 507 U.S. 619, 635–38 (1993).

- Rule against federal habeas review of state criminal convictions unless prisoner has properly exhausted state remedies.[275]
- Rule against federal habeas review of state criminal convictions supported by independent state ground.[276]
- Background norm that habeas remedies are informed by traditions of equity jurisprudence.[277]
- Miscarriage of justice exception. Principle that a prisoner presumptively has a judicial forum to present claims of actual innocence.[278]
- ***Immigration.*** Construe ambiguities in deportation statutes in favor of noncitizens.[279]
- Ambiguities or uncertainties in criminal laws referenced in immigration statutes should be resolved in favor of noncitizens.[280]
- Judicial deference to executive branch interpretations is especially appropriate in immigration cases, because the statutory scheme is so complex and often implicates foreign relations.[281]
- Strong preference for simple, categorical rules, given the nation's overburdened immigration system.[282]
- ***Indian Law.*** Rule that Indian sovereignty is limited to Indian tribe members and designated tribal territories.[283] Presumption

---

[275] O'Sullivan v. Boerckel, 526 U.S. 838, 845 (1999).

[276] Sanchez-Llamas v. Oregon, 548 U.S. 331 (2006); Massaro v. United States, 538 U.S. 500, 504 (2003); Wright v. West, 505 U.S. 277, 289 (1992); Coleman v. Thompson, 501 U.S. 722, 729 (1991).

[277] Holland v. Florida, 560 U.S. 631, 646 (2010); Munaf v. Geren, 553 U.S. 674, 693 (2008).

[278] McQuiggin v. Perkins, 133 S.Ct. 1924, 1931–32 (2013); Calderon v. Thompson, 523 U.S. 538 (1998). The leading case is Schlup v. Delo, 513 U.S. 298, 327–28 (1995).

[279] INS v. St. Cyr, 533 U.S. 289, 320 (2001); INS v. Cardoza-Fonseca, 480 U.S. 421, 449 (1987). This canon is applied with an unusual level of unpredictability and may be on the wane. Compare, e.g., INS v. Elias-Zacarias, 502 U.S. 478 (1992).

[280] Carachuri-Rosendo v. Holder, 560 U.S. 563, 581 (2010); Leocal v. Ashcroft, 543 U.S. 1, 11 n.8 (2004).

[281] Scialabba v. Cuellar de Osorio, 134 S.Ct. 2191, 2203 (2014) (plurality opinion); INS v. Aguirre-Aguirre, 526 U.S. 415, 424–25 (1999).

[282] Moncrieffe v. Holder, 133 S.Ct. 1678, 1690–01 (2013).

[283] Michigan v. Bay Mills Indian Community, 134 S.Ct. 2024 (2014); Atkinson Trading Co. v. Shirley, 532 U.S. 645 (2001).

against criminal jurisdiction by an Indian tribe over a nonmember.[284]

- Presumption that states can tax activities within their borders, including Indian tribal activities,[285] but also presumption that states cannot tax on Indian lands.[286]
- Indian tribes cannot be sued without explicit congressional authorization, and to abrogate such immunity Congress must "unequivocally" do so.[287]
- Presumption against national "diminishment" of Indian lands.[288]
- Longstanding assertion of state jurisdiction over Indian lands creates justifiable expectations of sovereign authority.[289]
- Presumption that party cannot invoke federal jurisdiction until exhausting her remedies in Indian tribal courts.[290]
- ***Labor Law.*** Rule against statutory interference in labor-management discipline disputes.[291]
- ***Patent Law.*** Patent law should be applied liberally to reward ingenuity and discourage infringements.[292] But patent law reflects a balance between rewarding innovation and allowing the market to take advantage of innovations once introduced.[293]
- Strong presumption that abstract ideas and laws of nature are not patentable.[294]

---

[284] Duro v. Reina, 495 U.S. 676, 693–94 (1990).

[285] Cotton Petroleum Corp. v. New Mexico, 490 U.S. 163, 174 (1989).

[286] Oklahoma Tax Comm'n v. Sac and Fox Nation, 508 U.S. 114 (1993); County of Yakima v. Confederated Tribes & Bands of the Yakima Indian Nation, 502 U.S. 251, 268 (1992).

[287] Michigan v. Bay Mills Indian Community, 134 S.Ct. 2024, 2030–32 (2014); C&L Ents., Inc. v. Citizen Band Potawatomi Tribe of Okla., 532 U.S. 411, 418 (2001). The leading case is Santa Clara Pueblo v. Martinez, 436 U.S. 49, 58 (1978).

[288] Hagen v. Utah, 510 U.S. 399 (1994).

[289] City of Sherrill, New York v. Oneida Indian Nation of New York, 544 U.S. 197 (2005); Hagen v. Utah, 510 U.S. 399, 421 (1994).

[290] Iowa Mut. Ins. Co. v. LaPlante, 480 U.S. 9, 15–17 (1987).

[291] Eastern Associated Coal Corp. v. UMW Dist. 17, 531 U.S. 57 (2000).

[292] Commil USA, LLC v. Cisco Sys., Inc., 135 S.Ct. 1920 (2015); Bilski v. Kappos, 561 U.S. 593 (2010).

[293] Kimble v. Marvel Entertainment, LLC, 135 S.Ct. 2401 (2015).

[294] Alice Corp. Pty. Ltd. v. CLS Bank Int'l, 134 S.Ct. 2347 (2014); Mayo Collaborative Servs. v. Prometheus Labs., Inc., 132 S.Ct. 1289 (2012); Bilski v. Kappos, 561 U.S. 593 (2010).

- Strong presumption that inventor (and not her or his employer or grantor) is the party entitled to patent the invented product.[295]
- Practice and precedent of Patent Office are persuasive evidence of statutory meaning in this area, given the much greater competence of that Office.[296]
- ***Pensions.*** Presumption that Employee Retirement Income Security Act of 1974 (ERSA), the federal pension-protection law, should be interpreted consistently with the common law of trusts.[297]
- ERISA reflects a balance of competing congressional purposes, i.e., protection of plan benefits for employees, but without discouraging employers from offering pension plans.[298]
- ***Securities Law.*** Federal securities laws should be read in light of the congressional purpose to insure honest securities markets and promote investor confidence.[299]
- Securities law disclosure rules should be applied under an objective standard, i.e., how they would be understood by a "reasonable investor."[300]
- Private cause of action to enforce § 10(b) and Rule 10b-5, created by courts, should be interpreted narrowly.[301]
- ***Taxation.*** Narrow interpretation of exemptions from federal taxation.[302] Presumption against taxpayer claiming income tax deduction.[303]

---

[295] Board of Trustees, Leland Stanford Junior University v. Roche Molecular Sys., Inc., 563 U.S. 776 (2011).

[296] Festo Corp. v. Shoketsu Kinzoku Kogyo Kabushiki Co., 535 U.S. 722 (2002).

[297] Tibble v. Edison Int'l, 135 S.Ct. 1823 (2015).

[298] Fifth Third Bancorp v. Dudenhoeffer, 134 S.Ct. 2459, 2470 (2014); Conkright v. Frommert, 559 U.S. 506, 517 (2010); Varity Corp. v. Howe, 516 U.S. 489, 497 (1996).

[299] Chadbourne & Parke LLP v. Troice, 134 S.Ct. 1058, 1067 (2014); United States v. O'Hagan, 521 U.S. 642, 658 (1997).

[300] Omnicare, Inc. v. Laborers Dist. Coun. Constr. Ind. Pension Fund, 135 S.Ct. 1318 (2015). The leading case is TSC Indus., Inc. v. Northway, Inc., 426 U.S. 438, 445 (1976).

[301] Janus Capital Group, Inc. v. First Derivative Traders, 131 S.Ct. 2296 (2011); Stoneridge Investment Partners, LLC v. Scientific-Atlanta, Inc., 552 U.S. 148, 167 (2008); Central Bank of Denver, N.A. v. First Interstate Bank of Denver, N.A., 511 U.S. 164 (1994).

[302] United States v. Burke, 504 U.S. 229 (1992) (Souter, J., concurring in the judgment); United States v. Wells Fargo Bank, 485 U.S. 351, 357 (1988).

[303] INDOPCO, Inc. v. Commissioner, 503 U.S. 79 (1992).

- Presumption that tax valuation statutes follow majority approach, and that departures from the majority approach would be signaled with clear statutory language.[304]
- ***Veterans' Benefits.*** Veterans' benefits statutes be construed liberally for their beneficiaries.[305]

[304] Limtiaco v. Camacho, 549 U.S. 483 (2007).

[305] Henderson ex rel. Henderson v. Shinseki, 562 U.S. 428 (2011); King v. St. Vincent's Hosp., 502 U.S. 215 (1991).

Table of Cases

Index

References are to Pages